Learning Problems & Learning Disabilities: Moving Forward

Howard S. Adelman
University of California, Los Angeles

Linda Taylor
Los Angeles Unified School District

Brooks/Cole Publishing Company
Pacific Grove, California

Two young ones playing restaurant:
"How do you want your steak?"
"Medium."
"I'm sorry, we only have large."
To those whose answers make us think.

Brooks/Cole Publishing Company
A Division of Wadsworth, Inc.

Printed in the United States of America

10   9   8   7   6   5   4   3   2   1

Library of Congress Cataloging-in-Publication Data
Adelman, Howard S.
    Learning problems and learning disabilities : moving forward /
Howard S. Adelman, Linda Taylor.
        p.   cm.
    Includes bibliographical references and index.
    ISBN 0-534-18756-0
    1. Learning disabilities — United States.   2. Learning disabled
children — Education — United States.   3. Learning disabled —
Education — United States.   I. Taylor, Linda (Linda L.)   II. Title.
LC4705.A36   1992   92-9363
371.9′0973 — dc20   CIP

Sponsoring Editor: *Vicki Knight*	Cover Photo: *Lee Hocker*
Marketing Representative: *Diana Rothberg*	Art Coordinator: *Lisa Torri*
Editorial Assistant: *Heather Graeve*	Interior Illustration: *Kevin Opstedal and Lotus Art*
Production Editors: *Kay Mikel and Kirk Bomont*	Photo Coordinator: *Larry Molmud*
Manuscript Editor: *Judith Johnstone*	Photo Researcher: *Gail Meese*
Permissions Editor: *Marie DuBois*	Typesetting: *Graphic World Inc.*
Interior and Cover Design: *Sharon L. Kinghan*	Printing and Binding: *Arcata Graphics/Fairfield*

Part I: Gale Zucker. **Chapter 1:** 2, Mike Penney; 3, (both) Gail Meese/Meese Photo Research; 4, Robert Finken; 5, Gail Meese/Meese Photo Research; 12, Cleo Freelance Photo. **Chapter 2:** 18, Jeff Albertson/Stock Boston; 26, (top) Cathy Watterson, (bottom) Gail Meese/Meese Photo Research; 27, Sunrise/Trinity Photos; 33, Gail Meese/Meese Photo Research. **Part II:** 38, Gale Zucker. **Chapter 3:** 40, Robert Finken; 44, Gail Meese/Meese Photo Research; 52, Mike Penney; 60, Martha Tabor/Working Images Photographs. **Chapter 4:** 66, Robert Finken; 69, Art Phaneuf; 77, Mike Penney; 81, Gail Meese/Meese Photo Research; 83, (top) Gale Zucker, (bottom) Ulrich Tutch; 84, Cleo Freelance Photo; 88, Michael Siluk. **Chapter 5:** 98, Martha Tabor/Working Images Photographs; 102, Mike Penney; 111, Gale Zucker; 115, Martha Tabor/Working Images Photographs; 120, Elizabeth Hamlin/Stock Boston. **Chapter 6:** 126, James L. Shaffer; 129, Martha Tabor/Working Images Photographs; 134, Gail Meese/Meese Photo Research. **Chapter 7:** 140, Mike Penney; 150, Gail Meese/Meese Photo Research. **Part III:** 154, Gale Zucker. **Chapter 8:** 156, Martha Tabor/Working Images Photographs; 159, Gail Meese/Meese Photo Research; 164, 173, Martha Tabor/Working Images Photographs. **Chapter 9:** 176, Chuck Wyrostok/AppaLight; 179, Cleo Freelance Photo; 184, Gail Meese/Meese Photo Research; 185, The Bettmann Archive; 189, Robert Finken; 193, (top) James. L. Shaffer, (bottom) Gail Denham. **Chapter 10:** 196, MacDonald/Envision; 200, Cleo Freelance Photo; 203, Elizabeth Crews/Stock Boston; 205, Martha Tabor/Working Images Photographs; 213, (top left, bottom left), Martha Tabor/Working Images Photographs; (top right, bottom right) James L. Shaffer. **Chapter 11:** 226, Mike Penney; 233, Gail Denham; 244, Mike Penney. **Chapter 12:** 252, Virginia Bensing. **Part IV:** 268, Mike Penney. **Chapter 13:** 270, NASA/Johnson Space Center; 272, (top left and right, bottom right) Gail Meese/Meese Photo Research, (bottom left) Robert Finken; 276, 277, Gail Meese/Meese Photo Research. **Chapter 14:** 284, Brooks/Cole Photo.

Preface

"What can I do to help the children in my class who have learning problems?" the teacher asked with a note of despair.

Before either of us could respond, someone shouted, "Why don't we talk about improving schools to keep kids from having learning problems?"

It was more a statement than a question, and the feeling was intense. Some of the audience agreed loudly. Others, more concerned about the specific type of learning problems called learning disabilities, felt general school improvements would not do the job. They called for more special programs. And so it goes whenever learning problems are discussed!

This book is concerned with a broad range of learning problems. It also offers an overview and a context for understanding that subgroup of learning problems known as learning disabilities. The work is an outgrowth of our two earlier books, which focused mainly on learning disabilities—while attempting to place the concept within a broader perspective. Our change in emphasis is consistent with evolving directions in psychology and education and reflects 25 years of ongoing collaboration with students who have had learning problems and our colleagues in school districts and universities.

The world around us is changing at an exponential rate—and so must the way learning problems are approached. In the future, the emphasis must be on a comprehensive understanding of such problems.

We all are called upon to do something about the many individuals who have trouble learning academic skills, and we will need a broad understanding of what causes learning problems (including learning disabilities) and what society in general and schools in particular need to do about them. It is time to move forward, putting learning disabilities firmly into perspective as one type of learning problem, and approaching all learning problems in the context of fundamental ideas about learning and teaching.

To these ends, this book focuses on a wide spectrum of learning problems and emphasizes new directions. It is intended for students preparing for professional careers, and also for anyone seeking to broaden their orientation to learning problems and learning disabilities.

In Part 1, we offer perspectives for understanding the nature and scope of learning problems and learning disabilities and point out what is involved in dealing with such problems comprehensively.

Part 2 provides an overview of intervention, stressing each phase of the process, the type of programs offered from preschool through adulthood, approaches to assessment, and ideas for improving current practices.

In Part 3, the focus is on specific ideas and procedures for personalizing instruction and providing remediation, emphasizing the importance of matching motivation and development, providing a comprehensive curriculum, and using a sequential and hierarchical approach to teaching.

Part 4 discusses the processes and problems involved in moving forward to comprehensive practice and research.

Part 5 contains a specially prepared set of twenty "readings" to provide a more detailed look at the topics of (1) learning disabilities, (2) assessment, (3) teaching, and (4) the process of intervention as it relates to individuals and society. This unusual feature is intended to ensure that certain specialized topics (such as learning disabilities) and basic concepts and information (on topics such as assessment) are covered, but in a way that does not disrupt the flow of the main text. Beyond providing additional coverage and resource material, you will find a range of issues presented to stimulate your thinking. Although the readings all have been placed in Part 5, each can be read at any time that seems appropriate. You are referred to these readings throughout the text and at the end of chapters with the suggestion that you Read More About It.

Throughout, we stress the importance of viewing learning problems in a broad context and understanding learning disabilities as one of several types of learning problems. We focus on motivational and developmental differences, deficiencies, and dysfunctions. We discuss a variety of causal factors, and current and evolving intervention approaches. Although this is not a methods text per se, we provide a general orientation to methods, with enough specifics to allow the reader to join in the process of moving forward to prevent and correct learning problems. We pay particular attention to the many issues that must be addressed by practitioners and researchers interested in advancing the field.

Specifically, our intent is to

- present a comprehensive view of the causes of learning problems—differentiating learning disabilities as one special subgroup
- discuss intervention from an interactional/transactional perspective—stressing the need to change learning environments as well as to provide individual remediation
- emphasize the key role of motivation—especially intrinsic motivation—in improving interventions
- address motivational and behavioral problems as ongoing concerns in dealing with all learning problems
- approach intervention from a least intervention needed perspective with a societal approach

And from these viewpoints we describe

- a broad continuum of programs ranging from prevention to treatment of chronic problems
- a sequential approach to all classroom instruction that begins with personalization and moves on to remediation only when necessary

- a hierarchical approach to remediation that encompasses direct instruction and treatment of underlying problems

Throughout you will also find references to works you can consult for a deeper look at a specific topic.

As you proceed, keep the following questions in mind:

What are the different *types* of learning problems?
What is the best way to *prevent* such problems?
What is the best way to *help* those with such problems?

A Note on Using the Book to Personalize Learning

The twenty readings included in the text provide a variety of ways to personalize learning for individuals who are at different levels or who have different career goals, as well as a starting point for pursuing and expanding special interests.

For example:

Individuals interested specifically in learning disabilities will want to read *Learning Disabilities in Historical Perspective* to gain a sense of the field's history.

Readers who have not been introduced to concepts such as reliability, validity, norms, and standards may need to read *Technical Concerns About Assessment*.

For persons beginning to think more about theoretical foundations for teaching, there is the reading on *Theories of Instruction and Models of Teaching*.

And, there are readings to stimulate thinking and discussion about ethical concerns, cultural differences, socialization and helping interventions, and barriers to working with parents and colleagues.

While the chapters are meant to be read in order, the readings should be pursued in ways that fit your specific needs and interests. And, since needs and interests change over time, some of the material may continue to be a useful resource over the years.

Acknowledgments

We owe so much to so many that we cannot begin to name them all. Instead, we take this opportunity to acknowledge an enormous debt to our colleagues and to the youngsters with whom we have worked over the years; what they have taught us is reflected throughout this volume.

In preparing the book, significant contributions were made by the editorial staff at Brooks/Cole and by external reviewers sought out by Managing Editor Vicki Knight. Although anonymous reviews were forwarded us, we are now in a position to thank the following individuals for their helpful and encouraging feedback: Dr.

Ginger Blalock, University of New Mexico; Dr. Harry Dangel, Georgia State University; Ms. Rebecca B. Evers, Northern Illinois University; Dr. Charles Hughes, Penn State University; Dr. Elliott Lessen, Northern Illinois University; Dr. Gayle A. Mayer, University of Texas at El Paso; Dr. Regina H. Sapona, University of Cincinnati; and Dr. Cheryl A. Utley, The Juniper Gardens Children's Project.

Howard S. Adelman
Linda Taylor

Brief Contents

PART 1 *LEARNING PROBLEMS AND LEARNING DISABILITIES*   **1**

    1 *Introductory Perspectives*   *2*

    2 *Causes*   *18*

PART 2 *INTERVENTION: AN OVERVIEW*   **38**

    3 *Intervention Concepts and Learning Problems*   *40*

    4 *Assessing Learning Problems*   *66*

    5 *Program Considerations from Preschool Through Adulthood*   *98*

    6 *Who Decides?*   *126*

    7 *Toward Improving Intervention*   *140*

PART 3 *PERSONALIZED INSTRUCTION AND REMEDIATION*   **154**

    8 *Matching Motivation and Development*   *156*

    9 *Curriculum Content: Basics Plus*   *176*

    10 *The Process of Teaching*   *197*

    11 *Remediation*   *226*

    12 *Evaluating Effectiveness*   *252*

PART 4 *GETTING OUT OF THE BOX*   **268**

    13 *Moving Forward: A Sense of Direction*   *270*

    14 *Use What You Have Learned*   *284*

PART 5 *READ MORE ABOUT IT*   **288**

    I. *On Learning Disabilities*   *290*

    II. *On Assessment Tools and Technical Concerns*   *340*

    III. *On Teaching*   *354*

    IV. *On the Individual and Society*   *390*

    References   *431*

    Name Index   *463*

    Subject Index   *471*

Contents

PART 1 *LEARNING PROBLEMS AND LEARNING DISABILITIES* **1**

CHAPTER 1 *Introductory Perspectives* **2**

Learning Problems or Learning Disabilities? 3
What is a Learning Disability? 6
  Controversy over Characteristics 6
  Controversy over Definitions 7
Placing Learning Disabilities in Perspective 11
  Learning Problems as the Context for Understanding Learning Disabilities 11
  Learning and Teaching as the Context for Understanding Learning Problems 11
  Society as the Context for Teaching and Learning 13
  Type I, II, and III Problems 13
Moving Forward 15
  Forward to Basics 15
  Toward a Comprehensive Approach 15
Summing Up 16

CHAPTER 2 *Causes* **18**

The Problem of Compelling Clues 19
  Errors in Logic 19
  Causes and Correlates 20
Causal Models 20
  Human Functioning: A Transactional Model 20
  The Transactional Model as an Umbrella 22
  Behaviorist Perspectives on Cause 23
Learning Problems: The Common Case 25
The Special Case of Learning Disabilities 27
  Factors Causing Central Nervous System Problems 28
  How the CNS is Affected and Learning is Disrupted 29

Learning and Behavior Problems   35
Summing Up   35

PART 2   *INTERVENTION: AN OVERVIEW*   **38**

CHAPTER 3   ***Intervention Concepts and Learning Problems***   **40**

A Broad Focus   41
Defining Intervention   42
Broadening the Focus of Intervention   43

Contemporary Interventions for Learning Problems   45
Overview   45
The Many Purposes of Assessment   49
Contrasting Orientations to Remediation   53
Eclecticism   55

Least Intervention Needed   56
Mainstream versus Special Settings   57
Labeling: Is It Necessary?   58
Needs Come First   59
Regular and Special Education   61

No Magic Bullets   62
Summing Up   64

CHAPTER 4   ***Assessing Learning Problems***   **66**

Facets of Assessment   67
Identification   67
Placement   68
Planning Specific Changes   70
Evaluating Intervention   73
Other Factors Shaping Assessment   75

Fundamental Concerns About Prevailing Practices   75
Problems of Interpretation   77
Biasing Factors   79
Ethics   86
Meeting Minimal Standards   90

Beyond Conventional Practices   91
Preassessment Interventions   91
Focal Point   92
Single versus Multi-Stage Decision Making   93
Interventionist Assessment   93

Summing Up   94

CHAPTER 5   *Program Considerations from Preschool Through Adulthood   98*

    Prekindergarten   99
        Prevention   99
        Early-Age Interventions   101
    Elementary Students   104
        Redesigning Regular Instruction   104
        Early School Adjustment Problems   113
        Enhancing Teacher Learning   116
        Special Resources for Severe Problems   118
    Adolescents and Adults   119
        Special Concerns   119
        Special Programs   121
    Summing Up   123

CHAPTER 6   *Who Decides?   126*

    Parental Consent and Due Process   127
    Children's Assent   130
        Competence   130
        Paternalism   131
    Demystification   131
    Conflicts over Decisions   133
        In Whose Best Interests?   134
        Helping and Socialization   135
    The Politics of Decision Making   136
    Summing Up   138

CHAPTER 7   *Toward Improving Intervention   140*

    The Process of Improving Intervention   141
        Building Models   141
        Experimenting and Problem Solving   144
    Broadening the Focus   146
        More than Children   146
        More than Diagnosis and Treatment   146
        More than Remediation   146
        More than Individualization   147
        More than Basic Skills and Direct Instruction   149
        More than Changing People   150
    Sequential Decisions   151
    Summing Up   151

PART 3 *PERSONALIZED INSTRUCTION AND*
REMEDIATION   **154**

CHAPTER 8 *Matching Motivation and Development*   **156**

Interaction of the Learner with the Environment   *157*
The Learner   158
The Environment   159
Transactions and the Match   160

Matching Motivation   *163*
Motivation and Learning   163
Key Components of Motivation: Valuing and Expectations   165
Overreliance on Extrinsics: A Bad Match   167

Matching Development   *170*
Variations in Developmental Patterns   170
Key Performance Dimensions   172

Personalization   *173*
Summing Up   *174*

CHAPTER 9 *Curriculum Content: Basics Plus*   **176**

Focusing on Motivation   *177*
Enhancing and Expanding Intrinsic Motivation   179
Overcoming Avoidance Motivation   180
A Few Curriculum Implications   183

Forward to Basics: Basics Plus   *184*
Toward a Comprehensive Curriculum   *187*
Remediation in Perspective   187
Developmental Tasks and General Domains of Learning   189
Enrichment   192

Summing Up   *194*

CHAPTER 10 *The Process of Teaching*   **196**

Mobilizing the Learner   *197*
Options   198
Learner Decision Making   199
Continuous Information on Progress   199

Facilitating Motivated Learning   *202*
Environmental Setting   203
Structure   205
Activities, Techniques, and Motivated Practice   207

Least-Intervention Teaching   214
Personalizing Classrooms   215
    Key Assumptions and Major Elements   216
    Sequential and Hierarchical Framework   217
    Case   219
    Moving Toward Personalization   222
Summing Up   223

CHAPTER 11   *Remediation*   226

When Is It Needed?   227
What Makes Remediation Different?   227
Criteria for Implementing Remediation   229
    Motivational Problems   229
    Developmental Problems   229
Content Focus   231
    Perceptual-Motor Problems   231
    Language and Psycholinguistics   232
    Math   232
    Cognitive Prerequisites   233
    Learning Strategies and Reasoning   234
    Social and Emotional Functioning   235
    Motivation   235
    Interfering Behavior   236
Remedial Methods   236
Levels of Remediation   241
Sequencing Remediation   243
Summing Up   246

CHAPTER 12   *Evaluating Effectiveness*   252

What is the Program Trying to Accomplish?   253
    Whose Rationale? Whose Judgment?   254
    Program Purposes and Evaluation   255
    Breadth of Program Focus and Evaluation   256
Measuring What's Happening   258
    What Is Done Currently?   258
    What Is Evaluation?   262
    Steps in Evaluation Planning   262
Summing Up   265

PART 4   *GETTING OUT OF THE BOX*   268

CHAPTER 13   *Moving Forward: A Sense of Direction*   270

Differentiating Among Learning Problems   271
  Keeping Learning Disabilities in Perspective   272
  A Causal Continuum   273
Reconceiving and Expanding Intervention   275
  Motivation as a Primary Concern   275
  A Societal Approach   277
  Integrating Programs in a Catchment Area   280
Accountability and Change   280
  Accountability and Evaluative Research   280
  The Problem of Change   281
Summing Up   282

CHAPTER 14   *Use What You Have Learned*   284

PART 5   *READ MORE ABOUT IT*   288

SECTION I   *On Learning Disabilities*   290

I.1 Learning Disabilities in Historical Perspective   291
*I.2 CNS Function and Assessment of Minor Dysfunction
  Environment   304*
I.3 Controversial Treatments and Fads   309
I.4 Remedying Learning Disabilities: Prevailing Approaches   314
I.5 Screening for Learning Disabilities   323
*I.6 Assessment for Learning Disabilities' Diagnosis, Placement, and
  Program Planning   328*

SECTION II   *On Assessment Tools and Technical Concerns*   340

II.1 Procedures and Instruments for Assessing Learning Problems   341
II.2 Technical Concerns About Assessment   349

SECTION III   *On Teaching*   354

III.1 Theories of Instruction and Models of Teaching   355
III.2 Enhancing Motivation and Skills in Social Functioning   362
III.3 Intrinsic Motivation and School Misbehavior   365
*III.4 Learner Options and Decision Making to Enhance Motivation and
  Learning   369*
III.5 Fernald's Techniques in their Motivational Context   380

SECTION IV   *On the Individual and Society*   **390**

    IV.1 Ethical Concerns About Negative Effects   391

    IV.2 Whose Interests Are Being Served?   395

    IV.3 Toward Services with an Informed Consumer Orientation   400

    IV.4 Involving Parents in Schooling   410

    IV.5 Social Control   413

    IV.6 Cultural and Individual Differences as Barriers to Working Relationships   418

    IV.7 Managing and Preventing School Misbehavior   422

References   431
Name Index   463
Subject Index   471

Learning Problems and Learning Disabilities

What the best and wisest parent wants for his own child
that must the community want for all of its children.
Any other idea . . . is narrow and unlovely.

Dewey (1966, p. 7)

A s we have seen in Part 1, interventions for learning problems range from prevention programs to highly specialized placements and treatments. The concept of intervention includes assessment and referral activities and, along the way, some of this activity results in a diagnosis of learning disability.

Just as professionals differ in how they approach the matter of cause, they differ in their orientations to intervention. In Part 2 and the related readings, ideas that shape the nature and scope of intervention are reviewed. First we highlight the general nature of intervention, specifically emphasizing contemporary approaches and dominant orientations relevant to learning problems. This provides a broad introduction to basic concepts about intervention, including assessment. Then follows a more detailed discussion of assessment and the range of available programs. Chapter 4 explores prevailing approaches to assessing learning problems, with a specific focus on (a) the many facets of assessment activity, (b) concerns and limitations related to prevailing practices, and (c) recent efforts to go beyond conventional approaches. Then in Chapter 5 we offer a perspective on the range of programs available from preschool through adulthood.

Permeating all interventions for learning problems are fundamental concerns about informed consent, due process, and conflicts of interest. Chapter 6 introduces these topics in relation to the decision to intervene. Finally, we explore ideas for broadening the focus of contemporary intervention practices.

As you proceed, remember your objective is to understand both what is commonly done and how current practices can evolve to make intervention more effective.

CHAPTER 1

Introductory Perspectives

Learning Problems or Learning Disabilities?

What Is a Learning Disability?

Controversy Over Characteristics

Controversy Over Definitions

Placing Learning Disabilities in Perspective

Learning Problems as the Context for Understanding Learning Disabilities

Learning and Teaching as the Context for Understanding Learning Problems

Society as the Context for Teaching and Learning

Type I, II, and III Problems

Moving Forward

Forward to Basics

Toward a Comprehensive Approach

Summing Up

Someone is in trouble . . .

At school each day the words go by,
* too quickly to make sense.*
So attention turns from reading
* to avoidance, pain, pretense.*

Learning Problems or Learning Disabilities?

When someone has trouble learning, it is tempting to describe the person as having a learning disability. But not all learning problems are learning disabilities. Let us introduce you to David, James, Matt, and Mara. They are composites of individuals we have encountered over the years. We will refer to them many times throughout this book.

DAVID

To hear his parents tell the story, having David diagnosed as learning disabled was almost as bad as finding that he had a fatal disease. They were horrified.

David entered kindergarten at age five with the same eagerness and cheerfulness his older brother and sister had shown. There was no question in anyone's mind about his future. There would be kindergarten, followed by brief hitches in elementary and secondary school, honors at a good university, and finally a profession.

By the end of second grade, however, the family's expectations were changing. David was still a nonreader. He hated school. His teacher described him as her worst behavior problem. He was tested by a school psychologist, who diagnosed him as learning disabled.

What had happened to David's eagerness and promise? What convinced the psychologist that he was learning disabled? Could the problem be corrected? What about his future?

JAMES

"We adopted James — a beautiful child, with curly hair and flawless skin — when he was 5. Clearly he had been hurt by the loss of his parents and two years in foster homes. When first approached, he had a look of fear like that of a frightened animal.

After a few months, James seemed to adjust well to his new home, and we all grew to love each other. While quieter than Jenny, our 8-year-old, he joined in all activities readily and ably.

We enrolled James in school when he was 6. School brought the challenge of letters and numbers, and a new identity: learning disabled. At first we were shocked. We had seen no signs of learning problems at home. We wondered if it could be an emotional reaction. The tests apparently indicated a perceptual-motor problem and other signs of neurological dys-

(continued)

JAMES (continued)

function. We decided we would do everything we could to help him overcome his handicap.

For the next six years, James had special tutoring and support at school. It helped, but not enough to let him catch up with the others. Teacher after teacher described him as immature, impulsive, and easily distracted or confused. By the time he got to junior high, James was convinced he couldn't do it. Gradually the self-doubt led to frustration and then to anger. He lashed out at everyone. Soon he was in trouble with the law—stealing, fighting, hitting a teacher, doing drugs.

As soon as he was 16, James dropped out of school. They were glad to see him go."

James is now 18. He works when and where he can. He's worried about his future. So are we.

MATT

I am 13 years old and learning
disabled. I have had problems along time.
People say I am smart but I lak eny
ability and I am tired of trying.
My parrents tryed to help me,
but I dont deserve there support
or concern, I am just not worth
it. I do not get allong with
people eneywhere and never have been
able to. I am affraid of every one
and hate being told to wake up
or come out of my dreemworld.
I dont know how to deel with
eneything eneywhere.

MARA

Jack Floyd, M.D.
10 Main Street
Bryant, Arizona

Re: Mara Jackson
Age 8 yrs.

Dear Jack:

Thank you for referring Mara for a psychological evaluation.

My full report is attached. By way of summary, I met with her and her mother on January 5 and 6. First I interviewed Mrs. Jackson, who reported that Mara was suffering from reading and writing difficulties and poor coordination. The mother thinks Mara is simply lazy but wonders about the possibility of some sort of disability. Apparently Mara tends to be argumentative at home, especially with her younger brother. She is described as having a strong personality and as being quite a "stinker" at times. She also apparently can be quite affectionate.

With regard to past problems, the mother states there were no special traumas, physical or emotional, except that Mara has appeared to be somewhat upset by her father's frequent business trips. Since you have an extensive file on her developmental, medical, and family history, there is no need to review such matters here.

The school history is checkered. She went to preschool at 3½ with no reported difficulties. In kindergarten she was in continual conflict with her teacher, but in first grade the teacher apparently worked very well with Mara. Second grade, and now the first half of third grade, have been almost complete disasters. Besides poor academic performance, she has gotten into frequent fights and often refuses to go to school.

To assess the nature of Mara's problems, I administered a psychological test battery consisting of the Wechsler Intelligence test (WISC-III), the Woodcock-Johnson Psychoeducational Battery, the Goldman-Fristoe-Woodcock Test of Auditory Discrimination, the Bender Visual-Motor Gestalt Test, and several personality tests—and I made some observations while interacting informally with her in the play room. My conclusions are as follows:

Mara is a nice-looking girl of average height and weight. She entered the test situation somewhat apprehensively, but I was able to calm her anxiety and get her focused on the tasks with little difficulty. She performed in the average range on the IQ test, with some unevenness in her performance on both the verbal and nonverbal subtests. Her achievement scores were at the first-grade level, and it is therefore not surprising she is having difficulty at school. The pattern of her performance leads me to a diagnosis of learning disabilities and to recommend special remedial help as soon as possible. In this connection, I have given the mother the names of several agencies and private tutors. Since Mara also shows signs of emotional upset and seems to have an intensive rivalry with her younger brother, I also recommended they be separated as much as possible and that family counseling be pursued.

Mara should have the benefit of retesting in about a year to evaluate progress.

Thanks again for the referral.

Sincerely yours,

George P. Blanc, Ph.D.
Licensed Psychologist

What Is a Learning Disability?

Obviously, David, James, Matt, and Mara have problems—but should their problems with learning be called learning disabilities? Although this may seem like an easy question, every effort to answer it has given rise to controversy.

Controversy Over Characteristics

If you know anyone who has been diagnosed as learning disabled, you probably have wondered about the symptoms of learning disabilities. Like David, James, Matt, and Mara, such people clearly have trouble learning certain things—but so do people without learning disabilities. These four individuals may be immature, disorganized, impulsive, distractible, inflexible, or awkward—but so are people who do not have learning disabilities. They may be hyperactive, emotionally upset, and generally disruptive—but so are many people who have no problem learning. Which characteristics are unique to learning disabilities?

Lists of characteristics or symptoms of learning disabilities have been distributed widely by learning disability organizations, and they frequently turn up in popular magazines. Such lists are based on early descriptive studies and summaries (see Feature 1-1).

One characteristic of persons currently in programs for learning disabilities that is not found in nonlearning-problem populations is *severe academic underachievement.* As outlined in the United States' federal regulations, this "characteristic" is the major inclusive criterion for identifying specific learning disabilities.

A team may determine that a child has a specific learning disability if: (1) the child does not achieve commensurate with his or her age and ability levels in one or more areas [seven of which are specified—oral or written expression, listening comprehension, basic reading skill or comprehension, mathematics calculation or reasoning] when provided with learning experiences appropriate for the child's age and ability levels; and (2) the team finds that a child has a severe discrepancy between achievement and intellectual ability in one or more of [these] areas. (*Federal Register,* 1977, p. 65083)

How severe the discrepancy between achievement and intellectual ability must be and how it should be measured are difficult questions. Think about two individuals, both one year below grade level in reading as measured by a standard achievement test. If one of them has a very high IQ and the other a very low IQ, do both have a severe discrepancy? What if they both have an average IQ, but one is in the ninth grade and the other is in the second grade?

A variety of formulas have been proposed to deal with the problem of defining a severe discrepancy. None has found wide acceptance, however, and specific procedures and criteria for determining a severe discrepancy continue to vary from one locale to another.

One problem hindering research on characteristics and specific symptoms is the disagreement among experts as to what a learning disability is. The term has been used for persons whose learning problems have very different causes and whose remedial needs differ greatly. Programs serving the "learning disabled" often contain persons with so many different types of learning problems that the main thing these individuals have in common is that they do not perform well in learning situations. In such programs, one can find almost every characteristic described so far.

Controversy Over Definitions

Ever since the term *learning disabilities* was popularized in the early 1960s, there has been controversy over how it should be defined (see Feature 1-2). The definition proposed by the National Advisory Committee on Handicapped Children was given official status throughout the United States when it was incorporated

Feature 1-1   Controversy Over Characteristics

Textbooks, journal articles, and organizations concerned with learning disabilities, as well as articles in magazines and newspapers, frequently offer lists of characteristics and symptoms. The sources for such lists are descriptive studies and expert opinion. All such lists are controversial.

One of the most widely cited early listings was generated by a government-sponsored task force in the 1960s (Clements, 1966). After reviewing the many and varied descriptions cited in the literature, the panel of experts identified ten characteristics it viewed as general symptoms: (1) hyperactivity, (2) perceptual-motor impairments, (3) emotional lability, (4) general coordination defects, (5) disorders of attention, (6) impulsivity, (7) disorders of memory and thinking, (8) specific learning disabilities, (9) disorders of speech and hearing, (10) equivocal neurological signs and encephalographic irregularities.

Because the above list is so abstract and general, subsequent lists have tended to itemize specific problem behaviors and present them as symptoms. Examples include:

1. reversals of letters, words, and numbers (called *strephosymbolia*, which means "twisted symbols")
2. mistakes in identifying left and right
3. not having well-established preferences when using one's hands and feet (often called *laterality* or *mixed dominance problems*)

4. clumsiness
5. writing illegibly
6. difficulty blending speech sounds
7. leaving out or adding speech sounds
8. difficulty with abstractions
9. high degree of activity or agitation (often called *hyperactivity*)

Clearly, these characteristics indicate problems that should not be ignored. Moreover, such characteristics are frequently found among people with learning problems. But, there is no evidence to support the view that these are symptoms that differentiate learning disabilities from other types of learning problems.

Controversy will continue until well-designed studies clarify which characteristics and symptoms are unique to persons with learning disabilities. In the 1980s, research underscored but did not resolve the controversy (for example, Cone, Wilson, Bradley, & Reese, 1985; Fuerst, Fisk, & Rourke, 1989; Keogh, Major-Kingsley, Omori-Gordon, & Reid, 1982; Kirk & Chalfant, 1984; Lyon, 1985; Lyon & Flynn, 1991; McKinney, 1988, 1989; Shepard, Smith, & Vojir, 1983). Future research must focus not only on persons at specific ages with and without learning problems but also must differentiate learning disabilities from other types of learning problems and then clarify specific subtypes.

(with minor modifications) into federal legislation in 1969. As stated in federal statute (U.S. Public Law 94-142—the Education for All Handicapped Children Act of 1975), individuals with specific learning disabilities are those who have

a disorder in one or more of the basic psychological processes involved in understanding or in using language, spoken or written, which may manifest itself in an imperfect ability to listen, think, speak, read, write, spell, or to do mathematical calculations. The term includes such conditions as perceptual handicaps, brain injury, minimal brain dysfunction, dyslexia, and developmental aphasia. The term does not include children who have learning problems which are primarily the result of visual, hearing, or motor handicaps, of mental retardation, or emotional disturbance, or of environmental, cultural, or economic disadvantage. (*Federal Register,* 1977, p. 65083)

Feature 1-2   *Popularizing "Learning Disabilities": Historical Note*

In the 1960s, the term *learning disabilities* began to take the place of such terms as "minimal brain damage," "minimal cerebral dysfunction," "perceptual impairment," "neurological handicap," and "learning disorders." William Cruickshank (Cruickshank, Bentzen, Ratzeburg, & Tannhauser, 1961) and Samuel Kirk (1962) usually are credited with starting the trend toward widespread use of the term *learning disabilities.*

As related by Kirk and Gallagher (1979, p. 287):

The term *learning disability* became popular when the Association for Children with Learning Disabilities (ACLD) was organized under the name in 1963. During the period just prior to that, parents throughout the United States became concerned because their children who were not learning in school were rejected from special education since they were not mentally retarded, deaf or blind, or otherwise handicapped. Local parent groups were organized. Parent-sponsored schools were initiated. They were called by different names such as schools for the neurologically handicapped, brain injured, aphasoid, dyslexic, and perceptually handicapped. Parent organizations met in Chicago in 1963 to discuss their mutual problems, one of which was the need for a national organization and an appropriate name.

Discussing the problem and the difficulties of labels for these children, Kirk (1962) explained that sometimes classification labels block out thinking. It is better, he told the conference, to state that a child has not learned to read than to say the child is dyslexic. He continued that it may be more scientific to say "a child has not learned to talk" than to say the child is aphasic or brain injured. He advised that a name should be functional and that if the parents were interested in research on the relation of the brain to behavior, they could use a neurological term. He suggested further that if they were interested in service to their children, it might be preferable to use a term related to teaching or learning and that a term such as *learning disability* might be preferable to some currently used terms such as *cerebral dysfunction* or *brain injured.*

The term *learning disabilities* struck a receptive chord with the parent groups since it implied teaching and learning and since they were interested primarily in service for their children. They selected the name Association for Children with Learning Disabilities, and from that point on, learning disabilities became a new category of exceptional children and crept into federal, state, and local legislation.

While useful for legislative purposes, this definition has been criticized since it was first proposed. In particular: (1) Use of the term *children* was seen as inappropriately excluding adolescents and adults; (2) the phrase *basic psychological processes* was seen as too vague and became the focus of debates between advocates of direct instruction and those concerned with treating underlying processing disabilities; (3) the list of inclusive conditions (for example, perceptual handicaps, minimal brain dysfunction) was seen as out-dated and ill-defined; and (4) the "exclusion" clause was seen as contributing to misconceptions (that is, that learning disabilities cannot occur in conjunction with other handicapping conditions, or environmental, cultural, or economic disadvantage).

Controversy over the federal definition has led to proposals for a revised definition. Two prominent examples are seen in the products of the National Joint Committee for Learning Disabilities (Hammill, Leigh, McNutt, & Larsen, 1981) and the Association for Children and Adults with Learning Disabilities — now called the Learning Disabilities Association of America (Association for Children with Learning Disabilities, 1985). After a series of compromises, the revised version circulated by the National Joint Committee for Learning Disabilities (NJCLD) has been most publicized. As finalized in 1989, that definition reads:

> Learning disabilities is a general term that refers to a heterogeneous group of disorders manifested by significant difficulties in the acquisition and use of listening, speaking, reading, writing, reasoning, or mathematical abilities. These disorders are intrinsic to the individual, presumed to be due to a central nervous system dysfunction, and may occur across the life span. Problems in self-regulatory behaviors, social perception, and social interactions may exist with learning disabilities but do not by themselves constitute a learning disability. Although learning disabilities may occur concomitantly with other handicapping conditions (for example, sensory impairment, mental retardation, serious emotional disturbance) or with extrinsic influences (such as cultural differences, insufficient or inappropriate instruction), they are not the result of those conditions or influences.

Learning Disabilities in Historical Perspective (p. 291) includes further discussion about the problem of defining learning disabilities and a phrase-by-phrase analysis of the rationale underlying the NJCLD definition.

While addressing criticisms inherent in the federal definition, the NJCLD's definition has also sparked controversy. In particular, the statement that the problem is "presumed to be due to a central nervous system dysfunction" has not pleased those who want the term *learning disabilities* applied to any factor that produces inefficient learning. It should be emphasized, however, that the field of learning disabilities essentially was created to address learning problems caused by a central nervous system (CNS) dysfunction. Moreover, when there has been movement away from tying learning disabilities to CNS dysfunctioning, the term has been overused to the point where it is applied to almost any type of learning problem.

For example, a study by Shepard and Smith (1983) found that only 28 percent of those diagnosed and placed in learning disability programs met stringent criteria for learning disabilities. Another 15 percent were seen as meeting weak criteria. The remaining 57 percent appeared to be misdiagnosed (for example, the students were slow learners, nonfluent in English, had minor behavior problems, or manifested other handicapping conditions).

Despite its limitations, the federal definition has been defended as useful in meeting the educational needs of large numbers of students with severe learning problems. Certainly, the definition has been used effectively to justify funds for programs for many who otherwise might not have received special services.

However, while we want to give special help to those who need it, we cannot ignore the fact that their learning problems undoubtedly resulted from many different causes. The tendency to ignore this fact has resulted in a ludicrous situation where estimates of the prevalence of learning disabilities range from zero to 70 percent (see Feature 1-3). Another result has been to compromise the integrity of research and practice.

As long as some people think there is no such thing as a learning disability and others use the term to label every learning problem, confusion and controversy will reign (Swanson, 1991). It is time to move forward, putting learning

Feature 1-3   How Many People Have Learning Disabilities?

Some experts believe that no more than 1 percent of the school population really have learning disabilities. Using expert estimates, the U.S. Department of Education initially used a 3 percent figure in making policy decisions. But sometimes figures as high as 30 percent of all students are cited. In a study of expert opinion, estimates of prevalence ranged from zero to 70 percent, most respondents giving figures between zero and 3 percent (Tucker, Stevens, & Ysseldyke, 1983).

Why the different estimates? Mostly it is because different definitions and criteria are used in identifying people as having learning disabilities.

Although there is no consensus on how many people should be so identified, at least we have some figures for discussing how many currently are. Not surprisingly, the trend was for the numbers to increase very rapidly after government funding for learning disabilities became available. Shortly after the passage of legislation in the United States in 1969, 120,000 students were identified as having learning disabilities; by 1970, the figure rose to 648,000 (Grant & Lund, 1977). Federal government figures are available for 1976 through 1987 to show how many individuals

(ages 3 to 21) received special services for learning disabilities. Over the years, there was an increase from 797,212 to 1,926,097 (U.S. Department of Education, 1988). This last figure represents 4.8 percent of the total school population, preschool through twelfth grade.

The 1988 National Health Interview Survey of Child Health, conducted by the National Center for Health Statistics, presents data from parents in the United States. Findings indicate 6.5 percent of all children aged 3 to 17 were reported as having learning disabilities and 5.5 percent of those between 6 and 17 years old were reported as attending special classes or schools because of their learning disabilities (Zill & Schoenborn, 1990).

Recent figures indicate that the number diagnosed has gone far beyond the figures projected in the 1960s and 1970s. The fact is that, in a relatively short period, those diagnosed as having learning disabilities have become by far the largest percentage of students currently in special education programs. As might be expected, these trends not only have raised concerns but have also resulted in calls for policies and practices to reserve the most costly services for those with the most severe problems.

disabilities firmly into perspective as one type of learning problem and approaching all learning problems in the context of fundamental ideas about learning and teaching.

Placing Learning Disabilities in Perspective

Although reliable data do not exist, most would agree that at least 30 percent of the public school population in the United States have learning problems. Throughout this book, we approach the field of learning disabilities with that large group in mind, and we limit the term *learning disabilities* to one specific subtype found among the larger group.

Moreover, we consider all learning problems in the context of basic ideas about learning and teaching. We believe that to move forward in dealing with all learning problems requires a fundamental appreciation of how to foster learning among persons with and without internal disabilities. And, because sociopolitical and economic factors have such a pervasive influence on learning and teaching, we approach these topics within a societal context.

Learning Problems as the Context for Understanding Learning Disabilities

There are valid reasons for wanting to differentiate among individuals who have learning problems. One reason is that some learning problems can be prevented; another is that some learning problems are much easier to overcome than others. However, differentiating is not easy. As noted earlier, severity is the most common factor used to differentiate learning disabilities from all other learning problems. However, there is also a tendency to rely heavily on how far an individual lags, not only in reading, but also in other academic skills. Thus, besides severity, there is concern about how pervasive the problem is. Specific criteria for judging severity and pervasiveness depend on prevailing age, gender, subculture, and social-status expectations. Also important is how long the problem has persisted.

In the final analysis, the case for learning disabilities as a special type of learning problem is made from the perspective of learning problems in general. Throughout the book, we maintain this perspective in discussing cause, assessment, correction, and prevention.

Learning and Teaching as the Context for Understanding Learning Problems

Although learning is not limited to any time or place, problems in learning are recognized most often in the classroom. Why do people have so many learning problems? What can we do to make things better? We need to understand both the factors that lead to learning and those that interfere with it. One critical set of such factors has to do with teaching, both in and out of schools.

From the perspective of learning and teaching, another way to differentiate among learning problems is to identify those caused primarily because of the way things are taught. Given that there are schooling-caused learning problems, they ought to be differentiated from those caused by central nervous system dysfunctioning (that is, learning disabilities). When we do this, it becomes clear that the prevention of some learning problems requires changing some school practices. Individuals with learning disabilities may require something more in the way of help.

We hasten to add that the fundamentals of teaching apply in helping anyone with a learning problem. Moreover, quality teaching can be seen as providing a necessary context for approaching all learning problems. And excellence in teaching is best understood in the context of how people learn.

As Jerome Bruner (1966) has stated: "The single most characteristic thing about human beings is that they learn." This is not to say that all learning is the result of direct teaching. High-quality teaching encourages learning beyond that which can take place during any lesson.

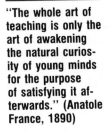

"The whole art of teaching is only the art of awakening the natural curiosity of young minds for the purpose of satisfying it afterwards." (Anatole France, 1890)

For individuals with severe learning problems, an important key to overcoming their problems is pursuit of learning outside of the teaching situation. Poor readers, for example, are unlikely to become good readers if the only time they read is during reading instruction. Throughout this book, basic ideas about learning and teaching provide the context for discussing learning problems in general and learning disabilities in particular. A specific focus is on what mobilizes and maintains an individual's pursuit of learning.

Society as the Context for Teaching and Learning

Education is a social invention. All societies design schools in the service of social, cultural, political, and economic aims (Coles, 1987; Hurn, 1985; Tyack, 1979). Concomitantly, socialization is the aim of a significant portion of the teaching done by parents and other individuals who shape the lives of children. This is especially the case for populations labeled as problems. Because society has such a stake in teaching and learning, it is critical to discuss these topics within a societal context.

Society shapes the content and context of teaching, the definition of learning problems, and the way teachers are held accountable for outcomes. The field of learning disabilities exemplifies these points. It was created and is maintained through political processes (see Feature 1-2). Prevailing definitions and prominently proposed revisions are generated through political compromises. Guidelines for differentiating learning disabilities from other learning problems, for planning what students are taught, and for evaluating what they learn—all are established through political processes.

Moreover, as Nicholas Hobbs (1975a) has stated:

> Society defines what is exceptional or deviant, and appropriate treatments are designed quite as much to protect society as they are to help the child. . . . "To take care of them" can and should be read with two meanings: to give children help and to exclude them from the community. (pp. 20–21)

Inevitably, exploration of teaching and learning and of learning problems and disabilities touches upon education and training, helping and socializing, democracy and autocracy. Schools, in particular, are places where choices about each of these matters arise daily. The decisions made often result in controversy.

It is only through understanding the role society plays in shaping teaching practices and research that a full appreciation of the limits and the possibilities of ameliorating learning problems can be attained. Thus, we try to maintain a societal perspective throughout this book.

Type I, II, and III Problems

In most cases, it is impossible to be certain what the cause of a specific individual's learning problem might be. Nevertheless, from a theoretical viewpoint it makes sense to think of learning problems as caused by different factors. (This is discussed in detail in Chapter 2.)

By way of introduction, think about a random sample of students for whom learning problems are the *primary* problem (that is, the learning problem is not the result of seeing or hearing impairments, severe mental retardation, severe emotional disturbances, or autism). What makes it difficult for them to learn? Theoretically, at least, it is reasonable to speculate that some may have a relatively *minor* internal disorder causing a *minor* central nervous system (CNS) dysfunction that makes learning difficult even under good teaching circumstances. These are individuals for whom the term *learning disabilities* was created. In differentiating them from those with other types of learning problems, it may help if you visualize learning disabilities as being at one end of a learning problems continuum. We call this group Type III learning problems.

At the other end of the continuum are individuals with learning problems that arise from causes outside the person. Such problems should not be called learning disabilities. Obviously, some people do not learn well when a learning situation is not a good one. It is not surprising that a large number of students who live in poverty and attend overcrowded schools manifest learning and psychosocial problems. Problems that are primarily the result of deficiencies in the environment in which learning takes place can be thought of as Type I learning problems.

To provide a reference point in the middle of the continuum, we can conceive of a Type II learning problem group. This group consists of persons who do not learn or perform well in situations where their individual differences and vulnerabilities are poorly accommodated or are responded to with hostility. The learning problems of an individual in this group can be seen as a relatively equal product of the person's characteristics and the failure of the learning and teaching environment to accommodate to that individual.

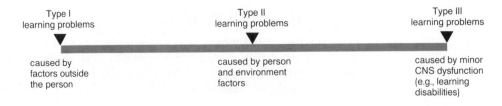

Failure to differentiate learning disabilities from other types of learning problems has caused a great deal of confusion and controversy. Currently, almost any individual with a learning problem stands a good chance of being diagnosed as having learning disabilities. As a result, many who do not have disabilities are treated as if the cause of their problems was some form of personal pathology. This leads to prescriptions of unneeded treatments for nonexistent internal dysfunctions. It also interferes with efforts to clarify which interventions do and do not show promise for ameliorating different types of learning problems. Ultimately, keeping learning disabilities in proper perspective is essential to improving both research and practice. Therefore, throughout the text, we use the term *learning problems* to encompass the full continuum of learning problems and limit the term *learning disabilities* to Type III problems.

Moving Forward

Besides maintaining a broad perspective on learning problems, it is essential to design interventions that move forward (not backward) to basics and move toward comprehensive and integrated programs.

Forward to Basics

Every time a new report is published on the deficiencies of public education there is a call to go "back to basics." The problem with this recipe for improving education is that, while basics are essential, it would be a mistake to go back to old ideas about teaching that weren't very effective in the first place (such as an overemphasis on rote learning and practice). Good teaching involves accommodating a wide range of individual and subgroup differences, strategies that make skill learning meaningful, and the ability to bring subject matter to life.

Furthermore, it is important not to limit one's view of basics to reading, writing, and arithmetic. Today's complex world requires additional basic skills, especially the abilities to solve problems and to interact effectively with others.

People such as David, James, Matt, and Mara need programs that are built on a foundation of forward-looking views about how and what to teach with respect to learning problems in general and learning disabilities in particular. To these ends, this book stresses such ideas as the importance of matching motivation and development, providing a comprehensive curriculum, enhancing and expanding intrinsic motivation, overcoming avoidance motivation, practicing least-intervention teaching, personalizing classroom instruction, and approaching remediation from a sequential and hierarchical perspective.

Toward a Comprehensive Approach

Another aspect of moving forward is to ensure that society's approach to learning problems is a comprehensive one. This involves policies that create a full continuum of programs—ranging from prevention to treatment of chronic problems (see

Figure 1-1   *From Prevention to Treatment: A Continuum of Programs for Learning, Behavior, and Socioemotional Problems*

Intervention Continuum	Types of Activities
Prevention	1. Primary prevention to promote and maintain safety and health
	2. Preschool programs
Early-age intervention	3. Early school adjustment
	4. Improvement of ongoing regular support
Early-after-onset intervention	5. Augmentation of regular support
	6. Specialized staff development and interventions prior to referral for special education and other intensive treatments
Treatment for chronic problems	7. System changes and intensive treatment

Figure 1-1) and procedures that tie the programs together so they can function in a coordinated and integrated way.

To date, there have been experimental demonstrations of promising programs at every level of the continuum represented in Figure 1-1. However, each program exists as an independent entity; that is, the approach is a piecemeal one. As a result, there is no place where the full continuum has been pursued in an integrated way.

To ensure that a comprehensive approach is appreciated, we highlight a full range of programs and suggest ways to move forward toward an integrated approach.

Summing Up

Discussions of learning problems and disabilities are inevitably plagued by confusion and controversy. This occurs because professionals disagree about how to define the various types of learning problems and how to differentiate among them in practice. This state of affairs has restricted progress in creating effective approaches to helping those who need it.

With a view to accelerating progress, we have adopted a broad perspective of learning problems in which persons with learning disabilities are viewed as one group among several placed on a learning problems continuum. Along the continuum, Type I learning problems are conceived as caused by factors outside the person; Type II learning problems are seen as caused by the interaction of factors outside the person and individual differences and vulnerabilities; Type III learning problems are defined as caused by minor central nervous system dysfunctioning and as warranting the term *learning disabilities.*

We have also adopted a perspective that approaches all learning problems from the context of basic ideas about learning and teaching and that recognizes their societal context. In doing so, we want to convey a forward-looking and comprehensive orientation for understanding the causes of learning problems and to suggest strategies for prevention and treatment.

Chapter 2 presents a look at causes.

Do you, or does anyone you know, have a learning problem?

If so, jot down a brief description of what you know about the problem. If you don't know such an individual or are uncertain about how to proceed with your description, answer the following questions from general information you have acquired about learning problems.

1. Who first identified the problem, and on what basis?
2. Does the person have learning problems in all situations or just in certain situations related to specific types of learning?
3. Are there alternative explanations for the person's problems other than that the individual has a disability?
4. If not, what is the evidence for the belief that there is a disability?
5. If the individual has behavioral or emotional problems as well as a learning problem, are the problems seen as separate or related?

Learning Disabilities in Historical Perspective (p. 291) To keep learning disabilities in proper perspective as one type of learning problem, it is helpful to understand the roots of what has become known as the LD field. Therefore, we have included an overview of the LD field's evolution and a compilation of comments from a survey of prominent LD professionals about the field's future.

Specific topics covered are:

- phases of the field's development
- intervention strategies
- parent and professional organizations
- legislation
- litigation
- the changing sociopolitical climate
- the ongoing controversy over definitions
- future directions for theory, research, practice, and training

Causes

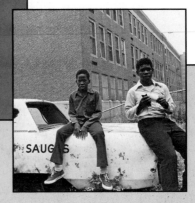

The Problem of Compelling Clues

Errors in Logic

Causes and Correlates

Causal Models

Human Functioning: A Transactional Model

The Transactional Model as an Umbrella

Behaviorist Perspectives on Cause

Learning Problems: The Common Case

The Special Case of Learning Disabilities

Factors Causing Central Nervous System Problems

How the CNS Is Affected and Learning Is Disrupted

Learning and Behavior Problems

Summing Up

*In the last analysis, we see only what
we are ready to see. We eliminate
and ignore everything that is not part
of our prejudices.*

Charcot (1857)

What causes learning problems in general, and learning disabilities in particular? In this chapter, we look first at the problem of understanding cause and effect and at general models that shape thinking about the causes of human behavior. Then, using a broad model, we explore the causes of Type I, II, and III learning problems.

The Problem of Compelling Clues

At one time there was a tribe of South Pacific Islanders who believed that lice were responsible for keeping a person healthy (Chase, 1956). They noticed that almost all the healthy people in the tribe had lice, while those who were sick had no lice. Thus it seemed reasonable to them that lice cause good health.

A teacher-in-training, working with children who have learning problems, notices that most of them are easily distracted and more fidgety than students without learning problems. They are also less likely to listen or to do assignments well, and they often flit from one thing to another. The new teacher concludes that there is something physically wrong with these youngsters.

Every day we puzzle over our experiences and, in trying to make sense of them, arrive at conclusions about what caused them to happen. It is a very basic and useful part of human nature for people to try to understand cause and effect. Unfortunately, sometimes we are wrong. The South Pacific Islanders didn't know that sick people usually have a high fever, and, since lice do not like the higher temperature, they jump off!

The teacher-in-training is right in thinking that some children with learning problems may have a physical condition that makes it hard for them to pay attention. However, further training and experience will show that there are a significant number of students whose attention problems stem from a lack of interest, or from the belief that they really can't do the work, or from any number of other psychological factors.

Errors in Logic

Because it is so compelling to look for causes, and because people so often make errors in doing so, logicians and scientists have spent a lot of time discussing the problem. For example, logicians have pointed out the fallacy of assuming (as the Islanders did) that one event (lice) caused another (good health) just because the first event preceded the second. We make this type of error every time we *presume* that a person's learning problems are due to a difficult birth, a divorce, poor nutrition, or other factors that preceded the learning problem.

Another kind of logical error occurs when one event may affect another, but only in a minor way, as part of a much more complicated set of events. There is a tendency to think people who behave nicely have been brought up well by their parents. We all know, however, of cases in which the parents' actions seem to have very little to do with their child's behavior. This can be especially true of teenagers, who are strongly influenced by their friends.

When I read the obituary column, I wonder why people always seem to die in alphabetical order.

A third logical error arises when two events repeatedly occur together. After awhile, it can become impossible to tell whether one causes the other or whether both are caused by something else. For instance, frequently children with learning problems also have behavior problems. Did the learning problem cause the behavior problem? Did the behavior problem cause the learning problem? Did poor parenting, or poor teaching, or poor peer models cause both the learning and behavior problems? The longer these problems exist, the harder it is to know.

Causes and Correlates

In trying to understand learning problems, researchers and practitioners look for all sorts of clues, or correlates. When faced with compelling clues, it is important to understand the difference between causes and correlates. *Correlates* are simply events that have some relation to each other: lice and good health, no lice and sickness, learning and behavior problems. A *cause* and its effect show a special type of correlation, one in which the nature of the relationship is known. Some events that occur together (that is, are correlates) fit so well with "common sense" that we are quick to believe they are cause and effect. However, we may overlook other factors important to understanding the actual connection.

Some correlates are particularly compelling because they fit with current theories, attitudes, or policies. In general, once a problem is seen as severe enough to require referral for treatment, any other problem or unusual characteristic or circumstance attracts attention. Often these other problems, characteristics, or circumstances seem to be connected by some cause-effect relationship. The more intuitively logical the connection, the harder it is to understand that they may not be causally related. They are compelling clues, but they may be misleading.

Causal Models

Many factors shape thinking about human behavior and learning and the problems individuals experience. It helps to begin with a broad transactional view, such as currently prevails in psychological theory.

Human Functioning: A Transactional Model

Before the 1920s, psychology was dominated by models of human behavior that viewed the determinants of learning primarily as a function of a person (for example, the characteristics with which the individual was born). With the rise of behaviorism, there was a model shift that emphasized the determinants primarily as a function of the environment (for example, the stimuli and reinforcers one encountered).

Times have changed. The prevailing model for understanding human functioning today is a transactional view that emphasizes the reciprocal interplay of person and environment. This view is sometimes referred to as *reciprocal determinism* (Bandura, 1978).

Let's apply a transactional model to a learning situation. In teaching a lesson, the teacher will find that some students learn easily, and some do not. Even a good student may appear distracted on a given day.

Why the differences?

A commonsense answer suggests that each student brings something different to the situation and therefore experiences it differently. And that's a pretty good answer—as far as it goes. What gets lost in this simple explanation is the nature of the differences and the fact that each student is continuously changing and so is the situation and that the changes influence each other.

Essentially, a learner brings to a learning situation both

- *capacities and attitudes* that have been accumulated over time, and
- *current states of being and behaving.*

These transact with each other and also with the learning environment.

The learning environment consists not only of

- *instructional processes and content,* but also
- *the physical and social context* in which instruction takes place.

Each part of the environment also transacts with the others.

The outcome of all these transactions may be positive learning or learning problems. Because the nature of the transactions can vary considerably, so can the outcomes. In general, the types of outcomes can be described as:

- deviant learning—capacities and attitudes change and expand, but not in desirable ways

I WISH I HAD ASKED MORE QUESTIONS WHEN I WAS YOUR AGE.

HOW COME?

SO I COULD ANSWER MORE OF YOURS.

- disrupted learning—interference with learning and possibly a decrease in capacities
- delayed and arrested learning—little change in capacities
- enhanced learning—capacities and attitudes change and expand in desirable ways

The Transactional Model as an Umbrella

Professionals working with individuals who have learning problems tend to use models that view the cause of an individual's problems as either within the person or coming from the environment. Actually, two person-oriented models have been discussed widely: (1) the disordered or "ill" person, the medical model; and (2) the slow-maturation model. In contrast, the environment model has emphasized the notions of inadequate and pathological environments. We will discuss each of these views later in the chapter.

It has long seemed strange to us that the prevailing view of behavior and learning reflects a transactional model, while the view of problems remains dominated by person or environment models. We are not suggesting that these models always lead to wrong conclusions. As indicated in Chapter 1, some individuals' problems are due primarily to something wrong within them, and other people do have problems because of factors they encounter in their environment. But what about those whose problems stem from both sources?

It might seem reasonable to continue to use person models and environment models and simply add the transactional model to cover those cases where problems stem from both person and environment. However, a transactional view encompasses the other models and provides the kind of comprehensive perspective needed to differentiate among learning problems.

Think again about a continuum of Type I, II, and III learning problems. This time we'll add the locus of *cause*—the primary source of the instigating factors. As portrayed in Figure 2-1, at one end are problems caused by the environment; at the other end are problems caused by factors within the person; in the middle are problems stemming from a relatively equal contribution of both sources. Remem-

Figure 2-1   A Continuum of Learning Problems Reflecting a Transactional View of the Locus of Primary Instigating Factors

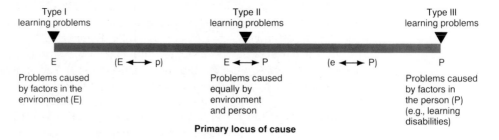

ber, this is a continuum. Thus, at each point between the extreme ends, environment and person transactions contribute in varying degrees to a problem. Toward the environment end of the continuum, environmental factors play a bigger role, with person variables playing a smaller role (represented as E < --- > p). Toward the other end, person variables account for more of the problem (thus e < --- > P).

The continuum generated by using a transactional model encompasses a full range of learning problems, including learning disabilities. From this perspective, a transactional view provides an umbrella under which the causes of all learning problems can be appreciated. A list of specific instigating factors that can cause learning problems based on a transactional view would fill the rest of this book. Table 2-1 is offered as an alternative.

Behaviorist Perspectives on Cause

Not all professionals are concerned about what originally instigated a learning or behavior problem. Many practitioners have adopted the view that initial causes often cannot be assessed; and even if they could, little could be done about the cause once the problem exists. Furthermore, behaviorists see appropriate remediation procedures as based on assessing current functioning and contributing factors — not on assessment of initial causes. That is, behaviorists view remediation as focused *solely* on (1) helping the individual acquire learning skills and strategies that should have been learned previously and on (2) eliminating factors that *currently* are contributing to problems.

Advocates of a behaviorist perspective tend to argue against defining learning disabilities in terms of causal factors. Many prefer a broad definition that includes anyone of at least average intelligence who is having difficulty learning despite appropriate motivation and adequate instruction.

In stressing the tendency of behavioral practitioners to put aside the matter of initial causes of learning and behavior problems, we do not mean to imply that behaviorist thinking ignores the causes of human behavior. The behaviorist literature provides detailed descriptions of the factors that determine how people learn and act. A considerable body of work explores how environmental events can selectively reinforce and shape actions, thoughts, and feelings. And although some behaviorists disagree about how to describe the determinants of behavior (see Ross, 1985), they agree that the description should be in psychological rather than neurological terms (see Mahoney, 1974; Skinner, 1974).

At the same time, behaviorists are concerned about current factors that interfere with effective learning and performance. For example, the current existence of poor study habits or the absence of particular skills and strategies for learning may be identified as causing poor attention to a task or failure to remember something that was apparently learned. In attempting to correct ongoing problems, the assumption is that the inappropriate habits can be

Table 2-1   Factors Instigating Learning Problems

Environment (E) (Type I problems)	Person (P) (Type III problems)	Interactions and Transactions Between E and P* (Type II problems)
1. Insufficient stimuli (e.g., prolonged periods in impoverished environments; deprivation of learning opportunities at home or school such as lack of play and practice situations and poor instruction; inadequate diet)	1. Physiological insult (e.g., cerebral trauma, such as accident or stroke; endocrine dysfunctions and chemical imbalances; illness affecting brain or sensory functioning)	1. Severe to moderate personal vulnerabilities and environmental defects and differences (e.g., person with extremely slow development in a highly demanding, understaffed classroom, all of which equally and simultaneously instigate the problem)
2. Excessive stimuli (e.g., overly demanding home or school experiences, such as overwhelming pressure to achieve and contradictory expectations)	2. Genetic anomaly (e.g., genes that limit, slow down, or lead to any atypical development)	2. Minor personal vulnerabilities not accommodated by the situation (e.g., person with minimal CNS disorders resulting in auditory perceptual disability enrolled in a reading program based on phonics; very active student assigned to classroom that does not tolerate this level of activity)
3. Intrusive and hostile stimuli (e.g., medical practices, especially at birth, leading to physiological impairment; conflict in home or faulty child-rearing practices, such as long-standing abuse and rejection; migratory family; language used in school is a second language; social prejudices related to race, sex, age, physical characteristics, and behavior)	3. Cognitive activity and affective states experienced by self as deviant (e.g., lack of knowledge or skills such as basic cognitive strategies; lack of ability to cope effectively with emotions, such as low self-esteem)	3. Minor environmental defects and differences not accommodated by the individual (e.g., student is in the minority racially or culturally and is not participating in many school activities and class discussions because he or she thinks others may be unreceptive)
	4. Physical characteristics shaping contact with environment and/or experienced by self as deviant (e.g., visual, auditory, or motoric deficits; excessive or reduced sensitivity to stimuli; easily fatigued; factors such as race, sex, age, unusual appearance that produce stereotypical responses)	
	5. Deviant actions of the individual (e.g., performance problems, such as excessive errors in reading and speaking; high or low levels of activity)	

*May involve only one (P) and one (E) variable or may involve multiple combinations.

overcome and the missing skills can be learned. The implication is that if there is a neurological or psychological disorder that is continuing to handicap the individual's efforts to learn, intervention cannot directly correct the underlying disorder. However, the skills and strategies the individual is taught are seen as either counteracting the disorder or helping the individual compensate for the handicap (Kazdin, 1984).

Other contributing factors may be any of the instigating factors indicated in Table 2-1 that continue to have a negative effect on current functioning. For example, a student may be a rather passive learner at school (for example, not paying adequate attention) because of physical and emotional stress caused by inappropriate child-rearing practices, illness, poor nutrition, and so forth. Obviously, practitioners concur that the presence of such factors should be assessed and corrected whenever feasible.

Learning Problems: The Common Case

Given that learning is a function of the transactions between the learner and the environment, it is understandable that certain groups would have higher rates of Type I learning problems. One such group consists of individuals living in poverty.

According to 1985 data, children under age 6 were the group with the greatest percentage (23 percent) living in poverty in the United States. (The overall poverty rate was 14 percent; people age 65 and over had 13 percent in poverty.) In terms of ethnicity, 50 percent of all African American and 20 percent of Latino children lived in poverty (U.S. Bureau of the Census, 1986, p. 27). It is acknowledged widely that poverty has a high correlation with school failure and high school drop out (National Center for Education Statistics, 1983; Rumberger, 1987). Poverty also is associated with delinquency and teenage pregnancy (Ekstrom, Goertz, Pollack, & Rock, 1986; Hodgkinson, 1989; Rutter & Giller, 1983).

Young children living in poverty have less opportunity to develop the initial capabilities and attitudes most elementary school programs require. At best, most poor families simply do not have the resources to provide the same preparatory experiences for their children as those who are better off financially. At worst, those in urban ghettos reside in the type of hostile environment that can generate so much stress as to make school adjustment and learning excessively difficult.

Thus, in comparison to students coming from middle- or higher-income families, those living in poverty come to school with capacities and attitudes that may not match the demands made of them. The mismatch may be particularly bad if the individuals have recently migrated from a different culture, do not speak English, or both. There is a poignant irony in all this. Children of poverty often have developed a range of other cultural, subcultural, and language abilities that middle-class–oriented schools are unprepared to accommodate, never mind capitalize upon. As a result, many of these youngsters struggle to survive without access to their strengths. It should surprise no one that a high percentage of these youngsters soon are seen as having learning problems, and (through circumstances to be discussed in subsequent chapters) may end up diagnosed as having learning disabilities.

Of course, a youngster does not have to live in poverty to be deprived of the opportunity to develop the initial capabilities and attitudes to succeed in elementary-school programs. There are youngsters who in the preschool years develop a bit slower than their peers. Their learning potential in the long run need not be affected by this fact. However, if early school demands do not

What are they developmentally ready to learn?

accommodate a wide range of developmental differences, the youngsters are vulnerable. When a task demands a level of development they have not achieved, they cannot do it. For example, youngsters who have not yet developed to a level where they can visually discriminate between the letters b and d are in trouble if the curriculum demands they do so. And months later, when their development catches up to that curriculum demand, the reading program has moved on, leaving them farther behind. Given what we know about the normal range of developmental variations, it is no surprise that many of these youngsters end up having problems (that is, Type II learning problems).

The Special Case of Learning Disabilities

In contrast to common learning problems, learning disabilities are defined as stemming from a minor central nervous system (CNS) dysfunction. That is, the term is used to account for neurologically based learning problems that are subtle, and not the result of gross brain damage or the kind of severe CNS dysfunction associated with major disorders such as cerebral palsy. As you read on, remember that the factors discussed in this section can, but do not always, cause

CNS problems and when they do, the effects may be so minimal as to have no effect on learning.

Factors Causing Central Nervous System Problems

Factors that can cause CNS problems and lead to learning disabilities may be grouped into four categories: (1) genetic, (2) prenatal (before birth), (3) perinatal (during birth), and (4) postnatal (after birth).

Genetic.   Some genetic syndromes (for example, neurofibromatosis) appear to have a high probability of leading to learning problems. The transmission of such genetic abnormalities may produce abnormal brain structures, dysfunctional patterns of CNS maturation, biochemical irregularities, or a high risk for diseases that can impair the brain. When any of these occur, learning problems may follow. However, research has not demonstrated that genetic defects are a high-frequency cause of specific learning disabilities (see Feature 2-1). More commonly, events in the first stages of life have been identified as leading to learning disabilities (Colletti, 1979; Shaywitz, Cohen, & Shaywitz, 1978; Touwen & Huisjes, 1984).

Prenatal (before birth).   Factors suggested as resulting in CNS malfunctioning before birth include:

- Rh factor incompatibility
- exposure to disease, such as German measles
- deficiencies in the mother's diet, such as vitamin or mineral deficiencies

Feature 2-1   Are Learning Problems Genetically Caused?

When a child with a learning problem has a parent who also has a learning problem, there is a tendency to believe the problem is inherited. This is unfortunate, since more often than not similar environmental factors have caused the problem for both the parent and the child.

The nature of learning experiences and attitudes about learning are often similar for parents and their children. For example, children often go to schools similar to those their parents attended. Parents often recreate the home environments they experienced as children. If books and reading were not important in the home where the father and mother grew up, the parents may not make much of an effort to provide books or to encourage their children to spend much time reading.

In general, parents teach their attitudes and beliefs to their children in daily encounters. If parents don't like to read, or think of themselves as having a learning problem, their children may adopt the same attitudes. A child may interpret these attitudes as family traits and choose to model them. Thus what is passed on is a *learned* behavior and not a genetic trait.

As yet there is little evidence that genetic transfer of learning problems is a widespread phenomenon (Olsen, Wise, Conners, Rack, & Fulker, 1989; Pennington & Smith, 1988; cf. Smith, 1986; Smith, Pennington, Kimberling, & Ing, 1990).

- illnesses of the mother, such as diabetes, kidney disease, hypothyroidism, emotional stress
- exposure to radiation, such as X rays
- use of certain drugs and medication by the mother
- excessive use of cigarettes or other substances by the mother that may produce a shortage of oxygen

Because many of these prenatal factors contribute to premature birth, premature infants (those less than 5½ pounds) are especially at risk for a variety of illnesses that may affect CNS development.

Perinatal (during birth).   During labor and delivery, events can occur that may result in physical damage or oxygen deficiency affecting brain tissue. Perinatal factors, however, are infrequently the primary causes of learning disabilities. Those perinatal events that may cause problems include:

- intracranial hemorrhaging during labor, due to prolonged passage through the birth canal
- injury from forceps delivery
- deprivation of oxygen when the umbilical cord is wrapped around the infant's neck
- negative effects from drugs used to induce labor or control postnatal hemorrhaging

Postnatal (after birth).   Many factors in subsequent stages of life may cause CNS malfunctions. To simplify things, they may be discussed in terms of events or conditions that lead to

- destruction or deterioration of brain tissue, or
- biochemical irregularities that cause poor connections between brain cells or result in abnormal brain development.

Specific examples of these kinds of events and conditions are head injuries, strokes, tumors, ingestion of toxic substances, poor nutrition (such as vitamin deficiencies), hypoglycemia, severe and chronic emotional stress, glandular disorders (such as calcium and thyroid imbalances), and diseases and illnesses (such as meningitis and encephalitis) that cause prolonged high fevers.

How the CNS Is Affected and Learning Is Disrupted

It is relatively easy to suggest a variety of ways in which the brain fails to function appropriately and thus causes learning disabilities. Many theories have been offered. However, the more we learn about CNS functioning, the more some theories are seen as too simplistic (see Feature 2-2).

Any factor that leads to hormonal, chemical, or blood-flow imbalances may instigate CNS trouble. However, only a few things are likely to have more than

Feature 2-2   Cerebral Dominance and Mixed Laterality: Historical Note

Remedial approaches based on the dominance of one side of the brain over the other exemplify a simplistic theory that was very popular at one time. For most of this century, many believed that a major cause of learning problems was the failure of one hemisphere to develop dominance over the other. The seeds for this idea were planted in the late nineteenth and early twentieth centuries, when it was found that for most people the left hemisphere was primarily responsible for language functioning. This led to a widespread view that the left was the dominant hemisphere and that the right hemisphere was subordinate and somewhat inferior.

The dominant hemisphere was also thought to determine which side of the body would be favored, especially with regard to handedness. Because the right side of the body was seen as controlled by the left hemisphere (viewed as dominant for most people), the fact that most people are right-handed was attributed to left-hemisphere dominance.

Based on these ideas, the theory was proposed that appropriate development of left-hemisphere dominance would be reflected in a consistent preference for the right side of the body with regard to the use of hands, eyes, ears, and feet. Many individuals with learning problems did not show such a consistent pattern. Instead they had a mixed pattern, such as a preference for right hand and left eye or left hand and right eye. This pattern came to be called *mixed* or *confused dominance* or *mixed laterality* and was believed to be the result of a failure to develop cerebral dominance (for example, see Orton, 1937).

A variation on this theory focused specifically on those who were left-handed. Left-handedness seemed to be an indication that the right side of the brain was establishing primacy for language functions; thus, the learning problems of left-handed persons were the result of the inability of the nondominant right hemisphere to perform language functions adequately (Delacato, 1966).

Remedial programs based on such ideas were created. The intent was to help individuals develop a dominant cerebral hemisphere through activities designed to establish a consistent (nonmixed) pattern of laterality or left-hemisphere dominance for language. These programs lasted quite a while before their validity was seriously questioned. The first evidence that raised concern about these programs was that many good learners showed mixed laterality patterns. Then came the finding that handedness is not a good indicator of which hemisphere is dominant. Finally, there was a breakthrough in awareness about areas of right-hemisphere dominance. Now it is recognized that both hemispheres have areas of dominance. In particular, the right hemisphere has dominance for nonverbal functions as well as having the ability to assume dominance for language functions in certain cases.

With the decline of theories about left-hemisphere dominance, there has been a shift in explanations about mixed laterality. The mistake in looking at laterality as a symptom was in stressing the mixed pattern. The current view is that problems arise not from mixed laterality and its causes, but from a lack of well-established preference. For example, if a youngster has not established habitual use of a dominant hand because of lack of regular practice, he or she is likely to have difficulty with writing or catching a ball. This does not mean that the lack of established preference is causing the learning problem. If learning problems are present, they and the failure to establish satisfactory preference may both be due to slow maturation or other CNS problems.

a temporary effect. When the effects are more than temporary, they take the form of CNS destruction or deterioration, delayed neurological maturation, development of abnormal brain structures, or malfunctioning of connections between brain cells.

Brain injury and dysfunction. Nerve cells in the brain (neurons), once destroyed, cannot be restored. It is comforting to note, however, that the human brain is estimated to have 12 billion neurons, and that as many as 10,000 die a natural death every day without apparent negative effect on brain functioning. Thus, a small amount of damage can occur without severe consequences. In cases of brain injury, the nature and scope of dysfunction appears to depend in part on the amount of tissue damage. For example, as long as enough cells remain undamaged, there are instances where nondamaged cells take over new functions. Also important in determining the effects of brain injury are its location and the stage of CNS development at the time (see Feature 2-3).

When there is uneven learning of a particular skill such as reading, specific areas of the brain are suspected to be malfunctioning (Bakker, Bouma, & Gardien, 1990). For instance, some youngsters readily recognize letters when asked to point them out but have trouble reading them without prompting. Or they may have difficulty understanding that certain groups of letters mean the same thing as the words they speak. In such cases, experts may attribute the reading problem

Feature 2-3   *Recovery from Brain Damage*

Most people have heard of individuals who lost the ability to speak or read because of stroke, head injury, or surgery. Sometimes these losses are temporary; that is, after the immediate effects of the event wear off there is spontaneous recovery of skills. For others, where the extent of brain damage is considerable, there is reason to think the functions may be lost forever.

There have been instances, however, where people regained lost abilities through diligent rehabilitation efforts. In the most dramatic instances, significant relearning of lost skills occurred after surgeons removed an entire section of the brain (for example, one lobe). As a result of such cases and of research with animals, theories have been proposed about the ability of healthy brain cells to take over the functions of damaged ones. For example, in some cases where the left hemisphere of the brain was damaged, the right hemisphere was able to take over many language functions.

What remains less clear are the factors that make recovery of lost functions possible. Age seems to be one such factor. Adults tend to make a poorer recovery than children. However, just how old one has to be before recovery is impossible has not been established. One reason for children's better recovery may be that their nervous systems are continuing to grow and various areas of their brains have not yet become dedicated to particular functions. The poorer recovery of adults may be due to a decreased efficiency, associated with age, in establishing new transmission connections between neurons. The nature of rehabilitation efforts may also make a difference in the degree of recovery. Distinguishing the remedial approaches that work awaits further research.

to a brain malfunction and refer to it as *dyslexia*. (To the regret of many, the term *dyslexia* has come to be applied to almost any reading problem, rather than to the particular subset of reading problems caused by CNS dysfunctioning.)

One theory of dyslexia suggests that factors such as oxygen deprivation (anoxia) produce damage to cells in the association centers of the brain, the parietal and parietal-occipital lobes. Damage to these areas is believed to result in a specific inability to associate symbols with meaning but not to interfere with the recognition of symbols (Rabinovitz, 1959, 1968).

Damaged brain cells can interfere with communication along neural pathways. Such communication between brain cells is known as *neural impulse transmission*. It is an electrochemical process that is essential to effective learning and performance.

Impulse-transmission problems occur when a neuron is prevented from communicating with others or when the speed of transmission is inappropriate (too rapid or too slow). Dysfunctions in neural impulse transmission usually are the result of endocrine malfunctions and chemical imbalances.

If brain cells cannot communicate fully, then development, learning, and performance will be affected. This may be the case for individuals who appear to have extremely high activity levels and difficulty sustaining attention. One hypothesis suggests that when brain cells are damaged, neurotransmitter chemicals usually are destroyed as well. When there is not enough of the chemical to inhibit transmission, it becomes too rapid (Wender, 1976). Another hypothesis proposes that overly rapid transmissions occur when the points of connection between neurons (that is, synapses) are so insensitive to chemical inhibitors that they do not adequately slow down transmission (Kinsbourne & Caplin, 1979).

As might be imagined, research to test hypotheses about CNS dysfunctioning is difficult. Efforts in this direction include postmortem studies of brain anomalies of individuals who had reading problems (Galaburda, 1985, 1989; Vellutino, 1987) and investigations of families and twins in search of genetic trends (DeFries & Decker, 1982; La Buda & DeFries, 1988). Researchers also are capitalizing on recent technical advances that allow for indirect viewing of brain structure and function, namely computed tomography (CT-scan), positron emission tomography (PET-scan), magnetic resonance imaging (MRI) and the use of spectoscopy with MRI, as well as procedures for monitoring brain wave activity through computer-assisted brain electrical activity mapping (BEAM). Although some studies have suggested the promise of these techniques, there have been cautions about limitations (Begley, 1988; Coles, 1987; Duane, 1986; Duffy & McAnulty, 1985; Obruzut & Boliek, 1991).

Developmental lag.   Not all theories about neurological causes focus on CNS *dysfunction*. Any of the environmental or personal instigating factors cited in Table 2-1 can delay the rate of CNS maturation.

It is widely hypothesized that persons whose neurological development is disrupted or is comparatively slow will lag behind their peers, especially in the

David struggling.

early formative years. This slow development often is referred to as *maturational* or *developmental lag* (Duane, 1989; Goldstein & Myers, 1980; Koppitz, 1973; Rutter, 1983). According to this view, children whose neurological development is not the same as that of others their age are not ready to learn the same tasks as the majority of their peers. At school, children who are lagging considerably behind others find that most classrooms cannot wait for them to catch up. It is this fact, not the developmental lag by itself, that is seen as the instigating factor leading to learning problems.

For instance, the first-grade reading curriculum begins with the assumption that all students have a certain level of auditory and visual perceptual capability. Auditory and visual perception differ from auditory and visual acuity. *Acuity* is a matter of sharpness and depends on the sensitivity of one's sense organs (for example, an eye that can clearly see shapes and forms). *Perception* is the psychological process by which a person organizes and makes sense out of incoming sensory information. A child may have 20/20 vision (perfect acuity) but not be able to discriminate (perceptually distinguish) differences among letters.

CNS Function and Assessment of Minor Dysfunction (p. 304) outlines the functions of the cerebral cortex and the problems of assessing minor CNS dysfunctions.

If David (see Chapter 1) has not yet developed such capabilities at the expected level, chances are he will not be able to handle parts of the reading lessons *at the expected time.* As the teacher moves on to teach the next lesson, he falls further behind. A year or so later, his neurological development will advance to a point where he has the necessary physiological capability. Unfortunately, he will have missed learning important basic skills. In such cases (and in many cases in which CNS malfunctions produce only temporary disruptions in learning), subsequent learning problems are no longer due to the initial CNS factors. They are caused by the fact that the individual is missing certain skills that are prerequisites for subsequent learning.

The sequence of events discussed to this point, beginning with instigating factors, is diagrammed in Feature 2-4. This sequence becomes complicated after a CNS disorder causes learning problems. More often than not, the learning problems themselves cause more problems, and subsequent development, learning, and performance are disrupted. The impact on the individual can extend into

Feature 2-4   Sequence of Events Related to Problems in CNS Functioning and Development

The sequence of events related to CNS disorders begins with a *primary* instigating factor that produces the disorder (see accompanying diagram). In turn, the disorder can produce a handicap. In the case of disrupted learning resulting from a CNS disorder, such a handicap has come to be called a *learning disability.* It is seen as disrupting learning in specific areas (for example, in associating meaning with symbols). As a result, the individual has trouble performing in learning settings, such as reading instruction at school.

Quite commonly, the performance problems and others' reactions to these problems have a negative psychological impact on the individual. These negative psychological effects are often referred to as an *emotional overlay* to the learning problems.

The combination of performance problems and problems stemming from negative psychological effects often cause the learning problems to become worse. That is, these factors become *secondary* instigating factors leading to further handicapping conditions that cause specific learning problems to become wide-ranging performance and behavior problems.

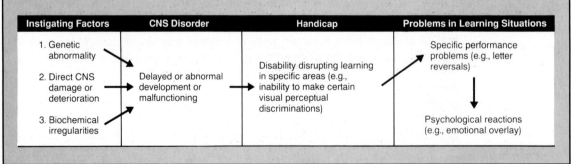

all areas of learning and can be responsible for a variety of negative emotions, attitudes, and behaviors.

Learning and Behavior Problems

Individuals with learning problems frequently manifest behavior problems and vice versa. In terms of cause, a person who is having trouble learning may start to misbehave as a reaction to the learning problem, and the behavior problems also get in the way of learning. Furthermore, both sets of problems may appear simultaneously and stem from the same or separate causes. Given all this, it is not surprising that there is considerable confusion about the relationship between learning and behavior problems.

A particular concern arises around behavior and learning problems that are associated with high activity levels. Individuals with this configuration of problems may be assigned formal diagnostic labels such as *attention deficit disorder (ADD)* or *attention deficit-hyperactivity disorder (ADHD)*. One view of those assigned these labels attributes their problems to neurological factors (see Silver, 1990); another perspective sees the cause of such problems in interactional terms (Murphy & Hicks-Stewart, 1991).

From a causal perspective, we think it useful to view behavior problems in transactional terms just as we have done with learning problems. That is, a continuum of Type I, II, and III behavior problems can be conceived as portrayed in Figure 2-1. Thus we see diagnostic terms such as ADD or ADHD applying only to Type III problems (attention deficits and hyperactivity caused by factors within the person). Currently, however, the diagnostic labels are used as indiscriminately as the term *learning disabilities.* We suggest that the labels are inappropriately applied to many behavior problems—namely, those caused primarily by the impact of the environment (Type I problems) or the transaction between person and environment (Type II problems).

It is important to remember that an individual can have more than one problem; that is, the person may manifest hyperactivity as well as learning disabilities.

The strong relationship between learning and behavior problems makes it essential that practitioners, researchers, and policymakers strive to understand this association. A transactional model of cause can provide a useful framework for doing so.

Summing Up

What causes learning problems? The question is considerably easier to ask than to answer. Some theorists point to CNS problems that can disrupt learning, others stress psychological factors, still others emphasize causes related to environmental influences. We have suggested the value of viewing such problems from the perspective of a transactional model that can act as an umbrella for thinking about a full range of learning problems and their causes. Such a broad perspective can guide researchers in the difficult task of providing evidence to pinpoint the variety of factors causing Type I, II, and III learning problems.

Despite the absence of a satisfactory body of etiological research, practitioners are called upon each day to differentiate among learning problems (and to diagnose learning disabilities) and pursue ways to correct them. This brings us to the topic of intervention, which is addressed in Part 2.

The following item was reported in a large metropolitan newspaper:

> St. Louis, Mo. (UPI)   Being neurotic has its advantages. A study of 434 white males by Washington University, St. Louis, showed the neurotics among them earned about 23 percent higher salaries than those diagnosed as well. The results of the survey were reported in a recent issue of *American Family Physician.* Researchers also found that the neurotics had significantly higher ratings for full-time employment, IQs, and total years of schooling.

1. Does this report seem to imply causal connections?
2. Are there other, perhaps more logical, explanations for the reported outcomes?
3. Which of the following explanations seems most plausible?
   - High IQ is the cause of more years of schooling, which leads to higher salaries and full employment.
   - More years of schooling led to higher scores on IQ tests as well as to higher paying jobs and better employment opportunities.
   - Being neurotic leads to higher salaries and better employment opportunities.
4. In this context, what do you think about the use of the label *neurotic?* How do you think the researchers were able to determine that the individuals studied were neurotic?

CNS Function and Assessment of Minor Dysfunction (p. 304) Theories about learning disabilities have suggested possible dysfunctions in each of the major parts of the brain. Most current theories focus on cerebral cortex dysfunctions. Therefore, to encourage you to read more about this specific topic, we have outlined

- the functions of the cerebral cortex, and
- problems related to attempts to assess minor central nervous system dysfunctioning — especially the difficulties associated with measuring "soft signs."

Intervention:
An Overview

What the best and wisest parent wants for his own child
that must the community want for all of its children.
Any other idea . . . is narrow and unlovely.

Dewey (1966, p. 7)

A s we have seen in Part 1, interventions for learning problems range from prevention programs to highly specialized placements and treatments. The concept of intervention includes assessment and referral activities and, along the way, some of this activity results in a diagnosis of learning disability.

Just as professionals differ in how they approach the matter of cause, they differ in their orientations to intervention. In Part 2 and the related readings, ideas that shape the nature and scope of intervention are reviewed. First we highlight the general nature of intervention, specifically emphasizing contemporary approaches and dominant orientations relevant to learning problems. This provides a broad introduction to basic concepts about intervention, including assessment. Then follows a more detailed discussion of assessment and the range of available programs. Chapter 4 explores prevailing approaches to assessing learning problems, with a specific focus on (a) the many facets of assessment activity, (b) concerns and limitations related to prevailing practices, and (c) recent efforts to go beyond conventional approaches. Then in Chapter 5 we offer a perspective on the range of programs available from preschool through adulthood.

Permeating all interventions for learning problems are fundamental concerns about informed consent, due process, and conflicts of interest. Chapter 6 introduces these topics in relation to the decision to intervene. Finally, we explore ideas for broadening the focus of contemporary intervention practices.

As you proceed, remember your objective is to understand both what is commonly done and how current practices can evolve to make intervention more effective.

CHAPTER 3

Intervention Concepts and Learning Problems

A Broad Focus
  Defining Intervention
  Broadening the Focus of Intervention

Contemporary Interventions for Learning Problems
  Overview
  The Many Purposes of Assessment
  Contrasting Orientations to Remediation
  Eclecticism

Least Intervention Needed
  Mainstream versus Special Settings
  Labeling: Is It Necessary?
  Needs Come First
  Regular and Special Education

No Magic Bullets

Summing Up

There is nothing as practical as a good theory.

Kurt Lewin

When his parents were told that David should be placed in a special class, they were not surprised. They had noticed some distressing things at home and had been told by his teachers about other problems. Of course they were concerned — and they were in disagreement about what to do:

MOTHER: I want David to stay in regular classes so he won't feel different from his friends.

FATHER: But he already feels different. He knows he can't do things as well as the others. He says he feels dumb.

MOTHER: He might feel worse in a special class. And besides, he'll miss out on a lot of information and experiences his friends will get.

FATHER: That might be true, but what if keeping him in the regular program prevents him from overcoming his problems or makes them worse? This is the time to help him. We can't afford to waste any time.

MOTHER: I see that, but what will they do in a special class that can't be done in regular ones? Aren't there other treatments?

FATHER: The special teachers have learned special ways to teach children. Other treatments may help, but the school says he will still need special instruction.

Picture yourself as one of David's parents. You want the best for your son, but you really don't know much about the approaches used in treating such problems. You need an overview. In this chapter, a broad introduction to intervention (including assessment) is provided through an exploration of the general nature of intervention and the prevailing approaches used to remedy learning problems.

A Broad Focus

Intervention is something everyone does, but few people take the time to analyze it. In approaching learning problems, some professionals think of assessment, diagnosis, and referral as distinct from intervention. This tends to limit use of the term *intervention* to teaching or treatment, but in so doing the intervening nature of assessment, diagnosis, and referral is not fully appreciated. All intervention (including procedures to assess, refer, and diagnose) involves decision-making processes, and each decision is a potentially life-shaping event. The intent, of course, is to produce benefits. But not all interventions are beneficial, and every intervention has the potential for negative side effects. For these reasons, it is useful to define intervention broadly. Further, it is essential to appreciate how much intervention activity is shaped by the way the term is defined and by the assumptions made about who or what is its focus.

Defining Intervention

It is natural for professionals to stress benefits in defining intervention. For example,

> Intervention is a general term that refers to the application of professional skills to maintain or improve a child's potential for ongoing healthy development. (Suran & Rizzo, 1979, p. 79)

> Methods used to intervene are described as "designed to help people change for the better." (Kanfer & Goldstein, 1991, p. 1)

With reference to problems, a more neutral definition describes intervention as

> any directed action upon the deviance predicament between child and community. (Rhodes & Tracy, 1972, p. 28)

On a less positive note, critics have accentuated the fact that intervention is an "interference into the affairs of another" (Illich, 1976; Szasz, 1969).

Various definitions agree that intentional intervention refers to planned actions intended to produce desired changes in existing (usually problematic) conditions of persons or environments. To leave it at that, however, is to ignore some important matters (Adelman & Taylor, 1988). An expanded definition of intervention is needed. In developing such a definition, the following ideas should be considered:

1. Because interventions must be applied flexibly, efforts to produce changes often reflect unplanned, as well as planned, actions.
2. Such actions may or may not produce change. If they do, some outcomes may be unintended, and some may be negative.
3. To avoid a pathological bias, we need to think about desired changes not only in terms of problems but also with reference to nonproblematic conditions.
4. To expand thinking in terms of a transactional view of learning, the focus should be not only on the individual or the environment but also on the transactions between person and environment.

For our purposes, *intentional interventions* are the planned (and unplanned) actions that result from a desire to produce changes in existing problematic or nonproblematic conditions of a system (person, environment, or the transactions between both). Such actions may or may not produce changes, and if they do, some may be unintended.

Why bother with all this? The importance of broadening the definition can be seen in the following implications:

- There is less chance that negative outcomes and positive side effects will be ignored (because the definition stresses that some intervention actions and changes may be unintended).
- The relevance of positive growth and enrichment activities and outcomes are highlighted (because of the focus on nonproblematic conditions).
- The importance of considering changes in organizations and societal institutions is underscored (because change is not defined simply in terms of the individual).

In sum, a broad and neutral definition of intervention helps maintain a perspective that avoids overemphasizing person-pathology while recognizing the potential for intervention to do harm. With this expanded definition, intervention encompasses the entire range of responses to individuals or groups seeking educational or psychosocial help. This contrasts markedly with the tendency to view existing conditions as problematic and residing within the individual.

Broadening the Focus of Intervention

It is easy to fall into the trap of thinking that interventions for learning problems should always be directed at the individual. This happens because definitions tend to be person centered and because person-centered models of cause and correction dominate professional thinking. One result is that most of what is written about such problems focuses intervention on individuals.

Focusing only on individuals tends to limit assumptions about what is wrong and what needs to change. Adopting a transactional view instead suggests a fuller set of options with respect to who or what should be the object of change (see Figure 3-1). Such a set of options is essential in dealing with the full continuum of learning problems (Types I, II, and III).

Figure 3-1 Focal Points for Intervention

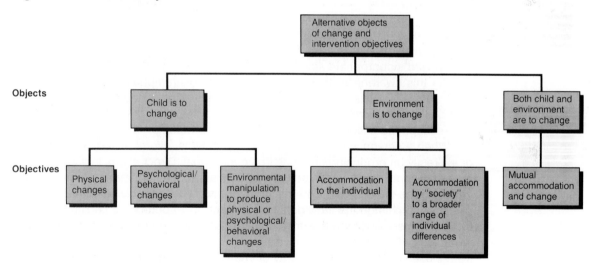

Examples of types of intervention:

Physical changes—medication, special diet

Psychological/behavioral changes—psychotherapy, counseling, teaching, training

Environmental manipulation—behavior change strategies, such as altering reinforcement patterns

Accommodation to individual—environment (home/classroom) change strategies designed to increase the range of acceptable options, to accommodate interests, response styles, and capabilities

Accommodation by "society"—policy actions designed to increase the range of acceptable options for all persons in a particular setting or throughout the society

Mutual accommodation—family therapy, school consolation, policy actions designed to optimize intervention

How can James's mother best help him?

We know that professionals are aware that there are cases where an individual's learning problems arise because the environment (home, school, society) has applied inappropriate standards or has limited choices. But we suggest that, despite this awareness, there is a tendency to overemphasize interventions focused on individuals. For instance, interventions that do address the need for changes in the environment often stress the manipulation of reinforcers to control and reshape the actions of those with learning problems.

When a person is identified as having problems, efforts usually focus directly or indirectly on producing changes in the individual. Direct efforts include remediation, psychotherapy, and medically related approaches. Indirect efforts include changing the way parents and teachers interact with the individual. Interventions designed to change the individual may be the most appropriate choice for some. However, the environment sometimes needs to change in ways that accommodate rather than modify individual differences. These environmental changes differ from those used as an indirect way of changing the individual.

Because the distinction is so important, the difference between environment *manipulation* and environment *change* is worth underscoring. For example, teaching James's mother behavior-control strategies is not the same as helping her to see the implications of offering James other options when appropriate. Instructing parents and teachers to be more discriminating in their use of reinforcement contingencies is an indirect way of changing the child. It is not the same as helping them to make appropriate changes in their expectations about what is acceptable behavior, performance, and progress, or changing their disciplinary practices.

When the cause of the problem is in the environment, the most appropriate intervention, where feasible, is to change the environment. The change may be to alter situations hostile to the individual or, stated differently, to accommodate either a specific individual or a wider range of individual differences. Such changes can be seen as preventive in the full sense of the term (Caplan, 1964; Cowen, 1986).

With the rise in popularity of interactional approaches to psychological intervention, especially family therapy, there has been greater emphasis on making both the individual and the environment focal points of change (Alexander & Malouf, 1983; Cook, Howe, & Holliday, 1985; Goldstein, 1988; Patterson, 1986). It remains to be seen whether this trend will result in an expanded focus on environment changes per se.

The implications of broadening the focus of intervention (as presented in Figure 3-1) are immense. For one, environments and the transactions between persons and environments become a primary concern for assessment and correction. Efforts to prevent problems expand to include programs that encourage accommodation of a wider range of individual differences in schools and society. And this broad perspective works against the presumption that most learning problems are caused by CNS dysfunctions.

Contemporary Interventions for Learning Problems

Interventions for learning problems take a variety of forms. Although each may be discussed separately, it is essential not to lose sight of the entire picture.

Overview

Figure 3-2 graphically presents the various types of general intervention tasks and services associated with learning problems. The range of activity is extensive, and every facet requires rational planning and decision making. The nature of each task will become clearer as we progress through the book; this section provides only a brief introduction.

It would have been nice if David's problem had been prevented—or at least identified and treated soon after it appeared. In Chapter 5 we discuss how prevention and early-intervention programs are evolving and show considerable promise. When such programs are completely effective, the need for further services is eliminated. Even in less successful cases, the impact of problems may at least be eased.

Prevention programs also provide a vehicle for early screening. When a problem is identified, the individual may be referred for screening follow-up in the form of further assessment and consultation, which sometimes includes prereferral intervention. Alternatively, the person may be referred directly to one or more special service programs.

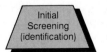

In David's case, his learning problem finally became severe enough for his second-grade teacher to refer him to the school psychologist. In effect, this was David's initial screening process. Formal screening to identify learning disabilities goes well beyond such spontaneous referrals, however. In the United States,

Figure 3-2   *Intervention Activity Associated with Learning Problems*

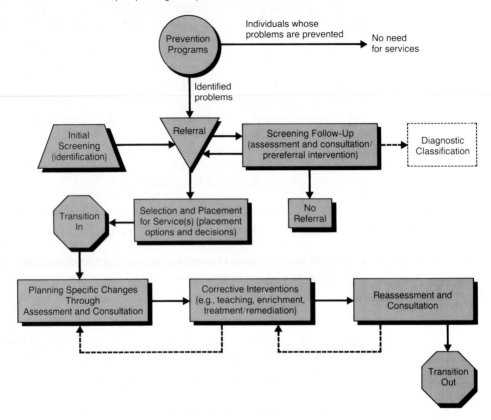

All major intervention tasks and services are based on a rationale and
require planning for implementation and evaluation.

development of large-scale child-find (screening) programs is mandated by law.
All such screening is supposed to be followed by referral for an intensive assessment and consultation.

Screening Follow-Up
(assessment and consultation/
prereferral intervention)

As is typical in such cases, David's teacher — and then
the psychologist — approached the problem with the
presumption that he should be the focus of intervention. Thus, the follow-up assessment and consultation
consisted primarily of psychoeducational testing, and resulted in a diagnosis of
learning disabilities and a referral for special help.

Alternatively, David's teacher might have been offered consultation to explore
a variety of strategies to see if formal testing was necessary. This could have
helped maintain David in the regular classroom, or at least have provided additional data regarding his special needs. This process of consultation, support, and
informal assessment is called *prereferral intervention.* Three specific models of

prereferral intervention are one-to-one consultation, teacher assistance teams, and peer collaboration (Chalfant, Pysh, & Moultrie, 1979; Fuchs, 1991; Graden, Casey, & Christenson, 1985; Johnson & Pugach, 1991). These interventions are meant to improve response to the learning problem by the regular classroom teacher and are seen as a good way to reduce the number of students tested, diagnosed, and referred to special programs. Optimally, prereferral consultation can result in a student's staying in the regular classroom because the teacher has learned new ways to work with the problem. Minimally, such activity can add assessment data that lead to increased validity of diagnoses and referrals. In David's case, however, there was no effort to explore ways in which the teacher might better address the problem. David was diagnosed and recommended for special placement.

> Selection and Placement for Service(s) (placement options and decisions)

To improve intervention planning and evaluation, Public Law 94-142 included guidelines requiring a multidisciplinary team to prepare a written individualized education program (an IEP) for each student seen as possibly having a disability. The team also provides a mechanism for case management. For example, at referral the team can encourage prereferral interventions; team members do additional, multidisciplinary assessment; they write up a specific program plan and arrange for placement and monitoring of progress (Cruickshank, Morse, & Grant, 1990).

Once diagnosed as having a learning disability, an individual is eligible for services not necessarily available to those with other types of learning problems. For school-age youngsters, any of the following decisions may be made:

- *Class placement.* The student may be kept in regular classes or placed in a special classroom for all or part of the day.
- *Private remedial school.* If there is a need for a special class that the public school cannot provide, the student may leave the school and attend a private remedial school (using public funds for tuition).
- *Extra help.* If the student is kept in regular classes, a collaborative teacher may be brought in at selected times to provide special instruction, or the student may go to a special class part of the day. After-school tutoring may be considered, instead of the other arrangements, or to supplement them.
- *Ancillary services.* In addition to educational services, counseling, psychotherapy, or speech therapy may be recommended for the student. Physicians and other medically related specialists may recommend medication, special diets, vision correction, or various other clinical services. (As discussed in *Controversial Treatments and Fads,* p. 309, many of these have been challenged.)

"Will you do my homework for me?"

"No. It wouldn't be right if I did it."

"That's OK. I don't get them all right either."

For adolescents and adults, options also may include service programs designed to prepare the individual for a vocation or a career. These options may encompass career counseling, job training, and work-study programs that take into account the individual's special needs. Because few classroom programs are designed for adults with learning disabilities, those who are not enrolled in special college programs often find that their options for remedial instruction are limited to a clinic's tutorial program or private tutoring.

It should be stressed that, although eligibility for many services requires assignment of a diagnostic label, the types of services just described may be as appropriate (or inappropriate) for anyone with a learning problem. Moreover, because the procedures currently used to diagnose learning disabilities are highly fallible, the possibility that David has been misdiagnosed cannot be ignored.

Given available options, selection and placement decisions have to be made. In David's case, the school psychologist described all the options and recommended placing him in a special class. In the end, David's parents decided the psychologist "knew best." No one asked for David's views, however, and they were not considered. (Later, David indicated that he would not have chosen to be placed in a special class.) The IEP team reviewed the psychologist's recommendations and made the final decision on his eligibility for the special program.

 Once a decision was made to enroll David, the matter of transition arose. Many practical and psychological barriers (for example, transportation and funding; fear and anxiety) can interfere with an individual following through on a referral or making a successful adjustment to a new program. A decision to try a service is no guarantee that it will be pursued, and when it is, the program may be experienced as uninviting or even hostile. Increasingly, professionals recognize the importance of interventions that help ensure successful transitions. These include providing detailed activities, stressing personal contacts, and providing social support. Doing these things can smooth over follow-through and program adjustment difficulties.

At another level of transition (from school to postschool), legislation for educating individuals with disabilities has made it mandatory for the IEP to specify needed *transition services.* Transition services are specified as

> a coordinated set of activities for a student, designated within an outcome-oriented process, which promotes movement from school to postschool activities including postsecondary education, vocational training, integrated employment (including supported employment), continuing and adult education, adult services, independent living or community participation. The coordinated set of activities shall be based upon the individual student's needs, taking into account the student's preferences and interests, and shall include instruction, community experiences, the development of employment and other postschool adult living objectives, and, when appropriate, acquisition of daily living skills and functional vocational evaluation. (Public Law 101-476, enacted in 1990)

Such a transition plan is to specify "interagency responsibilities or linkages (or both) before the student leaves the school setting" and is to be made annually beginning no later than age 16 (earlier when appropriate).

Planning Specific Changes Through Assessment and Consultation

After David enrolled in the program, assessment and consultation efforts centered on guiding each specific intervention toward accomplishing intended outcomes. Each day's activity was shaped by ongoing assessment and decision-making processes. These processes are discussed in detail in the next chapters and related readings.

Corrective Interventions (e.g., teaching, enrichment, treatment/remediation)

Although corrective interventions for learning problems usually are grouped into remediation or treatment, they generally involve a complex set of remedial, treatment, teaching, and enrichment activities. We discuss the prevailing orientations to remediation and treatment in a subsequent section and in the readings; teaching and enrichment are explored in Part 3.

Reassessment and Consultation

After David has been in the special class for a while, it is essential to use information regarding his daily performance to evaluate previous decisions, as well as his progress and current problems. In particular, the focus of reassessment activity is on such matters as:

1. Was the diagnosis of learning disabilities valid?
2. Was the initial decision to pursue special class placement a good one?
3. Is he making progress?
4. Is anything interfering with progress?
5. Are there any negative side effects?

Eventually, the questions will arise:

6. Has the program accomplished its objectives?
7. Has it done all it can?

And, at some point, decisions will have to be made about leaving this program. For the most part, the ongoing assessment data used for daily planning will be sufficient to help in making such decisions.

Transition Out

When an individual is ready to leave a program, practical and psychological barriers may arise. For example, David may need help in overcoming anxiety about returning to a regular program; he may need to learn specific survival skills if he is to succeed in the mainstream. And, as noted above, if he is ready to leave school, extensive steps must be taken to ensure a good postschool transition.

The Many Purposes of Assessment

People are involved in assessment many times each day. Although such assessments are not as formal or systematic as those performed by professionals, the process is the same: they gather information and formulate judgments (and eventually make decisions based on the assessment).

Among some professionals, assessment is referred to as diagnosis, diagnostic testing, or screening. These terms, following medical usage, imply that procedures (commonly tests, ratings, and interviews) are used to look for and label an individual's problem and, perhaps, to analyze it and prescribe treatment. Unfortunately, in education and psychology, this person-centered, problem-focused approach perpetuates a narrow view of learning and behavior problems.

Assessment does not have to be restricted to persons; environments and person–environment transactions can be assessed as well. With learning problems, however, assessment continues to be viewed in terms of screening and diagnosis and is shaped primarily by the presumption that problems stem from and belong to targeted individuals.

Assessment does not have to be restricted to problems; strengths and interests can also be identified and may be important in correcting problems. Prevailing practices, however, continue to deemphasize assessment of such positive attributes.

Definition.   To avoid the limitations and conceptual baggage associated with medically related language, the term *assessment* increasingly has been adopted. Formally defined, assessment is the process by which attributes of phenomena are *described* and *judged*. Descriptions take the form of data gathered by formal and informal measures, such as tests and observations of behavior or settings. Judgments take the form of interpretive conclusions about the meaning of data, such as whether a phenomenon is good or bad, above or below standard, pathological or not.

In practice, the overall aim of assessment is to describe and make judgments as an aid to decision making. The judgments may represent a conclusion about the past (such as what caused a problem), a statement about the present (such as how severe a problem is), or a prediction about the future (such as how much the problem will improve as a result of intervention).

Functions.   As seen in Figure 3-3, we have grouped the major purposes of psychoeducational assessment into four categories of function. These four functions represent the types of decisions for which such assessment may be useful.

1. *Identification.* Data are used to help find and label phenomena of interest. The focus may be on a person, the environment, or both, and may or may not be on problems.

2. *Selection.* Data are used to help make decisions about general changes in status. These usually are discussed as placement decisions, but they also encompass decisions about changes in environments. Specifically, these are decisions about the general nature and form of needed intervention (for example, educational, psychological, or medically oriented treatments; placement in a special setting; changes in the organization of a classroom or school).

3. *Planning for specific change.* Data are used to decide about immediate and short-term objectives and procedures for accomplishing long-term goals. Examples are specific plans or prescriptions for any given day's intervention.

Figure 3-3   *Assessment Processes and Purposes*

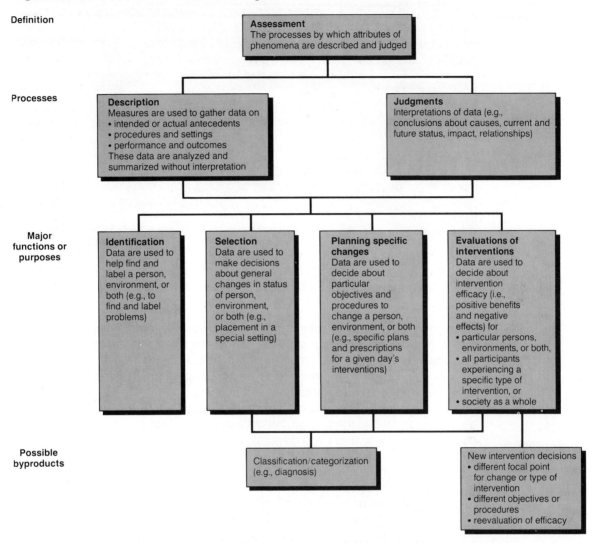

4. *Evaluation of intervention.* Data are used to decide intervention effectiveness based on positive and negative outcomes. Decisions may be made with reference to the impact on (a) particular persons or environments or both, (b) all experiencing a specific intervention, or (c) society as a whole.

In addition to the labeling related to identification, categorization of phenomena (that is, assignment of a classification label) may occur as a byproduct of any of the other three assessment functions.

An example may help clarify the preceding points. Achievement tests are often used to assess reading performance in a given school. The number of right and wrong answers provides a description of performance on a given set of items at a

Observing problems and progress to plan for tomorrow.

given time. Based on these descriptive data, a variety of judgments are likely to be made. They will be based on available norms and prevailing standards.

Different judgments will be made about individuals with identical scores who differ in age. Different judgments may be made about groups living in economically advantaged and disadvantaged communities.

Decisions will be made about whether to assign diagnostic labels to individuals and programs judged to be performing poorly. That is, an individual might be labeled as having a learning disability; a school could be labeled as failing to do its job.

Decisions will be made as to whether some individuals and schools should be helped, and if so, specific plans may be formulated. At a later date, achievement test data again will be used to evaluate performance.

As the example indicates, the same form of data may be used for

• *identification* (for example, finding and labeling individuals and programs),
• *selection* (for example, deciding whether an individual needs special services, or whether a class, school, or district should consider different approaches to instruction),
• *planning for specific changes* (for example, deciding what a given individual should be taught and what specific approach to instruction should be adopted),
• *evaluation* (for example, deciding whether an individual's progress and a school's reading program are adequate).

Choices about what data to gather and what to exclude are guided by the types of judgments and decisions to be made. For instance, as the above example stresses, there are a variety of practical and policy decisions for which assessment data may be helpful. Given the nature and scope of such decisions, it is well to remember that assessment can shape a life as surely as any other form of intervention.

Contrasting Orientations to Remediation

Approaches to remedying learning problems in general, and learning disabilities in particular, have been described extensively in books and journals. At first glance, the variety of teaching models, strategies, and techniques appears overwhelming. One hears about diagnostic-prescriptive teaching, direct instruction, precision teaching, clinical and remedial teaching, behavior modification, metacognitive and learning strategies approaches, pedagogical and psychotherapeutic approaches, and so forth. Despite the variety, approaches to remediation can be grouped into two general and contrasting orientations — underlying versus observable problem approaches (see Table 3-1).

Underlying problems.   This orientation is based on the assumption that most learning problems are symptoms of an underlying problem. For example, cognitive deficits or emotional distress often are identified as underlying learning problems. In the case of learning disabilities, the underlying problem is seen as biological, namely a minor CNS dysfunction. The underlying CNS dysfunction is seen as interfering with processes (for example, short-term memory, selective attention) required to learn effectively and efficiently. As discussed in Chapter 2, over time this state of affairs is seen as affecting development (slowing it down or producing developmental anomalies). In turn, this interferes with acquiring certain prerequisites (for example, visual and auditory perceptual discriminations) needed for learning to read, write, and so forth. Failure to acquire these prerequisites impedes subsequent learning and performance.

As outlined in Table 3-1, those who pursue an underlying problem orientation to learning problems (including learning disabilities) attempt to address a range of motivational and developmental differences and disabilities that disrupt learning. When underlying problems appear resistant to remediation, individuals are taught ways to compensate for a specific disability.

Although the primary overall concern is with underlying problems, classroom programs also provide instruction to teach students age-appropriate school and life skills (especially readiness skills). Strategies also are designed to minimize behavior that interferes with classroom instruction.

The roots of this orientation are found in medical, psychotherapeutic, and educational concepts. Thus, the resulting corrective interventions usually are built on diagnostic testing designed to analyze perceptual, motoric, cognitive, language, and social-emotional functioning, with informal assessment of motivation. In addition, for purposes of diagnosis, neurological or psychoneurological testing may be done. Intervention objectives are stated in nonbehavioral as well as behavioral and criterion-referenced terms. Instructional strategies are eclectic, drawing on psychotherapeutic principles and a variety of teaching models. Thus intervention emphasizes rapport building to reduce anxiety and increase positive

Table 3-1 **Contrasting Orientations to Remediation**

	Underlying Problem Approaches	Observable Problem Approaches
PRIMARY OVER-ALL CONCERN	Motivational and developmental differences and disabilities that disrupt learning	Age-appropriate unlearned skills

SPECIFIC AREAS OF CONCERN

	Motivation • reactive motivation problems • proactive motivation problems Development • perceptual problems • motoric problems • cognitive problems • language problems • social problems • emotional problems Compensatory strategies for overcoming areas of continuing disability	School/life knowledge and skills • readiness (for learning) skills (including strategies for learning) • basic language/reading and math • academic content areas • life adjustment skills (including social and vocational skills)
SECONDARY CONCERN	Enhancing intrinsic motivation Age-appropriate skills (i.e., school/life knowledge and skills)	Interfering behaviors (e.g., poor impulse control, lack of sustained attention)
TERTIARY CONCERN	Interfering behaviors	

PROCESS COMPONENTS

ASSESSMENT

	Construct-oriented assessment of developmental and motivational functioning for program planning and evaluation	School curriculum-based assessment of sequential skills for program planning, monitoring, and evaluation

FORM OF OBJECTIVES

	Nonbehavioral, as well as behavioral and criterion-referenced objectives	Behavioral and criterion-referenced (observable) objectives

REMEDIAL RATIONALE AND METHODS

	Therapeutic-oriented with eclectic instruction (primary emphasis on establishing rapport through interpersonal dynamics and use of a variety of teaching models) • counseling and psychotherapy • expanded options/choices for learning • minimized coercion • enhanced interpersonal options • accommodation of a wide range of motivational and developmental differences • exercises intended to correct developmental anomalies and accelerate lagging development • eclectic instruction related to age-appropriate unlearned skills • eclectic instruction related to compensatory strategies • eclectic strategies for reducing interfering behaviors	Behavior change interventions (primary emphasis on establishing control over behavior through manipulation of reinforcers and instruction in cognitive self-direction and monitoring) • direct instruction to teach missing skills • behavior management to reduce interfering behaviors

involvement, traditional learning principles (for example, mastery learning, reinforcement theory), contemporary views of cognitive strategy instruction, use of social interaction, and so forth.

Observable problems.   As outlined in Table 3-1, a contrasting view sees no value in assuming an underlying problem. Instead, this view assumes that individuals with learning problems simply haven't yet learned the skills they need. Those who hold this view stress a primary concern with age-appropriate, unlearned skills and with the use of direct instruction to teach observable skills.

For instance, based on a student's grade and age, proponents of this approach focus assessment on knowledge and skills through analyses of the school curriculum and daily life tasks. Upon identifying missing skills, criterion-referenced (behavioral) objectives are formulated. In classrooms, intervention also is designed to deal with behavior that interferes with classroom instruction. Strategies emphasize direct and systematic teaching and behavior management drawing on behavior change principles.

The roots of this orientation are in behavior and cognitive behavior-modification concepts. Thus, direct behavior change strategies are stressed (for example, eliciting and reinforcing specific responses, and instruction in cognitive self-direction and monitoring).

As applied in the classroom, both orientations have had to contend with the fact that a significant number of students with learning problems also manifest motivational and behavior problems that interfere with remedial efforts. It is not uncommon for such students to be inattentive and argumentative. In adopting strategies for classroom management, even those who are concerned with underlying problems have tended to use behavior change strategies (for example, manipulating reinforcement contingencies) to control interfering behavior.

Adding general learning strategies.   Because neither remedial orientation has been particularly effective over the long run, there has been a trend on the part of proponents of both to evolve their strategies to include contemporary cognitive concepts and methods. This has given rise to a major emphasis on general learning strategies. This added focus involves teaching strategic and efficient strategies for learning and remembering. Proponents of the prevailing orientations have adapted this approach to fit their own views. That is, among those with an underlying problem orientation, some see learning strategies as another group of underlying abilities that may require remediation. Others see teaching such strategies as a way for an individual to compensate for an area of dysfunction. Advocates of direct instruction view the strategies as another set of skills the learner already should have learned and needs to be taught.

Remedying Learning Disabilities: Prevailing Approaches (p. 314) discusses contrasting orientations to remediation with specific respect to learning disabilities.

"What's your orientation?"

"Whatever works."

Eclecticism

Increasingly, when asked their orientation, professionals in education and psychology seem to be answering, "I am eclectic."

Eclecticism can be a very healthy thing, especially when related to learning problems, where there is so much to learn that interveners cannot afford to be dogmatic. But eclecticism takes many forms. We distinguish three:

1. *Naive eclecticism.* There is a tendency among practitioners simply to keep their eyes open for every new idea that pops up. If it appeals to them, they adopt it with little concern for whether it is valid or consistent with other practices they use. It is this casual and undiscriminating approach that stimulates fads and results in the negative reaction against eclecticism.

2. *Applied eclecticism.* After years of practice, professionals find that certain practices don't work and should be avoided, and some are useful in certain situations but not others. They also come to identify a large number of procedures that fit their philosophy and orientation.

3. *Scholarly eclecticism.* Through systematic theoretical and philosophical analyses and research, some professionals evolve a set of procedures that is comprehensive, integrated, and consistent.

Experienced practitioners who pursue "clinical teaching," for example, tend to be eclectic. *Clinical teaching* is a term used to describe the day-by-day process followed by most remedial teachers. The process can be diagrammed as follows:

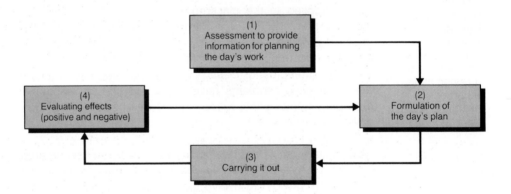

The evaluation provides much of the assessment data for planning the next session. The evaluation findings are supplemented with additional assessment if necessary, and the cycle continues. It is not the cycle alone that makes experienced remedial teachers eclectic, however; it is the fact that they have acquired at least an applied, and sometimes a scholarly, understanding of what is likely to work or not work with a specific individual.

Least Intervention Needed

In making general decisions about intervention, most professionals would agree that the least needed is preferable (Kanfer & Goldstein, 1990). For example, if a youngster can be helped effectively in the regular classroom by the regular teacher, putting the individual in a special education program is unnecessary and undesirable.

The principle of "least intervention needed" and the related idea of placement in the "least restrictive environment" provide a guideline for those who prescribe intervention. The guideline can be stated as follows:

> Do not disrupt or restrict a person's opportunity for a normal range of experiences more than is absolutely necessary.

The guideline recognizes that very disruptive or restrictive interventions tend to narrow an individual's immediate and future options. The negative results can include poor self-concept, social alienation, and loss of career or other life opportunities.

Four topics are particularly germane in thinking about providing the least intervention needed.

1. Should an individual in need of help be kept in the mainstream or placed in a special setting?
2. Is diagnostic labeling necessary?
3. Is the least restrictive environment (LRE) always the best way to meet the individual's needs?
4. Can regular education meet the needs of all learners?

Mainstream versus Special Settings

Special classrooms tend to segregate "handicapped" persons from others. For this reason, the law in the United States requires placement in the "least restrictive environment" for all students with disabilities, including those diagnosed as having learning disabilities. This is to ensure that they are educated in a regular environment along with students who do not have disabilities and in the school they would regularly attend—unless there is a compelling educational reason for not doing so. The idea that such students should be educated as much as possible with students who do not have disabilities is called *mainstreaming* (sometimes referred to as *inclusive education*). The point is to keep students in the mainstream of public education rather than segregating them in special classes or institutions.

As a placement aid, lists have been formulated that describe a continuum of placements ranging from least to most restrictive (see Figure 3-4). Obviously the least restrictive "placement" is to keep people in regular situations, using special assistance only as needed. Thus a decision to place a student in a special class is somewhat more restrictive than keeping the individual in a regular class, and full-day placement in a special class is even more restrictive. The most restrictive placement would be assignment to a special school or institution. By law, in the United States, schools must have a continuum of alternative placements for students with disabilities.

The ideas of least intervention needed and placement in the least restrictive environment are rooted in "the principle of normalization" (Bank-Mikkelsen, 1968, 1976; Wolfensberger, 1972). This principle raises concerns over labeling and

Figure 3-4   A Continuum of Placements Ranging from Least to Most Restrictive

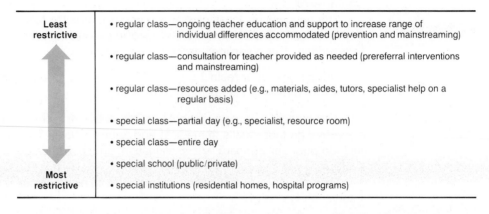

Least restrictive ↑ ↓ **Most restrictive**	• regular class—ongoing teacher education and support to increase range of individual differences accommodated (prevention and mainstreaming) • regular class—consultation for teacher provided as needed (prereferral interventions and mainstreaming) • regular class—resources added (e.g., materials, aides, tutors, specialist help on a regular basis) • special class—partial day (e.g., specialist, resource room) • special class—entire day • special school (public/private) • special institutions (residential homes, hospital programs)

supports mainstreaming and deinstitutionalization. In the United States, such ideas also are consistent with the Regular Education Initiative (REI), or General Education Initiative (GEI).

The General Education Initiative, and earlier calls for noncategorical programming, arose as a reaction to the proliferation of separate educational programs for each special education group (learning disabilities, mental retardation, emotional disturbance). The various attempts to revamp special education have underscored deficiencies and negative consequences of current practices and policies. For example, critics suggest that current procedures lack reliability and validity, fail to distinguish specific treatment needs appropriately, lead to a fragmentation of services and professional training, and result in a "bounty hunter" mentality (Hobbs, 1975a, 1975b, 1980; Jenkins, Pious, & Peterson, 1988; Morsink, Thomas, & Smith-Davis, 1987; Reynolds, Wang, & Walberg, 1987). These criticisms are bolstered by the view that current forms of special programming produce insufficient benefits to warrant special placements (Gartner & Lipsky, 1987; Glass, 1983; Jenkins et al., 1988; Leinhardt & Pallay, 1982; Slavin, Madden, Karweit, et al., 1991; Stainback & Stainback, 1984).

Opponents of fundamental efforts to revamp special education warn that too much normalization will lead to inequities (Fuchs & Fuchs, 1988; Kauffman, 1989). Specifically, they argue that many students will suffer whenever regular teachers lack the skills and time required to deal effectively with the diversity of educational needs in their classrooms. In addition, they stress that support for special education will be jeopardized because the general public, elected officials, policymakers, judges, administrators, and so forth will not appreciate special individual needs. To bolster their argument, they point out that just such negative consequences arose in England and Wales when disability categories were abolished (Feniak, 1988).

Labeling: Is It Necessary?

Assignment of a label such as *learning disabilities* plays a major role in decisions to treat individuals specially. As a result, diagnostic labels have been a target of criticism (National Association of School Psychologists, 1986). In addition to the above concerns, such labeling has played a key role in segregating children with physical, cognitive, social, and emotional differences—including a disproportionate number from minority groups (Copeland, 1983; Heller, Holtzman, & Messick, 1982; MacMillan, Hendricks, & Watkins, 1988).

From a transactional perspective, present labeling practices are criticized for presuming that most learning and behavior problems are caused by pathology within the individual (Hobbs, 1975a). This perspective downplays the possibility that many individuals assigned special education labels have problems initially caused (and perhaps maintained) by environmental factors. And, systematically downplaying the environment's role keeps intervention narrowly focused on individual change (that is, strategies to increase coping and adaptation by individuals). Whether intended or not, this results in deemphasizing interventions designed to alter environments and systems so they can accommodate a wide range of individual differences.

It should be stressed, however, that not all critics of current diagnostic practices are against labeling in some form (Wang & Walberg, 1988). Many want to replace current categories with a system that identifies special individual needs (1) only as such needs become relevant to providing an appropriate education and (2) through a process and terminology that have direct relevance to intervention and that minimize negative consequences (for example, Type I, II, and III learning problems).

Given the scope of concerns, dissatisfaction with current labels and diagnostic procedures is quite understandable and appropriate. Calls for improvement in classification and identification systems certainly are warranted and timely. Calls for eliminating all classification and identification, however, are premature. We hasten to add that to argue for classification is not to argue for tying all forms of special help to formal diagnoses. Classification is essential to scientific research and basic to efforts to improve interventions.

Needs Come First

There has been much support for the idea of using the least intervention and for descriptions of least restrictive placements. There are, however, some problems. For instance, the least restrictive setting may be the most restrictive in the long run if it cannot meet the needs of the individual.

Take the case of Joel and his friend Jesse. In sixth grade, they were in the same class, and both were behind in their reading. It was decided to keep them in a regular sixth-grade classroom and provide special tutoring in class for an hour a day. Joel has a learning disability and is reading at no better than the second-grade level; Jesse has no disability and is reading at the fifth-grade level. Both respond reasonably well to the tutoring. Jesse also begins to perform satisfactorily during other times of the day. Joel continues to have trouble learning at other times, and he also tends to be a behavior problem. While the intervention plan keeps both students in the mainstream, someone is bound to ask,

Does Joel need to be placed in a special class?

Might it be better to place Joel temporarily in a special classroom that can be more responsive to his educational needs so that he can overcome his problems and then return to the mainstream?

The argument continues,

After all, isn't it much *less restrictive* in the long run to get intensive treatment so the problem can be overcome as quickly as possible? In so many cases, what might seem like the less restrictive approach may mean added years of involvement in special treatments, and the results may not even be as good.

Opponents of special class placements would answer,

Those are good points, but the evidence suggests that special classrooms are not particularly effective.

And, they say,

Some never do get to go back to mainstream programs after being placed in special schools and institutions.

Placement decisions clearly are difficult!

It is assumed that placement will be in the least restrictive, but also most effective, environment. A short stay in a more restrictive placement may be more effective than a long stay in a minimally restrictive, but less effective, program. In general, the relatively small number of individuals with severe problems are the most likely candidates for the more restrictive placements.

Besides the least restrictive environment guideline, financial support and program availability can be major factors in deciding school placements. Indeed, there is a trend toward approaching educational placements as an administrative rather than a remedial arrangement. For example, efforts to return students from special schools and classes to regular programs (mainstreaming) generally have not been paired with improvements in the ability of regular programs to serve the special needs of such students. Thus, students have been shifted from one setting to another without significant attention to whether the new setting contains adequate resources for appropriate remediation.

One final note about placement in special settings: It is widely recognized that all decisions to place individuals in special settings need regular review to detect placement errors and to determine how effective remediation is.

Regular and Special Education

Clearly, the matter of least intervention needed goes right to the roots of the difference between regular and special education. One way to look at the difference is to see regular education classes as trying to serve as wide a range of people as they can. Those people whom regular educators cannot serve appropriately need special education in some form (see McCann, Semmel, & Nevin, 1985). The less the regular education program can do, the more the need for special education. The unanswered questions are:

- What range of individual differences can regular education programs serve under *optimal conditions?*
- What range of individual differences can regular education programs serve under *typical conditions?*

Most regular programs probably could handle a greater range of individuals than they do. To do so, however, some changes in these programs are needed. For those who argue that mainstreaming can work well for many exceptional students, a basic assumption is that most regular classroom programs must be changed before they can be successful with such students. These changes include additional materials, equipment, and procedures, and some training for the teacher in how to use them.

Changes also are recommended in staffing and support patterns and staff–student ratios, so that a teacher has more time to devote to those with special needs. Examples of these changes are team teaching and the addition of aides or tutors (including peer tutors). The right pattern and ratio certainly will vary depending on the number of students with special needs and severe problems. In addition, there is likely to be a call periodically for consultation and specialist help in and out of the classroom (for example, resource teachers — reading and speech specialists to assess student problems and clarify needs). Finally, it may still be necessary for certain students (those with Type III learning problems) to have some special help outside their classroom daily.

If regular classrooms are not changed, the potential value of mainstreaming cannot be fairly tested. The longer regular classrooms stay as they are, the more call there will be for placements in special education programs.

No Magic Bullets

Controversial Treatments and Fads (p. 309) discusses concerns associated with vision training, colored lenses, stimulant medication, special diets, megavitamin therapy, CNS training, and vestibular treatment.

Ethical Concerns About Negative Effects (p. 391) highlights (a) dilemmas that arise when diagnostic and remedial practices produce negative consequences, and (b) ethical principles relevant to such practices.

Medical researchers warn that it is a mistake to think about medication as if it worked like a magic bullet. They say many people tend to think that, once administered, a drug speeds directly to its target and cures the problem. Medication is imagined to disappear upon entering the body and to reappear magically at its goal where it performs its work and again disappears. This belief fosters a tendency to ignore such facts as: (1) drugs can cause damage as they go through the body, and (2) drugs don't necessarily stop having effects as soon as they have done the work they are intended to do (Lennard, Epstein, Bernstein, & Ransom, 1970).

We all dream of miracle cures, but most of us recognize that quick and easy treatments for difficult problems are rare. Still, when we are involved, the hope for a miracle is strong. This makes us a bit too receptive to those claiming to have an effective answer and a bit too ready to ignore possible harmful effects of treatments (see Feature 3-1).

There are no magic bullets in remedying learning problems. All approaches can do harm as well as good.

It's customary to speak of the unwanted consequences arising from treatment as "negative side effects." This term makes it sound as if the harmful effects are inconsequential. Negative consequences indeed may be trivial, but they also may be life-shaping—physically, psychologically, economically, and socially.

Commonly discussed potential negative consequences of assessing and correcting learning problems include:

- invasion of privacy
- errors of identification
- stigmatization
- segregation and social isolation
- limitation of current and future opportunities
- overdependence on others
- creation of self-fulfilling prophecies
- burdensome financial costs

Ethical practitioners, of course, try to minimize negative consequences and try to ensure that benefits outweigh harm. Controversy arises when there is a disagreement about whether a given negative consequence should be tolerated at all and whether benefits outweigh harm.

Harmful effects have a way of coming back to haunt professionals. Professionals who downplay negative consequences of intervention and professions that allow the public to become overdependent on them may be pleased with the response at first. However, there often is a backlash when the public becomes disappointed and disenchanted because of the repeated failure of the professionals to live up to their expert images. Such backlash is seen in the increasing malpractice suits in medicine and psychology and in the demands for accountability and excellence in education.

Feature 3-1   On Harmful Effects

When treatments are suggested for bothersome problems that have no proven cure, most of us are tempted to try them. This is especially so when the treatment is intuitively appealing and advocated by someone who seems to have expertise. The attitude "What harm can it do?" operates whenever possible harm is not obvious or well publicized.

Use of diets and megavitamins for those diagnosed with learning disabilities and attention deficits and hyperactivity seem to many people to have no potential harmful effects. Indeed, advocates of such treatments tend to claim this is so.

Concerned physicians, however, raise cautions (Sieben, 1977; Silver, 1987). Sieben stresses special diets may cause

- a person to feel different from others;
- family conflict when parents must insist that a child follow the diet;
- elimination of foods that have positive effects (for example, antioxidant preservatives that may inhibit carcinogens);
- a person to use failure to follow the diet as an excuse for ongoing problems; or
- other, potentially more effective actions to be ignored.

Megavitamins may cause

- edema (watery swelling) of the brain (large doses of vitamin A),
- kidney stones (mass doses of vitamin C), or
- liver damage (vitamin B_6 and nicotinic acid).

Neither the positive nor harmful effects of diets and megavitamins have been studied adequately. Without appropriate evidence, the concerns remain simply concerns, just as the promises remain simply promises.

Even treatments with fairly well-publicized harmful effects may produce additional unexpected negative outcomes. For example, those who prescribe stimulant medication usually point out possible side effects such as appetite loss, sleeplessness, irritability, and retardation of physical growth. However, most are unlikely to warn of a potential relationship to Tourette's syndrome. This hereditary syndrome is characterized by multiple repetitive tics and uncontrollable verbalizations that often, but not always, include cursing (Bronheim, 1991). In 1983, a report was published in *The Journal of the American Medical Association* on research done at Yale University suggesting that about 15 percent of children with Tourette's might not have developed the syndrome if stimulant drugs had not been used to treat hyperactivity and attention problems. The implication is that those with a family history of Tourette's may be particularly at risk when stimulant medication is prescribed. Further study is needed, but the point is clear.

Besides surprising harmful effects, some consequences are so subtle and pervasive that they creep into our lives without our awareness. Critics of institutionalized professional activity such as Ivan Illich, R. D. Laing, Irving Goffman, and Thomas Szasz have warned about such hidden consequences. For example, society's way of thinking about learning problems is shaped subtly by professional activity. The public is led to think about individual differences (quirks) as problems; problems are thought of as disorders within people rather than as trouble with the way society functions. Such thinking leads to treatments focused on changing people rather than institutions and to overreliance on medical, psychological, and educational professionals for answers (Illich, 1976).

Summing Up

David's parents have been confronted with a dilemma. David seems to need special help to succeed at school. There are decisions to be made: some by the family, some by those who provide special help.

One set of options involves deciding about services, places where remediation and treatment will be carried out, and who should carry out the options. The choice may be to pursue special education services in or out of special classrooms and schools; medically related and psychotherapeutic treatments also may be chosen. In all cases, decisions are guided by the idea of using the least intervention needed. But David's parents find this is not an easy guideline to use.

The other set of decisions involves the form that help should take each day. For example, two contrasting remedial orientations have dominated programming. Each orientation is based on different assumptions about what must be done to help students like David.

It should be clear by now that contemporary remedial and treatment approaches can be complex and controversial. Because assessment plays such a major role in all this, Chapter 4 offers a more detailed discussion of the multiple facets of assessment, highlighting prevailing approaches, concerns, and new directions.

Take a few minutes to think about your own views regarding intervention.

1. If you had a problem requiring a psychologist or a medical doctor, would you want her or him to follow the principle of least intervention needed?
2. Would you want the psychologist to have an underlying or observable problem orientation?
3. What about the M.D.? What type of orientation should he or she have?

Remedying Learning Disabilities: Prevailing Approaches (p. 314) explores major approaches to remedying learning disabilities from contrasting orientations:

1. Underlying problem approaches are discussed in terms of their focus on
   - perception
   - motor functioning
   - language
   - general cognitive functioning

2. Observable problem approaches are discussed in terms of their focus on
   - observable skills and objectives
   - direct instruction

Controversial Treatments and Fads (p. 309) contains some interventions specifically developed for Type III problems (learning disabilities) that are controversial. The discussion briefly reviews the following:

- optometric vision training
- Irlen's colored lenses
- stimulant medication (such as Ritalin)
- special diet
- megavitamin therapy
- CNS training
- vestibular treatment

Ethical Concerns About Negative Effects (p. 391) points out that potential negative effects are facts of life for practitioners. The dilemmas are difficult and complex, and there are no easy answers. However, there are some concepts and principles that can help. We have outlined three topics:

- balancing costs versus benefits
- understanding the complexity of fairness
- applying the concept of informed consent

Assessing Learning Problems

Facets of Assessment
   Identification
   Placement
   Planning Specific Changes
   Evaluating Intervention
   Other Factors Shaping Assessment

Fundamental Concerns About Prevailing Practices
   Problems of Interpretation
   Biasing Factors
   Ethics
   Meeting Minimal Standards

Beyond Conventional Practices
   Preassessment Interventions
   Focal Point
   Single- versus Multi-Stage Decision Making
   Interventionist Assessment

Summing Up

We cannot perceive unless we anticipate, but
we must not see only what we anticipate.

Neisser, 1976 (p. 43)

Much time and effort is devoted to identifying individuals with learning problems and deciding what to do with them. As an integral part of the process, professionals give tests, carry out interviews, and make observations and ratings.

Attitudes toward prevailing assessment practices vary considerably. They are defended and cursed with equal vigor. Professionals are often confused by contradictory claims about the validity of a procedure. To the novice, it must be even more bewildering. Chapter 3 introduced the many purposes of assessment; this chapter is devoted to a more detailed discussion of this key component of intervention. Here we focus on each facet of assessment, emphasizing its uses, abuses, and limitations, and noting some contemporary trends.

Facets of Assessment

At the turn of the twentieth century, Alfred Binet and his co-workers undertook the task of developing assessment procedures to identify children unable to profit from regular instruction. Since that time, use of such procedures has been viewed as both necessary and desirable; this has led to a tremendous proliferation of assessment practices. However, as formal assessment practices became popular, widespread, and profitable, major concerns and controversies arose. This section details the four functions of assessment introduced in Chapter 3 (see Figure 3-3, p. 51).

Identification

Assessment for Learning Disabilities' Diagnosis, Placement, and Program Planning (p. 328) reviews (a) assessment approaches used to diagnose, place, and plan programs for persons with learning disabilities, and (b) concerns that have been raised about certain practices.

Identifying individuals with learning problems is an intriguing detective job. Increasingly there are calls for large-scale searches for "underachievers," "school failures," "high challenges," or "individuals at risk," and of course for those with learning disabilities. As a result, screening designed to find and label those with learning problems, particularly young children, has become widely accepted.

The current ethos stresses that a person manifesting a problem ought to have professional help. Parents, teachers, doctors, legislators, and judges usually see it as their duty to refer the person to a professional helper. Such referrals often are based on informal assessment and thus are an informal type of screening.

Formal screening to identify persons who have problems or who are "at risk" is accomplished through individual or group assessment procedures. Group procedures are usually first-level screens that are expected to overidentify problems (that is, they identify many persons who do not have significant problems). Errors are supposed to be detected by follow-up assessments (see Feature 4-1).

Placement

The major practical objective of identifying problems is to correct them. Thus the ultimate value of finding problems depends on the nature of subsequent placement and corrective interventions.

As suggested in Chapter 3, placement considerations for individuals with learning problems involve understanding the problem's general nature and having information on available interventions. Once these matters are clarified, the placement process itself has three aspects:

- determining the general nature and form of interventions needed,
- deciding which of these to pursue, and
- from the service provider's perspective, deciding whom to serve.

Each of these is discussed below.

Screening for Learning Disabilities (p. 323) stresses the nature and scope of screening practices and what research suggests about the state of the art.

Nature and form of intervention needed.   One of the most profound intervention decisions involves whether an individual should remain in the current setting or transfer to another. Such a decision is based on whether the person's problem is viewed as mild to moderate or severe and pervasive, and whether it is related to learning, behavior, or emotional functioning.

In some cases, adequate data for assessing severity and pervasiveness may come from information provided by those who have observed the individual's functioning in various settings (classroom, home, and recreation centers). When such information is not adequate, additional data can be gathered through psychoeducational testing, which may have been administered as part of the identification process.

When data indicate that a person is not making appropriate progress, what-

Feature 4-1   Concerns About Screening

Referrals based on informal assessment are commonplace. How people decide where to refer is an interesting—and sometimes controversial—matter. The literature that emphasizes a societal context suggests that referral is shaped by the status of both the referrer and the person being referred. Socioeconomic status, race, education, age, and sex of both the referrer and those referred can be major biasing factors. (We have more to say about factors that bias assessment later in this chapter.)

Even when referrals are based on formal screening instruments, there is reason for concern. We have mentioned the tendency to over-identify problems. In addition, screening proce-

dures are often misused. For example, when data from first-level screening tests and rating scales are used to make tentative classifications and prescriptions, the labels and analyses are sometimes allowed to become definitive statements about an individual's status and needs. Given the low validity of first-level screens, especially those used with infants and primary grade children, this is unfortunate. At best, most screening procedures provide a preliminary indication that something may be significantly wrong. When diagnostic classifications and specific prescriptions are to be made, we need to use assessment procedures with greater validity.

"Of course, there are limits to what different people are capable of achieving, but we should make no uninformed assumptions about what these limits are." (Stevenson & Stigler, 1992, p. 223)

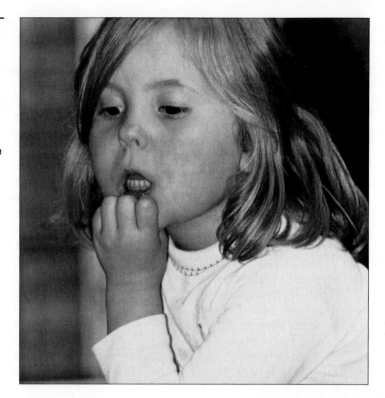

ever the cause, the tendency is to consider use of special services and place-ments. Persons with severe and pervasive problems are often placed in special population settings such as special classrooms and institutions. Mild to moderate problems are supposed to be dealt with in normal population settings (that is, the mainstream) — either through modifying it somewhat or adding extra (ancillary) services or both. Placement decisions focus first on major intervention needs, then on which, if any, ancillary interventions seem indicated. In many cases, decisions about ancillary activity are best made after major interventions are given an ade-quate trial and found to be insufficient.

Ancillary interventions can involve

1. extra instruction such as tutoring
2. enrichment opportunities such as projects, learning by discovery, arts and crafts, and recreation
3. psychologically oriented treatments such as individual and family therapy
4. biologically oriented treatments such as medication

Assessment data for making decisions about extra instruction involve little more than an indication from a learner or teacher that current instructional time and resources are insufficient. Decisions to offer enrichment opportunities are not based on assessment data but on theory or belief about the value of such activity. The same is true of most psychological and biological interventions.

Client decision making.   Recent years have seen increasing interest in consumer concerns. In Chapter 6 we highlight a variety of ethical and legal issues that have been raised about the role of clients in decision making.

Assessment can provide basic information for consumers about such matters as: What is available? What best meets the consumer's needs in terms of location, cost, and type of intervention? and How can the consumer get admitted to a desired program? Unfortunately, even when a broad range of resources is available, as in large urban centers, systematic information is rarely presented to aid consumers in selecting services.

Professional and agency decisions.   Once an application is made to a professional or agency, the focus shifts from the consumer to the service provider. Service providers use assessment data as aids in making placement decisions. Sometimes applicants are rejected because they do not fit established eligibility criteria. At other times, acceptable applicants must be rejected because too many have applied. Discussion of whom to select stresses data on type, severity, and pervasiveness of problem—and sometimes data on demographic factors.

Placement decisions involve institutional or individual values or both (Cronbach & Gleser, 1965). Data and criteria used in accepting and rejecting applicants usually reflect institutional values. For example, a professional or an agency may want only persons whose characteristics are viewed as maximizing the service's efficacy, efficiency, or reputation. Thus selection may favor one sex, or individuals from certain backgrounds, or those with learning problems who are not hard to handle behaviorally.

It should be noted that the literature on placement accuracy is sparse. Moreover, validation studies are not reliable. If a person placed in a service does not improve, it may be unclear whether this was due to

1. selecting the wrong type of intervention,
2. the intractability of the problem, or
3. the way the intervention was implemented.

Given the likelihood of error, as well as other factors that can make a placement unsatisfactory, placement decisions must be reassessed regularly.

Planning Specific Changes

Prevailing assessment procedures for planning the specifics of an intervention reflect contrasting views toward remediation. They also reflect differing views about how to design instruction.

Remedial orientations shape assessment practices.   Advocates of a particular orientation will usually argue for their procedures and sometimes argue against those reflecting other orientations. To understand why requires some knowledge of opposing views about what is to be remedied.

Essentially, current assessment practices have been dominated by the two remedial orientations discussed in Chapter 3—approaches emphasizing either

Remedying Learning Disabilities: Prevailing Approaches (p. 314) discusses contrasting orientations to remediation with specific respect to learning disabilities.

underlying problems or direct instruction of observable skills. As the emphasis on metacognitive (general learning) strategies has evolved, this has generated additional ideas about remedying learning problems. Each orientation defines remedial needs in different terms and thus specifies assessment differing in nature and scope.

(a) Underlying problems. Advocates of the underlying problem orientation (sometimes called the *process* or *diagnostic-prescriptive model*) postulate that learning problems result from disabilities related to specific areas of development. Thus they focus on assessing such concepts as perceptual, motor, linguistic, and memory functioning as a basis for planning treatment. They assume underlying problems must be corrected or compensatory strategies must be acquired before basics such as reading can be learned.

The ultimate value of the underlying problem orientation is yet to be determined. Available tests and research based on this orientation have been criticized severely (see reviews by Arter & Jenkins, 1979; Coles, 1978). In response, it has been argued that such criticism is not evidence that the basic premises of the underlying problem orientation are invalid (Colarusso, 1987; Snart, 1985). The poor validity of a given test says little about the theory upon which it is based. Recognizing this, some critics have directed their arguments against the theoretical assumptions of the approach (Carnine & Woodward, 1988). However, recent emphasis on cognitive and temperament components of learning problems has revitalized the theoretical underpinnings of this orientation and renewed interest in developing remedial and assessment approaches aimed at underlying problems.

(b) Observable problems. Those oriented to direct instruction of what is observable are concerned with specific knowledge and skills (including traditional readiness-prerequisite skills). They concentrate on what has not yet been learned by the individual. That is, they assess, teach, and reteach such basics as reading, language, mathematics, and social skills. Their skill-oriented assessments tend to use standardized achievement tests; unstructured, informal skill diagnostic tests; observation of daily performance; and criterion-referenced evaluations.

The observable nature of what is assessed has made this orientation attractive to those who write education agency guidelines. As a consequence, many such guidelines have been written in ways that shape the formulation and evaluation of programs in behavioral terms.

Advocates for focusing on underlying problems argue that such dysfunctions can interfere with learning skills and that, by ignoring underlying problems, direct instructors prevent some individuals from making progress. Motivation theorists, on the other hand, criticize both orientations for ignoring factors such as avoidance and anxiety. As to observable skills themselves, there has been controversy about what skills should be assessed and about whether all assessed skills need to be taught formally.

(c) Strategy problems. Those who pursue metacognitive (general learning) strategies emphasize the awareness and control learners can produce over the learning process. That is, the focus is on the ways an individual thinks about how to learn (one's awareness of strategies for learning and one's ability to direct one's thinking about how to learn). Some interveners stress metacognitive skills (Brown

& Campione, 1986); others distinguish metacognitive knowledge from metacognitive experiences (Flavell, 1985; Garner, 1987).

The most used procedures in assessing metacognitive knowledge and cognitive monitoring are verbal interviews and error detection. Assessment procedures are chosen for their relevance to school learning and for their ease of use (Harris & Pressley, 1991; Wiener, 1986; Wong, 1991). Such procedures have been criticized both methodologically and conceptually (for example, problems of reliability and validity related to interviews, debates over what strategies can and should be taught).

The interest in cognitive components underlying learning problems goes beyond metacognitive knowledge and cognitive monitoring (Swanson, 1988). In what is called the dynamic assessment movement (see Feature 4-2), a variety of cognitive skills and processes have been identified as appropriate for remedial intervention (Campione & Brown, 1987; Feuerstein, 1979).

We do not expect that issues surrounding current orientations to remediation will be resolved in the near future. Although specific instruments may be discredited, advocates of each orientation will continue to use assessment procedures that reflect their remedial approach and will continue to criticize each other. At the

Feature 4-2   *The Dynamic Assessment Movement*

The term *dynamic assessment* was coined by Feuerstein (1980). During the 1980s, the desire to use more interventionist approaches to assessment coalesced into what has come to be called the dynamic assessment movement. Dynamic assessment can be seen as a reaction to static (conventional psychometric) approaches to measuring intelligence. Static approaches are criticized for treating IQ as a trait rather than a score, thereby equating it with learning ability and ignoring the nature of cognitive development and functioning and the influence of handicapping conditions and cultural bias. Static approaches and techniques are also criticized as too limited for planning interventions.

The dynamic assessment movement wants to go beyond conventional psychometric techniques. It is interested in determining "the operation of basic psychological processes presumed responsible for acquisition of the information requested on standard tests" (Campione & Brown, 1987; p. 82).

Feuerstein and his colleagues (Feuerstein, Rand, Jensen, Kaniel, & Tzuriel, 1987) stress that their approach to dynamic assessment provides data not only on cognitive functioning but also on

"structural cognitive modifiability . . . the very structural nature of the cognitive processes that directly determine cognitive functioning in more than one area of mental activity" (pp. 42–43). Their intent is to assess the efficiency of specific cognitive processes, not just measure enhanced performance or the magnitude of response to instruction (see Haywood, Brown & Wingenfeld, 1990; Lidz, 1987).

Because dynamic assessment involves prompting and teaching, it is also used to identify intervention approaches that seem to work well for the individual. Thus the products of the assessment are seen as providing information on both what and how to teach. In order to gather such data, the process is designed and implemented as an intervention to improve performance. Improved performance is interpreted as an indication of the learner's real capability as well as the ability to change (learning potential).

Because the content focus of dynamic assessment is on underlying processes, critics of the underlying problem orientation have attacked the movement. In doing so, they reiterate arguments that the measures and theoretical assumptions lack validity.

same time, advocates of environmental and transactional models can be expected to escalate their criticism and propose alternative assessment procedures.

Matching instruction to the learner.   Differing views about how to design instruction for specific learners also lead to divergent assessment perspectives. For instance, concern has been raised that assessment for individualized, as contrasted with personalized, instruction results in an inadequate instructional design (Adelman & Taylor, 1983a; 1986).

Individualization typically emphasizes detecting a student's deficiencies by monitoring daily performance and then modifying instruction to address the deficiencies. Approaches like dynamic assessment attempt to assess the best teaching approach for a given child. In most cases, however, a major shortcoming of assessment based on individualized instruction is that it overemphasizes developmental deficiencies and underemphasizes motivation—especially intrinsic motivation. This is not surprising, given how little systematic attention researchers and practitioners have paid to the concept of intrinsic motivation.

In contrast, the concept of personalization could broaden the focus of assessment. *Personalization* encompasses individualization by stressing the importance of designing intervention to match not only current learner capabilities but also levels of motivation, and especially intrinsic motivation. This latter emphasis is seen as critical, given the degree to which intrinsic motivation can profoundly affect current, as well as long-term, performance and learning (Adelman, 1978; Adelman & Taylor, 1990; Deci & Chandler, 1986). Thus a major implication of personalization is that systematic procedures are needed to address motivation.

All formal and informal procedures used to assess and prescribe specific treatment plans raise basic concerns (Salvia & Ysseldyke, 1991). Many experts suggest that among problem populations a person's performance is often affected by low motivation or high anxiety. When this is the case, the findings are "contaminated." Under such circumstances, it is impossible to know whether failure to demonstrate an ability represents a real deficiency; thus it is easy to misprescribe treatment.

It is easy, for example, to make the mistake of planning to teach skills that a person has already acquired—instead of helping the individual overcome psychological problems that interfere with performance. Also, concerns have been raised that comprehensive remedial plans need to go beyond what can be readily assessed by prevailing practices. Finally, it has been stressed that assessment may be viewed as only one facet of making intervention decisions.

Evaluating Intervention

It is not uncommon to hear professionals say, "If it works, use it!" Unfortunately, there is rarely adequate evidence about what really works in the long term. One reason that conflicting orientations exist is the difficulty of measuring what works and what doesn't. A considerable amount of research has been reported; however, measurement and other research methodology problems have made it impossible to prove the worth of the programs studied (Tindal, 1985).

Nevertheless, assessment plays a major role in efforts to answer the basic question: Are interventions for learning problems effective? Although some may prefer to ignore this question, two facts make this impossible. One, evaluative research is essential to improve interventions. Two, this is an age of accountability, and evaluation is increasingly mandated by legislation, government regulations, and funding agencies. It is easy to mandate accountability. Unfortunately, such mandates ignore the fact that current evaluation practices are terribly inadequate (see Feature 4-3). Thus, while mandated evaluation goes on continually, comprehensive and valid evaluation is rare.

Chapter 12 discusses evaluating interventions. At this point, it is sufficient to indicate that evaluation involves determining the worth or value of something (Stake, 1967, 1976). In formal terms, we define evaluation as *a systematic process designed to describe and judge the overall impact and value of an intervention for purposes of making decisions and advancing knowledge.*

More specifically, the goals and objectives of evaluation include the following:

- to describe and judge an intervention's (a) rationale, including assumptions and intentions, and (b) standards for making judgments
- to describe and judge an intervention's (a) actual activity, including intended and unintended procedures and outcomes, and (b) costs (financial and negative effects)
- to make decisions about continuing, modifying, or stopping an intervention for an individual or for all those enrolled in a program

Feature 4-3   Evaluation Problems and Issues

Problems arise because of limitations in measurement capability. Unfortunately, many of the measurement instruments are not highly reliable or valid. Furthermore, because of accountability pressures there has been an overemphasis on measuring immediate behavioral outcomes. This is unfortunate, because many desirable program outcomes are not easily translated into immediate behaviors (for example, self-concept, attitudes toward learning, problem-solving capabilities, creativity) and thus are deemphasized in planning and evaluating programs. Comprehensive evaluation requires a range of valid procedures, and development of such procedures requires considerable financial commitment. Because of the costs, evaluation remains a token item in most budgets.

Issues about evaluation arise because of different views about its appropriate focus (Is it sufficient to gather data on person variables?

Should long-term outcomes be measured as well as immediate effects?) and about the best way to gather and interpret data (What specific measures and design should be used? Should there be emphasis on minimizing the negative effects of evaluation?). Because of differing views, issues arise over whose perspective should determine the evaluation focus, methods, and interpretation. Should the views of teachers, parents, students, researchers, or funding agencies prevail? Stated more boldly, whose biases or vested interests should prevail? (We have more to say about biases later in the chapter.)

Finally, we note that decisions as to what and how to evaluate are made by those administering or funding a program. Currently, there is little student or parent involvement in such decisions and, not surprisingly, there is little emphasis on client–consumer judgments of whether a program has value.

- to advance knowledge about interventions to improve (a) practices, (b) training, and (c) theory

The information needed to meet these purposes comes from comprehensive evaluations that include both immediate and long-term program data. Commonly, programs are evaluated using learner-centered paper-and-pencil tests of ability and performance, reports (including grades), and systematic interviews and observations of behavior. However, because such practices are so limited when it comes to assessing complex performance, a trend has evolved toward what is being called "authentic" assessment (Archibald & Newman, 1988; Linn, Baker, & Dunbar, 1991; Wiggins, 1989). The focus of this trend is on performance-based evaluation using such procedures as essays, open-ended responses, responses to computer simulations, interview data, and analyses of student journals and work that is accumulated over time in a portfolio.

Procedures and Instruments for Assessing Learning Problems (p. 341) presents an outline listing by category frequently cited approaches for assessing psychoeducational problems.

Other Factors Shaping Assessment

In addition to having four major purposes, activity related to assessment occurs in phases, and differs in terms of focus and types of procedures used (see Table 4-1). Moreover, there are a variety of options in deciding what and how to assess.

For example, stimulus-and-response conditions may differ in terms of the number of variables assessed, their complexity, and whether they are simulated or natural. Variations also occur with respect to (a) how ambiguous and subjective the stimuli are, (b) how well standardized the administration procedures are, (c) how obtrusive the procedures are, and (d) how much they cause unintended reactions. There are also important considerations about similarities and differences between the assessor and the assessed (for example, in terms of race, cultural background, socioeconomic status, and gender).

Although we recognize that such variations in practice influence both the form of assessment activity and the findings, there is little agreement and considerable concern about their impact.

Fundamental Concerns About Prevailing Practices

Reviewers have been consistent in noting that most assessment practices for learning problems raise major concerns with respect to their validity as diagnostic and prescriptive tools (Coles, 1987; Fewell, 1991; Reynolds & Kaiser, 1990; Salvia & Ysseldyke, 1991). On a broader level, there has been concern over the way conventional assessment practices perpetuate an unsatisfactory status quo.

By understanding some fundamentals, one can appreciate the importance of new approaches that are designed to go beyond prevailing practices. In the preceding discussion, we alluded to a variety of concerns. This section takes a more systematic look at

- problems affecting interpretation of assessment data
- factors that bias assessment
- ethical concerns

Table 4-1   Nature and Scope of Assessment Activity

I. *Functions and purposes of assessment*
   A. **Identification**
      1. Screening and referral
      2. Diagnostic labeling
      3. Nonpathological attributes
   B. **Selection/placement**
      1. Clarification of options
      2. Client decisions about general changes in status
      3. Professional and agency decisions to accept or reject applicants
   C. **Specific planning for change**
      1. Detailed objectives
      2. Detailed procedures
   D. **Evaluation of interventions**
      1. Individual efficacy
      2. Efficacy for all participants
      3. Impact on society

II. *Major phases related to assessment*
   A. **Preparatory decisions about what is to be assessed** (implicit or explicit rationale for assessment activity)
   B. **Description** ("measurements" of specified variables and serendipitous data gathering, followed by analyses and descriptive summaries)
   C. **Judgments** (interpretations)
   D. **Communication and decision making with reference to assessment purposes**

III. *Focus of assessment*
   A. **Focal point**
      1. Person(s) — individuals or groups of individuals
      2. Environment(s)
      3. Person–environment transactions
   B. **Nature of phenomena**
      1. Problematic–nonproblematic conditions
      2. Observable–inferred
      3. Proximal–distal
      4. Historic–current–future expectations
   C. **Levels**
      1. Molecular–molar analyses of persons
      2. Primary, secondary, tertiary contextual analysis
      3. Transaction of person–environment
   D. **Areas or domains**
      1. Biological and psychological processes
      2. Motor and verbal functioning
      3. Physical environment
      4. Social environment
      5. Transaction of person–environment

IV. *Types of procedures and instruments* (standardized, semi-standardized, or unstandardized)
   A. **Interviews and written personal reports** (responses to oral or written questions, inventories of items, etc.)
   B. **Observations**
   C. **Verbal and performance measures** (objective instruments such as achievement tests; projective instruments such as thematic pictures; instruments developed by teachers, psychologists, and MDs that have not been formally and technically standardized)
   D. **Biological tests** (electrorecording devices, chemical analyses)
   E. **Available records and data** (analyses of current or cumulated records related to person, environment, transactions; analyses of natural performances and products, such as portfolio assessment)

"The ideal day in the lives of elementary school children balances physical, social, and intellectual activity, allows children opportunities for gaining a sense of accomplishment and competence, has both structure and freedom, and gradually evolves—so that what is expected of children follows their developmental progress." (Stevenson & Stigler, 1992, p. 71)

Problems of Interpretation

Decisions about what data to gather are determined by views about what we want to assess. However, the actual data provide only a description of observed behavior. We do not directly observe intelligence or perception or attention deficits or minimal CNS dysfunctioning. Instead, we see responses to stimuli, or noncompliance with rules and directions (test answers or refusal to do a task), or reports of poor performance and misbehavior. Thus, concerns arise about the following:

Inadequate descriptions of a phenomenon
- Does the procedure provide information relevant to the types of interpretations and judgments we want to make?
- Does the procedure measure what it says it does?
- Only what it says it does?
- All of what it says it does?
- Does it provide new information?

Invalid interpretations and judgments of phenomena
- Are inferences justified?
- Are appropriate norms and standards available?

Invalid decisions
- How relevant are the data with respect to the decisions to be made?

Setting out to assess cognitive deficiencies, for example, we want to be able to discuss findings in terms of such deficiencies and to judge the nature and scope of deficiencies based on appropriate norms and standards.

Reliability and validity.   Deficiencies with regard to reliability and validity generate controversy not only about what findings mean but about the value of assessment per se. Obviously it is important for a procedure to be reliable (that is, to provide consistent and reproducible findings). Fortunately, reliability can be determined in a relatively technical and objective way. Unfortunately, many procedures used to assess learning problems are not highly reliable.

Validation of a procedure is not so straightforward; it requires a great deal of rational and subjective activity. As Cronbach (1970) stressed with respect to assessing constructs,

> construct validity is established through a long-continued interplay between observation, reasoning, and imagination. . . . The process of construct validation is the same as that by which scientific theories are developed. (p. 142)

Because determining a procedure's validity is difficult and costly, assessors find themselves having to use the best that is available, even though the best may not be very good. The inevitable result has been criticism of procedures and decisions based on them.

Norms and standards.   Given the same set of findings, people still arrive at different conclusions. Why? Often because they use different standards in interpreting what they see. The term *standards* refers to values, theoretical ideas, and the empirical bases used to make judgments. The judgments often are about whether a problem exists, whether something is good or bad, and whether what was assessed is consistent with some theory.

Norms are empirical standards (not value or theoretical statements). That is, norms are a set of findings that can be used for purposes of comparison. (Are the current findings higher, lower, or the same as the earlier findings? How much higher or lower?) Formal norms are based on research and systematic observation. In practice, any set of findings (including nonsystematic observations over years of professional practice) might constitute the norms with which to compare assessment data.

Norms and standards are the major referents in interpreting assessment data. When norms are inadequate, or when there is no consensus regarding standards, interpretations become controversial. To understand this, it is important to appreciate the nature of the interpretive or judgmental process in assessment, which requires an appreciation of the way standards and norms are used.

After formal or informal norms are used, it is commonplace to apply value-based standards to make judgments. This can happen so quickly that it may not be apparent. For example, a score from a test or rating scale that falls outside some predetermined average may be quickly translated into a judgment that the performance indicated significant underachievement, developmental lag, or pathology. This is understandable, especially with tests of achievement and measures of development. However, it is important to note that a judgment has been made. The use of norms, of themselves, does not lead to a judgment.

Technical Concerns About Assessment (p. 349) presents a fuller discussion of the concepts of reliability, validity, norms, and standards.

All in all, controversy seems inevitable, given that assessors must rely on inadequate procedures and given the lack of consensus about standards (Buros, 1974; Coles, 1987; Schrag & Divoky, 1975). And the criticism is justified when professionals proceed in uncritical ways. As Buros (1974) noted, practitioners

> seem to have an unshakable will to believe the exaggerated claims of test authors and publishers. If these users were better informed regarding the merits and limitations of their testing instruments, they would probably be less happy and successful in their work. The test user who has faith—however unjustified—can speak with confidence in interpreting test results and making recommendations. The well-informed test user cannot do this; [this person] knows that the best of our tests are still highly fallible instruments which are extremely difficult to interpret with assurance in individual cases. Consequently, [the user] must interpret test results cautiously with so many reservations that others wonder whether [s]he really knows what [s]he is talking about. (p. xxxvii)

Biasing Factors

Potential for bias in assessment is great. Indeed, some degree of bias is inevitable. In this instance, we are not concerned with the prejudiced and stereotypic thinking of an individual, but with factors that affect large numbers of assessors and cause them to react in systematically biased ways.

Bias (that is, selectivity and distortion) affects both the descriptive and judgmental phases of assessment. Systematic bias stems from a weak knowledge base and from psychological and societal factors that affect the information available to the assessor and the way that information is processed.

Weak knowledge base. To comprehend why some degree of selectivity and distortion is inevitable, one need only recognize that assessors primarily look for what they have come to understand are the important aspects of phenomena. They cannot really afford to do otherwise. There is no time to describe everything, and random sampling of complex phenomena tends to produce random findings and little understanding of what is assessed. Thus, whether explicitly stated or not, each assessor is guided by some underlying rationale.

What does an assessor's rationale consist of? Usually the assessor has some theory or model about what and how something is to be assessed. If there is widespread consensus about the assessor's rationale, descriptions and judgments probably will not be seen as biased. That is, where there appears to be a strong base of knowledge related to a phenomenon and how to measure it (for example, X rays of broken bones), there will be little controversy over methods and conclusions. And, whatever selectivity and distortion are present will not be readily apparent.

In contrast, when theory and research are viewed as inconclusive, there will be diverse and competing models and methods. Assessors will differ, often markedly, in the rationales shaping their practices. They will try to draw on the available (albeit weak) knowledge base. However, because no model, orientation, or trend will be dominant, even professionals from the same discipline can be expected to be guided by different ideas. Under such circumstances, assessors will look for different data, perhaps use different methods, and often arrive at different conclusions about the same phenomena. Moreover, it should not be too surprising that there will be a tendency to find and interpret data in ways that are consistent with one's theories.

A weak knowledge base means that research is only in its early stages and cannot resolve debates over which ideas and practices are correct. When there is a weak knowledge base, the factors underlying a practice's acceptance appear to be its compelling "logic" and intuitive appeal, or the proselytizing capability of its adherents. Many pioneering assessment practices that lack validity have become institutionalized through training programs, unsupported expert opinion, publishing company sales campaigns, and so forth. Such practices prevail until a strong body of research not only documents their inappropriateness but also is used effectively to undermine their institutionalized support. (However, even when there are data suggesting a given practice is ineffective or even harmful, the findings may not be accepted. Widespread testimony claiming a practice's validity can overwhelm arguments against its use.)

Currently, psychology and education are dominated by relatively weak theories and methods for measuring causes and correcting problems. This ensures ongoing controversy among those who hold competing assessment rationales. Selection and distortion continue to be inevitable.

Coexistence of contradictory perspectives does not mean that each enjoys equal status. A model may be in vogue, but vogues change. For example, for some time a pathological perspective (medical or disordered-person model) dominated psychoeducational assessment practices. Only in recent years has this view been challenged sufficiently to allow nonpathologically oriented assessment procedures to evolve.

With reference to the case of David, the weak knowledge base affected everyone involved in making the decisions. While the teacher knew David was not performing as well as others in the class, she didn't know why or what to do about it. She recalled some of the "symptoms" she had learned about in education courses and recognized these in David. This led her to feel justified in referring him for help.

The psychologist duly noted David's symptoms. She administered the standard assessment procedures used by the school district. Her diagnosis and recommendations were based on the view that persons who test significantly below grade level on an achievement test and who score at least average on an IQ test can be diagnosed as having a learning disability and might have a minimal brain dysfunction. Because David was a poor reader and did not do well on a test of visual perception, she thought he might be dyslexic.

David's parents felt confused about the problems. They recalled various TV programs and magazine articles dealing with learning disabilities, dyslexia, and brain damage. They were further mystified, yet strangely reassured, by the information provided by the school's "experts." In the end, they agreed to all the recommendations because they didn't think there was an alternative.

As for David, neither his parents nor the school personnel were certain about what to tell him or how to talk with him about the nature of the problem.

David struggles on.

Psychological bias.   In addition to bias that stems from the knowledge base, there is selectivity and distortion from psychological factors that affect the information available to the assessor and the way that information is processed. A few examples will illustrate this point.

As a general principle, the more complex and comprehensive the phenomena assessed, the more difficult it is to obtain an adequate sample of data. Although reasons for this may be strictly procedural and practical (lack of instruments, time, and so forth), sometimes the difficulty is due to an assessor's cognitive, perceptual, and motivational functioning. An example of one such psychological factor, of potentially great importance in understanding the bias in assessment, comes from attribution theory.

Those who assume the role of gathering data, especially professional assessors, can be described as *observers* of phenomena. Persons observed can be designated as *actors*. In discussing perceptions of the causes of behavior, attribution theorists have suggested a pronounced tendency for observers and actors to perceive the causes of an actor's behavior in different ways. Specifically, as hypothesized by Jones and Nisbett (1971), "there is a pervasive tendency for actors to attribute their actions to situational requirements, whereas observers tend to attribute the same actions to stable personal dispositions" (p. 80). There seems to be a corresponding tendency to believe that the observers' (assessors') perceptions are objective and accurate, while the perceptions of those assessed (actors) are subjective and biased.

Systematic observer–actor differences have been interpreted as arising from (a) information availability and processing, and (b) motivation — including self-serving interpretations (Bradley, 1978; Miller & Ross, 1975; Monson & Snyder, 1977). Research has found observer–actor differences consistently enough to warrant speculation that this might be an important biasing factor in assessment. For example, a great many assessors may be predisposed to look for, and localize, causes of psychoeducational problems within those who manifest the problems, the students. In contrast, students may tend to attribute cause to teachers, peers, or task difficulty. If this is to be expected as a result of psychological influences, how can one know whose perceptions are correct? Perhaps both are biased and incorrect. Selectivity and distortion in assessment that results from actor–observer differences in perception clearly needs further investigation (Compas, Adelman, Freundl, Nelson, & Taylor, 1982; Compas & Adelman, 1981).

Professional role demands are also potential factors causing selectivity and distortion. Psychologists and educators are under constant pressure to demonstrate greater competence than current knowledge warrants. This pressure often leads professionals to overstate expertise. In turn, their public declarations then lead them to defend, and subsequently believe in, these unsubstantiated theories and practices. Other individuals oversell their expertise, not for ego-defensive reasons, but for ego-enhancing purposes, including such self-serving objectives as attaining status and financial rewards.

As these examples suggest, the cognitive–perceptual–motivational predispositions of assessors can combine in complex ways to shape their actions and conclusions.

In the case of David, the teacher, psychologist, and his parents started out with the assumption that something was wrong with him. Thus it is not surprising that what they looked for and found were problems within David. Then, it seemed only logical to help him deal with *his* problems.

Societal bias.   Prevailing social values define what is exceptional, deviant, or a problem, and how it should be dealt with. These values are translated into governmental policies that determine which psychoeducational problems are attended to and which practices are encouraged. As many writers have suggested, interventions are designed as much — and perhaps more — to serve and protect society's interests as they are to help an individual. In particular, it has been argued that the best developed assessment practices, especially widely used tests, are primarily a reflection of society's need to foster and protect its own interests.

Chase (1977) presents the position that society, for self-serving purposes, has perpetuated biological explanations for problems that require social solutions. Kamin (1974) proposes that IQ tests have been used in ways that support "the belief that those on the bottom are genetically inferior victims of their own immutable defects." He further suggests:

The courts have ruled that some testing procedures result in racially discriminating practices.

How will her test scores be used?

the consequence has been that the IQ test has served as an instrument of oppression against the poor—dressed in trappings of science, rather than politics. . . . The poor, the foreign born, and racial minorities are shown to be stupid [and] born that way. The underprivileged are today demonstrated to be ineducable, a message as soothing to the public purses as to the public conscience. (p. 2)

Similarly, Coles (1978) argues that the "biologizing" of social problems has resulted in the positing of

organic causalities for poverty, aggression, and violence, as well as for educational underachievement. . . . By positing biological bases for learning problems, the responsibility for failure is taken from the schools, communities, and other institutions and is put squarely on the back, or rather within the head, of the child. Thus, the classification (assessment leading to the diagnosis of learning disabilities) plays its political role, moving the focus away from the general educational process, away from the need to change institutions, away from the need to rectify social conditions affecting the child, and away from the need to appropriate more resources for social use toward the remedy of a purely medical problem . . . a classic instance of what Ryan (1971) has called "blaming the victim." (p. 333)

What is being boldly stated by such writers is that society has a large stake in how the causes and corrections of psychoeducational problems are understood. Bias stemming from society's values seems so ubiquitous a phenomenon that someone (source unknown) has formulated the "law of selective attention to data." This "law" postulates that the greater the ideological relevance of research or assessment findings, the greater the likelihood that involved professionals will selectively pay attention to the data gathered.

Prevailing biases are reflected in mandatory programs and in research and development activity supported by government. Because societal bias so pervasively shapes perceptions, it is likely that most people are unaware of the selectivity and distortion built into government supported practices. This lack of awareness, of course, makes it difficult to counter the bias.

In the case of David, a teaching assistant in the classroom had noticed that two other children seemed equally inattentive and were falling behind in their work. The others, both girls, stared quietly at their books and drew little attention to themselves. David, on the other hand, got a bit noisy when bored and tapped his pencil, flipped pages, and talked to others at his table. Since she was concerned with sex role discrimination, the assistant wondered whether noisy boys were more likely than quiet girls to be referred for testing and special programs. More generally, she wondered whether such a societal bias might be a significant factor in learning disabilities being seen as primarily a boy's problem (see Feature 4-4).

In general, there seems to be a widespread impression that existing assessment procedures are better than they are. This impression contributes to an

Feature 4-4
Why Are More Boys than Girls Diagnosed as Having Learning Disabilities?

It is important to keep in mind the full range of possible causes, rather than to assume that most learning problems are related to neurological troubles. Only from a broad perspective can one appreciate the difficulty of adequately explaining such facts as the overall higher incidence of learning problems among males (and low-income minority groups) and the underachievement patterns that appear among females in their later schooling. For example, available data indicate that 72 percent of those diagnosed as having learning disabilities are boys (U.S. General Accounting Office, 1981; also see Finucci & Childs, 1981). Those who believe current diagnoses of learning disabilities are accurate tend to explain the sex differential in terms of biological differences.

One set of theories stresses sex differences in neurological development and specialization of the cerebral hemispheres (Dalby, 1979). Another explanation suggests that, on the average, males have larger heads at birth than females, and this greater size increases the probability of difficult births and higher rates of oxygen deprivation causing brain damage.

In contrast, those who believe that a significant number of males are misdiagnosed as having learning disabilities tend to look for explanations outside the central nervous system. They hypothesize, for instance, that the source of many males' learning problems and of the underachievement patterns of many girls in their later schooling can be traced to differences in cultural expectations. Many boys come to school with experience that tends to make them more interested in highly active pursuits than in quiet academic activity. As they get older, many girls are expected to behave in ways that play down their academic capabilities.

Comparable points about psychological, socioeconomic, cultural, and political factors have been made about the high incidence of learning problems among children reared in poverty.

unquestioning use of certain procedures in making major psychoeducational decisions. Methodological deficiencies (in terms of reliability, validity, and norms) should raise sufficient concerns about such practices. Moreover, the weak knowledge base underscores concerns about (1) what is actually being assessed, (2) overreliance on tests, (3) the low utility of data gathered with respect to decision making, and (4) what factors actually play the most significant role in arriving at a particular type of decision. In this section, we have also stressed that current procedures may be biased. Awareness of such bias underscores that, in many instances, it is the assessor's rationale (rather than valid findings) that guides and shapes assessment decisions. Obviously, work is needed to improve assessment procedures and counteract the problems of selectivity and distortion that permeate current assessment practices.

Ethics

Impetus for ethical and related policy concerns about negative aspects of assessment has come from reported misuses and abuses of test data. Criticism has come from political conservatives, liberals, and civil libertarians. At the center of the controversy is the traditional tension between society's rights, responsibilities, and needs, and individuals' rights and freedoms. Critics have argued that individual rights and liberties are not sufficiently safeguarded and have pushed for greater legal protection of rights and due process. This is leading to improvements in consent procedures.

Another line of ethical criticism and policy concern stresses the errors, costs, and negative side effects of assessment. Some critics cite psychological, social, economic, and possible physical harm to individuals; others point out that subgroups are discriminated against; a few have raised the specter that the quality of life in society may be significantly lowered by institutionalizing assessment practices. In contrast, some professionals underscore that it is an ethical responsibility of professionals to use assessment practices to maximize benefits for individuals and society.

The widespread use of assessment to define learning problems is ample indication of belief in its benefits. In this section, however, we highlight the two most prominent areas of ethical concern — privacy rights and negative consequences of assessment.

Privacy.   There is a dual concern about privacy rights: invasion of privacy and misuse of information. These concerns arise when the information is considered highly sensitive and could lead to diagnoses and evaluations that are perceived negatively. The situation is especially volatile when assessment is carried out primarily to serve societal or institutional objectives.

Power to assess — to obtain and use information about others — is power to shape lives. Legally and ethically, there is a need to keep such power in check. At issue is the nature of the control people ought to have over the gathering and disclosure of information about themselves. In other words, when should society be able to mandate assessment if, in the process, it infringes on individual rights? This is an aspect of the broader concern over when society should be allowed to coerce individuals and, thereby, deny a variety of rights and freedoms (Adelman & Taylor, 1988; Robinson, 1974). From this issue springs a variety of questions. What kind of information is it reasonable to gather on an individual? What safeguards exist with respect to the collection and use of highly personal and sensitive information? What types of records should be kept and who should have access to them? What restrictions should be placed on how information can be used? Is parental consent sufficient when children don't want to be assessed?

The complexity of ethical concerns is well illustrated when individuals come for help. A request for help may be seen as consent to gather data on anything the assessor sees as relevant. Given adequate theory and evidence about what is relevant, it would be a relatively clear-cut matter to explain what is needed and why as a basis for eliciting informed consent. Unfortunately, the state of knowledge regarding psychoeducational problems is not sophisticated enough to specify absolutely what information is needed. Thus assessors develop their own criteria. Some feel free to follow their intuition about anything that seems significant at the moment. Although well meaning, they may pry into painful areas of a person's life to gather data that may be irrelevant. Such data may amount to little more than gossip. Insignificant and invalid data can be even more harmful when used inappropriately (for example, to prescribe treatment).

For a variety of political and legal reasons, many school systems have moved away from presumptions of consent. In the United States, this movement has been accelerated by federal law (for example, the Family Educational Rights and Privacy Act of 1974). The apparent result has been that (1) less assessment data are gathered and circulated in schools, (2) consent is sought more frequently when a need for assessment exists, and (3) due process is emphasized with respect to student and parent access to records and for complaints and corrections of data that may be inappropriate or in error.

Critics caution, however, that the burden of protecting rights still falls mostly on those assessed. Consumer advocates advise students or parents to object if they dislike either what is asked or the procedures. When they do so, however, they run the risk of being refused services or having the objection interpreted as defensiveness, hostility, or lack of cooperation.

The situation is further complicated where procedures have become routinized and institutionalized. Under such circumstances, those involved may see neither a rights issue nor a need for consent. For example, physicians, psychologists, educators, and a variety of other personnel in schools, clinics, and agencies routinely administer tests and questionnaires with little or no explanation about why the information is needed or about any limitations with respect to the procedures' validity. When procedures have become a natural part of an institution's operations, those administering them may be genuinely unaware of invading privacy or coercing people. Those who are assessed may assume that the experience must be essential, and any discomfort is to be borne silently.

Negative consequences.   As stressed in Chapter 3, every major intervention has some negative consequence. Assessment is no exception. It is customary to speak of ''negative side effects,'' but this wording tends to ignore errors and

**How might socio-
political-economic
factors affect what
happens to her
at school?**

economic costs and is more appropriately applied to minor and perhaps low-probability phenomena. Negative consequences encompass the range of potentially significant harm that may occur.

Negative consequences, such as extreme anxiety, may occur during the assessment process or may be an immediate or long-term outcome. It is widely recognized that persons who are assessed and labeled may be stigmatized, isolated, and excluded from important experiences, and that this may negatively affect motivation and hinder full and healthy development. Evidence suggests that certain subgroups are more likely than others to experience such negative effects (Copeland, 1983; Heller et al., 1982; MacMillan, Hendicks, & Watkins, 1988; Swanson & Watson, 1982). Civil rights hearings and court cases have highlighted the intentional and unintentional cultural and sex-role bias of formal assessment (see Feature 4-5). Unfortunately, little data exist on the frequency of negative consequences (including inevitable errors) or about financial costs to individuals and to taxpayers. Concerns about costs are increasing. For example:

> In the case of testing to identify children in mildly handicapped categories, the costs of assessment and staffing procedures use up half of the extra per-pupil resources available *without any evidence that pro forma administration of tests adds to the scientific integrity of placement decisions.*

Feature 4-5   The Changing Sociopolitical Climate

Throughout the 1970s and 1980s, judicial decisions were an important sociopolitical factor influencing legislation, policy making, and practice. In the courts, parents and advocacy groups pushed for the rights of those with disabilities and equality of education and fought discrimination (for example, see *Litigation and special education*, 1986).

Hobson v. Hansen (1969)   This was the first major case raising questions about placement in special education. The court ruled that using test scores to group students into "tracks" was unconstitutional because it discriminated against blacks and the poor.

Diana v. State Board of Education (1970)   Here was a case in which the use of tests to place students was again challenged. Diana, a Spanish-speaking student in Monterey County, California, had been placed in a class for mildly mentally retarded students because she had scored low on an IQ test given to her in English. The court ruled that Spanish-speaking children should be retested in their native language to avoid errors in placement.

Mills v. D.C. Board of Education (1972)   Seven school-age students had been excluded from school because of handicaps. The school district claimed it did not have the money needed to provide an appropriate education for them. The landmark decision in this case established that children with disabilities should be given a free and suitable public education and cannot be excluded for financial reasons.

Pennsylvania Association for Retarded Citizens (PARC) v. Commonwealth of Pennsylvania (1972)   Like the *Mills* case, this was a class-action suit that declared that all children have the right to a free and appropriate education.

Larry P. v. Riles (1972)   Larry P. was a black student in California, and his complaint led to an expansion of the ruling in the *Diana* case. The court ruled that schools are responsible for providing tests that do not discriminate on

the basis of race. In the class-action case of *PASE v. Hannon* (1980), however, the judge stated he could find little evidence of bias in the test items. The *Larry P.* case also set a precedent for the use of data indicating disproportionate placement of minority groups as prima facie evidence of discrimination. However, subsequent cases have undermined this precedent (*Marshall et al. v. Georgia* [1984] and *S-I v. Turlington* [1986]).

Le Banks v. Spears (1976)   The decision in this case helped spell out the nature of a suitable or appropriate education for those with disabilities.

Burlington School Committee v. Department of Education (1985)   The U.S. Supreme Court ruled that parents who place their disabled child unilaterally into a private school are entitled to tuition reimbursement after a court determines the placement was appropriate under Public Law 94-142 and the public school placement was inappropriate.

Honig v. Doe (1988)   The U.S. Supreme Court ruled that Public Law 94-142 prohibits schools from unilaterally excluding students with disabilities from the classroom for dangerous or disruptive conduct growing out of their disabilities. Normal nonplacement-changing procedures, including temporary suspensions for ten school days, are allowed. This case appears to overrule the case of *Victoria L. v. District School Board* (1984), which did allow for unilateral placement of a dangerous disabled student pending review proceedings.

In many ways, it is unfortunate that litigation is necessary. But it is. Current legislation may mandate rights, but as Meyen (1982) has stated, it "does not guarantee that compliance will be enforced" (p. 9). Moreover, it seems that many questions about the appropriate treatment of those who do not "fit in" are so unsettled and unsettling as to require adjudication.

[Research shows] there is a very high correspondence between initial teacher referrals and final placement decisions, with all the testing in between serving to justify placement. At least half of the children labeled by schools as learning disabled [LD], by far the largest category of handicap, are misidentified. Rather than fitting the original definition of LD, they are more aptly described as slow learners, linguistically different children, misbehaving boys, children who are absent or whose families move too frequently, or as average learners in above-average contexts. (emphasis added, Shepard, 1990; p. 23)

Illich (1977) and others have warned that the cost to society may be more than financial. He has argued that overreliance on professionals leads to an alarming incapacity among individuals and natural support systems to cope with problems. The rapid rise in number of children diagnosed as having learning disabilities, and the highly specialized (and sometimes inappropriate) treatments prescribed may be a most poignant example of such effects.

From a practical perspective, concern over negative consequences generally centers on how to minimize negative effects and be certain that benefits outweigh harm. Often at issue is whether the positive outweighs the negative. There does seem to be widespread agreement, however, about the following guidelines:

1. Assessors are obligated at least to be aware of potential negative consequences, such as immediate and long-term harm to individuals, groups, and society.
2. Where consent is sought, assessors are required ethically and often legally to inform prospective consenters of potential positive and negative consequences.
3. As they attempt to maximize benefits, assessors are obligated to minimize potential negative effects.
4. Assessors are expected not only to look for data that confirm hypotheses about problems, they also must *actively* seek disconfirming evidence.
5. Although they cannot follow a student around to prevent self-fulfilling prophecies, they are expected to take steps to correct and guard records and equip students and parents to protect and advocate for themselves.
6. Assessors are expected to acknowledge whenever findings are inconclusive and not rationalize or dismiss uncertainties and incongruities in findings.

Meeting Minimal Standards

Although critics have consistently raised concerns, there are few who would argue that a procedure should not be used until it is perfected (if it ever could be). The consensus is that, despite inadequacies, many assessment tools can provide useful information to inform decision making—if they are properly chosen and used. But what constitutes proper choice and use?

At the very least, most will agree that assessment procedures should meet the minimal standards set forth by the American Psychological Association and the American Educational Research Association (see "Standards for Educational and Psychological Tests"). From an ethical and legal perspective, a practice should do more good than harm. In this context, it has been argued that some psychometric and rating-scale procedures used for massive screening are used in ways that produce so many false-positive errors that they probably cause more harm than good and should not be used (Adelman, 1989). In California, based on the *Larry P. v. Riles* court decision, the Los Angeles Unified School District has taken the extreme position of placing a moratorium on the use of IQ test data in special education placement decisions.

When assessment procedures are seen as meeting minimal standards and providing useful information, there is still the problem that data gathered may be limited and perhaps erroneous. There are no satisfactory solutions for these problems. A common suggestion is that additional data be gathered that might at least disconfirm false-positive findings. Ethically, it has been stressed that all concerned parties should be alerted to the limitations of the findings and the tentative nature of recommendations and conclusions based on the data. With respect to gathering disconfirming data, there is growing advocacy for viewing decision making as a multi- rather than single-stage process.

Beyond Conventional Practices

In this section, we explore four directions for change advocated by those who have been critical of conventional practices.

Preassessment Interventions

Critics concerned about premature person-focused assessment have argued that major efforts to improve programs should come first. In this context, we recall Hobb's (1975a) views on screening.

> Ideally, special screening programs to identify health problems and develop-mental difficulties of children should not be necessary. All children regardless of economic status should be able to participate in a comprehensive health maintenance program. (pp. 90–91)

We would add that, once children arrive in kindergarten and the elementary grades, they should be provided with comprehensive psychoeducationally ori-ented school programs. That is, the need for screening is secondary to the need to evolve classroom programs to match learners' levels of motivation and devel-opment. Advocates suggest that preventive and early-age intervention programs can reduce the number of learning and behavior problems, provide improved in situ screening to identify those who continue to require special help, and thereby reduce the need for special assessment.

As indicated in preceding chapters, there are a substantial number of advocates for improving programs as the first step in a screening sequence for learning problems (see Feature 4-6). In essence, they argue that, prior to assessment, programs to ameliorate learning problems should (a) enhance regular learning and instruction for all children, and (b) remedy problems that arise as soon as possible and with the least intervention needed. It is recognized that accomplishment of these goals requires broadening the psychoeducational nature of regular school interventions (personalizing instruction) and increasing the availability of support mechanisms for academic learning (volunteer aides, peer tutoring, computers). Proponents also stress the need for programs to train and provide consultation and peer collaboration opportunities for teachers regarding what interventions to pursue before referring a student for special education (prereferral interventions).

Focal Point

There is general concern that the focus of prevailing assessment procedures encompasses too narrow a range of factors. This criticism is being voiced more strongly as new models emerge; these models challenge the prevailing view that sees learning problems in terms of *person* variables (that is, in terms of pathology or lack of readiness). Competing models focus on the *environment* (also emphasizing either pathology or deficiencies) or the *transactions* between person and environment.

Of the three models, only the person model has been used extensively. Its focus has been on assessing physiological and psychological correlates of pathology, developmental deficits, or both. But, as can be seen in texts on special education and neuropsychological assessment, this focus has been restricted to a highly delimited set of variables associated with behavior and learning (Gaddes, 1985; Salvia & Ysseldyke, 1991; Swanson & Watson, 1982). Some researchers have suggested broadening the range of assessed correlates to include social skills, temperament and cognitive style, and a variety of cognitive and metacognitive variables (Swanson, 1991). The focus of remedial planning and evaluation has broadened to encompass such variables. And there is increasing pressure to counter trends toward "skill and drill" assessment and teaching so as to avoid narrowing the curriculum and to foster higher-order thinking. One such trend has been called *authentic* or *performance assessment.*

Because of dissatisfaction with the prevailing person-oriented model, the work

Feature 4-6   Proposed Research on Preassessment Intervention

Despite ongoing advocacy for improving programs as a first step in screening (Johnson & Pugach, 1991), the idea remains relatively uninvestigated. One type of study needed would upgrade a representative sample of preschool, kindergarten, and primary school programs across socioeconomic groups to improve personalized and remedial instruction. The proportion of children subsequently found to manifest problems in these settings would then be compared with those in a matched control sample of standard programs. Data from this comparison would indicate the efficacy of the experimental settings in preventing some types of problems.

Identification of learning problems in each classroom would involve no more than establishing criteria for daily performance and noting those who do not meet the criteria over a period of several weeks. Students in the experimental and control samples could be followed into the upper elementary grades to determine the degree to which false-positive and false-negative identifications were made. After this first study, a second could determine whether identification sensitivity and specificity are improved by adding formal assessment screening procedures to the experimental programs.

of researchers who focus on the environment has taken on some prominence. These investigators assess home and school variables to clarify the role they play in learning problems in general and learning disabilities in particular (Barclay, 1983; Fraser & Walberg, 1991; Freund, Bradley, & Caldwell, 1979; Lloyd & Blandford, 1991; Moos, 1979).

Going a step further, transaction-oriented investigators hope to determine the degree to which the interplay of person and environment must be accounted for in understanding cause and correction (Adelman, 1970–71; Bandura, 1978; Coles, 1987; Sameroff, 1985). Those who have adopted a transactional (interactional, reciprocal determinist) orientation have incorporated, not rejected, the other two models.

Single- versus Multi-Stage Decision Making

Although some assessors find it necessary or convenient to assess and make decisions in one or two sessions, such a single-stage approach is a matter of concern. For example, it is generally acknowledged that, after a potential problem has been identified, subsequent steps must be taken to confirm or disconfirm it. (Critics warn that diagnoses and placement decisions often are made solely on the basis of first-level screening data.) Furthermore, even when the best available assessment procedures are used, initial decisions about placement and special programming may be in error and should be confirmed or disconfirmed through monitoring performance as the individual pursues daily tasks.

Similar arguments have been raised about ways to improve diagnosing learning disabilities and learning disability subgroups. For instance, researchers suggest that identifying those whose learning problems are due to CNS trouble requires filtering them out through sequential assessment (Adelman, 1971; Lindsay & Wedell, 1982; Wissink, Kass, & Ferrell, 1975). Increasingly, sequential or multi-stage assessments are advocated as one way to work on improving decision accuracy, including reducing the number of persons wrongly diagnosed as having learning disabilities.

Interventionist Assessment

Conventional, psychometric approaches and techniques raise a variety of validity concerns. A common example already noted is that, under formal assessment conditions, poor performance among problem populations may be due to low or negative (avoidance) motivation resulting from high anxiety or negative attitudes. These factors, and cultural differences, may negatively affect the performance of persons from certain cultural backgrounds. That is, the assessment results for such persons are seen as contaminated and thus cannot be taken at face value. These critics argue that it is impossible to know whether failure to demonstrate specific knowledge, abilities, or skills represents a real deficiency. The implications for research and intervention are profound.

Within the psychometric tradition, efforts to deal with this criticism stress accounting for contaminants when interpreting findings, improving task content and administration to reduce biasing conditions (including frequent reassessments), and going beyond standardized administration to assess how much more the individual can do (for example, allowing additional time, adding a brief prompting or teaching facet to the process). Going a step further, those in the dynamic assessment movement argue for alternative procedures designed to determine how much more the individual can do when comprehensively prompted and taught. This is a highly interventionistic approach to assessment. The assessor is "an active intervener who monitors and modifies the interaction with the learner in order to induce successful learning. The learner is prodded, directed, and reinforced into a role of active seeker and organizer of information" (Lidz, 1987; pp. 3–4).

To underscore the fundamental direction involved here, it is useful to contrast conventional practices with what can be described broadly as interventionist assessment. The term *interventionist* goes beyond dynamic assessment to encompass a wide variety of activities designed to determine whether a person can perform at a higher level. Interventionist assessment is designed to move beyond the nondynamic/static approach found in typical psychometric testing. The assessor actively "tests the limits" to encourage increased performance. This often takes the form of an assess–teach–reassess approach, involving a reasonable interval of time for learning to take place.

Critics raise questions about the underlying assumptions and the validity of interpretations made by interventionist assessment. For example, they question whether deficient functions found in cognitive processes can be modified to a significant extent during an assessment procedure. With respect to the validity of interpretations, they also charge that performance changes may primarily reflect motivational rather than cognitive change.

Advocates of interventionist assessment approaches state that the intent is not to replace but to supplement prevailing assessment procedures (Lidz, 1987; Palincsar, Brown, & Campione, 1991). They stress they are seeking data not available through prevailing approaches (for example, data on performance capability in a teaching situation, and information on teaching approaches that appear to be effective with the learner).

Summing Up

Assessment is a broad-based concept. The term has been adopted to encompass narrower, medically related processes such as diagnosis, screening, and diagnostic testing. Formally defined, assessment is the process by which attributes of phenomena are described and judged. Descriptions take the form of data gathered by formal and informal measures, such as tests and observations of behavior or settings. Judgments take the form of interpretive conclusions about the meaning of data.

Psychoeducational assessment encompasses four major purposes:

1. identification (including screening)
2. selection (including placement)

3. planning for specific change
4. evaluation of intervention

Choices about what data to gather and what to exclude are guided by the types of judgments and decisions to be made (diagnostic classification, placement, remediation).

Controversy surrounds prevailing approaches to assessing learning problems. Although some of the controversy is about the deficiencies and limitations of specific procedures, broader concerns and criticism have been directed at the way assessment is used to shape research and practice and related policy decisions. Even when relatively objective assessment data are used, subsequent decisions often are extremely subjective. This is not surprising, given that most decisions involve considerations that go well beyond the availability of valid data. More often than not, complex social–political–economic value questions are involved. Indeed, in some cases seemingly relevant data are ignored in order to arrive at a decision that the decision makers see as viable and beneficial (Woodhead, 1988). Thus controversy is inevitable, and as Thorndike and Hagen (1977) have aptly stated, "The wisdom of the decider is crucial" (p. 20).

What should be clear by this point is that assessment for identification, placement, program planning, and evaluation is a complex matter. Moreover, the state of the art is seriously restricted. Thus, despite the importance of all four assessment functions, prevailing assessment procedures

- do not have sufficient validity to warrant large-scale programs aimed at early identification;
- are not capable of producing appropriate differential diagnoses and placements for persons with learning problems;
- misprescribe remediation, deemphasize the importance in program planning of a person's strengths and interests, and narrow the focus of school curricula; and
- inappropriately shape evaluation and eventually redefine and limit objectives.

Furthermore, overemphasis on assessment practices that focus on persons hinders development of procedures for assessing the role of the environment. As a result of the bias toward localizing problems within persons, interventions tend to be person-centered. Almost by presumption, environmental variables are exonerated as causal factors and as the focal point of intervention.

In spite of the deficiencies of prevailing practices, each day professionals are called upon to assess and make decisions about individuals with learning problems. Unfortunately, for now they must do so using a relatively weak knowledge base.

The need for improved practices is evident. Fortunately, recent research has pointed to promising approaches that go beyond conventional procedures. There may be major concerns about the state of the art, but there can be no doubt that persons with problems can and must be helped. And, because learning problems are a life-long concern, such help must be available to persons of all ages. Chapter 5 highlights program considerations from preschool to postschool.

I. Think about a test on which you received a low grade:

1. Was the test a reliable and valid way to find out what you had learned?
2. How do you explain the fact that you received a low grade?
3. What type of attributions do you think the grader made about your test performance?
4. What do you think is the best way to assess what you have learned?

II. Engage a group of friends in a discussion about the pros and cons of using labels such as learning disabilities and placing those with learning problems in special classes.

Explore any concerns group members have about current assessment procedures that are used for diagnosis and placement.

Is the use of college admission tests an example of using assessment for identification and selection?

On Assessment Tools

Technical Concerns About Assessment (p. 349) This contains a brief overview of basic concepts that are central to understanding how good an assessment procedure is. The four topics are:

- reliability
- validity
- norms
- standards

Procedures and Instruments for Assessing Learning Problems (p. 341) As a special resource, this (a) provides a list of specific assessment procedures and instruments frequently used in assessing psychoeducational problems, and (b) gives references for finding and evaluating them.

On Learning Disabilities

Assessment for Learning Disabilities' Diagnosis, Placement, and Program Planning (p. 328) With respect to diagnosing, placing, and planning programs for learning disabilities, this

- reviews assessment approaches, and
- highlights concerns about certain practices.

Screening for Learning Disabilities (p. 323) Searching for learning disabilities is both common and controversial. The discussion stresses

- the nature and scope of screening practices, and
- what research suggests about the state of the art.

Remedying Learning Disabilities: Prevailing Approaches (p. 314) This explores major approaches to remedying learning disabilities through contrasting orientations: It discusses (1) underlying-problem approaches, with their focus on perception, motor functioning, language, and general cognitive functioning, and (2) observable-problem approaches, with their focus on observable skills and objectives, and direct instruction.

Program Considerations from Preschool Through Adulthood

Prekindergarten
>   *Prevention*
>   *Early-Age Interventions*

Elementary Students
>   *Redesigning Regular Instruction*
>   *Early School Adjustment Problems*
>   *Enhancing Teacher Learning*
>   *Special Resources for Severe Problems*

Adolescents and Adults
>   *Special Concerns*
>   *Special Programs*

Summing Up

*Before one can begin to change a condition
one must believe in the possibility of change.*

Lauter and Howe, 1970

Interventions for learning problems extend across the life span from prenatal care to adult programs. Some are broad-band programs designed to help a wide range of learning problems; others are narrowly focused on individuals seen as having learning disabilities. There are many methods books on learning problems and learning disabilities that describe such programs and the specific methods used (references are provided in Chapter 11). Here we offer you a broad perspective on the nature and scope of programs that relate to a full continuum of learning problems (Type I, II, and III problems). In the process, we provide enough detail to convey a sense of the educational reform agenda that has emerged because of dissatisfaction with public education. Included in this agenda is an emphasis on redesigning regular education so that fewer individuals will require special education, and rethinking special education so that all those who need special help are appropriately served.

Prekindergarten

As outlined in Chapter 2, there are a variety of genetic, prenatal, perinatal, and postnatal factors that can lead to variations in development and problems with learning. Because the seeds are planted early, early intervention is indicated; it is a key application of the principle of least intervention needed.

Early intervention is understood to encompass three different stages where it can still be hoped to precede a problem's becoming chronic (see Figure 1-1, p. 16):

- before the problem begins (prevention)
- when children are very young (early-age intervention)
- as soon as feasible after the onset of a problem (early-after-onset)

Prevention

A proactive approach to addressing learning problems involves doing something to prevent them. Thus, in addition to improving prenatal care, there is increasing emphasis on providing programs for young children. Some of these are broad-band programs designed to reach as many people as possible (for example, public health campaigns, community-based parent education, television programs such as *Sesame Street*). Others are designed for designated groups seen as high-risk populations.

For our purposes here, the term *high risk* is used for children who

- are born prematurely or who manifest significant early health problems,
- live in impoverished or hostile environments,

- manifest serious lags in development, or
- manifest serious adjustment problems.

Some high-risk children are easier to identify than others. In the easy cases, procedures are used to find and refer them to special programs. However, because there are spurts and plateaus in human development, it can be difficult to differentiate problems from normal variations (see Feature 5-1). When identification is difficult, rather than screening for individual problems, broad-band prevention programs are indicated. Broad-band, primary prevention for learning problems promotes and maintains family planning and the well-being of infants in utero, as well as their safety and physical and mental health after birth.

Two major forms of preventive intervention are advocated widely. One is the provision of pre-, peri-, and neonatal care, such as prenatal and well-child clinics and infant immunization outreach services. A second form is community educa-

Feature 5-1   *Visual Perceptual Development*

Given that normal variations make it difficult to sort out genuine problems from individual developmental differences, it is critical to understand normal developmental fluctuations. As an example, here is a brief look at visual perception. For more, you may want to move on to a basic psychology text on human development.

Perception is the recognition and interpretation of what our senses pick up. Developmental research has learned a great deal about infant perception. For example, most babies start to notice shapes, colors, and patterns at about 2 months, but it takes until 3 or 4 months before they seem able to recognize changes in color and shape, distinguish three-dimensional figures, and respond to motion. Also, around 3 months, infants show preference for familiar rather than novel sights; over time they slowly start to respond to somewhat new stimuli. It takes up to 24 months—and later for some—for totally unfamiliar stimuli to hold their attention.

To obtain a sense of the relationship between visual perception and learning to read and write, let's skip to around age 3. From this age until about 7, there are major variations in visual ability to perceive differences in rotated or reversed forms. Even by age 7, only 85 percent can accurately point to their own left and right sides (Nichols & Chen, 1981). Normal variations in abil-

ity to make certain visual perceptual discriminations may continue as late as age 9. The early maturational advantage of girls over boys probably is at play here as well.

Given the general variations in development, it is not surprising that, as children between 3 and 9 start to learn to read and write, most make similar errors. For example, some write letters backwards (especially those that are mirror images of each other) or reverse letters. And, given sex differences in maturation (as well as the influence of sociocultural learning), it is not surprising that the errors continue to occur over a longer period for boys than girls. Because of the nature of visual perceptual development, however, few children continue to make such errors past age 9.

"Should making errors associated with visual perception be seen as a learning problem? Should young children who make such errors be seen as high risks?" If teachers and parents are willing to accommodate such errors as individual differences in development, the answer is no—at least until about age 9. However, there usually comes a point where the school curriculum demands that such errors no longer occur. Then the erring student operationally becomes a learning problem; indeed, for a reasonable time before age 9 the child can be viewed as at risk.

tion, such as parent programs to improve infant/child nutrition and physical safety and to increase stimulation.

Health and safety maintenance and problem prevention programs have relevance for reducing all learning problems, including learning disabilities, among all segments of the population, and they are particularly important for those who live in poverty. For instance, it has been reported that, while the incidence of lead poisoning in the United States is 7 percent, it is over 15 percent in some poverty pockets (Berwick & Kamaroff, 1982). As Keogh, Wilcoxen, and Bernheimer (1986) note:

> Based on the national figure of 7 percent, lead poisoning causes an additional 13 cases of learning disability and 1.4 cases of mental retardation in every thousand children. Lead-abatement and lead-screening programs reduce these figures to 7 cases of learning disability and 0.6 cases of mental retardation. Corresponding figures for inner-city areas would be approximately double, given the incidence of 15 percent for these areas. (p. 299)

Thus, environmental protection programs designed to reduce lead toxicity clearly make a significant contribution to the prevention of learning disabilities.

Early-Age Interventions

Perhaps the most familiar early-intervention programs related to learning problems are early-age interventions, and probably the best known of these are day care and early education programs. Other examples of early-age interventions include programs to educate parents about lead poisoning, about cognitive stimulation activities for babies who experienced prenatal anoxia, and about low-birth-weight and premature infants (Bromwich, 1981; Tjossem, 1976). These interventions can prevent some youngsters from being diagnosed as having learning disabilities and others from developing learning problems. They are early interventions in that they begin problem correction at an early age, usually very soon after onset, thereby minimizing the severity and pervasiveness of subsequent problems. Most of these programs fall into the category known as *secondary prevention.*

Health programs and educational interventions designed for young children from low socioeconomic and other high-risk populations, and for mild to moderately handicapped children, certainly contain some youngsters at risk for a diagnosis of learning disabilities. However, learning disabilities are widely diagnosed only after youngsters display major difficulty learning to read, write, spell, or do arithmetic. Thus it is rare to see anyone with a diagnosis of learning disabilities before the latter part of the first grade. Prior to age 7, early-intervention programs are for youngsters who are seen to be at risk for a wide range of learning problems—not necessarily learning disabilities.

As we have stated, probably the most widespread early-age intervention occurs in early education programs. By enhancing individual capabilities, these programs can minimize the impact of current and subsequent environmental deficiencies and personal vulnerabilities. A good example is Head Start.

Getting off to a good start.

The curriculum for young, at-risk children may aim at fostering development in a combination of areas (perceptual, motoric, language, cognitive, social, and emotional). Usually there are activities related to gross and fine motor skills, language (especially communication skills), visual and auditory perception and memory (discrimination and integration), basic cognitive and social competence (problem solving and self-help skills, cooperative social interactions), and positive self-concept.

In the United States, legislation in the 1960s stimulated initiation of a variety of early education programs, including programs for children with disabilities (Hebbeler, Smith, & Black, 1991; Swan, 1980, 1981). By the early 1980s, over 350 early education demonstration projects for those with special needs had been funded. Even so, by the late 1980s only about half the states had legislation mandating educational services for children with disabilities at ages 5 and under; moreover, available figures suggest that only about half of all children with disabilities in the 3 to 5 age group were in early education programs.

In general, data on early-age interventions for students with special needs support the benefits of such activity. They do not, however, clarify specific factors that make interventions effective (Cowen, 1986; Guralnick, 1991; Kagan, 1990; Lakebrink, 1989; Lee, Brooks-Gunn, Schnur, & Liaw, 1990; Mitchell, Seligson, & Marx, 1989; Silver & Hagin, 1990; Slavin, Karweit, & Madden, 1989; White, 1985–86; Zigler, 1987). Findings do suggest that the longer and more intense the program, the more positive the effects in terms of measures of intelligence, language, and academic achievement (see Feature 5-2).

So far, the data on long-term benefits of early education are sparse. One longitudinal investigation, the Perry Preschool follow-up study, has reported long-term benefits for a high-risk sample of economically disadvantaged African Americans whose IQs ranged from 60 to 90. Findings gathered when these individuals were 19 indicate they had had significantly less need for special education programs than a comparison group not in the special preschool program (Berrueta-Clement et al., 1984).

Although data on early childhood education are promising, conclusions must be made cautiously. As Zigler (1987) stresses in arguing against mandating schooling for all 4-year-olds:

- Findings about the success of early education programs primarily reflect benefits for economically disadvantaged children.
- Successful programs differ from "standard school fare" in that they usually provide primary health and social services in addition to remedial academic programs. That is, they include important elements not found in most programs.

In cautioning against compulsory early education, Zigler does advocate that the option be made available to everyone. However, he stresses that the programs

Feature 5-2   *What Constitutes a High Quality Early Education Program?*

In judging quality, the National Association for the Education of Young Children (1983) cites the following essential elements:

1. physical environment
2. health and safety
3. nutrition and food service
4. administration
5. staff qualifications and development
6. staff–parent interaction
7. staff–child interaction
8. child–child interaction
9. curriculum
10. evaluation

Few would dismiss any of these, but some see the listing as insufficient. For instance, the staff of the frequently cited Perry Preschool project state:

Style of program operations is the additional ingredient necessary to ensure high quality. The style . . . is manifested in the skillful blending of program elements. . . . Elements of particular importance are as follows: curriculum implementation, parent involvement, staff supervision, inservice training provision, teacher planning time, staff relationships, ongoing evaluation, and administrative leadership. These elements are not rigidly tied to a "right" way of doing things: for example, it is not as important which curriculum is chosen, as *that* a curriculum model is chosen to guide program operations. (Berrueta-Clement, Schweinhart, Barnett, Epstein, & Weikart, 1984; pp. 109–110)

More specifically, Schweinhart and Weikart (1989) state:

The principal characteristic of a good early childhood development program . . . is that children initiate their own learning activities—choosing them within a framework created by the teacher and carrying them out as they see fit, unconstrained by the teacher's definition of the "correct" answer or the "correct" use of materials. Child-initiated activity is distinguished from random activity by its purposefulness; it is distinguished from teacher-directed activity by the fact that the child controls what happens. (pp. 85–86)

should primarily offer recreation and socialization with a secondary focus on developmentally appropriate educational curricula.

Elementary Students

Once children arrive in kindergarten and the elementary grades, prevention and early-intervention programs for learning problems are primarily based in schools and have a twofold focus:

- to enhance regular learning and instruction of all students
- to remedy problems that arise as soon as possible and with the least intervention needed

In this section, we discuss four things relevant to accomplishing these goals. First, we explore ideas about broadening the psychoeducational nature of regular school interventions. Second, we discuss ideas for increasing support for academic learning. Third, we note programs for teachers regarding interventions to pursue before referring a student for special education. Fourth, after all that can be done has been done to improve regular education, the focus shifts to special resources for severe problems. Embedded in this sequence is the notion that by redesigning regular education there will be fewer Type I and II learning problems to deal with; and, by improving special education, there will be better opportunities for helping persons with Type III problems (learning disabilities). Moreover, the emphasis on comprehensive change is in keeping with current policy directions stressing a multifaceted attack on educational and psychosocial problems. (See Figure 1-1, p. 16, about the continuum of programs for addressing problems.)

Redesigning Regular Instruction

After centuries of formal schooling, there is still no consensus on the best approach for classroom teaching. Walberg (1991) argues that direct, didactic teaching has the best track record. He calls such an approach *conventional teaching* and describes it as encompassing "(a) daily review, homework check, and, if necessary, reteaching, (b) rapid presentation of new content and skills in small steps, (c) guided student practice with close teacher monitoring, (d) corrective feedback and instructional reinforcement, (e) independent practice in seatwork and homework, and (f) weekly and monthly review" (p. 44).

Citing the Gage and Needels (1987) analysis of teaching methods, Walberg (1991) states:

It is important to retain well implemented conventional teaching as a major option for improving education. It works moderately well in attaining conventional criteria of academic progress, and it does not require extraordinary teacher preparation, materials, and facilities. Although other methods [discussed] have shown larger effects on special criteria they are designed to

Theories of Instruction and Models of Teaching (p. 355) highlights the views on teaching of Maria Montessori, Jean Piaget, Jerome Bruner, B. F. Skinner, Carl Rogers, and Robert Gagné. Also outlined is Joyce and Weil's approach to synthesizing ideas about instruction into four major "families" or models of teaching.

accomplish, they lack conventional teaching's long history. Many such inno- vations have come and gone, and conventional teaching remains the perva- sive method in schools in low- and high-income countries. (p. 44)

Despite its long history, however, there are large segments of the population for whom direct, didactic instruction has not worked (Goodlad, 1984; National Commission on Excellence in Education, 1983). This has led to calls for a major restructuring of schooling to improve leadership and training, order and manage- ment, and instructional procedures and supports (Berliner, 1984; Brophy & Good, 1986; Purkey & Smith, 1983; Rosenshine & Stevens, 1986; Stevenson & Stigler, 1992).

The following discussion focuses on educational changes advocated to en- hance regular instruction. Specifically, we explore ideas for (a) changing schools and (b) changing classroom instruction. We approach these topics from the perspective of preventing as many learning problems as possible.

Good ideas and missionary zeal are sometimes enough to change the thinking of individuals; they are rarely, if ever, effective in changing compli- cated organiza- tions (like the school) with tra- ditions, dynam- ics, and goals of their own.

Sarason, 1971 (p. 213)

Changing schools.   As a first step in enhancing regular instruction, it is useful to look at ideas for improving the school as a whole (see Elmore & Associates, 1990; Schlechty, 1990). Thus we begin by reviewing factors that have been associated with "effective" schools.

Based on an accumulated body of research, lists have been formulated of characteristics found in schools that are relatively more effective than others with which they have been compared. For instance, Edmonds's (1979, 1981) influential listing emphasizes

- strong administrative leadership
- high expectations for student learning
- discipline and school order
- basic skills acquisition
- monitoring student progress through measured indicators of achievement

The following factors have been added by others (Good & Brophy, 1986; Phi Delta Kappa, 1980; Purkey & Smith, 1983, 1985; Rutter, 1981):

- a sense of teamwork in the school
- an emphasis on academic work and homework
- effective parental involvement
- teacher influence and control

Lists of individual characteristics do not convey a full picture. To emphasize that the whole is greater than the sum of its parts, specific subsets of effective-school characteristics have been designated as indicators of school climate, culture, and ethos (respectively by Brookover, Beady, Flood, Schweitzer, & Wisenbaker, 1979; Purkey & Smith, 1985; and Rutter, 1981).

Approaching the matter from a different perspective and drawing on a different body of research, Walberg (1991) generated a list of learning "productivity" fac- tors. He categorized his nine factors into three groups:

- student aptitude
  ability/achievement
  development (age/maturation)
  motivation or self-concept
- instruction
  amount of time students engage in learning
  quality of instructional experience
- psychological environments
  "curriculum of the home"
  morale or climate of classroom social group
  peer group outside school
  minimum leisure TV viewing

We see that, unlike the effective-school factors, Walberg emphasizes the learner's capabilities and attitudes and a wider range of environmental factors outside the school. Recognition of the transactional nature of learning is implicit in the approach.

Lists of effective-school and productive-learning factors are helpful as long as there is awareness of the limitations of the research and the theoretical and philosophical rationales upon which they are based (Witte & Walsh, 1990). Used cautiously, such factors provide an important stimulus for discussing ways in which schools might change. And schools must change, or the number of learning problems will continue to grow, inundating special education programs with so many students they will be unable to serve those most in need (those with Type III problems).

Applied uncritically, however, the emphasis on effective-school factors can produce serious harm—especially to those students who have learning problems. We must be careful not to overestimate the value of specific characteristics, and to recognize that each of these rather abstract ideas (for example, strong administrative leadership) can be interpreted in very different ways.

In schools with low academic test scores and a high incidence of problem behavior, the entire school program requires rehabilitation. Interventions for this purpose rely heavily on a dynamic principal who is given additional resources and empowered to initiate major variations in school district policy. In some cases the school is given special status, as has happened with magnet programs and other schools of choice.

The magnet approach in East Harlem has been cited by the media as a promising example of the dramatic metamorphosis possible for schools in trouble. Schools with differing specialties (science, the arts, sports) were created and parents and children offered a choice among them. This allowed each school to portray itself as a special place of opportunity. As a result, their programs are valued by more and more parents and students, and school personnel have a sense of renewal. Moreover, the changes seem to have stimulated feelings of hope and a sense of community and commitment on the part of students, parents, and school personnel.

Perhaps more typical of future directions is a rehabilitative effort in the Los

Angeles Unified School District called Project Intervention that began in 1987. The pilot project is a "plan of action designed to prove that all children can learn when the conditions of learning are at an optimum." New principals were recruited for ten poverty-area schools. Immediate changes included a reduction in teacher–pupil ratio to 20 to 1 for the primary grades, establishment of formal planning and training periods for teachers, a mentor teacher program, an extended school year for students, teachers, and administrators, and parent education programs.

Of course, modifying schools is difficult and time-consuming, and there is no guarantee that substantive changes will occur or that changes will lead to more effective instruction (Barth, 1990; Sarason, 1990). Thus another alternative for a student who is not doing well is to move to another school. Sometimes a move to another regular school that is functioning better, or to an alternative school (such as a magnet school), can go a long way toward solving the immediate problems of a student.

Changing classrooms.   Curriculum content, processes, and intended outcomes in conventional programs are designed to match a relatively narrow range of individual differences. Many of these programs also reflect a limited understanding of human psychology. Moreover, because a major emphasis is on socialization, there is a tendency to rely on strategies for controlling behavior rather than procedures for fostering positive attitudes toward learning and school. (Given the pervasive emphasis on socialization, it is ironic how often schools are ineffective in preventing, managing, and correcting deportment and adjustment problems.)

Because conventional teaching does not accommodate individual differences well, those who can't keep up suffer. Moreover, because conventional practices overemphasize behavior control at the expense of enhancing intrinsic motivation for learning, they may be both a cause and an ongoing contributor to the large number of learning and behavior problems seen in the schools. Such practices need to be modified.

Approaches for redesigning classrooms stress practices for accommodating a wider range of individual differences. Highlighting these approaches, we explore

- individualized instruction
- personalized instruction
- providing more time for individual and small group instruction

(a) **Individualized instruction.** Most efforts to accommodate individual differences have stressed the traditional idea that it is important to meet learners where they are. In regular classrooms, this has meant individualizing instruction.

The vast number of programs described as individualized attests to the concern over the narrow range of differences accounted for in classrooms and the desire to improve the situation (Joyce & Weil, 1986; Snow, 1986; Wang & Walberg, 1985). Unfortunately, the term *individualization* is used indiscriminately, and modifications made to accommodate differences vary markedly. They range from simply enabling students to proceed at their own rate to allowing for major differences in what and how much is to be learned at a given time and in what standards are used in judging quality of performance. They also vary as to matters such as how time for learning is used, how learning and performance are evaluated and graded, and the degree to which classroom structure provides support and guidance toward autonomy as contrasted to overemphasizing control. In general, the term *individualization* is used to describe any approach designed to improve the match between instructional practices and a particular student's capabilities.

Individualization is seen as an essential but not always sufficient step in countering learning problems. Typically, the process involves starting students at their current level of functioning, allowing them to proceed at their own pace, monitoring daily performance on learning tasks, and then modifying instruction as necessary.

Programmed materials and computer-aided instruction are examples of efforts to individualize direct instruction. Another widely discussed process that attempts to place and pace students individually is called *mastery learning* (Bloom, 1982). This is a direct-instruction approach that emphasizes a standardized step-by-step curriculum, assessment to properly place the student, self-pacing, and evaluation using criterion-referenced objectives. Finn (1989, July 12), in his analyses of Japanese mathematics instruction (specifically the Kumon method), makes an important observation about their version of mastery learning. He notes that instruction does start at the student's current level of functioning and moves each one along individually. The student is pushed as fast as possible, and if progress is too slow, the youngster is told to put in more time and effort.

Probably the most discussed program for individualizing regular classroom instruction to better accommodate students with disabilities is the Adaptive Learning Environments Model (ALEM). ALEM was designed to make school a place where each child can effectively master basic skills in academic subjects, and to foster self-responsibility for learning, coping, and managing behavior in the classroom (Wang, 1980; Wang, Peverly, & Randolph, 1984). This multifaceted approach includes

1. a prescriptive learning component consisting of hierarchically organized basic skills curricula that students pursue at their own pace
2. an open-ended exploratory learning component
3. classroom management procedures emphasizing teacher feedback, reinforcement, and positive interactions with students
4. a family involvement program
5. a flexible organizational structure that allows for multi-age grouping and team teaching (Wang, Gennari, & Waxman, 1985)

Thus it represents a major effort to adapt the standard curriculum to emphasize individualized instruction and exploratory learning; remediation and therapy, when needed, are provided by specialists and aides working in the classroom. Such an individualized approach is especially important to the success of mainstreaming students with disabilities (Wang & Walberg, 1985).

Because of political and methodological concerns, controversy surrounds ALEM (Fuchs & Fuchs, 1988; Wang & Walberg, 1988). Lost in this controversy has been the value of the program as a stimulus for discussing ways to make regular instruction accommodate a wider range of individual differences.

Metacognitive strategies represent another major approach to developmental differences in the classroom. As mentioned in Chapter 4, their focus is on the ways a person thinks about how to learn (the individual's awareness of strategies for learning, the ability to direct thinking about how to learn). To address functional differences, metacognitive approaches encourage students to learn general strategies that direct and organize learning and also to self-manage and self-monitor their learning.

Building on metacognitive strategies, advocates of *dynamic instruction* have argued for a more interactive approach to enhancing instruction. Specifically, they stress the value of interacting in a structured way to (a) accurately assess a student's range of functioning, (b) model learning strategies and guide initial practice, and (c) in general, find the best teaching approach (Feuerstein, 1979; Palincsar & Brown, 1984). Feuerstein, for example, focuses on children at risk for learning problems; his Learning Potential Assessment Device (LPAD) employs trial and appraisal teaching (involving a variety of teaching strategies) to determine how a child learns best. The findings are used to modify the instructional program to better accommodate the youngster's current learning capabilities.

Cooperative learning also has been used to help account for individual differences (Bohlmeyer & Burke, 1987; Johnson & Johnson, 1986). This approach places students in small groups so they can learn how to work cooperatively with others as they help each other pursue academic objectives. The process individualizes instruction by assessing developmental levels, assigning students to groups who are at different levels (having each work at their own level and at their own pace), and encouraging students to help each other. If problems persist, the teacher is consulted.

(b) Personalized instruction. In attempting to meet students where they are, individualized instruction has focused primarily on differences in students' developmental abilities. As widely practiced, individualization has overemphasized differences in ability and underemphasized differences in motivation, especially intrinsic motivation. Given that most views of learning and instruction address motivational as well as developmental differences, it seems a major oversight not to have addressed them in an equally systematic way. This oversight may account for the limited effectiveness of the many individually oriented approaches to instruction.

When motivational differences are not addressed, instruction may be aimed at an unreceptive student. This is especially true for those who have difficulty learning at school. Efforts to improve instruction must mobilize students and keep them mobilized. The term *personalized* can be used to distinguish this approach from individualized programs that do not address motivational differences in a comprehensive way (Adelman, 1971). Moreover, personalization has been treated as a psychological idea rather than simply a set of procedures (Adelman & Taylor, 1983a). This is because addressing motivation comprehensively requires that each learner's perception of how a program meets her or his interests and abilities be the primary focus. The evidence is clear that people experience environments differently based on what is important to them. As Lazarus (1991) emphasizes in his review of cognition, motivation, and emotion, "what is important or unimportant to us determines what we define as harmful or beneficial" (p. 352).

A personalized approach begins by working on establishing a student's motivational readiness to learn and then ensuring that learning activities are developmentally appropriate. To maximize motivational readiness, special efforts are made to accommodate individual differences in intrinsic motivation. Emphasis then moves to maintaining motivation by enabling the student to play a major role in planning and implementing learning activity and evaluating outcomes. Specific elements of personalized instruction are discussed in Chapter 10.

(c) More time for personal instruction. Two major ways to increase time for individual work, especially with those having trouble, are to (a) increase the pool of people and technical resources for providing instruction or (b) reduce class size. The first approach often focuses on offering tutorial help (Allen, 1976; Berger, 1981; Cohen, 1986; Gartner, Kohler, & Reissman, 1971; Gerber & Kauffman, 1981; Topping, 1986).

Tutoring. Based on a research review of one-to-one tutoring, Wasik and Slavin (1990) concluded that "one-to-one tutoring of low-achieving primary-grade students is without a doubt one of the most effective instructional innovations avail-

Personal interest is a powerful motivator for learning.

able" (p. 22). They caution, however, that there is no magic involved; "for tutoring to be maximally effective, it must improve the quality of instruction, not only increase the amount of time, incentive value and appropriateness to students' needs" (p. 25).

The competence of the tutor in establishing a positive working relationship with the student and knowing how to help the student learn determines the quality of instruction. In this regard, it is relevant to note that there are major variations in the way tutoring is provided. Tutors may be volunteers or paid; may be peers, older students, adult nonprofessionals, paraprofessionals, or professionals; or may be computers (see Feature 5-3). Tutoring can vary in where it takes place (in or out of the classroom); when it is offered (during or after school hours); how long a session is, how often it is given, and whether it is provided individually or in a small group (2 to 3 students).

One particularly ambitious and comprehensive example of an academic tutoring approach is reported by Melaragno (1976). Through a project called the Tutorial Community, cross-age and same-age tutoring was introduced as a major component in an elementary school's instructional program. The approach stressed four types of tutoring:

1. *intergrade tutoring,* in which upper-grade students tutor primary students
2. *interschool tutoring,* in which junior-high students teach upper-grade elementary students

3. *inter- [and intra-] class tutoring,* in which students at the same grade level assist each other
4. *informal tutoring,* in which older students serve as playleaders for younger students on the playground, help with projects, and go along on field trips

The concept of a tutorial community conceives of tutoring as more than a supplement for instruction or remediation. Tutoring becomes a means by which the entire student body can aid and be aided and a sense of community can be established.

Reducing class size. Tutoring is also the linchpin of a multifaceted elementary school approach developed by Slavin and his colleagues (Slavin, Madden, Karweit, Livermon, & Dolan, 1990). However, another major aspect of the program is reducing class size.

Called Success for All, the program includes an emphasis on one-to-one tutoring in reading, research-based reading methods carried out with a reduced class size, frequent assessment, enhanced preschool and kindergarten programs, family support, and other interventions to prevent learning problems. With respect to the tutoring, certified and experienced teachers are used. They take a student out of class for 20 minutes during social studies and work to support the reading curriculum.

During regular reading periods, the tutors become additional reading teachers so that class size is reduced to 15 students. This can be seen as a form of team teaching, which is a time-honored way of reducing the number of students a

Feature 5-3   *Computer as Tutor*

Computer-assisted instruction has become more feasible with the increasing availability of personal computers and promising programs. Obviously, computer programs have all the advantages and most of the disadvantages of direct instruction. That is, they can assess needs, provide tasks that are at an appropriate developmental level, allow students to proceed at their own pace, provide feedback on performance, and record progress. And, initially, they seem to have some value in motivating students. However, after the novelty wears off, the relentless emphasis on skill instruction can become tedious. Also, if a student doesn't understand an underlying concept, the programs are not designed to deal with the problem.

There are a variety of studies attesting to the promise of computer-assisted instruction for students with learning problems (Cohen, Torgesen & Torgesen, 1988; Goldman & Pellegrino, 1987; Male, 1988; Mather, 1988; Slavin et al., 1989).

Computers also have been used as a research tool in investigating ways to detect errors in diagnosing learning disabilities (Adelman, Lauber, Nelson, & Smith, 1989).

Programs are available to help a student learn and practice basic academic skills and problem solving; some of these are in the form of computer games to enhance their motivational value. In addition, use of word processing programs provides a student the opportunity to prepare written assignments with greater ease. More important, access to the computer for pleasure and for creative writing can help a student pursue personal interests while obtaining valuable language experience. Even computerized games have promise in facilitating basic cognitive development (Greenfield, 1984).

Computers obviously are a powerful tool. As with all tools, they can be misused. It is up to the teacher to be certain a good program is chosen and is used only so long as it is productive.

teacher must instruct at a given time. It also adds some flexibility in accommodating students' individual differences. (It is worth noting that students in the Success for All program are grouped for reading instruction according to reading level rather than age or grade. Moreover, the program emphasizes cooperative learning activities built around partner reading. The curriculum emphasis for kindergarten and first grade is on language skills, auditory discrimination, sound blending, and use of phonetically regular minibooks.)

The idea of reducing class size is, of course, controversial because of the costs involved. Odden (1990) offers a policy-oriented analysis of research related to the cost-effectiveness of reducing class size as a way of enhancing instructional effectiveness. He concludes that reducing class size is not warranted throughout a school system because it would cost more than it would accomplish. However, reductions are indicated for targeted populations. In particular, reduced class size is seen as a promising way to help elementary school students at the first signs of learning and behavior problems.

Clearly there is much work to be done in expanding the accommodation of individual differences in the classroom as a way to enhance instruction. It may not be evident, however, that the problem of improving instruction has been analyzed in cultural and sociopolitical, as well as psychoeducational, terms. Those who view the problem in such terms argue that a satisfactory solution requires a fundamental transformation in the nature of public education. Minimally, this calls for making schools truly pluralistic institutions. To achieve such a goal requires development of sociopolitical strategies and a reform agenda (for example, see Biklen & Zollers, 1986).

Early School Adjustment Problems

Redesigning regular instruction is not sufficient for dealing with adjustment problems that interfere with students' learning at school. For example, successful adjustment at school depends not only on having the necessary skills and behaviors to learn but also on the characteristics of the classroom situation to which the student is assigned. Students need greater capability and higher motivation to succeed in demanding programs. In contrast, even students with skill and motivational deficiencies may adjust well in programs that accommodate individual differences and remedy minor deficits.

To meet the needs of students with school adjustment problems, there has been a push to include mental health "basics" in school curricula (Long, 1986). Examples include programs to

- enhance self-concept (California Task Force Report, 1990)
- promote social competency, coping, and problem solving (Bond & Compas, 1989)
- train empathy (Feshbach, 1984)
- increase cooperative behavior (Wright & Cowen, 1985)

These efforts represent only a small part of decades of work aimed at improving the mental health climate in schools through curriculum change, teacher training, direct services, and consultation and collaboration (Bond & Compas, 1989; Conoley & Conoley, 1990; Zigler, Kagan, & Muenchow, 1982).

School adjustment problems are a common concern, but major programs to address such problems are rather uncommon. A few examples will illustrate the potential scope of such interventions.

From the late 1970s, the Kindergarten Intervention Program (KIP) has addressed school adjustment problems through a classroom-based approach (Munn, McAlpine, & Taylor, 1989). The process involves identifying students who are manifesting significant school adjustment or psychosocial problems. Identification involves daily teacher observation over a few weeks. Once students are identified, a three-component intervention is used to address their problems. The first component involves use of volunteer aides (college students, parents, senior citizens). These individuals are recruited, trained, and supervised to work directly in the classroom with identified students for 3 to 5 hours a week. The intent is to provide someone who will offer additional psychosocial and educational support. The second component emphasizes increased parent involvement in dealing with their child's school adjustment problems. The third component is teacher consultation, provided by mental health professionals in the form of one-to-one interchanges for problem solving and inservice education. Emphasis is on the general needs of at-risk youth in the classroom and on planning and implementing systematic steps to enhance the motivation and success of the targeted students.

Along similar lines, but much better known, is the school-based program created by the Primary Mental Health Project (Cowen, 1980; Cowen & Hightower, 1990). This widely adopted program encourages (a) prompt detection of early school adjustment problems, (b) establishment of specific intervention objectives, (c) adding resources to carry out interventions, and (d) broadening the remedial focus in kindergarten and early elementary classrooms to help students adjust to school. As adopted in California (Primary Intervention Program, 1987), the pro-

**Expanding
resources through
volunteer help.**

gram is offered for kindergartners and those in grades 1 through 3. Identification is
made through screening by mental health professionals, interviews with parents,
and teacher input. Once a child is identified, a child aide (a trained paraprofes-
sional) is assigned to work 30 to 40 minutes once a week with the student in a
specially designed and equipped playroom at the school. Supervision is provided
by a mental health professional. The aide may work with the youngster individually
or in small groups; the intent is to foster healthy self-concepts, develop social
skills, and bring school work up to potential.

School adjustment problems are common among newcomers, such as students just starting school and those who move into a new school. Special attention
is needed for newcomers lagging in the area of social development, those who are
recent immigrants, and for non-native speakers of English.

The problem of newcomers is just beginning to receive the attention it warrants (Jason, Betts, Johnson, Smith, et al., 1989). Programs to address the adjustment problems of newcomers fall into the category of "transition-in" interventions
(see Chapter 3). One proposed approach would create permanent changes at a
school, both to minimize negative experiences during the transition-in process and
to ensure positive outreach (Adelman & Taylor, 1991). The intervention has two
phases. Specific components of the first phase are (a) a school-wide welcoming
atmosphere — including a positive reception by the office staff, a welcoming packet
containing greetings and information, and a special conference with the principal
and teacher; (b) newcomer orientation activities for students and parents;
(c) personal invitations and support for joining relevant ongoing activities; and

*We do not know
to what extent we
can be of help. . . .
We do not present
ourselves as ex-
perts who have
answers. We have
much to learn
about this helping
process. . . . To-
gether we may be
able to be of help
to children.*

*Sarason et al.
(1960)*

(d) immediate linking with others (for example, peer pairing) to create a social support network. Phase two of the process identifies and provides interventions for newcomers manifesting significant school adjustment or psychosocial problems. Identification involves daily teacher observation over the first few weeks. Once a student is identified, the three-component intervention described earlier in relation to the Kindergarten Intervention Program is used to address problems.

Enhancing Teacher Learning

Implied in any effort to improve schools and classrooms is the idea of teachers' learning on the job. Stated more strongly, enhancing teacher learning is central to any strategy for improving education. From a financial perspective, much of the effort must take the form of conventional inservice courses and workshops. However, there are examples of innovative approaches that provide teachers with personalized opportunities for learning how to improve instruction and deal with problems. These include

- problem consultation
- modeled and guided change

Problem consultation.   Consultation in schools is a collaborative problem-solving intervention. Consultants enter into such a collaboration with the intent of improving the nature of intervention activity that others will implement (Caplan, 1970; Conoley & Conoley, 1990; Gutkin & Curtis, 1990; Meyers, 1981).

Consultants deal with both the educational and psychosocial aspects of students' problems. They focus on designing direct interventions, as well as facilitating referral for special services. Although much school consultation focuses on individual student problems, this need not, and probably should not, be the case. Collaborative, problem-solving consultation can be used to improve classroom, school, or district-wide programs both by overcoming problems and by enhancing positive development.

Truly collaborative problem solving requires considerable skill. Even when consultation is sought, and those seeking the consultation are highly motivated, consultants must be adept at (a) initiating and maintaining a mutually respectful working relationship and (b) facilitating the problem solving. Consultants must be committed to sharing their expertise in ways that enable those seeking consultation to solve future problems on their own (Pugach & Johnson, 1989; Zins, Curtis, Graden, & Ponti, 1988).

Consultation for those who are not motivated to solve problems raises additional concerns. Such persons may be only passive participants in the problem-solving process, and unlikely to follow through on potential solutions. In such cases, the consultant also needs to understand how to deal with reactive and proactive barriers to problem solving. Common barriers arise from differences in economic background, current lifestyle, skin color, culture, sex, power, status, or professional training. Such differences can, of course, be complementary and helpful — as when staff from different disciplines learn from each other.

Collaborative consultation holds particular promise for helping teachers learn new ways to work with learning and behavior problems, thus reducing referrals for special education. Three models of "prereferral interventions" provide good examples:

One-to-one consultation. Here a consultant is responding to a teacher's request to refer a youngster for special help (Graden, Casey, & Christensen, 1985). Consultation at this point may introduce additional ways the teacher could meet the student's needs. Only if the new interventions prove ineffective is referral pursued.

Teacher assistance team. The teacher requesting special help for a student meets with an informal team of school personnel to brainstorm and problem solve (Chalfant & Pysh, 1983). Such a team might consist only of other regular teachers or may include special education teachers and resource professionals. Again, the intent is to identify additional intervention strategies that might allow the youngster to progress without special help.

Peer consultation. This process is conceived of as a structured dialogue among peers. Several regular teachers are assigned to meet and develop ways to work more effectively in the classroom. Specific metacognitive strategies, such as self-questioning and summarizing, are formally taught and used to guide development of problem-solving skills (Johnson & Pugach, 1991).

As the above examples suggest, the aim of consultation goes well beyond solving a particular problem. It provides an important vehicle for personalized, on-the-job teacher education aimed at broadening the range of individual differences accommodated in regular classes.

Modeling and guiding change.   One result of consultation is that teachers are expected to try new interventions. This often means they must learn new skills. Such learning probably is best accomplished when teachers (a) can observe how others effectively handle problems in the classroom and (b) have adequate opportunities for guided practice. Unfortunately, neither of these elements tend to be available to teachers as they pursue on-the-job learning (and the first element often was lacking in their preservice education as well).

One approach developed along these lines involves use of master teachers to model and guide new practices (Adelman, 1972). The approach encompasses four overlapping steps carried out in four- to seven-week cycles. During each cycle, a master teacher goes from classroom to classroom, helping other teachers learn more effective procedures for coping with learning and behavior problems. The master teacher can work with three teachers in a school during each cycle.

Step 1: *Demonstration and discussion* (2 to 3 weeks). The cycle begins with a discussion to clarify what is to be demonstrated and the process to be used. Then, for a day or two, the master teacher observes in each classroom (usually during academic instruction such as the reading period). After the observation days, the master teacher takes responsibility for instruction during that period for about two weeks. This provides a model of procedures to be learned and frees the teacher to observe. Before and after each day's demonstration, the master teacher explains the rationale for what is modeled and explores alternative ideas and procedures. When problems arise, problem-solving strategies are discussed and modeled. (In some cases, a few readings may also be recommended.) During this step, the teacher has the daily opportunity to observe a master demonstration and discuss the process personally and in depth for about two weeks—and to do all this in his or her own classroom.

Step 2: *Initial guided practice* (1 to 2 weeks). After approximately two weeks (sooner if the teacher is ready), guided practice is initiated. While the master teacher continues to have primary responsibility for the lesson, the regular teacher practices aspects of what has been demonstrated. During this step, the master teacher will observe the practice and provide immediate guidance and support, including additional demonstrations.

Step 3: *Guided total implementation* (1 to 2 weeks). After one to two weeks of guided practice, the regular teacher resumes full responsibility for teaching. The master teacher observes and meets daily for discussion. If necessary, additional demonstrations are provided. (At this point the process resembles traditional supervised teaching, but the dynamics are different because of what has gone before.)

Step 4: *Follow-up.* As the master teacher moves on to begin a new training cycle, a time is established for follow-up consultation (observation and discussion and even additional brief demonstrations if necessary). The follow-up period lasts no more than a month.

Clearly, there are a variety of ways to improve inservice education for teachers. Unfortunately, the trend remains one of overreliance on general inservice workshops. If regular education is to be improved significantly, we suggest there will have to be a greater emphasis on personalized on-the-job learning.

Special Resources for Severe Problems

At some point, students' problems become too severe for most regular classroom teachers to handle without the direct assistance of another professional. Such assistance may come from another regular teacher, a specialist teacher, or specialists in mental health, medicine, and so forth. It may take the form of educational remediation or therapeutic treatments. Needed from the professional is not only a set of appropriate skills but also the time to work with the student and perhaps the student's parents. Optimally, such services should already be available at the school or should be brought there when needed.

For students with learning problems, resource teachers exemplify one of the most important special resources. Beyond consultation, a resource teacher brings master skills for working with one or more students in or outside the regular classroom (Marston, 1987–88). Mental health professionals can be particularly helpful in exploring the motivational bases for learning problems and the implica-

tions for dealing with motivational problems (Taylor & Adelman, 1990). Available evidence suggests that effective on-the-job teacher training and use of special resources can reduce the number of students referred for special education (Graden, Casey, & Bonstrom, 1985; Lloyd, Crowley, Kohler, & Strain, 1988). We must remember, however, that there comes a time for some students when intensive special education programs and placements are warranted (that is, they become the least intervention needed).

Adolescents and Adults

If a learning problem is not corrected by the end of elementary school, the problem becomes more profound in many ways. Then it requires an additional range of special programs. In this section, we first explore some of the special concerns confronting those with learning problems as they get older; then we outline a range of programs for dealing with these concerns.

Special Concerns

Individuals vary considerably as to how stressful the transition from childhood to adulthood is (Powers, Hauser, & Kilner, 1989). During adolescence, rapid changes occur in all areas of development simultaneously. Besides the demanding physical changes that take place between childhood and adulthood, individuals are confronted with a myriad of sociocultural expectations, especially from family and friends. These are potent influences shaping the many evolving views of self (such as gender, role, performance expectations, and feelings of competence).

Havighurst's (1972) outline of eight central developmental tasks provides a useful framework for appreciating the special concerns of individuals during this period:

- accepting one's physique and sexual role
- establishing new peer relationships

A potential drop-out?

- attaining emotional independence from parents
- achieving assurance of economic independence
- choosing and preparing for an occupation
- developing intellectual skills and concepts necessary for civic competence
- acquiring socially responsible behavior patterns
- building conscious values that are harmonious with one's environment

How well prepared adolescents are to accomplish each developmental task is reflected in their subsequent growth and shapes the adults they become. For example, those from low-income and minority backgrounds may experience considerable difficulty because of early deprivations and discrimination (Dao, 1991; Gibbs, Huang, & Associates, 1989). Similarly, those who have experienced significant learning problems in elementary school may be ill-prepared to cope appropriately. They lack prerequisite skills and may also have developed negative attitudes toward school and academic learning. Those who are poorly prepared to master the developmental tasks of adolescence and adulthood are vulnerable to a host of social and emotional problems.

All indicators suggest that learning problems are a major concern in secondary schools and beyond. Although figures on school dropout rates are controversial, it is clear that in many schools serving students from low-income, minority backgrounds over 50 percent of those who start ninth grade do not graduate (Rumberger, 1987). The best evidence available suggests that many of these students have learning problems (Rumberger, 1987; Finn, 1989). Poor learning is characteristic even of many who do graduate. For example, a study in Chicago found that only 47 percent of students enrolled in ninth grade in 1980–81 graduated in 1984, and only 15 percent of those who graduated could read at or above the national average (Designs for Change, 1985). Data on literacy in the United States suggest that over 50 percent of 17-year-olds who don't drop out of school are no better than semiliterate (able to handle less than 75 percent of simple reading material encountered daily); among students from low-income, minority backgrounds the figures are higher (National Assessment of Educational Progress, 1976).

As to students diagnosed as having disabilities, statistics indicate schools are providing special programs for increasing numbers of adolescents and adults. In the United States, individuals in the age range of 12 through 17 represent 41 percent of all students receiving special education services, with another 5 percent accounted for by those 18 through 21. Unfortunately, the data also indicate that less than half of these students graduate with a high school diploma (U.S. Department of Education, 1988).

We hasten to emphasize that individuals are resilient and often show inner strength and develop their own talents, even when early experiences have been negative. There are endless examples of those who have succeeded despite serious disabilities or growing up in hostile environments or even performing poorly in school.

The cure for adolescence is to live through it.

D. W. Winnicott

However, we cannot take much comfort in exceptions, and must not leave matters entirely to chance. To increase the number who do succeed, a variety of special programs have been proposed.

Special Programs

Obviously, the approaches for improving learning at the elementary level are relevant for secondary schooling. There are, in addition, specific programs that adolescents and adults need because of the impact of years of problems, the nature of the developmental tasks confronting them, and the shortened time available for access to government-supported help.

These additional programs for older students and adults do raise dilemmas. For example, in addition to having regular needs (regular curriculum or living requirements), the skill deficiencies of older individuals call for programs of intensive remedial instruction to help them catch up. But it is clear that many do not catch up, and time should be spent teaching them ways to compensate for problems. Many also need special preparation to meet requirements for graduation and future employment or additional schooling. Finally, there are those who require additional support in the form of counseling and help with transitions.

Over and above the regular demands of adolescence and adulthood, all these special needs take time and resources and, given the limited quantity of both, priorities must be set. This is true for the individual and for those trying to help, and it is true whether efforts are made to meet the needs through regular programs or by establishing special ones.

Given that priorities will determine availability, the range of options includes the following:

- emotional support (psychological counseling)
- intensive remediation
- instruction related to other types of life skills (problem-solving skills, establishing effective interpersonal relationships)
- vocational and career education (including work-study programs)
- graduation testing preparation (for minimal competency testing or tests to qualify for a graduate equivalent degree)
- counseling and special preparation for postsecondary education
- transition planning and support
- adult mutual support and advocacy groups

Feature 5-4   Postsecondary Education and Vocational Training

Postsecondary and vocational programs for students with learning problems are fundamental avenues to enhanced futures. Programs designed specifically for persons with learning disabilities are opening the way for all who have not done well in secondary schools. Such programs are relatively new and remain rather controversial.

For some time, it was widely assumed that so few students with learning disabilities were interested in going to college that special programs for them were not needed. Data from the 1970s and 1980s counteracted this assumption. After that, it was speculated that students with learning disabilities could not survive in college even with special help. This view was bolstered by figures showing how few of those who began college actually graduated. To rebut this argument, it has been emphasized that even when special programs are offered, the tendency is to promise more than is delivered; thus, students are not getting the support necessary for success.

That special programs at the college level are costly and difficult to set up is also a factor that tends to cause resistance. The issue is one of priorities. Given that only so much money is available, should it be used to bolster existing, regular programs—or should it be used to create additional services for those who need special help to survive in college? (For more on this topic and guides to colleges that make provision for students with learning problems, see Liscio, 1985; Mangrum & Strichart, 1988; Sclafani & Lynch, 1989; Vogel, 1985, 1987.)

More controversial than postsecondary programs has been the topic of vocational training. The roots of the issue are found in the type of menial jobs that many vocational programs have emphasized for those who have not done well academically. Critics say such programs often demean and underutilize the potential of those enrolled and certainly limit their options for the future.

To deal with the criticism, the trend seems to be toward increasing the range of career and vocational options for which training is made available. Lack of money and resources and the demands of the job market, of course, are barriers to this reform. Therefore, critics are pessimistic about improvement and remain concerned about who is counseled into such programs. (For more on this topic, see Halpern, 1992; Miller & Schloss, 1982; Okolo & Sitlington, 1986; Phelps, Chaplin, & Kelly, 1987; Rusch & Phelps, 1987; Scott, 1991).

What is actually available tends to be much less than the above and tends to be more available to targeted groups, such as those at risk for dropout or those diagnosed as having a learning or other disability (see Feature 5-4).

Summing Up

Because the seeds of learning problems are planted early, programs have been designed to intervene as early as possible. Some prevention programs aim at promoting health care and safety beginning even before birth. The most widespread early intervention, however, is that of early education programs.

As children move into elementary school, efforts to deal with learning problems focus on redesigning regular instruction by making schools more effective overall and expanding the range of individual differences accommodated in the classroom. In addition, programs to deal with school adjustment problems seem particularly important. To enable regular teachers to reduce learning problems, personalized on-the-job learning and special resources are indicated.

All signs suggest that learning problems continue to be a major concern in secondary schools and beyond. Because of the impact of years of problems, the developmental tasks confronting them, and the limited time remaining for access to funded help, adolescents and adults require a range of additional programs. Unfortunately, what is available for them tends to be restricted to a few targeted groups.

Overall, the various approaches discussed in this chapter demonstrate an impressive array of programs that can be used to address learning problems. However, as long as they are pursued in a piecemeal fashion, they can only make modest inroads into the complex psychosocial and educational factors that underlie learning problems.

As noted in Chapter 1, a comprehensive perspective on intervention points to the importance of attacking problems with a full range of integrated community- and school-based programs. As Kagan (1990) stresses in her policy analysis, "three linked strategies . . . offer hope [of moving] from well-intentioned, piecemeal programs to comprehensive services that reach new standards of excellence. . . . These include (1) moving from 'programs to systems' models; (2) moving from a particularistic to universal vision; and (3) moving from short- to long-term commitments" (p. 17).

In the long run, a comprehensive, coordinated attack has the potential to be not only more effective but also less costly. The problem is that in the short run comprehensiveness is expensive. Until society and its policymakers are ready to expend the necessary resources, programs to address learning problems must continue to do whatever they can to provide students, parents, and teachers with the support they desperately need.

Indeed, each day professionals are called upon to screen, diagnose, place, and provide remediation and treatment for learning problems. It is one of the ironies of daily practice that professionals often are called upon to do more than they know, and at other times to know more than they can do. Yet do we must. Decisions must be made and programs carried out. However, we must keep in mind that interventions can have negative as well as beneficial effects. Therefore, intervention decisions need to be made in an informed manner, with consideration for the rights and interests of all concerned. Chapter 6 is devoted to an overview of fundamental concerns related to making intervention decisions.

Given the years you have spent in school, you probably have some views about how regular instruction should be redesigned.

List your top ten changes, and see how they compare with those discussed in this chapter.
Ask your friends about their top ten changes.

Theories of Instruction and Models of Teaching (p. 355) provides a glimpse of the various efforts that have been made to synthesize ideas about instruction and teaching. You will read a bit about

- the Montessori Method
- Piaget's ideas on how intellect develops
- Bruner's ideas on the processes of education and instruction
- Skinner's technological approach
- Rogers's humanistic approach
- Gagné's attempts to weave ideas about essential conditions for learning into a theory of instruction
- Joyce and Weil's framework for cataloguing models of teaching

Who Decides?

Parental Consent and Due Process

Children's Assent

Competence

Paternalism

Demystification

Conflicts over Decisions

In Whose Best Interests?

Helping and Socialization

The Politics of Decision Making

Summing Up

Deciding what is best for a child often poses a question no less ultimate than the purposes and values of life itself.

Mnookin, 1985

Despite Superintendent Brown's apprehension, her school board decided that the district would give a battery of screening tests to all incoming kindergartners to find any who have learning problems.

"Easier said than done," complained the superintendent to the board. "You know the concerns I have about such testing, and I'm not the only one. I'm sure there will be a reaction from teachers and the community."

The decision to implement a screening program or any other intervention raises the question: Who should be involved in making intervention decisions?

Disregarding concerns raised by the superintendent and others, the screening program was carried out. And, based on the test findings, Matt's parents were informed that his scores indicated a need for special help. To be certain, further assessment was done. The results again indicated problems. His parents were told Matt should be placed in a special class.

This placement decision raises such questions as the following:

- Does the school have the right to place Matt in a special class even if the parents don't agree with the decision?
- Does Matt have any say in the matter?

The above questions arise whenever decisions are made to intervene. Each encompasses major legal and ethical concerns related to the topic of consent (see Feature 6-1). This chapter is an introduction to such concerns.

Parental Consent and Due Process

There was a time not so long ago when assigning students to special programs was done matter-of-factly. Most professionals believed they knew who needed help and what help was needed. It was a relatively simple matter to inform those involved that a problem existed and what was to be done. Growing awareness of rights and of the potentially harmful effects of treatment led to safeguards. Currently, consent is not taken for granted.

Parent and student involvement have become prominent considerations in designing screening, diagnosis, and placement practices in the schools. Parent organizations and child advocates have insisted that parents be involved in any decision that might have a profound effect on the course of a child's life. With respect to special education, this fact is reflected in the "procedural safeguards" associated with the passage of Public Law 94-142. These safeguards are rooted in the legal concept of due process as established in the Fourteenth Amendment to the federal constitution.

Due process protects people's rights; procedural safeguards are meant to help guarantee that everyone is treated fairly. The special education procedural safeguards are meant to ensure that parents are involved in decisions regarding testing and placement of their child. That is, such interventions are not supposed to take place without parental consent.

Some of the safeguards spelled out in law are the following:

1. Parents must be notified whenever the school plans to conduct a special evaluation of their child.
2. Parents have the right to refuse consent for such an evaluation. (However, the school district has the right to a legal hearing to prove it is needed. Should parents want a special evaluation and the school refuses to provide it, parents can seek a legal hearing.)
3. Parents have the right to:
   • review the procedures and instruments to be used in any evaluation
   • be informed of the results and review all records
   • obtain an independent educational evaluation to be considered in any decisions
4. Parents must be notified whenever the school wants to change their child's educational placement, and they have the right to refuse consent for such a change. (Again, the school district can ask for a legal hearing to overrule the parents' decision; and parents who are unable to convince the school to provide the special placement they want can also seek such a hearing.)

All notifications and explanations are to be given in the parents' primary language or other primary mode of communication.

Feature 6-1   Informed Consent

Levine (1975) enumerates the basic information that should be communicated and understood. These items include clarifying the purpose of the procedures (why the person is there; what the person will be doing), describing risks and benefits, spelling out alternatives, assuring the individual that participation is not required, and eliciting and answering all questions.

To make sure it is understood, such information may need to be presented in a variety of ways. Repeated verbal or written communications, translations, media presentations, question-and-answer follow-ups to evaluate whether information was understood, feedback from other consumers—all may be relevant at various times.

The emphasis on information, and the very term *informed consent,* may sometimes lead to greater emphasis on giving information than on ensuring true consent. As Biklen (1978) says of the term:

It suggests that the key element of consent is the provision of information to people who are giving consent. Consent is a legal concept that has been referred to and implicitly defined in court cases and in legislation. It has three major aspects: capacity, information, and voluntariness. All three elements are equally relevant to any consent procedure or decision. Simply stated, one must have the ability to give consent in order to do so; one must have adequate information to do so in a knowledgeable way; and one must be free from coercion or any other threat to one's voluntariness. (p. 99)

**Talking *to* parents
or talking *with*
parents?**

Beyond concerns raised by special education processes, contacts between teachers and parents raise concerns about the type of life-shaping decisions that occur and how they are made. Take, for example, the case of Jose.

Jose's family had come to the United States four years ago. His father worked as a gardener; his mother worked in the garment district. Neither parent was fluent in English (mother less so than father).

Jose's parents were called to school because of his misbehavior in the classroom. The teacher (who did not speak Spanish) informed them that she was having to use a range of behavioral management strategies to control Jose. However, for the strategies to really work, she said it was also important for the parents to use the same procedures at home. To learn these "parenting skills," the parents both were to attend one of the six-week evening workshops the school was starting. They were assured the workshop was free, was available in English or Spanish, and there would be child care at the school if they needed it.

After meeting with the teacher, Jose's father, who had reluctantly come to the conference, told his wife she should attend the workshop, but he would not. She understood that he saw it as her role—not his—but she was frightened; they fought about it. They had been fighting about a lot of things recently. In the end, she went, but her resentment toward her husband grew with every evening she had to attend the training sessions.

Over the next few months, the mother attempted to apply what she was told at

Involving Parents in Schooling (p. 410) discusses parents' key role in their child's education, barriers to participation, and intervening to enhance parent involvement in schooling.

the workshop. She withheld privileges and confined Jose to periods of "time out" whenever he didn't toe the line. However, she felt his conduct at home was not that bad—it was just the same spirited behavior his older brothers had shown at his age. Besides, she knew he was upset by the increasingly frequent arguments she and her husband were having. She would have liked some help about what to do, but she didn't know how to get it.

Instead of improving the situation, the control strategies seemed to make Jose more upset; he "acted out" more frequently and with escalating force. Soon his mother found he would not listen to her and would run off when she tried to do what she had been told to do. She complained to her husband. He said it was her fault for pampering Jose. His solution was to beat the youngster.

To make matters worse, the teacher called to say she now felt that Jose should be taken to the doctor to determine whether he was hyperactive and in need of medication. This was too much for Jose's mother. She did not take him to the doctor, and she no longer responded to most calls and letters from the school.

Jose continued to be a problem at school, and now at home too, and his mother didn't know what to do about it or who to turn to for help. When asked, Jose's teacher describes the parents as "hard to reach."

Children's Assent

Young people's involvement in decision making is only beginning to be discussed seriously. For example, there is increasing discussion of the need to obtain the minors' assent in addition to parental consent.

Interest in civil rights in the late 1960s, and related advocacy of minors' rights in education and mental health, has led to greater consideration of the rights of children and adolescents to be involved in making decisions that affect them. Concomitantly, long-standing controversies have reemerged about the risks and benefits of young people's involvement in decision making and their competence to make appropriate decisions. Two related concepts are explicitly or implicitly part of the debate: the question of children's decision-making competence and the problem of paternalism.

Competence

Stated directly, the question of competence asks: To what degree is an individual capable of understanding the factors that go into making an appropriate decision (about a given intervention)?

There is little in the way of satisfactory research on the degree to which individuals at various ages and with various problems have such capabilities. Available findings suggest that minors, including those diagnosed as having learning disabilities, may be able to participate in placement decisions considerably before late adolescence—which is the earliest age most professionals have accepted for encouraging such participation. However, the age at which minors clearly are able to decide for themselves remains to be established, as must differences in decision-making competence between minors and adults (Melton, Koocher, & Saks, 1983; Taylor, Adelman, & Kaser-Boyd, 1984, 1985).

Paternalism

The problem of paternalism reflects the fact that parents, professionals, and various representatives of society have special responsibilities for minors. In carrying out such responsibilities, they must have the right to make certain decisions for children and adolescents. When these paternalistic decisions produce little complaint or reaction from those affected, or when major health and safety matters are at stake, paternalism is unlikely to be seen as a problem.

However, suppose a 14-year-old does not want to be placed in a special class. Should the student be compelled? Currently, students have no legal say until they are 18. Only the parents (or a special advocate) can argue for or against the placement.

Are 18-year-olds more competent to decide than 14-year-olds? Maybe. But an 18-year-old may be as incompetent as a 14-year-old with respect to making the decision. For that matter, some parents are seen as ill-equipped to make placement decisions. And, of course, it also is possible that by age 14 some individuals have developed the competence to decide such matters for themselves.

Legal age aside, there is little agreement about how to determine competence for decision making or about whether a competent minor should be able to overturn some paternalistic decisions. In general, then, competence and paternalism are at the heart of most arguments against seeking minors' consent or assent.

Those favoring increased involvement of minors in decision making also argue that the process can produce major benefits. For one, individuals who feel the choice was theirs can be expected to have higher levels of commitment and motivation with respect to decisions that are made. Thus consent can be seen as an important prerequisite to positive participation. Moreover, if competence to make decisions increases with experience and learning, then participation in the process should help to increase competence for making future decisions (Adelman, Kaser-Boyd, & Taylor, 1984). In contrast, not participating in decision making may undermine motivation and competence. We have more to say about these matters in Parts 3 and 4.

Demystification

One of the most basic ethical obligations in any field is to be honest and to avoid conflicts of interest. Besides providing relevant information as part of informed-consent procedures, this also means making a major attempt to avoid deceiving or mystifying others. Activity designed to inform, clarify, or correct misinformation is called *demystification.*

Currently the general public is confused about the nature of learning problems in general and learning disabilities in particular. Assessment and treatment practices can be a mystery. Even professionals seem uncertain about what to call individuals with learning problems and about how valid some procedures are. Widespread use of jargon and failure to clarify the limits, uncertainties, and controversial nature of many practices not only fails to inform but also tends to deceive and mystify. The failure to demystify the public probably accounts, in part, for the many fads and panaceas that have plagued us.

Arguments against efforts to explain matters to clients and the general public often stress that nonprofessionals don't have the ability to understand the complexities of professional practices or that they are not really interested (Feature 6-2). To counter the latter argument, it has been pointed out that one of the most frequent formal complaints from clients and consumers is about practitioners who fail to explain the limitations and uncertainties of the procedures they use.

Practices that mystify, such as overselling expertise, tend to undermine people's ability to take care of themselves. People come to think that if they go to professionals their problems will be solved; they begin to believe that the only way to solve such problems is to go to professionals. A negative consequence of the failure of practitioners to demystify their activity is that people in our culture are evolving an unhealthy reliance on professionals. Many in our society believe that they are incompetent to deal with problems in certain basic areas of personal and interpersonal functioning without the services of a professional (Illich, 1976). This, of course, is good for business; but it raises serious ethical concerns about self-serving tendencies on the part of professionals.

The range of ethical considerations we have outlined barely scrapes the surface. In coming years, professionals in education, psychology, medicine, and so forth will be grappling with these concerns and many others (Stephens, 1985). At the least, they must deal more systematically with the following ethical responsibilities:

Feature 6-2   Mystification

"If there is, in fact, an area in which one does know things that the client doesn't know, it is extremely easy to believe that one knows generally what is best for the client.... In addition there is the fact ... the client has a serious problem or concern which has rendered the client weak and vulnerable. This, too, surely increases the disposition to respond toward the client in a patronizing, paternalistic fashion. The client of necessity confers substantial power over his or her well-being.... Invested in all of this power both by the individual and the society, the ... professional responds to the client as though the client were an individual who needed to be looked after and controlled, and to have decisions made for him or her ... with as little interference from the client as possible" (Wasserstrom, 1975, pp. 21–22).

"The parents of a child who has been labeled and is physically, psychologically, or academically deficient are usually avid consumers of ideas that promise help. These parents are struggling to understand what may be incomprehensible. But answers come easy, and all too often they are given by individuals with well-lubricated ethics in a forceful, professional, quasi-scientific and logical manner" (Pihl, 1975, p. 23).

Toward Services with an Informed Consumer Orientation (p. 400) presents specific examples of consumer-oriented services for persons with learning problems.

1. The obligation to be aware of potential negative consequences, such as immediate and long-term harm to individuals, groups, and society.
2. The obligation (ethically and often legally) to inform prospective clients of potential positive and negative consequences.
3. The dual obligation to minimize potential negative effects and maximize potential benefits during intervention.
4. The obligation to anticipate subsequent negative consequences and to take steps to counter them—especially by preparing clients to protect themselves.
5. The obligation to acknowledge when intervention outcomes (including assessment findings) are inconclusive and to avoid rationalizing and dismissing uncertainties and incongruities.

Understanding ethical concerns is no guarantee that persons will behave ethically. Indeed, ethical considerations often appear to be honored more in discussion than in practice. Ultimately, ethical practice is a matter of individual understanding, conscience, and action.

Conflicts over Decisions

When interests coincide, there is unlikely to be much concern about who makes decisions. When interests conflict, however, who decides becomes a critical matter. In most situations, decision making is controlled by those with the most authority and power. In this sense, a decision to intervene is a sociopolitical one.

In the cases of David, James, Matt, or Mara, a great many intervention decisions were made over the years. Inevitably, because of the number of interested parties affected by the decisions, conflicts arose.

With most learning intervention decisions, there are at least three interested parties besides the student: family, teachers, and policymakers (such as principals, school boards, and funding agencies). When a decision is not acceptable to one or more of these parties, the dilemma can only be resolved if one party prevails or if all compromise. Let's look at an example.

When James was 15, he felt strongly that he no longer wanted to stay in a special class. The special class made him feel stigmatized, and he didn't see that he was making any progress. He wanted to try regular classes and have a tutor help him. His parents and teacher, however, both thought that he wouldn't be able to handle the work. Furthermore, they believed that, rather than making him feel better about himself, the experience would only make him feel worse. An additional concern was that the school did not provide tutoring for those in regular classes.

Because both the parents and the teacher were in agreement, it was decided they "knew best"—so James spent another year in the special class. It was a disastrous year in which he did no real work and got into a lot of trouble. As soon as he was 16, he insisted on dropping out of school; his parents and the school were so frustrated that they simply went along with this decision. Looking back, they all wondered if some compromise should have been worked out when he wanted to leave the special class.

James's mother tries to help.

What compromises? Several might have been considered:

- James could have spent some time each day in regular classes and some in the special program where tutoring could have been provided.
- He could have been offered a one-semester trial period in carefully selected regular classes with some volunteer tutoring (from community resources or advanced students).
- The transfer could have been approved, with the provision that James first work with his teacher to identify any missing prerequisites essential for survival in the regular program and then work on acquiring these skills over a specified time period (no more than an additional semester).

Other compromises probably have occurred to you. Whether any would have worked is uncertain. What is obvious is that the decision to ignore James's choice did not lead to positive outcomes and had a negative effect on his motivation to overcome his problems. A compromise that he saw as an effort to help him pursue his best interests might have mobilized him toward positive activity.

As the example illustrates, differences in perception lead people to different decisions. Sometimes the perceptions differ because the same information is not available to all interested parties; sometimes the perceptions are shaped by the fact that the parties have differing interests.

In Whose Best Interests?

James almost always made decisions in terms of what he saw as his best interests. However, his parents and teacher thought many of his decisions reflected current fancies rather than his long-range best interests. (It is common for adults to see minors as unable to delay gratification.) Because of this, they usually overruled James's decisions.

Are parents' decisions always in a youngster's best interests? Obviously not. Are a professional's decisions inevitably in a client's best interests? Unfortunately, no. But, because notions about what is best in the long run are based on judgment, it is not surprising that parents feel they are more competent to make decisions than their children, even after their children become adults. (Don't additional years of experience and training make for better judgments?) And professionals often prefer, or are expected, to make major intervention decisions for clients.

Parents and professionals have the legal power to control decision making. "Remember," they say from a legal-paternalistic perspective, "we are responsible for looking out for the youngster's/client's best interests." Thus there is a tendency for family members or professionals to make decisions for persons with learning problems — except when the individual's decisions are those with which they agree or see as unimportant. Certainly James's parents felt they knew best. Ironically, over the years there were many times when James's parents found themselves pushed into accepting the school's recommendations, even though they believed some other action should have been tried.

The degree to which family members and professionals actually make the best decisions is a matter still to be clarified by researchers. There are also philosophical and political issues tied up in all this that should not be ignored.

> *Society defines what is exceptional or deviant, and appropriate treatments are designed quite as much to protect society as they are to help the child. "To take care of them" can and should be read with two meanings: to give children help and to exclude them from the community.*
>
> *Hobbs, 1975a*
> *(pp. 20–21)*

Helping and Socialization

When decisions are being made about intervention, each interested party may be operating in the interests of the person with the learning problem or in their own interests. When James's parents and teacher decided he should stay in the special program rather than return to regular classes, they felt their decision was in James's best interests. But were other interests involved as well? For example, were the parents concerned that they would have the added cost of paying for a special tutor if James were in a regular class? Was the teacher concerned about keeping enough students enrolled in special programs? Were the adults more interested in socializing James than in addressing the concerns and interests he expressed?

While the views of those with problems may be the same as those who are responsible for their care, there is often a conflict of interests. One way to understand this is in terms of differences between the socializing role of parents and professionals (in a philosophical and political sense) and the role they have in helping those who have problems.

For example, the responsibilities for socializing the young include making decisions that ensure youngsters learn the skills and behaviors needed to become contributing members of society. Responsibility for helping encompasses pursuing decisions that maximize the interests of the individual even when they are inconsistent with society's agenda. A common problem when individual interests conflict with the essential needs of the society is that individual interests tend to be suppressed. Whether this happens depends on who makes the decisions.

Whose Interests Are Being Served? (p. 395) presents further discussion of concerns about conflicting interests and helping vs. socialization.

For instance, one of the reasons society establishes schools is to socialize the young. Teachers are hired to carry out this agenda. Such an agenda may or may not be in the best interests of a given student. To ensure that the "right" decisions are made (those in society's best interests), school personnel control decision making. Thus they maintain the school's socialization agenda. It is from this perspective that one can best understand why schooling is compulsory, the way in which grades are used, and the one-sided nature of a school's decision-making processes.

When a student has a learning problem, however, teachers are often caught in a dilemma. They want to help the student overcome the problem, so they tend to think in terms of helping relationships. But because schools are designed to socialize, teachers are supposed to reflect a socialization, rather than a helping, agenda. Often the result is that, rather than helping, the procedures frustrate the student and teacher and increase avoidance motivation and negative reactions.

A helping relationship requires putting the individual's interests over those of the society when there is a conflict. It often means trying procedures not associated with socialization that maximize pursuit of the individual's interests while deviating from society's socialization agenda.

The Politics of Decision Making

When ideas and interests conflict, who decides becomes profoundly important (see Feature 6-3). The problem of conflicting interests is reflected in our extensive concern about society's ability to exercise control through psychological and

Feature 6-3   The Power to Decide

"In our culture, parents traditionally have been given broad authority to decide what is best for their children. Within the family, parents have legal power to make a wide range of important decisions that affect the life of the child. Although there are limits to this parental power—for example, parents are held responsible by the state for their child's care and support—children themselves have generally had much less liberty than adults. Children are not normally entitled to their own earnings and do not have the power to manage their own property. Moreover, persons younger than certain statutory age limits are not allowed to vote, hold public office, work in various occupations, drive a car, buy liquor, or be sold certain kinds of reading material, quite apart from what they or their parents might wish.

This traditional allocation of power is now being questioned from two very different perspectives. Some reformers believe young people should have broader legal rights to decide things for themselves, independent of their parents' desires. Child liberators want more power of decision given to the child. Others are equally critical of parental power, but from a very different angle. Their concern arises not from the notion that children should have a greater voice in their own affairs, but rather from their feeling that parents all too often provide inadequately for their children's needs. These reformers often push for the expansion of government programs that they claim are necessary to protect children" (Mnookin, 1985, pp. 511–512).

educational interventions (Adelman & Taylor, 1986, 1988; Coles, 1978; Robinson, 1974; Schrag & Divoky, 1975). At one extreme, it is argued there are times when society must put its needs before individual rights by pursuing certain interventions designed to maintain itself (for example, compulsory education). At the other extreme, it is argued that interventions that jeopardize the individual's rights (coercion, invasion of privacy) are never justified. For many persons, however, neither extreme is acceptable, especially where minors are involved.

Without agreeing or disagreeing with a particular position, one can appreciate the importance of the debate. Specifically, it serves to heighten awareness that

- no society is devoid of some degree of coercion in dealing with its members (no right or liberty is absolute) and that such coercion tends to be seen as especially justified in intervening with minors and those with problems
- interventions for learning problems can be used to serve the vested interests of subgroups in a society at the expense of other subgroups (to deprive minorities, the poor, females, and legal minors of certain freedoms and rights)
- informed consent and due process of law are central to the protection of individuals when there are conflicting interests at stake (about who or what should be blamed for a problem and thus be expected to carry the brunt of corrective measures)

This sensitivity to conflicts is essential if minors are to be adequately protected from abuse by those with power over them.

Control of decision making is usually maintained by those with the greatest authority in a situation. This is a questionable practice when those in authority have no legitimate basis for assuming power or have interests that conflict with those of other participants. The former circumstance includes instances when professionals assess and prescribe outside their area of competence or in areas where the state of knowledge precludes anyone having sufficient expertise; it also includes cases where professionals inappropriately assume the consent of participants. The latter circumstance encompasses instances where professionals' values or financial interests are in conflict with those seeking services and when society pursues its rights and responsibilities at the expense of the rights and liberties of individuals.

It is when ideas and interests conflict that the political facets of intervention are underscored. Power conflicts and imbalances are apparent when those with authority succeed in having their vested psychological, social, political, or economic interests prevail over the objections of those less powerful.

Authority stems from psychological and social–political–economic factors that may or may not be institutionalized. Political facets of intervention are not limited to power imbalances stemming from legislated authority. We see the overt political facets of intervention where interventions are mandated by organizational (government, school, industry) policies and when, for example, assessment data are used for planning, evaluating, and policy-making purposes. Covert political facets are potentially present in all other intervention activity. Any power imbalance may be detrimental to the interests of one or more parties.

Concerns are raised about the decision-making role of clients — especially those presumed to be less than competent (such as those with learning problems). Increasingly, professionals debate the role such persons and their advocates should play in decision making (Melton, Koocher, & Saks, 1983; Mnookin, 1985; Taylor & Adelman, 1986). Court cases and various advocacy programs reflect efforts to ensure protection for those denied a decision-making role. We can expect improved guidelines to emerge soon that will clarify both the legitimate bases for denying individuals decision-making power and the protections safeguarding their interests when others have decision-making authority.

Because overt and covert power imbalances appear inevitable, stringent protection of individual rights is essential. There must be understanding of, and commitment to, ethical principles by professionals and society as a whole if abuses are to be constrained.

Summing Up

Given the life-shaping nature of interventions for learning problems, each decision made is clearly of major significance. And, because each decision is so important, the matters of who makes it and on what bases take on major significance.

In this chapter, we have highlighted issues and problems related to the matter of who decides. Understanding the concerns requires an appreciation of the question of competence, the problem of paternalism, the importance of demystification, and the politics of decision making.

Because of the many legal and ethical concerns related to who decides, due-process safeguards are essential. Central to such procedural protection is the concept of informed consent.

USE WHAT YOU'VE LEARNED

Parents, teachers, psychologists, and many others debate whether minors should be involved in making decisions. Some say minors don't have the competence to weigh all the information and outcomes that are involved in making good decisions. Others say minors, especially those with problems, will take advantage of situations where they are given a choice and make decisions that are not in their best interests.

In support of involving minors in decision making, some suggest that there are many decisions minors are competent to make for themselves and others that they can participate in making. Furthermore, they point out that it is through the process of making decisions and experiencing their consequences that one develops the ability to make better decisions.

• Take a few minutes to think through where you stand on this issue.

- If you lean toward favoring minors' involvement in decision making, do you have greater reservations about the matter where the minors have been identified as having learning problems? Why or why not?

Whose Interests Are Being Served? (p. 395) notes that there are always situations in which the interests of individuals with learning problems come into conflict with the needs of social systems, and discusses the problem of conflicting interests in greater detail. Topics include

- conflicting interests
- helping vs. socialization interventions
- coercive intervention

Toward Services with an Informed Consumer Orientation (p. 400) illustrates three examples of consumer-oriented services for learning problems:

- a community resource helpline
- a referral system
- an initial assessment and consultation approach

The services described — all designed to demystify consumers by keeping them well-informed — reflect the growing concern over mystification by professionals.

Involving Parents in Schooling (p. 410) points out that positive parent participation in the education of their children has been found to benefit student achievement, attitudes, and aspirations. Enhancing parent involvement includes

- overcoming barriers
- inviting greater participation
- facilitating positive involvement
- maintaining ongoing interest

Toward Improving Intervention

The Process of Improving Intervention
   Building Models
   Experimenting and Problem Solving
Broadening the Focus
   More than Children
   More than Diagnosis and Treatment
   More than Remediation
   More than Individualization
   More than Basic Skills and Direct Instruction
   More than Changing People
Sequential Decisions
Summing Up

*Do not follow where
the path may lead.
Go, instead, where
there is no path
and leave a trail.*

Anonymous

Learning problems are complex. To address the full continuum (Types I, II, and III) requires sophisticated intervention models. Research and theory related to learning problems are evolving beyond the ideas seen in prevailing practices. There is growing appreciation that solutions must be based on complex and systematically linked ideas about the nature of learning, learning problems, and intervention. Many professionals have contributed ideas to expand our thinking about intervention. The following brief discussion is a bridge from the general overview of Parts 1 and 2 to the specific intervention steps presented in the rest of the book.

The Process of Improving Intervention

Solutions to complex problems emerge slowly from a great deal of thinking, exploration, and problem solving. Experience can suggest an idea, and one idea may lead to another. Gradually, ideas that complement each other are linked into models for new approaches.

Building Models

The ongoing debate over models upon which to build intervention highlights the fact that intentional interventions are rationally based (Adelman & Taylor, 1985; Heshusius, 1989; Joyce & Weil, 1986; Westman, 1990). That is, underlying such activity there is a rationale—whether or not it is explicitly stated.

A *rationale* is a framework of assumptions outlining and shaping the nature of intervention aims and practices. It consists of views derived from philosophical, theoretical, and empirical sources. In fields focusing on special populations and problems, a rationale includes general orientations or "models" of the causes of problems, of tasks to be accomplished, and of appropriate processes and outcomes of intervention.

Although rationales direct intervention, there is little evidence that they are systematically formulated and explicitly stated by the majority of professionals. Even when not explicitly stated, however, an underlying rationale guides professionals' thoughts and actions.

The nature and scope of intervention rationales have been discussed by those who study intervention. For instance, Bruner (1966) stated that instructional interventions reflect "a theory of how growth and development are assisted by diverse means" (p. 1). Rossi and Freeman (1982) stress that interventions are based on hypotheses drawn from causal and predictive studies, from theories, and from clinical impressions. And Howard and Orlinsky (1972) indicate that underlying psychotherapeutic intervention is "some conception of *human nature* or personality (the material to be worked with), *human fulfillment* (the ideal to be sought), *human vulnerability* (psychopathology), of *therapeutics,* and of the therapeutic *profession.* Taken together, they comprise . . . the Therapeutic Belief-Value Complex" (p. 617).

Because intervention rationales both guide and limit the nature of subsequent activity, they have major ramifications for outcomes. As Brickman and his colleagues (1982) suggest, "each set of assumptions has characteristic consequences for . . . competence, status, and well-being . . . [and] the wrong choice . . . will undermine effective helping and coping" (p. 368).

Not all intervention models are equal. Some reflect a higher level of scholarly sophistication; some cover a broader range of relevant considerations; some have greater philosophical, theoretical, and empirical consistency. But a model's sophistication, breadth, and consistency are not the only important considerations. We must be concerned about systematic bias that can arise from dominating models. For instance, the models dominating interventions for learning problems in general, and learning disabilities in particular, reflect biases that suggest that the cause of the problem is within the individual, and that the focus of intervention is on changing the individual. This colludes with tendencies to play down the fundamental role of the environment (school programs) as a major cause and thus as a primary focus for efforts to correct the problem. Moreover, basic socialization (teaching specific skills) remains one of the most pressing intervention objectives — even though this is often counterproductive to helping individuals and limits the nature and scope of their education.

One effort toward improving the way in which we think about interventions for complex problems involves describing activity as a series of interrelated phases, tasks, and steps. Take, for example, decisions about screening, placement, and specific program planning as discussed in the preceding chapters. It would be handy to do the assessment related to all these decisions at once. But that would ignore many of the concerns just outlined. After screening has identified a potential problem, it is essential to take additional steps to confirm or disconfirm it. Only then can *initial* placement considerations and *preliminary* remedial and treatment plans be considered. And only after specific plans are initiated can the appropriateness of the placement decisions and intervention plans be evaluated through daily assessment (see Figure 7-1). Such sequential and interventionist assessments show promise for improving intervention decision making.

As another example of expanding thinking by conceiving intervention in sequential as well as hierarchical terms, let's look at remedial strategies. Hewett, for instance, drawing from several developmental theories, was an early advocate of applying hierarchical models to remedial instruction (Hewett & Taylor, 1980). He outlined competence to learn as developing through six hierarchical levels encompassing abilities to

1. attend,
2. respond,

3. order stimuli,
4. explore,
5. interact socially, and
6. master complex skills and ideas.

Based on this hierarchy, he outlined lists of observable skills to guide assessment in detecting missing ones that then became specific objectives for direct instruction. Despite the limitations of direct instruction, the notion of conceiving remedial needs in a hierarchical way is a useful one.

Thinking in terms of phases, tasks, steps, sequences, and hierarchies requires care to avoid the pitfall of rigid linear implementation. Sometimes steps can be taken one at a time in a straightforward sequence. More often, however, intervention involves jumping around—skipping a step, repeating another, and so forth. Sometimes new steps must be added and old ones abandoned. The order in which skills are listed is not necessarily the order in which they are best learned. And, of course, many skills may be learned without formal instruction.

We are talking about the value of building and expanding models and theories to guide program development and research. Obviously thinking in these terms requires some mental juggling and flexibility. Equally obvious is that such thinking is essential to moving forward in efforts to ameliorate learning problems.

Figure 7-1   Screening, Placement, and Specific Planning as a Complex Sequence

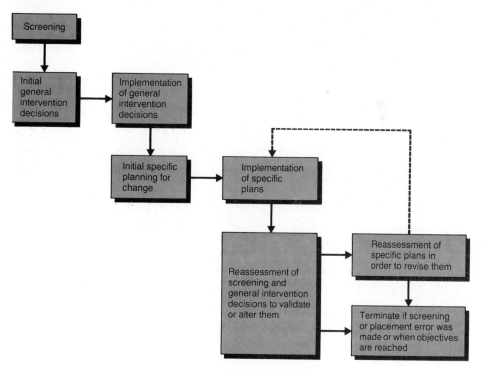

Experimenting and Problem Solving

Efforts to develop new ideas and link them together involve a great deal of research. Unfortunately, the term *research* has come to convey such abstract activities that it seems irrelevant to many practitioners. Thus their energy, experience, and insight are lost to researchers.

Perhaps it would help to think about research as primarily concerned with exploration and problem solving. Practitioners do both in their daily work. Teachers, remedial specialists, and clinicians begin with their best estimate of what is

Feature 7-1   Key Steps and Tasks in Problem-Solving Intervention

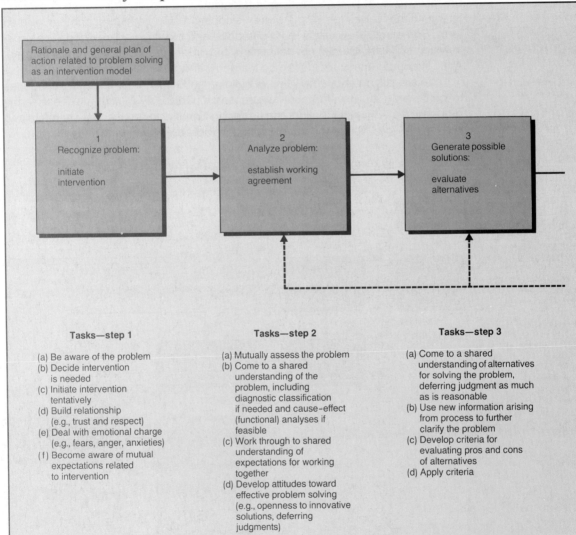

Tasks—step 1

(a) Be aware of the problem
(b) Decide intervention is needed
(c) Initiate intervention tentatively
(d) Build relationship (e.g., trust and respect)
(e) Deal with emotional charge (e.g., fears, anger, anxieties)
(f) Become aware of mutual expectations related to intervention

Tasks—step 2

(a) Mutually assess the problem
(b) Come to a shared understanding of the problem, including diagnostic classification if needed and cause–effect (functional) analyses if feasible
(c) Work through to shared understanding of expectations for working together
(d) Develop attitudes toward effective problem solving (e.g., openness to innovative solutions, deferring judgments)

Tasks—step 3

(a) Come to a shared understanding of alternatives for solving the problem, deferring judgment as much as is reasonable
(b) Use new information arising from process to further clarify the problem
(c) Develop criteria for evaluating pros and cons of alternatives
(d) Apply criteria

wrong and what will effectively resolve an individual's learning problem. As they work with the problem, they continually appraise what is happening. If things are not going well, they look for clues to guide their next efforts. They pursue the exploratory and problem-solving processes of experimentation and trial and appraisal until the problem is resolved or until they run out of ideas (see Feature 7-1). Whether or not such practitioners realize it, their problem-solving approach is the essence of research.

Much important data on what works and what doesn't are discovered through daily exploration and problem solving in the classroom and the clinic. What makes

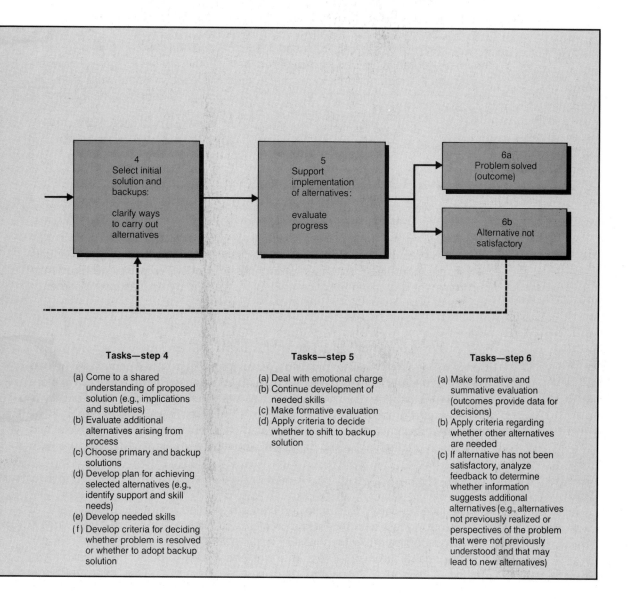

Tasks—step 4

(a) Come to a shared understanding of proposed solution (e.g., implications and subtleties)
(b) Evaluate additional alternatives arising from process
(c) Choose primary and backup solutions
(d) Develop plan for achieving selected alternatives (e.g., identify support and skill needs)
(e) Develop needed skills
(f) Develop criteria for deciding whether problem is resolved or whether to adopt backup solution

Tasks—step 5

(a) Deal with emotional charge
(b) Continue development of needed skills
(c) Make formative evaluation
(d) Apply criteria to decide whether to shift to backup solution

Tasks—step 6

(a) Make formative and summative evaluation (outcomes provide data for decisions)
(b) Apply criteria regarding whether other alternatives are needed
(c) If alternative has not been satisfactory, analyze feedback to determine whether information suggests additional alternatives (e.g., alternatives not previously realized or perspectives of the problem that were not previously understood and that may lead to new alternatives)

the data more than an interesting set of anecdotes is the care with which interventions are carried out and described and the systematic way in which positive and negative findings are sought and reported. Systematic and cautious reports of case results—positive and negative—help advance knowledge.

Broadening the Focus

Practitioners are becoming more and more aware that there are many ideas they cannot ignore if they want to do a better job helping those with learning problems. It is becoming clear that the focus of intervention has been too narrow.

Greater attention is currently being paid to the full age range of those experiencing learning problems. The need to go beyond the concepts of diagnosis, treatment, remediation, and individualized instruction is stressed. There is growing awareness of the importance of expanding prevailing views about what are basic skills and how they should be taught. It is becoming evident that much more is needed than simply pursuing strategies to change people.

In Chapter 3, we discussed the importance of broadly defining and broadening the focus of intervention. In this section, we expand on that discussion.

More than Children

Over time we have become aware that learning problems remain for many adolescents and adults, often despite the best efforts of professionals and parents. Thus it has become imperative to reformulate policies and practices and advocacy groups and professional training to avoid discriminating against older individuals with learning problems. We see the emphasis broadening to include more than children in the increased attention paid to postsecondary education and career or vocational programs.

More than Diagnosis and Treatment

Concerns about prevailing practices for diagnosis and treatment have helped clarify that there is more to diagnosis than objective assessment and there is more to treatment than the day-by-day activity of a teacher or therapist. Such activity is only part of a broader set of intervention activities or tasks (see Figure 3-3). All major programmatic tasks are interrelated, and each requires a rationale and formulation of planning, implementation, and evaluation phases (see Figure 7-2).

More than Remediation

Special interventions for learning problems are called remediation, treatment, or therapy. Obviously, when there is a problem, intervention is needed. However, it is dangerous for the entire emphasis in working with an individual to be on remedying the referral problem. Programs that stress only problem remediation can deprive a person of other important experiences and can be overwhelmingly tedious and disheartening (see Feature 7-2).

Figure 7-2   Phases of Intervention

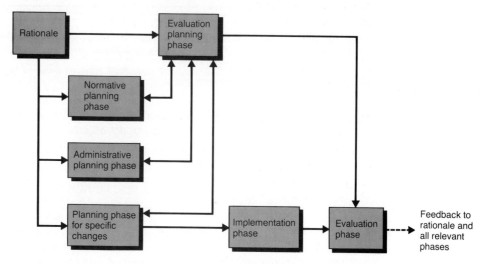

Schools have the responsibility, not only to help students overcome learning problems, but also to facilitate ongoing development and provide opportunities for creative growth. The fact that a student has a problem learning to read doesn't alter the fact that he or she probably wants to learn a variety of other things (Swift & Lewis, 1985). To find the time for remediation, it may be tempting to set aside other learning opportunities, but this deprives students of other experiences and may negatively affect their attitudes toward school, teacher, and themselves. The strong emphasis on mainstreaming students with handicaps is one prominent manifestation of the concern about such negative effects.

More than Individualization

Ask what's wrong with putting Matt into a regular classroom and probably the answer will be that the program will not be "individualized" enough. Ask "What does Mara need?" Chances are the answer will be "individualized instruction." James? David? "Individualized instruction."

Individualized instruction has become the standard for remedying learning problems. It represents a major improvement over the days when few serious attempts were made to treat learners as individuals. There are, however, tremendous variations among individualized programs, and almost all of them ignore some essential individual differences.

Individualized programs propose to meet learners where they are. This generally means that activities are planned with reference to an individual's current developmental status and performance capabilities. For example, if a fifth grader is reading at a second-grade level, functioning in math at a fourth-grade level, and so forth, the program is supposed to be designed to take these levels into account. Moreover, if students with the same level of skill learn at different rates, the program is supposed to allow for this. Increasingly it is stressed that differences in motivation also ought to be accounted for in a highly systematic way.

Feature 7-2   More than Remediation

There is growing appreciation for the importance of providing opportunities to work in areas of special strength and interest for students diagnosed as having learning disabilities. Answering the question "What happens when all the needs of the child are not addressed due to a preoccupation with academic deficit?" Baum and Kirschenbaum (1984) report the case of Neil:

Neil, a junior in high school, was failing his subjects. He was disgusted with school and was exhibiting symptoms of depression requiring weekly visits to a psychologist. His teachers described him as lazy, claiming he could do better if only he would apply himself. A typical comment was, "When I talk to Neil, he has so much to offer. However, he just doesn't produce."

On his own, Neil had acquired a wealth of knowledge about music, religion, psychology, and photography. He pursued his extracurricular interests with enthusiasm and persistence. His major interest during this time was photography.

He had not received much praise for his creativity. Instead, he had been regularly criticized for poor academic work.

The school did try to capitalize on his interest in photography—but at first did so in a manipulative way.

When Neil's school tried to incorporate his interest in photography into academic assignments, he rebelled to the extent of temporarily abandoning photography. Instead of attracting him to academics, Neil was "turned off" to photography for months. He wanted to enjoy his photographic ability unfettered by the expectations of school.

The one major success for Neil in high school apparently occurred when he was finally given the opportunity to pursue his interest in photography at school—in ways he defined for himself.

Once Neil had defined a personally chosen task, he became alive and motivated. He became an investigator of a problem real to him, and the product that resulted has indeed had an impact on others.

Unfortunately, this experience appears to have been the exception rather than the rule.

Neil finished high school, but decided not to go to college. Four months after graduation, he said "Now that school is out, I finally have time to learn." He talked about several contemporary history books he was reading, even though he had hated history in school.

Neil's experiences dramatically illustrate the importance of considering the whole child. It can be profoundly destructive to a student's self-esteem to be labeled and treated only in terms of a learning disability when, in addition, a student may be exhibiting gifted behaviors that are equally worthy of attention.

Within the school setting, with its fixed time periods, predetermined curricula, isolated subject areas, and teacher accountability with regard to students' minimal competencies, gifted behaviors often go unrecognized.

What is needed, then, is *information* about the talents of these children. Usually, the folders of learning-disabled students are filled with notations concerning the things they *can't* do in school. Their strengths are overshadowed by problematic weaknesses that consume the school's well-intentioned energies and attention.

Attention needs to be given to strengths (in their own right) as well as weaknesses, rather than simply working *through* strengths to get to weaknesses. (pp. 92–98)

Because the term *individualization* has become so identified with accommodating individual differences in developmental capability, the term *personalization* has been proposed to encompass attempts to meet learners where they are—developmentally and motivationally.

More than Basic Skills and Direct Instruction

The three Rs certainly are a basic concern in any learning problem program. But they are not the only *basic* skills, nor are basic *skills* a sufficient curriculum in such programs.

Similarly, there are times when direct instruction of observable skills is indicated. However, such a process neither reflects a sufficient approach to instruction nor an appreciation of the range of learning that can occur without direct instruction.

Besides reading, writing, and arithmetic, the capability to solve problems, relate to others, and make appropriate decisions are now recognized as essential life skills. These aspects of basic human functioning require the ability to analyze problems, weigh alternatives, and figure out how to accomplish daily tasks and deal effectively with other people.

Even expanding the definition of basic skills, however, does not result in a broad enough scope. We all have skills we choose not to use in certain circumstances. We all could acquire other useful skills, but choose not to do so. What we do is influenced strongly by our attitudes.

Two major problems with back to basics movements have always been that the advocates define basics in terms of a limited range of skills (the three Rs) and approach the learning of skills without sufficient appreciation for the role of attitudes (or motivation) in learning and instruction. An expanded view, including other basic skills and a strong emphasis on intrinsic motivation for learning, suggests not going backwards but going *forward to basics.*

What is the best way to arrange the environment to optimize learning?

More than Changing People

As already discussed, the prevailing models for thinking about learning problems have been person-centered and pathologically oriented. Behaviorist and ecological thinking helped to stress an alternative that recognizes that significant numbers of learning problems stem from pathological or inadequate environments.

Interactional and transactional views of human behavior have offered an even broader way to understand the full range of learning problems. Such models recognize that problems may be due primarily to something within the individual or something in the environment or something related to the transactions between both.

Increasingly, environmental and transactional models are influencing thinking about the cause of learning problems and related interventions. The implications of such models are far reaching.

It is easy to fall into the trap of thinking that interventions for learning problems should always be directed at a specific individual. Adopting a transactional view points to an expanded set of options regarding who or what should be the object of change (see Figure 3-1).

Profound implications arise when we expand the range of objects that are to be the focal point of intervention. For one, environments and the transactions

Figure 7-3   Intervention Guidelines for Individuals with Learning Problems

First	If Necessary
1. Provide an appropriate match between the learner and the learning environment	Remedy individual problems
2. Try general, enriched, and least disruptive solutions	Try specialized treatments and settings, maintaining them only as long as needed
3. Use assessment and consultation to screen, place, plan, and evaluate	Use assessment to diagnose and then to find diagnostic errors
4. Make decisions and plans with those involved using careful analysis of alternatives	Proceed temporarily without their participation until they can or will decide
5. Look for simpler explanations before assuming there is a learning disability	Look for disorders after simpler explanations have been systematically ruled out

between persons and environments become primary concerns for assessment and corrective interventions. Problem prevention efforts expand to include programs that encourage accommodation of a wider range of individual differences in school and society. The broadened perspective works against presumptions about dysfunctions within people as the source of most learning problems.

Sequential Decisions

In moving forward to improve intervention, the principle of least intervention needed still provides a useful starting point. Based on this principle, intervention guidelines for those with learning problems can be organized into five sequential steps (see Figure 7-3).

With such guidelines in mind, our objective in Part 3 is to explore specific concepts and steps for developing broad-based intervention approaches for learning problems.

Summing Up

Efforts to advance knowledge about learning problems require taking prevailing ideas and connecting them with new ones. In making such connections, it is helpful to think in terms of building models and theories that emphasize sequences and hierarchies of intervention phases, tasks, and steps. Thinking in such comprehensive and systematic ways guides exploration of new directions and improves problem solving.

A review of evolving trends suggests a move toward

- programs that address the problems of adolescents and adults as well as children;
- an expanded and systematically integrated set of intervention tasks, steps, and phases implemented in sequential and hierarchical ways;
- greater emphasis on facilitating ongoing development and providing opportunities for creative growth in addition to remediation;
- personalization as a process that goes beyond individualization to meet learners where they are developmentally and motivationally;
- an emphasis on basics that goes beyond the three Rs, beyond skills, and beyond direct instruction to include problem solving, decision making, basic attitudes, and motivated learning;
- environmental and transactional models of human behavior and learning that provide a broader intervention focus; and
- expanding the focus of intervention beyond individuals to include changing the environment to accommodate rather than modify individual differences and, where appropriate, simultaneously pursuing changes in both the environment and the individual.

In Part 3, prevailing approaches are integrated with evolving trends to clarify specific concepts and practices for working with learning problems.

In study courses, a sequential, cognitive strategy often taught is the SQ3R (Survey Q 3R) method. The procedure involves use of the following five steps in reading textbook material:

1. Survey
2. Question
3. Read
4. Recite
5. Review

Briefly, the steps involve the following activity:

1. *Surveying* means initially taking a quick look at a book's preface and table of contents to find out what the book covers. Then, you leaf through it, page by page, to get a sense of how it's laid out and what it contains. In particular, you read headings and summaries and look at pictures and graphs, reading their captions.

When it comes time to read a particular assignment, you again survey the assigned material, but more thoroughly than before. Special attention is paid to headings so you can see how the material is outlined and organized. (What are the main topics and subtopics?)

Surveying provides a roadmap that shows what the important points of interest are.

2. *Questions* are basic to learning. They direct, guide, and help bring meaning to the process. There are two major sources of questions in textbook material. (Ask yourself: What are the two major sources of questions?)

If a teacher has assigned questions or the text contains questions at the end of the chapter, read them carefully and think about them before reading the chapter. Whether or not there are assigned questions, make up your own.

You can do this by asking questions about each heading before reading a chapter and again before reading the specific section. You can also do so when key statements are made (as we demonstrated earlier). For example, as you approach Chapter 8, notice it is entitled "Matching Motivation and Development." You might ask What does matching mean? Why is it worth doing? et cetera.

Before reading, you may have some ideas about the answers for some of the questions. As you read, you can compare your ideas with those presented.

3. *Reading* is an obvious step. Or is it? Reading needs to be done actively. (Remember all the times you have gotten to the end of a page and wondered what you have just read! That's passive reading.) As you read, be answering the questions you have identified.

4. *Recitation* helps to keep you reading actively. Stop regularly (after each paragraph, if necessary) and try to answer the relevant question(s) you have identified for the section. If you don't have a question, simply recite the important points covered in the material you just read. If you can't recite, it's time to formulate a question and reread the material.

5. *Reviewing* means taking another look at what you've read. As you skim over the headings once more, think through the questions and recite the answers. You will quickly find out what you remember and what you don't.

Reviews are done regularly—beginning as soon as you've finished a chapter. Rereading is done whenever you remember too little of the material. Several reviews are recommended (at spaced intervals before an exam) rather than one long cram session.

Try the SQ3R strategy as you approach the next chapter. Afterwards evaluate whether you continued to use the strategy related to this book and other texts.

If you did continue to use it, think about the reasons you did so.

If you didn't, think about why not.

PART 3

Personalized Instruction and Remediation

Let the main object . . . be as follows: To seek and to find a method of instruction, by which teachers may teach less, but learners learn more; by which schools may be the scene of less noise, aversion, and useless labour, but of more leisure, enjoyment, and solid progress.

Comenius (1632)

Teaching is a fascinating and somewhat mysterious process. Is it an art, or is it an activity that most people can learn to do? It is certainly an activity that many people do every day. Helping someone grow, develop, and learn is one of the most basic forms of human interaction. In some form, we've all been taught. And we've all experienced the satisfaction of succeeding in helping others learn and the frustration when they don't "get it."

Frustration is a common feeling when teaching and learning don't go smoothly. The frustration often leads us to conclude that there's something wrong with the people we're trying to help. After all, we explained it right; they should have understood it. And the fact that they didn't usually is seen as indicating a lack of effort ("They would have if they had really been trying") or a lack of ability ("They would have if they were smarter or not handicapped by a brain dysfunction").

Sometimes the frustration isn't just with a particular individual; it is with the poor school performance of large numbers of children and adolescents and with the vast amount of adult illiteracy. Such frustration leads to conclusions that something is wrong with the schools ("We need to get back to basics!"), or with certain groups of people ("These youngsters do badly because their parents don't value education"), or with both.

The frustration surrounding learning problems is understandable. And where there is frustration, it is not surprising that there are accusations and blaming. But blaming does not solve the problem. The solution is to be found, in part, in improving the ways in which basic knowledge and skills are taught.

Chapter 8 discusses the importance of matching motivation and development, and personalizing interventions in and out of classroom settings. In Chapters 9, 10, and 11, we focus on teaching and remediation for individuals with learning problems. Discussions emphasize the importance of a comprehensive curriculum, motivation as an initial focus in improving the match, personalizing classroom programs, and sequential steps in remedying learning problems.

Throughout Part 3, a variety of concepts and specific steps and procedures are explored. Because evaluation plays a key role in studying interventions, Part 3 ends with a brief presentation on evaluating programs.

Matching Motivation and Development

Interaction of the Learner with the Environment

The Learner

The Environment

Transactions and the Match

Matching Motivation

Motivation and Learning

Key Components of Motivation: Valuing and Expectations

Overreliance on Extrinsics: A Bad Match

Matching Development

Variations in Developmental Patterns

Key Performance Dimensions

Personalization

Summing Up

Motivation does not reside exclusively within the child or within the setting. It depends on a match or interplay between the two.

Smith, Neisworth, and Greer, 1978

"I hate reading!" Mara is having lots of trouble learning to read, and she's not about to spend any more time doing it than she has to.

What came first—the learning problem or her negative attitude? It's hard to be sure. But it isn't hard to understand that Mara's present efforts in the classroom and on tests are influenced both by her poor skills and by her negative attitude.

Does she have a learning disability? We don't want to make a mistake in answering this question, and we do want to help her learn to read. So our first step is to find a situation in which Mara will really try to learn. If she's so angry or scared that she holds back or just goes through the motions, we won't see what she can do; we'll only see the abilities she wants to show us. The less she shows of what she can do and the less effort she puts into learning, the more we are likely to see false symptoms. Because the information available is not good data for arriving at a diagnosis, we might prematurely conclude that someone like Mara has a learning disability. She may or may not. One of the tasks in working with her will be to help clarify the matter. A big part of the job, then, is to provide a program in which Mara will want to learn. This will help us to see what type of learning problem she has, and it will help her take a big step toward overcoming it.

Of course, the environment must do more than affect Mara's attitudes toward learning. It must also be a good match for her current levels of competence and style of performance. Thus the first step in working with Mara and other students with learning problems is to meet them where they are, motivationally and developmentally. How to accomplish the first step requires understanding the interactions between learners and learning environments.

Interaction of the Learner with the Environment

When asked to do course evaluations, students in the same class generally vary in their opinions. Some say the course was too demanding, others say it was easy; some think it was too loosely organized, others see it as highly structured; some enjoyed student interchanges in class, others thought listening to students talk a waste of time.

Evaluation of what the students learned during the course will also indicate differences. The range may extend from those who learned a lot to those who learned relatively little. From our discussion so far about learning and teaching as a transactional process, it should be clear that such differences in learner perceptions, needs, and outcomes are to be expected. A transactional viewpoint suggests such variations are inevitable.

Remember, a learner brings to a learning situation both

- *capacities and attitudes* that have been accumulated over time, as well as
- *current states of being and behaving.*

These transact with each other and also with the learning environment.
The learning environment consists not only of

- *instructional processes and content,* but also
- *the physical and social context* in which instruction takes place.

Each part of the environment also transacts with the others.

Also recall that, while the general intent of these transactions is to produce positive learning, learning problems are a common outcome. That is, as we saw in Chapter 2, the results of the transactions between the learner and the environment may not only be (1) enhanced learning, but also (2) deviant learning, (3) disrupted learning, and (4) delayed and arrested learning.

Let's look a bit more closely at the learner and the environment and how they interact to produce a good or bad match for learning.

The Learner

Mara comes to every learning situation with certain accumulated capacities and attitudes. She is also affected by her current physiological and psychological states. With her innate qualities providing a foundation on which to build, Mara has acquired a variety of abilities, expectations, and values over the years. These accumulated capacities and attitudes, in turn, provide the foundation upon which all subsequent learning is built.

Although her capacities and attitudes establish a foundation for Mara's learning, she does not enter the classroom in the same condition or state each day. She may be well rested or tired, well nourished or hungry, ready to listen or preoccupied with thoughts of what happened earlier or with plans for later in the day. She may feel happy, sad, or angry.

Stop reading for a minute and tune in to your own experience. You may be tired, hungry, bored, preoccupied, or distracted by what's going on in the room. It's easy to see that your current physiological and psychological state affects your concentration and learning.

Concerns about poor diet and health habits, allergic reactions to foodstuffs, frequent illnesses, and arousal and orienting responses reflect an appreciation of the importance of the current *physiological* state of the learner. Similarly, concerns about fear of failure, high levels of anxiety, and anger toward teachers and school reflect an awareness of the importance of the learner's *psychological* state.

Somewhat less obvious is the fact that people appear to be influenced by their own actions, which then further influence the way they think and feel (see Bandura, 1978). If you notice that you are fidgeting or are having trouble keeping your eyes open in class, you try to understand why. If it is a hot day and the lecture is dull, you may conclude that the temperature in the room is too high or that you

Mara brings her uniqueness to every learning activity.

are bored. And, of course, your actions produce changes in the learning environment; if you nod off, the teacher is likely to react.

Given that Mara's background is similar to that of some individuals and differs from that of others, we can make some general assumptions about why she is having trouble learning. Like all generalities, however, they may be wrong in her particular case. To go beyond assumptions, tests may be administered in an attempt to measure her accumulated capacities and attitudes and current states. Because of the limitations of available tests, additional assessment strategies are constantly being developed as part of ongoing learning programs. As discussed in the following chapters, these strategies include ongoing analyses of a learner's direct statements, actions, and performance under conditions of high intrinsic motivation to learn.

The Environment

When you think about the learning environment, your tendency may be to think first about features directly associated with instructional processes and content—especially materials, personnel, activities, and equipment. The context of instruction may also strongly influence learning (see Feature 8-1 and Table 8-1). Before going on, look around you and decide how well the environment you're in lends itself to reading this text. If it's less than optimal, what changes may make it better?

Available research indicates the important role that the *physical* context plays in learning. The ease with which a student can see the chalkboard, the comfort of the furniture, the spaciousness or crowding, and the temperature in the room are only a few of the physical features that may influence learning. Perhaps more influential is the *social* context. For a school-age youngster, the teacher and other adults in the school are extremely vivid features of the environment. Competition for attention, fear of embarrassment, desire to be praised, interest in what others are doing—all are part of the social experience in a classroom that affect learning.

In addition to the physical and social contexts are the instructional processes and content presented to the learner. As discussed in Chapter 7, the intent in many programs is to individualize instruction to match aspects of the learner's accumulated capacities. Additional steps to match instructional processes and content to the motivation of the person also play an important role in learning.

Although many of the features of instruction and its physical and social contexts are easy to measure, the key aspect—the learner's perception of the situation—is difficult to assess (see Fraser & Walberg, 1991; Lloyd & Blandford, 1991; Moos, 1979).

Transactions and the Match

Poor learning environments are ones in which the transactions between learner and environment produce undesirable outcomes. This can be thought of as a bad match between the learner and the environment. There are three different forms that a bad match may take: unchallenging, overdemanding, and overwhelming.

Feature 8-1   The Many Contexts of Learning and Instruction

When we talk about the learning environment, it would be a mistake to think only about classrooms and schools. It would also be a mistake to think of each environment as a distinct and separate place. There are layers of environments that interact with one another and with learners. For convenience, we think about them as they are depicted in the accompanying diagram.

To clarify the point, the learner in the classroom obviously experiences the physical and social climate created by the teacher and other students, plus the materials, equipment, furniture, lighting, and general decor (the primary environment). At the same time, there is bound to be an effect generated by such factors as the size, general condition, and decor of the school, the composition and values of the student body, and the socioeconomic level, racial composition, and values of those living in the surrounding neighborhood (the secondary environment).

There are also the effects of the values, beliefs, standards, customs, and political policies of the society and culture (city, state, and nation). This tertiary level of environment may seem far removed from the daily classroom learning environment. The reality, however, is that factors such as political policies are some of the most powerful determinants of the types of resources and services made available to both problem and nonproblem learners.

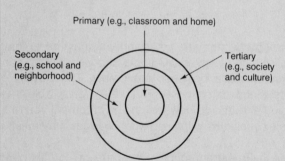

Primary (e.g., classroom and home)

Secondary (e.g., school and neighborhood)

Tertiary (e.g., society and culture)

Table 8-1   Environmental Variables that Can Influence Learning

---

I. *Setting and context characteristics*
   A. **Organizational format**
      (e.g., personal patterns, client/
      student groupings)
   B. **Locale, nature, and scope**
      (e.g., geographic context, architec-
      tural features, availability and use of
      materials and furnishings, popula-
      tion "density")

   C. **Climate**
      (e.g., perceptions of physical, social,
      intellectual, political, and moral atmo-
      sphere)

II. *Characteristics of the participants*
   A. **Formal role identification**
      (e.g., intervener, client, student, par-
      ent, societal agent, association with
      specific organizations)
   B. **Demographics**
      (e.g., urban/rural, ethnicity, socio-
      economic status, sex and age distri-
      bution, association with specific groups)

   C. **Individual differences in current
      motivation and development**
      (e.g., competence, commitment,
      perceptions of self and others)
   D. **Criteria and standards used in
      judging person characteristics**
      (e.g., absolute or relative standards
      about good-bad, normal-abnormal,
      success-failure; psychological,
      socioeconomic-political criteria; cutoff
      points altering the number of false-
      negatives and false-positives)

III. *Task–process–outcome characteristics*
   A. **General features**
      1. Quantitative (e.g., amount to be
         accomplished; sequencing, dura-
         tion, pacing, and rate; number of
         persons required or involved)
      2. Qualitative (e.g., underlying rationale;
         intrinsic and extrinsic value; co-
         operative or competitive; actual
         and perceived difficulty)
   B. **Specific types, areas, and levels
      of tasks and outcomes**
      (e.g., current system tasks; prereq-
      uisites needed to perform current
      tasks; remediation; development;
      enrichment)

   C. **Specific processes**
      1. Procedural methods and models
         (e.g., helping or socialization;
         mechanistic-behavioral, industrial,
         humanistic; role of participants;
         nature of structure)
      2. Tools (actions/experiences/
         materials) (e.g., communication,
         practice, learning; printed material
         such as texts and workbooks; au-
         diovisual — including computer-
         presentations; games)
      3. Techniques (e.g., variations in the
         characteristics of a tool or the way it
         is applied, such as varying intensity,
         duration, patterning, and cueing;
         systematic or unsystematic feed-
         back, rewards, punishments)

Some environments seem to offer little or no challenge to the learner. No new learning takes place when a person can consistently use already acquired capacities in responding to a learning environment. If this situation continues for any significant length of time, important areas of learning will not expand.

In contrast, a rather common situation is one in which learners perceive the environment as demanding more than they want to give in terms of ability and effort. Under such circumstances learning may occur, but not usually the type that is desired. When asked to practice her reading, Mara doesn't always argue about the matter. There are times when her transactions with the environment are attempts to find other ways of getting around the demand. In her search for ways to avoid assignments, she learns a great many new ways to manipulate and distract others.

Thus she is learning new skills all the time—but probably not those most of us view as desirable. What she is learning is sometimes called *deviant behavior*.

Sometimes individuals find themselves in environments where the demands are so great that they cannot find any way to deal with the situation. If they must stay in this demanding environment for a long time, they not only stop functioning, but they may also start to *decompensate* (experience a decrease in their accumulated capacities). For instance, because of his learning problems, James increas-

Feature 8-2
Learning as a Function of Person-and-Environment Transactions

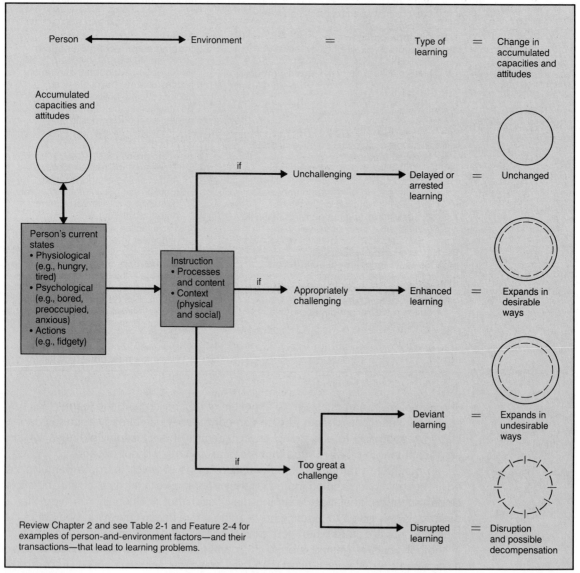

Review Chapter 2 and see Table 2-1 and Feature 2-4 for examples of person-and-environment factors—and their transactions—that lead to learning problems.

ingly experienced strong feelings of anxiety and embarrassment each day at school; he felt criticized and socially isolated from other students. Whenever something new was to be learned, James knew he would have trouble. He tried to hide within himself. Not only could he not cope with the new tasks, but he also became uncertain about what he had already learned. He began to be uncertain of words he once could read and spell, and he no longer risked reading them aloud or writing them. Soon his progress was entirely disrupted.

Given a reasonably adequate learning environment, most of us readily learn at least what is minimally expected. In such instances, the transactions between the environment and the learner have produced a desirable, if not always optimal, outcome (see Feature 8-2). In theory, optimal learning occurs when the match between learner and environment results in an interaction in which learners want to and are able to make full use of their accumulated capacities. That is, the learning environment and the individual's developmental and motivational capacities differ just enough that the learner sees the task as a challenge that can be achieved and that is worth pursuing.

Remember the last time an abstract idea suddenly became clear? Or you finally figured out how to solve a puzzle? These magical moments of insight and learning occur when the learner–environment match is optimal or close to it. Such moments don't have to be infrequent or accidental. The more we understand about creating a learning environment that matches an individual's motivation and developmental level, the more that appropriate learning will occur.

Matching Motivation

Mara doesn't want to work on improving her reading. Not only is her motivational readiness low, but she also has a fairly high level of avoidance motivation for reading.

In contrast, David is motivationally ready to improve reading skills, but not in the ways his teacher proposes. He has high motivation for the outcome but low motivation for the processes prescribed for getting there.

Matt often gets very motivated to do whatever is prescribed to help him learn to read better, but his motivation starts to disappear after a few weeks of hard work. He has trouble maintaining a sufficient amount of continuing motivation.

James appeared motivated to learn, and he did learn many new vocabulary words and improve his reading comprehension on several occasions over the years he was in special school programs. His motivation to read after school, however, has never increased. It was assumed that as his skills improved, his attitude toward reading would too. But it never has.

Motivation and Learning

What the preceding examples show is that

• motivation is a prerequisite to learning, and its absence may be a cause of learning problems, a factor maintaining such problems, or both

What's motivating him?

- individuals may be motivated toward the idea of obtaining a certain learning outcome but may not be motivated to pursue certain learning processes
- individuals may be motivated to start to work on overcoming their learning problem but may not maintain their motivation
- individuals may be motivated to learn basic skills but maintain negative attitudes about the area of functioning and thus never use the skills except when they have to

Obviously, motivation must be considered in matching a learner with a learning environment. What's required is

- developing a high level of motivational readiness for overcoming the learning problem (including reduction of avoidance motivation) — so the learner is mobilized
- establishing processes that elicit, enhance, and maintain motivation for overcoming the problem — so the learner stays mobilized
- enhancing motivation as an outcome so that the desire to pursue a particular area, such as reading, increasingly becomes a positive intrinsic attitude that mobilizes learning outside the teaching situation

An increased understanding of motivation clarifies how essential it is to avoid processes that make students feel controlled and coerced, that limit the range of options with regard to materials, and that limit the focus to a day-in, day-out emphasis on the problem to be remedied. From a motivational perspective, such processes are likely to produce avoidance reactions among students and thus reduce opportunities for positive learning and for development of positive attitudes (Adelman, 1978; Adelman & Taylor, 1983b, 1990; Deci & Ryan, 1985).

Key Components of Motivation: Valuing and Expectations

Two common reasons people give for not bothering to learn something are "It's not worth it" and "I know I won't be able to do it." In general, the amount of time and energy spent on an activity seems dependent on how much the activity is valued by the person and on the person's expectation that what is valued will be attained without too much cost (see Stipek, 1988).

Valuing.   What makes something worth doing? Prizes? Money? Merit awards? Praise? Certainly! We all do a great many things, some of which we don't even like to do, because the activity leads to a desired reward. Similarly, we often do things to escape punishment or other negative consequences that we prefer to avoid.

Rewards and punishments may be material or social. For those with learning problems, there has been widespread use of such "incentives." Rewards often have taken the form of systematically giving points or tokens that can be exchanged for candy, prizes, praise, free time, or social interactions. Punishments have included loss of free time and other privileges, added work, fines, isolation, censure, spanking, and suspension. Grades have been used both as rewards and punishments.

Because people will do things to obtain rewards or avoid punishment, rewards and punishment are called *reinforcers*. Because they generally come from sources outside the person, they often are called *extrinsic*.

Extrinsic reinforcers are easy to use and can have some powerful immediate effects on behavior; therefore, they have been widely adopted in the fields of special education and psychology. Unfortunately the immediate effects are limited to very specific behaviors and are often short term. Moreover, as seen in the next section, extensive use of extrinsics seems to have some undesired effects. And sometimes the available extrinsics simply aren't powerful enough to get the desired results.

External reinforcement may indeed get a particular act going and may lead to its repetition, but it does not nourish, reliably, the long course of learning by which [one] slowly builds in [one's] own way a serviceable model of what the world is and what it can be.

Bruner, 1966
(p. 128)

Although the source of extrinsic reinforcers is outside the person, the meaning or value attached to them comes from inside. What makes some extrinsic factor rewarding to you is the fact that you experience it as a reward. And what makes it a highly valued reward is that you highly value it. If you don't like candy, there is not much point in our offering it to you as a reward. Furthermore, because the use of extrinsics has limits, it is fortunate that we sometimes do things even without apparent extrinsic reason. In fact, a lot of what we learn and spend time doing is done for intrinsic reasons. Curiosity is a good example. Our curiosity leads us to learn a great deal. Curiosity seems to be an innate quality that leads all of us to seek stimulation and avoid boredom.

We also pursue some things because of what has been described as an innate striving for competence; people seem to value feeling competent. We try to conquer some challenges, and if none are around, we usually seek one out.

Of course, as we discuss in the next section, if the challenges confronting us seem unconquerable or make us too uncomfortable (for example, too anxious or exhausted), we try to put them aside and move on to something more promising.

Another important intrinsic motivator appears to be an internal push toward self-determination. People seem to value feeling and thinking that they have some degree of freedom in deciding what to do. And people seem to be intrinsically moved toward establishing and maintaining relationships with others. That is, people tend to value feelings of being interpersonally connected (Deci & Chandler, 1986).

Expectations.   We may value something a great deal, but if we believe we can't obtain it without paying too great a personal price, we are likely to look for other valued activities and outcomes to pursue. Expectations about these matters are influenced by previous experiences.

Areas where we have been unsuccessful tend to be seen as unlikely paths to valued extrinsic rewards or intrinsic satisfactions (Harackiewicz, Sansone, & Manderlink, 1985). We may perceive failure to be the result of our lack of ability, or we may believe that more effort was required than we were willing to give. We may also feel that the help we needed to succeed was not available. If we perceive that very little has changed with regard to these factors, our expectation of succeeding at this time will be rather low.

Learning environments that provide a good match increase expectations of success by providing a learner with the support and guidance he or she wants and needs (Koestner, Ryan, Bernieri, & Holt, 1984).

So we see that what we value interacts with our expectations, and motivation is one product of this interaction. Within some limits (which we need not discuss here), high valuing and high expectations produce high motivation, while high valuing and low expectations produce relatively weak motivation.

David greatly values the idea of improving his reading. He is unhappy with his limited skills and knows he would feel a lot better about himself if he could read. But, as far as he is concerned, everything his reading teacher asks him to do is a waste of time. He's done it all before, and he still has a reading problem. Sometimes he will do the exercises, but just to earn points to go on a field trip and to avoid the consequences of not cooperating. Often he tries to get out of doing his work by distracting the teacher. After all, why should he do things he is certain won't help him read any better?

High expectations paired with low valuing also yield low approach motivation. Thus, the oft-cited remedial strategy of guaranteeing success by designing tasks to be very easy is not as simple a recipe as it sounds. Indeed, the approach is likely to fail if the outcome (improved reading) is not valued or if the tasks are experienced as too boring or if doing them is seen as too embarrassing. In such cases, a strong negative value is attached to the activities, and this contributes to avoidance motivation.

Throughout this discussion of valuing and expectations, we have emphasized that motivation cannot be determined solely by forces outside the individual. Others can plan activities and outcomes to influence motivation and learning; how the activities are received determines the outcome. It is necessary to appreciate this when designing a match for optimal learning (see Feature 8-3).

Overreliance on Extrinsics: A Bad Match

A growing appreciation of the importance of a learner's perceptions has led researchers to some very important findings about undesired effects that can result from overreliance on extrinsics.

Would offering you a reward for learning about learning problems make you more highly motivated? Maybe. But a reward might also reduce your motivation in the future. Why might this happen?

You might perceive the proposed reward as an effort to control your behavior. Or you may see it as an indication that the activity needs to be rewarded to get you to do it. Such perceptions may start you thinking and feeling differently about what you have been doing. First, you may resent the effort to control (or bribe) you. Or you may begin to think there must be something wrong with the activity if we have to offer a reward for doing it. Also, once the course is over, you may come to feel

Feature 8-3   Is It Worth It?

In one small town, there were a few youngsters who were labeled as handicapped. Over the years, a local bully had taken it upon himself to persecute them. In a recent incident, he sent a gang to harass one of his classmates who had just been diagnosed as having learning disabilities. He told the youngsters they could have some fun calling the boy a "retard."

Day after day in the schoolyard the gang sought the boy out. "Retard! Retard!" they hooted at him.

The situation became serious. The boy took the matter so much to heart that he began to brood and spent sleepless nights. Finally out of desperation he told his teacher about the problem, and together they evolved a plan.

The following day when the little ones came to jeer at him he confronted them, saying, "From today on I'll give any of you who calls me a 'retard' a quarter." Then he put his hand in his pocket and, indeed, gave each boy a quarter.

Delighted with their booty, the youngsters naturally sought him out the following day and began to shrill, "Retard! Retard!"

The boy looked at them, smiling. He put his hand in his pocket and gave each of them a dime, saying, "A quarter is too much. I can only afford a dime today."

The boys went away satisfied because, after all, a dime was a dime. However, when they came the next day to hoot, the boy gave them only a penny each.

"Why do we get only a penny today?"

"That's all I can afford."

"But two days ago you gave us a quarter, and yesterday we got a dime. It's not fair!"

"Take it or leave it. That's all you're going to get."

"Do you think we're going to call you a 'retard' for one lousy penny?"

"So don't."

And they didn't. (Adapted from a fable presented by Ausubel, 1948.)

that the topic is not worth pursuing any longer because we are no longer going to reward you.

Any of these thoughts and feelings may cause you to shift the intrinsic value you originally placed on learning about the topic. The point is that extrinsic rewards can undermine intrinsic reasons for doing things (Lepper & Greene, 1978). Although this may not always be a bad thing, it is an important consideration when deciding to rely on extrinsic reinforcers (see Feature 8-4).

You might want to think about how grades affect your motivation.

- Do good grades increase your motivation?
- Do poor grades increase or decrease your motivation?
- Do you feel that you're working for a grade or to learn?
- If you took a course on a pass/fail basis, instead of for a grade, do you think it would affect your motivation?

Because of the prominent role they play in school programs, grading and other performance evaluations are a special concern in any discussion of the overreliance on extrinsics as a way to reinforce positive learning. Although grades are often said to be simply "informative" about how a student is doing, many, if not most, students perceive each grade as a reward or punishment. Many teachers do use grades to try to control behavior. Sometimes parents add to a student's perception of grades as extrinsic reinforcers by giving a reward for good report

Feature 8-4   Rewards: To Control or Inform?

"Rewards are generally used to control behavior. Children are sometimes rewarded with candy when they do what adults expect of them. Workers are rewarded with pay for doing what their supervisors want. People are rewarded with social approval or positive feedback for fitting into their social reference group. In all these situations, the aim of the reward is to control the person's behavior—to make him continue to engage in acceptable behaviors. And rewards often do work quite effectively as controllers. Further, whether it works or not, each reward has a controlling aspect. Therefore, the first aspect to every reward (including feedback) is a controlling aspect.

"However, rewards also provide information to the person about his effectiveness in various situations. When Eric received a bonus for outstanding performance on his job, the reward provided him with information that he was competent and self-determining in relation to his job. When David did well at school, his mother told him she was proud of him, and when Amanda learned to ride a bike, she was given a brand new two-wheeler. David and Amanda knew from the praise and bicycle that they were competent and self-determining in relation to school and bicycling. The second aspect of every reward is the information it provides a person about his competence and self-determination.

"When the controlling aspect of the reward is very salient, such as in the case of money or the avoidance of punishment, [a] change in perceived locus of causality . . . will occur. The person is 'controlled' by the reward and he perceives that the locus of causality is external." (Deci, 1975, pp. 141–42)

GOSH, MRS. THOMPSON, I WAS READY TO
LEARN MATH YESTERDAY. TODAY I'M READY
TO LEARN TO READ.

cards. (For one of the authors, it was a nickel for a "B" and a dime for each "A," but that was forty years ago; the going rate today has to be much higher to be highly valued as a reward.)

We all have our own horror stories about the negative impact of grades on ourselves and others. In general, grades have a way of reshaping what students do with their learning opportunities. In choosing what to study, students strongly consider what grades they are likely to receive. As deadlines for assignments and tests get closer, interest in the topic gives way to interest in maximizing one's grade. Discussion of interesting issues and problems related to the area of study gives way to questions about how long a paper should be and what will be on the test. None of this is surprising, given that poor grades can result in having to repeat a course or being denied certain immediate or long-range opportunities. Grades are a good example of how systems that overemphasize extrinsics may have a serious negative impact on intrinsic motivation for learning. And, if the impact of current practices is harmful to those who are able learners, imagine the impact on students with learning problems!

The point is that learning involves matching motivation. Matching motivation requires an appreciation of the importance of a learner's perceptions in determining the right mix of intrinsic and extrinsic reasons for learning. It also requires understanding the key role played by expectations of success. When a good match is achieved, negative attitudes and behaviors tend to decrease. They are replaced by an expanding interest in learning, new feelings of competence and self-determination, and an increase in the amount of risk taken in efforts to learn. Specific intervention strategies for matching motivation are discussed in Chapter 9.

Matching Development

Matching motivation is a first objective in creating an optimal match for learning. However, matching motivation is difficult without simultaneously matching the learner's level of development. This point may already be clear from our discussion of expectations and the key role they play in determining motivation. If Mara can't do the learning activities, she has little motivation to proceed.

Let's consider the matter of matching the learning environment to development (see Feature 8-5). To understand some of the complexities, it is important to appreciate the variability of development. Therefore we begin by discussing variations in developmental patterns. Then we turn to the topic of key performance dimensions used to measure individual differences in development.

Variations in Developmental Patterns

The primary historical emphasis in programs for learning disabilities has been on problems in perceptual, motor, and language and related cognitive development. Problems in social and emotional development, for the most part, were seen as secondary concerns until recently. Currently, we recognize that persons with learning problems may have difficulty functioning in one or more of these six areas.

Although difficulties in developmental functioning may be caused by CNS trouble, failure to account properly for individual differences can also cause such difficulties (Simmons, 1992). This occurs when others' expectations result in demands that go beyond a person's stage of development.

Causality aside, there are important differences in the way people develop. Although most of us finally reach at least some minimal level of competence in each area of development, we do so at different rates. For example, it has been widely noted that, on the average, girls develop verbal abilities earlier than boys. Among both sexes, in the years when youngsters are first learning to read, there appear to be relatively large individual differences in a number of areas of development. This is the case, for example, with regard to the minimal level of visual perceptual ability needed for discriminating among letters and words. Again we stress that such natural differences are only problems when situations and events place demands on individuals to do things that are beyond their current level of development in a given area (see Dalby, 1979). Whatever the reason, it is clear that people vary with regard to developmental patterns. In facilitating learning, we must try to match a person's current capacities in all areas of development. This means accounting for areas in which development clearly is lagging and for areas in which development has kept up with or surpassed the norm.

In first grade, James's visual perception and language functioning developed more slowly than that of most of the others in his class. However, he was a very bright and sociable youngster who related well to children and adults. If the teacher had replaced his group participation with individual remedial exercises, he would have been cut off from the few times during the school day when he could demonstrate his competence and experience school as an enjoyable place (see Feature 8-6).

In general, although it is useful to discuss specific areas of development, it is the overall pattern that must be considered in creating a good match between the learner and the environment. And the pattern, as it can be observed, reflects both accumulated capacities and attitudes.

Feature 8-5   Matching Development and Instruction

The literature on learning and learning problems offers a range of discussions on how to provide instruction to meet developmental deficits and differences. Here are three major examples.

1. *Modifying learners to match instruction.* Education has a tradition of working with learners to prepare them for what the learning environment expects of them. Early education, kindergarten, and first-grade programs are devoted in great measure to teaching school readiness skills.

The trend toward teaching general learning strategies exemplifies this tradition. The focus of this trend has been on teaching strategies and skills for coping with assigned tasks and social situations at school. Although different strategies have been developed, probably the most popular are cognitive behavior-modification techniques. For instance, there are approaches that stress teaching students "cognitive strategies" in efforts to enhance their attention and organize their thinking on tasks such as reading.

2. *Modifying instruction to match learners.* There is a growing emphasis on the importance of efforts to match teaching to the developmental level of the learner. Sometimes the focus is on matching specific observable skill levels, sometimes it is on pervasive "aptitudes."

For example, since learners differ in their ability to conceptualize, it has been proposed that those with a low conceptual level be given tests with a high degree of structure, while those with a high conceptual level be allowed to work with a low or intermediate level of structure (Hunt & Sullivan, 1974; Miller, 1981).

Corinne Smith (1991) presents a comprehensive approach to matching tasks and settings to the skills of individuals diagnosed as learning disabled. She stresses matching tasks and instructions to the student's attention, speed of processing information, need for practice, strongest modalities, cognitive style, and learning strategies. To match such developmental differences among students, Smith proposes that teachers replace current analyses of the order in which skills should be taught with analyses of learning tasks that reflect a variety of learner dimensions she identifies as critical.

3. *Modifying environments, persons, or both.* This chapter's approach to establishing a good match for learning does not presume that the learning environment is essentially fixed or that the goal of instruction at each stage is to prepare the learner for the next level of development. The approach does emphasize modifying instruction and the learning environment. In doing so, it looks beyond levels of development to consider the learner's motivation. Moreover, because learning is understood to result from the ongoing transactions between the learner and the learning environment, we recognize that a change in either or both may be appropriate at any given time.

Key Performance Dimensions

Psychologists and educators interested in individual differences have found it useful to stress four key performance dimensions when measuring the pattern of human functioning (Gagné, 1967):

- *rate* — the pace at which the person performs (given three second-graders, one reads a sentence in five seconds, another reads the same sentence in two seconds, the third takes ten seconds)
- *style* — preferences with regard to ways of proceeding (one likes to hold his book up when reading, another prefers to leave it resting on the desk, the third doesn't care which position the book is in but likes to have her feet up when she reads)
- *amount* — quantity of work the person does (during quiet reading time, one of the students stops after reading three or four assigned pages, another stops after the teacher is no longer watching, the third reads as much as he can before the period ends)
- *quality* — care, mastery, and aesthetic features demonstrated in performance (three students will be found to differ in how well they understand what they read and in how much the practice period improved their skills)

Remember that rate, style, amount, and quality of performance not only reflect levels of developmental competence but also are influenced by levels of motivation to perform. Therefore, efforts to assess a learner's skills in any area of development often are confounded by motivation — especially among individuals

Feature 8-6   Strengths and Weaknesses

Sometimes the problem of matching a learner's pattern of development is equated with focusing on strengths and weaknesses. This is understandable since both topics deal with differences in developmental functioning — areas that are well developed and those that are not. However, the two matters are not the same.

The issue of whether to focus on strengths or weaknesses initially arose as part of the underlying-problem orientation. The argument centers on whether remedial approaches should (1) attempt to build up weak areas of development (underlying abilities) or (2) teach students to compensate for deficits by relying on areas of strength.

Those who advocate building up deficiencies in underlying abilities assume that underlying deficits are interfering with the learning of basic school subjects; they also assume they can ac-

curately identify and facilitate the development of such deficiencies in ways that improve overall learning. Those who advocate relying on strengths assume that basic school subjects such as reading can be learned even though use of major facets of human functioning (identified as the weak underlying abilities) are ignored.

Some practitioners have tried to settle the issue by advocating a strategy that combines both approaches. While this may appear to be a pragmatic solution, the combined strategy has been criticized as ignoring the fact that the assumptions of the two approaches are in conflict.

Whether or not weak areas of development reflect underlying deficits, they must be accounted for in efforts to personalize learning. Similarly, strong areas of development must be accounted for, both to facilitate continuing development and to maintain and enhance motivation.

To each according to ability? To each according to need?

whose previous failures make them relatively unmotivated to perform on formal measures.

Specific intervention strategies for matching development as well as motivation are discussed in Chapters 10 and 11.

Personalization

By this point it should be clear why it is important to match motivation and development in facilitating the learning of David, James, Matt, Mara, and others with learning problems. However, you may not yet quite understand what is involved. Therefore, before moving on to a more detailed discussion in Chapters 9 and 10, we want to refer again to the concept of personalization (Adelman, 1971).

Personalization can be viewed as a psychological construct. We use the term to denote that it is how the *learner* experiences the learning environment that determines whether it is an effective match. That is, the environment is a good match only if the learner perceives it as a good match.

Matt and Jerry both are in Mr. Phillips's fifth-period class. Jerry may not say so spontaneously, but the class seems to fit him very well. He likes most of what he does in class each day, and he finds it just challenging enough (not too easy and not too hard). All indications suggest he experiences his classroom as a good match motivationally and developmentally.

Matt finds few things to like about the class. Although the teacher has planned remedial activities that Matt is able to do rather easily, they don't interest him. He is bored and feels unhappy. From his perspective, the learning environment is not a good one.

In general, the emphasis on how the learner perceives the match and on matching *both* development and motivation distinguishes a personalized intervention from other individually oriented approaches.

Because learning is an ongoing, dynamic, and interactive process, a learning environment must continually change to match changes in the learner. Jerry perceives the environment as personalized and responds by learning; the changes in him usually call for changes in the environment so that he will continue to perceive it as personalized. There must be an ongoing series of transactions and mutual changes on the part of the learner and the learning environment.

Thus important procedural objectives of personalized intervention are to provide enough options with respect to content, activities, and outcomes so that the learner finds those that are most likely to be a good motivational and developmental match. With this in mind, and recalling the guideline of least intervention needed, we present a framework of sequential and hierarchical strategies in Chapters 9 through 11.

Summing Up

Adopting a transactional perspective makes it clear that learning and learning problems are a function of the match between what the learner brings to the learning environment and what the environment offers and demands. A good match exists when learners perceive the environment as supporting what they can and want to learn.

Although the concept of the match has been presented here in connection with learning problems, it applies to all teaching. Indeed, if early schooling were more personalized, a significant number of learning problems could be prevented.

Interview a friend about a few of her or his current classes. Get a rating of the degree to which each class is perceived as a good or bad match. Remember to get separate ratings for motivation (valuing, expectations of success) and current patterns of development.

- If the match is perceived as not too good, ask for some specific examples of why this is the case.
- Ask your friend for some specific ideas about what should be changed to make it a good match for him or her.
- Finally, ask how many others in the class your friend thinks might agree that such changes would improve the match for them.

When you are finished, you will have conducted an empirical test of the validity of what you read in this chapter. What are your conclusions?

Curriculum Content: Basics Plus

Focusing on Motivation
  Enhancing and Expanding Intrinsic Motivation
  Overcoming Avoidance Motivation
  A Few Curriculum Implications
Forward to Basics: Basics Plus
Toward a Comprehensive Curriculum
  Remediation in Perspective
  Developmental Tasks and General Domains of Learning
  Enrichment
Summing Up

TEACHER: *Do you understand the questions?*
MATT: *Sure. The questions are easy. It's the answers that are hard to figure out.*

Curriculum content is a critical and controversial element in any effort to match a learner's motivation and development. It is particularly controversial in programs for individuals with learning problems. Thus, before moving on to discuss the processes of teaching and remediation, we must take a brief look at curriculum.

The curriculum for individuals diagnosed as having learning disabilities tends to be rather limited in scope. Individual Education Plans (IEPs) often stress goals and objectives bearing only on identified problems. Putting aside the matter of the inaccuracy of many such prescriptions, notice how narrow the focus can become if one is not careful.

As to more common learning problems, some people claim schools have become too soft on students and are offering too many nonessential and inappropriate courses. They demand that schools get back to basics.

Like so many catch-all phrases, "back to basics" means different things to different people. For some, it means returning to the way they themselves were taught to read and write—it worked for them, and they don't see why it shouldn't work for everyone. Others mean that the schools should stop wasting time (and money) teaching courses in value clarification, sex education, poetry, and the like. In both cases, there may also be a demand for stricter discipline and regimentation ("All this motivation talk is a lot of hooey; what some of these kids need is a good swift kick in the pants").

Both the problem focus of remediation and the push back to basics tend to have a constricting effect on curricula. In this chapter, the focus is on the importance of a broad curriculum that systematically addresses motivational as well as developmental considerations. Although we emphasize elementary and secondary classroom programs, the ideas and strategies have also been used in clinical settings and with adults.

Focusing on Motivation

"How many psychologists does it take to change a light bulb?"
"Only one. But the bulb has to want to change."

This old joke has the ring of truth about it. Individuals who don't want to change represent a special challenge to professionals, parents, and friends alike. Concerned persons commonly lament that students aren't motivated and don't put enough time and effort into their schoolwork. It is implied that teachers and parents should motivate and, if necessary, demand better learning and performance. Most people agree that motivation is a major problem in schools. They don't agree, however, on what to do about it (see Feature 9-1).

Good teachers may present lessons that are seen as excellent by most observers. But it is almost inevitable that a particular lesson will not appeal to everyone. For those who aren't interested, the lesson's intended objectives are not likely to be accomplished very well. To meet the objectives in such cases, a teacher must focus first on student motivation. Despite the teacher's best efforts, students with learning problems often are not motivated to work on improving basic skills.

Mr. Johnson is confronted with a "chicken-and-egg" dilemma. He understands, at least intuitively, that if he could improve Mara's skills he might enhance her motivation for reading. Thus, he proceeds with basic reading-skill instruction in ways designed to ensure that she can do the work successfully. However, Mara either refuses or just goes through the motions with each assigned activity. He soon realizes that, besides not improving her motivation to read, he is increasing her avoidance. What is he to do? He can't just ignore her skill deficits; but he doesn't want to increase her avoidance of reading.

Most individuals with learning problems do want to overcome their problems. Mara doesn't like having problems with her reading, and she would love to be a good reader. What she hates—and tries to avoid—is her remedial reading program.

Feature 9-1   Should School Learning Be Interesting?

A mother said to me not long ago, "I think you are making a mistake in trying to make school-work so interesting for the children. After all, they are going to have to spend most of their lives doing things they don't like, and they might as well get used to it now."

Every so often the curtain of slogans and platitudes behind which most people live opens up for a second, and you get a glimpse of what they really think. . . . Is life nothing but drudgery, an endless list of dreary duties? Is education nothing but the process of getting children ready to do them? . . . One would expect that people feeling this way about their own lives would want something better for their children, would say, in effect, "I have somehow missed the chance to put much joy and meaning into my own life; please educate my children so that they will do better."

Well, that's our business, whether parents say it or not. (Holt, 1964, pp. 160–61)

Writers like Holt have suggested that those who call for increased pressure on students to learn seem to be operating more on a training than an educational model. They seem to be equating the process of education with processes designed to teach people selected sets of skills (addition and multiplication facts, vocabulary words, typing, driving). They fail to recognize that even such skills as these are learned best when a person is intrinsically motivated to practice them and to understand underlying concepts—as contrasted, for example, with being forced to practice and memorize skills by rote.

There can be no doubt about the usefulness of the training model. If one can exercise control, people and animals can be trained to perform certain behaviors. Such an approach, however, may not be the best way to proceed in teaching children to read and do math. In fact, such an approach may be counterproductive if an additional objective is to establish an attitude of growing interest that continues beyond the course of instruction.

Think about all the people who have been trained to do math fundamentals and who "hate" math. (Many of these people are now teaching math; many others have major learning problems related to math.) There is nothing, intrinsically, to hate about math. It seems likely that the training approaches used to teach math skills have negatively affected many people's motivation for learning math and pursuing activities that involve its use.

What changes in the curriculum would help her?

With regard to motivation, the task in helping students like Mara seems to be twofold. First, the learning environment should be designed to enhance her intrinsic motivation for learning. Then, if she still shows signs of avoidance in overcoming problems, the program must focus on the reasons for her avoidance.

If it is granted that motivation is of major importance in learning, in general, and learning problems, in particular, then a commitment to correcting learning problems requires instructional reforms that stress motivation. The following discussion explores what might be involved in such a direct focus on motivation.

Enhancing and Expanding Intrinsic Motivation

Let's start with the assumption that a prerequisite for learning at school is the student's perceptions that the time and effort required to learn effectively and behave appropriately at school are worthwhile. From our discussion in Chapter 8, remember that what a person values (intrinsically/extrinsically) interacts with expectations about what will happen, and motivation is one product of the interaction. It is as if the learner thinks in terms of such questions as the following:

- Are the tasks worth doing? (valuing)
- Can I do them? (expectations)

The answers determine whether the tasks are pursued or avoided and whether a little or a lot of effort and ability is expended. Psychologists refer to this view of motivation as the expectancy-times-value (E $\times$ V) theory.

Enhancing Motivation and Skills in Social Functioning (p. 362) contrasts social-skills training programs with curricula approaches designed to improve interpersonal problem solving by focusing on both motivation and development.

In recent years, theorists interested in the motivational role played by thoughts and feelings have discussed many factors that influence people's valuing and expectations (Stipek, 1988; Weiner, 1980). The growing body of theory has many implications for understanding and working with learning problems. One very basic implication is how easy it is to mistake a lack of motivation for a lack of skills. In contrast, we recognize that individuals with learning problems can display amazing effort, and progress, under conditions of high intrinsic motivation to learn. If classroom programs ignore these facts, not only may instruction fail to capitalize on motivation, but motivation also may be undermined. Moreover, students may appear to know less than they do, and time will be wasted teaching them what they already know. These are some of the reasons it is so important to focus first on enhancing and expanding current areas of intrinsic motivation.

All students probably have some areas in which they are highly motivated to learn and other areas in which their motivation is at least positive and will increase if encouraged. It also can be expected that, given the opportunity, they will develop new interests.

Thus, as a first step, learning environments should be designed in ways that maintain currently high motivation, enhance budding motivation, and expand areas of interest. This means establishing learning environments that help students to identify intrinsic reasons for learning and overcoming problems. In doing so, there will be times when it is necessary to reduce external demands to perform and conform.

Overcoming Avoidance Motivation

Sometimes a focus on enhancing and expanding motivation is sufficient. Students find the curriculum captures and holds their interest, and they proceed to learn. Where this step is insufficient, the program must expand to include a focus on avoidance motivation and related problem behaviors (see Feature 9-2). Regardless of the type of learning problem, a significant amount of the problem behavior seen among students may be the result of avoidance motivation. Students who have failed extensively at school are unlikely to expect to succeed with schoolwork or to value it. Indeed, they probably have a strong dislike for schoolwork.

When people dislike an activity, but are pushed to do it, they are likely to protest or to try to avoid the activity (Brehm & Brehm, 1981). If the protest or direct efforts to avoid are unsuccessful, an individual can be expected to react in increasingly negative ways.

Because of his many experiences of failure at school, David tends to perceive learning situations as threatening. Even before he knows much about a situation, he expects to have difficulty coping. Thus he feels vulnerable, fearful, and sometimes angry at being pushed into such situations.

David would like to avoid the situations, and if he can't do so directly, he tries indirect ways, such as diverting the teacher to a discussion of other matters. When he can't manipulate the situation effectively, he engages in various misbehaviors. This often leads to a power struggle with the teacher, which ends up with David being sent to the principal or home.

After a number of such experiences, David has developed some rather strong negative expectations and attitudes about school and teachers and has learned a rather large range of behaviors to protect himself from what he perceives as bad situations. Unfortunately, the more he displays such behavior, the more those around him tend to think of him as emotionally disturbed.

A great deal of the negative behavior of persons like David may reflect reactions to immediate school pressures (see Feature 9-3). Those with long or intense histories of problems at school are likely to develop general expectations that most classroom experiences will be hurtful. Given such a general expectation, a student may approach all school situations looking for the worst and thus perceiving it. Even when a teacher offers "exciting" new opportunities, they may not be readily seen. (This, of course, can be frustrating to a teacher who has spent a great deal of time developing new procedures to enhance motivation.)

Feature 9-2   Motivation Problem Subgroups

In working with learning problems, we have found it useful to identify subgroups of motivation problems. We have found it one thing to work with students who have minor avoidance tendencies toward learning literacy skills; it is quite another thing to work with those who have major avoidance tendencies. It is even harder to work with those who have found interfering behaviors to be attractive alternatives to school learning and who even view such behaviors as signs of competence.

For instance, truancy, peer interactions including gangs and drug culture, and baiting authority are much more interesting and exciting to some adolescents than any learning activities the school is offering. In these instances, efforts to enhance motivation toward overcoming skill deficiencies generally aren't too successful. What is needed are strategies for correcting the motivation "problems" *directly,* and *before* efforts to remedy academic and developmental deficits. For example, if a student strongly values and feels committed to behaviors that interfere with classroom learning, procedures are needed to counter this commitment. Similarly, procedures are needed to modify the perceptions of students who strongly expect to fail or who believe that success is beyond their control.

In identifying motivation problems, look for the following:

Group A—those who want to attend school and learn some, but not all, of the basic skills demanded.

Group B—those who want to attend school and learn all or some of the basic skills but do not greatly value the procedures currently used to teach basics or do not expect to succeed with them. This group is further divided into (a) those who are willing to discuss and explore alternative learning processes, and (b) those who are not.

Group C—those who want to attend school but do not want to be taught or to learn what the program currently demands. This group also is divided into (a) those who are willing to discuss and explore alternative learning opportunities, and (b) those who are not. (This subgroup includes a large number of adolescents who come to school primarily for peer interactions, and some students who have such major fears of failure that they avoid all discussion of their problem.)

Group D—those who do not want to attend school.

This view of motivation problems underscores that for some students motivation is a problem and in some cases may be as much of a problem as a lack of basic skills.

Feature 9-3 Motivation and Misbehavior

Mara hates reading and refuses to do her assignments. James drops out of school. David is seen as a behavior problem. Matt withdraws into himself.

Youngsters with learning problems frequently display a range of behaviors that are seen as inappropriate and troublesome. Such behavior can reflect proactive (approach) or reactive (avoidance) motivation. Noncooperative, disruptive, and aggressive behavior patterns that are proactive tend to be rewarding and satisfying to an individual because the behavior itself is exciting or because the behavior leads to desired outcomes (peer recognition, feelings of competence or autonomy). Intentional negative behavior stemming from such approach motivation can be viewed as *pursuit of deviance.*

Of course, misbehavior in the classroom is of-

ten reactive, stemming from avoidance motivation. These behaviors can be viewed as *protective reactions.* That is, students with learning problems can be seen as motivated to avoid and to protest against being forced into situations in which they cannot cope effectively. For such students, many teaching and therapy situations are perceived in this way. Under such circumstances, individuals can be expected to react by trying to protect themselves from the unpleasant thoughts and feelings that the situations stimulate (feelings of incompetence, loss of autonomy, negative relationships). In effect, the misbehavior reflects efforts to cope and defend against aversive experiences. The actions may be direct or indirect and include defiance, physical and psychological withdrawal, and diversionary tactics (see accompanying figure for a graphical representation of this).

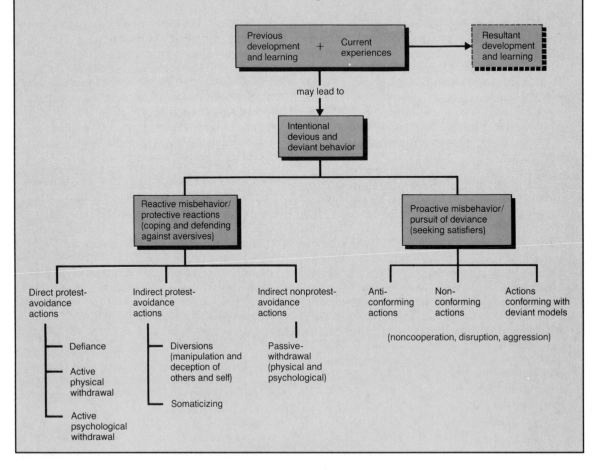

Intrinsic Motivation and School Misbehavior (p. 365) explores the importance of understanding the motivational underpinnings of school misbehavior, with a special emphasis on intrinsic motivation.

Learner Options and Decision Making to Enhance Motivation and Learning (p. 369) discusses the topic of providing learners with options regarding content, process, and likely outcomes and facilitating student decision making.

Remedying Learning Disabilities: Prevailing Approaches (p. 314) presents contrasting orientations to remediation specifically for learning disabilities.

It is helpful to understand the reasons for avoidance motivation and, more generally, the motivational underpinnings for school misbehavior. Whatever the reasons, however, there are times when efforts to enhance motivation do not sufficiently eliminate behaviors interfering with classroom learning. At such times, the next step is to change any environmental factors that seem to be producing the individual's negative reactions. In particular, this involves making certain that external demands to perform and conform are truly minimized. This strategy is intended to reduce interfering behavior to a level at which the teacher and student can at least work together. The focus is then on efforts to help the student identify areas in which vulnerability and distress won't be felt and in which she or he indicates motivation to learn.

A Few Curriculum Implications

Concern with intrinsic motivation shifts the focus of curriculum planning away from a preoccupation with behavioral objectives. Skills and behaviors, however, are not ignored. A motivational focus just stresses the importance of developing motivational readiness and continuing motivation to learn and to overcome problems. In general, consideration is given to how to enhance and expand an individual's valuing and expectations of success in important areas of learning.

Concern focuses on such matters as the following:

- Does David perceive the environment as filled with positive opportunities for learning or as something that he is forced to endure?
- If it is only to be endured, does he perceive himself as being able to do so with minimal discomfort, or does he expect it to be a very painful experience?
- Does he have a strong attraction to do something else with his time?

Accurate answers to such questions would tell us a lot about why David behaves as he does and would give us some hints about what to do to help him overcome his problems. When it is clear that motivation is playing a key role in David's problems, formulation of motivation-oriented objectives is indicated.

But how can we know the answers to such questions? To do so, we would have to know what David is thinking and feeling.

With motivation as our focus, assessment takes on a new direction. What does David think and feel about his school program? What is it that Mara sees as worth learning? What other things does she see as worth considering? Why does she say she hates reading? Assessment of motivation relies heavily on a continuing series of dialogues with a student. At first the focus is on finding out what the student wants to learn at school; once the program is under way, progress and problems are discussed.

Given that these matters are assessed, program planning must consider each of them. Planning must also consider what else a student might be likely to perceive as worthwhile learning opportunities. Optimally, all program decisions should be made in ways that don't undermine feelings of competence, self-determination, and relatedness and that do heighten a sense of personal choice, responsibility, and commitment (Deci & Ryan, 1985). As interveners increasingly

**David still strug-
gling.**

recognize the importance of accounting for motivational differences and problems, the implications for instruction are slowly being spelled out.

The most fundamental implications are that if we are to minimize reactive avoidance of learning (see Feature 9-3) the curriculum must not be perceived by the student as some unattainable goal or as lacking in worth. Stated positively, the test of a good curriculum for a student with learning problems is that the student perceives the content, processes, and likely outcomes as worth pursuing and as attainable without excessive strain.

Teachers are finding themselves spending increasing amounts of time adapting "mainstream" curriculum materials to match students with problems (Kameenui, 1991). To save teachers time and effort, there is a need for a greater range of motivationally and developmentally appropriate curriculum materials.

Forward to Basics: Basics Plus

As long as there have been schools, there has been criticism of schools. In 1632, Comenius noted:

> For more than a hundred years much complaint has been made of the unmethodical way in which schools are conducted, but it is only within the last thirty that any serious attempt has been made to find a remedy for this state of things. And with what result? Schools remain exactly as they were.

Backwards to basics?

We read almost daily of falling achievement test scores, rising illiteracy rates, and lack of respect for school property and personnel. The cry is for competency tests and excellence in education. Remedies proposed include back to basics, increased discipline, longer school days, longer school years, and more homework.

Many who talk about back to basics don't actually mean going back to old methods. They just want a greater amount of time devoted to teaching the three Rs and a few other basics, such as science. Also, they often want to introduce ways to make teachers more accountable for poor student performance. There's no question that people need to learn basic skills. What's controversial and at issue are the questions: What is basic? How are the skills best learned? and What should be offered in the way of other learning opportunities? (See Feature 9-4.)

The answers to these questions as reflected in the demand to get back to basics do not take into account the experience of those who have learning problems. Many individuals with learning problems have been taught by the very procedures advocated by the back-to-basics movement. Thus, rather than a reactive back-to-basics approach, the need is to go forward to basics and to develop programs that offer basics plus (see Carnine, 1991).

In recent years, psychology and education have made important advances in facilitating learning, and it seems naive and wasteful to ignore all that has been learned. A leap back to old-fashioned methods not only ignores important new ideas but also falsely assumes the old methods really worked.

You may believe that you are a good reader because you were taught by a specific approach, say, phonics. Some of your friends believe they are good readers because they learned by a whole-word (look-say) method. Whatever method worked for you is probably the one you think should be used for others.

If you did a study, however, you would find that almost every method used has *not* worked for a significant number of people. Experts acknowledge that teaching reading is much more complex than has been implied in teacher-education courses on how to teach reading. Experts also *disagree* about what is the best way to teach reading in public schools (Adams, 1990).

The terms *forward to basics* and *basics plus* are meant to convey the following points:

- Basic skills involve more than the three Rs and cognitive development. There are many important areas of human development and functioning, and each con-

Feature 9-4   What's Basic?

Once upon a time, the animals decided that their lives and their society would be improved by establishing a school. The basics identified as necessary for survival in the animal world were swimming, running, climbing, jumping, and flying. Instructors were hired to teach these activities, and it was agreed that all the animals would take all the courses. This worked out well for the administrators, but it caused some problems for the students.

The squirrel, for example, was an "A" student in running, jumping, and climbing but had trouble in flying class—not because of an inability to fly, for she could sail from the top of one tree to another with ease, but because the flying curriculum called for taking off from the ground. The squirrel was drilled in ground-to-air take-offs until she was exhausted and developed charley horses from overexertion. This caused her to perform poorly in her other classes, and her grades dropped to "D"s.

The duck was outstanding in swimming class—even better than the teacher. But she did so poorly in running that she was transferred to a remedial class. There she practiced running until her webbed feet were so badly damaged that she was only an average swimmer. But since average was acceptable, nobody saw this as a problem, except the duck.

In contrast, the rabbit was excellent in running but, being terrified of water, he was an extremely poor swimmer. Despite a lot of makeup work in swimming class, he never could stay afloat. He soon became frustrated and uncooperative and was eventually expelled because of behavior problems.

The eagle naturally enough was a brilliant student in flying class and even did well in running and jumping. He had to be severely disciplined in climbing class, however, because he insisted that his way of getting to the top of the tree was faster and easier.

It should be noted that the parents of the groundhog pulled him out of school because the administration would not add classes in digging and burrowing. The groundhogs, along with the gophers and badgers, got a prairie dog to start a private school. They all have become strong opponents of school taxes and proponents of voucher systems.

By graduation time, the student with the best grades in the animal school was a compulsive ostrich who could run superbly and also could swim, fly, and climb a little. She, of course, was made class valedictorian and received scholarship offers from all the best universities. (Benjamin [1949] credits George H. Reeves with giving this parable to American educators.)

tains "basics" that individuals may need help in acquiring. Moreover, an individual may require special accommodation in any of these areas.

- Motivational considerations play a major role in the acquisition of basic skills. Instruction should stress procedures that provide for a range of meaningful options, personal decision making, and useful feedback. Such processes can underscore intrinsic reasons for learning the skills, eliminate overemphasis on extrinsics, and provide for motivated practice. Individual differences in motivation may also require special accommodations.
- Facilitating learning involves varying three major areas of the learning environment and program: the setting (physical and social), program (structure and activities), and teacher techniques.
- Remedial procedures must be added to instructional programs for certain individuals, but only after appropriate nonremedial procedures for facilitating learning have been tried.

Toward a Comprehensive Curriculum

Theories of Instruction and Models of Teaching (p. 355) highlights the views on teaching of Maria Montessori, Jean Piaget, Jerome Bruner, B. F. Skinner, Carl Rogers, and Robert Gagné. Also outlined are Joyce and Weil's approach to synthesizing ideas about instruction into four major "families" or models of teaching.

By now, we hope it is clear that adequate intervention for any student with a learning problem must go beyond remediation; it must encompass facilitation of ongoing development and provide enrichment activities as well. And more is at stake than teaching the three Rs and higher order thinking. The focus must be on a variety of areas, types, and levels of instruction and learning.

As we have suggested, many forces shape decisions about what should be taught and how to teach. Because of the value conflicts inherent in these matters, final decisions are made through formal and informal political processes. Decisions about curriculum content influence decisions about the process of teaching, and vice versa. This reciprocal influence is clear from analyses of models of teaching and "theories" of instruction and conceptions of curriculum (McNeil, 1990). What also seems clear from such analyses is that narrow conceptions of curriculum content and teaching processes limit the futures of the young.

Let's summarize and then build a bit more on what we already have suggested about the nature of a curriculum for individuals who experience learning problems.

Remediation in Perspective

Given that teaching is an imperfect process, a particular individual's poor performance may be as much a teaching problem as it is a learning problem. That is, until one is certain that the program is a good match for the student's current levels of motivation and development, the trouble may just as easily be seen as stemming from the program as from the student. Applying the least-intervention-needed principle to the students involved suggests to us that the most appropriate time to pursue remedial objectives and procedures is after efforts have been made to personalize the program as much as is feasible.

Ideally, then, the first step is to personalize the curriculum. One major purpose of personalizing learning is to mobilize learners to perform as well as they can. In this way, those without significant underlying problems will be seen as able to learn and the process of identifying those with underlying problems (learning disabilities) and their specific curriculum needs becomes easier and less prone to error.

As underlying problems associated with learning become evident, there may be a need to focus on more than one level of intervention. That is, remediation can be seen as focused on one or more of the following three levels:

Level A: Age-appropriate life tasks (basic knowledge and skills and interests). Once motivation and development are matched appropriately, individuals with learning problems (including some diagnosed as having learning disabilities) may have no difficulty learning. Such individuals can simply continue to catch up in their basic skills and pursue the regular curriculum. Of course, the teaching process and even the regular curriculum content should differ from that associated with previous poor learning and performance. This level of focus usually will be sufficient for the early stages of Type I and II problems.

Level B: Missing prerequisites. Some individuals may not have acquired certain prerequisite (readiness) skills or may not have acquired an interest in learning to read, do math, or understand science. Those who have not learned to order and sequence events or follow learning directions will need to develop such skills before they are likely to be successful in learning to read and do math. If the person doesn't see much point in learning the three Rs, such interests must be developed. This level of intervention remains necessary only until we have facilitated acquisition of specific missing prerequisites.

Level C: Interfering factors. There are three types of interfering factors—disabilities, negative motivation, and interfering behaviors. If an individual has trouble learning skills in a personalized learning environment even after missing prerequisites are addressed, it seems reasonable to explore the possibility of underlying problems. One such problem might be that internal learning mechanisms are not functioning effectively (the individual has a learning disability). Other individuals do not respond positively for a variety of social and emotional reasons. They display a range of behaviors and interests that are incompatible with pursuing learning in most classrooms, and they usually are not interested in one-to-one instruction. At this level of intervention, the focus shifts to clinical remediation or to psychotherapy and behavior-change strategies designed to help the individual overcome whatever is interfering with learning.

There has been a tendency to redefine and constrict the curriculum once an individual is identified as having a learning problem. For example, remedial programs often focus primarily on a limited range of factors related to basic skills and pay relatively little attention to other opportunities that enhance learning. Always working on one's problems and trying to catch up can be a grueling experience. One has to be tremendously motivated (and perhaps a bit masochistic) to keep working on fundamentals and problem areas day in and day out. Picture yourself

What are some of the reasons a student might be bored at school?

with no other courses but basic requirements and those that you find extremely hard; how would you feel about going to school each day?

Limiting the focus to remediation presumes the learner cannot learn when motivated to do so and risks making the whole curriculum rather deadening. Broadening the focus to an increased range of developmental tasks and enrichment activities not only can balance the picture a bit but also may prove to be the key to finding better ways to help an individual overcome problems. A comprehensive curriculum is essential to minimize students' delay in accomplishing major developmental tasks that are not affected by learning problems.

We have more to say about the specific nature of remediation and strategies for offering remedial help in Chapter 11.

Developmental Tasks and General Domains of Learning

When one moves beyond basic academics and beyond technological approaches to teaching skills, curriculum decisions involve complex philosophical arguments about the role schooling should play with respect to individuals and society. These matters are as important in planning programs for those with learning problems (including Type III problems) as they are for those without problems.

Most public school curriculum guides and manuals reflect efforts to prepare youngsters to cope with what may be called *developmental* or *life tasks.* Reading, math, biology, chemistry, social studies, history, government, physical education, sex education—all are seen as preparing an individual to take an appropriate role in society as a worker, citizen, community member, and parent.

Table 9-1   Outline of Goals of Education

The following outline was developed by the Evaluation Technologies Program at UCLA's Center for the Study of Evaluation. Cognitive, affective, and psychomotor outcomes across all areas of development are reflected in the list. The outline illustrates the broad range of outcomes and content that may be appropriate in any school program, including programs for students identified as having learning disabilities.

I. Affective and personality traits
   A. *Personal temperament*
      1. Self-assertion
      2. Emotional stability
      3. Responsibility and self-control
   B. *Socialization*
      1. Social awareness
      2. Social values and conduct
   C. *Attitudes, values, and motivation*
      1. School orientation
      2. Self-esteem
      3. Achievement motivation
      4. Interests

II. Arts and crafts
   A. *Valuing art*
      1. Appreciation of art
      2. Internalization of art
   B. *Producing art*
      1. Representational skill in art
      2. Expressive skill in art
   C. *Understanding art*
      1. Art analysis
      2. Developmental understanding of art

III. Career education
   A. *Career values and understanding*
      1. Knowledge of vocations and careers
      2. Interest in vocations and careers

IV. Cognitive and intellectual skills
   A. *Understanding and reasoning*
      1. Classification
      2. Comprehension of information
      3. Logical reasoning
      4. Spatial reasoning
   B. *Creativity and judgment*
      1. Creativity
      2. Evaluative judgment
   C. *Memory*
      1. Rote memory
      2. Meaningful memory

   D. *Foreign language skills*
      1. Reading comprehension in a foreign language
      2. Knowledge of elements of a foreign language
      3. Conversation in a foreign language
      4. Writing in a foreign language
   E. *Valuing foreign language and culture*
      1. Cultural insight and values
      2. Enjoyment and appreciation of a foreign language

V. Language arts
   A. *Writing skills*
      1. Spelling
      2. Punctuation and capitalization
      3. Grammatical skills in writing
      4. Penmanship
      5. Purpose and organization in writing
      6. Expression in writing
   B. *Reference and study skills*
      1. Reference and library skills
      2. Personal study skills and habits

VI. Mathematics
   A. *Understanding math*
      1. Knowledge of numbers and sets
      2. Knowledge of numeral systems and number principles
      3. Knowledge basic to algebra
   B. *Performing arithmetic operations*
      1. Whole number computation
      2. Computation with fractions
      3. Decimal and percent computation
   C. *Applying and valuing mathematics*
      1. Solution of word problems
      2. Personal use and appreciation
   D. *Geometry and measurement skills*
      1. Knowledge of geometric objects and relations
      2. Measurement knowledge and skills
      3. Use of tables, graphs, and statistical concepts

SOURCE: This material is also presented in CSE Elementary School Test Evaluations, 2nd ed. (Los Angeles: Center for the Study of Evaluation, UCLA, 1976), edited and prepared by R. Hoepfner, M. Bastone, V. Ogilvie, R. Hunter, S. Sparta, C. Grothe, E. Shari, L. Hufano, E. Goldstein, R. Williams, and K. Smith. The original source is out of print but can be retrieved through the ERIC system (ED 143670).

VII. Music
- A. *Valuing music*
  1. Appreciation of music
  2. Internalization of music
- B. *Performing in music and dance*
  1. Singing
  2. Instrument playing
  3. Dancing
- C. *Understanding music*
  1. Music analysis
  2. Developing understanding of music

VIII. Perceptual and motor skills
- A. *Sensory perception*
  1. Visual and tactile perception
  2. Auditory perception
- B. *Psychomotor skills*
  1. Fine motor skills
  2. Gross motor skills

IX. Physical education and health education
- A. *Sports skills*
  1. Athletic skills and physical condition
  2. Sports knowledge
- B. *Valuing physical education*
  1. Sportsmanship
  2. Sports enjoyment and participation
- C. *Health habits and understanding*
  1. Health and safety behavior and attitudes
  2. Knowledge of health factors
  3. Knowledge of life functions
  4. Knowledge of human sexuality
- D. *Understanding hazards and diseases*
  1. Knowledge of safety precautions
  2. Knowledge of habit-forming substances
  3. Knowledge of disease and disability

X. Reading
- A. *Reading readiness skills*
  1. Listening
  2. Speaking
  3. Word attack skills
- B. *Familiarity with literature*
  1. Recognition of literary devices and qualities
  2. Knowledge of literature
- C. *Reading with understanding*
  1. Recognition of word meanings
  2. Reading comprehension
- D. *Reading interpretation and criticism*
  1. Oral reading
  2. Reading interpretation
  3. Critical reading

- E. *Valuing literature and language*
  1. Response to literature and language
  2. Personal use of reading and language

XI. Religion and ethics
- A. *Understanding religion*
  1. Knowledge of own religion
  2. Knowledge of religions of the world
- B. *Personal ethics and religious belief*
  1. Ethical code and practice
  2. Religious belief and practice

XII. Science
- A. *Investigating the environment*
  1. Scientific observation and description
  2. Generalization and hypothesis formulation in science
  3. Experimentation
- B. *Understanding science*
  1. Knowledge of different life forms
  2. Knowledge of ecology
  3. Knowledge of physical science
  4. Knowledge of the foundations of science
- C. *Valuing and applying science*
  1. Science interest and appreciation
  2. Application of scientific methods in everyday life

XIII. Social studies
- A. *Understanding history and civics*
  1. Knowledge of history
  2. Knowledge of government and civics
  3. Knowledge of current events
- B. *Understanding geography*
  1. Knowledge of physical geography
  2. Knowledge of anthropology and cultural geography
  3. Knowledge of economic processes and geography
- C. *Understanding social relationships*
  1. Knowledge of family life
  2. Knowledge of social control and conflict
  3. Knowledge of social groups
- D. *Valuing and applying social studies*
  1. Social studies interest and appreciation
  2. Citizenship
  3. Ethnic and cultural appreciation

Some have argued, however, that schools should do more than prepare individuals for social roles (McNeil, 1990). On the one hand, those with a humanistic orientation have argued for curricula that allow individuals to maximize their individual growth and personal integrity. On the other hand, there are those who want schools to stress societal needs over individual interests with a view to social reform and reconstruction.

These are matters that must be explored as decisions are made about curriculum content. However, to avoid bogging down in philosophical debate here, we can pursue a comprehensive curriculum for those with learning problems by following the lead of those who have viewed educational goals as fostering major facets of human development.

Over the years, efforts have been made to discuss developmental tasks related to perceptual-motor activity, cognition, language, and social and emotional functioning. Educators have tried to combine these areas of human functioning into three general categories referred to as the cognitive, affective, and psychomotor domains (Bloom, Englehart, Furst, Hill, & Krathwahl, 1956; Kibler, Barker, & Miles, 1970; Krathwahl, Bloom, & Masia, 1964). Each domain is seen as encompassing a wide range of instructional content and outcomes (see Table 9-1).

Whatever areas of human functioning are stressed, the "developmental" curriculum is divided into sequential blocks and spread over the years a youngster is in school. The timing for teaching a specific curricular block depends on data about when most students will need, and appear able to learn, the material and on a variety of practical matters.

Of course, not every area is given the same degree of emphasis. Instruction in some areas and for some students is designed to achieve a relatively high level of mastery and depth of understanding. For example, higher levels of competence are expected for reading than for physical prowess; students planning to go to college are expected to develop higher levels of competence than those who are not. Some topics are presented simply because it is felt that students should be aware of them.

Programs overemphasizing basics risk deemphasizing other important areas of human functioning. They stress basic cognitive skills and knowledge and the level of overall competence that should at least minimally be expected of an individual. Obviously, however, because of the range of developmental tasks, more is required for successful daily functioning than a minimal level of literacy in the three Rs and basic academic subjects such as science and history.

Enrichment

Enrichment goes beyond basics and beyond minimal levels of competence. In some people's minds, enrichment consists of extracurricular activities, something to be done only if time is left after basics are mastered. Others see enrichment as elite activities to be reserved for high-IQ, talented students. In either case, the expectation is that what is learned will be something extra, and often something that is hard to identify. Enrichment comprises opportunities for exploration, inquiry, and discovery related to topics and activities that are not part of the expected

Basics plus!

developmental curriculum. Opportunities are offered but need not be taken. If they are taken, no learning objectives may be specified. It is assumed that much will be learned and, equally as important, that it will be accompanied by a greater sense of the value of instruction and the joy of pursuing knowledge.

Enrichment activities often are more attractive and intriguing than those offered in the developmental curriculum. In part, this is because they are not required, and individuals can seek out those that match their interests and abilities. Enrichment activities also tend to be responsive to students; whatever doesn't keep their attention is replaced.

Because so many people think of enrichment as a frill, it is not surprising that such activities may be overlooked for individuals having trouble with developmental tasks. After all, these persons are seen as needing all the time that is available for "catching up." This view seems to be in error. The broader the curriculum, the better the opportunity for creating a good motivational match and for facilitating learning throughout an important range of developmental tasks and remedial needs.

Summing Up

Facilitating the learning of basic knowledge and skills begins with an understanding of which basics are to be taught and what is involved in teaching them. In this chapter, we have emphasized that (1) the basic knowledge and skills needed by most individuals, with or without learning problems, involve more than the three Rs and cognitive development, and (2) in facilitating the learning of such basics, motivational considerations play a major role. This means programs must offer a broad curriculum that includes not only remedial instruction in deficit areas but also programs to enhance development and enrich daily learning.

In addition, whatever the initial cause of the learning problem, an individual with longstanding basic-skill problems is likely to have negative feelings and thoughts about instruction, teachers, and schools. The feelings include anxiety, fear, frustration, and anger. The thoughts may include strong expectations of failure and vulnerability and low valuing of many learning activities. Such thoughts and feelings can result in avoidance motivation or low motivation for learning and performing in many areas.

Low motivation leads to half-hearted effort. Avoidance motivation leads to avoidance of activities. Individuals with avoidance and low motivation often also are attracted to socially disapproved activities. Poor effort, avoidance behavior, and active pursuit of disapproved behavior interfere with the remediation of learning problems.

Sometimes these interfering behaviors decrease when systematic efforts are made to enhance and expand motivation. When this proves not to be the case, special remedial procedures are necessary. The objectives of such strategies have been introduced in this chapter; the processes for accomplishing them are discussed in detail in Chapters 10 and 11.

Make a list of what you think are essential things to learn for a person diagnosed as having learning disabilities.

Assume that such a person will need to spend time remedying his or her learning problems and therefore will not have enough time to pursue all the things on your list.

- Which ones would you cross off?
- Why did you list the ones you did?
- How did you decide which ones to cross off?

If you haven't already done so, read:

Theories of Instruction and Models of Teaching (p. 355) for a glimpse at how Piaget, Bruner, Skinner, and Rogers viewed curriculum content and at Gagné's and Joyce and Weil's efforts to synthesize ideas about instruction and teaching.

Then, read about curricula designed to address motivational considerations in helping individuals with learning and behavior problems in the following:

Enhancing Motivation and Skills in Social Functioning (p. 362) contrasts social-skills training programs to curricula approaches designed to improve interpersonal problem solving by focusing on both motivation and development.

Intrinsic Motivation and School Misbehavior (p. 365) underscores the importance of understanding the motivational underpinnings of school misbehavior. The specific focus is on the intrinsic motivation concepts of self-determination, competence, and relatedness vis à vis proactive and reactive intentional misbehavior.

Learner Options and Decision Making to Enhance Motivation and Learning (p. 369) explores motivational considerations in designing curricula for students with learning and behavior problems. Emphasis is on providing learners with options regarding content, process, and likely outcomes and on facilitating student decision making.

Remedying Learning Disabilities: Prevailing Approaches (p. 314) presents contrasting orientations to remediation specifically for learning disabilities.

The Process of Teaching

Mobilizing the Learner
  Options
  Learner Decision Making
  Continuous Information on Progress

Facilitating Motivated Learning
  Environmental Setting
  Structure
  Activities, Techniques, and Motivated Practice

Least-Intervention Teaching

Personalizing Classrooms
  Key Assumptions and Major Elements
  Sequential and Hierarchical Framework
  Case
  Moving Toward Personalization

Summing Up

> *I suspect that many children would learn*
> *arithmetic, and learn it better, if it were illegal.*
>
> **John Holt, 1989**

As stressed in Chapter 8, curriculum content is learned as a result of transactions between the learner and environment. The essence of the teaching process is that of creating an environment that can first mobilize the learner to pursue the curriculum and then maintain that mobilization, while effectively facilitating learning.

Mobilizing the Learner

No teacher has control over all the important elements involved in learning. Indeed, teachers actually can affect only a relatively small segment of the physical environment and social context in which learning is to occur. Because this is so, it is essential that teachers begin with an appreciation of what is likely to affect a student's positive and negative motivation to learn. For example, they need to pay particular attention to the following points:

- Optimal performance and learning require motivational readiness. Readiness is no longer viewed in the old sense of waiting until an individual is interested. Rather, it is understood in the contemporary sense of offering stimulating environments that can be perceived as vivid, valued, and attainable.
- Teachers not only need to try to increase motivation—especially intrinsic motivation—but also to avoid practices that decrease it. For example, overreliance on extrinsics to entice and reward may decrease intrinsic motivation.
- Motivation represents both a process and an outcome concern. For example, the program needs to be designed to maintain, enhance, and expand intrinsic motivation for pursuing current learning activities as well as learning beyond the lesson.
- Increasing motivation requires focusing on a student's thoughts, feelings, and decisions. In general, the intent is to use procedures that can reduce negative and increase positive feelings, thoughts, and coping strategies. With learning problems, it is especially important to identify and minimize experiences that maintain or may increase avoidance motivation.

The point about minimizing experiences that have negative associations deserves special emphasis. Students with learning problems may have developed extremely negative perceptions of teachers and programs. In such cases, they are not likely to be open to people and activities that look like "the same old thing." Major changes in approach are required for the student to notice that something has changed. Exceptional efforts must be made to have these students (1) view the teacher as supportive (rather than controlling and indifferent), and (2) perceive content, outcomes, and activity options as personally valuable and obtainable.

Three major intervention implications are that a program must provide for

- a broad range of content, outcomes, and procedural options, including a personalized structure to facilitate learning

- learner decision making
- ongoing information about learning and performance

Such procedures are fundamental to mobilizing learners in classroom programs.

Options

If the only decision Mara can make is between reading book A, which she hates, and reading book B, which she loathes, she is more likely to avoid making any decision than to be pleased that she has a choice. Even if she chooses one of the books over the other, the motivational effects the teacher wants are unlikely to occur. Thus: *Choices have to include valued and feasible options.*

Mara clearly doesn't like to work on her reading problem at school in any way. In contrast, David wants to improve his reading, but he doesn't like the programmed materials the teacher presents to him to work on each day. James would rather read about science than the adventure stories his teacher has assigned. Matt will try anything if someone will sit and help him with the work. Thus: *Options usually are needed for (a) content and outcomes, and (b) processes and structure.*

Every teacher knows a classroom program has to have variety. There are important differences among students as to the topics and procedures that currently interest or bore them. In programs for students with learning problems, more variety seems necessary than in classes for those without learning problems.

Moreover, among those with learning problems are a greater proportion of individuals with avoidance or low motivation for learning at school. For these individuals, few currently available options may be appealing. How much greater the range of options needs to be depends primarily on how strong avoidance tendencies are. In general, however, the initial strategies for working with such students involve the following:

- further expansion of the range of options for learning (if necessary, this includes avoiding established curriculum content and processes)
- primarily emphasizing areas in which the student has made personal and active decisions
- accommodation of a wider range of behavior than is usually tolerated

Learner Decision Making

From a motivational perspective, one of the basic instructional concerns is the way in which students are involved in making decisions about options. Critically, decision-making processes can lead to perceptions of coercion and control or to perceptions of real choice (being in control of one's destiny, being self-determining). Such differences in perception can affect whether a student is mobilized to pursue or avoid planned learning activities or outcomes.

People who have the opportunity to make decisions among valued and feasible options tend to be committed to follow through. In contrast, people who are not involved in decisions often have little commitment to what is decided. If individuals disagree with a decision that affects them, they may also react with hostility.

Thus essential to programs focusing on motivation are decision-making processes that affect perceptions of choice, value, and probable outcome. Optimally, we hope to maximize perceptions of having a choice from among personally worthwhile options and attainable outcomes. At the very least, it is necessary to minimize perceptions of having no choice, little value, and probable failure.

Three special points about decision making among individuals with learning problems should be noted. First, it is well to remember that the most fundamental decision some of these individuals have to make is whether they want to participate or not. That is why it may be necessary in specific cases temporarily to put aside established options and standards. Before some students will decide to participate in a proactive way, they have to perceive the learning environment as positively different—and quite a bit so—from the one in which they had so much failure.

Second, decisions are based on current perceptions. As perceptions shift, it is necessary to reevaluate decisions and modify them in ways that maintain a mobilized learner.

Third, effective and efficient decision making is a basic skill, one that is as fundamental as the three Rs. Thus, if an individual does not do it well initially, this is not a reason to move away from learner involvement in decision making. Rather, it is an assessment of a need and a reason to use the process not only for motivational purposes but also to improve this basic skill.

Continuous Information on Progress

Because of the potential negative impact of an overemphasis on extrinsic rewards and punishment, teachers, psychologists, and parents need to be very careful how they provide students with information on their progress (see Feature 10-1). Obviously, this information needs to highlight success. Feedback should also

We all know how to talk *to* young people. Talking *with* them is another matter.

Learner Options and Decision Making to Enhance Motivation and Learning (p. 369) discusses providing learners with options regarding content, process, and likely outcomes and facilitating student decision making.

stress effectiveness in making decisions and relate outcomes to the student's intrinsic reasons for learning. Handled well, the information should contribute to students' feelings of competence, self-determination, and relatedness and should clarify directions for future progress.

Feedback can be provided during formal or informal conferences. At such times, products and work samples can be analyzed; the appropriateness of current content, outcomes, processes, and structure can be reviewed; and agreements and schedules can be evaluated and revised if necessary.

Regardless of the form in which feedback is given, emphasis should be on clarifying progress and effectiveness; avoid procedures that may be perceived as efforts to entice and control. To these ends, self-monitoring techniques and record keeping are especially helpful; close supervision and external rewards are procedures to be used sparingly.

Dialogues are the easiest and most direct way to know about learners' views of the match between themselves and the program. Many students are ready to say what's working well for them and what isn't.

Some students may not yet have the ability to self-evaluate satisfactorily; others may be motivated to make excuses, overstate how well they are doing, or avoid discussing the matter at all. That students have trouble with self-evaluation is not a reason to return to procedures that stress close supervision and decision making by others. Rather, the problems these students are experiencing become an important focus for intervention.

Feature 10-1 Evaluative Feedback and Variations in Perception

Why do people arrive at different conclusions about progress and about the reasons for ongoing problems? Sometimes because they perceive events differently.

For example, social psychologists interested in the "attributions" people make about the causes of behavior have stressed that there are some systematic ways that people differ in their perceptions. Research has shown that there is a general tendency for observers to perceive the behavior of others in terms of internal dispositions or traits. "He failed the test because he's lazy (or stupid)." "She's a success because she works very hard (or because she's very smart)." Referring to the same actions, the people carrying out the behaviors have a tendency to blame problems they experience on factors in the environment (for example, poor teaching, hard tasks, bad luck) and to credit their successes to their efforts or ability.

Why? Theorists suggest that sometimes it is because people are operating on the basis of different information. This is especially true when one person has information not available to the other, as is often the case for observers as contrasted to those who are actively involved in an event. For instance, when you do poorly on a test because you didn't have time to study, you may be the only one who knows the reason. Others may think it was because you didn't care to put in the time or that you have difficulty understanding the material. In this instance, the observers lack a key bit of information.

However, the different information affecting perceptions may also be due to the perceiver's level of competence and particular philosophical or political interests. That is, people often are selective in what they see because of their motivation or their capacity to understand.

In general, then, differences in evaluation of progress and problems may reflect differences in the information that is actually available to the decision makers or differences in what information they choose to notice and stress. Understanding such factors can be helpful. Let's take an example.

Matt wants to improve his spelling. From various options, he has chosen to learn five interesting words each day, which he will pick for himself from his experiences at school or at home. He agrees to bring a list of his five chosen words to school each day.

On the first day, Matt shows up without his list. "I lost it," he explains. The next day, still no list. "We had to go visit my grandmother; she's sick."

Naturally, Ms. Evans, his teacher, is suspicious. She knows that many students with learning problems use elaborate excuses and blame everything but themselves for their poor performance. Her first thought is: Matt is telling tales. He really doesn't want to work on his spelling. He's lazy. Probably I should assign his spelling words.

But then she thinks: Suppose he's telling the truth. And even if he isn't, what will I accomplish by accusing him of lying and by going back to procedures that I know were unsuccessful in working with him before? I must work with what he says and try to help him see that there are other ways to cope besides saying he will do something and then giving excuses for not following through.

Ms. Evans tells Matt: "I want you to think about your program. If you don't want to work on spelling, that's OK. Or if you want to choose another way to work on it, we can figure out a new way. I won't check up on what you do. When we meet, you can just let me know how you're doing and what help you want."

Matt seemed greatly relieved by this. The next day he told Ms. Evans that he'd decided to find his five words at school each day, and he'd like some help in doing so.

When students are not motivated to be appropriately self-evaluative and self-directive, they need opportunities to find out how valuable these skills can be to them. Sometimes all they need is to feel that it's safe to say what's on their minds. If they already feel safe and just haven't acquired the skills, self-monitoring and regular record keeping provide a good framework for moving toward competence.

Facilitating Motivated Learning

For motivated learners, facilitating learning involves (1) maintaining and possibly enhancing motivation, and (2) helping establish ways for learners to attain their goals. We want to help the individual learn effectively, efficiently, and with a minimum of negative side effects.

Sometimes all that is needed is to help clear the external hurdles to learning. At other times, facilitating learning requires leading, guiding, stimulating, clarifying, and supporting. Although the process involves knowing when, how, and what to teach, it also involves knowing when and how to structure the situation so that people can learn on their own (Joyce & Weil, 1986).

Specifically, the teacher can be viewed as trying to accomplish nine comprehensive procedural objectives:

1. establishing and maintaining an appropriate working relationship with students (for example, through creating a sense of trust, open communication, providing support and direction as needed)
2. clarifying the purpose of learning activities and procedures, especially those designed to help correct specific problems
3. clarifying the reasons procedures are expected to be effective
4. clarifying the nature and purpose of evaluative measures
5. building on previous learning
6. presenting material in ways that focus attention on the most relevant features of what is to be learned (modeling, cueing)
7. guiding motivated practice (for instance, suggesting and providing opportunities for meaningful applications and clarifying ways to organize practice)
8. providing continuous information on learning and performance (as discussed earlier)
9. providing opportunities for continued application and generalization (for example, concluding the process by addressing ways in which the learner can pursue additional, self-directed learning in the area, or can arrange for additional support and direction)

The focus in facilitating learning is not on one procedure at a time. Teachers usually have some overall theory, model, or concept that guides them to certain procedures and away from others. In general, procedures and content are tightly interwoven, with procedures seen as means to an end. In this connection, it is frequently suggested that learning is best facilitated when procedures are perceived by learners as good ways to reach their goals.

What makes learning exciting?

Because there is no proven set of procedures and principles for facilitating learning, our emphasis is on synthesizing current ideas. For example, see Feature 10-2, and review the outline in Table 8-1 (p. 161) for key factors relevant to facilitating learning. Also review the discussion of matching the learner's current levels of motivation and development (see Chapter 8).

With these ideas in mind, let's explore the topics of learning–environment characteristics, structure, activities, techniques, and motivated practice.

Environmental Setting

Psychologists studying the effects of settings on behavior have drawn attention to the importance of various physical and social factors in learning contexts (Altman, 1975; Rutter, 1983; Walberg, 1991). Examples of widely discussed factors that can have negative effects include crowding, lack of privacy, and environments that are extremely ill-equipped or poorly arranged.

There are less dramatic factors in classroom settings, however, that if ignored can have a profound negative effect on efforts to facilitate learning. For instance, Matt is small in stature and needs a special-sized desk and chair; James is left-handed, and at many times during his schooling he lacked appropriate materials (for example, left-handed scissors and examples of how to write left-handed); David and Mara both need a work space that cuts down on visual distractors when they are doing written tasks at their desks.

In general, key setting and context characteristics can be thought about in terms of three questions:

- What are the composition and organization of the teaching personnel and learners?
- What are the nature and quality of the physical surroundings? (for example, architecture, materials, furnishings, design, color, lighting, temperature control)
- How is the setting perceived? (for example, physical, social, intellectual, political, and moral atmosphere)

Let's look at a few brief examples of each of these.

The quality of facilitation depends on the presence of a teacher who has both competence and time. Assuming reasonably competent teaching, the number of students, their characteristics, and the length of time they spend with a teacher remain major concerns. In general, the greater the number of students, the more critical is the ratio of students to personnel (for example, teacher, aides, resource specialists). This factor can become even more critical if a large percentage of the students have learning or behavior problems (Odden, 1990).

For students both with and without problems, one-to-one instruction is sometimes necessary. Some things are learned best in the context of a group, especially when the group is selected because its characteristics can facilitate what is to be learned. Furthermore, the composition of the class shapes its dynamics and thus can profoundly affect efforts to facilitate learning. Of particular importance is the presence of positive or negative leaders and models. Working with others one likes or admires may change learning experiences from mediocre to exceptional.

The quality of the physical surroundings also plays an important role. Think about the impact on teachers and students of run-down buildings in urban ghettos as contrasted to the attractive new buildings found in most suburban areas. And what about the impact of being assigned to a segregated, special program within a larger school setting? Furthermore, think of the difference of having or not having a wide range of appropriate curriculum materials available.

Whether the environment appears good or bad to others is less important than how it appears to the learner. As we have stressed, the learner's perceptions of the

Feature 10-2   Factors Relevant to Facilitating Learning

Efforts to synthesize ideas for facilitating learning draw upon what is currently known about human function in such areas as motivation, attention, information processing, decision making, and interpersonal dynamics. These psychological constructs encompass such topics as the role of realistic goals, choice, commitment, incentives, curiosity, striving for competence, schedules of reinforcement, negative consequences, feedback, expectation and set, intensity and vividness, cues, stimuli covariation, life circumstances, active participation, massed versus distributed practice, overlearning, memory and assimilated schemata, group dynamics in informal and formal settings, sense of community, task focus versus ego-oriented communication, leadership styles, and more.

Working together can make learning better.

setting are among the most important determinants of whether it is experienced as facilitative.

Structure

Another way to view the setting variables is in terms of the structure they provide to facilitate learning (Adelman & Taylor, 1983a; McGrath, 1972). In talking about structure, some people seem to see it as all or nothing; that is, they see a program as structured or unstructured. Moreover, there has been a tendency to equate structure simply with limit setting and control.

When a student misbehaves in a classroom setting, it is common for observers to say that the youngster needs "more structure." Sometimes the phrase used is "clearer limits and consequences," but the idea is the same. The youngster is seen as being out of control, and the need perceived by the observer is for more control.

Most teachers wish it were that easy. There comes a point when efforts to use external means to control behavior can become incompatible with developing the type of working relationship that facilitates learning. This happens when a teacher sees no choice but to isolate a student (for example, "time out"). Using the term *structure* to describe extreme efforts to control behavior tends to ignore this point.

Structure involves communication, support, direction, and the types of limits or external controls that facilitate learning and performance. The point is to facilitate learning, not just control behavior.

Obviously, it is not possible to facilitate the learning of youngsters who are out of control. Equally obvious, however, is that some procedures used to control behavior also interfere with efforts to facilitate learning. A teacher cannot teach a youngster who is suspended from school, and the youngster may be less receptive to the teacher when the suspension ends. A youngster on medication to control behavior may be less of a behavior problem, but may be so sedated that she or he does not learn any better than before the pills were prescribed.

Structure is the type of support and direction available to the learner. Such support and direction can be provided in little or great amounts. Furthermore, how much structure is offered can vary from task to task. Finally, support and direction include clarifying information and limits (external controls).

Feature 10-3   *Structure and Working Relationships*

There appears to be a belief among some teachers that a tight and controlling structure must prevail if students are to learn. This view is caricatured by the teacher's maxim "Don't smile until Christmas!" Good structure allows for active interactions between students and their environment, and these interactions are meant to lead to a relatively stable, positive, ongoing working relationship. How positive the relationship is depends on how learners perceive the communications, support, direction, and limit setting. Obviously, if these matters are perceived negatively, what may evolve in place of a positive working relationship is avoidance behavior.

Some students—especially those who are very dependent, are uninterested, or who misbehave—do need a great deal of support and direction initially. However, it is essential to get beyond this point as soon as possible.

As long as a student does not value the classroom, the teacher, and the activities, then the teacher is likely to believe that the student requires a great deal of direction. We stress that the less the student is motivated, the more it is necessary to teach and control behavior, and the less successful the whole enterprise of schooling appears to be. Conversely, the more the student is motivated, the less it is necessary to teach and control, and the more likely the student will learn.

To facilitate a positive perception, it is important to allow students to take as much responsibility as they can for identifying the types and degree of support, direction, and limits they require. In providing communication, it is important not only to keep students informed but also to interact in ways that consistently convey a sense of appropriate and genuine warmth, interest, concern, and respect. The intent is to help students "know their own minds," make their own decisions, and at the same time feel that others like and care about them.

To achieve these objectives, a wide range of alternatives must be available for support and direction so students can take as much responsibility as they are ready for. Some students request a great amount of direction; others prefer to work autonomously. Some like lots of help on certain tasks but want to be left alone at other times.

When a continuum of structure is made available and students are able to indicate their preferences, the total environment appears less confining. Although we see this as positive, it does tend to make many observers think they are seeing an *open classroom* or *open structure,* as these terms are widely understood. This is not necessarily the case. The main point of personalizing structure is to provide a great deal of support and direction for students when they need it and to avoid creating a classroom climate that is experienced by students as tight and controlling. Such an approach is a great aid in establishing positive working relationships.

Social Control (p. 413) discusses the excessive use of power, limits, and expert role playing in teaching students who have learning and behavior problems.

Cultural and Individual Differences as Barriers to Working Relationships (p. 418) focuses on how differences related to sex, skin color, social class, language, and so forth can interfere with accomplishing goals and explores ideas about overcoming such barriers.

Ideally, the type and degree of support and direction should vary with the learner's needs at the moment. Some activities can be pursued without help, and should be, if the learner is to attain and maintain independence. Other tasks require considerable help if learning is to occur. Although teachers are the single most important source of support and direction in classrooms, aides, other students, and volunteers all can help come closer to the ideal of varying structure to meet learners' needs.

Figuring out the best way to provide support and direction is one of the most important problems a teacher faces in building a working relationship with a student. The problem is how to make the structure neither too controlling and dependency-producing nor too permissive. The teacher does not want to create an authoritarian atmosphere, and no teacher wants to be pushed around. Although a facilitative working relationship may not have to be positive and warm, the literature tends to support the value of these qualities (Kanfer & Goldstein, 1990). Most teachers find that a positive working relationship requires mutual respect; a warm working relationship requires mutual caring and understanding (see Feature 10-3).

Activities, Techniques, and Motivated Practice

The amount of structure offered during the pursuit of learning activities is especially important when providing support and direction to facilitate learning. Some degree of structure is inherent in all planned activities; when more structure is needed, a teacher may introduce activities, employ a variety of techniques, or both. The intent is to increase attractiveness and accessibility and decrease avoidance and distraction with respect to the planned activity.

Although any experience can be a learning activity, not all activities are meant to be vehicles for learning something new. Some are primarily designed for practice, to solidify and consolidate learning. Practice activities present a special concern because they often involve the type of drill that people find dull and prefer to avoid.

Activities.   The range of available learning and practice activities is tremendous. For teaching reading, language, and math skills alone, there are a staggering number of packaged and published materials and "programs." Some activities can be used with a variety of content and techniques. Others (such as programmed materials) prescribe content and outcomes, incorporate a particular set of techniques, and reflect specific theories and ideas about the nature of instruction.

Because there are so many possible activities, it is necessary to try to group or categorize them. One early effort listed about 180 activities, organizing them into eight groups: visual, oral, listening, writing, drawing, motor, mental, and emotional (Burton, 1962). Another early effort focused on activities learners can do independently (Darrow & Van Allen, 1961). These were categorized into four groups (activities for searching, organizing, originating, and communicating) to underscore the purpose of the activities.

Looking at learning disabilities, Lerner (1988) groups activities into a combination of developmental and academic learning areas. She delineates hundreds of exercises, games, and materials for use in efforts to improve

1. *preacademic learning,* which includes motor development (for example, gross and fine, body-image and awareness) and academic readiness skills (for example, auditory perception and phonological awareness, visual perception and memory, tactile and kinesthetic perception, and integration of perceptual systems)
2. *oral language* (for example, listening and speaking)
3. *reading* (for example, word recognition, building fluency, and comprehension)
4. *written language* (for example, written expression, spelling, and handwriting)
5. *mathematics*
6. *social and emotional behavior* (for example, developing social competencies, building self-esteem and emotional well-being, and behavioral management strategies)

See Feature 10-4 for an example of the activities Lerner has compiled for preacademic learning and motor development problems.

As these examples suggest, one useful way to distinguish among activities is in terms of their purpose. Although this approach is straightforward and simple, it does not convey the complexities involved in making decisions about which activities to use.

Minimally, classroom activities should be differentiated in terms of

• *purpose* (for example, to facilitate learning, practice, creative expression, communication, exploration, recreation, entertainment)
• *form* (for example, printed material such as texts, workbooks, library materials; writing and performing; one-to-one and group discussions; role playing; games; machines, tools, instruments, equipment—including video and computers)
• *source* (for example, commercially made; resources found in the community; intervener-made materials)
• *provider* (for example, costs covered by school, teacher, parents, public library, community agencies; labor provided by teacher, volunteers)

Practical decisions about activities are shaped by their source (many manufactured materials are costly). Cost aside, many decisions about the form and purpose of activities are fundamentally related to philosophical, psychological, and political views of the teaching process. For example, if you believe the best learning takes place through carefully controlled and sequenced instruction, you are unlikely to choose discovery-oriented learning activities.

Whatever the orientation, the job of matching learner motivational and developmental levels is made easier when multiple sources of activities can be drawn upon and when multiple forms are used. The place to begin is with as much commercially made material as can be purchased. Inevitably, however, some material has to be adapted for students with learning problems—especially for those with learning disabilities. For example, rather than using an entire workbook or computer program, a teacher may find only a few activities appropriate for a given student. Furthermore, in pursuing appropriate activities, teachers of students with learning problems must be prepared to use a variety of techniques.

Techniques.   In developing and using activities to facilitate learning, teachers often want to make them more attractive and accessible and to minimize interfering factors (factors that lead to avoidance and distraction). This is accomplished through various techniques.

Techniques alter the structure provided for an activity. The same activity can be pursued under different degrees of support and direction by varying the amount of cueing and prompting given to the learner. Some variations are ''built in'' at the time an activity is developed (such as special formatting in published materials); others are added as the activity is pursued.

Feature 10-4   Activities for Academic and Developmental Problems

Lerner (1988) organizes activities for learning disabilities into six categories of teaching strategies related to areas of development and academic learning. Two examples illustrate her approach.

In categorizing activities for teaching mathematics, she begins by defining three categories: concepts, skills, and problem solving. Each category is further divided into subcategories, and then for each subcategory, she offers various activities. For instance, she offers the following activities related to mathematics concepts:

1. Classification and grouping activities (for example, sorting games, matching and sorting, tasks involving recognition of groups of objects)
2. Ordering activities (for example, tasks involving serial order relationships, walking on number lines and number blocks, pattern games)
3. One-to-one correspondence activities (for example, pairing/matching/aligning one object with another)
4. Counting (for example, activities that combine counting with motor activity)
5. Recognition of numbers (for example, activities that incorporate techniques such as color coding and multisensory materials)
6. Motor activities (for example, varied counting materials such as an abacus, beans, and play

money; puzzles, pegboards, and form boards; measurement activities)

For motor development problems, Lerner compiles activities related to the following three subcategories:

A. Gross motor
   1. Walking activities (for example, forward, backward, sideways, and variations; animal walks; steppingstones; line and ladder walks)
   2. Balance beam (for example, forward, backward, sideways, and variations)
   3. Other (for example, skateboard, balance board, stand-up, jumping jacks, hopping, bouncing, galloping steps, hoop games, rope skills)
B. Body image and body awareness
   (for example, point to and touch body parts, the robot, Simon Says, puzzles, life-sized drawings, Twister, water activities)
C. Fine motor
   1. Throwing and catching (for example, objects, ball games)
   2. Eye-hand coordination (for example, tracing, cutting, stencils, lacing, paper-and-pencil activities, playing jacks)
   3. Chalkboard (for example, dot-to-dot, geometric shapes, letters and numbers)

Table 10-1   Categorizing Techniques

I. Techniques to enhance motivation
  A. *Nurturance* (including positive regard, acceptance and validation of feelings, appropriate reassurance, praise, and satisfaction)
  Specific examples:
  - eliciting and listening to problems, goals, and progress
  - making statements intended to reassure students/clients that change is possible
  - increasing the number of interpersonal, but nonauthoritarian and nonsupervisory, interactions
  - increasing the frequency of positive feedback and positive public recognition
  - reducing criticism, especially related to performance
  - avoiding confrontations

  B. *Permission* for exploration and change (including encouragement and opportunity)
  Specific examples:
  - increasing availability of valued opportunities
  - establishing and clarifying appropriate expectations and "set"
  - modeling expression of affect (self-disclosing) when relevant
  - encouraging pursuit of choices and preferences
  - reducing demand characteristics such as expanding behavioral and time limits, reducing the amount to be done

  C. *Protection* for exploration and change (including principles and guidelines — rights and rules — to establish "safe" conditions)
  Specific examples:
  - reducing exposures to negative appraisals
  - providing privacy and support for "risk taking"
  - making statements intended to reassure clients when risk taking is not successful
  - reducing exposure to negative interactions with significant others through eliminating inappropriate competition and providing privacy
  - establishing nondistracting and safe work areas
  - establishing guidelines, consistency, and fairness in rule application
  - advocating rights through statements and physical actions

  D. *Facilitating effectiveness* (see techniques for enhancing sensory intake, processing, decision making, and output)

II. Techniques for sensory intake, processing, decision making, and output
  A. *Meaning* (including personal valuing and association with previous experiences)
  Specific examples:
  - using stimuli of current interest and meaning
  - introducing stimuli through association with meaningful materials, such as analogies and pictorial representation of verbal concepts, stressing emotional connections
  - presenting novel stimuli
  - participating in decision making

  B. *Structure* (including amount, form, sequencing and pacing, and source of support and guidance)
  Specific examples:
  - presenting small amounts (discrete units) of material and/or information
  - increasing vividness and distinctiveness of stimuli through physical and temporal figure-ground contrasts (patterning and sequencing), such as varying context, texture, shading, outlining, use of color
  - varying levels of abstraction and complexity
  - using multisensory presentation
  - providing models to emulate, such as demonstrations, role models
  - encouraging self-selection of stimuli
  - using prompts and cues, such as color coding, directional arrows, step-by-step directions
  - using verbally mediated "self"-direction ("stop, look, and listen")
  - grouping material

- using formal coding and decoding strategies such as mnemonic devices, word analysis and synthesis
- rote use of specified study skill and decision-making sequences
- allowing responses to be idiosyncratic with regard to rate, style, amount, and quality
- reducing criteria for success
- using mechanical devices for display, processing, and production, such as projectors, tape recorders, and other audio visual media, typewriters, calculators, computers
- using person resources such as teachers, aides, parents, peers to aid in displaying, processing, and producing

C. *Active contact and use* (including amount, form, and sequencing, and pacing of interaction with relevant stimuli)

Specific examples:

- using immediate and frequent review
- allowing for self-pacing
- overlearning
- small increments in level of difficulty, such as in "errorless training"
- using play, games, and other personally valued opportunities for practice
- role playing and role taking
- using formal reference aids, such as dictionaries, multiplication charts
- using mechanical devices and person resources to aid in interactions

D. *Feedback* (including amount, form, sequencing and pacing, and source of information/rewards)

Specific examples:

- providing feedback in the form of information/rewards
- immediate feedback provided related to all processes and/or outcomes or provided on a contingency basis (reinforcement schedules or need)
- peer and/or self-evaluation
- using mechanical monitoring and scoring

III. **"Technical methods."** Sometimes groups of techniques are combined into comprehensive and complex sets of tools (activities/experiences/materials and techniques). Despite the fact they are complex methods, they usually are referred to simply as techniques as they are communicated from intervener to intervener.

Specific examples:

- kinesthetic techniques (Fernald, 1943)
- desensitization and relaxation techniques (Wolpe, 1958)
- problem-solving strategies (see Chapter 7)
- reciprocal teaching (Palincsar & Brown, 1984)

Note: While we have attempted to conceptualize discrete categories, the examples are not mutually exclusive.

We define *techniques* as planned variations in the characteristics of a tool or the way it is applied, the immediate intent of which is to increase attraction and accessibility and decrease avoidance and distraction.

From a psychological perspective, techniques are intended to enhance

- motivation (attitudes, commitment, approach, follow-through),
- sensory intake (perceptual search and detection),
- processing and decision making (evaluation and selection), and
- output (practice, application, demonstration).

In Table 10-1, techniques are categorized in terms of the aspects of human functioning they are intended to enhance.

To further clarify these points, an extended analysis of a specific remedial approach is presented in the accompanying reading entitled *Fernald's Techniques in their Motivational Context* (p. 380). The technical method analyzed is one that has long been used with individuals with learning disabilities. The discussion illustrates that the approach incorporates techniques that address all four of the above objectives (that is, the method has potential for enhancing motivation, sensory intake, processing and decision making, and output). Similar analyses could be made of other special remedial approaches, including older methods such as the multisensory approach developed by Gillingham and Stillman (1966) and the current widespread emphasis on direct instruction (Carnine, Silbert, & Kameenui, 1990).

Motivated practice.   The idea of motivated learning and practice is not without its critics: "Your points about motivation sound good. I don't doubt that students enjoy such an approach; it probably even increases attendance. But—that's not the way it really is in the world. People need to work even when it isn't fun, and most of the time work isn't fun. Also, if people want to be good at something, they need to practice it day in and day out, and that's not fun! In the end, won't all this emphasis on motivation spoil people so that they won't want to work unless it's personally relevant and interesting?"

Learning and practice activities may be enjoyable. But even if they are not, they can be viewed as worthwhile and experienced as satisfying. We recognize that there are many things people have to do in their lives that will not be viewed and experienced in a positive way. How we all learn to put up with such circumstances is an interesting question, but one for which psychologists have yet to find a satisfactory answer. It is doubtful, however, that people have to experience learning basic knowledge and skills as drudgery in order to learn to tolerate boring situations!

In response to critics of motivated practice, those professionals who work with learning problems stress the reality that many students do not master what they have been learning because they do not pursue the necessary practice activities. Thus, at least for individuals experiencing learning problems, it seems essential to facilitate motivated practice.

One of the most powerful factors keeping a person on a task is the expectation of feeling some sense of satisfaction when the task is completed. For example, task persistence results from the expectation that one will feel smart or competent while performing the task—or at least will feel that way after the skill is mastered.

Within some limits, the stronger the sense of potential outcome satisfaction, the more likely practice will be pursued even when the practice activities are rather dull. The weaker the sense of potential outcome satisfaction, the more the practice activities themselves need to be positively motivating.

Minimally, facilitating motivated practice requires establishing a variety of task options that are potentially challenging—neither too easy nor too hard. However, as we have stressed, the processes by which tasks are chosen must lead to perceptions on the part of the learner that practice activities, task

Doing.

Listening.

Looking.

Asking.

outcomes, or both are worthwhile, especially as potential sources of personal satisfaction.

The following examples illustrate ways in which activities can be varied to provide for motivated learning and practice. Because most people have experienced a variety of reading and writing activities, the focus here is on other types of activity.

Learning and practicing by

1. *Doing*
   - using movement and manipulation of objects to explore a topic (using coins to learn to add and subtract)
   - dramatization of events (historical, current)
   - role playing and simulations (learning about democratic versus autocratic government by trying different models in class; learning about contemporary life and finances by living on a budget)
   - actual interactions (learning about human psychology through analysis of daily behavior)

- applied activities (school newspapers, film and video productions, band, sports)
- actual work experience (on-the-job learning)

2. *Listening*
   - reading to students (to enhance their valuing of literature)
   - audio media (tapes, records, and radio presentations of music, stories, events)
   - listening games and activities (Simon Says; imitating rhymes, rhythms, and animal sounds)
   - analyzing actual oral material (learning to detect details and ideas in advertisements or propaganda presented on radio or television, learning to identify feelings and motives underlying statements of others)

3. *Looking*
   - directly observing experts, role models, and demonstrations
   - visual media
   - visual games and activities (puzzles, reproducing designs, map activities)
   - analyzing actual visual material (learning to find and identify ideas observed in daily events)

4. *Asking*
   - information gathering (investigative reporting, interviewing, and opinion sampling at school and in the community)
   - brainstorming answers to current problems and puzzling questions
   - inquiry learning (learning social studies and science by identifying puzzling questions, formulating hypotheses, gathering and interpreting information, generalizing answers, and raising new questions)
   - question-and-answer games and activities (twenty questions, provocative and confrontational questions)
   - questioning everyday events (learning psychology by asking about what people value and why)

These activities can be pursued in one-to-one or group interactions. From a motivational perspective, friends often work particularly well together on projects. Friends with common interests can provide positive models and support that enhance productivity and even creativity.

Least-Intervention Teaching

Highly motivated individuals tend to learn a lot more than teachers can teach. In this sense, the form of teaching that requires the least intervention needed is self-teaching. Thus, in applying the least-intervention principle to daily teaching processes, it is useful to conceive them as ranging from learner-initiated to teacher-dominated processes (see Figure 10-1).

As conceived, the processes that involve the least intervention are those in which learners self-select outcomes and learn on their own; the greatest degree of

Figure 10-1   Nature and Source of Intervention

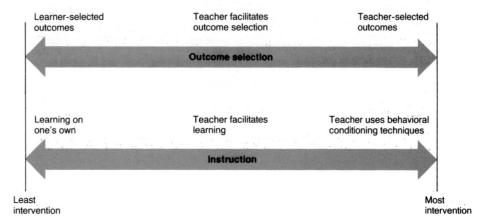

intervention occurs when the teacher selects the outcomes and uses behavioral conditioning techniques to accomplish desired ends. Obviously, variations in degree of intervention occur when the source and nature of intervention differ for outcome selection and instruction. For example, in most classrooms, teachers select most outcomes, which then are learned through teacher facilitation.

Students with different types of learning problems vary in how much teacher intervention they need with respect to different areas of learning. And teachers vary considerably in their attempts to apply the principle of least intervention needed. Thus, it is to be expected that classroom programs—and specific facets of such programs—vary considerably in the degree to which teaching practices are restrictive, intrusive, and disruptive of natural learning processes.

Personalizing Classrooms

Efforts to apply the least-intervention principle to classroom teaching raise many problems. This is especially the case when classes contain large numbers of students, when many of the students have learning and behavior problems, and when resources are inadequate. It would be foolish to suggest that such circumstances do not make the teacher's task seem impossible at times.

In recent years, the term *burnout* has been used to describe the exhaustion and discouragement teachers often experience when confronted with students who do not seem to want to learn. Obviously the situation could be improved by reducing teacher–student ratios and increasing availability of appropriate resources. Unfortunately, progress in this regard is likely to be somewhat slow and limited.

The concept of personalization provides a key to ways to facilitate learning with increased effectiveness under less than optimal conditions. Such increased effectiveness can reduce burnout. Personalizing a classroom program is not easy, and it is not without its problems. But personalization is no harder than many other current approaches and has the potential to be a lot more satisfying for teachers and students at both the elementary and the secondary level.

Key Assumptions and Major Elements

As defined in Chapter 8, *personalization* stresses the importance of a learner's perception of how well the learning environment matches her or his motivation and development. Personalized programs are built on the following assumptions:

- Learning is a function of the ongoing transactions between the learner and the learning environment.
- Optimal learning is a function of an optimal match between the learner's accumulated capacities and attitudes and current state of being and the program's processes and context.
- Matching a learner's motivation must be a prime objective of the program's procedures.
- Matching the learner's pattern of acquired capacities must also be a prime procedural objective.
- The learner's perception is the critical criterion for evaluating whether a good match exists between the learner and the learning environment.
- The wider the range of options that can be offered and the more the learner is made aware of the options and has a choice about which to pursue, the greater the likelihood that he or she will perceive the match as a good one.
- Besides improved learning, personalized programs enhance intrinsic valuing of learning and a sense of personal responsibility for learning. Furthermore, such programs increase acceptance and even appreciation of individual differences, as well as independent and cooperative functioning and problem solving.

Curiosity is a basic propensity in human functioning. The desire to explore, discover, understand, and know is intrinsic to people's nature and is a potentially central motivator of the educational process. Yet all too frequently, educators, parents, and policymakers have ignored intrinsic motivation and viewed education as an extrinsic process, one that must be pushed and prodded from without.

(Deci & Ryan, 1985)

The following are the major elements of personalized programs:

- regular use of informal and formal conferences for discussing options, making decisions, exploring learner perceptions, and mutually evaluating progress;
- a broad range of options from which the learner can make choices with regard to types of learning content, activities, and desired outcomes;
- a broad range of options from which the learner can make choices with regard to facilitation (support, guidance) of decision making and learning;
- active decision making by the learner in making choices and in evaluating how well the chosen options match his or her current levels of motivation and capability;
- establishment of program plans and mutual agreements about the ongoing relationships between the learner and the program personnel; and
- regular reevaluations of decisions, reformulation of plans, and renegotiation of agreements based on mutual evaluations of progress, problems, and current learner perceptions of the "match."

Sequential and Hierarchical Framework

The figure in Feature 10-5 presents a sequential and hierarchical framework that can guide efforts to provide a good match and determine the least intervention needed for individuals with learning problems, including learning disabilities. As can be seen, the first step focuses on changing the classroom environment. The

Feature 10-5 Sequences and Levels in Providing a Good Match and Determining Least Intervention Needed

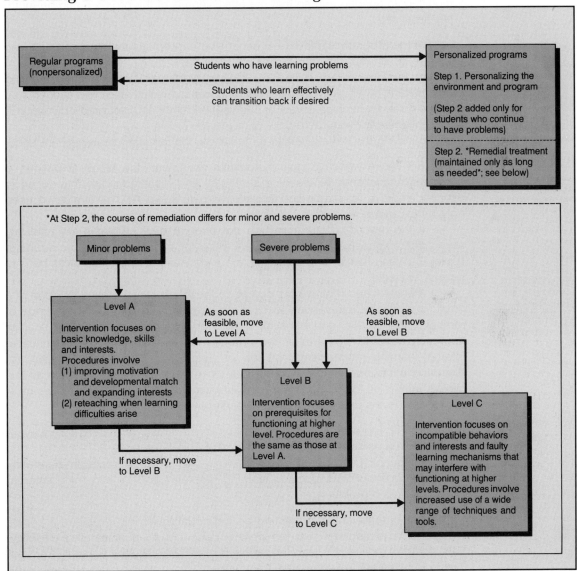

changes are meant to make the program more responsive to learner differences in motivation and development. The next step provides remedial treatment as needed.

Specifically, *Step 1* involves

- establishing a learning environment with a broad array of options
- assisting each student to sample from the range of options and then to make some initial decisions about which ones will be pursued (the primary basis for the choices made is the learner's view of what seems to be a good match)
- monitoring and evaluating effectiveness so that the initial decisions can be modified as needed and so that the effectiveness of the program can be mutually assessed

Ideally, if the program is effective in enhancing appropriate learning, this first step would be continued until the learner "catches up."

Step 2 is introduced only if the learner continues to have some learning problems or in other ways does not respond well to the first step. This second step involves three hierarchical levels of intervention focus as discussed in Chapter 9 and highlighted in Feature 10-5.

In pursuing the three levels of remediation, the following strategies are used:

1. For those whose ongoing problems are minor, the range of options is expanded and alternative teaching strategies and techniques are introduced in efforts to improve the match and facilitate learning (Level A). This strategy is used only when, and as long as, it is needed.

2. If the preceding strategies are not enough or if problems are relatively severe, the emphasis is on identifying and pursuing missing learning prerequisites (Level B). When this level of activity is no longer needed, the focus shifts back to Level A strategies.

3. If Level A and B strategies do not do the job, treatment takes the form of a one-to-one clinical intervention focused on interfering factors. A broad range of remedial, therapeutic, and behavior-change approaches are tried. The specific approach depends on whether the problem is identified as (a) dysfunction in internal learning mechanisms, (b) low or negative (avoidance) motivation, (c) disruptive social and emotional behaviors, or (d) lack of interest. As soon as this clinical work is no longer necessary, the intervention focus shifts back to the most appropriate levels and strategies listed earlier.

A graphic representation of the various levels, types, and areas for intervention focus in a personalized classroom is offered in Feature 10-6.

The sequential and hierarchical framework also provides a sequential strategy for detecting errors in diagnosing learning problems and for screening different types of learning problems:

- If Step 1 is sufficient in correcting an individual's learning problem, it seems reasonable to suggest that the person does not have a learning disability. Instead, the individual's learning problem may have resulted primarily from the inadequacies of the learning environment.

- If Levels A and B of Step 2 are sufficient, the individual is probably a learner whose natural variations in development or whose minor physical or psychological vulnerabilities require considerably more accommodation than current regular programs provide.
- If Level C of Step 2 is necessary and the problem does not appear to be caused by social or emotional factors, it may well be that the individual has learning disabilities stemming from a minor CNS dysfunction.

Case

It was a hard decision, but David and his parents decided he should go to a private school to correct his learning problem. Among those they looked into was one that emphasized personalized learning. When they visited the program, they observed

Feature 10-6   Levels, Types, and Areas of Intervention

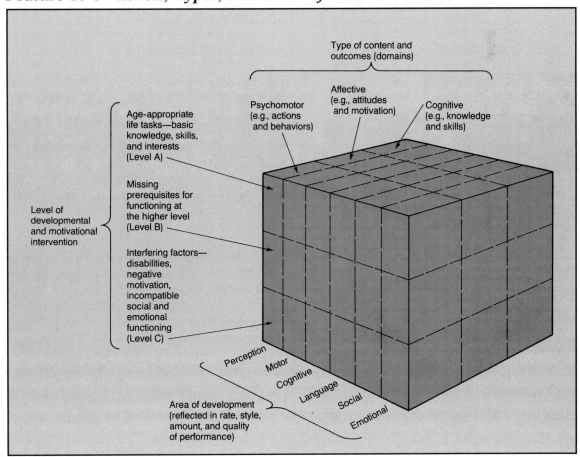

a variety of learning options that they were encouraged to explore. After visiting several programs, David was asked which he preferred. His decision was to try the personalized program.

In early September, a meeting was arranged with his prospective teacher, Ms. Hopkins. She used this first meeting to engage David in a discussion of his interests, things he was good at, and what he hadn't liked about his previous school experiences. Then, she described, demonstrated, and helped David sample as many of the available learning activities as time allowed, highlighting those related to his interests.

Before he left that day, David indicated to Ms. Hopkins and his parents the specific activities he was interested in pursuing during his first week at school. The program he scheduled consisted of an enrichment class in anatomy dissection, a group focusing on chicken incubation, a guitar class, a soccer class, and participation on the school newspaper. Somewhat tentatively he also indicated a desire to improve his math skills. In all, he had scheduled activities covering 2½ hours a day. Therefore, his school day was initially scheduled to last just that long.

Because the activities did not include a reading program, David's parents were concerned. Ms. Hopkins explained that the main focus for now was to let David find that learning at school was something worth doing. "We don't want to make the mistake of just recreating the program you left; after all, it was not working for David."

Each day of David's first week, Ms. Hopkins talked with him several times. Sitting next to him, she informally continued the dialogue begun at their first meeting. David indicated that most of the activities were going fine, but the guitar class was not what he had thought it would be, and he was still not sure about the math. The guitar class was dropped, and the time was devoted to helping him explore other options.

As agreed at the first meeting, David, his parents, and Ms. Hopkins had another formal meeting at the end of the week. They discussed how the program was shaping up and other concerns. David and his parents were pleased with the way things had begun. He really liked the dissection class; he had replaced guitar with a drawing and oil painting class; the school newspaper was his favorite activity. Math was still not quite satisfactory; however, one of the other students who was good at math had agreed to help him. Because they were just getting started, David wanted a few more days to see how it would work out. If nothing else, the alliance was a good one since the other student had helped David enter a circle of friends quickly. David had also agreed to let Ms. Hopkins know anytime he was getting bored and restless so that they could find a good activity rather than letting him fall into old patterns of daydreaming or distracting others.

As the meeting was ending, the parents again expressed concern about David's reading. Ms. Hopkins again stressed that the first step was to help David experience school as a positive learning environment and that as he became involved in various learning experiences there would be plenty of opportunities to help him improve his basic skills. "For example," she pointed out, "David's decision to be on the school newspaper means he spends three hours a week planning what the paper will include and another three hours carrying out reporter assignments and writing up articles."

The program continued to work well over the next few weeks. New activities were added, and his school day was increased to 4½ hours. Then two problems cropped up. David started to arrive at school a half hour late several days a week, thereby missing most of his creative writing class. Moreover, toward the end of the day he would begin to pick on another student, disrupting both their programs.

As soon as she noted the pattern of behavior, Ms. Hopkins arranged a special meeting with David. He wasn't too eager to talk about the problems. To engage him, Ms. Hopkins said: "Look, I'm not asking about these things to trap you or blame you or punish you. After all, I didn't send you to the office or call your parents, did I? I just figured something was wrong, and I thought it would be a good time to show you how you can work on solving a problem rather than suffering with it. Let me show you how we do it."

David was a bit surprised that the teacher wasn't "coming down on him." And he was intrigued when she went to the blackboard, wrote "Problem Solving Steps," and made three columns, headed "Problem," "Alternatives," and "Pros and Cons." "Let's look at the reasons you get here late," she said. He repeated the excuses he had given over the past few weeks — traffic jams and oversleeping. "Anything else?" she asked. David shrugged. Ms. Hopkins smiled, "Sometimes students come late because they don't like what's scheduled."

"Well," said David, "sometimes I don't feel like doing creative writing."

They went on to look at some ways he might handle the problems he had noted: catching an earlier bus, asking his parents to help him not oversleep, looking at ways to make creative writing more enjoyable, and having another activity planned that he could do whenever he didn't feel like doing what was scheduled.

"Each of these ideas has some good points and bad points," Ms. Hopkins noted. "Let's list some of them." She offered a couple; David added some more. Then she asked, "Well, now that you've had a chance to think the problem through, do you want to try any of these ways to solve it?" He chose the ideas of looking for ways to make creative writing more enjoyable and having other activities he could do when he didn't feel like doing what was scheduled.

"You did a great job on this, David. Perhaps you can think about the other problem in the same way, and let me know in a day or two if you come up with some ideas for handling it. If you need help solving it, I'll be glad to work on it in the same way we did this one."

During the next few weeks, Ms. Hopkins used informal daily contacts to follow up with David. They found that one of the things that made creative writing a problem for him was the need to come up with new topics each day. They hit upon the idea of his writing a continuing story and using his drawing skills to illustrate it.

With regard to his second problem, David reported that he would like to stop the conflict with the other student, but he just didn't know how to do it. Because this had been noted as a longstanding problem for David, Ms. Hopkins took the opportunity to suggest that he might like to join a group that was working on how to deal with such problems.

As the year progressed, David's program was reviewed and revised regularly. He was given a lot of options to choose from and made a lot of decisions for himself. By November, he was attending school full time. By midyear, his program consisted of a varied set of activities, including reading instruction. From all reports, he was enjoying school and regaining his self-confidence.

The March conference with David and his parents was a happy one. David felt he had made good progress and continued to like his program. However, he missed going to school with his neighborhood friends and expressed an eagerness to return to public school the next fall. His parents were pleased with his progress and his attitude and were anxious for him to get back to public school too. However, they were worried that it might be too soon. Their concerns were explored, and it was agreed that David would plan some work that would enable everyone to see whether he was now ready to handle public school.

For the next two months, David pursued a regular school program. He had subjects and texts similar to those in public school; he increased his homework time and took weekly quizzes on what he studied. He wrote a special term paper to practice the skills involved in such activity. Along with other students preparing to return to public school, he spent an hour a day learning "survival skills." These included study skills and interpersonal problem solving with teachers and other students. Because David was now highly motivated to learn such skills, things that had been "learning problems" and avoided in the past were learned quickly. It turned out he already had many skills he had seemed to lack.

Day after day, David's motivation to learn at school increased, and the range of what he wanted to learn expanded. Ms. Hopkins now could focus on facilitating his quest for learning. She always looked forward to the time when "problem" students gained enough motivation that she could help them experience the sense of competence that comes from valued learning. For Ms. Hopkins, teaching was not simply a job, but a labor of love. She helped her students learn to read and write and to use their skills to explore the wonders of the world. She never stopped being intrigued with what made the process of teaching work—when it did.

Moving Toward Personalization

What does it take to personalize a classroom? First of all, the teacher must expect and value individual differences in students' motivation and development. The teacher also must be willing to offer available resources as options and help students make decisions among these learning alternatives. The emphasis in such decision making must be on encouraging students to pursue what they perceive as a good match in terms of learning activities and structure. And as new information about what is and isn't a good match becomes available, there must be a willingness to revise decisions.

When a teacher is highly motivated to personalize a classroom program, both the students and the teacher have to become accustomed to the special elements of the approach. Thus it is usually necessary to move toward personalization through a series of transition steps (see Table 10-2). In general, this means developing an appropriate variety of learning options to offer as a starting point,

Table 10-2   Transition Steps Toward Personalizing Classrooms

I. Preparing the class
   A. Giving an enthusiastic explanation to the class of the why, what, when, and how of the intended changes (e.g., with emphasis on the special personal opportunity of the new approach for them)
   B. Identifying available options and increasing the variety to reflect the range of interests and capabilities present in the class
   C. Teaching students to be relatively self-sufficient at times and to ask others for help when necessary (e.g., a range of independent activities are introduced and students are shown how to use them, how to move toward other tasks on their own, and how to use aides, peers, and volunteers for support and direction when the teacher is working with others)
   D. Recruiting aides, peers, and volunteers and teaching them how to provide help that may be needed by class members when the teacher is occupied with others
   E. Making trial runs to evaluate if students, aides, etc., can function effectively while the teacher holds individual conferences; continuation of development of self-sufficiency and trial runs until class is at least minimally effective in this regard
   F. Giving demonstrations and opportunities to sample learning options
   G. In first conferences, focusing on discussing each student's interests and strengths, available options, other options each would like to have available, and amount of structure the individual views as needed; first conferences should be oriented particularly to building a sense of valuing the opportunity to interact with the teacher in making program decisions
   H. Over the first weeks, focusing also on working with students, aides, and volunteers to develop additional learning options in keeping with students' specific requests

II. Additional conditions to facilitate individual conferences and small-group and one-to-one facilitation of learning
   A. Establishing a quiet area where others will not interfere or be distracted
   B. Scheduling such sessions when other students are involved in independent activities or there is sufficient help available
   C. Establishing record keeping and information procedures for use by both student and teacher (e.g., objective checklists, records from last conference, products, work samples, test materials)

III. Ending the transition phase
   A. Establishing working agreements with each student about learning plans (e.g., intended outcomes, procedures, and products, needed support and direction)
   B. Establishing procedures for regular individual conferences with students to improve, evolve, and expand the quality of the learning activities
   C. Establishing procedures for implementing remediation if necessary

facilitating student understanding of what the new approach involves, and establishing procedures so that some students can work independently while the teacher pursues one-to-one and small-group interactions.

Summing Up

As a leading writer of the twentieth century, John Steinbeck was asked to address a convention of teachers. Part of what he said to them was the following:

> School is not easy and it is not for the most part very much fun, but then, if you are very lucky, you may find a teacher. Three real teachers in a lifetime is the very best of luck. My first was a science and math teacher in high school, my

second a professor of creative writing at Stanford and my third was my friend and partner, Ed Rickets.

I have come to believe that a great teacher is a great artist and that there are as few as there are any other great artists. It might even be the greatest of the arts since the medium is the human mind and spirit.

My three had these things in common—they all loved what they were doing. They did not tell—they catalyzed a burning desire to know. Under their influence, the horizons sprung wide and fear went away and the unknown became knowable. But most important of all, the truth, that dangerous stuff, became beautiful and very precious (1955, p. 7).

It is well to acknowledge that great teaching rises to the level of art. At the same time, it is essential to understand as much about the process as can be learned.

Regardless of curriculum content, the process of teaching starts with mobilizing the learner. This involves providing for

1. a broad range of content, outcomes, and procedural options—including personalized structure
2. learner decision making
3. ongoing information about learning and performance

With a mobilized learner, the emphasis is on maintaining mobilization while pursuing methods that provide an appropriate match with the learner's current levels of motivation and development.

In this regard, the concept of personalization provides a model for the process of teaching that can help prevent learning problems and identify true learning disabilities. Applied in the primary grades, the outlined sequential and hierarchical approach to teaching could significantly reduce the number of problems and their negative impact. Finally, as will become evident in the next chapter, personalization provides an important foundation for remediation.

Interview some friends about music lessons, and find out how many were forced to take instrumental music lessons as children.

- How many learned to play well?
- How many came to dislike the lessons and the practicing and dropped out as soon as they could?
- How many professional musicians do you think had to be regularly forced to practice?

We have stressed the importance of learner options and decision making through-out Chapters 8, 9, and 10. Detailed examples on how such learner involvement can be accomplished are provided in *Learner Options and Decision Making to Enhance Motivation and Learning* (p. 369), where the emphasis is on providing options regarding content, process, and likely outcomes and facilitating student decision making, especially for students with problems.

By way of contrast, the way in which efforts designed mainly to control behavior interfere with empowering learners is discussed in *Social Control* (p. 413). Those teaching students who manifest learning and behavior problems increasingly are confronted with problems related to the concept of social control. Three topics are explored: the *excessive* use of power, limits, and expert role-playing.

Cultural and Individual Differences as Barriers to Working Relationships (p. 418) focuses on how differences related to sex, skin color, social class, lan-guage, and so forth can interfere with accomplishing goals and explores ideas about overcoming such barriers.

Remediation

When Is It Needed?

What Makes Remediation Different?

Criteria for Implementing Remediation
Motivational Problems
Developmental Problems

Content Focus
Perceptual-Motor Problems
Language and Psycholinguistics
Math
Cognitive Prerequisites
Learning Strategies and Reasoning
Social and Emotional Functioning
Motivation
Interfering Behavior

Remedial Methods

Levels of Remediation

Sequencing Remediation

Summing Up

A Brief Bibliography on Remedial Methods

The pessimist says that a 12-ounce glass containing 6 ounces of drink is half empty— the optimist calls it half full. I won't say what I think the pessimist would say about research and practice in special education at this point, but I think the optimist would say that we have a wonderful opportunity to start all over!

Scriven, 1981 (p. 10)

Remediation is an extension of general efforts to facilitate learning. Thus, before a remedial focus is introduced, the best available nonremedial instruction will be tried. Optimally, this means trying procedures to improve the match between the program and a learner's current levels of motivation and development. A significant number of learning problems may be corrected and others prevented through optimal, nonremedial instruction.

There does come a time, however, when remediation is necessary for some individuals. In this chapter we sketch the criteria for deciding who needs it, the general features of remediation, and the focus and form of remedial methods. For those of you ready to move on to detailed discussions of remedial methods, there are references at the end of the chapter.

When Is It Needed?

Stated simply, an individual needs remediation when the best nonremedial procedures are found to be ineffective. As we have suggested, remediation is used for motivation problems and for those who have difficulty learning or retaining what they have learned.

Because remediation in all areas usually is unnecessary, as much learning as possible will probably continue to be facilitated with nonremedial approaches. Besides facilitating learning, such procedures provide an essential foundation and context for any remedial strategy, especially if they are valued by the learner.

What Makes Remediation Different?

Techniques and materials designated as remedial often appear to be very different from those used in regular teaching. However, the differences often are not as great as appearance suggests. Some remedial practices are simply adaptations of regular procedures. This is even the case with some packaged programs and materials especially developed for problem populations. In general, regular and remedial procedures are based on the same instructional models and principles (Gagné, 1985; Joyce & Weil, 1986).

Because all teaching procedures are based on the same principles, the question is frequently asked: "What's so special about special education?" The answer to this question involves understanding (1) the factors that differentiate remedial from regular teaching, and (2) the special task of special education. The following six factors differentiate remedial from regular teaching:

Sequence of application. Remedial practices are pursued after the best available nonremedial practices have been found inadequate.

Teacher competence and time. Probably the most important feature differentiating remedial from regular practices is the need for a competent teacher who has time to provide one-to-one instruction. While special training does not necessarily guarantee such competence, remediation usually is done by teachers who have special training. Establishing an appropriate match for learners with problems is difficult. Indeed, a great deal of this process remains a matter of trial and appraisal. Thus there must be additional time to develop an understanding of the learner (strengths, weaknesses, limitations, likes, dislikes). There must also be access to and control over a wide range of learning options.

Outcomes and content. Along with basic skills and knowledge, other content and outcome objectives are often added. These are aimed at overcoming missing prerequisites, faulty learning mechanisms, or interfering behaviors and attitudes.

Processes. Although instructional principles underlying remedial and nonremedial procedures do not differ, remediation usually stresses an extreme application of the principles. Such applications may include reductions in levels of abstraction, intensification of the way stimuli are presented and acted upon, and increases in the amount and consistency of direction and support—including added reliance on other resources. Of course, special settings (outside regular classrooms) are not the only places such processes can be carried out.

Resource costs. Because of the types of factors already cited, remediation is more costly than regular teaching (allocations of time, personnel, materials, space, and so forth).

Psychological impact. The features of remediation already mentioned are highly visible to students, teachers, and others. Chances are they are seen as "different" and stigmatizing. The psychological impact of remediation is thus likely to have a negative component. The sensitive nature of remediation is another reason it should be implemented only when necessary and in ways that result in the learner's perceiving remediation as a special and positive opportunity for learning.

Changing the individual while leaving the world alone is a dubious proposition.

Neisser, 1976 (p. 183)

Special educators also have the responsibility to clarify whether general educators share the same basic concerns. Special educators are asked to take on an additional concern. Their responsibility is to clarify whether general answers to educational matters are adequate for everyone and, if not, how the answers should be modified to account for specific subgroups of learners. Until much more is known about how to meet the needs of those who are not well served by regular classroom programs, a role for remedial teaching and special education will certainly remain.

Criteria for Implementing Remediation

To determine who needs remediation, one must have ongoing assessment that detects when individuals are having learning problems. The process should focus on motivational as well as developmental needs, and specify criteria for deciding when a problem exists.

Motivational Problems

As we have stressed, a key step in assessing remedial needs is to ensure that teaching matches the student's current levels of motivation and development. If the student remains unengaged in learning basics such as reading and math, remediation must first address the motivational problem.

From one remedial orientation, the problem may be addressed by continuing to focus instruction directly on basic skills, using extrinsic reinforcers in the effort to mobilize the student. Alternatively, the lack of mobilized learning can be treated as an underlying motivation problem. In either case, the immediate remedial problem is the student's negative motivation.

Assessment, of course, continues after remediation is implemented. At some point, we need to decide whether remediation has been effective. For example, take the choice to continue with some form of direct instruction and extrinsic reinforcement: Subsequent assessment must determine, not only if there has been significant improvement in the immediate retention of skills and knowledge, but also whether there has been long-term maintenance and generalized application in other areas. If not, treating the underlying problem deserves consideration. The rationale for doing so is threefold: (a) the direct instruction may have been unproductive because of the motivational problem; (b) continued emphasis on direct instruction risks increasing avoidance motivation and reactive misbehavior; and (c) the probability of eventual benefits may be increased by temporarily setting aside an unproductive area of instruction. In place of ineffective reading instruction, for example, the student might be offered counseling and alternative classroom learning opportunities, especially those that are likely to result in the rediscovery of personal reasons for learning to read. (We have discussed the remedial focus for motivational problems in preceding chapters and related reading.)

In sum, the first criterion for remediation is the learner's disinterest (lack of engagement) in optimally presented learning opportunities. Such a finding indicates a motivational problem. (How interveners work on solving the problem depends on their orientation to remediation.)

Developmental Problems

Students who appear generally engaged in learning at school may become candidates for remediation when they are not performing up to standards in a particular instructional area. Standards for evaluating academic progress include measures of rate, amount, and quality of learning.

There are two major difficulties in applying performance standards to decide whether to initiate remediation. The first difficulty is determining whether the standards are appropriate. If performance standards are unrealistically high for a given individual, they should be modified before evaluating the need for remediation. The second difficulty arises in defining specific criteria for judging whether the individual's performance is so poor as to warrant remediation.

Given that a student is mobilized to learn and instruction is appropriately designed to accommodate the learner's capabilities, there is little difficulty identifying those who are not learning. The difficulties arise when an individual is learning, but not as well as most other students in the classroom.

One trend in such cases has been to apply the notion of criterion-referenced objectives to assess learning. The simplicity of this approach masks several controversial matters. For one, the teaching process and ultimately what is taught may be inappropriately reshaped because of the pressure to specify objectives as readily measured concrete behaviors. For another, while it is easy to determine what objectives are not attained, it is not easy to determine what criteria should be used for deciding remediation is needed. For instance, in checking retention of instruction, what criterion should be used to indicate a learning problem: Below 90 percent retention? Below 75 percent? Below 50 percent? And, given common fluctuations in retention, is remediation indicated after the first test shows below-standard performance, or does a pattern have to be established over several tests? Finally, the data say nothing about why the student performed below the specified level.

At present there are no agreed-upon criteria for initiating remediation in moderate cases. As rough guidelines for assessment, the following seem reasonable: Before any assessment for a learning problem, efforts should have been made to ensure the student is mobilized to learn and instruction is appropriately designed to accommodate the learner's capabilities. Then, retention should be checked immediately after instruction and several days later. If a pattern emerges over several weeks of difficulty retaining at least 75 percent of what initially appeared to be learned, remediation seems warranted.

In the section of this chapter on levels of remediation, we offer additional operational criteria for deciding when to shift from a focus on current tasks to teaching missing prerequisites and, finally, to working on interfering factors.

Content Focus

Not surprisingly, because of the primary emphasis on problematic conditions of persons, the outcomes sought usually are identified as problems in specific areas of functioning. Thus the following problem (or content) areas usually are major remedial concerns. (Some prominent historical names and controversies associated with each of these areas are highlighted in *Learning Disabilities in Historical Perspective,* p. 291.)

We want to provide a quick conceptual picture of the range of content areas that are the focus of remedial activity. Each area deserves an extensive review; at the end of the chapter you are directed to works about remediation of reading and other language functions, math, motor functioning, reasoning, and social functioning.

Perceptual-Motor Problems

Some of the most prominent programs during the 1940s and 1950s focused on perceptual-motor problems. Indeed, the early evolution of the field was dominated by such interventions and by those persons associated with them. The general content focus has been on

- motor skills and patterns
- perception (ability to recognize and interpret sensory stimuli)
- perceptual-motor integration (organization and coordination of sensory stimuli with motor activity and use of motor activity to monitor and correct perceptions)
- relationship of motor and perceptual development to more complex cognitive development

Note that perceptual problems differ from sensory acuity problems (a person may have 20/20 vision and thus be able to receive visual stimuli well, but still have trouble interpreting what is seen).

In response to concerns about perceptual-motor functioning, remedial activities have been directed at improving

- laterality and directionality
- body image and differentiation
- balance and posture
- locomotion
- gross and fine motor coordination
- ocular control
- figure-ground perception
- constancy of shape
- position in space
- spatial relationships
- perceptual-motor coordination
- auditory and visual integration
- tactile and kinesthetic integration
- multisensory integration
- rhythm
- agility
- strength, endurance, flexibility
- catching and throwing

Controversial Treatments and Fads (p. 309) discusses concerns associated with vision training, colored lenses, stimulant medication, special diets, megavitamin therapy, CNS training, and vestibular treatment.

In addition to the psychoeducational focus on perceptual-motor problems, a range of controversial treatments are in use that are aimed at affecting physiological functioning (vision training, colored lenses, medication, diets). See *Controversial Treatments and Fads* (p. 309) for a discussion of these.

Language and Psycholinguistics

The 1940s and 1950s also saw a group of prominent programs and pioneers stressing language remediation. The general content focus since then has been on

- listening skills
- speaking skills
- reading skills
- writing skills
- spelling skills
- grammar
- usage (written expression)
- processing abilities underlying language

In response to concerns about language development and psycholinguistic functioning, remedial activities have been directed at improving

- basic skills in each of the content focus areas (for reading, the focus might be on sound-symbol associations, word recognition, phonics and structural analysis, and comprehension)
- underlying abilities in each of the content focus areas (for reading, the focus may be on such factors as phoneme perception and phonetic representation in short-term memory; or, more generally, the concern may be with a "phonological core deficit")

As linguists and psycholinguists improve our understanding of language and communication, the areas of focus for remediation are expanding.

Math

Only recently have comprehensive remedial efforts been made with respect to mathematics. The general focus has been on

- computational skills
- conceptual processes associated with quantitative relationships

In response to concerns about math performance, remedial activities have been directed at improving functioning related to

- shape and size discrimination
- sets and numbers
- one-to-one correspondence
- counting
- place value
- number-combination knowledge
- computational aids
- graphs, charts, maps
- measurement
- money and time concepts
- word problems
- algorithms
- algebraic addition
- geometric relationships
- descriptive statistics

Language is rooted in our personal experiences.

Remediation to improve math skills also often focuses on prerequisite skills, underlying abilities, and compensatory tools related to perceptual-motor development, language, cognition, and motivation.

Cognitive Prerequisites

Concerns about cognitive prerequisites have expanded greatly in recent years with the reemergence of cognitive psychology. The work of Piaget, Bruner, Vygotsky, and many others has contributed greatly to efforts to understand what factors may be worthy of remedial concern. The general content focus has been on

- attentional skills (short-term and sustained voluntary attention)
- memory (organization/coding, storage/retention, and retrieval of information)
- conceptual skills (cognitive structuring of perceived stimuli and operations to order, sequence, classify)

In response to concerns about deficiencies in cognitive prerequisites, remedial activities have been directed at improving

- attention to tasks
- following directions
- rote memory
- short-term or immediate memory
- serial or sequential memory
- long-term memory
- spatial or temporal sequential ordering
- classification to understand relationships

Remedying Learning Disabilities: Prevailing Approaches (p. 314) reviews contrasting orientations to remediation for learning disabilities.

In addition, prerequisites for cognitive development, such as motivation and perceptual, motor, and language development, are relevant.

Maria Montessori was an early advocate of focusing specifically on development of cognitive prerequisites. Her ideas are reflected in many remedial programs for basic skills. One example is her emphasis on teaching arithmetic and science and on the use of concrete materials representing abstract principles.

With the increasing interest in attentional and memory problems related to learning disabilities, these areas are becoming a major focus of remediation. Efforts to improve attention and memory usually stress ways to improve learning efficiency. The objectives are to learn specific skills and strategies, including ways to compensate for any disabilities.

Learning Strategies and Reasoning

Along with the trend toward viewing learning problems as the result of inefficient learning, there has been an increasing emphasis on the notion that poor learners have deficiencies in general learning strategies and reasoning. These students are seen as needing to learn to (1) think about how to learn, and (2) use what they have learned. The general content focus is on

- pacing and timing
- thinking and questioning
- organizing, structuring, and integration
- problem solving

In response to concerns about deficiencies in learning strategies and reasoning, remedial activities have been directed at improving

- study strategies
- strategies for describing and judging phenomena
- strategies for grouping and classifying phenomena (for example, noting sameness)
- hypothesis testing
- problem analysis
- self-monitoring and evaluating
- strategies for generating alternatives
- strategies for evaluating options
- strategies for differentiating and generalizing
- use of visual and verbal imagery

Work in this area has stressed teaching any strategy that can help the individual acquire, organize, store, retrieve, and use information. Such a focus appears most appropriate for those who are of at least average intelligence, who are reading at a third-grade level or better, and who can deal with abstract as well as concrete tasks (Alley & Deshler, 1979; Deshler & Schumaker, 1986).

Furthermore, if such instruction is to produce learning strategies that are maintained and generalized and if higher-order thinking is to be enhanced, intervention must minimize fragmented curricular approaches and rote learning of facts and metacognitive skills. To these ends, there have been renewed calls for integrative curricula approaches (Carnine, 1991).

Social and Emotional Functioning

Social and emotional problems were an early concern to those dealing with learning problems. With the emergence of the learning disabilities field, social and emotional problems were pushed temporarily into the background. Currently there is a reemergence of interest in their relationship to the causes and correction of learning problems. The general content focus has been on

- interpersonal functioning (for example, social perception)
- intrapersonal functioning (for example, self-concept)

In response to concerns about social and emotional functioning, remedial activities have been directed at improving

- awareness of self
- awareness of others
- mastery of interpersonal skills
- empathy
- choice and decision making
- coping and adaptation
- assertion
- intrapersonal and interpersonal problem solving
- cooperative learning

Remedial ideas dealing with social and emotional functioning draw on the psychological literature focusing on such phenomena as self-concept, anxiety, dependency, aggression and withdrawal, social perception, interpersonal relationships, and moral development. Particularly influential has been the vast literature on psychotherapy and behavior change (Westman, 1990).

Motivation

Although motivation has always been a concern to those who work with learning problems, the stress is usually on how to use extrinsics to mobilize the learner and maintain participation. There is a recent emphasis on the relationship of learning problems to deficiencies in intrinsic motivation. The general content focus has been on

- increasing feelings of self-determination
- increasing feelings of competence and expectations of success
- increasing feelings of interpersonal relatedness
- increasing the range of interests and satisfactions related to learning

In response to concerns about deficiencies in intrinsic motivation, remedial activities have been directed at improving

- awareness of personal motives and true capabilities
- learning to set valued and appropriate goals
- learning to value and to make appropriate and satisfying choices
- learning to value and accept responsibility for choice

Current work in psychology has brought renewed attention to motivation as a central concept in understanding learning and learning problems. This work is just beginning to find its way into applied fields and programs for persons with learning and related problems.

Managing and Preventing School Misbe-havior (p. 422) explores approaches ranging from prevention to discipline and use of logical consequences.

Interfering Behavior

Throughout the 1950s and 1960s, it became evident that remediation, especially in the classroom, was often delayed because so many individuals with learning problems also manifested behavior problems. Such individuals were frequently described, not only as learning disabled, but also as hyperactive, distractable, impulsive, behavior disordered, and so forth. Their behavior patterns were seen as interfering with efforts to remedy their learning problems, and the conclusion was that such interfering behaviors would have to be eliminated or minimized in order to pursue remediation. The focus has been on any actions of an individual that compete with the intended focus of remediation.

Besides trying to reduce the frequency of deviant and disruptive actions directly, programs have been designed to alter such behavior by improving

- impulse control
- selective attention
- sustained attention and follow-through
- perseverance
- frustration tolerance
- social awareness and skills

Variations in focus derive from the ways in which interfering behaviors are viewed. Some professionals see the problem as a skill deficiency and have tried to improve the situation through instruction. Others see the problem as a matter of control and have addressed it through the use of control techniques. For those children diagnosed as hyperactive or as having attentional deficit disorders with hyperactivity, a number of controversial nonpsychoeducational interventions also have been advocated (such as the use of stimulant drugs or special diets to avoid chemical additives in food).

Remedial Methods

Discussions of remedial procedures often begin with concerns about remedial classroom settings. "Isn't it harmful to segregate a student in a special class-room?" "Shouldn't everyone be kept in the mainstream of education?"

Whether remedial approaches should be administered in special or regular classrooms is a secondary consideration and one that, for now, is best decided pragmatically. The primary consideration is to provide students with a teacher who has the competence, time, and resources to facilitate learning appropriately. If such conditions are available in regular classrooms, it is always preferable not to segregate students just because they need remedial help (Topics in Early Child-hood Education, 1990).

The problem of knowing what works.   Some special remedial methods are based on specific theoretical formulations about the nature of an individual's learning problem. For example, procedures emphasizing stimulus bombardment, stimulus simplification, modality isolation, or multisensory integration have been designed for particular types of problems. What usually are referred to as "theories" of remediation are the rationales, orientations, and models used in developing remedial strategies. In general, such theories reflect views about faulty learning mechanisms and stress ways to improve sensory intake, processing and decision making, and output (review Table 10-1, p. 210).

Advocates of many remedial procedures have argued that their approach is needed to deal with some interfering factor within the learner. The factor may be seen as an underlying processing deficit, a motivational or emotional problem, a developmental delay in selective attention, inefficient use of learning strategies causing poor retention, or whatever. When a procedure is applied and an individual improves, advocates of the approach naturally believe that the progress validates the procedure. They also tend to believe the approach has corrected the underlying problem and see this as supporting their assumption about what caused the learning problem in the first place.

In contrast, when a procedure is applied and the individual doesn't improve very much, advocates of the approach tend to suggest either that it wasn't applied properly or that a different underlying factor must have been causing the problem. Those who favor competing ideas and methods see the procedure's lack of effectiveness as evidence that it and its underlying rationale are both invalid!

Generally ignored in these skirmishes is the fact that, when an approach appears to be effective in any particular instance, there is no way to be very confident about the reason. For one thing, adequate research usually will not have been conducted, and therefore, events other than the approach may well have been responsible for the outcome. Even when satisfactory evaluative research has been carried out, there inevitably are other competing explanations for the procedure's effectiveness that will not have been adequately explored. For instance, analysis of most remedial methods suggests that they not only have the potential to influence the factor they were designed to affect (processing deficits, selective attention) but also have the potential to enhance motivation and to facilitate performance. Thus, before the approach can be credited with correcting any assumed underlying factor, these other factors must be ruled out.

Illustrations of contrasting orientations.   Again, the range of remedial methods is too extensive to review here. The two following examples illustrate differences between methods designed to address observable problems and those aimed at underlying problems. (Remember, references for further reading on remediation are included at the end of the chapter.)

(a) Direct instruction—a focus on observable problems. In reaction to remedial methods that emphasize underlying problems, there has been a growing emphasis on procedures that keep remediation focused on observable skills and behaviors. These approaches to remediation are not particularly concerned with *why* someone is having trouble learning to read, write, or do math. The assumption is that the person can learn the skills if the right teaching approach is used.

One of the most cited observable-problem approaches is called *direct instruction (DI)*. (Because the roots of DI are in the behaviorist tradition, its basic features are the same as those found in directed teaching, mastery learning, curriculum-based assessment and instruction, or applied behavior analysis.) Names associ-

I TOLD HER THE DOG ATE MY
HOMEWORK. SO SHE GAVE MY DOG AN F.

ated with the development of DI procedures include Sigfried Engelmann, Carl Berieter, Wesley Becker, Douglas Carnine, Joseph Jenkins, and many more (Carnine, Silbert, & Kameenui, 1990).

Direct instruction "is based on task analysis and features systematic and explicit instruction of academic skills such as language, reading, and mathematics, with a goal of maximizing academic learning time. The instructional procedures of DI, like the content, are direct; it is teacher managed and fast paced, utilizing a highly structured presentation of material with frequent opportunities for student response and reinforcement of correction" (Lovitt, 1989, p. 407).

More specifically, DI focuses on the skills an individual is having trouble learning, for example, reading vocabulary. Based on an analysis of the skills and tasks related to learning to read vocabulary words, DI offers a sequential list of skills and related tasks. This list provides a basis for assessing what students already know and what they need to learn. The assessment prescribes the step-by-step sequence for directly teaching missing skills through activities that emphasize drill and repetition. Eventually, instruction focuses on integrating what has been learned into a fluent set of reading and comprehension skills.

A major example of DI is seen in the Distar Reading Program (Engelmann & Bruner, 1984), designed to develop beginning skills. This basal reader series uses a highly structured decoding program (a synthetic phonics approach) that begins by teaching the student to combine isolated sounds into words. The teacher usually works with a small group of students for a 30-minute period each day. The program proceeds in small, sequential steps, and the teacher is expected to praise students for progress at each step. Progress is measured using criterion-referenced tests. For older students (grades 4 through 12), there is a similar program called the Corrective Reading Program (Engelmann, Becker, Hanner, & Johnson, 1978).

Over the years, research has suggested positive immediate outcomes but poor maintenance and generalization of the skills learned. In addition, there has been a rift among proponents of direct instruction. Some professionals have reacted against the emphasis on teaching skills in isolation and have argued for a more holistic approach (Poplin, 1988). Myers and Hammill (1990) argue that "most successful practitioners probably employ a good mix of each approach" (p. 44).

(b) Multisensory instruction—a focus on underlying problems. Multisensory

approaches have a long and distinguished history in the remediation of learning problems in general and learning disabilities in particular (Fernald, 1943; Gillingham & Stillman, 1966). Grace Fernald viewed many reading and language problems as due to the fact that the methods used in public schools were not adapted to the needs of certain individuals. In particular, she saw some individuals as "thinking" in auditory or kinesthetic terms. In some cases, she assumed this may have been due to brain dysfunction. However, unless the ability to learn was completely disrupted, she believed that the only thing interfering with the individual's progress was the failure of instructional methods to account for the way the individual learned best. She also recognized that learning problems almost inevitably produced emotional problems.

Because the prevailing procedures used in schools stressed auditory and visual modalities, Fernald argued that an approach that also emphasized kinesthetic and tactile modalities would benefit those who learned best through such senses. She developed a series of technical steps and stages, incorporating multisensory learning, to help individuals learn and practice skills related to basic school subjects.

We discuss Fernald's approach in some detail in *Fernald's Techniques in Their Motivational Context* (p. 380); here is a brief summary of key elements.

In working with severe learning problems, Fernald found it useful to begin with methods that involved a multisensory (tracing) approach for learning words. From this beginning, she moved systematically to procedures used widely in teaching anyone to improve vocabulary. In all, she delineated four overlapping stages through which she took individuals with reading problems.

All the stages are similar, in that each new word to be learned is identified by the student, usually in the context of intrinsically motivated activity (see Feature 11-1). That is, at any of the stages, words the student does not know are discovered as the individual reads and writes while pursuing a self-determined activity. Students are told to let the teacher know when they encounter an unknown word while reading, or when a word is needed in writing. No effort is made to teach the words at this point; they are simply read to or written for the student. This is done to avoid disrupting the student's flow, enjoyment, and satisfaction in reading and writing. By agreement, a temporary record is made of those words the student wants to consider learning. (Obviously, the same type of strategy can be used to assess and plan instruction for a wide range of other skill deficiencies, like deficiencies in punctuation, capitalization, grammar.)

The stages also are similar because they all call for simultaneously looking at (visualizing) and saying (vocalizing) the word that is being learned and because they prescribe immediate and subsequent practice and review.

The stages differ as follows:

Stage 1   Visual-auditory-kinesthetic-tactile — tracing words the teacher has written on tracing slips

Stage 2   Visual-auditory — no tracing, but continued use of tracing slips with teacher-written words, then making the transition to teacher-written words on flashcards

Stage 3   Visual-auditory—use of words in print rather than teacher-written words

Stage 4   Independent learning—use of reference material, generalization, inference, and other analytic and synthesizing skills to learn new words

Although Fernald specified four stages, these stages blend one into the other. Essentially, they form a continuum ranging from the extreme remedial strategy of Stage 1 to the very general educational approaches used in Stage 4.

(c) Some commonalities. The preceding examples illustrate that techniques and materials designated as remedial often have much in common with regular teaching practices. In fact, all special remedial procedures can be re-analyzed in terms of how they affect motivation, attention, and performance. Thus, regardless

Feature 11-1   Remedial Methods

Although best known for the specific remedial techniques she developed, Grace Fernald's (1943) general orientation to remediation provides many important insights regarding the application of remedial methods.

Fernald stressed that all techniques (including her kinesthetic approach) should be applied within the context of intrinsically valued learning activities. She was concerned that the activities be ones that could be done successfully and would not add to emotional upset. The major emphasis she placed on such matters has unfortunately been widely ignored by those who have adopted the kinesthetic technique. Fernald advocated an overall methodological stance toward teaching and learning with some specific techniques to help when individuals had special difficulty; she underscored the importance of changing the fixed and emotionally disruptive way in which children tend to be taught in schools. Take for example, what she said about written language problems:

> Many children fail to learn to spell because the methods used by the schools actually prevent them from doing so. These children are forced to write over and over again words they do not know, until bad habits are fixed. The child knows he is not writing [the] words correctly and is emotionally upset on this account. When he gets back . . . written work with misspelled words marked in red and with disparaging remarks concerning [the] attempts to write, the negative attitude becomes estab-

lished as part of the total problem. As a matter of fact, it is much more important that a child should love to write than that he should write in perfect form. To teach spelling in such a way that the development of form takes the joy and life out of writing is a futile process. (p. 13)

Over the years, the kinesthetic techniques described by Fernald for remedying reading problems have been tried by many teachers around the world. Not surprisingly, specific research findings have been inconclusive. But, for the most part, those who use the steps say they are very effective for many students. Ironically, at the clinic school that Fernald founded, kinesthetic techniques were used more sparingly than in other settings where Fernald techniques are advocated. We often use the approach for its value in enhancing motivation, attention, and performance, rather than with any thought that the youngster is a "kinesthetic thinker." That is, the novelty and the high degree of support and direction provided by the specific steps that a learner follows are seen as useful for individuals with a variety of learning problems.

More important is that, whenever we use techniques advocated by Fernald or anyone else, we do so in the context of activities that emphasize intrinsically worthwhile learning. This has always been an essential ingredient of the Fernald method, and it may be one of the most important features of any remedial method. Unfortunately, research on the effectiveness of remedial methods has tended to ignore this point.

of the problem for which a remedial practice has been developed, it may prove to be a useful aid for a variety of problems. For instance, a procedure developed for use in perceptual-motor training can be a novel and effective activity for improving skills in listening and in following directions.

By re-analyzing procedures in terms of general instructional principles, we can greatly increase the variety of alternatives available for remediation. Most remedial procedures available on the market and discussed in the literature can be readily adapted, and many more procedures can be created, by anyone who understands what is involved in facilitating learning. Much remedial instruction can be accomplished using only paper and pencil and commonly available objects.

While all remedial activities are intended to correct a problem, compensate for a problem, or both, there is considerable debate as to what is correctable, what needs to be compensated for, and what compensatory strategies are appropriate and effective. At this point, the pragmatic position suggests that, if direct approaches do not appear to remedy the problem, compensatory approaches should be tried. There are two ways to help a learner compensate for a deficit. The teacher can change the demands to accommodate the learner's handicap, or the learner can be taught a strategy to self-initiate whenever needed, or both approaches can be employed. If neither direct nor compensatory approaches work, it seems reasonable, as discussed in the next section, to move to the level of addressing underlying problems.

Levels of Remediation

As outlined in Chapter 9, specialized psychoeducational procedures to facilitate learning can be applied at any of three levels:

Level A — age-appropriate life tasks (basic knowledge, skills, and interests)
Level B — missing prerequisites needed to function at Level A
Level C — factors interfering with learning

Age-appropriate life tasks.   Current life tasks involve a variety of basic knowledge, skills, and interests as part of day-by-day living at school, home, and on the job. These include reading (see Feature 11-2), writing, interpersonal and intrapersonal problem solving, and so forth.

At this level, remediation essentially involves reteaching — but not with the same approach that has just failed. Alternative ways must be used to present material the student has had difficulty learning. This is accomplished by further modifying activities in ways likely to improve the match with the learner's current levels of motivation and development. Throughout Part 3, we have discussed how this is done.

You may recall we pointed out that teachers can use a range of environmental factors to influence the match (review Table 8-1, p. 161). Also remember that many techniques can be used to vary environmental factors for purposes of enhancing (1) motivation, (2) sensory intake, (3) processing and decision making, and (4) output (review Table 10-1, pp. 210–211).

Prerequisites.   At this level, the focus is on identifying missing prerequisites and teaching them. The types of prerequisites that may be missing are outlined in Feature 11-3. Procedures are the same as those already described for facilitating learning related to current life tasks.

Interfering factors.   At this level, we must face the possibility of faulty learning mechanisms. As discussed in Part 1, a variety of underlying problems have been suggested as interfering with learning. Remedial approaches are designed to overcome such deficiencies by directly correcting the problems or indirectly compensating for them. Prevailing approaches to remedying interfering factors are discussed in Chapter 3 (for example, see Table 3-1, p. 54), as are commonly used remedial activities. Also see the references at the end of this chapter.

Feature 11-2   *Remediation of Reading Problems*

Remedies for dyslexia are still more likely to emanate from cuckoo land than from the research literature. (Stanovich, 1991a, p. 79)

What does the research literature say about remedial reading? A synthesis suggests that in the early stages of regular reading instruction the emphasis should be on teaching skills for word recognition and decoding (phonics), connecting spoken and written language, and reading for meaning. Moreover, children who are read to and individuals who read a good deal on their own are most likely to become good readers (Adams, 1990; Chall, 1983a, 1983b).

In terms of teaching materials, the emphasis is on appropriate basal texts, supplemented with story and information books. For example, Chall, Jacobs, and Baldwin (1990) state:

We do not recommend . . . a reading program that follows an extreme—one that focuses only on a more highly structured reading system, with little time for reading, or one that uses only trade books, dropping explicit teaching of skills. (pp. 151–152)

Although research on computer-assisted instruction has been limited, eventually it may be possible to relegate some of the skill instruction to interactive computers. Given a comprehensive approach to regular instruction, what should be done with a student who still has problems learning? Pronouncements based on the research literature are less satisfactory in this regard. Some writers have underscored the importance of mobilizing the learner, notably by use of what has been called the *language experience approach* or an *integrated language approach.* This orientation to teaching reading attempts to build on a learner's cognitive, language, and sociocultural background (Bartoli & Botel, 1988; Fernald, 1943; Stauffer, 1980).

There also is concern about how to deal with areas of vulnerability or dysfunction. It has been suggested that instruction be redesigned for such persons to build on strengths and minimize weaknesses, at least temporarily. For example, if an individual has difficulty making auditory perceptual discriminations, it may be necessary to avoid overrelying on instruction in phonetic analysis. This argument in no way denies the importance of phonological awareness and phonics skills. It simply suggests that some individuals may have to compensate for an auditory perceptual weakness by relying more initially on learning vocabulary through visual or multisensory means. It also suggests that overemphasizing instruction in the area of weakness may negatively affect feelings of competence and create a negative attitude toward reading and schooling.

For those with severe learning problems and learning disabilities, typical classroom approaches to reading instruction require some of the types of modification described in this chapter.

Sequencing Remediation

When a youngster has a learning problem at school, the teacher and student must decide whether instruction in that area should be delayed until learning might be easier. For instance, the need for such decisions is common with young children (5- to 8-year-olds) whose perceptual development may be slower than average for their age group. This strategy may also have to be considered with adolescents and adults who are so anxious or so unmotivated that they are not ready to pursue learning vigorously in a particular area. Remediation is most productive with students who express a desire for help.

When remediation is indicated, the teacher may focus on any of the three levels described. However, the sequence and level differ depending on whether the student has minor and occasional problems or severe and pervasive problems. The process involves the following sequence.

Feature 11-3   Prerequisites

In general, individuals should have the following important prerequisites if they are to benefit appropriately from instruction in the three Rs.

A. **Language**
1. Expressive—working vocabulary and ability to speak clearly and plainly enough to be understood
2. Receptive—ability to understand what is said
3. Use—ability to use at least simple sentences and to express ideas, thoughts, and feelings; understanding of the relationship between spoken and written language

B. **Perception**
1. Visual discrimination—ability to discriminate differences and similarities in letters, words, numbers, and colors and to see the relationship of a part to a whole
2. Auditory discrimination—ability to discriminate differences and similarities in sounds of letters

C. **Cognition and Motivation** (including attentional, memory, and conceptual skills)
1. Interest in what is being taught
2. Ability and desire to follow simple directions

3. Ability and desire to stay at the desk for sufficient periods of time to complete a simple classroom task
4. Ability and desire to remember simple facts
5. Ability and desire to answer questions about a simple story
6. Ability and desire to tell a story from a picture (associate symbols with pictures, objects, and facts)
7. Ability and desire to stay focused on material (pictures, letters, words) presented to the class by the teacher
8. Ability and desire to solve simple task-oriented problems
9. Ability and desire to tolerate failure sufficiently to persist at a task
10. Ability and desire to make transitions from one activity to another
11. Ability and desire to carry on with a task over several days
12. Ability and desire to accept adult direction without objection or resentment
13. Ability and desire to work without constant supervision or reminders
14. Ability and desire to respond to normal classroom routines
15. Ability and desire to suppress tendencies to interrupt others

"Treat people as if they were what they ought to be and you help them become what they are capable of being." (Goethe)

For learners with minor or occasional problems, the initial focus is on facilitating learning related to current tasks and interests and on expanding the range of interests. The procedures involve (1) continued adaptation of methods to match and enhance current levels of motivation and development, and (2) reteaching specific skills and knowledge when the student has difficulty. (This level of focus is Level A in Feature 10-5, a portion of which is reproduced in Feature 11-4.)

If the problem continues and is assessed as severe, the focus shifts to assessment and development of missing prerequisites (Level B) needed for functioning at the higher level. Again procedures are adapted to improve the match, and reteaching is used when the learner has difficulty. If missing prerequisites are successfully developed, the focus returns to Level A.

The intent in proceeding in this sequential and hierarchical way is to use the simplest and most direct approaches first when problems appear minor. However, if available data indicate the presence of severe and pervasive motivation or developmental problems, instruction at Level B is begun immediately.

And if help at Level B is not effective, the focus shifts to Level C. Only at this level is the emphasis on factors that may interfere with functioning—that is, incompatible behaviors and interests or dysfunctional learning mechanisms.

At Level C, there is increased and intensified use of a wide range of psycho-educational techniques (see Table 10-1, p. 210). As soon as feasible, the focus shifts back to prerequisites (Level B) and then on to current tasks and interests (Level A). These remedial strategies are used whenever and as long as necessary.

Even among those with pervasive and severe problems, there are likely to be some areas in which the learning problem is not severely handicapping. These are areas in which learning can proceed without remediation or, at least, in which remediation can be focused more directly on Level B or A. In such cases, an individual would be pursuing learning at several levels at once.

A couple of examples may help further clarify this sequential and hierarchical approach to remediation.

Larry had a minor reading problem; Joan's problem was somewhat more severe. Mr. Johnston's first efforts to help Larry improve his reading skills involved a variety of reteaching strategies. The activity focused on current reading tasks in which Larry had indicated an interest. The reteaching strategies were not simply a matter of trying more of the same (more drill, for example). He tried alternative procedures ranging from commonly used explanations, techniques, and materials (such as another example or analogy, a concrete demonstration, a memorization strategy) to less common, specialized, *remedial* techniques (such as a multisensory method).

After working on this level for a week, Mr. Johnston found that over the preceding years Larry had not learned a number of prerequisites widely viewed as reading-readiness skills. For example, Larry had difficulty following directions in-

Feature 11-4   *Sequencing of Hierarchical Strategies*

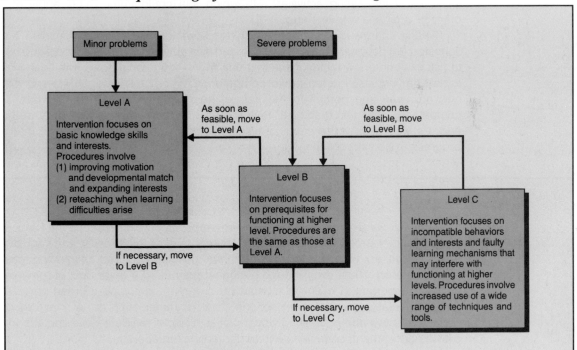

volving more than one point at a time, and he had problems ordering and sequencing events described to him. He also seemed to have little awareness of the relationship between the spoken and the printed word. As he assessed these problems in his daily work with Larry, Mr. Johnston pointed them out, and they agreed to include them as a major focus of instruction.

With other students, Mr. Johnston had found that once the missing prerequisites were learned, they had little problem learning basic reading skills. This turned out to be the case with Larry.

Joan's situation proved to be more difficult. Because her problem was more severe, Mr. Johnston had focused from the start on absent reading prerequisites. As he worked with her over a period of several weeks, he found that she had trouble learning most of the prerequisites he taught her and retained only a small amount of what she learned. Thus, he moved on to try to detect any dysfunctional learning mechanisms that might be interfering with her learning.

Over a period of weeks, it became clear that Joan was having widespread difficulty discriminating sounds and was continuing to have severe trouble recalling what she had learned the day before. Rather than have her continue to experience failure, Mr. Johnston shifted the focus of instruction. The time usually spent on reading instruction was devoted to helping overcome her learning handicaps. Activities she wanted to do were identified; as she had trouble, he worked with her using techniques that stressed multisensory involvement. To improve her retention, he encouraged her to take smaller amounts, and together they identified a variety of interesting activities with which she could immediately apply and practice what she was learning.

At first Joan was hesitant to try things at which she had failed earlier. Mr. Johnston did not push. He followed her lead and at the same time encouraged her to risk exploring new things. Note that one of Mr. Johnston's goals with Joan was to help her increase her feelings of competence. When he first began working with her, however, she perceived the special help as another sign of her lack of competence, and this made her feel worse. Such a reaction is common. In the end, as was usually the case with such students, Mr. Johnston found Joan's progress to be slow but steady.

Summing Up

In Chapter 9, we stressed that remedial programs often tend to reduce the focus of instruction by narrowing the curriculum. As important as the three Rs and cognitive development are, other basic areas of human development and functioning must not be ignored. Thus, even though a student may need a great deal of remediation, it is important to maintain a balanced program—including a broad range of developmental and enrichment options. That is, remediation is not intended to replace effective and interesting opportunities that can facilitate development and provide enrichment; special help is added only as needed.

In general, the task of regular and remedial teachers is the same—facilitating learning. For motivated learners (with and without learning problems), this involves (1) maintaining and possibly enhancing motivation, and (2) helping establish ways for learners to attain their goals.

This chapter presented remediation as an extension of nonremedial processes for facilitating learning. We have focused on the criteria for deciding when such a special focus is needed, reviewed the major features that differentiate remediation from regular teaching, outlined the problems remedial strategies are designed to address, and explored the nature of remedial methods and applications.

Remedial strategies involve no new principles of instruction. What makes such approaches appear different is their rationale, the extreme degree and consistency with which they must be applied, and their application on levels of functioning other than current life tasks. How well remediation works and why it does—when it does—remains unclear. What may make any remedial procedure work is the fact that it is different from those a student has already tried and found ineffective. Special procedures have the benefit of being novel and thus having motivation- and attention-inducing value.

As a general stance regarding remedial activity, we concur that learning problems and learning disabilities "cannot be corrected or 'cured' by a specific teaching method or training technique. It is imperative that teachers have a wide range of instructional materials and techniques at their disposal and that they are imaginative and flexible enough to adapt these to the specific needs of their pupils" (Koppitz, 1973, p. 137).

We would add, however, that effective flexibility and imaginativeness in facilitating learning stem from a sound understanding of what is involved in personalizing regular and remedial instruction.

Now that you've read about specific ways to intervene with individuals having learning problems, what do you think?

- Are interventions such as teaching an art, or are they something most people can learn to do?
- Why do you think so?

Remedying Learning Disabilities: Prevailing Approaches (p. 314) explores major approaches to remedying learning disabilities through contrasting orientations:

1. Underlying-problem approaches are discussed in terms of their focus on
   • perception
   • motor functioning
   • language
   • general cognitive functioning
2. Observable-problem approaches are discussed in terms of their focus on
   • observable skills and objectives
   • direct instruction

Controversial Treatments and Fads (p. 309) notes that some interventions specifically developed with Type III problems (learning disabilities) in mind are controversial. The discussion briefly reviews controversies about:

• optometric vision training
• Irlen's colored lenses
• stimulant medication (such as Ritalin)
• special diet
• megavitamin therapy
• CNS training
• vestibular treatment

Managing and Preventing School Misbehavior (p. 422) discusses intervention for school misbehavior in terms of three phases:

• efforts to prevent and anticipate
• actions to be taken during misbehavior
• steps to be taken afterward

A Brief Bibliography on Remedial Methods

Summaries of Remedial Methods

Hammill, D. D. & Bartel, N. R. (1990). *Teaching students with learning and behavior problems* (5th ed.). Boston: Allyn & Bacon.

Kirk, S. A. & Chalfant, J. C. (1984). *Academic and developmental learning disabilities.* Denver: Love Publishing.

Lerner, J. W. (1988). *Learning disabilities: Theories, diagnosis, and teaching strategies* (5th ed.). Boston: Houghton Mifflin.

Mercer, C. D. & Mercer, A. R. (1987). *Teaching students with learning problems.* Columbus, OH: Merrill.

Smith, C. R. (1991). *Learning disabilities: The interaction of learner, task, and setting* (2nd ed.). Boston: Allyn & Bacon.

Wallace, G. & Kauffman, J. M. (1986). *Teaching children with learning and behavior problems.* Columbus, OH: Merrill.

For more detailed presentations of practices related to improving functioning in specific areas, see the following.

On Perceptual-Motor Development

Cratty, B. (1986). *Perceptual and motor development in infants and children* (3rd ed.). Englewood Cliffs, NJ: Prentice-Hall.

On Language and Psycholinguistics

Aukerman, R. C. (1984). *Approaches to beginning reading.* New York: Wiley.

Bangs, T. E. (1982). *Language and learning disorders of the preacademic child (with curriculum guide).* Englewood Cliffs, NJ: Prentice-Hall.

Bartoli, J. S. & Botel, M. (1988). *Reading/learning disability: An ecological approach.* New York: Teachers College Press.

Berry, M. (1980). *Teaching linguistically handicapped children.* Englewood Cliffs, NJ: Prentice-Hall.

Burns, P. C. (1980). *Assessment and correction of language arts difficulties.* Columbus, OH: Merrill.

Cazden, C. B. (1988). *Classroom discourse.* Portsmouth, NH: Heinemann.

Fernald, G. M. (1943). *Remedial techniques in basic school subjects.* New York: McGraw-Hill. Reissued in 1988 by PRO-ED.

Harris, A. J. & Sipay, E. R. (1990). *How to increase reading ability: A guide to developmental and remedial methods* (9th ed.). New York: Longman.

Heath, S. B. (1983). *Ways with words.* New York: Cambridge University Press.

Mann, V. & Ditunno, P. (1990). Phonological deficiencies: Effective predictors and further reading problems. In G. Pavlides (Ed.), *Perspectives on dyslexia: Cognitive language and treatment* (Vol. 2). New York: Wiley.

Soifer, R., Irwin, M. E., Crumrine, B. M., Honzaki, E., Simmons, B. K. & Young, D. L. (1990). *The complete theory-to-practice handbook of adult literacy: Curriculum design and teaching approaches.* New York: Teachers College Press.

Stauffer, R. G. (1980). *The language experience approach to the teaching of reading* (2nd ed.). New York: Harper & Row.

Wiig, E. H. & Semel, E. M. (1984). *Language assessment and intervention for the learning disabled* (2nd ed.). Columbus, OH: Merrill.

Zinsser, W. (1988). *Writing to learn.* New York: Harper & Row.

On Math

Baroody, A. J. (1989). *A guide to teaching mathematics in the primary grades.* Boston: Allyn & Bacon.

Bley, N. S. & Thornton, C. A. (1989). *Teaching mathematics to the learning disabled* (2nd ed.). Austin, TX: PRO-ED.

Cawley, J. F. (Ed.). (1985). *Practical mathematics: Appraisal of the learning disabled.* Rockville, MD: Aspen.

Connolly, A. J. (1988). *Key math — Revised.* Circle Pines, MN: American Guidance Service.

Ginsburg, H. P. (1989). *Children's arithmetic: How they learn it and how you teach it* (2nd ed.). Austin, TX: PRO-ED.

Reisman, F. K. & Kaufman, S. H. (1980). *Teaching mathematics to children with special needs.* Columbus, OH: Merrill.

On Cognitive Prerequisites, Learning Strategies, and Higher Order Thinking

Baron, J. & Brown, R. V. (Eds.) (1991). *Teaching decision making to adolescents.* Hillsdale, NJ: Erlbaum.

Carnine, D. (1991). Curricular interventions for teaching higher order thinking to all students: Introduction to the special series. *Journal of Learning Disabilities, 24,* 261–269.

Ceci, S. J. (Ed.) (1986). *Handbook of cognitive, social, and neuro-psychological aspects of learning disabilities.* Hillsdale, NJ: Erlbaum.

Day, B. D. (1988). *Early childhood education: Creative learning activities* (3rd ed.). New York: Macmillan.

Deshler, D. D. & Schumaker, J. B. (1986). Learning strategies: An instructional alternative for low-achieving adolescents. *Exceptional Children, 52,* 583–590.

Engelmann, S., Davis, K. & Davis, G. (1986). *Your world of facts I: A memory development program.* Tigard, OR: CC Publications.

Gelzheiser, L. M., Solar, R. A., Shepherd, M. J. & Wozniak, R. H. (1983). Teaching learning disabled children to memorize: A rationale for plans and practice. *Journal of Learning Disabilities, 16,* 421–425.

Glover, J., Ronning, R. & Bruning, R. (1990). *Cognitive psychology for teachers.* New York: Macmillan.

Harris, T. L. & Cooper, E. J. (Eds.) (1985). *Reading, thinking, and concept development.* New York: College Board.

Mastropieri, M. A., Scruggs, T. E. & Levin, J. R. (1985). Mnemonic strategy instruction with learning disabled adolescents. *Journal of Learning Disabilities, 18,* 94–100.

Montessori, M. (1964). *The Montessori method.* New York: Schocken Books.

Trapani, C. (1990). *Transition goals for adolescents with learning disabilities.* Boston: College-Hill Press.

On Social and Emotional Functioning, Motivation, and Interfering Behavior

Canfield, J. & Wells, H. (1976). *100 ways to enhance self-concept in the classroom.* Englewood Cliffs, NJ: Prentice-Hall.

Cartledge, G. & Milburn, J. F. (Eds.) (1986). *Teaching social skills to children: Innovative approaches* (2nd ed.). New York: Pergamon.

Dangel, R. F. & Polster, R. A. (1988). *Teaching child management skills.* New York: Pergamon.

Deci, E. L. & Ryan, R. M. (1985). *Intrinsic motivation and self-determination in human behavior.* New York: Plenum.

Dinkmeyer, D. & Dinkmeyer, D., Jr. (1982). *Developing understanding of self and others — revised* (DUSO). Circle Pines, MN: American Guidance Service.

Elardo, P. & Cooper, M. (1977). *Aware: Activities for social development.* Menlo Park, CA: Addison-Wesley.

Johnson, D. W., Johnson, R. T., Holubec, E. J. & Roy, P. (1984). *Circles of learning: Cooperation in the classroom.* Alexandria, VA: Association for Supervision and Curriculum Development.

Mcintosh, R., Vaughn, S. & Zaragoza, N. (1991). A review of social interventions for students with learning disabilities. *Journal of Learning Disabilities, 24,* 451–458.

Purkey, W. & Novak, J. *Inviting success: A self-concept approach to teaching and learning.* Belmont, CA: Wadsworth.

Slavin, R. E. (1990). *Cooperative learning: Theory, research, and practice.* Englewood Cliffs, NJ: Prentice-Hall.

Stipek, D. J. (1988). *Motivation to learn: From theory to practice.* Englewood Cliffs, NJ: Prentice-Hall.

Wlodkowski, R. J. & Jaynes, J. H. (1990). *Eager to learn: Helping children become motivated and love learning.* San Francisco: Jossey-Bass.

CHAPTER 12

Evaluating Effectiveness

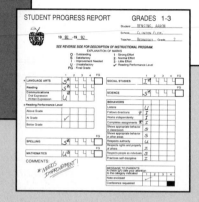

What Is the Program Trying to Accomplish?

Whose Rationale? Whose Judgment?

Program Purposes and Evaluation

Breadth of Program Focus and Evaluation

Measuring What's Happening

What Is Done Currently?

What Is Evaluation?

Steps in Evaluation Planning

Summing Up

TEACHER: *Yes, Matt, what is it?*
MATT: *I don't want to scare you, but my Dad says if I don't get better grades someone is due for a spanking.*

Accountability! It's becoming an increasingly familiar topic. More than that, it's an increasingly common demand. Everybody agrees that professionals should be accountable, but there are major disagreements about what it means. Unfortunately, in fields such as education, psychology, and medicine, evaluation is not a simple matter. Accountability for professionals working with learning problems means that they must show that their work is effective. But effective in what way? To what degree? At what cost?

It is not uncommon to hear professionals say, "If it works, use it!" This statement suggests that, in choosing their practices, they use effectiveness as a yardstick. Unfortunately, there is rarely adequate evidence about what really works. It is one thing to want and need accountability; it is quite another to work out a satisfactory way to decide whether a program is any good. Accountability is as easy to demand as evaluation is difficult and costly to carry out.

As we explore the approaches to evaluation and concerns about it, some will be familiar to you because we have already discussed them in relation to other assessment practices. Many evaluation concerns are basic to any assessment effort. Remember: Evaluation is one of the major purposes for which assessment is used (review Figure 3-3, p. 51).

What Is the Program Trying to Accomplish?

A program may be evaluated simply in terms of whether it accomplishes its intended outcomes. People, however, also tend to evaluate a program in terms of whether they agree with what it is trying to do.

What a program intends to do is reflected in its rationale. Programs with different rationales may look alike in some ways, but they will certainly differ in important ways. Thus evaluations of a program usually reflect judgments about the appropriateness of its rationale—particularly about the major ways in which its rationale makes it different from other programs. All psychoeducational programs are designed with the hope that the individuals served will be able to cope effectively with day-to-day demands; they intend to do something positive and to minimize negative side effects.

Some programs, however, focus on a narrow range of basic academic skills; others stress a broad range of goals related to motivation and development. When you don't agree with a program's rationale, you will not likely approve of the program—even if evaluation data indicate it is effective.

Whose Rationale? Whose Judgment?

Everyone may agree that the following statements are true:

- People need to learn to read, write, and do basic mathematical computations.
- Remedial procedures should be used to help individuals overcome learning and behavior problems.
- A remedial program should improve a person's skills, so that the individual can function as effectively as those without learning problems.

As program details are worked out, however, it often becomes clear that different individuals and groups have very different ideas about what they want accomplished and how they want it done.

Whose Interests Are Being Served? (p. 395) discusses the problem of conflicting interests and presents helping and socialization interventions.

Reading programs, for instance, obviously teach reading. However, daily objectives and procedures can differ tremendously. One program may be designed by the program staff primarily to teach a set of basic reading skills; little time may be spent on activities for increasing enjoyment and valuing of reading. Thus specific skills are taught, and evaluation focuses on whether they are learned. Little attention is paid to whether students' enjoyment and pursuit of reading outside of school increases or decreases.

Another program may be concerned both with skills and with enjoyment of reading. Thus both skills and attitudes are evaluated.

There are a variety of persons and agencies with different vested interests who make decisions about programs (see Feature 12-1). Whether they are sophisticated, directly involved, or have any control over the situation, each interested party is likely to have beliefs and values about what a program should be doing and how to evaluate and judge its worth. The more diverse the perspectives of the interested parties, the more the likelihood of conflict (Strupp & Hadley, 1977).

Feature 12-1   Parties Who Directly or Indirectly Shape a Program's Rationale and Evaluation

I. Directly involved interested parties

A. *Subscribers* — private individuals and representatives of organized bodies who are seeking intervention for themselves, others, or both

B. *Objects to be changed* — individuals and those in settings who seek change or are referred by others

C. *Interveners* — those who, in addition to whatever self-interests are involved, may base their activity on the stated desires or interpreted needs of subscribers, the objects of change, or both

II. Indirectly involved interested parties (those whose influence has the potential to produce a major impact on the intervention)

A. *Immediate or primary environmental influences* — family, friends, employers, teachers, coworkers, local representatives of funding sources

B. *Secondary and tertiary environmental influences* — governmental agents related to health, education, welfare, and law enforcement; professional and lay organizations; theorists, researchers, and instructors; that is, those who lobby for, underwrite, study, evaluate, and teach about intervention.

Figure 12-1   Helping and Socialization

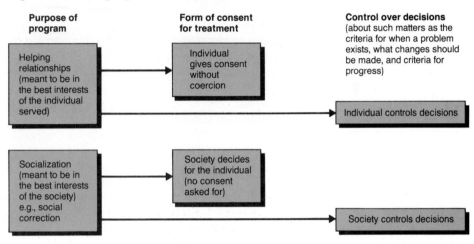

Conflict among interested parties always highlights issues of the appropriateness of the program's goals and of the criteria used in judging its effectiveness. Moreover, conflict always underscores the concern over whose perspective should prevail and the need for processes to decide the matter. When there are no established procedures for determining whose perspective should prevail, program planning is usually shaped by the beliefs and values of those with greatest authority in the situation.

Program Purposes and Evaluation

One basic conflict that often arises concerns the question of whether a program's rationale and evaluation should primarily reflect the interests of the individual enrolled in the program or the interests of society. For example, a very important concern in programs for problem populations is the degree to which a program is intended to *help* individuals or to *socialize* them. When the intent is socialization, programs are designed to accomplish society's aims and are evaluated from the perspective of society's standards. Helping programs are designed to meet the individual "client's" needs and are evaluated in terms of the standards of the client or the client's advocates (see Figure 12-1).

Programs for individuals with problems are established to meet varying and, at times, conflicting needs and ends. Differences in objectives particularly arise when programs are designed to meet the interests of society rather than the interests of the "client." Society's interests, of course, are the primary consideration in school programs that enroll students with learning and behavior problems. That is, school systems are established by society as socializing agencies, with helping services added when feasible.

Parents of students experiencing problems generally want a greater emphasis on helping, but usually also value the school's socializing functions—especially when their youngster's problems include bad behavior. In contrast, students do not often like the socializing facets of schooling and usually don't see school programs as designed to be helpful.

Ironically, many students diagnosed as having learning disabilities are individuals who have not responded to the socialization efforts of public schools and have been singled out for remediation because of it. Moreover, many students' learning problems go uncorrected because so much teacher effort is devoted to procedures designed only to establish social control. All of this should not be surprising. Students with learning problems are often hard to control. And, even though individuals with learning problems need help, schools are not established to create helping relationships.

Nevertheless, the needs of such individuals lead many parents and students to believe that their school programs should become more help-oriented. This view often brings them into conflict with those whose responsibility it is to maintain the school's socialization agenda. When there is conflict, a great deal of valuable time and energy can be wasted as parents, students, teachers, and administrators engage in a struggle over whose rationale, interests, and criteria are to prevail. (Factors differentiating helping relationships from socialization are highlighted in Figure 12-1.)

The key to differentiating between helping relationships and socialization depends on whose interests are being served. Helping relationships are defined as serving the individual's interests; socialization serves the interests of society. Sometimes there is no conflict of interests; often there is. When there is, the conflicting parties may hold very different views about the appropriate aims of a program and the criteria and standards that should be used in identifying problems, prescribing what should be done, and judging effectiveness.

Another basic conflict arises between proponents of underlying- and observable-problem orientations. You will recall that, although each orientation intends to remedy an individual's learning problems, they set about doing so in very different ways and with very different initial objectives and timetables.

From a motivational perspective, conflicts also arise when programs stress only developmental problems and ignore motivation and attitudes. Similarly, from a transactional perspective, conflicts arise when programs ignore the need for environmental changes and focus only on changing individuals—especially when major problems in the school and home environments have been identified.

Obviously, the program's purposes may be judged as inappropriate prior to any measure or judgment of program effectiveness. Moreover, data on effectiveness may be gathered in terms of the program's intentions or in terms of anything else the evaluator thinks is important.

Breadth of Program Focus and Evaluation

As the discussion to this point indicates, evaluation should be used to determine (1) if one agrees with what the program is trying to accomplish, and (2) how well the program is achieving the full range of outcomes desired. The less a program is trying to achieve, the easier it is to determine these matters. It is so hard to evaluate most school programs because they are trying to accomplish many different things. Not coincidentally, however, the longer that a program is the focus of formal evaluation, the less it may try to accomplish. At least this appears to be one of the negative effects of the big push toward behavioral and criterion-referenced objectives as ways to improve accountability.

Behaviorist-oriented instructional objectives and other naive accountability trends often put the cart before the horse. That is, the emphasis on evaluation is so strong that the primary focus of instruction shifts from the program's rationale (for example, long-range aims) to a limited set of objectives that can be measured immediately. As greater attention is paid to what can be measured, the breadth of instructional focus is often reduced (see Feature 12-2).

Thus, if one is not careful, the desire for data on effectiveness can result in programs being redesigned to pursue only that which can currently be measured.

Feature 12-2   *Specifying Remedial Outcomes for Evaluation*

Because of increasing demands for accountability, the primary focus in preparing IEPs for students with learning problems tends to be on remedial outcomes. Furthermore, the prevailing emphasis is on specifying them in terms of behavioral and criterion-referenced objectives.

These trends no doubt are a major aid in efforts to evaluate whether remedial outcomes are accomplished. However, the tendency to limit the focus to remediation ignores the school's responsibility to facilitate ongoing development and to provide enrichment opportunities. An overemphasis on remediation also can be counterproductive to overcoming problems if the program involves little more than a set of laborious and deadening experiences.

In general, the danger is that important intervention aims and goals will be lost in the emphasis on designing *all* program plans to meet highly concrete and easily measurable objectives. Not all of the complex long-range aims a program must pursue can be stated as immediate behavioral objectives; nor should they be. Attitudes, motivation, and creative functioning in the arts and sciences, for example, do not lend themselves to discussion as simple behaviors.

For the most part, only a relatively limited set of skills can be specified in highly concrete, behavioral terms, and even in these instances it may not be desirable to do so for instructional purposes. Besides the fact that specifying everything in this way would result in far too many objectives to teach, the trend also contributes to an overemphasis on teaching at the expense of learning.

A teacher's job is to facilitate a student's efforts to learn—not to establish a program in which everything to be learned must be taught. The point of evaluation is to sample the broad range of what has been learned—not to measure a limited range of skills that have been taught. Although it is worth making the job of evaluation as easy as possible, this should not be done in ways that limit the learning opportunities of individuals who are evaluated.

Finally, specifying and evaluating remedial outcomes keeps the focus on individuals and the changes they are to make. This contributes to the tendency to ignore environmental and program changes. Obviously, at times the environment, or specific interactions between individuals and the environment, are the appropriate objects of change. It seems unfortunate that current approaches to evaluation have become another force colluding with narrow models of the causes and correction of learning and behavior problems.

This is a negative form of teaching to the test, because in the process many important things may be ignored simply because they will not be evaluated.

Comprehensive evaluation should stress the full scope of desired aims. That is, even if certain processes and outcomes are not easily measured, they still need to be evaluated as well as possible, and they need to be kept in the forefront in discussions about a program's worth. (For example, is the program leading to greater interest, desire, and participation in learning on the part of students?) Evaluations of a program must first address the question: Is what the program is trying to accomplish appropriate? The frame of reference for such evaluations may be the program's rationale or what others think the program should be doing. Generally, this means clarifying such matters as: Who or what is to be the focal point of intervention—a person, the environment, or both? and What changes are desired?

After judging the appropriateness of what is expected, the program's intended breadth of focus should guide efforts to evaluate effectiveness. However, at this time not everything can be measured in a technically sophisticated way. This means that some things will be poorly measured, or simply reviewed informally. Obviously this is less than satisfactory. Still, it is better to focus on the entire gamut of program aims than to adopt evaluation approaches that inappropriately reduce the focus of instruction and evaluation.

With this as background, we now turn to the topic of measuring what's happening.

Measuring What's Happening

One of the reasons that conflicting remedial orientations exist is the difficulty of validly measuring what works and what doesn't. A considerable amount of research has been reported. However, measurement and other research methodology problems have made it impossible to prove the worth of the programs studied (Tindal, 1985; Kavale & Forness, 1985).

In recent years, the increasing demand for accountability, especially from funding agencies, has led to mandated program evaluations. It is easy to mandate such accountability. Unfortunately, such mandates ignore the fact that current evaluation practices are terribly inadequate. Thus, while mandated evaluation goes on continually, comprehensive and valid evaluations are rare.

What Is Done Currently?

Most commonly, programs are evaluated using paper-and-pencil tests of ability and performance, self-reports and interviews, and systematic observations of behavior. (Examples are cited in *Procedures and Instruments for Assessing Learning Problems,* p. 341.) Besides test scores, professionals rely heavily on grades and ratings. Unfortunately, many of the measurement instruments used are not highly reliable or valid. Accountability pressures have led to an overemphasis on measuring immediate, behavioral outcomes, and many important facets of a program are not easily measured (self-concept, attitudes toward learning, problem-solving capabilities, creativity).

Usually, decisions as to what and how to evaluate are made by those administering or funding the program. Currently, there is little student or parent involvement in such decisions, and not surprisingly, there is little emphasis on consumer judgments of a program's value. The small amount of long-term follow-up research and the problems with the research that has been done simply reflect the extreme cost and difficulty of doing such studies (Haring, Lovett, & Smith, 1990; Horn, O'Donnell, & Vitulano, 1983). As a result, most evaluations reported in the literature

Feature 12-3   *How Effective Is Remediation? How Effective Is Evaluation?*

After reviewing a set of long-term studies, Spreen (1982) concluded that

> most children who are referred for a learning or reading disability do not catch up. In fact, their disability is likely to become worse with time. In addition, remedial instruction has not been shown to improve the prognosis for these children (p. 483).

Similarly, citing the results of a recent longitudinal study (Rissman, Curtiss, & Tallal, 1990; Tallal, 1988, 1990), Bashir and Scavuzzo (1992) state, "there is little evidence of 'catch-up' of academic abilities" (p. 57).

Horn, O'Donnell, and Vitulano (1983) reviewed 24 of the long-term outcome studies on learning disabilities. The studies go back to 1960. The reviewers found that neither the outcome data nor the procedures used to gather the data were particularly good. Therefore they caution against interpreting the body of findings as indicating that remediation is ineffective. They conclude that until better evaluations are conducted such a pessimistic conclusion would be unfortunate and premature.

To support conclusions about the poor quality of evaluation practices, Horn and his colleagues cite major methodological problems related to samples and the lack of appropriate control and comparison groups. They also note that decisions to measure different outcomes often lead to very different conclusions about effectiveness.

In connection with samples, for instance, they note a lack of precise descriptions of populations studied and procedures used to select samples.

In addition, they found it was common to compare quite dissimilar samples (in terms of problem severity and demographics such as age and socioeconomic status). Moreover, they found that emphasis on total group functioning tended to mask possible gains by subgroups.

The reviewers also point out that one of the most important decisions in evaluative research involves choosing which outcomes to measure. They identify three major classes of outcomes used to measure effectiveness in the studies they reviewed: (1) measures of educational/vocational attainment, such as grades, years of schooling, occupation; (2) tests of basic skill areas, such as achievement or perceptual functioning; and (3) indices of behavior/emotional functioning, such as parent reports of problems or symptoms. Based on their analyses, they emphasize that these different outcome measures produce different findings and thus result in differing conclusions about program effectiveness.

Horn and his colleagues conclude that

> while it does appear that LD persons have enduring deficits in basic skills areas, their relatively good educational/vocational outcome indicates that many persons are able to compensate for their continued deficits. . . . The challenge for future research is to identify the kinds of compensatory strategies that contribute the most to helping which particular subgroups of LD persons achieve satisfactory educational and vocational goals while minimizing emotional and behavioral difficulties. (p. 554)

have been narrowly focused. Because of this, there is continuing criticism of current evaluation purposes and practices and complaints that practices are judged unfairly (see Feature 12-3).

Clearly, it is not possible to be sure about the long-term effectiveness of current interventions. If any conclusion is to be drawn, it cannot be overly optimis-

Feature 12-4   A Framework for Evaluation

A framework formulated by Robert Stake (1967) provides a useful example of the models used by evaluators. Stake's framework offers a graphic and comprehensive picture of various facets of evaluation and how they relate to each other (see accompanying figure).

In brief, Stake emphasizes that "the two basic acts of evaluation" are description and judgment. Descriptions take the form of data gathered by formal or informal means. Judgments take the form of interpretive conclusions about the meaning of the data, such as whether a procedure is good or bad, a student is above or below norm, a behavior is pathological or not. In practice, judgments are used for purposes of decision making. When it comes to deciding specifically what to describe and judge, evaluators often are guided by their understanding of the decisions to be made at the conclusion of the evaluation.

Stake stresses that proper program evaluation requires data and criteria for analyzing the degree to which

- conditions anticipated prior to the program (antecedents), planned procedures (transactions), and intended outcomes are consistent with the program rationale and are logical in relation to each other; and
- intended antecedents, transactions, and outcomes actually occur.

An example may help further clarify Stake's framework for evaluation. Let's use Mara's reading program to illustrate each cell of the matrix shown here.

Rationale
Her teacher has decided that, because Mara's auditory functioning seems stronger than her vi-

sual abilities, he will teach her phonics as a way to improve her reading.

Intents
Antecedents: The teacher knows that Mara has the ability to learn phonics and that he taught her vowel sounds on Monday.

Transactions: He plans to teach her initial consonant sounds on Wednesday.

Outcomes: He decided she should be able to reproduce vowel and initial consonant sounds during a review test on Friday.

Observations
Antecedents: The teacher notes Mara did not put much effort into learning the vowel sounds on Monday.

Transactions: Because of a field trip on Thursday, there was not enough time for her to practice the sounds she had learned on Monday and Wednesday.

Outcomes: On Friday's review, Mara was unable to reproduce half of the sounds she had been taught.

Standards
Antecedents: The teacher expects Mara to be motivated enough to put in the effort to learn whatever he teaches as long as the material is not too difficult.

Transactions: He considers the procedures used to teach the material to be extremely good ones, and he has found them effective for about 90 percent of the students in the class.

Outcomes: On Friday's review, other students in the class reproduce 95 percent of the sounds correctly.

tic. In general we suspect that, where a particular approach is found reasonably effective, it is because the majority of individuals in the program have Type I or Type II learning problems (that is, do not have true learning disabilities). It is important to remember that significant numbers of people are misdiagnosed as having learning disabilities. Because this is so, it is easy to fall into the trap of

Judgments

Antecedents: Looking back to Monday, the teacher judges his work with Mara as having been unrealistic. He now thinks that, if she was not motivated to work, she was not really learning what he was teaching.

Transactions: Besides not particularly wanting to do the lesson on Monday, Mara tells him that she did not understand the lessons on either day.

Outcomes: Mara's inability to reproduce half the sounds was judged unsatisfactory and was seen as the result of unrealistic teaching practices.

In general, the types of data Stake's framework indicates should be gathered can provide a wealth of information for use in describing and judging programs and making decisions about ways to improve them.

Layout of Statements and Data to Be Collected by the Evaluator of an Educational Program

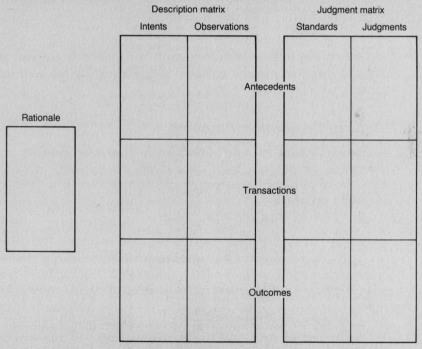

SOURCE   Adapted from "The countenance of educational evaluation," by Robert Stake, *Teachers College Record*, Vol. 68, No. 7 (April, 1967), pp. 523-540, Figure 1. Reprinted with permission.

thinking that positive program findings are evidence that the intervention is effective for learning disabilities; in fact, the program may only be successful with those who have been misdiagnosed! Furthermore, it is easy to make the mistake of thinking that a successful outcome is due to a specific intervention. It may be that a variety of other interventions designed to produce the same outcome would have been just as effective.

What Is Evaluation?

Essentially, evaluation involves determining the worth or value of something (Stake, 1967, 1976). For purposes of this discussion, *evaluation* is defined as a systematic process designed to describe and judge the overall impact and value of an intervention for purposes of making decisions and advancing knowledge.

Specifically, the goals and objectives of evaluation include the following:

Evaluation practiced at the highest level of the state-of-the-art is one means of speeding up the processes that contribute to human and social progress.
Rossi, Freeman, & Wright, 1979

- to describe and judge an intervention's (1) rationale, including assumptions and intentions, and (2) standards for making judgments
- to describe and judge an intervention's (1) actual activity, including intended and unintended procedures and outcomes, and (2) costs (financial, negative effects)
- to make decisions about continuing, modifying, or stopping an intervention for an individual or for all those enrolled in a program
- to advance knowledge about interventions to improve (1) practices, (2) training, and (3) theory

The information needed to meet these purposes comes from comprehensive evaluations that include both immediate and long-term program data. The full range of data that may be gathered is suggested by the particular evaluation framework adopted (see Feature 12-4).

Steps in Evaluation Planning

Awareness of steps involved in planning an evaluation provides another way to understand the process. Such steps reflect the necessity of making decisions about the focus of the evaluation, its specific objectives, and appropriate methodology and measures.

One formulation of key steps follows.

1. *Clarification of the intended use to be made of the information.* Most important at this step is awareness of who wants the information and why they need it (what types of decisions they need to make). Also, it is important to anticipate the reactive impact—politically and motivationally—of evaluation processes and findings.

2. *Understanding of the program's rationale.* Often the program's rationale is clarified as part of step 1 because evaluation data generally are used to make judgments related to the program's rationale. This may not be the case, however, when the evaluation is designed to judge the program with reference to some standard set of basic objectives. This occurs, for example, when the same stan-

I CAN HARDLY READ YOUR HANDWRITING. YOU MUST LEARN TO WRITE MORE CLEARLY.

AW, WHAT'S THE USE! IF I WRITE ANY CLEARER, YOU'LL COMPLAIN ABOUT MY SPELLING.

dardized test of reading is administered in all schools. Of course, even in such cases, it may be desirable to evaluate whether a program is accomplishing the other things that it has set out to do.

3. *Formulation of evaluation questions.* The matters to be evaluated are translated into a set of major questions. For example: How effective is procedure A, versus B, for students with severe learning problems? Are students more motivated to learn in special or in regular classes? Because all programs are likely to have some negative effects, one standard question always is: What negative impact does the program produce?

Few, if any, major interventions can claim to have no negative features. A contemporary example is the increasing recognition of the potential negative consequences, both physical and psychological, of treating "hyperactivity" with stimulant drugs. Another example is the increasing levels of dependency on teachers that is a byproduct of many remedial approaches.

Even when negative consequences are known, often little attention is paid to them; of course, many are undoubtedly unknown because so little effort has been made to detect them. Obviously there is little justification for ignoring negative effects, and indeed to do so is unethical. Consequently, evaluation efforts must include a direct focus on all major negative consequences that can be anticipated; evaluative research must also be directed at finding unexpected negative outcomes.

4. *Specification of data to be gathered.* For each major question, it is necessary to specify relevant descriptive data to be gathered (intended and unintended antecedents, transactions, and outcomes). At this point, specific instructional objectives are noted, along with the other matters about which data are to be gathered. The more things that are of interest, the more we have to settle for

samples of information. Often it is not feasible to gather all the data desired (because of time, money, personnel).

5. *Specification of procedures.* Further problems in gathering desired data arise as one attempts to specify procedures. Sometimes there is a good test or other measuring instrument; sometimes only weak procedures are available; sometimes there is no currently feasible way to get the information. Thus decisions about the data to be gathered are shaped first by what one wants to know and then by practical considerations. As indicated in Chapter 4, the limitations associated with procedures for directly assessing complex performance have resulted in a trend toward "authentic" assessment (analyses of essays, open-ended responses, responses to computer simulations, interview data, student journals and portfolios).

6. *Specification of a design.* An evaluation design is used so that data can be gathered and interpreted appropriately. When someone asks how good a program is, the judgment made is based on the available data and related to some standard of comparison. A sound design ensures that appropriate data are gathered on the program under evaluation and that there is also a set of data for use as standards in judging the findings.

7. *Designation of time and place for data collection.* These matters are determined in part by the design, and in part by practical factors such as resource availability.

Feature 12-5
The Power of Evaluation to Shape Schooling Inappropriately

Elementary school students almost invariably regard mathematics as the most important subject in the curriculum—not because of its elegance, but because math has the most homework, because the homework is corrected the most promptly, and because tests are given more frequently than in any other subject. The youngsters regard spelling as the next most important subject, because of the frequency of spelling tests. "To a pupil," Professor White explains, "the workload and evaluation demands obviously must reflect what the teacher thinks is important to learn." (Silberman, 1970, p. 147)

Similarly, with the increasing demands for accountability, teachers quickly learn what is to be tested and what is not, and gradually place greater emphasis on teaching what will be on the tests. Over time what is on the tests comes to be viewed as what is most important. Because only so much time is available to the teacher, other things are deemphasized, and often get dropped from the curriculum. If allowed to do so, accountability procedures have the power to reshape the entire curriculum.

What's wrong with that? Nothing—if what is being evaluated reflects everything we want students to learn in school. But this is not the case.

Current accountability pressures reflect values and biases that have led to evaluating a small range of basic skills, and doing so in a narrow way. For students diagnosed as LD, this means their school programs have been increasingly restricted to improving skills they lack. As a result, they are cut off from participating in learning activities that might increase their interest in overcoming their problems, and indeed might open up opportunities for them and enrich their future lives.

One major evaluation concern not reflected in these steps involves decisions about what role various interested parties should play. For example, as suggested in step 2, there may be different rationales about what should be evaluated. When this is the case, whose rationale should prevail? At almost every step, evaluators will be influenced by this decision.

Another evaluation concern not specifically addressed in the preceding steps involves decisions about ethical matters associated with evaluation. Many of the ethical concerns are similar to those that arise in assessment and treatment. At each step, evaluators must be concerned with how to minimize possible bias, conflicts of interest, and negative consequences that can arise from evaluation itself (see Feature 12-5).

Summing Up

Evaluation is a key to the future.

Evaluation is a difficult process, which many would prefer to avoid; but it is a process that can improve programs, protect consumers, and advance knowledge.

In point of fact, everyone evaluates the programs with which they come in contact. Teachers judge whether their own and others' programs are going well. Students are quick to formulate likes or dislikes of teachers and school programs. Administrators will tell you which programs they think are working and which aren't.

Whenever anyone decides that a program is or isn't a good one, an evaluation is being made. Many times such evaluations simply reflect an individual's or group's informal observations. At other times, however, the judgments reflect careful data gathering and analyses and the use of an appropriate set of standards. Sometimes the judgments reflect differences in opinion about what a program should be doing; sometimes the judgments are about the degree to which the program is being effective.

Systematic efforts to evaluate programs involve decisions about

- the focus of evaluation (person or environment, immediate objectives versus long-range aims)
- whose perspective is to determine the evaluation focus, methods, and standards to be used (the views of teachers, parents, students, or funding agencies)
- the best way to proceed in gathering and interpreting data (specific measures, design)

In making such decisions, concerns arise because

- what can be evaluated currently is far less than what a program may intend to accomplish
- inappropriate bias and vested interests can shape what is evaluated, thereby influencing whether a program is seen as good or bad
- evaluation processes can produce a variety of negative effects (over time what is

evaluated can reduce and reshape a program's intended aims; evaluation can lead to invasion of privacy, undermine the ability of students and professionals to self-evaluate, and so forth)

Unfortunately, many professionals caught up in the day-by-day pressure of providing programs for individuals with problems feel that evaluation is just one more unnecessary chore. It just takes time away from carrying out the program. Indeed, programs often get into trouble because everyone is so busy "doing" that there is no time to evaluate whether there might be a better way. One is reminded of *Winnie-the-Pooh:*

> Here is Edward Bear, coming downstairs now, bump, bump, bump, on the back of his head behind Christopher Robin. It is, as far as he knows, the only way of coming downstairs, but sometimes he feels that there really is another way, if only he could stop bumping for a moment and think of it (A. A. Milne, 1926, p. 1).*

There is an obvious need for professionals to improve their practices and to be accountable. There is an equally obvious need to improve current evaluation practices. Because evaluations can as easily reshape programs in negative as well as positive directions, it is essential that such practices be improved and that accountability pressures not be allowed to narrow a program's focus. This is especially important for special education programs in which there is already the tendency to limit evaluation to specific remedial objectives.

Finding out if a program is any good is a necessity. But in doing so, it is wise to recognize that evaluation is not simply a technical process. Evaluation involves decisions about what and how to measure, and these decisions are based in great part on values and beliefs. As a result, limited knowledge, bias, vested interests, and ethical issues are constantly influencing the descriptive and judgmental processes and shaping the decisions made at the end of the evaluation.

Ultimately, the decisions made affect not only individuals with learning problems but also the entire society.

---

*From *Winnie-the-Pooh*, by A. A. Milne. Copyright 1926 by E. P. Dutton, renewed 1954 by A. A. Milne. Used by permission of Dutton Children's Books, a division of Penguin Books USA, Inc.

1. Write down what you think are the most important things that should be taking place to facilitate learning in a classroom. (In a sense, you will be stating your rationale for what makes a program good.)
2. Observe a classroom for an hour.
3. Write down your observations as follows:
   a. Divide your paper into two columns—label the left-hand column "Descriptions" and the right-hand column "Judgments."
   b. Write down your descriptions in the left-hand column before making any judgments. (This may be a bit harder than you imagine at first. As you write out the descriptions of what you saw, keep asking yourself: Have I excluded all judgments?)
   c. Write your judgments in the right-hand column. (You will be making good–bad statements; be certain you think in terms of degree—how "good" or "bad.")
4. Look over your judgments and think about why you decided what you did. This will help you get in touch with the standards you are using and the factors that led you to adopt these particular standards. You might give particular thought to the following:
   a. Are the standards you are using appropriate to every classroom situation?
   b. Are they more appropriate for classrooms serving students who don't have learning problems than they are for students who do have problems?
   c. Do your standards reflect what you found was effective in your own schooling?
   d. Do you think you tend to assume that what worked for you—or what you now believe would have been a better approach for you—should be used with everybody else?
   e. If so, how might such an assumption be a problem?

Whose Interests Are Being Served? (p. 395) explores the problem of conflicting interests. The focus is on

- helping
- socialization
- coercive interventions

PART 4

Getting Out of the Box

classic puzzle involves the following nine dots:

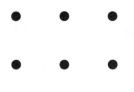

Can you connect all nine dots with four straight lines without removing your pencil from the page or retracing any line? Most people do not solve this puzzle. We hope you can, but in case you have trouble, here is a hint. The solution requires being able to see beyond the dots—to get out of the nonexistent square box—and see the problem from a different perspective.

Got it now? (If not, see the answer at the end of Chapter 13, p. 283.)

In a sense, the problem of the nine dots is a metaphor for moving practice and research forward in ways that will improve things for those with learning problems. Prevailing trends have boxed in the way people think about such problems. The concept of learning disabilities has been applied so inappropriately that it has almost become synonymous with all learning problems. School programs for such problems are dominated by remedial approaches. Programs outside of schools are few and far between. Little attention has been paid to connecting existing programs with each other.

It is time to get out of the box!

In Chapter 13, we summarize some key perspectives covered in the preceding chapters and suggest some directions for moving forward. Chapter 14 encourages you to reflect on any new perspectives you may have acquired.

Moving Forward: A Sense of Direction

Differentiating Among Learning Problems

Keeping Learning Disabilities in Perspective

A Causal Continuum

Reconceiving and Expanding Intervention

Motivation as a Primary Concern

A Societal Approach

Integrating Programs in a Catchment Area

Accountability and Change

Accountability and Evaluative Research

The Problem of Change

Summing Up

If you don't care much about where you get to,
it doesn't matter which way you go.

From an intervention perspective, two overlapping matters can be seen as fundamental in improving efforts to prevent and correct learning problems:

- differentiating among the various types of problems
- reconceiving and expanding intervention approaches

When differentiating among problems, it is essential to keep the concept of
learning disabilities in perspective. A step in this direction can be accomplished by
thinking of learning problems along a causal continuum.

When modifying interventions, several trends seem worth pursuing. One is to
establish motivation as a primary concern. A second is to expand the range of
programs beyond teaching. A third is to develop ways to coordinate and integrate
the expanded range of programs within appropriate geographical catchment
areas. All this represents an ambitious agenda for moving forward.

Differentiating Among Learning Problems

By now the importance of differentiating among problems should be evident.
Unfortunately, there has been little conceptual and empirical work designed to
evolve a valid classification scheme for learning problems. Such a scheme is
needed, first to differentiate among major types of learning problems, and then to
conceive subtypes (such as learning disabilities) within each major category. In
the absence of a theory-based classification scheme, efforts to identify key diagnostic criteria, assessment procedures, and corrective strategies are often misdi-
rected.

It is clear, for example, that persons with learning problems differ not only in
terms of functioning but also in the causes of their problems. As a result, those
individuals found in one program or research sample often differ in important (but
unidentified) ways from those found in another—confounding efforts to compare
and generalize. The failure to account for these differences has been one of the
most significant factors undermining prevention, remediation, research, and training and the policy decisions shaping them. For example, because of differing
causes, it has been difficult to arrive at valid conclusions about unique intervention
needs, and to find what works for individuals with special problems (such as
learning disabilities). This lack of differentiation has also resulted in an overinterpretation of poor research, widespread misdiagnosis, and limited intervention
effectiveness.

Although reliable data do not exist, few would disagree that at least 30 percent
of the school population in the United States are experiencing significant learning
problems. As long as almost any individual with a "garden variety" learning
problem stands a good chance of being diagnosed as having LD, there will be a
tendency to treat most learning problems as if they had the same cause. Failure to

**Learning problems?
Certainly! Learn-
ing disabilities?
*What do you think?***

differentiate cause can result in the prescription of unneeded specialized treatments for those who do not have disabilities, and may lead to profound misunder-
standing of which interventions have promise for actual disabilities.

Moreover, failure to differentiate underachievement caused by neurological
dysfunction from that caused by other factors has been cited as a major deterrent
to important lines of research, and is certainly a threat to the very integrity of the LD
field. Because of the diagnostic problem, much research purporting to deal with
LD samples has more to say about learning problems in general than about
learning disabilities.

With learning problems so poorly differentiated and with prevalence and incidence estimates so questionable, it is not surprising that many individuals are
misdiagnosed as having learning disabilities. It also is not surprising that there has
been a significant backlash against the concept of learning disabilities, manifested
in specific criticism of current practices and policies. Indeed, lack of agreement
about definition and about who should be diagnosed as having LD has caused
some to question whether there is such a thing as a learning disability and whether
there is a need for the field of special education. The danger in these positions, of
course, is that researchers and practitioners may lose sight of learning problems
caused by minor CNS dysfunction and deemphasize the fact that regular educators are limited in what they can accomplish without specialized help.

Keeping Learning Disabilities in Perspective

As a way of reducing the confusion caused by varying definitions and criteria for
learning disabilities (LD), some have recommended that specific markers such as

demographic, personality, and programming variables be reported on every sample (Keogh, Major-Kingsley, et al., 1982). However, this recommendation, along with efforts to identify LD subtypes (Lyon & Flynn, 1991; McKinney, 1988; Rourke & Strang, 1983), overlooks the confusion caused by accepting current samples as if they had been diagnosed validly. By starting with a group already diagnosed as having learning disabilities, the researchers skip the more fundamental problem of differentiating LD from other types of learning problems. Such activity works against conceptual clarity and tends to collude with trends to treat all learning problems as if they were learning disabilities.

As we have discussed, the key to identifying learning problems caused by minor CNS dysfunctions (learning disabilities) involves assessing neurological dysfunction. Unfortunately, available methodology precludes doing this in a valid manner; that is, existing neurological and psychoneurological procedures lack validity for diagnosing LD. As a result, the majority of currently diagnosed individuals have been so labeled based mainly on assessment of relatively severe underachievement—the causes of which remain undetermined (Chalfant, 1985; Coles, 1987; Shaywitz, Escobar, et al., 1992). Obviously, then, just because someone has been assigned the LD label is not currently sufficient indication that the individual has an underlying dysfunction. Nevertheless, it remains scientifically valid to conceive of a subset of learning problems (albeit a small one) that are neurologically based.

A Causal Continuum

Clearly, a classification scheme that puts learning disabilities into proper relationship to other learning problems would help in many ways. Of course, no simple typology can do justice to the complexities involved in classifying learning problems for purposes of research, practice, and policymaking. However, as discussed in Part 1, even a simple conceptual classification framework based on a transactional view of causality can be a useful starting point.

For example, we have suggested a continuum of different types of learning problems based on a transactional view. As outlined in Chapter 2 (see Figure 2-1, p. 22), such a continuum ranges from problems caused by factors outside the individual (Type I problems) to those caused by factors within the individual (Type III problems), with problems stemming from a relatively equal contribution of both sources falling in the middle (Type II problems).

Subtypes can be formulated within groups at each end of the continuum. For example, subtypes for the Type III category might include not only learning disabilities, but learning problems arising mostly from other personal disorders, such as serious behavioral or emotional disabilities or developmental disruptions (see Figure 13-1). In formulating subtypes, basic dimensions such as problem severity, pervasiveness, and chronicity obviously also play an important role.

There are, of course, tremendous practical problems involved in making differential diagnoses along such a continuum. This fact does not preclude using the conceptual classification scheme as an aid to understanding (1) the variety of

Figure 13-1   Categorization of Psychoeducational Problems Based on a Transactional View of Cause

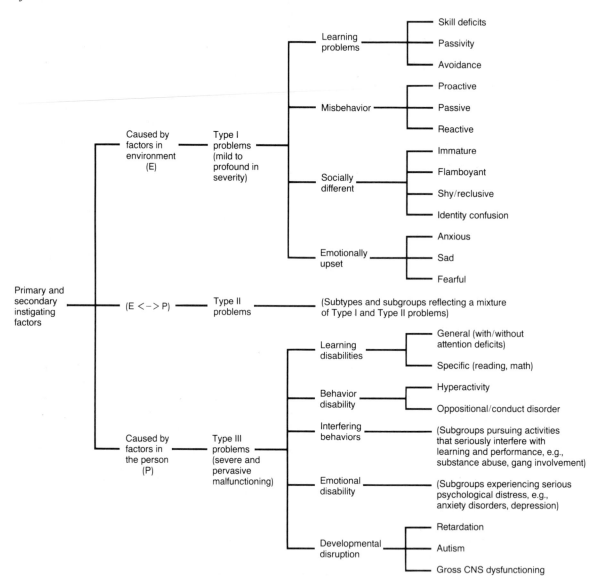

learning problems that confront practitioners and researchers, and (2) concerns that have arisen because of failure to operate within a broad framework.

Ultimately, differentiating among learning problems is essential to improving both research and practice. Practically and politically, the degree of indiscriminate diagnosis is an increasing source of embarrassment to those who focus on learning problems, and has inevitably produced backlash. More important, the failure to differentiate among learning problems means continued inappropriate use of the limited resources available for intervention and research.

Reconceiving and Expanding Intervention

Since the advent of the concept of learning disabilities, interventions for learning problems have primarily pursued a rather narrow special education orientation. As a result, they have relied exclusively on remedial practices designed mainly to address developmental concerns. Ironically, the weight of available evidence points to the limited efficacy of what has been tried in this regard (for example, Horn, O'Donnell, & Vitulano, 1983; Kavale & Forness, 1985; cf. Torgesen & Wong, 1986).

To move forward, practitioners and researchers must (1) broaden their approach to teaching, and (2) expand their view of intervention beyond teaching. With the former, it seems particularly important to focus on motivation as a primary intervention concern and in doing so to pursue a personalized, sequential, and hierarchical approach to teaching. Beyond teaching, it is important to think in terms of a societal approach encompassing an integrated continuum of preventive and treatment services.

Motivation as a Primary Concern

A transactional perspective suggests that prevention and correction of many learning problems requires general changes in systems and learning environments (modifying approaches to schooling and instruction). It seems likely that major benefits would accrue from modifying current instructional practices to better match individual differences not only in developmental capability but also in motivation. The focus on motivation probably needs to be given primary emphasis.

The theoretical concept of the match, as advocated by leading scholars such as Piaget, Bruner, Vygotsky, and J. McVickers Hunt, reflects a transactional view of learning and learning problems. Both individualized and personalized interventions are based on this concept. However, most individualized approaches primarily focus on accounting for individual differences in capability, while personalization has been defined as accounting for individual differences in both capability and motivation, especially intrinsic motivation.

Personalization represents an application of the principles of normalization and least intervention needed (which encompass the concept of "least restrictive environment"). Because learner perceptions are considered critical factors in defining whether the environment appropriately accounts for interests and abilities, personalization can also be viewed as a psychological construct.

Properly implemented, personalized instruction encompasses the types of procedures regular classroom programs need in order to improve mainstreaming and prereferral interventions. Therefore, such procedures should reduce the need

"If American children are not motivated to learn, could it be because they live in a society that does not recognize that its schools promote boredom and inattentiveness?" (Stevenson & Stigler, 1992, p. 26)

for remediation. They should also facilitate accurate identification of remaining remedial needs. Proper implementation of a personalized program seems a necessary step toward validly identifying those who may require more than accommodation of individual differences in order to learn effectively.

The motivational emphasis in a personalized program is designed to mobilize all learners. For many, matching current levels of motivation and development should be sufficient for learning (particularly for Type I learning problems). Others, while trying harder, will continue to have some problems (particularly for the Type III category). These latter individuals clearly need remediation. Depending on problem severity, such remediation involves one (or more) of the three hierarchical levels—ranging from a focus on observable to underlying problems. (Recall that Level A focuses on age-appropriate life tasks, Level B on missing prerequisites for learning, and Level C on factors that interfere with learning—see Feature 11-4, p. 245.)

Permeating procedures used to personalize and remedy intervention is a primary focus on motivation. This stresses

- overcoming negative attitudes
- enhancing motivational readiness for learning
- maintaining intrinsic motivation throughout the learning process
- nurturing the type of continuing motivation that results in the learner's engaging in related learning activity away from the teaching situation

"A person's willingness to expend effort depends on whether he or she believes the effect is worthwhile." (Stevenson & Stigler, 1992, p. 222)

Attending to these concerns is essential to maximizing maintenance, generalization, and expansion of learning. Failure to attend to these matters means approaching passive (and often hostile) learners with methods that confound diagnostic and research activity and that may just as readily exacerbate as correct learning and behavior problems.

In addition to prevention and correction, the type of personalized, sequential, and hierarchical approach just summarized has promise for identifying different types of learning problems and for detecting errors in diagnoses. For example, when only personalization is needed to correct a learning problem, it seems reasonable to suggest the individual does not have a learning disability. At the same time, when a highly mobilized individual still has extreme difficulty learning, the hypothesis that the person does have a disability may be somewhat safer.

A Societal Approach

Increasingly, policymakers are recognizing the importance of devising valid approaches to major psychoeducational and health problems that account for a range of social, economic, political, and cultural factors (see Feature 13-1). The potential array of preventive and treatment programs is extensive and promising and can be appreciated by grouping programs on a continuum from prevention through treatment of chronic problems. As outlined in Chapter 1, the activities encompass

- primary prevention to promote and maintain safety and physical and mental health (beginning with family planning)
- preschool programs
- early school adjustment programs
- improvement of ongoing regular support
- augmentation of regular support
- specialized staff development and interventions prior to referral for special help
- system change and intensive treatments

Feature 13-1   Social Factors

Drugs, poverty, immigration—all are implicated as factors leading to learning problems. In 1988, Florida found that 5.5 percent of 185,000 births were prenatally exposed to drugs including alcohol (Office of Policy Research and Improvement, 1989). Nationally, 10 percent of pregnant women report drug use during pregnancy, and available data suggest that as many as 375,000 infants are affected by substance use and abuse (National Association of Perinatal Addiction Research and Education, 1989). Although it remains to be seen how many exposed children will experience lasting problems, it is clear that a rapidly increasing number of special programs are appearing in response to predictions of severe and pervasive psychoeducational problems (National Association of Perinatal Addiction Research and Education, 1989; Shaywitz, Cohen, & Shaywitz, 1980).

Reed and Sautter (1990) note that as many as a million minors in the United States have no stable home or live on the street. Reporting on children in poverty, they state:

Poverty in America knows no boundaries, no geographic borders. The only common denominator for the children of poverty is that they are brought up under desperate conditions beyond their control—and for them, the rhetoric of equal opportunity seems a cruel hoax, an impossible dream (p. K-4).

Despite prevailing stereotypes, by the end of the 1980s about two-thirds of the poor in the United States were not from minority backgrounds, and almost 50 percent of poor children lived with both parents. Furthermore, families were the fastest growing group among the homeless, resulting in over 220,000 homeless children—with almost as many more living on the brink. Many of these were newly arrived immigrants. Projections indicate a worsening situation. Transiency and missed schooling, poor nutrition, poor medical care, exposure to hostile conditions, the inability to speak English, and lack of exposure to beneficial stimulation are not a prescription for learning to read and write in the United States (Bassuk, Rubin, & Lauriet, 1986; Gonzales, 1990). Again, some programs have appeared as society attempts to address these problems. However, they are few and far between, and as increasing numbers of children are found to have learning problems, it is the classroom teacher who is called upon to turn things around.

As Stoddard (1991) warns, "Teachers alone cannot solve the problem. . . . However, teachers joining with other professionals and the family can provide a comprehensive support system that enables families and children . . . to reach maximum potential." (p. 17)

Figure 13-2   *From Prevention to Treatment: A Continuum of Programs for Learning, Behavior, and Socioemotional Problems*

Intervention Continuum	Types of Activities

Prevention	1. Primary prevention to promote and maintain
	    • safety
	    • physical and mental health (beginning with family planning)

Early-age intervention	2. Preschool programs
	    • day care
	    • parent education
	    • early education (encompassing a focus on psychosocial and mental health problems)
	
	3. Early school adjustment
	    • personalization in primary grades
	    • parent participation in problem solving
	    • comprehensive psychosocial and mental health programs (school-based)

Early-after-onset intervention	4. Improvement of ongoing regular support
	    • specified remedial role for regular classroom teachers
	    • parent involvement
	    • comprehensive psychosocial and mental health programs (school-based—all grades)
	
	5. Augmentation of regular support
	    • academic (e.g., reading teachers, computer aided instruction, volunteer tutors)
	    • psychosocial (e.g., staff and peer counselors, crisis teams)
	
	6. Specialized staff development and interventions prior to referral for special education and other intensive treatments
	    • staff training/consultation
	    • short-term specialized interventions

Treatment for chronic problems	7. System changes and intensive treatment
	    • rehabilitation of existing programs
	    • special education services
	    • referral to and coordination with community mental health services

Unfortunately, implementation of the full continuum of programs with an extensive range of activities does not occur in most communities, and what programs there are tend to be offered in a fragmented manner.

Although competition for limited public funds works against expanding programmatic activity, policymakers are coming to see the relationship between limited efficacy and the tendency for complementary programs to operate in isolation. For instance, physical and mental health programs generally are not coordinated with educational programs; a youngster identified and treated in early education programs who still requires special support may or may not receive systematic help in the primary grades; and so forth. Failure to coordinate and follow through can be counterproductive, undermining immediate benefits and working against efforts to reduce subsequent demand for costly treatment programs. Limited efficacy seems inevitable as long as interventions are carried out piecemeal. Thus there is an increasing thrust toward moving beyond piecemeal strategies to provide comprehensive, integrated programs (Hodgkinson, 1989; Kagan, 1990; Kagan, Rivera, & Parker, 1990; Kean, 1989; Kirst, 1991).

Integrating Programs in a Catchment Area

The range of programs cited in Figure 1-1 are elaborated in Figure 13-2. Each can be seen as integrally related, and it seems likely the impact of each could be exponentially increased through collaborative integration. Indeed, it may be that a major breakthrough in the battle against learning and behavior problems will only result when the full range of programs is implemented in a comprehensive and integrated fashion.

To accomplish a comprehensive, societal approach requires a consortium representing key programs in appropriate geographical catchment areas. The task of such a consortium is to develop, coordinate, and evaluate an integrated approach to the entire range of interventions, as graphically represented in Figure 13-2.

Accountability and Change

Ideas for change are relatively easy to formulate. Producing change is quite a bit harder. For a variety of reasons, systems tend to resist change. But there are ways to overcome such resistance. One somewhat naive strategy has been simply to demand accountability; another approach has been to address the problem of change as a major intervention concern.

Accountability and Evaluative Research

In the simplest sense, professionals who carefully adhere to ethical guidelines are being accountable. For example, they are careful not to oversell their expertise or to mystify the general public. In addition, when data are insufficient to support widespread use of an intervention or when data suggest potential negative effects, such professionals proceed with extreme caution (for example, unvalidated procedures are so described and used only in controlled, experimental ways). In general, they do their best, and they believe the outcomes are the best that can be expected under the circumstances.

Other than adhering to ethical principles, some professionals would prefer to ignore the topics of accountability and program evaluation. Two facts make this impossible. One, this is an age of accountability; evaluation increasingly is mandated by legislation and government regulations. Two, evaluative research is essential to the improvement of interventions.

There can be no doubt that professionals concerned about learning problems must be accountable. However, the ways to implement accountability are not all positive.

As discussed in Chapter 12, it is best to pursue evaluation in a comprehensive way. Comprehensive evaluation requires a large set of valid procedures, and the development of such procedures requires a large financial commitment. Some legislators act as if all they have to do is demand accountability. For the most part, they have not shown readiness to underwrite the costs of planning and implementing comprehensive evaluation research. Thus accountability usually remains a token item in program budgets, and those mandating it generally do not see that they have only created another dilemma for those trying to deal with learning problems.

As Goodlad (1984) has noted about education:

> "Accountability" is a good word. *Webster's Third* defines it as both "capable of being accounted for" and "subject to giving an account." In the second sense, state legislators and policy makers, including those at the district level, have been diligent in seeking to make others educationally accountable but have been restrained with respect to their own responsibility for articulating priorities based on careful studies of need and sound educational concepts. . . . [Instead] we have been told frequently in recent years that people want to go back to an earlier, simpler time in our history when the 3 Rs were the sole expectation for schools. . . . there never was such a time. I doubt that this time has come now. (pp. 49–50)

Indeed, the need is to move forward — not backward. An important means for doing so is to turn the demand for accountability into comprehensive programs of intervention research and development. That is, given the limited funds available for accountability and intervention research, it makes sense to combine both objectives so that it will be feasible to underwrite bold innovations and long-term evaluations. As Head Start and the space program both demonstrated, boldness and extensive financial underwriting are essential if major breakthroughs are to be made.

The Problem of Change

Once intervention research and development suggests an approach, the problem arises of adoption by ongoing programs. Existing programs often resist change. In most cases, introduction of desirable innovations requires carefully planned and implemented strategies.

According to those who study organizations, creation of an appropriate climate for change requires at least the following conditions:

- appropriate incentives for change (intrinsically valued outcomes, expectations of success, recognitions, rewards)
- procedural options, so that those who are expected to implement change can select one they see as workable

Those involved in trying to produce significant changes in schools and communities should remember the immortal words (of whoever said them first): "Illegitimati non carborundum!"

Translation: "Don't let the bastards grind you down!"

- mechanisms to facilitate the efforts of those responsible for installing change (participatory decision making, special training, resources, rewards, procedures designed to improve organizational health)
- agents of change who are perceived as pragmatic rather than as idealistic
- realistic pacing—not trying to accomplish too much too fast (facilitating readiness, planned transition or phasing in of changes)
- appropriate feedback regarding progress of change activity
- ongoing support mechanisms to maintain changes as long as they remain appropriate

Some of the preceding points may seem familiar—at least, they should. We have stressed similar points when discussing the concepts of facilitating learning through personalization.

Summing Up

In this chapter we have identified two overlapping fundamental matters to be addressed in improving efforts to prevent and correct learning problems: (1) differentiating among the various types of problems, and (2) reconceiving and expanding intervention approaches. Some of the changes suggested as ways to help the field move forward include (a) developing a broadly conceived classification framework that keeps the concept of learning disabilities in perspective, (b) incorporating motivation as a primary intervention concern, (c) expanding the range of programs beyond teaching, and (d) developing ways to coordinate and integrate an expanded range of programs within appropriate geographical catchment areas. Finally, we have stressed the importance of combining the limited funds available for research and program accountability so that bold innovations can be properly implemented, evaluated, and adopted.

Use Figure 13-2 as a guide to check whether a complete continuum of programs are available in your community.

1. Within each category, what types of specific programs are offered?
2. How many programs work together in a coordinated and integrated way?

This is the solution to the puzzle on page 269:

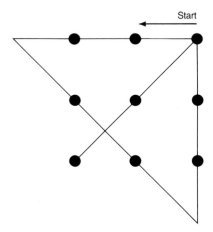

CHAPTER 14

Use What You Have Learned

I hear, and I forget;
I see, and I remember;
I do, and I understand.

(Old Chinese proverb)

> In discussing anatomy, one seventh grader wrote: "Anatomy is the human body made up of three parts, the head, the chest, and the stummick. The head holds the skull and the brains, if there is any. The chest holds the liver, and the stummick holds the vowels, which are *a, e, i, o, u,* and sometimes *w* and *y.*"

Obviously, it can take a while for any learner to effectively assimilate the many basic things that she or he has been studying.

The preceding chapters offered a great deal of information and proposed many ideas. Either you will soon forget most of what you have read or you will assimilate the material, making it part of the way you view things in the immediate future. Which of these two possibilities takes place probably depends on the degree to which you have reason to use what you have learned in the days to come.

One reason for using the material could be that someone asks what you think about some of the issues and problems of individuals with learning problems. If so, what might they ask?

What follows are 12 questions that reflect basic concerns about learning problems and learning disabilities that people often ask or think they should ask. Use a blank sheet of paper to answer each question. If you want to review material for a particular question, we have noted some relevant sections in the book. Additional material on each topic can be found by using the index.

Remember, there are no simple answers to these questions.

1. "I've heard that *learning disabilities* is a special term that should not be used as a catch-all label for everyone who has a learning problem. Who should be diagnosed as having a learning disability?" (Take another look at Chapters 1 and 2; also see the readings *On Learning Disabilities.*)

2. "What causes learning problems?" (Review Chapter 2; also see the readings *On Learning Disabilities.*)

3. "What are some concepts and steps that can be applied in following the principle of using the least intervention needed in helping those with learning problems?" (Chapters 3 and 7 are a good place to begin in thinking about this matter.)

4. "Is there any way to prevent learning problems?" (See Chapters 5 and 13.)

5. "How are learning problems corrected?" (A good place to begin in thinking about this topic is with Chapters 5, 7, and 8; also see the readings *On Teaching.*)

6. "My youngster's school says they're going to start a program to identify learning disabilities in kindergarten. I've heard that some professionals are

concerned about such screening programs. Should I encourage my child's school to screen for learning disabilities in kindergarten? Why or why not?'' (See Chapter 4; also review *Screening for Learning Disabilities.*)

7. "My child has just been placed in a special class for learning disabilities. We hope it will help. Can it hurt?'' (See Chapter 3; *Ethical Concerns About Negative Effects.*)

8. "In working with motivational problems, what are some alternatives to commonly used behavior modification strategies?'' (See Chapter 8; *Intrinsic Motivation and School Misbehavior; Dealing with School Misbehavior.*)

9. "The teacher says my kid could learn but doesn't seem to want to. I asked what she was going to do about it. She said all she could think of was to start rewarding him only when he did his work. Isn't there something more she should be trying?'' (A good place to begin is with Chapter 8; also see *Learner Options and Decision Making to Enhance Motivation and Learning.*)

10. "I've heard that not everyone with learning problems needs special remediation and that those who do should not be placed in special classes. Who does need remediation and what is the best way to provide for such special needs?'' (See Chapters 8 through 11.)

11. "Because of all the learning problems, there was an editorial in the newspaper calling for greater accountability on the part of educators. The idea seems right, but there was a letter in response to the editorial that said there are serious problems with the way accountability is carried out. What are these problems?'' (See Chapters 12 and 13.)

12. "Next year I begin teaching in a regular elementary school classroom. What can I do to help students who are having trouble learning? What should I do if I think a student has a learning disability?'' (See Chapters 3 through 5; Chapters 8 through 11; *On Learning Disabilities; On Teaching; On the Individual and Society.*)

If you tried the study skill activity outlined at the end of Chapter 7 (the SQ3R method), how did it work out for you?

How do you understand this outcome?

Many people who are taught such study skills or skills for memorizing material or who go through other skills-training approaches do not continue to use them over the long run. That is, they learn the skills, may use them briefly, and then give up using them.

Why do you think this happens? (Think in terms of the relationships between motivation and learning and performance discussed in Part 3.)

PART 5

Read More About It

*T*he following readings have been especially prepared for this text. Four areas are covered: learning disabilities, assessment tools and technical concerns, teaching, and the process of intervention in general as it relates to individuals and society. In addition to providing broader coverage and resource material, the perspectives are offered to stimulate your thinking.

SECTION I *On Learning Disabilities*

I.1 Learning Disabilities in Historical Perspective   291
I.2 CNS Function and Assessment of Minor Dysfunction   304
I.3 Controversial Treatments and Fads   309
I.4 Remedying Learning Disabilities: Prevailing Approaches   314
I.5 Screening for Learning Disabilities   323
I.6 Assessment for Learning Disabilities' Diagnosis, Placement, and Program Planning   328

SECTION II *On Assessment Tools and Technical Concerns*

II.1 Procedures and Instruments for Assessing Learning Problems   341
II.2 Technical Concerns About Assessment   349

SECTION III *On Teaching*

III.1 Theories of Instruction and Models of Teaching   355
III.2 Enhancing Motivation and Skills in Social Functioning   362
III.3 Intrinsic Motivation and School Misbehavior   365
III.4 Learner Options and Decision Making to Enhance Motivation and Learning   369
III.5 Fernald's Techniques in Their Motivational Context   380

SECTION IV *On the Individual and Society*

IV.1 Ethical Concerns About Negative Effects   391
IV.2 Whose Interests Are Being Served?   395
IV.3 Toward Services with an Informed Consumer Orientation   400
IV.4 Involving Parents in Schooling   410
IV.5 Social Control   413
IV.6 Cultural and Individual Differences as Barriers to Working Relationships   418
IV.7 Managing and Preventing School Misbehavior   422

SECTION I

On Learning Disabilities

I.1 Learning Disabilities in Historical Perspective

I.2 CNS Function and Assessment of Minor Dysfunction

I.3 Controversial Treatments and Fads

I.4 Remedying Learning Disabilities: Prevailing Approaches

I.5 Screening for Learning Disabilities

I.6 Assessment for Learning Disabilities' Diagnosis, Placement, and Program Planning

I.1   Learning Disabilities in Historical Perspective

The term *learning disability* became popular in the 1960s. In the late 1960s, learning disability texts began to appear. In 1968 the first issue of the *Journal of Learning Disabilities* was published. The foundation for the field, however, was laid much earlier. From around the turn of the century, the field evolved through research and practice in clinics and classrooms, through efforts of special interest groups, and through political action. That evolution has shaped what is happening today in the LD field and will continue to influence its future.

In the Clinic and the Classroom

Although the field of learning disabilities did not exist before the 1960s, the foundation had been laid for over a 50-year period by influential clinicians and researchers. Their impact is reflected in the extensive emphasis in the early LD texts on perceptual-motor and language/psycholinguistic disabilities and on the use of behavior modification strategies (see Feature 1).

The Clinical Legacy

During the late nineteenth and early twentieth centuries, studies of brain-damaged adults led to a variety of theories about how the brain functions to produce specific behaviors. Over the first half of the 1900s, clinicians in education, psychology, medicine, and related fields working with clients with brain damage or severe learning problems, or both, pioneered remedial theories and practices. Their focus was primarily on perceptual-motor and language disabilities. In the 1960s it was these theories and therapy-oriented practices that shaped the field. It was these clinical diagnostic and treatment practices that were presented in textbooks, and thus it was these practices that were taught to professionals-in-training.

Feature 1   Phases in the Development of the LD Field

Wiederholt (1974), in his brief historical summary, suggests that three types of disorders shaped most of the development of the field: disorders of spoken language, of written language, and of perceptual and motor processes. Furthermore, he divides the evolution of the LD field into three phases.

Wiederholt describes the first phase of historical development as the *foundation phase* (up to about 1930). This period was characterized by early studies of brain-behavior relationships with brain-damaged adults. Theoretical formulations were proposed regarding the nature and cause of learning disabilities. The prominent pioneers were Goldstein, Strauss, Werner, and Orton.

Second was the *transition phase* (1930–62), during which attempts were made to translate theoretical formulations into remedial practices.

During this phase, the work of Wepman, Myklebust, Kirk, Fernald, Cruickshank, Frostig, and Kephart predominated.

Third, the *integration phase* (from 1963 on) is described as reflecting a merging of information into comprehensive diagnostic-remedial practices. During this phase, the number of professionals in the field has grown quickly, and there have been new attempts at theoretical formulations, further proliferation of diagnostic-remedial approaches, and rapid escalation of basic and applied research.

Lerner (1988) adds a fourth *contemporary phase* (beginning in 1980). This emerging phase has encompassed trends toward serving a wider age range, providing services across special education categories, mainstreaming, expanding use of computer technology, and increasing organizational activity.

Let us briefly introduce some of the most prominent pioneers of what have been called the perceptual-motor and language/psycholinguistic approaches to the LD field. (Basic works by most of the individuals presented are listed in the references at the end of the book.)

The perceptual-motor approach   Kurt Goldstein (1939) provides a good starting point for discussing perceptual dysfunctioning as a basis of learning disabilities. Working with brain-injured veterans after World War I, he found them to be hyperactive and easily distracted. They had difficulty separating "figure" and "ground," separating the important from the unimportant, dealing with abstractions, and delaying responses to stimuli. Many nineteenth-century clinical investigators influenced his work, and, in turn, his clinical research provided a major foundation for several pioneers of the learning disabilities field.

Alfred Strauss and Heinz Werner migrated to America from Germany in 1937. First at the Wayne County Training School and then at the Cove Schools for brain-injured children, they and colleagues who joined them (Laura Lehtinen, Newell Kephart) pursued a highly influential line of work. They applied Goldstein's observations to their research differentiating brain-injured from non-brain-injured retarded children. They recommended reducing unessential stimuli and increasing multisensory inputs in teaching.

Strauss and Lehtinen developed additional educational strategies designed to facilitate perceptual organization. These included the use of special materials and teaching strategies to compensate for areas of weakness and to capitalize on strengths. They also stressed the value of analyses of specific task performance as a basis for educational plans.

Kephart's work with Strauss applied the view that motor and perceptual development are the bases for later conceptual learning. Kephart designed techniques to enhance gross motor and perceptual-motor functioning of "the slow learner in the classroom." He was particularly concerned with body image, balance, locomotion, perceptual-motor coordination, and use of physical sensations as feedback to the learner.

William Cruickshank (Cruickshank et al., 1961), a student of Strauss and Werner, further refined the educational methods employed by Strauss and

Lehtinen. His work focused especially on distractibility and hyperactivity in children, including those functioning in the normal range of intelligence. He stressed reduced environmental stimuli and use of multisensory methods and structured educational programming. Many of his students have gone on to play important roles in the development of the field (for example, Daniel Hallahan, Norris Haring).

Marianne Frostig established the Frostig Center of Educational Therapy where, from the 1950s well into the 1970s, she developed and disseminated the Developmental Test of Visual Perception and a program of workbook materials for training "visual perception." The test and training materials were extremely popular until the mid-1970s, when influential research reviews challenged the validity of the idea of training perceptual processes.

A few others in the perceptual-motor tradition whose remedial ideas subsequently became prominent include Gerald Getman, Ray Barsch, Glen Doman and Carl Delacato, Jean Ayres, and Bryant Cratty.

The language/psycholinguistic approach   Starting a bit earlier than the work of Strauss and his colleagues, two different — but highly influential — lines of remedial thinking had begun. One line was initiated by Samuel T. Orton, a professor of psychiatry at the University of Iowa; the other was begun by Grace Fernald, a professor of psychology at what is today the University of California, Los Angeles.

From 1928 to 1948, Orton studied the reading processes of brain-injured adults and concluded that the specific location of damage was critical. This led to neurological views about the causes and correction of reading problems, some of which are no longer held. However, Orton's emphasis on reading problems due to language deficits provided a major contrast to the perceptual-motor tradition. He advocated an approach to reading instruction that involved the use of individually paced phonics with kinesthetic aids that is still widely used. His influence also continues to be felt through the Orton Society's conferences and journal.

Fernald established her clinical laboratory in 1921. Her work focused on a variety of remedial approaches for all basic academic skills. She stressed that learning could be improved by enhancing the vividness of stimulus inputs. A major way to do this was through multisensory methods in teaching language, reading, spelling, writing, and math. Also toward this goal, she stressed meaningful content, high-interest activities, and learning as a function of the whole person. Her work is widely cited and used today, and the clinic-laboratory she founded continued to pioneer new approaches into the 1980s.

In the 1950s, the language/psycholinguistic tradition continued to expand with the emergence of two additional remedial approaches. One approach was given special impetus by the work of Samuel A. Kirk; the other approach followed the lead of Helmer R. Myklebust.

Kirk and his colleagues developed the Illinois Test of Psycholinguistic Abilities (ITPA) in the 1950s and 1960s. The test was specifically designed to guide remedial instruction. Despite questions about the validity of training psycholinguistic abilities, specific training programs continue to be developed to correct disabilities identified by the test. Beyond the ITPA, Kirk's work and leadership have influenced a large number of colleagues and policymakers. In the immediate years after the LD label was formally adopted, his students from his years at the University of Illinois played a prominent role in shaping the field.

Myklebust worked initially with deaf children, and this work led to his interest in the development of auditory or receptive language. As interest grew in language-related learning disabilities, his work was seen as particularly promising. Myklebust's strengths as a theorist and researcher provided an important model for the emerging field of learning disabilities.

In the 1960s, Doris Johnson and Myklebust, working at Northwestern University, developed an approach to remediation that advocated specific training procedures designed to strengthen deficit areas and teach through intact sensory modalities. Their comprehensive notions of what was involved in remedying learning disabilities set an influential standard for those who followed.

Methods developed in relation to the perceptual-motor and psycholinguistic approaches came under attack in the 1970s (Arter & Jenkins, 1977; Hammill & Larsen, 1974a, 1974b; Mann, 1971). Such underlying-abilities (or processing) approaches were criticized along philosophical and empirical lines. Criticism of processing views arose at a time when the behavioral approach, with its emphasis on teach-ing observable skills through direct instruction, was on the ascendancy. The field was soon polarized.

The Behavioral Approach

As classroom teachers tried to apply the LD practices that had been developed in clinical settings, more often than not a plaintive cry was heard: "I'm so busy dealing with behavior problems I don't have time to teach." LD teachers found that they had been trained to do something about a student's learning problems but had not been adequately prepared to cope with the behavior problems such students often displayed. It was understandable that they now wanted special training in how to control the students long enough to get them to sit down and learn.

In the 1960s and throughout most of the 1970s, behavior modification was the most frequent prescription for teachers asking how to deal with behavior problems in the classroom. Such techniques had been found useful in controlling certain behaviors of persons diagnosed as emotionally disturbed and retarded. In response to teachers' needs, behavior modification researchers and practitioners designed strategies for use in classroom management. These strategies soon dominated the training in many programs.

As the emphasis on behaviorist principles and techniques spread throughout the LD field, the ideas were applied not only to classroom management but also to practices for remedying problems in learning academic skills. This trend accelerated in the 1970s and the early 1980s with the adoption of "applied behavioral analysis," "directive instruction," "precision teaching," and "cognitive behavior modification" methods.

Again, we offer a brief introduction to a few of the most prominent names that have come to be associated with introducing the behavioral approach into LD classroom programs. (Basic works by most of the individuals presented are cited in the reference list at the end of the book.)

Throughout the 1950s and 1960s, the ideas of Edward Thorndike, B. F. Skinner, and other reinforcement theorists and behaviorists were translated into programs for a wide range of educational and behavior problems (Bijou & Baer, 1967; Risley & Baer, 1973). In the field of special education, ideas for classroom application developed by Richard

Whelan, Norris Haring, Ogden Lindsley, and Frank Hewett were especially influential and exemplify approaches seen in many current programs for those with learning and behavior problems.

Richard Whelan developed a highly structured behavior modification–oriented classroom program for severely disturbed children in the late 1950s and into the 1960s. The focus was both on improving behavior and on academic remediation. His work provided one of the first comprehensive and sophisticated efforts to apply behavior modification in managing and programming an entire classroom of disturbed children.

Norris Haring, a student of Cruickshank's, also developed a program emphasizing operant conditioning principles and a highly structured environment to improve behavior and academic problems. Working with E. Lakin Phillips in the 1950s and then joining forces with Whelan in 1962, he contributed to the refined use of operant methods in classrooms.

Ogden R. Lindsley, who had studied with Skinner, joined Haring at the University of Kansas in the early 1960s. He brought with him an interest in the problem of precise measurement of behavior for use in planning instruction. The approach he developed and called *precision teaching* involves identifying specific behaviors, counting and charting performance, and using the data to plan subsequent remediation. The system has also been influential in establishing procedures for program evaluation.

The work of applied behavior analysts (Lindsley, 1964; Bijou, 1970) and other educational theorists (Bloom, 1978) led to what has come to be called *direct instruction.* Practitioners of this approach assume that even if a person has a learning disability, the only thing that can be done is to teach the skills the individual needs to learn. Moreover, they view skill instruction as hierarchical and best accomplished through use of behavioral change strategies.

Direct-instruction advocates fought with those advocating processing approaches throughout the 1970s, and the fight was responsible for a variety of major rifts in the LD field (see Kavale & Forness, 1985).

Just before the war between advocates of the underlying-abilities and direct-instruction approaches, Frank Hewett, working at UCLA and in a nearby school district during the early 1960s, designed what he called the "engineered classroom" for emotionally disturbed children. His approach combined behavior modification methods and a developmental sequence of educational goals to "engineer" success. Subsequently, he replaced the concept of "engineering" success with that of "orchestrating" success. In doing so, Hewett placed greater emphasis on the importance of attitudes, feelings, and self-concepts. His creative approach to remediation and his detailed descriptions of his work resulted in widespread application. Although developed in the context of classrooms for emotionally disturbed children, the breadth and evolving nature of his work made it of special interest to the LD field.

Hewett's shift from "engineering" to "orchestrating" classroom programs reflected a general shift among behaviorists. In the 1970s, it became evident to many who used behavior modification strategies that M&Ms and token reinforcers were useful only for controlling a few behaviors, and when used with some individuals they weren't useful at all. When it came to correcting severe learning and behavior problems, individuals' attitudes and emotions kept getting in the way. New strategies were needed to deal with such thoughts and feelings. One immediate response was to modify behavior modification, and thus the field of cognitive behavior modification evolved.

The early efforts of Virginia Douglas (1972) and Donald Meichenbaum (1977) are representative of the trend toward use of cognitive behavior modification concepts and methods. To control behavior and improve learning, they stressed teaching children to use cognitive cues, ranging from "stop, look, and listen" to more complex strategies. Such self-instructions are said aloud at first but in later stages of instruction students are taught to say them to themselves.

In the field of learning disabilities, the emphasis on cognitive and metacognitive functioning led to the "general learning strategies approach" (Deshler & Schumaker, 1986). The focus of this continuing trend is on teaching strategic and efficient skills for learning and remembering. Examples include self-questioning, rehearsal and review, and cueing memory.

Trends in the 1980s

All the emphasis on cognition and general learning strategies paved the way for an evolved cognitive processing approach based on information-processing models (Kolligan & Sternberg, 1987; Samuels, 1987; Swanson, 1987; Torgesen & Wong, 1986). As a result, renewed emphasis emerged with respect to assessing deficiencies related to cognitive functioning and using strategies to correct these problems.

Another trend in the 1980s saw renewed interest in social and emotional functioning growing out of increasing concerns about the social functioning and development of those diagnosed as having learning disabilities. In particular, social and life-skills training programs burgeoned.

The 1980s also saw a reaction to the widespread emphasis on direct instruction and its companion "curriculum-based assessment." Ironically, one of the criticisms used against early underlying-abilities approaches by advocates of direct instruction was that processing models risked fractionalizing learners by conceiving their problems as specific ability deficits. By 1990 a similar criticism was being widely leveled at direct instruction. One leading critic (Heshusius, 1991) argued that direct instruction is not a model for instructing human beings, but only an isolated set of measurement and control procedures superimposed on, but unrelated to, the actual phenomena of human learning. In place of direct instruction, there was a call for a return to holistic approaches with their emphasis on the learner as a functioning whole and a motivated discoverer of meaningful skills and knowledge (Bartoli, 1990; Heshusius, 1982, 1986, 1989; Iano, 1987; Poplin, 1988). In counterpoint, behavioral principles have been defended vigorously (Forness, 1988; Forness & Kavale, 1987; Kimball & Heron, 1988).

Consistent with a holistic view and preceding the reaction to direct instruction was a renewed interest in models of intervention that included a focus on intrinsic motivation and on learner-environment transactions. Past tendencies to overemphasize remedial needs were countered by stressing the importance of enhancing development in nonproblem areas and providing opportunities for enrichment (Adelman & Taylor, 1983a, 1986).

As the difficulty of correcting learning problems became evident in the 1980s, there was increased concern about what happens as children with learning problems grow into adolescents and adults with learning problems. The concern became particularly urgent as the movement toward minimal competency testing spread (Hall & Gallagher, 1984). When such testing was required for high-school graduation or college entrance, steps were advocated for special preparation of students diagnosed as having learning disabilities. In addition, proposals were made for appropriate modifications in test administration as a way of meeting the special needs of these students. Concomitantly, career education became an important focus. Besides high-school vocational programs, new college programs were developed for such students to enable them to qualify for a wider range of, and better, jobs (Mangrum & Strichart, 1988).

Parents and Professionals Organize

Also of major importance to the LD field has been the development of special organizations by those concerned about learning disabilities. As has been common in fields involving children's mental health and special education, parents were the first to organize.

The oldest organization is The Orton Dyslexia Society, founded in 1949 and named after Samuel T. Orton, who was one of the pioneers of the language approach. However, it was not until the early 1960s that local groups of parents banded together to form a national organization using the term *learning disabilities*.

At a conference in Chicago in 1963, the Association for Children with Learning Disabilities (ACLD) was formed. The organization rapidly became a major lobbying group and played a key role in creating the new field. In 1979 the group changed its name to the Association for Children and Adults with Learning Disabilities in recognition that learning disabilities are not just a problem of childhood; it also established a Learning-Disabled Adult Committee. In the late 1980s, the name was changed once more to the Learning Disabilities Association of America (LDA).

By 1968 professionals had also established a learning disabilities organization. Within the Council for Exceptional Children (CEC), they formed the Division for Children with Learning Disabilities (DCLD). The organization grew rapidly in its first decade, and in 1978 published the first issue of its journal, the *Learning Disability Quarterly*. Like the ACLD, the professional group saw that a name change would signal the group's growing recognition that the field had been paying insufficient attention to learning disabilities among adolescents and adults. Thus in 1981 it became the Council for Learning Disabilities (CLD). Because of growing dissatisfaction with certain regulations of the governing organization, a voting majority of CLD members decided to withdraw the group from CEC; and on June 30, 1983, CLD became an autonomous organization. On July 1, 1983, CEC approved establishment of the Division for Learning Disabilities (DLD) to replace the now-autonomous CLD.

With the proliferation of organizations came a need for a mechanism for coordination and cooperation. In 1975 six major organizations concerned with learning problems established the National Joint Committee for Learning Disabilities (NJCLD). By the end of the 1980s, eight organizations were represented: the American Speech-Language-Hearing Association, Learning Disabilities Association of America, Council for Learning Disabilities, Council for Exceptional Children's Division of Learning Disabilities, International Reading Association, National Association of School Psychologists, Division for Children with Communication Disorders, and The Orton Dyslexia Society.

In response to the need for an organization that would bring together major researchers in the field, the International Academy for Research in Learning Disabilities (IARLD) was formed in the latter half of the 1970s. This organization consists of "a rigorously selected group of the world's leaders in learning disabilities" (Cruickshank, 1983, p. 193).

Organizations concerned with learning disabilities do not exist in a vacuum. They draw from and contribute to the work of all those who are concerned about the rights and needs of special populations. In fact, the effectiveness of such organizations has been largely due to coordinated lobbying that has influenced legislation.

Legislation and Financial Support

A stormy history led to legislation and funding for programs for persons with learning disabilities. It grew out of centuries of social reform and judicial decisions in education in general, and in the education of exceptional individuals in particular.

The immediate legislative history is the result of a sociopolitical climate that emerged in the United States in the 1960s. During this period, both general and special education became national priorities. This occurred partly out of fear of an apparent shift in the balance of power between the United States and the USSR, partly out of a desire to create a Great Society, partly as the result of special-interest lobbying, and partly from litigation in the courts.

The 1960s and 1970s were a time of great change in programs for children, the poor, and the handicapped. In the Congress of the United States and in federal courtrooms, events were taking place that were unprecedented. As Goodlad (1984) notes, the Eighty-Eighth Congress, the "Education Congress," in 1964 enacted the Equal Opportunities Program of the Civil Rights Act and the Economic Opportunity Act. The new laws provided support for vocational and technical education, teaching the handicapped, prevention of delinquency, desegregation, early learning opportunities for young children in disadvantaged areas, and much more.

> The 89th Congress extended most of these commitments in the astonishing and unprecedented Elementary and Secondary Education Act of 1965. Title I was designed to assist school districts with their momentous tasks of helping children from low-income families in school and giving them there the kind of education thought to be needed. Title II provided for the purchase of books — in both public and private nonprofit elementary and secondary schools. Titles III and IV provided funds for linking the educational resources of communities and for comprehensive programs of research, development, and dissemination of knowledge through the collaborative efforts of universities, public schools, private nonprofit educational agencies, and state departments of education. Title V put money directly into state departments of education for strengthening their increasingly compelling leadership responsibilities. To effect all of this, the budget of the Office of Education was increased by $1,255,000,000 for fiscal 1966. (Goodlad, 1984, pp. 3–4)

In 1963 the Congress of the United States passed Public Law 88-164, the first law to provide federal support for educating the "handicapped." At that time, however, learning disabilities as a type of handicap were not formally recognized, which is not surprising because the term was just being introduced. Still, as has been noted: "Under P.L. 88-164, the federal government did in fact provide assistance to many pupils we would now consider to be learning disabled, under the mandate to provide support for 'crippled or other health impaired.' Such children were then typically diagnosed as brain injured, minimally cerebral palsied, aphasic, or perceptually handicapped'' (Mann, Cartwright, Kenowitz, Boyer, Metz, & Wolford, 1984).

Along with official legislation came the establishment of the National Advisory Committee on Handicapped Children and several task forces that attempted to clarify the status and needs of certain special education populations (Chalfant & Scheffelin, 1969; Clements, 1966; Haring & Miller, 1969). The experts participating in these groups soon concluded that learning disabilities should be included as a category of handicap under the law. Their analyses and recommendations, along with the general climate in the country and the lobbying of parents' organizations, led to Congressional action.

With passage of the Children with Specific Learning Disabilities Act by Congress in 1969, the concept and the field were given the government's official stamp of approval. The Congress also provided a major economic base of support. By 1970 learning disabilities were becoming one of the most frequently identified problems among official handicapping conditions.

Legislation for the handicapped particularly benefited from the social climate of the 1970s (see Feature 4-5, p. 89). Whereas in the 143 years between 1827 and 1970 only 114 federal laws were passed that focused on the handicapped, in the five years between March 1970 and March 1975, 61 such laws were enacted (Weintraub, Abeson, Ballard, & La Vor, 1976). The three landmark acts during these five years were (1) Section 504 of the Rehabilitation Act of 1973, (2) Public Law 93-380, the Education of the Handicapped Amendments of 1974, and (3) Public Law 94-142, the Education for All Handicapped Children Act of 1975. This last law was intended to guarantee that every youngster (from ages 3 to 21) diagnosed as handicapped would receive a free and appropriate education; it indicated certain procedural protections for their rights; and it specified procedures to identify and plan instruction with a view to strengthening special education programming.

In the 1980s Congress updated and extended these acts; it passed the Rehabilitation Amendments Act of 1986 (Public Law 99-506), reauthorized the Education of the Handicapped Act (in 1983 and 1986), and added a new Amendments Act in 1986 (Public Law 99-457). Of particular importance was the emphasis on ensuring that the full rights and protections established in Public Law 94-142 were applied to handicapped children ages 3–5 as of 1990. Also stressed was the importance of the family in planning an appropriate program from birth on. The focus on infants and preschoolers has resulted in a shift from Individual Education Plans (IEPs) to Individual Family Service Plans (IFSPs) for young children.

On July 26, 1990, the Americans with Disabilities Act (Public Law 101-336) was signed into law in the United States. This act extends civil-rights protections to individuals with disabilities in private-sector employment, all public services, public accommodations, transportation, and telecommunications. It is anticipated that this act will have a significant impact on adolescents and adults diagnosed as having learning disabilities as they pursue employment opportunities and grievances about discrimination.

On October 30, 1990, the Education of the Handicapped Act Amendments of 1990 was signed into Public Law 101-476 with a new name—Individuals with Disabilities Act. Throughout the amendments, the word *handicapped* was replaced with the term *individuals with disabilities.*

As a direct result of federal legislation and funding, the LD field and related training, program development, and research flourished in the late 1960s and throughout the 1970s. One of the first effects was seen at universities and colleges, where training programs to prepare professionals to specialize in learning disabilities burgeoned.

Between 1971 and 1980, 97 Child Service Demonstration Centers were established (Mann et al., 1984). There was at least one center in every state and one in Puerto Rico. Besides providing services to those with learning disabilities, these programs aided in training and in program research and development activity. Relatedly, the group of model demonstrations known as the Handicapped Children's Early Education Programs (HCEEP) were established with the aid of federal support (de Weerd, 1984).

To focus on major concerns confronting the field, five university-based Learning Disabilities Research Institutes were funded across the United States during the 1970s. The institutes focused on (1) learning-disabled adolescents and on learning strategies (University of Kansas), (2) processing deficits in the three Rs (Teachers College, Columbia University), (3) social competence and communication (University of Illinois, Chicago Circle), (4) cognitive theory and the control of attention (University of Virginia), and (5) assessment-identification-placement practices (University of Minnesota). A summary of the institutes' work is available in *Exceptional Education Quarterly* (1983). Their efforts contributed to an increased appreciation of the issues surrounding the field and the directions that needed to be pursued.

Despite the fact that federal law in the United States provides for educating handicapped individuals from age 3 to 21, the early preoccupation of the field was clearly with children. Throughout the 1970s and 1980s, however, increasing attention has been paid to learning disabilities among adolescents and adults. This has resulted in efforts to provide and improve programs for such persons in secondary schools and colleges and has created renewed interest in career and vocational education to meet the needs of those with learning disabilities.

In the first half of the 1980s, federal involvement declined in fields such as learning disabilities. The immediate impact was a major decrease in support for the types of demonstration, training, and research activities described here. The federal administration's stated intent was that local and state governments and private philanthropy take over important public services where the federal government left off. However, socioeconomic and political conditions worked against such a development.

Changing Definitions

In reviewing the literature, Hammill (1990) found a total of 11 different definitions that previously had been seriously considered or currently have prominence. As discussed in Chapter 1, the dominant definition has been the one enacted into Public Law 94-142. The source of that definition is credited to the efforts of Samuel Kirk beginning in 1962.

By the late 1970s, dissatisfaction with the "federal" definition led the National Joint Committee for Learning Disabilities (NJCLD) to formulate a new one. In developing their definition, the NJCLD wanted one that was

basically a *theoretical statement* specifying the delimiting characteristics of conditions called learning disabilities. These attributes had to be broad enough to include all known examples of learning disabilities, yet narrow enough to permit the distinction of learning disabilities from other conditions. The purpose of the definition was to establish learning disabilities theoretically—not to set up specific operational criteria for identifying individual cases. Important as operational criteria may be to school placement, research subject selection, and funding practices, the theoretical statement must come first, because it serves as a guide for generating actual objective identification procedures. To be practical, the abstract contents of the definition must be implemented in administrative rules and regulations. (Hammill et al., 1981, pp. 338–39)

The NJCLD's definition was formally proposed in 1981, with the dissent of one of its participating organizations (the Learning Disabilities Association of America—then known as the Association for Children with Learning Disabilities). The board of directors of the dissenting group subsequently offered a revised version.

In 1987 an expanded version of the NJCLD definition was sent to Congress as part of a report from the federal Interagency Committee on Learning Disabilities (composed of representatives of 12 agencies of the Department of Health and Human Services and the Department of Education). This version added a reference to difficulties in acquiring and using social skills and appended attention deficit disorders to the list of concomitant handicaps.

In 1989, after additional discussions and compromises, the NJCLD offered a further revision. To minimize misinterpretation of the proposed definition, the NJCLD (1989) prepared a phrase-by-phrase rationale. Given its historical significance, we outline this rationale here.

- *Learning disabilities is a general term* (a global or generic term under which a variety of specific disorders can be conveniently and reasonably grouped)
- *that refers to a heterogeneous group of disorders* (disorders that are specific and different in kind and appear in the designated ability areas)
- *manifested by significant difficulties* (highly detrimental effects that handicap and seriously limit

performance of some key ability—because "mildly handicapped" often has been used as a synonym, the Committee stated that learning disabilities can be just as debilitating as any other handicapping condition such as cerebral palsy, mental retardation, or blindness)

- *in the acquisition and use of listening, speaking, reading, writing, reasoning or mathematical abilities* (the term applies only when a disorder has resulted in serious impairment of one or more of these abilities)
- *These disorders are intrinsic to the individual* (the source of disorder is within the person affected, not the result of economic deprivation, poor child-rearing practices, faulty school instruction, societal pressures, and so on; such factors may complicate identification and hamper treatment but are not considered the cause)
- *presumed to be due to central nervous system dysfunction* (a known or presumed CNS dysfunction has caused the learning disability—for example, sequelae of traumatic damage to tissues, inherited factors, biochemical insufficiencies or imbalances)

The last sentence is intended to spell out clearly not only that learning disabilities are intrinsic to the individual but also that the source of the problem is structural or functional within the central nervous system.

The controversy over definition continues (Bartoli, 1990; Morrison & Siegel, 1991; Siegel, 1989), despite the suggestion by some that a consensus is at hand (Hammill, 1990). And, despite the domination of the federal definition, available evidence suggests that a variety of definitions and criteria actually are used in diagnosing learning disabilities (see Feature 2). Clearly, much work remains to be done in developing and implementing a definition that can move the field forward (Adelman, 1992; Swanson, 1991).

Looking to the Future

In 1984, we undertook the task of surveying prominent LD professionals to clarify what they viewed as the most fundamental concerns facing the field. We wanted to begin a process that would stimulate more systematic thought and planning for the future.

We mailed the brief survey to persons listed as (1) editorial consultants to the *Journal of Learning Disabilities* and the *Learning Disability Quarterly,* (2) officers of the Council for Learning Disabilities (CLD), the Division of Learning Disabilities (DLD), and the Association for Children and Adults with Learning Disabilities (ACLD), (3) fellows and members of the International Academy for Research in Learning Disabilities (IARLD), and (4) authors of learning disability textbooks.

Although a few respondents expressed concern that perhaps there was no such thing as an LD field, or that there would be no LD field in the not-too-distant future, most accepted its existence and were concerned with improving the field. The range of problems and issues they wanted to see resolved reflects that concern.

Respondents cited the need for general improvements in theory, research, practice, and training. Improvement in the quality of theoretical analyses was seen as essential to upgrading research; better theory and research were seen as providing the foundation for improving practice, training, and policy, and as the key to maintaining the integrity of the field.

For the majority, concern about defining LD (arriving at a conceptual and operational consensus of just what constitutes a learning disability) was seen as basic to efforts to advance the field. At the same time, the conflicting views that make it so difficult to deal with the matter of defining LD were seen in the responses of those who want the definition broadened versus those who want it narrowed.

There were also expressions about the need for more and better programs to enhance public awareness, improve legislation, and reduce politicization of the field. As to who might provide guidance in resolving current problems and issues, it was implied that much of the field's future is in the hands of those working for government agencies, major research groups, the leaders of professional and lay organizations, and journal editors and editorial boards.

A sample of some of the specific concerns raised by respondents is provided here. For a more detailed presentation, see the original report (Adelman & Taylor, 1985b).

Theory and Research

The most fundamental theoretical concern expressed was that the field does not draw adequately on the theoretical advances of those disciplines relevant to understanding learning, learning problems, and their correction. Specifically cited was the need for systematic effort to

- clarify differences in paradigms and their implications for theory, research, and practice
- base LD theories on psychological and neurophysiological theories of normal human development and functioning

- incorporate transactional, cognitive, and motivational theories into discussions of LD
- develop and clarify (in developmental terms) psycholinguistic analyses of reading and writing
- clarify theoretical bases for intervention practices (assessment, instruction, treatment, service delivery systems, public education)

Deficiencies in theory and lack of agreement about what constitutes LD were seen as seriously

Feature 2 Varying Definitions

Research on how the term *learning disability* is defined by various experts indicates a variety of definitions in use (Frankenberg & Harper, 1987; Frankenberg & Fronzaglio, 1991; Mercer, Hughes, & Mercer, 1985; McNutt, 1986; Tucker, Stevens, & Ysseldyke, 1983). This results in great variations in who is diagnosed as having learning disabilities and is a major factor associated with the 140 percent increase during the 1980s in the number of students identified as LD (Reed & Sautter, 1990).

In one study (Shepard & Smith, 1983), the findings indicate that only 28 percent of those diagnosed and placed in LD programs met a stringent criterion for learning disabilities. Another 15 percent met weak criteria. The remaining 57 percent appeared to be misdiagnosed (were slow learners, persons nonfluent in English, persons with minor behavior problems, or persons with other handicapping conditions). Similar findings are reported by others (McLeskey & Waldron, 1991).

Even when school districts employ a very specific definition, students not meeting the definition have been declared to have learning disabilities by decision-making teams for administrative reasons (Mirkin, Marston, & Deno, 1982).

The degree of discrepancy between a child's achievement and intellectual potential is seen as an important criterion in diagnosing learning disabilities. The discrepancy is supposed to be severe. Each locale sets its own criteria for how large the discrepancy must be before it is considered severe. Some have adopted one or another

of various discrepancy formulas that have been developed.

In a study of eight widely cited discrepancy formulas (Forness, Sinclair, & Guthrie, 1983), the investigators used all eight formulas in diagnosing each individual in a sample of children with learning problems. Findings show the formulas vary greatly in the number of individuals identified as having a learning disability. One formula identified 10.9 percent of the children, while another identified 37 percent.

Because of varying definitions and criteria, students in one LD program often differ in very important ways from those in another program. This is also true of individuals included in different research studies. This variation hurts the field in many ways. Because research samples have been extremely different from each other, it has been very difficult to arrive at sound conclusions about the causes of learning disabilities and about the characteristics and intervention needs of those with learning disabilities. In turn, the lack of conclusive research has hurt efforts to improve service programs and to evolve public policy.

Leaders in the field have called for consistent reporting of descriptions of individuals in learning disabilities research and service programs as a way of reducing the confusion engendered by the varying definitions and criteria (Keogh, Major-Kingsley, et al., 1982). Along with this trend, increasing efforts are being made to identify subtypes among those diagnosed as having learning disabilities.

handicapping research. Research needs cited range from further clarifying who we are talking about to development and validation of effective and efficient identification procedures and corrective interventions (including preventive strategies) for all age levels. In this connection, major issues were raised about whether and when to broaden or narrow the theoretical focus that determines which correlates, hypotheses, and programming considerations are explored.

On a basic research level, primary concern was for continued investigation of brain-behavior relationships associated with LD (neurophysiological/neuroanatomical bases for LD and its manifestations). Other basic research concerns stressed the need for more study of information processing related to memory and attention problems and of language and psycholinguistic development related to learning to read and write.

Respondents also proposed investigation of a variety of correlates seen as likely to have major implications for intervention. Social competence, problem-solving deficiencies, child abuse, juvenile sexual trauma, familial patterns, sexual and cultural (including immigrant group) differences were noted specifically. The importance of developmental comparisons between the nondisabled and those with learning disabilities was frequently stressed.

Many concerns about applied research could not be readily separated from those pointing to immediate needs for improving daily practices. These are covered in the following discussion.

Practice

Four major areas of concern to practitioners were identified: subtyping, differential programming, expanding intervention focus and improving efficacy, and prevention and early intervention.

Subtyping Most frequently mentioned (by over half the respondents) was the necessity of developing valid procedures for differential diagnosis and subtyping (for defining, identifying, and classifying the subgroups to be served).

This concern included expression of the need for

1. theory-based activity directed at clarifying the relevant differences between LD and other handicapped individuals at all ages and within the group identified as LD (differentiating dyslexia

from other forms of LD, gifted LD from those with average intelligence)
2. developing valid assessment procedures and criteria for differential diagnoses

In this context, several issues were raised. One was whether to continue seeking agreement on what constitutes a severe discrepancy between aptitude and achievement or whether to develop other criteria for defining LD operationally. Another focused on the advisability of broadening the field by defining as LD any learning problem that is not readily understood.

Differential programming The next most frequently cited practitioner concern focused on the use of differential instruction and treatment. Included was recognition of the need to accommodate persons whose differences and disabilities interfere with their ability to meet conventional standards.

This concern encompassed expression of the need to develop and validate corrective intervention strategies and related assessment procedures for appropriately identified subgroups and to implement them in ways that remove or minimize stigma.

In the context of differential programming for major subgroups, the issue raised was whether the same ends could be accomplished by programming more effectively for individual differences. Paralleling this concern was the view that too many students are being labeled as LD and provided with special education resources who do not really need such specialized assistance (those able to learn satisfactorily if motivated and in programs that can accommodate a wide range of individual differences).

Expanding intervention focus and improving efficacy The third most frequently cited set of applied concerns stressed the need to expand the nature of intervention activity and improve efficacy through evaluation research. The major focus was on traditional and recently introduced practices (with particular reference to investigating factors that facilitate and interfere with efficacy). There was also considerable emphasis on creating new approaches.

Specifically cited were the need for

• expansion and improvement of academic, vocational, career, and self-help programs, especially for adolescents and young adults (a more comprehensive approach to providing services and programs to meet the range of problems and needs that arise at each stage of life for those with LD)

- emphasizing more than deficits (increasing the focus on interests, talents, and strengths of those with LD)
- expansion and improvement of services for LD in public-school settings
- development and validation of a greater variety of instructional procedures that minimize the drudgery of learning basic skills (use of microcomputers, increased range of program and personal options)
- development and validation of specific roles that family members can play in helping individuals with LD
- development and validation of procedures that improve the degree of generalization and maintenance of what students with LD are taught
- long-term follow-up studies to clarify LD treatment efficacy and postschool status with reference to subtypes (or at least contrasting mild with severe/profound problems)
- exploration of psychophysiological/neuropsychological interventions
- clarification of system variables that interfere with, or best facilitate, the learning of individuals with LD

Prevention and early intervention The fourth most frequently cited major area expressed the desire to prevent or at least identify and correct LD at an early age. Specified as needs were (1) increased research on genetic factors, at-risk individuals (infants, young children), and the onset of learning disabilities, (2) intervention and applied research focused on prereferral populations and on detection and intervention at preschool age and in primary grades, and (3) programs to better accommodate individual delays in development.

Training

In addition to higher standards in preparing LD practitioners and researchers, training concerns stressed the need to educate all professionals who have contact with the LD population, to broaden the range of functional consultation to health professionals and families, and to expand public education programs. The major training issue mentioned was the matter of categorical versus generic training and certification. In this connection, the validity of separate competency lists for training and certifying LD

professionals was questioned. The issue of categorical versus generic training, of course, is basic to the continuation of the LD field as a separate entity.

The following points about expanding training-program curricula were advocated:

- More emphasis should be given to what is actually known regarding the constitutional bases for LD and the range of specific disabilities among individuals labeled as LD.
- More attention should be given to behavioral facets of LD.
- The implications of developmental and motivational differences for understanding learning, learning problems, and the correction of such problems should be stressed.
- With respect to methods of practice, greater emphasis should be given to how to adapt and create corrective strategies rather than overrelying on conventionally accepted but unproven approaches.

Taken as a whole, the survey responses were interpreted as prescribing the following future agenda for the LD field. Now that the initial period of exploration and debate in the field is over, the time has come to strengthen conceptual formulations related to (1) identifying the causes of LD, (2) differentiating LD from other learning problems and differentiating among relevant subgroups of learning disabilities, and (3) intervening to ameliorate and prevent. Only with improved conceptualization can more sophisticated research and practical applications be pursued.

To accomplish such ends, there must be changes in training, including recruitment from among the best and the brightest. Professionals must be prepared to use and advance the latest in theoretical analyses and related basic and applied research approaches. Besides recruitment and training of new professionals, there remains a need to attract highly able professionals from a variety of disciplines who can help resolve fundamental concerns.

Finally, a field's survival probably depends as much as anything on the strength of organization and activity manifested by the groups who represent its interests. Formal organizations are a major source of advocacy of ideas and actions, and a major source of lobbying for recognition and support. As a field matures, its organizations must mature. The focus must move beyond the concern for immediate survival to an analysis of the fundamental obstacles to advancing the field's knowledge base and practices. And the analysis must be followed by coordinated action dedicated to overcoming the obstacles.

Building on Critical Analyses

In 1987 Gerald Coles published *The Learning Mystique: A Critical Look at "Learning Disabilities."* This stinging analysis generated intense controversy among professionals and the general public. The main concerns raised were familiar ones about overinterpretation of poor research, widespread misdiagnosis, and limited intervention efficacy. Coles's view is that these problems result from the narrow, biological theories that dominate the field and shape research, training, practice, and policy. He joined many highly respected professionals in cautioning that overreliance on biological explanations mystifies the general public, colludes with tendencies to "blame the victim," and undercuts political pressure on society to improve institutions and systems (such as regular education programs). Primary among his recommendations is the notion that the field should broaden its understanding of learning and learning problems to reflect an interactional theory.

Almost all of the major concerns presented by Coles had been raised by respondents to our 1984 survey of the field or in journal articles and textbooks. For example, it has been a longstanding and widespread concern that much of the research in the field has been poorly conceived, inadequately implemented, and inappropriately interpreted. The demand for improvement has included calls for a new epistemological base, an expanded theoretical focus, and refinements in methodology (Adelman & Taylor, 1985b; Heshusius, 1986; Kavale & Forness, 1985; Keogh, 1986).

There has been widespread agreement that currently diagnosis of LD is not based on valid assessment of neurological dysfunction. Available evidence suggests that the majority of students have been so labeled based only on assessment of relatively severe underachievement—the causes of which remain uncertain (Chalfant, 1985). Failure to differentiate underachievement caused by neurological dysfunctioning from that caused by other factors has been cited as a major deterrent to important lines of LD research and theory and a threat to the very integrity of the field. Because of the diagnostic problem, a large proportion of research purporting to deal with LD samples has more to say about learning *problems* than about learning *disabilities*.

The weight of available evidence also points to the limited efficacy of prevailing approaches to intervention (Horn et al., 1983; Torgesen & Wong, 1986). In this context, the failure to differentiate among types of problems and subtypes of disabilities has also been cited as undermining research and practice.

Since the concerns raised were not new, it seems that Coles's critique was so controversial because the criticisms were compiled into a format for widespread consumption and were presented with considerable passion. The reactions were equally passionate (see articles in the *Journal of Learning Disabilities,* May 1989). If nothing else, the heated interchange certainly indicates that at this stage of its evolution the LD field remains bloody but unbowed.

Summing Up

The field of learning disabilities is relatively young. It is a field full of controversy. As this brief history indicates, the field has evolved rapidly, and major shifts in professional organizations and government support suggest rapid ongoing change—but not necessarily progress.

I.2   CNS Function and Assessment of Minor Dysfunction

Student to friend: "The human brain is amazing. The only time mine stops functioning is when I'm called on in class."

Theories about learning disabilities have suggested possible dysfunctions in each of the major parts of the brain. For example, because the reticular formation, or reticular activating system, filters stimuli to the cerebrum, it has been suggested that some problems in attentiveness are due to cerebral overstimulation caused by dysfunction in this system. However, because the majority of current theories about learning disabilities are concerned with cerebral cortex dysfunctioning, we will focus our brief discussion on this area of the CNS (see Feature 1).

Cerebral Cortex

Although the roles of the two hemispheres of the cerebral cortex differ, some functions of the body, such as vision and hearing, involve both sides of the brain. For instance, the left hemisphere receives stimuli from the right visual field of each eye, and the right hemisphere receives stimuli from the left visual field of each eye. Motor movements also involve both sides: movement on the right side of the body is controlled by the left hemisphere and vice versa.

For most people, the left hemisphere is primarily concerned with language functioning and analytic thought; the right hemisphere is primarily, although not exclusively, concerned with nonverbal functioning, and processes information as a whole. Functions related to most fine arts (drawing, music, dance) are associated with the right hemisphere. While the right hemisphere tends to have nonverbal functions, it apparently can assume some language functions. For example, if a child is born with a defect in the left hemisphere or if the left side is damaged before about age 12, the right hemisphere may take over language functions.

When the left hemisphere is damaged to the point where language is affected, learning and performance are subsequently affected (problems may arise with reading, writing, and verbal communicating). When the damage is in the right hemisphere, it affects spatial imagery (understanding math concepts and performing fine and industrial arts).

Each hemisphere has (1) four major regions (the temporal, frontal, parietal, and occipital lobes), (2) separators between the regions (such as the angular gyrus, the lateral sulcus), and (3) related association areas. Efforts to map out regions of the brain related to specific behaviors have pinpointed areas in the cortex responsible for certain functions. For example, the parietal lobe is associated with reading and writing, and dysfunctions in areas of this lobe are thought to engender specific learning disabilities in reading and writing.

References are included at the end of this reading for those interested in further information about brain function as it relates to learning disabilities.

Assessing Minor CNS Dysfunction

If a differential diagnosis is meant to identify learning disabilities that are caused by a neurological problem, it is necessary to show that the CNS dysfunction is minor. (If there is a severe neurological problem, other diagnoses, such as gross brain damage or cerebral palsy, are more appropriate.) Such a differential diagnosis requires valid measurement of specific indicators of minor neurological dysfunction or immaturity. Unfortunately, although major CNS dysfunctions usually are identified with relative ease, it is not so easy for minor ones. To explain why this is so, and to further exemplify the problems of differential diagnosis, we turn to a brief discussion of assessing minor neurological dysfunctioning in general, and the concept of "soft signs" in particular.

Neurological Soft Signs

In medicine, the term *signs* refers to *objective* evidence of disease, such as detection of a specific virus. When a sign is found, the illness can be diagnosed readily.

Since the late 1940s, it has become increasingly commonplace for practitioners to diagnose minor neurological dysfunctions by finding "soft signs."

This trend has occurred because objective signs are not present for minor neurological dysfunctions.

What are called *soft signs* (or sometimes equivocal, borderline, or ambiguous signs) are not signs at all; they are symptoms. For instance, in general medicine, symptoms, such as nausea and dizziness, are *subjective* and may occur along with many types of illness. They may be interpreted differently by different professionals. What professionals do agree about with regard to the behaviors called *soft* *signs* is that these symptoms resemble those seen in brain-damaged individuals (see Feature 2).

Neuropsychological Assessment

Assessment of neurological soft signs primarily involves tasks of motor and sensorimotor integration (see end of reading for references). Findings from this type of assessment can be differentiated from findings that are considered more direct indications

Feature 1   Major Areas of the Brain and Their Functions

The brain and spinal cord are the two major components of the CNS. Brain activity is determined by the biological structure and electrochemical transmissions of the nervous system.

The brain consists of the brain stem, cerebellum, and cerebral cortex (cerebrum). The functions associated with each are:

1. *brain stem* — integrates heart and breathing rates, regulates motor reflexes, and houses the reticular activating system, which instigates electrical activity in the cerebral cortex

2. *cerebellum* — coordinates the voluntary muscle system and is involved in controlling balance and coordinating muscle movement

3. *cerebral cortex* — controls all conscious activity. It consists of two halves, the left and right hemispheres, which have different functions but are almost the same in construction and metabolism. They are connected by the corpus callosum, a large group of fibers, which serves as the channel of communication between the two halves.

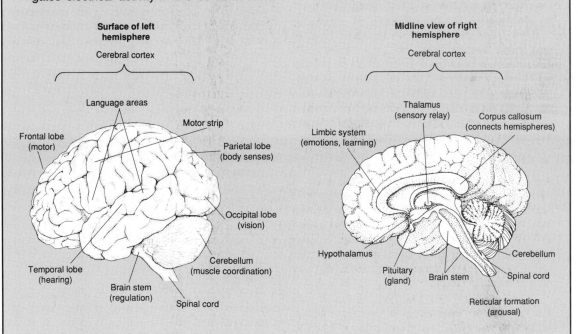

Illustration adapted from T. J. Teyler, "The Brain Sciences," in *Education and the Brain*, J. S. Chall and A. F. Mirsky, eds., Chicago: University of Chicago Press, 1978, p. 10. Reprinted by permission.

of brain status. For example, direct electrophysiological measures, such as the electroencephalogram (EEG), are useful in detecting gross brain dysfunctions. Unfortunately, such direct measures have had limited effectiveness in identifying minimal dysfunctions.

To improve assessment of CNS functioning, neu-ropsychological test batteries have been developed. These procedures attempt to go beyond assessing motor and sensorimotor integration by including measures of higher-level cognitive skills. With the rise in use of such batteries as standard ways to measure CNS dysfunction, there appears to be a tendency not only to expand the number and types

Feature 2   Soft Signs

Of the many procedures that may be used in a standard neurological exam, two examples follow.

As one check of oculomotor functioning, the examiner holds a finger in front of the youngster's eyes and then slowly moves it into the peripheral vision area on one side of the head and then on the other. Those tested are instructed to follow the movement only with their eyes and not move their heads. Anyone over the age of 5 is supposed to be able to do this successfully. Anyone older who persists in moving his or her head is seen as responding abnormally. One such abnormal response is called *nystagmus,* which is a condition in which both eyes slowly drift toward the periphery and then suddenly snap back (Curtis, Jacobson, & Marcus, 1972).

As a check on tactile and kinesthetic perception, those tested are asked to close their eyes. The examiner then touches the child on the left hand, on the right hand and left side of the face, and on the left hand and right side of the face. After each touch, the youngster is asked to identify the place of stimulation. The sequence is repeated four times. Again, those over 5 are supposed to be able to identify such stimuli with no more than one error out of the 12 touches.

Neurologists, of course, use medical terms in referring to tests for soft signs. For example, the second test described above is known as the test for simultanagnosia. Other soft-sign tests look for choreiform movements, mild dysphasias, borderline hyperflexia and reflex asymmetrics, finger agnosia, dysdiadochokinesis, graphesthesias, and so forth (Schain, 1972).

In using tests to detect soft signs, neurologists are looking for responses that are significantly, but not grossly, less than those expected for the age. The degree of performance deficit considered a problem, however, is not well established, and there is not yet a set number or pattern of soft signs that must be found before a diagnosis of learning disabilities can be made.

The logic behind the use of soft signs is reflected in a statement by William Gaddes in his 1985 book, *Learning Disabilities and Brain Function: A Neuropsychological Approach:*

> The confusion in defining MBD [Minimal Brain Dysfunction] stems from the common difficulty of identifying any borderline phenomenon. . . . Intense and localized brain damage in specific . . . areas will produce predictable deficits in adult behavior. . . . As we move along the continuum toward normal brain structure and function, however, we pass through a large number of children and adults who are not "brain damaged" and who, for no known reason, show many behavioral deficits similar to the brain-damaged patients, but in a much less intense way. These behavioral impairments (e.g., visual reversals, poor finger location, asymmetry of finger tapping, and a-stereognosis) are the soft signs, and their presence suggests very strongly that the person's brain and central nervous system has some minimal areas of dysfunction, although a standard neurological examination may have turned up nothing. (pp. 84–85)

Reviewers of research on soft signs indicate major problems in using these measures as indicators of minor CNS dysfunctioning (Taylor & Fletcher, 1983). Current evidence suggests caution when such measures are used to diagnose learning disabilities.

of tests but also to expand the number of soft signs.

In general, neuropsychological assessors attempt to measure

1. gross and fine motor coordination, including integrated motor acts (such as tying shoes, buttoning, placing the finger on the nose)
2. oculomotor functioning (such as eye-muscle control, relative diameter of the pupils)
3. postural control, gait, reflexes, and tremors (such as walking a straight line on tiptoes without awkwardness)
4. auditory and visual perception and related cognitive skills (such as recognition and discrimination of stimuli, reproduction of rhythmic patterns, discrimination of right and left, understanding and following simple commands, ability to make simple generalizations and deductions)
5. tactile and kinesthetic perception (such as ability to locate and discriminate sensations, movement detection)
6. speech and language functioning (such as articulation, ability to repeat and initiate verbal responses)
7. memory (such as immediate recall of verbal and nonverbal stimuli — with and without interference)
8. general looks and demeanor (such as physical characteristics)

In addition, some degree of effort often is made to assess basic skills in reading, writing, and arithmetic.

What neuropsychological assessors are seeking is any evidence of abnormal CNS functioning, including performance below expected age level. What they are measuring is overt behavior. When the behavior is not up to expectation, the part of the brain that is responsible for such behavior may not be functioning appropriately. Such a conclusion is likely to be most valid when other reasonable explanations can be ruled out. It helps if it can be shown that the behavior is not the result of psychological and sociocultural factors (such as emotional disturbance, or growing up in economically deprived circumstances). Another problem involves age or developmental expectations. For some of the behaviors being measured, there are disagreements about the point at which performance falls below what should be minimally expected of young children, especially those under age 7.

Summing Up

Each day individuals are diagnosed as having learning disabilities. When the intent of the diagnosis is to identify those whose current learning problems are caused by CNS or psychological dysfunction, then the diagnosis should be based on valid evidence of such dysfunction. Unfortunately, despite the compelling nature of the clues, current assessment procedures cannot always be relied upon to provide conclusive evidence of such dysfunctions.

Currently, research is being directed at improving methods to assess neurologically and psychologically based problems, and researchers remain optimistic about a breakthrough. For example, there is optimism about the promise of new devices for studying the brain, especially those that use computer technology (see Chapter 2).

While we await necessary advances in assessment, efforts to diagnose the causes of learning disabilities must proceed. Current regulations in the United States acknowledge this. Thus, in identifying those who should be diagnosed as having learning disabilities, regulations stress criteria related to severe underachievement and developmental immaturity, rather than focusing on CNS and psychological dysfunction. That is, present practices look more at symptoms than at causes in pursuing procedures for screening, placement, and correction. These practices were discussed in Chapter 3.

Further Readings

Should you be interested in further information about brain function and assessment as related to learning disabilities, see the following.

Barkley, R. (1983). Neuropsychology: Introduction. *Journal of Clinical Child Psychology, 12,* 3–5.

Chall, J. A. & Mirsky, A. F. (Eds.) (1978). *Education and the brain.* Chicago: National Society for the Study of Education.

Denckla, M. B., LeMay, M. & Chapman, C. A. (1985). Few CT scan abnormalities found even in neurologically impaired LD children. *Journal of Learning Disabilities, 18,* 132–35.

Gaddes, W. H. (1985). *Learning disabilities and brain function: A neuropsychological approach.* New York: Springer-Verlag.

Geschwind, N. & Galaburda, A. M. (1987). *Cerebral lateralization.* Cambridge, MA: MIT Press/ Bradford Books.

Hartlage, L. C. & Telzrow, C. F. (1983). The neuropsychological basis for educational intervention. *Journal of Learning Disabilities, 16,* 521–28.

Hiscock, M. & Kinsbourne, M. (1987). Specialization of the cerebral hemispheres: Implications for learning. *Journal of Learning Disabilities, 20,* 130–43.

Hynd, G. W. (1992). Neurological aspects of dyslexia: Comment on the balance model. *Journal of Learning Disabilities, 25,* 110–112.

Hynd, G. W. & Cohen, M. (1983). *Dyslexia: Neuropsychological theory, research, and clinical differentiation.* New York: Grune & Stratton.

Hynd, G. W. & Obrzut, J. E. (Eds.) (1981). *Neuropsychological assessment and the school-age child: Issues and procedures.* New York: Grune & Stratton.

Hynd, G. W., Marshall, R. & Gonzalez, J. (1991). Learning disabilities and presumed central nervous system dysfunction. *Learning Disability Quarterly, 14,* 283–96.

Levine, M. (1987). *Developmental variation and learning disabilities.* Cambridge, MA: Educator's Publishing Service.

Luria, A. R. & Majovski, L. V. (1977). Basic approaches used in American and Soviet clinical neuropsychology. *American Psychologist, 32,* 959–68.

Obrzut, J. E. & Boliek, G. A. (1991). Neuropsychological assessment of childhood learning disabilities. In H. L. Swanson (Ed.), *Handbook of assessment of learning disabilities: Theory, research, and practice* (pp. 121–46). Austin, TX: PRO-ED.

Plaistad, J. R., Gustavson, J. L., Wilkening, G. N. & Golden, C. J. (1983). The Luria-Nebraska Neuropsychological Battery—Children's Revision: Theory and current research findings. *Journal of Clinical Child Psychology, 12,* 13–21.

Rakic, P. (1988). Specification of cerebral cortical areas. *Science, 241,* 170–76.

Reitan, R. M. & Davison, L. A. (1974). *Clinical neuropsychology: Current status and applications.* New York: Winston-Wiley.

Reschly, D. J. & Gresham, F. M. (1989). Current neuropsychological diagnosis of learning problems: A leap of faith. In C. R. Reynolds & E. Fletcher-Janzen (Eds.), *Handbook of clinical child neuropsychology* (pp. 503–519). New York: Plenum.

Rie, H. E. & Rie, E. D. (Eds.) (1980). *Handbook of minimal brain dysfunction: A critical view.* New York: Wiley.

Rourke, B. P., Fisk, J. L. & Strang, J. D. (1986). *Neuropsychological assessment of children: A treatment-oriented approach.* New York: Guilford Press.

Snow, J. F., Hynd, G. W. & Hartlage, L. C. (1984). Differences between mildly and severely learning-disabled children on the Luria-Nebraska Neuropsychological Battery—Children's Revision. *Journal of Psychoeducational Assessment, 2,* 23–28.

Taylor, H. G. (1987). Childhood sequelae of early neurological disorders: A contemporary perspective. *Developmental Neuropsychology, 3,* 153–64.

Tranel, D., Hall, L. E., Olson, S. & Tranel, N. N. (1987). Evidence for a right-hemisphere developmental learning disability. *Developmental Neuropsychology, 3,* 113–27.

I.3 Controversial Treatments and Fads

If an individual is frequently sick or cannot see or hear well, there is an obvious need for medical attention. These problems may or may not be affecting learning, but treatment is well accepted and hardly controversial. There are, however, a range of medical and CNS treatments that, when used with individuals diagnosed as having learning disabilities, are quite controversial.

Vision Training

One ongoing controversy surrounds "vision training" for those who have learning problems (Keogh & Pelland, 1985). Vision training for those with learning problems is based on two related beliefs: one is that many learning problems are caused by faulty eye movements and poor organization of what is seen; the second is that vision training exercises will correct these faults and result in the individuals' overcoming their learning problems. Many optometrists offer such treatment; most ophthalmologists say such training is not worth the time, money, or effort.

Optometrists are trained to examine eye function and to prescribe corrective lenses, but they cannot treat eye diseases or prescribe medication. Some also offer activities they claim improve how the eyes move and function and how the individual organizes visual information. Some also claim such vision training will help those with learning problems. *Ophthalmologists* are medical doctors who specialize in treating eye diseases and injuries. They can also prescribe corrective lenses and could offer vision training if they believed it was helpful.

Critics argue that faulty eye movements and visual organization are not causes of learning problems; they suggest that such visual deficiencies often are simply side effects of learning problems. The growing consensus in the LD field is that the visual training procedures do little to help anyone overcome learning problems (Keogh & Pelland, 1985; Metzger & Werner, 1984).

Colored Lenses

An approach developed by a psychologist, Helen E. Irlen (1983), received a great deal of media attention in the late 1980s and early 1990s. Based on findings that some individuals have excessive retinal sensitivity to particular frequencies of the light spectrum, she postulates that such persons have a specific visual-perceptual dysfunction. Whiting (1985) describes the effects as causing print distortions (blurring or movement), particularly with black-and-white contrasting print. Whiting reports that these distortions are frequently associated with problems focusing for extended periods of time, eye strain, headaches, and poor attention span. Irlen calls the problem "scotopic sensitivity" and assesses such sensitivity with the Irlen Differential Perceptual Schedule. In a 1989 article, Irlen and Lass claimed that approximately 50 percent of those with reading disabilities (including dyslexia) have this problem.

To correct the sensitivity, she prescribes tinted lenses and the use of colored overlays to minimize print distortions. Irlen and her followers claim these techniques improve visual perception and the length of time a person can read, which in turn allows improved reading ability and elimination of related symptoms such as headaches and watery eyes (O'Connor, Sofo, Kendall, & Olsen, 1990; Robinson & Conway, 1990).

Critics warn that favorable discussions and findings reported in the literature are seriously flawed. Some express concern about whether scotopic sensitivity is a valid syndrome (Hoyt, 1990); all are concerned that the methodological flaws in the research done to date have been so pronounced as to make the findings worthless (Parker, 1990).

Stimulant Medication

A variety of drugs has been explored in connection with learning problems (Forness, Cantwell, Swanson, Hanna, & Youpa, 1991; Forness & Kavale,

1988). None is recognized officially by the Food and Drug Administration for treating learning disabilities. Nevertheless, many drugs are used with a view to improving cognitive functioning (Gadow, 1991).

Most commonly used for psychoeducational problems are stimulants such as Ritalin (methylphenidate), Dexedrine (dextroamphetamine), and Cylert (pemoline). These are used widely to treat those whose learning problems are associated with attention deficit disorders and hyperactivity. Prevalence studies (reviewed by Gadow, 1986) suggest that 1 to 2 percent (about a half million) of elementary-age children in the United States receive psychotropic drugs — usually stimulants — for hyperactivity. For those diagnosed with learning disabilities and in special education, approximately 10 to 20 percent receive psychotropic medication (typically Ritalin).

Part of the intrigue that surrounds the use of such drugs with this group stems from the question of how a stimulant makes highly active individuals less active. Although the impression has been created that such medication can be a major part of efforts to *cure* learning disabilities, the usual argument for its use claims much less. Advocates suggest that those given the medication will attend better and therefore learn better. Why this may happen has been widely debated. Both neurological and psychological explanations have been offered (Barkley, 1977; Whalen, 1989).

Research on use of medication has been extremely difficult to do because of sampling problems and difficulty in establishing proper experimental control conditions (Gadow, 1991; Pelham, 1986). Thus conclusions favoring widespread use are not based on satisfactory evidence. There does seem to be some immediate impact on children given relatively high doses. Some seem more controllable and productive on certain simple tasks that they tend not to do when off medication. However, there are no well-designed studies showing consistent evidence that this immediate impact leads to major improvements in reading or other academic learning (or even to getting along better with others over the long run).

Thus some students may *appear* to attend better to schoolwork; however, the evidence does not indicate that this translates into a major solution for learning problems. That is, stimulant medication has not yet been shown to have long-term effects on attention or to help students make major advances in overcoming their learning problems. Where it seems to have helped in the short run, the reason may be more psychological than physiological — thereby raising the possibility that the effects could be achieved without medication. Moreover, although not adequately researched, there is great concern over possible harmful effects, such as loss of sleep, weight loss, and even adverse effects on learning (Forness, Swanson, Cantwell, Youpa, & Hanna, 1992; Swanson, Cantwell, Lerner, McBurnett, & Hanna, 1991).

As with so many treatments of this type, in the absence of adequate research, the dominant view expressed in the literature and media shapes practice. The dominant view regarding medication is that it may help some children overcome their learning problems. Although critics argue that this view is misleading, it prevails. Thus stimulant medication remains a widely popular treatment.

Regardless of how the controversy is finally resolved, it is instructive to think about the impact the use of medication has had in shaping thinking about learning disabilities. This matter was addressed by journalists Peter Schrag and Diane Divoky (1975):

> It is nearly impossible to overestimate the role of the pharmaceutical houses in shaping medical and lay opinion about learning-disabled children. We are not talking here about their campaigns to convince practitioners and parents that medication — usually stimulant drugs — is the answer to problems in learning and behavior . . . but primarily about their part in creating the idea that any number of common childhood quirks are medical problems in the first place. The promotion of drugs to cure learning disabilities and related syndromes . . . is quite obviously related to the promotion of the ailments themselves. (pp. 56–57)

Special Diets and Megavitamin Therapy

Most people recognize that good nutrition is an important part of everyday living. It is also clear that some individuals are allergic to certain foods. Thus it is not controversial to suggest that poor nutrition or eating food that causes allergic reactions can cause other problems. Conflicts arise, however, with suggestions that people can overcome learning and behavior problems by means of the following:

- not eating certain things such as avoiding food additives, preservatives, and refined sugars (Feingold, 1976)
- taking doses of trace elements (calcium, sodium, iron, zinc, copper) to replace apparent deficiencies
- taking massive doses of vitamins (Cott, 1985)

As with research on medication, there is little evidence to support the preceding approaches (Baker, 1980; Haslam, Dalby, & Rademaker, 1984; Kavale & Forness, 1983; Mattes, 1983). Unlike the situation with medication, however, the dominant view remains one of skepticism about such treatments. As with medication, cautions are frequently raised about possible harmful effects (Sieben, 1977; Silver, 1987). Because of the poor quality of studies done to date, proponents argue that no valid conclusions can be drawn until methodologically sound research has been done.

Central Nervous System Training

In Chapter 2, we discussed efforts to retrain the brain when a person has lost certain functions because of brain damage. We also explored some of the efforts to retrain dominance and laterality.

Although the consensus seems to be that the functions of damaged and dysfunctioning areas of the brain can be taken over by other areas, it is not clear under what conditions this occurs. The success of individuals who have regained lost functions has reinforced the idea that the functioning of the central nervous system can be improved through training and "reprogramming." As a result, many treatment approaches are advocated. One of the most controversial with respect to treating learning disabilities has been that of "patterning" (Delacato, 1966; Doman & Delacato, 1968).

Patterning is based on the theory that poor neurological organization is the result of failure to pass through established developmental stages. To correct this problem, the treatment proposes to flood the sensory system with an intense program of stimulation designed to elicit a response from the motor system. Beginning at the earliest stages of motor development, exercises for physical and sensory stimulation have been designed to take the individual through successive stages of growth. In cases where the individual cannot do the exercises, the patterning is imposed (that is, the passive individu-

al's body is manually manipulated). The claim is that the exercises correct damage by inducing proper neural connections.

A variety of professional and parent organizations have issued statements of concern about the use of patterning as a treatment. For example, based on a review of available research, a statement from the American Academy of Pediatrics (1982) concluded that this treatment "offers no special merit, that the claims of its advocates are unproven, and that the demands on families are so great that in some cases there may be harm to its use."

Vestibular Treatment

The vestibular system's relationship to motion has made it a focal point in some explanations of problems such as poor balance and coordination, poor spatial orientation, and faulty eye movements. In turn, the presence of such symptoms (compelling correlates) in an individual with learning problems has been used to suggest that problems in the vestibular system can play a role in causing learning problems. Not surprisingly, once such a "cause" was identified, professionals started to advocate that it should be assessed and treated (Ayres, 1978; Levinson, 1980).

For example, Levinson (1980) has attempted to assess vestibular dysfunctions using "blurring speed" (passing words across the visual field until they could no longer be recognized). It has been argued that such a procedure tests visual performance rather than vestibular functioning. Ayres (1978) has developed treatment exercises that involve activities such as swinging, spinning, being rolled on a big ball, and so forth.

As in other areas of controversy, reports by advocates of the procedures suggest their promise, while other research on the various assessment and treatment approaches tend to be negative or inconclusive (Polatajko, 1985).

Fads and Irresponsible Claims

What makes all of the above approaches controversial is the tremendous disagreement among experts about underlying assumptions regarding

- how the CNS develops
- how current learning problems are connected to

the way the individual's CNS has developed and is functioning

- how specific treatment steps improve neurological functioning

Furthermore, there has been considerable concern over the potential harm that can arise from treatments that require so much commitment in terms of money, time, and effort.

The LD field has been particularly vulnerable to treatment fads and irresponsible claims of effectiveness (Rooney, 1991; Worrall, 1990). Four prominent reasons for this are discussed here.

First, the field is relatively young. When a field is new, there are not enough established, effective treatments available. Everyone is looking for *the* answer. Professionals look for every small clue that might suggest a useful treatment. They are not particularly looking for the reasons a practice may have an effect or whether effects are temporary and superficial. They don't particularly look for limitations and side effects. Often, premature statements are made about the promise of some training activity, test, material, drug, diet, or whatever. The media and individuals primarily interested in making money are always ready to exploit a proposed treat-

Feature 1   Media Example of a Fad

The following item appeared in *Newsweek,* October 8, 1973.

How Coffee Calms Kids
About five in every 100 U.S. grade school children suffer from hyperkinesis, a disorder marked by restlessness, disruptive classroom behavior, and inability to concentrate. In many cases, the condition can be controlled by the administration of stimulant drugs such as amphetamines that have a paradoxical calming effect on hyperkinetic youngsters and improve concentration. But the use of potent stimulants with children is controversial, mainly because they often produce side effects, which include a loss of appetite, insomnia, and abdominal pain. However, a South Carolina psychiatrist seems to have found a simple way out of this therapeutic dilemma: two cups of coffee a day may be as effective as drugs to calm the hyperactive child. Dr. Robert C. Schnackenberg happened upon the solution while taking the histories of hyperkinetic children at the William S. Hill Psychiatric Institution in Columbia, S.C. He was surprised to learn that an unusually high percentage of the youngsters regularly drank coffee. When he asked why, many of the children said the beverage had a calming effect and helped them in school. . . . Coffee drinking, Schnackenberg thinks, may account for the paucity of reports on hyperkinetic children in South America where many young-

sters drink the beverage. The disorder undoubtedly exists there, Schnackenberg says, but children may be "inadvertently treating their own symptoms."

Can you criticize the conclusions made in this article?
Sieben (1977) warns that

we must resist the temptation to follow each treatment fad willy-nilly. We must realize that newspapers and news broadcasts are poor sources of medical information. Simplistic new theories offer hope and have news value, but their refutation is a tedious and thankless task which holds little interest for such media. The burden of proof is on the promoter of a new theory. . . . To promote a hypothesis as fact without first submitting it to rigorous testing is a tremendous disservice to the patient and to the public . . . [and] an abuse of the very children we presume to be helping. . . . We should be alert for signs that a proposed treatment may be poorly substantiated. . . . We should be particularly careful in drawing conclusions from anecdotal case reports. . . . They afford fresh insights into familiar problems. Yet they are by their very nature biased, subjective, and impressionistic. . . . Such cases are provocative, but they do not establish the validity of new treatments. We have been misled too many times. (p. 147)

ment as long as there are eager consumers (see Feature 1). And, of course, those with problems are anxious for any help that the "experts" say is worth pursuing. As one writer succinctly notes:

> The parents of a child who has been labeled as physically, psychologically, or academically deficient are usually avid consumers of ideas that promise help. These parents are struggling to understand what may be incomprehensible. But answers come easy, and all too often they are given by individuals with well-lubricated ethics in a forceful, professional, quasi-scientific and logical manner. (Pihl, 1975, p. 23)

A second reason for the field's vulnerability to fads and irresponsible claims is that learning disabilities are poorly defined and identified. As long as so many types of learning problems can be identified as learning disabilities, it is easy to claim that any treatment that is effective with any learning problem may be effective with a learning disability.

Third, evaluating treatment effectiveness is extremely difficult. There are severe limitations to all efforts to evaluate a specific treatment. This is true for both positive and negative outcomes. As a result, it is not yet possible to base claims of treatment effects on comprehensive research. This is why placement and treatment choices reflect decision-makers' beliefs more than they do adequate research evidence. Without comprehensive evaluations of treatments, it is relatively easy for anyone to make positive claims as long as the approach they are pushing has an intuitive appeal. At the same time, the absence of adequate research findings makes it difficult to present conclusive arguments against such claims.

Finally, misinterpretations of reasons for positive outcomes are easy to make. Because a specific treatment takes place in the context of a variety of events and usually occurs over a period of time, many other factors besides the treatment may actually cause a positive change in a specific individual. For example, medical practitioners know that positive changes sometimes are the result of psychological factors rather than a specific treatment. In fact,

sometimes placebos (plain pills that look and taste like medication) are given in place of drugs when a doctor finds that a certain patient stops having symptoms simply by taking what he or she thinks is medication. (Well-designed treatment research must have a group that receives placebos; most of the research related to controversial treatments has not included such a group.) Getting older and maturing is another factor that can produce change regardless of treatment. When such factors operate, as they usually do for some individuals involved in any treatment, the tendency is to assume the specific treatment worked in these cases.

Apparent success leads to the recommendation of the treatment to others. The more enthusiastic and influential the recommenders, the more likely the word will spread about the promise of the treatment.

Summing Up

Treatments for learning disabilities are highly marketable commodities. To meet the growing demand for treatments to correct learning and behavior problems, an increasing number of persons, agencies, and companies are selling tests and programmed materials, training exercises, medication, and anything else that people can be convinced to buy.

If the sales pitch is good enough, people tend to ignore the limitations and potential harm of many practices. Ironically, some procedures come to be accepted as valid simply because they are so widely used. People seem to think that a practice must be good, or else why would so many textbooks discuss it, professionals offer it, companies sell it, legislative bodies endorse it, and consumers buy it. This type of validation has been jokingly called "market" or "cash" validity.

When there is a considerable amount of money that can be made if a treatment comes into vogue, it can be expected that special interests will help publicize the promise of their product. In such cases, it really becomes a matter of "buyer beware!"

I.4   Remedying Learning Disabilities: Prevailing Approaches

As discussed in *Learning Disabilities in Historical Perspective* (p. 291), remedial approaches for learning disabilities have been drawn from practices that were developed over the course of the twentieth century in clinics and classrooms. Thus, although practitioners in the LD field have adopted a variety of terms to describe their work, the major approaches can be grouped under the two contrasting orientations to remediation we discussed in Chapter 3 — underlying or observable problem approaches.

Underlying Problem Approaches

LD practitioners who use underlying problem approaches assume there is an internal dysfunction at the root of the learning problem. Both the initial and recent emphasis in the field has been to see the underlying problem as biological — namely, a minor CNS dysfunction. The underlying CNS dysfunction is seen as interfering with processes (such as short-term memory, selective attention) required to learn effectively and efficiently. As discussed in Chapter 2, over time this state of affairs is seen as affecting development (such as slowing it down or producing developmental anomalies). In turn, this interferes with acquiring certain prerequisites (such as visual and auditory perceptual discriminations) needed in learning to read, write, and so forth. Failure to acquire these prerequisites impedes subsequent learning and performance.

Lagging Development

To expand briefly on Chapter 2, lags in development (sometimes called maturational lags) are common and except in extreme cases are not matters of great concern. There are marked developmental differences both among people and within the same person with respect to sensory, perceptual, motoric, cognitive, language, social, and emotional functioning.

In most cases, there is no way to determine why some individuals develop at a slower (or for that matter at a faster) rate than others overall or in a particular area. But, it is commonplace for some individuals to lag behind at one time and eventually to catch up or even spurt ahead.

Learning problems arise when an individual has not yet developed sufficiently to meet age-related expectations and demands. This happens particularly in learning environments, such as school, and with respect to specific learning tasks, such as discriminating between letters, learning to write, and so forth. Such problems can make it more difficult for the individual to catch up. Overcoming such learning problems may be even harder if the initial lag in development was due to a CNS dysfunction.

Given the lack of diagnostic procedures to assess minor CNS dysfunctions validly, remedial decisions for young children generally are based on early indications of learning problems associated with lagging development. There have been frequent warnings about the difficulty of differentiating common fluctuations in development from those where the individual's developmental lag warrants a learning-disabilities diagnosis.

> Our clinical findings over the years since the term *learning disability* has come into vogue is that a large percentage of the boys and girls referred to our own clinical service as learning disabled have been children of apparently quite normal academic potential who simply were overplaced in school. In our opinion, these children are having trouble in school chiefly because they were started too soon — on the basis of their chronological age rather than their behavior age.
>
> Based on our clinical findings, we would urge all those involved with the process of education to make absolutely certain that they are not labelling any child as learning disabled who is immature or young for the grade he or she is in and who is thus failing simply because he or she is not ready for the work involved. (Ames, 1983, p. 19)

Developmental Anomalies

As also discussed in Chapter 2, development may be impeded or distorted because of brain injury or other factors causing CNS dysfunction (genetic abnormalities, endocrine malfunctions). Such factors may cause delayed neurological maturation, development of abnormal brain structures, or malfunctioning of connections between brain cells. Resulting problems may take the form of unusual behavior, difficulty in learning, or both. Obviously, developmental anomalies can be major factors interfering with efforts to teach.

Remedial Approaches

Remedial and treatment approaches used by those oriented to underlying problems include educational, psychological, and even some medically related strategies. As outlined in Table 1, those who pursue this orientation to learning disabilities attempt to address a range of developmental disabilities seen as disrupting learning.

Although the primary overall concern is with underlying problems, classroom programs also provide instruction to teach students age-appropriate school and life skills (especially readiness skills), and pursue strategies designed to minimize behavior that interferes with classroom instruction.

The roots of this orientation are found in medical, psychotherapeutic, and educational concepts. Thus the resulting corrective interventions usually are built

Table 1   Two Contrasting Remedial Orientations

	Underlying Problem Approaches	Observable Problem Approaches
PRIMARY OVERALL CONCERN	Developmental disabilities (lags and anomalies) that disrupt learning	Age-appropriate unlearned skills
	SPECIFIC AREAS OF CONCERN	
	Development • perceptual problems • motoric problems • language problems • general cognitive problems Compensatory strategies for overcoming areas of continuing disability	School/life knowledge and skills • readiness (for learning) skills (including strategies for learning) • basic language/reading and math • academic content areas • life adjustment skills (including social and vocational skills)
SECONDARY CONCERN	Age-appropriate unlearned skills (i.e., school/life knowledge and skills)	Interfering behaviors (e.g., poor impulse control, lack of sustained attention)
TERTIARY CONCERN	Interfering behaviors	
PROCESS COMPONENTS	**ASSESSMENT**	
	Construct-oriented assessment of developmental functioning for program planning and evaluation	School curriculum-based assessment of sequential skills for program planning, monitoring, and evaluation
	FORM OF OBJECTIVES	
	Nonbehavioral, as well as behavioral and criterion-referenced objectives	Behavioral and criterion-referenced (observable) objectives
	REMEDIAL RATIONALE AND METHODS	
	Therapy-oriented interventions (primary emphasis on establishing rapport through interpersonal dynamics) • exercises intended to correct developmental anomalies and accelerate lagging development • eclectic instruction related to age-appropriate unlearned skills • eclectic instruction related to compensatory strategies • eclectic strategies for reducing interfering behaviors	Behavior change interventions (primary emphasis on establishing control over behavior through manipulation of reinforcers and instruction in cognitive self-direction and monitoring) • direct instruction to teach missing skills • behavior management to reduce interfering behaviors

on testing designed to analyze perceptual, motoric, cognitive, and language functioning. In addition, for purposes of diagnosis, neurological or psychoneurological testing may be done.

Intervention is concerned specifically with underlying problems in four developmental areas: perceptual, motoric, language, and general cognitive functioning. Instructional objectives are stated in nonbehavioral as well as behavioral and criterion-referenced terms. Instructional strategies are eclectic, drawing on psychotherapeutic principles and a variety of teaching models. Thus they emphasize rapport building to reduce anxiety and increase positive involvement, traditional learning principles (mastery learning, reinforcement theory), contemporary views of cognitive strategy instruction, use of social interaction, and so forth. If all else fails, individuals are taught strategies for compensating for a specific learning disability (using multisensory techniques to learn words, mnemonic techniques to help with memorization).

Examples of approaches for psychoeducational remediation in the four specific developmental areas follow. Major medically related approaches and some controversies surrounding them are highlighted in *Controversial Treatments and Fads* (p. 309).

Perceptual-motor problems There is a long history of theory, intervention, and research in the LD field based on the view that underlying some learning problems (for example, in reading and writing) are perceptual and motor dysfunctions. These dysfunctions are believed to cause deficits in the ability to recognize and interpret sensory stimuli or in the ability to integrate such stimuli with motor activity. Major areas affected are seen as including auditory, visual, tactile, and kinesthetic perception and the integration of perceptions across areas and with motor patterns.

Kurt Goldstein, Alfred Strauss, and Heinz Werner are recognized as pioneers in working with such ideas. Later, Laura Lehtinen, Newell Kephart, William Cruickshank, and Marianne Frostig continued to emphasize this line of thinking; they developed remedial strategies that were used widely in the 1950s and 1960s.

For example, poor perception of body parts and functions has been attributed to CNS dysfunctions. In such cases, Cruickshank and colleagues (1961),

Kephart (1960), and others have advocated exercises to improve sense of body awareness and coordination. Such exercises start with simple tasks (identifying body parts in response to verbal cues); then they move on to more demanding tasks requiring controlled use of the body (catching, throwing, and walking special routes as directed).

The types of perceptual and related motor functions for which exercises have been developed or adapted include

- laterality and directionality
- balance and posture
- gross and fine motor coordination
- figure-ground perception
- position in space
- perceptual-motor coordination
- multisensory integration
- rhythm
- strength, endurance, and flexibility
- body image and differentiation
- locomotion
- ocular control
- eye-hand coordination
- constancy of shape
- spatial relationships
- auditory and visual integration
- tactile and kinesthetic integration
- agility

Because the exercises usually are designed for young children, practice is encouraged through use of gamelike activities, such as Simon Says, duck-, crab-, and elephant-walks, rabbit hops, hopscotch, angels in the snow, jumping rope, walking on balance boards, skating, skateboarding, copying, drawing, coloring, paper cutting and folding, and rhyming games.

Language-related problems Here, too, there is a long history of concern about underlying dysfunctions that interfere with language development and functioning (reading, writing, and speaking). Approaches developed by Samuel Orton and Grace Fernald in the 1920s often are mentioned as pioneer examples. It was not until the late 1950s and 1960s, however, that this area received major attention. During that period, Joseph Wepman, Samuel Kirk and his colleagues, and Helmer Myklebust and his colleague Doris Johnson focused attention on remedial approaches for disabilities underlying language learning problems.

For instance, there has been tremendous emphasis on the notion that CNS dysfunctions may interfere with the processes by which information from one or more senses is received and understood. Thus individuals with reading problems who are diagnosed as having learning disabilities often are hypothesized as having inadequate auditory or visual processing abilities. For example, a major area of study has been on deficiencies in perceiving the sounds of words (poor awareness of linguistic sounds). When this is the case, exercises are used to correct the problem, if possible. For the time being, at least, reading instruction is changed to avoid emphasizing the individual's auditory senses in favor of functionally stronger senses, including multisensory approaches.

The areas of underlying functioning related to language for which exercises have been developed or adapted include

- auditory and visual perception (awareness and processing)
- sound-symbol and visual-auditory associations
- conceptual understanding and classification
- auditory and visual memory
- speech production

Exercises include many of the activities cited above for improving perception; responding to rhythmic patterns; letter sound and phonics games; sorting and organizing; object and attribute identification tasks; direction following activities; recall of objects, designs, letters, and numbers.

In the 1980s and 1990s, renewed interest in instruction targeting language abilities and deficiencies has emphasized addressing phonological awareness, a hierarchy of metalinguistic skills related to the segmentation and manipulation of spoken language (Mann & Brady, 1988; Sawyer, 1992; Wagner & Torgesen, 1987). However, Hodgson (1992) offers a familiar note of caution about such activity:

> [Data reviewed question] whether the correlations that have been shown to hold between explicit knowledge of the phonological significance of orthographic units and word identification accuracy in the first 2 or 3 years of school may not be the direct pathway to mature, phonologically based reading that they have often been taken to be. . . . It may turn out that reading development is not entirely a creature of the exercise of general-skill-forming abilities over a simple set of explicit understandings. (p. 100)

General cognitive problems   With increasing theoretical activity related to cognitive development and function have come hypotheses about general cognitive problems underlying learning disabilities (Swanson, 1988). Early concerns about memory have been expanded to encompass problems related to automaticity, cognitive structures, cognitive style, and metacognition.

For example, CNS dysfunction may be seen as having disrupted development of knowledge and skills for approaching learning tasks effectively and efficiently. Or, the dysfunction may be responsible for passive or impulsive interactions with learning tasks. In this regard, there is an increasing concern about differences in cognitive style and temperament (Keogh & Bess, 1991).

All remediation designed to affect the way the individual thinks about pursuing learning can be viewed as involving metacognitive strategies. The prototype for such strategies comes from cognitive behavior-modification ideas introduced into LD classroom programs in the 1970s (Abikoff, 1979; Douglas, 1972; Meichenbaum, 1977, 1983). Initially, the approach stressed the importance of students' giving themselves directive messages and monitoring and evaluating their own progress. For instance, to teach students to attend more carefully in learning situations, the students were instructed to "stop, look, and listen." Broadly, the intention was to have them learn to define what had to be done, attend to the relevant parts of the task, reinforce themselves as they proceeded, and evaluate their accomplishments.

To teach such "cognitive strategies," (a) the teacher models the process by talking through the steps while doing a task, (b) the student does the task, with the teacher directing and talking through each step, (c) the student then repeats the task with self-directions, saying the steps aloud and eventually only whispering them, and finally (d) the student does the task without saying the directions aloud. What the student says may sound like this:

> OK, what is it I have to do? Copy these words. I should do it slowly so I won't make mistakes.

> Draw the line down—good—then to the right—that's it, now down. I'm doing fine so far. Remember to go slowly. Oh, oh. I was supposed to go down. That's OK. Just erase the line. Good. Even

if I make a mistake, I can go on. I have to draw a circle now.

Finished. I did it!

More generally, the approach has been to teach and model metacognitive strategies and arrange for practice in the form of rehearsal and review. For instance, cognitive-oriented strategies to improve memory have encompassed association techniques, mnemonic devices, and chunking (Mastropieri, Scruggs, & Levin, 1985). Such strategies emphasize use of visual or verbal mental images.

Strategies designed to improve the way the individual thinks about and approaches the process of learning encompass a range of general strategies for learning, lessons on specific ways to think about how one can improve learning through self-direction and monitoring, and modeling and guided learning to illustrate steps for learning and problem solving. (Many of the strategies resemble study-skills approaches.)

Strategies to alter passive or impulsive learning stress active, focused, self-directed, and monitored task involvement. For example, individuals with these problems are shown and encouraged to approach a learning task by (a) surveying it in order to gain a perspective and overview, (b) formulating questions, and (c) predicting or speculating about answers and outcomes. As they proceed, they are to pace reviews and rehearsal, to accommodate short attention spans, and to minimize passive involvement.

One example of a contemporary approach to cognitive-oriented remediation that stresses guided teaching is called "reciprocal teaching" (Palincsar & Brown, 1984). The method is based on Vygotsky's (1978) view that through social dialogue a child can participate in strategic activity that he or she does not completely understand. The process involves teachers and students in taking turns leading group discussions about a shared text. During the discussions, the process is structured through the use of four activities—predicting, questioning, summarizing, and clarifying—that are taught, modeled, and practiced as strategies.

Another example is seen in the extensive learning-strategies curriculum developed by the staff at the University of Kansas Institute for Learning Disabilities (Deshler & Schumaker, 1986; Schumaker, Deshler, & Ellis, 1986). Learning strategies have been defined as

"techniques, principles, or rules that will facilitate the acquisition, manipulation, integration, storage, and retrieval of information across situations and settings" (Alley & Deshler, 1979, p. 13).

Designed for adolescents, the curriculum has three major strands. The three strands are keyed to three curriculum demands that call on the student to (1) acquire information from written material (reading requirements), (2) identify and store important information (remembering and study techniques), and (3) demonstrate competence in written expression. Related to each curriculum demand are a set of general learning strategies. For example, six strategies are identified for the first curriculum demand listed above (strategies for word identification, visual imagery, self-questioning, paraphrasing, interpreting visual aids, and multipass—a review strategy). Finally, specific instructional steps are detailed for each learning strategy.

A major concern related to metacognitive instruction is that, rather than addressing underlying problems, strategies may become another set of observable skills that are not learned. That is, individuals with true learning disabilities may have as much trouble learning these strategies as they do learning other basic skills.

Observable Problem Approaches

Practitioners of observable problem approaches assume that even if a person has an underlying problem, the only thing that can be done from an instructional perspective is teach the skills the individual should be learning. In contrast to the underlying problem orientation, this view sees no value in assuming an underlying problem. Instead, the assumption is that individuals with learning problems simply haven't yet learned the skills they need. As we have discussed, those who hold this view primarily stress direct instruction of observable, age-appropriate, unlearned skills (review Table 1 and see Feature 1).

For instance, based on a student's grade and age, proponents of this approach focus assessment on knowledge and skills identified through analyses of the school curriculum and daily life tasks. Based on assessment of missing skills that should have been learned, behavioral and criterion-referenced objectives are formulated. In classrooms, intervention also is designed to deal with behavior that interferes with classroom instruction. Strategies emphasize direct and systematic teaching and behavior management drawing on behavior change principles.

Those who hold this view tend to subscribe to behaviorist and cognitive behaviorist models of instruction. Thus, they view skill instruction in terms of direct strategies for behavior change (eliciting and reinforcing specific responses, instruction in cognitive self-direction and monitoring).

Observable skills and objectives   The skills to be taught are seen building one on another. Lists of sequential skills, called *skill hierarchies,* have been developed in areas such as reading and math to identify which skills should be learned first, second, and so forth. These lists are presented as representing the developmental scope and sequence of skills to be learned. There also are lists of readiness skills that are seen as general prerequisites for most school learning. These include learning to listen, attend, follow directions, classify, relate to others, and so forth. (Some activities used to teach prerequisites are the same as those used in efforts to remedy underlying problems seen as interfering with learning such prerequisites.)

As indicated, assessment is used to identify missing skills, and these are specified as the intended outcomes for intervention. They are specified in the form of behavioral objectives (they are formulated in highly concrete behavioral terms) and criterion-referenced (they refer to a criterion for evaluating success). For instance: "Joe will decode unfamiliar vocabulary words from fourth-grade texts with 85 percent accuracy." Intended outcomes are carefully monitored as a basis for planning subsequent objectives.

Direct instruction   The process of direct instruction itself stresses use of curriculum-based assessment and monitoring, behavioral and criterion-referenced objectives, and operant conditioning and cognitive behavior-modification change strategies. To illustrate this orientation, it is useful to go back to programs that emerged around the middle of the twentieth century.

During the 1950s and 1960s, Richard Whelan, Norris Haring, E. Lakin Phillips, and Frank Hewett established classroom models based on behaviorist ideas of learning. In the 1960s and 1970s, an increasing number of learning disabilities classrooms adopted these models. Such approaches strongly emphasize establishment of environments in which desired behavior (observable skills appropriate to the student's level of functioning) can be elicited and then reinforced in a consistent manner.

For instance, first a student's most basic missing skills are identified; then relatively short tasks and exercises are provided to help the student acquire each skill. The student is told that he or she can earn rewards for working in a specified way. Thus, after perhaps 15 minutes of work, a student's efforts and

Feature 1   Contrasting Orientations

To illustrate one basic difference between the underlying and observable problem approaches, let's assume Mara has been having trouble learning beginning math skills. She is the only one in her class who can't count and group objects.

Underlying problem approaches would try to determine whether her learning problems were caused by developmental deficits, such as a deficit related to visual and auditory memory. If such a deficit is identified through assessment, remediation is likely to include exercises to improve short-term memory. These might involve Mara in doing such things as repeating tapped patterns, learning to use visual imagery, and so forth.

Those pursuing observable problem approaches would not be especially concerned with why Mara had not learned to count. They would assume she could learn the skills if a good direct teaching strategy was now used. Such a strategy would need to account not only for the math skills currently troubling Mara but also for any related observable readiness skills. Mara would then be directly taught all designated missing skills. Exercises might include games to help her memorize and recite the numbers 1 to 10, 11 to 20, and so forth.

accomplishments are evaluated and checkmarks, tokens, or some other "reinforcers" are given. Accumulated checkmarks or tokens are turned in at a specified time for a prize, a special activity, or for free time. If the student does not cooperate or misbehaves, he or she may lose a privilege. What the student obtains or loses (the positive and negative consequences) is seen as the actual reinforcement for the behavior. Reinforcement strategies have been described as (a) giving students something they want, (b) taking away something they want, (c) giving them something they don't want, and (d) taking away something they don't want to experience (Hewett & Taylor, 1980).

This early work was followed by "precision teaching" formulated by Lindsley (1964) and developed as "applied behavioral analysis" by colleagues such as Lovitt (1975a, 1975b; also see Alberto & Troutman, 1982) and by the directive teaching strategies of Stephens (1977). The emphasis on direct instruction and behavioral and criterion-referenced objectives also can be found in programmed materials for reading, language, and arithmetic such as DISTAR (Engelmann & Bruner, 1984).

Individual education plans Because observable problems are easier to monitor than underlying ones, approaches based on this orientation are appealing to program planners and evaluators. Thus, when legislation in the United States called for detailed, written individual educational planning (IEPs), a strong trend toward using these strategies developed.

Public Law 94-142 requires an IEP for each student with a learning disability. IEPs have rapidly become detailed prescriptions of content to be taught and outcomes to be achieved. A large proportion of these prescriptions are written in the form of behavioral and criterion-referenced objectives. This way of stating objectives tends to shape program content toward overemphasizing certain skills and toward using teaching processes that stress training rather than education (Heshusius, 1991). These points can be seen from the two relatively typical examples illustrated in Feature 2.

As can be seen from the examples, the IEPs provide no content or outcome options for the students. Moreover, teachers complained that the objectives poorly matched students' current motivational and developmental capabilities. In the case of the first student, the overriding need was that

he start to perceive school as a place that had something to offer him. He belonged to a street gang that was trying to convince him that school was a worthless experience; by following the IEP prescription, the teacher could not convince him otherwise.

The second student demonstrated tremendous creative talent in his cartooning and his creative stories. He had aspirations for a career in this area, and this was not out of line with his talent. His talent and career aspirations were ignored completely by the IEP and, indeed, the prescribed program left him no time for these important interests and strengths.

As legislation for individuals with disabilities has emphasized the importance of offering programs from birth on, the focus in planning programs has broadened from the individual to the family (Baily, Buysse, Edmondson, & Smith, 1992). Thus, rather than Individual Education Plans (IEPs), programs for infants and preschoolers prepare Individual Family Service Plans (IFSPs). Again, however, the trend is to focus on narrowly conceived objectives.

A Note on Classroom Management

Individuals with learning disabilities often manifest behavior problems as well. For this reason, learning disabilities teachers are as interested in classroom management strategies as they are in learning specific approaches to remediation. The problems they confront encompass a variety of behaviors associated with learning problems that interfere with classroom instruction and learning. These include poor impulse control, lack of sustained attention and follow-through, low frustration tolerance, and inappropriate interpersonal interactions.

In the 1960s when learning disabilities classrooms emerged in public schools, the underlying problem orientation dominated the scene. However, because such approaches were developed in clinical and research settings, the interventions did not address the matter of classroom management. Many teachers complained that instruction could not take place unless they could find a way to control their students' behavior.

To meet their needs, inservice programs offered training in classroom management. At the time, the prevailing techniques for managing problem behavior were behavior-change strategies of the type being used for populations with extreme problems (mental

Feature 2   IEPs: Two Typical Examples of Planning Gone Astray

The following is the Individual Educational Plan (IEP) of a 13-year-old student diagnosed as having learning disabilities—who also manifests severe behavior problems.

Annual goals	Short-term objectives	Evaluation
Behavior: develop appropriate modes of behavior	Will employ impulse control. Will submit a paragraph of 4 alternative ways in which inappropriate behavior could have been avoided.	Observation Product assessment
Math: demonstrate basic skills in mathematics	Will multiply a 3-digit no. by a 3-digit no. regrouping as necessary. Will divide a 3-digit no. by a 1-digit no. with and without a remainder.	Observation Product assessment
Reading: increase sight word vocabulary	Will recognize sight words from various content disciplines, e.g., Dolch & Core lists. Will maintain a booklet of synonyms, antonyms, and homonyms.	Observation Product assessment
Counseling: improve self-control	Will maintain self-control and comply with adult authority. Will share frustrations and feelings in counseling setting.	Observation

The following is the Individual Educational Plan (IEP) of a 16-year-old student diagnosed as having learning disabilities.

Annual goals	Short-term objectives	Evaluation
Math: develop consumer math skills	Will develop and learn shopping skills and learn to live within a budget. Will tell time to 1 hour with 100% accuracy.	Observation Product assessment
Behavior: develop ability to participate in small groups; develop ability to work on assignments	Will attend a small group for one class period. Will read aloud in group. Will work on teacher-assigned task independently for 15 min.; asking for help only when necessary.	Observation
Language arts: improve oral expression	Will moderate voice for expression. Will use complete sentences in spontaneous speech.	Observation
Improve sight vocabulary	Will increase sight vocabulary to 600 words. Will decode unfamiliar consonant-vowel-consonant words with 85% accuracy.	Product assessment
Counseling: increase sense of identity	Will identify feelings and formulate goals. Will express feelings and personal goals appropriately to others.	Observation

illness, autism, and profound retardation). As a result, many teachers ended up using an underlying problem orientation when working on students' developmental problems and an observable problem orientation in relation to students' behavior problems. This, along with the management orientation of IEPs, helped to institutionalize the observable problem orientation in the LD field.

Summing Up

In recent years, there has been a reaction to behavioral approaches. For example, direct instruction and curriculum-based assessment are criticized as an isolated set of measurement and control procedures superimposed on, and unrelated to, the phenomenon of human learning (Heshusius, 1991). The call is for a return to holistic approaches, with their emphasis on the learner as a motivated discoverer of meaningful skills and knowledge and a functioning whole (Bartoli, 1990; Heshusius, 1982, 1986, 1989; Iano, 1987; Poplin, 1988). In reaction to the criticism, behavioral principles have been defended vigorously (Forness, 1988; Forness & Kavale, 1987; Kimball & Heron, 1988). Besides bringing to the surface conflicting rationales underlying remedial practices, the need for the debate underscores increasing concern over the limited success of prevailing practices.

I.5   *Screening for Learning Disabilities*

Superintendent Brown was less than pleased. "We don't need to find any more learning disabled students!" The school board had just informed her of its decision to go ahead with a screening program for learning disabilities. "Our learning disabilities programs are already full!" she continued. "We can't afford any more special programs. Why look for more problems!"

One answer to the question, *"Why search for learning disabilities?"* may be that the law requires it. In the United States, for instance, legislative pressure for massive screening programs built rapidly in the 1960s and 1970s. The Social Security Act was amended in 1967 to require states to provide early and periodic screening, diagnosis, and treatment to all Medicaid-eligible children. Congressional action during the decade that followed continued to push for screening of special groups of children. The Education for All Handicapped Children Act of 1975 (Public Law 94-142) called for educational and related services from preschool through age 21; and the 1983 and 1986 Education of the Handicapped Amendments Acts (P.L. 98-199 and P.L. 99-457) placed primary emphasis on expanding and improving services to infants and preschoolers.

Some states have pursued massive child-find programs, and in the coming years, most states will consider such activity. In other countries, there has been rapidly escalating interest in such screening (Frankenburg, Emde, & Sullivan, 1985).

The desire to help children with special needs, reinforced by legislative mandate, already has made screening a large-scale and controversial enterprise. In the early 1980s, a national survey by the Minnesota Department of Education found 24 states had some form of comprehensive screening aimed at finding young children with problems. Available data indicate that specific practices vary greatly in their nature and quality, both across and within states (Gracey, Azzara, & Reinherz, 1984). Although well intentioned, it appears that the rush to establish screening programs has resulted in a climate where consumers and suppliers are less critical than they should be in evaluating the validity of procedures.

This is unfortunate, because large-scale screening programs are costly and there are always a significant number of errors and other negative consequences.

Underlying the legal push for screening is a desire to meet the special needs of all individuals with problems, regardless of age (Paget & Barnett, 1990). Obviously, there are very good reasons for seeking out problems. Identifying problems is essential for some forms of prevention and correction, and in such instances, screening can be seen as an ethical responsibility (Adelman & Taylor, 1984).

There are, however, also good reasons to be concerned about the effects of searching and the accuracy of findings. This is especially true of large-scale screening programs. Besides errors, such programs often are not followed up with needed services after problems are identified. Moreover, searching and finding individuals with problems shapes the nature of corrective intervention. With the focus on individuals, the tendency is to ignore interventions to change factors in the learning environment that may be creating individuals' problems.

Terminology

Before proceeding, let's get our terms straight. Because the main emphasis has been on finding children and helping them before they have too much failure at school, screening often is referred to as *early identification, early detection, early warning,* and even *prediction.* Such screening is directed at individuals with existing problems or those described as *high risk* or *at risk* for acquiring problems.

It is useful to differentiate the process of *predicting* who may eventually become a problem (high- or at-risk individuals) from the process of *identifying* existing problems. As the word *prediction* implies, the process of labeling a condition as high risk is a future judgment—an act of prophecy. Based on assessment of antecedent variables, future problems are hypothesized. In contrast, identification is the process by which current conditions are assessed to detect existing problems. Addition of the adjective "early" to form the term *early identification,* although appealing and widely used, can be confusing. In effect, the term tends to be used both for identification of problems *at an early age* and identification of problems *early after their onset.* And, often, it is used erroneously as a synonym for "prediction."

It also is important to differentiate between *screening* and *diagnosis.* Screening procedures usually are intended to survey large groups as a first stage in problem detection. These procedures are expected to have lower reliability and validity than those used for diagnostic classification or for generating a specific prescription. Indeed, the validity of most first-level screens is so low that they are expected to make a relatively large number of errors. At best, such screening is meant to provide a preliminary indication that something may be wrong. When diagnostic classification and specific prescriptions are desirable, assessment procedures of greater validity are required. Despite frequent warnings about the danger of blurring the distinction between screening and diagnosis, it is common for screening instruments to be misused.

Child-Find Procedures

Essentially, individuals are identified in at least one of four ways as potential learning problems or having learning disabilities. First, they may see themselves as having a problem. Second, informal observations made at home, school, or work may lead family, friends, teachers, or colleagues to suggest there is a problem. Third, formal assessment as part of regular checkups or treatment for other problems may result in a professional, for example an M.D., noting the possibility of learning disabilities. Fourth, large numbers of children may be screened as part of formal child-find programs. In all four instances, the individual may be referred to a diagnostician if a formal diagnosis is seen as necessary (see Feature 1). In the final case, sound practice calls for a follow-up individual assessment to detect errors; unfortunately, sometimes this step is ignored.

Our main focus here is on child-find programs because they are probably the most ambitious of all efforts to identify learning disabilities. We use the United States as an example because of legislation

mandating development of such programs. Minimally, by law, children already in school are to be identified; when feasible, efforts are to be made to find those about to enter school.

Besides funding, one of the biggest problems in developing appropriate child-find programs for learning disabilities is deciding on the characteristics of the individuals to be found. Development of criteria for use in diagnosing learning disabilities has been discussed in Part I. As indicated, federal guidelines specify minimal criteria related to a severe discrepancy between achievement and intellectual ability in various areas of academic performance. States and local school districts may add other criteria if they wish.

Besides specifying criteria, federal guidelines spell out procedures to be followed in applying the criteria and arriving at a diagnosis. The process involves a multidisciplinary team that minimally includes the student's regular teacher (or a qualified substitute), a qualified diagnostic examiner (such as a school psychologist), and a learning disabilities specialist. At least one member of the team, other than the student's regular teacher, is to observe the student's academic performance during class. After assessing the student, the team must prepare a written report clarifying

(1) whether the child has a specific learning disability
(2) the basis for making the determination
(3) the relevant behavior noted during observation
(4) the relationship of that behavior to the child's academic functioning
(5) the educationally relevant medical findings
(6) whether there is a severe discrepancy between achievement and ability that is not correctable without special education and related services
(7) the determination of the team concerning the effects of environmental, cultural, or economic disadvantage (*Federal Register,* 1977, p. 65, 083)

Not specified by the federal guidelines is how students are to come to the attention of the multidisciplinary team. That is, the guidelines do not discuss procedures for large-scale screening, and thus there is great variability in what is done (Gracey et al.,

1984). This is not surprising, because there is no well-validated procedure available. Good procedures are extremely difficult to develop. There is still no process that can correctly detect a high percentage of learning problems without making many false identifications.

A sense of the state of the art is provided by data from two surveys of prekindergarten screening. In Illinois, a statewide survey found 77 percent of the responding agencies used standardized but not well-validated instruments; 23 percent used locally developed, largely unvalidated procedures (Van Duyne, Gargiulo, & Allen, 1980). Similar findings come from a 1984 survey in Minnesota, the first state (in 1977) to offer comprehensive, free screening to all prekindergartners (Ysseldyke, Thurlow,

Feature 1   *Referral: The Hidden Screening Procedure*

Before any formal assessment, there often is an informal screening procedure. That procedure is *referral*. Most children and adolescents are referred for diagnosis and treatment by school and medical personnel and sometimes by the courts.

Teachers, physicians, and judges see many individuals who have problems, but they only refer a small number for psychoeducational diagnoses and treatment.

How do they choose who to refer? Sometimes they refer those they think can best profit from treatment; sometimes they choose those they especially like (or dislike).

There has been a great deal written about the possibility that racial, sexual, and class biases play a major role in referral processes. In general, individuals from nondominant (minority) groups in a society seem more likely than those in the dominant group to be identified and referred to programs for persons seen as "inferior" and "deviant." The fact that referral processes can be used in a way that hides prejudiced motives makes such processes controversial and of concern (Gerber & Semmel, 1984).

Another bias that affects referral processes is the tendency to see the causes of others' problems in terms of something "wrong" with the person observed. Referrers may be influenced by this tendency when they observe learning problems. They may assume the causes stem from something wrong inside the person (such as a learning disability) and therefore send the individual for diagnosis and treatment.

In contrast to observers' tendencies, the person involved may tend to see the problem as caused by some external factor, such as a poor teaching situation.

As discussed by *attribution* theorists,

> there is a pervasive tendency for actors [those observed] to attribute their actions to situational requirements, whereas observers tend to attribute the same actions to stable personal dispositions. (Jones & Nisbett, 1971, p. 80)

PROFESSOR: The reason students have trouble in my class is that they don't spend enough time studying. Some are simply lazy; others are too busy partying; some just don't care.

STUDENT: The reasons I'm having trouble in this class are that the lectures are boring and the reading is too hard. Also, the professors in my other courses all give so many assignments that I hardly have time to do any of my work very well.

Whose explanation is right? Often, it is impossible to tell without a great deal more information. However, we aren't concerned here with who turns out to be right. What's important to understand is that referrers may often operate with a psychological bias and so, in too many instances, may be ignoring environmental causes and "blaming the victim."

Attribution theorists would criticize prevailing referral processes as favoring causal models that see the cause and correction of learning problems only in terms of individuals (review Chapter 2). As suggested, such models tend not to pay sufficient attention to the role of environments in causing such problems or to the need for major changes in the environment as a part of efforts to correct learning problems.

O'Sullivan, & Bursaw, 1986). The survey reports the two most used instruments were the DIAL (Developmental Indicators of the Assessment of Learning) and the DDST (Denver Developmental Screening Test). The former has little empirical support for its reliability and validity (Lichtenstein & Ireton, 1984), and the latter was standardized in only one city and has overreferral rates as high as 44 percent (German, Williams, Herzfeld, & Marshall, 1982). Given this rate of overreferral, it is discomforting to note that the DDST is the screening instrument most often used by model childhood-education programs throughout the United States (Lehr, Ysseldyke, & Thurlow, 1986) and has even found its way to China (Chieh, Chu, Lu, Tang, & Wang, 1985).

Research findings and clinical observations indicate that youngsters with severe problems usually are identified readily by parents, pediatricians, and teachers without complex and costly screening devices (see Feature 2). Therefore it is not surprising that severe problems related to learning and behavior are also identified readily by screening devices.

Feature 2   Concerns About Screening Procedures

The desire to identify learning problems at an early age is easily understood. Prevention and intervention in the earlier stages of a problem can be more effective and economical than later remediation. Indeed, for some problems undue delay can make things considerably worse.

In contrast, arguments against screening are often misunderstood. Such arguments are raised primarily with respect to large-scale programs aimed at preschoolers and those in their first years in school. Don't make the mistake of thinking that critics of large-scale screening programs are arguing against efforts to prevent and correct problems. They, too, want to help.

One of their main concerns, however, is about the limitations of available procedures, especially for screening mild-moderate problems — which are by far the most numerous. Studies of how screening programs currently are run tend to support this concern.

Because so much emphasis has been placed on early-age screening, conclusions from research reviews in this area have special relevance for large-scale screening procedures. Reviewers report that the best available tests and rating scales generally are accurate in identifying only a moderate percentage of young (5- to 7-year-old) children who later have significant learning problems in school. In addition to missing individuals who subsequently do have problems, the procedures identify some whose current minor problems are not good predictors of later learning difficulties. The procedures are most accurate in identifying youngsters who currently have rather severe problems — that is, those who are so obviously experiencing problems that they are readily identified by parents, pediatricians, and teachers through informal observation! Only a small percentage of those who truly have learning disabilities are easily distinguished from others who have problems.

From another perspective, it has been suggested that the money spent on screening would be better used to improve preschool, kindergarten, and first-grade programs. Critics suggest that a very large proportion of those who are identified would never become persons with significant learning problems if their early schooling were redesigned. They also stress that commitment to large-scale screening programs tends to take attention away from the need to make system changes.

Hobbs's (1975a) conclusions are as relevant today as they were in the 1970s:

Every professionally competent report we have on early screening . . . strongly qualifies most assertions concerning the reliability, validity, or applicability of screening procedures . . . , especially for use in the early years of childhood. . . . Most serious developmental problems get picked up in routine clinical practice . . . or are identified by parents or other untrained observers; mild and moderate problems (by far the greatest number), however, are difficult to detect and assess even by well-trained professional people administering complete examinations with the best equipment. (pp. 92–94)

However, identifying severe problems is not the same thing as identifying learning disabilities. Some individuals with severe problems have learning disabilities, but many have other psychological problems or other biological problems. The relatively low incidence of learning disabilities (as compared to learning problems in general) means that anything less than highly accurate screening will make a large number of errors.

As indicated earlier, large-scale screening procedures for learning disabilities are meant to be only gross, first attempts at identification. They are expected to overidentify — that is, identify some individuals who do not have learning disabilities and some who don't even have significant learning problems. The errors are found later when each person is individually assessed (for example, by the multidisciplinary team as specified by federal guidelines).

In short, because large-scale screening procedures make so many errors, they are never supposed to be used to make specific diagnoses — not even tentative ones. When it comes time to make decisions about whether a person has a learning disability and about placements for remediation, the need is for assessment strategies that have greater diagnostic and prescriptive validity than is the case with available screening procedures.

Research

The dedication to screening for learning problems is reflected in an extensive research literature (Adelman, 1989; Badian, 1988; Barnes, 1982; Frankenburg et al., 1985; Jansky, Hoffman, et al., 1989; Lichtenstein & Ireton, 1984; Lipson & Wixson, 1986; Shaywitz, Escobar et al., 1992). Hundreds of studies have been reported over the past decade. Unfortunately, many were done so poorly that their results defy valid interpretation. The majority of studies have used psychometric tests, rating scales, and questionnaires (see *Assessment for Learning Disabilities' Diagnosis, Placement, and Program Planning,* p. 328), alone and in various combinations.

Three major models defining the focal point for intervention can be used in developing screening and diagnostic procedures. One model emphasizes person assessment, in terms of pathology (disorders and "illness") or lack of developmental readiness; another focuses on the environment (also emphasizing pathology or developmental deficiencies); and the third stresses the transaction of person and environment. Of the three models, only the first has been used extensively to guide screening research (Adelman, 1989).

Assessment of individuals focuses on a limited range of pathological indicators and developmental deficits. Lack of success with this approach has stimulated interest in adding specific home and school factors. This approach has the potential, not only to improve individual screening, but also to identify factors in the environment that should be changed.

As to criteria for determining how effective a screening procedure is, one must account for the ease with which serious problems are detected without formal screening. That is, the appropriate standard for judging the value of screening instruments should be their ability to identify individuals whose difficulties are not already recognized.

Summing Up

Because of the trend toward large-scale screening, we stress again that the evidence does not support use of existing psychometric or rating-scale procedures in massive screening for mild to moderate learning problems among infants, preschoolers, or kindergartners. The fact is that few of the available procedures meet even the minimal standards set forth by the American Psychological Association and the American Educational Research Association (see "Standards for Educational and Psychological Tests"). Such large-scale screening provides another example where pressure and enthusiasm for screening have led to inappropriate interpretations of research findings and premature application of new procedures.

I.6   Assessment for Learning Disabilities' Diagnosis, Placement, and Program Planning

As discussed in Chapter 4, widespread controversy surrounds assessment for learning disabilities. Some concerns stem from methodological, conceptual, and ethical issues and problems; others arise from social-political-economic considerations. A broad range of fundamental concerns must be understood and addressed in using assessment in practice and research.

In *Screening for Learning Disabilities* (p. 323), we addressed specific concerns about LD screening. Here the focus is on diagnosis, placement, and program planning specifically for learning disabilities.

Assessment for Diagnosis

For practitioners, the whole point of screening is to identify a problem so that it can be resolved. The point of screening specifically for LD is to treat those having such problems differently from those with other types of learning problems. While such differential treatment is not always available, the intent is there.

Before appropriate differential treatment can be given, a differential diagnosis must be made. Because there are different types of learning problems with different causes and remedies, it is important to differentiate among individuals who have one type or another. Differential diagnosis is the process by which a person is assigned to a particular category. To conclude that an individual should receive one diagnosis and not another, it is necessary to show the presence of a set of symptoms or signs unique to the diagnostic category.

Assessment procedures used in making a differential diagnosis should be keyed to a definition of learning disabilities and related criteria. When the definition and criteria stress central nervous system causes and resulting processing disabilities, the assessment should include procedures to detect the underlying problems. In contrast, if one is not interested in cause and underlying problems, one would stress definitions, assessment procedures, and criteria that focus only on observable problems and factors that contribute to such problems.

Because of controversy over definition, criteria, and related assessment procedures, currently assessors heavily rely on findings that (a) an individual should be diagnosed as having some problem other than learning disabilities (exclusionary criteria), and (b) the degree of underachievement is severe enough to qualify as indicative of LD. In addition, data are gathered on indicators of developmental immaturity and performance deficiencies—which are seen by some as related to underlying psychological processing dysfunctions.

Exclusion Data

Information is gathered regarding a variety of problems that may be the primary cause of the learning problem. As listed in federal guidelines (see Chapter 1), a diagnosis of LD is *not* given if any of the following are identified as the primary cause: (a) vision, hearing, and motor handicaps, (b) mental retardation, (c) emotional disturbance, and (d) environmental, cultural, or economic disadvantage.

Information about these matters often comes from existing school, medical, and psychological records. Where such information is inadequate, the data are sought through interviews, medical exams, and psychological tests.

One major difficulty in interpreting the information is lack of agreement about how severe any of the "exclusion" problems must be before a diagnosis of LD is ruled out. For example, how much loss of vision? Some say that to rule out a diagnosis of LD, visual acuity in the best eye must be poorer than 20/70 with glasses. What should be considered mental retardation rather than a learning disability? Some say that the person's individual intelligence test score (judged as valid by a qualified psychologist) must be 70 or below; others say 80 or below. What about environmental, cultural, and economic disadvantage? The current intent seems to be to avoid assigning a label of learning disabilities to those whose learning and performance problems reflect educational programs and testing procedures that have not appropriately considered an individual's background and native language.

Intelligence and Achievement Levels

Essentially, any of a number of standardized individual tests of intelligence and achievement in reading, math, and language may be administered (see Table 1 and *Procedures and Instruments for Assessing Learning Problems,* p. 341). All such tests have their limitations, especially when given to individuals with learning and behavior problems. In general, scores from the best available instruments are only moderately accurate for individuals from such populations. This is due to problems in test construction and administration, to psychological influences such as test-taking anxiety and motivation, and to other factors that can affect both the performance of the test taker and how assessors interpret subjective test responses (see Chapter 4 and *Technical Concerns About Assessment,* p. 349).

Because of the limitations of standardized psychoeducational tests, assessors and multidisciplinary teams reviewing LD diagnoses are encouraged to note other information, such as how individuals perform in the classroom or on the job, their motivation during testing, and so forth. Decisions regarding the inaccuracy of test findings often are based on judgments about such *in situ* behavior.

Scores on intelligence and achievement tests are used to determine how severe the discrepancy is between an individual's learning potential and current functioning. Determination of this discrepancy tends to be subjective.

In an effort to be more objective, many school districts have adopted one of a variety of discrepancy formulas that have been advocated (see Feature 1). However, critics of such formulas stress that the appearance of objectivity is countered by the fact that the formulas result in as many errors as the procedures they have replaced (Berk, 1984; Dangel & Ensminger, 1988; McLesky, 1989; Willson, 1987).

In part, errors in judging the severity of a discrepancy are due to the degree of error associated with intelligence and achievement scores. That is, when used with problem populations, such tests often produce invalid data on individuals. Also, an increase in error occurs when separate test scores are combined in discrepancy formulas (Berk, 1984; Stanovich, 1991b, 1991c).

Underlying Problems

Because of the controversies surrounding the assessment and correction of underlying problems, such as underlying psychological processes, federal guidelines do not specify that these must be assessed. Nevertheless, tests intended to assess such problems are administered quite routinely by diagnosticians. These are discussed in a subsequent section.

Testing

As part of the individual assessment used to arrive at a diagnosis of LD, a battery of tests is often administered. Although there is no standard battery, certain tests have been favored (see Table 1). At the same time, test reviewers have cautioned that all are severely flawed for use in diagnosing learning disabilities.

For example, even the best of the tests in technical terms, the long-established and recently revised Wechsler Intelligence Scales, have serious deficiencies as a diagnostic instrument. (Note: An instrument may be the best available, and still not be very good.) Intelligence testing using the Wechsler often is interpreted with respect to differences among the scales' various subtests. Large differences among the subtests have been interpreted as having major significance for diagnosis (and even for profiling strengths and weaknesses as a basis for remediation). Research has not supported such interpretations. The conclusion of researchers in this area is that the Wechsler scales "are not likely to be very useful in the diagnosis of LD or in its differential diagnosis" (Kaufman, 1981, p. 523). In addition—as discussed elsewhere in the text—the use of intelligence tests to diagnose and place students in special programs has been challenged as a discriminatory practice.

Labeling

"What's the use of their having names," the Gnat said, "if they won't answer to them?"

"No use to them," said Alice, "but it's useful to people who name them, I suppose. If not, why do things have names at all?" (Lewis Carroll, *Through the Looking Glass*)

What's in a name?

When it comes to diagnosis, the label assigned may profoundly shape a person's future. The labels attach names to problems. The names often imply what caused a problem and what to do about it. People tend to have strong images associated with specific labels and to act upon these images. Some-

Table 1   Tests Commonly Mentioned in Diagnosing Learning Disabilities

Area Tested	Tests
Intelligence	Wechsler Intelligence Scales (WPPSI, WISC-III, WAIS-R) or Stanford-Binet Intelligence Test
Intelligence and achievement	Kaufman Assessment Battery for Children (K-ABC)
Achievement (reading, math, mechanics of English, spelling)	One of the following: California Achievement Test Iowa Tests of Basic Skills Metropolitan Achievement Test Peabody Individual Achievement Test—Revised SRA Achievement Series Stanford Achievement Test Wide Range Achievement Test—Revised Woodcock-Johnson Psychoeducational Battery
Motor	One of the following: Bruininks-Oseretsky Test of Motor Proficiency Peabody Development Motor Scales
Perceptual-motor	One or more of the following: Bender Visual-Motor Gestalt Test Developmental Test of Visual-Motor Integration Developmental Test of Visual Perception Graham-Kendall Memory for Designs Purdue Perceptual-Motor Survey Southern California Perceptual-Motor Tests Motor-Free Visual Perception Test
Auditory perception	One of the following: Goldman-Fristoe-Woodcock Auditory Skills Test Battery Goldman-Fristoe-Woodcock Test of Auditory Discrimination Wepman Test of Auditory Discrimination
Language	One or more of the following: Detroit Test of Learning Aptitude—2 Goldman-Fristoe Test of Articulation Illinois Test of Psycholinguistic Abilities Peabody Picture Vocabulary Test Test of Written Language Test of Language Development—2 (primary, intermediate)
Social and emotional	One or more of the following: Childrens or Thematic Apperception Tests Childrens Depression Inventory House-Tree-Person (and other human figure drawings) Minnesota Multiphasic Personality Test Rorschach Sentence Completion Vineland Adaptive Behavior Scales
Neurological and psychoneurological	Specialists increasingly are using: Halstead-Reitan Neuropsychological Test Battery or Luria-Nebraska Neuropsychological Battery or Clinical assessment of soft signs

Note: The above data usually are supplemented with informal tests, questionnaires, and interviews with the referred individual and family members, as well as with a review of medical and school records. In addition, family members and teachers may be asked to provide rating data on a student using instruments such as the Child Behavior Checklist or the Connors Behavior Rating Scale. Finally, observations may be made in the home or at school.

times the images are useful generalizations; sometimes they are harmful stereotypes.

Some people think all labeling is a bad thing (National Association of School Psychologists, 1986). They point to many potential negative effects of assigning diagnostic labels such as learning disabilities:

> "The label stigmatizes the person. People tend to think less of a person who has a diagnostic label; they often avoid and act differently toward them. This may make a problem worse."

> "If you tell people they have problems, they often make your words come true."

> "When the label is wrong, serious errors in treatment can be made."

These are important concerns. Labeling a person can have negative effects. The possibility of negative effects is a good reason to be careful about how labels are used, and it may be a good reason to do away with a particular label. But it is not a good reason to stop diagnostic labeling.

Diagnostic labeling, like all classification in science, is essential. It is basic to communication and to efforts to solve problems. Society cannot hope to correct and prevent the various types of learning problems without some form of differential classification.

The problem is not to do away with labels, but to develop the most useful labels and minimize the negative effects that arise when they are used. One criterion of a "good" diagnostic label is that the label helps more than it hurts.

Although there is controversy over how the term *learning disabilities* is defined and applied, there seems to be consensus that the label itself is a good one for describing one major subtype of learning

Feature 1   Discrepancy Formulas

Despite all the criticisms of discrepancy formulas, they are used and, therefore, an example of one seems in order. The one developed by Myklebust (1968) provides a representative illustration. The formula yields an index of learning potential called a *Learning Quotient (LQ)*. The LQ is based on present achievement, called *Achievement Age (AA)*, as compared to expected achievement, called *Expectancy Age (EA)*.

This is expressed as the formula $LQ = \dfrac{AA}{EA}$.

Myklebust proposed that those whose LQ scores are 0.89 or below should be diagnosed as having learning disabilities. Because this figure was established without sufficient research, use of a higher- or lower-criterion score can rather easily be justified.

To show how the formula works, we can take the example of James. When he was 12, in grade 6.5, he was tested and found to have an IQ of 125. His reading test scores indicated a grade level of 5.5.

1. AA—To determine present achievement level, or Achievement Age, Myklebust's approach calls for adding 5.2 to James's achievement test score (5.5). So James's AA = 10.7.

2. EA—To determine his expected level of achievement, or Expectancy Age, the approach calls for combining mental age (MA), actual or chronological age (CA), and grade age (GA) and dividing by 3.

The MA is computed by multiplying his IQ score (125) by his chronological age (12) and dividing by 100. So James's MA = 15.

The GA is computed by adding 5.2 to his present grade level (6.5). So James's GA = 11.7.

Thus,

$$EA = \frac{MA + CA + GA}{3} = \frac{15 + 12 + 11.7}{3} = 12.9$$

3. LQ—Dividing 10.7 (AA) by 12.9 (EA) gives a learning potential or LQ score of 0.83.

By Myklebust's criterion of 0.89, James would qualify for a diagnosis of learning disabilities.

Obviously, discrepancy formulas can be used only with children who have learned to read well enough to produce a reasonably valid score on a reading test.

problem. However, some critics point out that, as this label is used in daily practice, a large number of persons are misidentified (Coles, 1987). From the perspective of these critics, the label should be used only for purposes of research and theory until the diagnosis can be made with fewer errors.

Mistaken Identity

School districts have identified many children as learning disabled simply because they did not perform at grade level. Many of these children are slow learners, culturally or linguistically disadvantaged, or have had inappropriate instruction. Anyone visiting the programs for learning disabled children will observe that most programs include children who are not the hardcore learning disabled. If this practice continues, the learning disability programs are in danger of becoming dumping grounds for all educational problems. (Kirk & Kirk, 1983, pp. 20–21)

A great many differential diagnoses of learning disabilities are made every day. Practitioners use the best procedures that are available. (Remember, best does not necessarily mean good.) Despite the best efforts, however, there are errors in diagnosis whether the focus is on neurological dysfunctioning or indicators of poor attention and memory.

Until there is an agreed-upon set of characteristics, symptoms, or signs for differentiating LD from other types of learning problems, a large number of misidentifications is inevitable. Soft signs and other behaviors seen as symptoms of minor cerebral dysfunctions or other psychological factors are compelling correlates, but they are insufficient evidence of the cause of an individual's learning problem (see Chapters 1 and 2 and *CNS Function and Assessment of Minor Dysfunction,* p. 304).

For example, what makes soft signs so compelling to diagnosticians is that they are found with significant frequency among individuals whose neurological disorders have been well established. However, researchers point out that the identified behaviors also are found with considerable frequency among persons whose problems are unlikely to be the result of neurological dysfunctioning and even among persons with no significant problems at all.

Misdiagnoses do continue to be a source of seri-

ous ethical and practical concern for practitioners and researchers. Inadequacies related to prevailing definitions and criteria and the poor validity of diagnostic procedures ensure that almost anyone manifesting a learning problem in school could, and many do, end up diagnosed as having learning disabilities. It is for this reason that those so labeled have become the biggest group of exceptional children. And, while this has made the field attractive to professionals and the general public, the magnitude of misidentifications also is the biggest threat to advancing knowledge about LD (and has produced significant political backlash).

Because there has been so much misidentification, individuals currently served in programs for LD and used in research studies differ in very important ways. Unfortunately, the prevailing tendency is to pay relatively little attention to spelling out these differences. As a result, most research purporting to deal with samples of individuals with LD is seriously compromised. The problem is compounded for all those studies that attempt to identify subtypes of learning disabilities (Lyon & Flynn, 1991). In effect, the literature on learning disabilities has much to say about learning *problems,* but its conclusions about learning *disabilities* are tenuous at best.

In general, it is one thing to theorize about learning disabilities; it is quite another to study the phenomenon. It is one thing to have a theory about what causes learning disabilities; it is quite another thing to be able to assess the cause of a particular individual's learning problem. This makes it particularly ironic that so many famous people who lived before the term *learning disabilities* was adopted have been assigned this label posthumously (see Feature 2).

Finding Diagnostic Errors

Mara's family was delighted to have her diagnosed as having a learning disability. Joseph, a high-school senior, wasn't quite so pleased, but he thought he could turn it to his benefit. We have probably known as many individuals who were content with the label as those who were upset by it.

For Mara, the label provided the family with public funds to help them pay for special programs. Many people would never be able to afford special help without such funds. Ask those who have been in similar circumstances, and they usually say they would have suffered considerably more without the label than with it.

Joseph plans to use the label to explain to college admissions officers why his reading and writing skills and some grades and admission test scores are so poor. He knows he is entitled to certain considerations because those diagnosed as having a learning disability are officially recognized as requiring special accommodation. Those who simply have learning *problems* receive no exceptions to admission criteria, nor are they usually offered individual remedial help or other special considerations after admission.

Despite the advantages people such as Mara and Joseph find in the diagnosis, they may be among those who have been misidentified. One of the most difficult problems confronting those who are trying to improve practice and research related to learning problems is that of identifying individuals erroneously diagnosed as having learning disabilities. The importance of finding the errors cannot be stressed enough; neither can ideas about how to do so (Adelman, 1989).

Those who argue that the errors must be identified don't want to deprive anyone of opportunities for help. Anyone who has a learning problem deserves as much help as possible. But there is more at stake than whether some individuals will qualify for special considerations. The large number of individuals misdiagnosed combined with the lack of procedures for finding these errors represents such a weak link in efforts to advance knowledge that it threatens the very existence of the field.

Currently the primary value of having a field devoted to learning disabilities is to lobby for those with LD and to help distinguish who does and who does not have such dysfunctions. The next major advances in knowledge about learning disabilities await the time when this subtype of learning problem can be isolated reliably. As more and more persons are indiscriminately declared as having LD, the public and its policymakers grow tired of the drain on special resources and cut back on support. Without support, the field cannot live up to its promise. Thus, to maintain its viability, the field must minimize misdiagnoses.

Cutting down on the number of errors in identification is also an important key to preventing many types of learning problems. Several researchers have suggested some type of filtering system for separating out those whose learning problems truly are due to LD (Adelman, 1971, 1989; Lindsay & Wedell, 1982; Wissink et al., 1975; Wedell, 1970). One proposed approach involves creating an optimal, nonremedial learning environment to find out if a significant number diagnosed as having learning disabilities can learn effectively under such circumstances. If they can, it becomes reasonable to argue that (1) these individuals did not actually have disabilities, and (2) similar individuals need not become learning problems if such optimal environments replace current classroom programs. Moreover, such programs might go far toward minimizing the emotional overlay that accompanies learning problems.

Such approaches eventually may lead to improvements in the diagnosis of LD and may even help distinguish several other significant subgroups within that category of handicap. At the very least, these strategies hold promise for reducing the number of persons wrongly diagnosed.

Assessment for Placement

Once a person is assessed as having a serious learning problem there is no question that special help must be provided. Let us assume that all options are available to the individual; the problem is to decide what types of help should be pursued.

Special class or not? Public or private setting? Stay in the regular class with extra help? These placement decisions are primarily made with information about what options are available. If a satisfactory educational program can be provided in the student's regular class, there is no reason to place the student elsewhere. (Of course, if this already were the case, it is unlikely the student would have been referred for help.) If an appropriate program cannot be provided somewhere in the public school system, then it becomes necessary to seek placement in a private setting.

What is an appropriate educational program? Minimally, an appropriate program is one with an apparently competent teacher who has time to give the type of one-to-one attention that the student requires. In keeping with the principle of least intervention needed, the idea has been set forth that an appropriate placement is the "least restrictive environment." The intent is to keep students with learning disabilities in the "mainstream" of public education. This appealing idea has been easy to accept in principle, but the implications for practice have proven to be rather difficult to turn into specific prescriptions for individuals.

Ancillary services? After major decisions are made about educational placement, decisions are made about which ancillary services, if any, seem appropriate. Often, the best assessment of the need for such services is made by waiting to see if the new educational placement is working and seems sufficient.

The decision that an individual should pursue

Feature 2   Edison, Einstein, and Rodin—Did They Have Learning Disabilities?

Did Albert Einstein really see the theory of relativity like this?

$$\exists = \mathsf{CM}^2$$

This is the claim made in an advertisement seen in a publication of a learning disabilities organization. The caption goes on to indicate that

Albert Einstein was dyslexic. Like many of the world's 7.5 million children with learning disabilities he was thought to be unintelligent by his teachers. . . . Fortunately, his parents placed him in a special school where he was taught in accordance with his disability. Otherwise he might never have gone on to achieve greatness.

In recent years, it has become fashionable to analyze the lives of famous people and to assign them a diagnostic label. Einstein, Thomas Edison, Auguste Rodin, and many other distinguished persons have been posthumously diagnosed as having learning disabilities.

What makes these particular historical figures likely candidates for posthumous diagnoses is that they had difficulties as children, and some did poorly at school. Edison was described in childhood as stupid and mentally defective; Rodin was seen as uneducable; Einstein apparently had a developmental lag with respect to speaking and later got into some trouble at school. These cases certainly show that developmental, learning, and schooling problems can plague even those with special genius. But should their problems be diagnosed as learning disabilities?

Take the case of Einstein, for example. Although his biographers agree that he was somewhat delayed in developing speech, there is no satisfactory evidence of a language *disability*. In fact, Einstein's reported fluency as an adult in composing German limericks and his acquisition of foreign language can be cited as evidence that he used language without apparent handicap after his earlier problems.

One of his biographers (Clark, 1971) specifically argued against the suggestion that Einstein's speech fluency difficulties as a child were due to dyslexia. "Far more plausible is the simpler explanation suggested by Einstein's son Hans Albert, who says that his father was withdrawn from the world as a boy . . . " (p. 10). Holton (1971–72) and Jakobson (1982) point out that Einstein himself accounted for his early problems by suggesting, "The words or the language, as they are written or spoken, do not seem to play any role in my mechanism of thought . . . I rarely think in words at all. A thought comes and I may try to express it in words afterward" (Jakobson, 1982, p. 140).

Significantly, none of his biographers mention reading problems or such difficulties as writing letters backward. In fact, Einstein was very advanced as a child, reading popular science books with what he later described as "breathless attention" (Hoffman & Dukas, 1972). At 13, he read and understood Kant's philosophical works. As for his school years, when he was 8, his mother wrote to her mother with pride that "yesterday Albert got his school marks. Again he is at the top of his class and got a brilliant record" (Hoffman & Dukas, 1972, p. 19). Einstein's main problem at school apparently was that he could not "sufficiently conceal his dislike for [his] teach-

ancillary treatment often is made less on the basis of valid assessment data than on decision makers' beliefs. For example, if the person making the decision believes that stimulant drugs or special diets or psychotherapy can help a person overcome a learning problem, such treatments are likely to be recommended. This is particularly true for a variety of controversial medically related interventions and the various fads that have plagued the field (see *Controversial Treatments and Fads,* p. 309).

Often, the assessment data gathered during the diagnostic process is sufficient for making general placement decisions. However, current law in the United States ties all such decision making to the

---

ers and their Draconian methods" (Hoffman & Dukas, 1972, p. 25).

In 1940, Einstein himself stated:

> When I was in the seventh grade at the Luitpold Gymnasium I was summoned by my home-room teacher who expressed the wish that I leave the school. To my remark that I had done nothing amiss he replied only "your mere presence spoils the respect of the class for me."
>
> I myself, to be sure, wanted to leave the school and follow my parents to Italy. But the main reason for me was the dull, mechanized methods of teaching. Because of my poor memory for words, this presented me with great difficulties that it seemed senseless for me to overcome. I preferred, therefore, to endure all sorts of punishments rather than to gabble by rote. (Hoffman & Dukas, 1972, p. 25)

In later years, he said:

> As a pupil, I was neither particularly good nor bad. My principle weakness was a poor memory and especially a poor memory for words and texts. . . . Only in mathematics and physics was I, through self-study, far beyond the school curriculum. (Erikson, 1982, p. 151)

As Einstein's recollections make clear, he had a lifelong history of challenging authority, thinking for himself, not thinking in words, and learning by his own means. And he had extremely high standards for himself. Consequently, his comments about poor memory for words must be judged in the context of these qualities. For example, his memory for words may have been "poor" as compared to his exceptional gifts for mathematics and physics. These qualities probably also account for his failure on his first college-entrance exam and the problems related to his first teaching position.

In short, while there is general agreement among his biographers that Einstein was somewhat delayed in developing verbal fluency, there is not satisfactory evidence to claim he had a verbal language disability and nothing to indicate that he was dyslexic. Indeed, despite his view (contradicted by other data) that he was neither a "particularly good or bad" student, he had excellent reading skills and was well read. Ironically, it is reported by his sister that he did have some minor problems with math computation in his early school years. However, his math grades over the years were high and, given his genius in mathematical concepts, it seems likely that any problem in this area was because he approached mathematics in ways that confounded those who attempted to have him work with simple addition and multiplication.

Given that professionals often cannot agree about a diagnosis of learning disabilities for individuals they have personally examined, it is not surprising to find controversy about assigning such a diagnosis to someone who died long before the concept of learning disabilities was conceived. While we understand there are positive motives for such posthumous diagnoses, we are concerned that history may be distorted in some cases. As the list of famous historical figures casually mentioned as having had learning disabilities grows, it seems increasingly important to exercise some caution in this regard. (See Adelman & Adelman, 1987, for more on this topic.)

process of developing an individualized educational program (IEP). It mandates that a specific program plan be formulated either at the time of placement or at least within 30 days of such decisions. Thus, whenever individualized educational programming is connected with placement decisions, a variety of tests and other assessment procedures may be used. It should be kept clear, however, that the data are needed for program planning—not for making the placement decisions per se.

Assessment for Program Planning

When it comes time to plan the specifics of a program, formal and informal assessment are essential. The procedures used include tests, observations, interviews, trial teaching, and so forth. As indicated, by U.S. law, a key administrative step is formulation of an IEP (see Feature 3).

Prevailing procedures related to LD have been shaped by the two dominant, contrasting orientations to remediation. Those concerned with underlying problems assess for deficits in such developmental areas as perception (for example, auditory, visual), cognition (for example, memory, language), and motor functioning in order to plan specific interventions. The types of instruments they have relied on are listed in Table 1. Poor performance on a set of subtest items is seen as indicating an underlying problem that should be improved (if it can be) through special treatment/training. This often takes the form of exercises to improve abilities, for example, to make visual or auditory discriminations. These exercises may differ from regular classroom tasks; for instance, they may involve discriminating abstract forms and patterns rather than specific letters and words. The assumption is that the exercises develop deficient underlying abilities and enable the individual to generalize successfully from the exercise to regular classroom tasks. If the underlying ability cannot be improved, the emphasis is on teaching individuals how to compensate for the handicap.

As already suggested, available research and logical analyses suggest that devices currently used to assess such areas are inadequate, especially for assessing problem populations. Research suggests that the special training exercises have not aided

learning to read, write, and do mathematics (Arter & Jenkins, 1977).

All this does not mean, however, that good tests of underlying problems and related remedial programs won't be developed (Kavale & Mundschenk, 1991). And the poor validity of a given test or remedial practice says nothing about the validity of the theory upon which it is based (Snart, 1985). The ultimate value of theories about underlying dysfunctions is yet to be determined. Thus it is well to be aware of the nature of assessment and remedial procedures based on such theory.

Those whose orientation is direct instruction of observable skills are concerned with specific knowledge and skills that have not been learned as yet by the individual. Thus, skill-oriented assessments use such procedures as standardized achievement tests, unstructured and informal skill diagnostic tests, observation of daily performance, trial teaching, and criterion-referenced evaluations.

No one skills-assessment instrument is mentioned in the literature more than others; *Procedures and Instruments for Assessing Learning Problems* (p. 341) provides a listing of representative examples. However, the processes called *criterion-referenced testing* (Hambleton, 1990), *curriculum-based assessment* (Shapiro & Derr, 1990), and *criterion-based measurement* (Blankenship, 1985; Deno, 1987; Fuchs, 1991; Fuchs, Hamlett, Fuchs, Stecker, & Ferguson, 1988; Shinn, 1989) represent the most highly structured and ambitious forms of skills assessment.

Although practitioners could make such assessments by daily observation of performance, diagnostic skill tests are used to provide information systematically. These approaches are designed to assess a variety of skills that a student is expected to learn. Tests are based on analyses of instructional goals and tasks. Assessed skills usually are grouped in terms of the sequence in which they are taught. Testing is used to evaluate progress and identify the skills the student apparently has not acquired.

For example, there are tests to assess readiness with respect to instructional programs that emphasize traditional reading instruction. One subtest focuses on readiness to learn phonics, with items assessing the student's performance in identifying, classifying, using, and producing alphabet-letter names, consonants, vowels, and their combinations. Using criteria reflecting what the student is expected to have learned, those who fall below criteria are seen as needing instruction and practice to develop missing skills. Such teaching takes the form of direct instruction, with an emphasis on workbooks and computer-aided instruction having specific objectives and exercises. The assumptions are that there is no underlying reason why the individual cannot learn such skills and that direct instruction is the best way to teach them.

As with testing underlying problems, diagnostic

Feature 3   The Individual Education Plan (IEP)

To improve intervention planning and evaluation, guidelines connected to Public Law 94-142 call for preparation of a written individualized education plan (an IEP) by a multidisciplinary team for each student seen as possibly having a disability. In addition to the written plan, the IEP process also is used for case management—from referral (encouraging prereferral interventions) going on to do multidisciplinary assessment, write the program plan, arrange placement, and monitor progress (Cruickshank et al., 1990).

A number of controversies have arisen around the IEP process. One has centered on the written plan itself.

The idea of writing out a specific plan is not controversial. Most practitioners feel that although this is a bit of a bother, it is reasonable for professionals to be open and accountable for their actions (Dudley-Marling, 1985).

What has become controversial is the manner in which government guidelines have tried to shape intervention rationales by stressing how intended outcomes should specifically be stated (Adelman & Taylor, 1983a).

The emphasis in current guidelines reflects the direct instruction of observable skills. That is, the trend has been toward "curriculum-based assessment" and writing all intended outcomes in the form of highly specific statements of observable behavior (behavioral or criterion-referenced objectives). Following behaviorist thinking, such an approach assumes that any long-range aim or goal (which can be a comprehensive and abstract outcome) is best achieved by listing each behavior or skill to be learned and then proceeding to teach it (Hambleton, 1990; Shapiro & Derr, 1990).

For instance, one long-range aim of schooling is to facilitate the development of children in a manner that prepares them to be effective citizens. A long-range goal related to this aim is to teach each student to read and write at a level adequate to participate in society (a level where they can hold a job). A great variety of objectives can be stated with respect to such a goal. One behavioral or criterion-referenced objective may be that "the student will learn to recognize 85 percent of a basic vocabulary list and correctly spell 60 percent of the words." Such objectives have been programmed for access by microcomputers for ease in generating the written plan.

Alone, objectives expressed in behavioral terms and including criteria for evaluation tend to look like a promising aid in planning and evaluating intervention. Critics concede that aspects of intervention can and should be spelled out in concrete ways. However, they also point out that students with a range of motivational, learning, emotional, and social problems are likely to require outcomes that cannot be translated appropriately into a set of simple behaviors and skills. Included are the many abstract outcomes of developing and changing attitudes and overcoming emotional blocks and other problems that may be interfering with learning. Attempts to state such outcomes as simple behaviors can end up as a list of objectives that have little connection with the intervention's intended long-range outcomes.

Many concerned theorists have cautioned that limiting programs to such simplistic objectives is, at best, irrelevant or perhaps a cruel hoax and, at worst, a dangerous reshaping of education (Heshusius, 1991; Shepard, 1991).

skill tests have their limitations, especially in assessing problem populations. The tests tend to yield inconsistent findings from one administration to another. Moreover, there is considerable controversy over what skills should be included in tests and programs because of fundamental arguments over what skills should be taught and when. And, because of test and performance anxiety and motivational considerations, there always is concern that skills identified as missing may have been acquired but not manifested during testing. Research suggests that skills learned through direct instruction are not maintained over time and do not generalize to the learning of more comprehensive knowledge and skills (Harris & Pressley, 1991; Heshusius, 1991).

In short, critics argue that such an approach to assessment for program planning assumes all skills require formal instruction. This fails to recognize that many basic skills are learned informally—in the course of daily experiences or while learning other things. Spoken language frequently is noted as an example of this informal learning. Those concerned about underlying problems maintain that the observable problem approach ignores the possibility that for some individuals there are factors interfering with learning skills.

As the above discussion suggests and *Remedying Learning Disabilities: Prevailing Approaches* (p. 314) further elaborates, there is little agreement about how best to remedy learning disabilities. Relatedly, there is considerable dissatisfaction with assessment procedures for program planning. In the long run, of course, such assessment cannot be any better than the interventions it prescribes.

Summing Up

Diagnosis, placement, and program planning must be done, and are done, every day. Whenever screening procedures are used, additional assessment and consultation must be done before a diagnosis of LD is made. Current criteria emphasize exclusionary factors, degree of underachievement, and symptoms of developmental immaturity. Because of problems related to such criteria, as well as controversies over definition and the deficiencies of diagnostic processes, misdiagnosis is rife. Correcting this problem is fundamental to advancing knowledge about LD.

In public schools in the United States, the diagnosis of learning disabilities means that an individual between the ages of 3 and 21 has the right to services, such as extra help and special teachers, that are not necessarily available to those with other types of learning problems. Decisions about which services should be provided are made on the basis of what is available and what seems most appropriate to those who are asked to make the decisions.

In keeping with the principle of providing the least intervention needed, the idea has been set forth that educational placements should be made in the "least restrictive environment." The intent is to keep students with learning disabilities in the "mainstream" of public education, but this has proven to be a rather difficult ideal to turn into specific prescriptions for individuals.

Over the years, assessment for program planning has been shaped largely by the two dominant orientations to remediation—underlying vs. observable problem approaches. However, as the IEP process has evolved, the trend has been toward reifying the latter. The result has been an overemphasis on assessing highly concrete skills and formulating plans in terms of behavioral objectives and direct instruction strategies.

Prevailing assessment procedures for diagnosis, placement, and program planning have been criticized as based on erroneous assumptions and as technically inadequate. Efforts to improve such assessment are seen as dependent on conceiving and successfully implementing more effective approaches to diagnosis and correction.

On Assessment Tools and Technical Concerns

II.1 Procedures and Instruments for Assessing Learning Problems

II.2 Technical Concerns About Assessment

II.1   Procedures and Instruments for Assessing Learning Problems

Assessment procedures are essential ingredients in most facets of practice and research. The demand for better procedures is great, and new procedures seem to appear at a faster rate than anyone can keep up with.

An estimated 250 million standardized tests are given each year in school settings. While most of these are routine achievement tests, a considerable amount of assessment is directed at diagnosing and planning for special populations.

An estimated 13 to 15 hours of professional time per person may be involved in assessment and decision making for individuals with psychoeducational problems (Ysseldyke & Algozzine, 1982). One observer has suggested the cost of such activity in school settings may be as much as $1800 for each targeted individual (Mirkin, 1980).

To document some of this activity, Thurlow and Ysseldyke (1979) surveyed 44 federally funded model learning disability programs. They found a great deal of variability in the tests used; they also found many instances in which tests developed for one purpose were being used for other purposes. Shepard and Smith (1983) reported that most tests used to identify learning disabilities in Colorado were technically inadequate. In general, those who have evaluated assessment activity related to learning problems are critical of the technical adequacy of prevailing procedures (Fuchs, Fuchs, Benowitz, & Barringer, 1987; Kavale & Mundschenk, 1991; Salvia & Ysseldyke, 1991).

Broadly speaking, the various types of assessment procedures used in the LD field tend to reflect the orientation of the practitioner. As discussed in Part 2, those who focus on CNS causes use assessment procedures that attempt to measure and prescribe treatment of underlying problems. In contrast, those who deemphasize initial causes tend to rely on assessment devices designed to identify and help plan corrective interventions for missing skills and learning strategies and for factors that may be currently interfering with correction.

In looking for assessment tools, practitioners find many worthwhile devices on the market. They also find more than a few that are not very good. The caution made by Buros (1974) is one we can all take to heart:

> At present, no matter how poor a test may be, if it is nicely packaged and it promises to do all sorts of things which no test can do, the test will find many gullible buyers. When we initiated critical test reviewing in the 1938 Yearbook, we had no idea how difficult it would be to discourage the use of poorly constructed tests of unknown validity. Even the better informed test users who finally become convinced that a widely used test has no validity after all are likely to rush to use a new instrument which promises far more than any good test can possibly deliver. Counselors, personnel directors, psychologists, and school administrators seem to have an unshakable will to believe the exaggerated claims of test authors and publishers. If these users were better informed regarding the merits and limitations of their testing instruments, they would probably be less happy and less successful in their work.
>
> The test user who has faith — however unjustified — can speak with confidence in interpreting test results and making recommendations.
>
> The well-informed test user cannot do this; [this person] knows that the best of our tests are still highly fallible instruments which are extremely difficult to interpret with assurance in individual cases. Consequently, [the user] must interpret test results cautiously with so many reservations that others wonder whether [the person] really knows what he is talking about. (p. *xxxvii*)

To identify what is available and find help in evaluating how good a procedure is, we can turn to a variety of sources. For example, a major resource is Buros Institute for Mental Measurements, which publishes the *Mental Measurement Yearbook*. This is a series of critical reviews and bibliographies of published psychometric tests. A companion work, Buros's *Tests in Print,* provides a comprehensive bibliography, by category, of tests used in psychology, education, and industry. The institute has a computerized system that can be accessed through bibliographic retrieval systems in libraries. Libraries also are a source for catalogues and survey summaries of unpublished research instruments (see, for example, Orvaschel, Sholomskas, & Weissman, 1980). Tests specifically designed for individuals manifesting learning and behavior problems are discussed in various texts (Salvia & Ysseldyke, 1991).

Hammill, Brown, and Bryant (1989) have developed a consumer's guide to tests in print. In addition, a variety of professional journals regularly discuss tests used to assess psychoeducational problems *(Journal of Assessment, Journal of Special Education, Remedial and Special Education).*

In Table 1 we list, by category, a range of procedures and instruments that are used for assessment of psychoeducational problems.

Table 1   Types of Procedures and Instruments Used in Assessing Psychoeducational Problems

I. Observations or Rating of Current Behavior (by parents, students, or professionals)

  A. *In natural settings such as classrooms, home, or free play situations*

    1. For prevention and identification

      a. Brigance Diagnostic Inventory of Early Development (Curriculum Associates)

      b. Learning Accomplishments Profile: Diagnostic Education—Revised (Kaplan School Supply Corp.)

      c. Child Behavior Rating Scale (Cassel, 1962)

      d. Denver Developmental Screening Test—Revised (Frankenburg, Dodds, Fandall, Kazuk, & Cohrs, 1975—LADOCA Publishing Foundation)

      e. Student Rating Scale (Adelman & Feshbach, 1971; Feshbach, Adelman, & Fuller, 1977)

      f. The Pupil Rating Scale Revised (Myklebust, 1981)

      g. Devereux Child Behavior Rating Scale, Devereux Adolescent Behavior Rating Scale, and Devereux Elementary School Behavior Rating Scale (Devereux Foundation)

      h. Developmental Profile II (Psychological Development Publications)

    2. For diagnosis, treatment planning, or evaluation

      a. Child Behavior Checklist and Profile (Achenbach & Edelbrock, 1983)

      b. Burks' Behavior Rating Scales (Burks, 1969)

      c. Conners Rating Scales (Abbot Laboratories)

      d. Revised Behavior Problem Checklist (Quay & Peterson, 1987)

  B. *In special assessment situations*

    1. For prevention and identification

      a. Early Detection Inventory (Follett Publishers)

      b. Gesell Developmental Tests (Ilg & Ames, 1964)

      c. Developmental Indicators for the Assessment of Learning—Revised (Childcraft Educational Corp.)

    2. For diagnosis, treatment planning, and evaluation

      a. Checklist for Student's Behavior (Smith, Neisworth, & Greer, 1978)

      b. While standardized measures are almost nonexistent, observation of behaviors during psychological and medical examinations tend to be the most heavily relied on data in confirming presenting problems

II. Interviews and Written Personal Reports (by parents, students, or professionals—responses to oral and/or written questions, or inventories of items, related to medical, psychological, educational, and socioeconomic background and status with emphasis on traumatic incidents and developmental problems)
Note: While some of the data elicited may be factual, there is undoubtedly an important bias toward subjective reinterpretation (Yarrow, Campbell, & Burton, 1970).

  A. *Histories*

    1. Medical information related to pregnancies and birth, illnesses, and injuries (Seidel & Ziai, 1975)

    2. Developmental information related to social, emotional, motor, language, and cognitive areas, e.g., Gesell's Illustrative Behavior Interview (Gesell & Amatruda, 1947)

    3. Diagnostic interviews for children and adolescents (Orvaschel, 1989)

    4. School history focusing on important events or patterns regarding school experiences (Wallace & Larsen, 1978)

    5. Family information including socioeconomic data, relevant medical, developmental, or school history of family members (Mercer & Lewis, 1977)

B. *Current status* (present concerns and perceived causes of problems)
   1. Medical status—current health status, recent illnesses, injury, or physical complaints (Schain, 1972)
   2. Developmental status—current social, emotional, motor, language, and cognitive status, e.g., Vineland Adaptive Behavior Scale (American Guidance Service)
   3. School status—current school problems and perspectives by all participants as to the causes and possible corrections
   4. Family status—current family events, living arrangements, impending changes

III. Verbal and Performance Measures

A. *For prevention and identification*
   1. de Hirsch Predictive Index (de Hirsch, Jansky, & Langford, 1966)
   2. The Satz Battery (Satz, Friel, & Rudegeair, 1976)
   3. Denver Developmental Screening Test (Frankenburg, Dodds, Fandall, Kazuk, & Cohrs, 1975—LADOCA Publishing Foundation)

B. *For diagnosis, treatment planning, evaluation*
   1. Cognitive area and aptitudes
      a. Wechsler Intelligence Scales, WPPSI, WISC-III, WAIS-R (The Psychological Corp.)
      b. Stanford-Binet Intelligence Test (Riverside Publishing)
      c. Boehm Test of Basic Concepts (Boehm, 1970)
      d. Detroit Tests of Learning Aptitude—2 (published by PRO-ED)
      e. Slosson Intelligence Test—Revised (Slosson Educational Publications)
      f. McCarthy Scales of Children's Abilities (The Psychological Corp.)
      g. Peabody Picture Vocabulary Test—Revised (American Guidance)
      h. Ravens Progressive Matrices (Ravens, 1956)
      i. System of Multicultural Pluralistic Assessment (Mercer & Lewis, 1979)
      j. Achievement tests such as the California Achievement Test (California Testing Bureau)
      k. Psychoeducational tests such as the Woodcock-Johnson Psychoeducational Battery (DLM/Teaching Resources)
      l. Kaufman Assessment Battery for Children—K-ABC (Kaufman & Kaufman, 1983)
      m. Learning Potential Assessment Device—a dynamic assessment instrument (Feuerstein, 1979; also see Palincsar, Brown, & Campione, 1991 for more on Dynamic Assessment)
   2. Academic achievement tests
      a. California Achievement Test (California Test Bureau)
      b. Stanford Achievement Test (The Psychological Corp.)
      c. Metropolitan Achievement Tests (The Psychological Corp.)
      d. Iowa Tests of Basic Skills; Tests of Achievement and Proficiency (Riverside Publishing)
      e. SRA Achievement Series (Science Research Associates)
      f. Gates-MacGinite Reading Tests (Teachers College Press)
      g. Wide Range Achievement Test—Revised (Jastak Associates)
      h. Peabody Individual Achievement Test—Revised (American Guidance Service)
      i. Psychoeducational tests such as Woodcock-Johnson Psychoeducational Battery (DLM/Teaching Resources)
      j. Kaufman Test of Educational Achievement—K-TEA (American Guidance Service)
      k. Skill diagnostic inventories, e.g., Criterion Reading (Hackett, 1971), Brigance Diagnostic Inventories (Curriculum Associates), and Diagnostic Mathematics Inventory/Mathematics System (CTB/McGraw-Hill)
   3. Perceptual-motor
      a. Bender Visual-Motor Gestalt Test (Bender, 1938–Western Psychological Services; see Koppitz, 1963, 1975, for scoring system)
      b. Developmental Test of Visual-Motor Integration (Follett Publishers)
      c. (Frostig's) Developmental Test of Visual Perception (Consulting Psychologists Press)
      d. Bruininks-Oseretsky Test of Motor Proficiency (American Guidance Service)
      e. Purdue Perceptual-Motor Survey (Merrill Publishing)
      f. Goldman-Fristoe-Woodcock Tests (American Guidance Service)
      g. Southern California Test Battery for Assessment of Dysfunction (Western Psychological Services)
      h. Visual Retention Test—Revised (The Psychological Corp.)

(continued)

(continued)

4. Language
   a. Goldman-Fristoe Test of Articulation (American Guidance Service)
   b. (Wepman's) Auditory Discrimination Test (Language Research Associates)
   c. Goldman-Fristoe-Woodcock Tests (American Guidance Service)
   d. Phonological Process Analysis (Weiner, 1979)
   e. Peabody Picture Vocabulary Test—Revised (American Guidance Service)
   f. Test of Adolescent Language—2 (PRO-ED)
   g. Tests of Language Development—2 (PRO-ED)
   h. Test of Written Language—2 (PRO-ED)
   i. Illinois Test of Psycholinguistics Abilities (Kirk, McCarthy, & Kirk, 1968)
   j. See achievement tests
   k. Reading readiness tests such as Metropolitan Readiness Tests
   l. Boder Test of Reading-Spelling Patterns (Grune & Stratton)
   m. Also see Johnson & Croasmum (1991)

5. Reading and math
   a. See achievement tests
   b. Diagnostic inventories such as the Brigance (Curriculum Associates), Woodcock Reading Mastery Test—Revised (American Guidance Service), Test of Mathematical Abilities (PRO-ED)
   c. Also on reading see Stanovich (1991) and on math see Baroody & Ginsberg (1991)

6. Social and emotional functioning
   a. Vineland Adaptive Behavior Scales (American Guidance Service)
   b. California Test of Personality (California Test Bureau)
   c. Kuder Personal Preference Record (Kuder, 1954)
   d. Goodenough-Harris Drawing Test (Harris, 1963)
   e. Childrens Apperception Test (Bellak & Bellak, 1965)
   f. Early School Personality Questionnaire (Coan & Cattell, 1970)
   g. Piers-Harris Children's Self-Concept Scale (Western Psychological Services)
   h. Coopersmith Self-Esteem Inventories (Center for Self-Esteem Development)
   i. Kohn Social Competence Scale (The Psychological Corp.)
   j. Social Skills Rating System (American Guidance Service)
   k. Walker-McConnell Scale of Social Competence and School Adjustment (PRO-ED)
   l. Personality Inventory for Children, Revised Format (Western Psychological Services)
   m. Also see Bryan (1991) on assessing social cognition and Keogh & Bess (1991) on assessing temperament

IV. Physiological Tests and Neuropsychological Exams

A. *Physical examination*—a nonspecialized exam including measurement of height, weight, head circumference, blood pressure, and exams of various physiological systems including visual acuity using Snellen wall or E charts

B. *Sensory acuity*—specialized tests
   1. Vision tests to assess acuity, refractive errors, nystagmus, faulty eye movement, color vision
      a. Keystone Visual Survey Service for Schools (Keystone View)
      b. Massachusetts Vision Test (Foote & Crane, 1954)
      c. Bausch and Lomb Orthorater
      d. Ishihara Color Blind Test (Ishihara, 1970)
   2. Hearing
      a. Sweep audiometry (discussed in Schain, 1972)
      b. Pure Tone Audiometry (see Northern & Downs, 1974)

C. *Neurological exam*
   1. Evaluation of mental status, speech, muscle tone, fine and gross motor control—"hard" neurological signs such as bilaterally exaggerated tendon reflexes, and various "soft" neurological signs such as confused dominance, asymmetrical reflexes, overflow or crossover movements (Obrzut & Boliek, 1991)
   2. Brain mapping, scanning, imaging (Duffy & McAnulty, 1985; Denckla, LeMay, & Chapman, 1985; Hynd & Willis, 1988; Coles, 1987)

D. *Neuropsychological tests*

Note: As distinct from neurological exams, neuropsychological exams involve a battery of tests measuring cognitive, sensory, and motor functioning and achievement, with the aim of relating performance to brain dysfunction (Hartlage & Golden, 1990; Obrzut & Boliek, 1991; Reitan & Davison, 1974)

1. Luria-Nebraska Neuropsychological Battery—Children's Revision (Golden, 1981)
2. Halstad-Reitan Neuropsychological Test Battery for Children (Reitan Neuropsychology Laboratory)
3. Selected subtests to measure sensation acuity and perception; motor, psycholinguistic, and cognitive functioning; attending; memory (Obrzut & Boliek, 1991)

E. *Special procedures to test hormonal, chemical, or structural defects* (Schain, 1972)

1. Brain scanning, mapping, and imaging
2. Metabolic tests, e.g., brain metabolism, ferric chloride test for PKU
3. Chromosomal studies

V. Available Records and Data

A. *Past*

1. Medical—reports from pediatricians, neurologists, other medical specialists
2. Psychological—test data, results, and reports from school psychologists or other professionals
3. Educational
   a. Review of past school products (written papers, projects)
   b. Reports from teachers and tutors
   c. Cumulative school records (grades, teacher comments, test scores, attendance, school health records)

B. *Current* (within the past three months)

1. Medical—report from the most recent physical and/or neurological exam
2. Psychological—test data, results, and reports from school psychologists or other professionals who have been consulted recently
3. Educational
   a. Review of current school products (written papers, projects)
   b. Reports from current teachers and tutors

VI. Environment Ratings Scales

A. *School*

1. The Instructional Environment Scales—prekindergarten and elementary (Ysseldyke & Christenson, 1987)
2. The Classroom Environment Scale (Consulting Psychologists Press)
3. Early Childhood Environment Rating Scale (Teachers College Press)
4. Quality of School Life Scale (Epstein & McPartland, 1976; Epstein, 1981)
5. Also see Toro et al. (1985) for social environmental predictors of elementary school adjustment, Heron & Heward (1982) on ecological assessment, Gable & Trout (1985) on assessing special education teaching processes, Gelzheiser & Leonard (1987) on assessing learning environment for math, and Fraser & Walberg (1991) on research for evaluating educational environments

B. *Home*

1. Home Observation for Measurement of the Environment (Caldwell & Bradley, 1984; Bradley & Rock, 1985)

Further Readings

The following list of references is provided as an aid in finding and evaluating assessment procedures.

Achenbach, T. M. & Edelbrock, C. (1983). *Manual for the child behavior checklist and revised child behavior profile.* Burlington, VT: Queen City Publishers.

Adelman, H. S. & Feshbach, S. (1971). Predicting reading failure: Beyond the readiness model. *Exceptional Children, 37,* 349–54.

Bellak, C. & Bellak, S. (1965). *Childrens apperception test.* Larchmont, NY: CPS.

Bender, L. (1938). *A visual-motor gestalt test and its clinical use.* American Orthopsychiatric Association Research Monograph. 3.

Boehm, A. E. (1970). *Boehm test of basic concepts.* New York: Psychological Corporation.

Bradley, R. H. & Rock, S. L. (1985). The HOME Inventory: Its relation to school failure and development of an elementary-age version. In W. K. Frankenburg, R. N. Emde, & J. W. Sullivan (Eds.), *Early identification of children at risk: An international perspective* (pp. 159–173). New York: Plenum.

Bryan, T. (1991). Assessment of social cognition: Review of research in learning disabilities. In H. L. Swanson (Ed.), *Handbook on the assessment of learning disabilities: Theory, research, and practice.* Austin, TX: PRO-ED.

Burks, H. (1969). *Burks' behavior rating scales.* El Monte, CA: Arden Press.

Caldwell, B. M. & Bradley, R. (1984). *Home observation for measurement of the environment.* Administration manual, revised edition. Little Rock, AK: University of Arkansas.

Cassel, R. N. (1962). *The child behavior rating scale.* Los Angeles: Western Psychological Services.

Coan, R. & Cattell, R. (1970). *Early school personality questionnaire.* Champaign, IL: Institute for Personality and Ability Testing.

Coles, G. S. (1987). *The learning mystique: A critical look at "learning disabilities."* New York: Pantheon Books.

de Hirsch, K., Jansky, J. & Langford, W. S. (1966). *Predicting reading failure.* New York: Harper & Row.

Denckla, M. B., LeMay, M. & Chapman, C. A. (1985). Few CT scan abnormalities found even in neurologically impaired learning disabled children. *Journal of Learning Disabilities, 18,* 132–35.

Duffy, F. H. & McAnulty, G. B. (1985). Brain electrical activity mapping (BEAM): The search for a physiological signature of dyslexia. In F. H. Duffy & N. Geschwind (Eds.), *Dyslexia: A neuroscientific approach to clinical evaluation.* Boston: Little, Brown.

Epstein, J. L. (Ed.) (1981). *The quality of school life.* Lexington, MA: Lexington Books.

Epstein, J. L. & McPartland, J. M. (1976). The concept and measurement of the quality of school life. *American Educational Research Journal, 13,* 15–20.

Feshbach, S., Adelman, H. S. & Fuller, W. (1977). Prediction of reading and related academic problems. *Journal of Educational Psychology, 69,* 229–308.

Feuerstein, R. (1979). *Dynamic assessment of retarded performers: The learning potential assessment device.* Baltimore: University Park Press.

Foote, F. M. & Crane, M. M. (1954). An evaluation of vision screening. *Exceptional Children, 20,* 153–61.

Frankenburg, W., Dodds, J., Fandall, A., Kazuk, E. & Cohrs, M. (1975). Denver developmental screening test, reference manual, revised. Denver: LA-DOCA Project and Publishing Foundation.

Fraser, B. J. & Walberg, H. J. (Eds.) (1991). *Educational environments: Evaluation, antecedents, and consequences.* New York: Pergamon Press.

Fuchs, D., Fuchs, L., Benowitz, S. & Barringer, K. (1987). Norm-referenced tests: Are they valid for use with handicapped students? *Exceptional Children, 54,* 263–271.

Gable, R. & Trout, B. (1985). Measurement of the teaching process in educational and treatment programs for exceptional youth. *Education and Treatment of Children, 8,* 297–320.

Gelzheiser, L. M. & Leonard, K. (1987). Assessing the learning environment for mathematics. *Journal of Reading, Writing, and Learning Disabilities International, 3,* 41–52.

Gesell, A. & Amatruda, C. S. (1947). *Developmental diagnosis: Normal and abnormal child development* (2nd ed.) New York: Harper & Row.

Golden, C. J. (1981). The Luria-Nebraska children's battery: Theory and formulation. In G. W. Hynd & J. E. Obrzut (Eds.), *Neuropsychological assess-*

ment and the school-age child: Issues and procedures. New York: Grune & Stratton.

Hackett, M. (1971). *Criterion reading: Individualized learning management system.* Westminster, MD: Random House.

Hammill, D. D., Brown, L. & Bryant, B. (1989). *A consumer's guide to tests in print.* Austin, TX: PRO-ED.

Harris, D. B. (1963). *Children's drawings as measures of intellectual maturity: A revision and extension of the Goodenough draw-a-man test.* New York: Harcourt, Brace & World.

Hartlage, L. C. & Golden, C. J. (1990). Neuropsychological assessment techniques. In T. B. Gutkin & C. R. Reynolds (Eds.), *The handbook of school psychology* (2nd ed., pp. 431–57). New York: Wiley.

Heron, T. E. & Heward, W. L. (1982). Ecological assessment: Implications for teachers of learning disabled students. *Learning Disability Quarterly, 5,* 117–25.

Hynd, G. W. & Willis, W. G. (1988). *Pediatric neuropsychology.* New York: Grune & Stratton.

Ilg, F. I. & Ames, L. B. (1964). *School readiness: Behavior tests used at the Gesell Institute.* New York: Harper.

Johnson, D. J. & Croasmum, P. A. (1991). Language assessment. In H. L. Swanson (Ed.), *Handbook on the assessment of learning disabilities: Theory, research, and practice.* Austin, TX: PRO-ED.

Kavale, K. A. & Mundschenk, N. A. (1991). A critique of assessment methodology. In H. L. Swanson (Ed.), *Handbook on the assessment of learning disabilities: Theory, research, and practice.* Austin, TX: PRO-ED.

Keogh, B. K. & Bess, C. R. (1991). Assessing temperament. In H. L. Swanson (Ed.), *Handbook on the assessment of learning disabilities: Theory, research, and practice.* Austin, TX: PRO-ED.

Kirk, S. A., McCarthy, J. J. & Kirk, W. D. (1968). *Illinois test of psycholinguistic abilities.* Urbana: University of Illinois Press.

Koppitz, E. M. (1963). *The Bender-Gestalt test for young children.* New York: Grune & Stratton.

Koppitz, E. M. (1975). *The Bender-Gestalt test for young children: Vol. II: Research and application, 1965–1973.* New York: Grune & Stratton.

Kuder, R. (1954). *Kuder personal preference record.* Chicago: Science Research Associates.

Mercer, J. R. & Lewis, J. F. (1977). *System of multi-cultural pluralistic assessment.* New York: Psychological Corporation.

Mirkin, P. K. (1980). Conclusions. In J. Ysseldyke & M. Thurlow (Eds.), *The special education assessment and decision making process: Seven case studies.* Minneapolis: University of Minnesota Institute for Research on Learning Disabilities.

Myklebust, H. R. (1981). *The pupil rating scale revised.* New York: Grune & Stratton.

Northern, J. L. & Downs, M. P. (1974). *Hearing in children.* Baltimore: Williams & Wilkins.

Obrzut, J. E. & Boliek, C. A. (1991). Neuropsychological assessment of childhood learning disorders. In H. L. Swanson (Ed.), *Handbook on the assessment of learning disabilities: Theory, research, and practice.* Austin, TX: PRO-ED.

Orvaschel, H. (1989). Diagnostic interviews for children and adolescents. In C. G. Last & M. Hersen (Eds.), *Handbook of child psychiatric diagnosis.* New York: Wiley.

Orvaschel, H., Sholomskas, D. & Weissman, M. M. (1980). *The assessment of psychopathology and behavioral problems in children: A review of scales suitable for epidemiological and clinical research (1967–1979).* DHHS Publication No. (ADM)80-1037. Washington, DC: U.S. GPO.

Palincsar, A. S., Brown, A. L. & Campione, J. C. (1991). Dynamic assessment. In H. L. Swanson (Ed.), *Handbook on the assessment of learning disabilities: Theory, research, and practice.* Austin, TX: PRO-ED.

Quay, H. & Peterson, D. (1987). *Revised Behavior Problem Checklist.* Coral Gables, FL: University of Miami.

Ravens, J. C. (1956). *Progressive matrices.* London: H. K. Lewis.

Reitan, R. M. & Davison, L. A. (1974). *Clinical neuropsychology: Current status and applications.* New York: Winston/Wiley.

Salvia, J. & Ysseldyke, J. E. (1991). *Assessment.* Boston: Houghton Mifflin.

Satz, P., Friel, J. & Rudegeair, F. (1976). In J. Guthrie (Ed.), *Aspects of reading acquisition.* Baltimore: Johns Hopkins.

Schain, R. J. (1972). *Neurology of childhood learning disorders.* Baltimore: Williams & Wilkins.

Seidel, H. M. & Ziai, M. (1975). Pediatric history and physical examination. In M. Ziai (Ed.), *Pediatrics.* Boston: Little, Brown.

Shepard, L. A. & Smith, M. L. (1983). An evaluation

of the identification of learning disabled students in Colorado. *Learning Disability Quarterly, 6,* 115–27.

Smith, R. M., Neisworth, J. T. & Greer, J. G. (1978). *Evaluating educational environments.* Columbus, OH: Merrill.

Stanovich, K. E. (1991). Reading disability: Assessment issues. In H. L. Swanson (Ed.), *Handbook on the assessment of learning disabilities: Theory, research, and practice.* Austin, TX: PRO-ED.

Thurlow, M. & Ysseldyke, J. (1979). Current assessment and decision making practices in model programs for learning disabled students. *Learning Disability Quarterly, 2,* 15–24.

Toro, P. A., Cowen, E. L., Weissberg, R. P., Rapkin, B. D. & Davidson, E. (1985). Social environmental predictors of children's adjustment in elementary school classrooms. *American Journal of Community Psychology, 13,* 353–64.

Wade, T. & Baker, T. (1977). Opinions and use of psychological tests: A survey of clinical psychologists. *American Psychologist, 32,* 874–82.

Wallace, G. & Larsen, S. C. (1978). *Educational assessment of learning problems: Testing for teaching.* Boston: Allyn & Bacon.

Weiner, F. (1979). *Phonological process analysis.* Baltimore, MD: University Park Press.

Yarrow, M. R., Campbell, J. D. & Burton, R. V. (1970). Recollections of childhood: A study of the retrospective method. *Monographs of the Society of Research in Child Development, 35,* No. 5.

Ysseldyke, J. E. & Algozzine, B. (1982). *Critical issues in special and remedial education.* Boston: Houghton Mifflin.

Ysseldyke, J. E. & Christenson, S. L. (1987). Evaluating students' instructional environments. *Remedial and Special Education, 8,* 17–24.

II.2   *Technical Concerns About Assessment*

How good are the assessment procedures outlined in *Procedures and Instruments for Assessing Learning Problems* (p. 341)? Some are terrible. Some are useful. Even the best are not good enough.

Many widely used assessment devices, even those that are commercially marketed, have technical deficiencies. To understand why this is so requires knowledge of what is meant by the concepts of reliability, validity, norms, and standards.

Assessment procedures (tests, rating scales, interview and observation schedules) produce descriptive data that vary in their degree of reliability and validity. In judging and interpreting the meaning of data, assessors use norms and standards that also vary in their reliability and validity.

What does it mean for an assessment procedure to be reliable and valid? What are norms and standards? Let's look at each of these matters.

Reliability

In common usage the term *reliability* refers to dependability, accuracy, and precision. As related to assessment, the concept is used to indicate how consistent and reproducible assessment data are.

Just as assessment is not limited to tests, the concept of reliability is relevant to all assessment activity. Furthermore, it is used to determine whether findings are consistent and reproducible over time, in different settings, despite differences in assessors. The concept is also used frequently to describe the consistency among procedures that claim to measure the same thing, such as several measures of intelligence.

Reliability, however, says nothing about what the procedure is measuring. The concept of validity deals with what the findings mean.

In technical terms, reliability refers to the degree a procedure is free of random error. Mathematically, reliability is presented as a number that varies from zero to one. This number is called a correlation or reliability coefficient. The coefficient for a totally unreliable procedure would be .00, perfect reliability is indicated by 1.0.

A common way to arrive at a reliability coefficient is to analyze the findings from several comparable administrations of an assessment procedure. Assuming what is being measured has not changed, the findings should be similar.

When the findings are not similar, it may be because of deficiencies in the procedure or because what is being measured has changed. On the other hand, highly reliable findings do not always mean that a procedure is technically sound; highly reliable findings can also be produced by biased administration or interpretation (nonrandom error).

No psychological assessment procedure is completely dependable or free from random error. With regard to tests, it has been pointed out that

> unless the test is perfectly reliable, and such instruments do not exist to the authors' knowledge, there is likely to be some margin of error in every test score. Indeed test theorists conceive that, were a hypothetical individual given the same test a great many times (assuming that learning and practice effects did not systematically change scores), there would be a range of score values observed, with the range being narrow for reliable tests and broad for unreliable tests. The examinee's "true" score would be the average of all the observed scores. This conception is an elaboration of the idea of reliability, and is presented in an easily comprehended manner in materials developed by test publishers such as the Educational Testing Service. Users of many of the tests published by this organization are advised to make decisions about individual students not in terms of the precise score obtained, but rather in terms of a band or interval extending on each side of the score. This "confidence band" is calculated on the basis of the reliability coefficient for the test and is to be interpreted as having a sufficiently high probability of including the student's true score. (Skager & Weinberg, 1971, pp. 121–22)

Validity

Valid data and decisions are the main concerns of assessors. The concept of validity applies both to assessment processes and to decisions based on assessment findings. If data are not highly valid, we cannot be very certain about what they mean. This leads to controversy and to a great many errors in interpreting the findings and making decisions.

Discussions of the validity of assessment procedures can be confusing. The concept relates to whether assessment and decision-making procedures are leading to meaningful

- descriptions of a phenomenon (Does the procedure measure what it says it does? Only what it says it does? All of what it says it does?)
- interpretations and judgments of a phenomenon (Are the inferences justified? How appropriate are the norms and standards?)
- decisions (How relevant are the data for the decisions that must be made?)

To understand the concept in more specific terms, we need to look at several of the related types of validity discussed in the assessment literature. Furthermore, while reliability is established in a relatively technical and objective way, validity usually is determined through a great deal of rational and subjective activity.

Three basic types of validity are

- content (How well does the procedure assess the knowledge, skills, and behavior it claims to measure?)
- criterion-related — including predictive, concurrent, and diagnostic validity (How well does the procedure assess the relationship between currently measured phenomena and future, concurrent, or past phenomena?)
- construct (How well does the procedure assess some theoretical concept, such as intelligence or anxiety?)

Content Validity

Content validity refers to how well the items on such procedures as standardized achievement tests and course exams actually sample learned skills, knowledge, and behavior. For example, several items that require adding two single-digit numbers may be used to test whether a youngster has learned this skill.

How do we know if a procedure has high content validity? We know because we or someone else makes a judgment that it does. In the example of adding single-digit numbers, the content validity of the items seems so evident that they are seen by

most people as appropriate on their "face value" — thus the term *face validity*. However, when a great many possible items can be included on a test, judgments about the content validity of many of them may be challenged. (Think about the items on any recent test you have taken; chances are you thought some were not a valid assessment of your knowledge and abilities.)

When more than face validity is necessary, judgments made by experts are used to establish content validity. However, the more comprehensive the content area to be assessed, the harder it is to sample and the more likely experts are to disagree.

Take any standardized achievement tests as an example. The content validity of such tests is almost always judged to be high. That is, a group of experts has designed and judged the items to be a good, representative sample of skills in a particular area such as reading. At the same time, inspection of the popular reading tests on the market shows they vary markedly in their content. All claim high content validity, yet they differ in many important ways. The experts clearly have different opinions about what the content of this type of test should be, and one suspects that each would disagree with the judgments of others. And since reading is an area in which content has been relatively well defined, the problems can only be greater in areas where knowledge and skills have not been clarified very well.

Even when there is expert consensus about the high content validity of a test, it may be a poor measure for some individuals and groups. For instance, a math test that requires reading directions or has a short time limit is a poor measure of what a person knows about arithmetic for any individual with a reading problem or anyone who works slowly.

In sum, statements about content validity reflect someone's subjective judgment. For most consumers, this means they must choose from among expert opinions. In doing so, it is helpful to have clearly in mind what one wants to assess and why as bases for discriminating among conflicting expert views.

Predictive, Concurrent, and Diagnostic Validity

Criterion-related (including predictive, concurrent, and diagnostic) validity refers to how well current assessment data can be used to help understand some future, present, or past concerns.

An example is assessment designed to predict

future school failure. To establish predictive validity in such a case, research must show a strong relationship between the data used to predict and some criterion representing subsequent school failure, such as poor grades or low achievement scores. As with reliability, correlation coefficients are used to indicate the strength of the relationship.

Criterion-related validity coefficients for comprehensive psychoeducational assessment procedures generally are not high. Coefficients as high as .60 are rare. Some assessment experts recommend that procedures with coefficients as low as .30 can still be useful (Garrett, 1954; Guilford, 1956).

Decisions as to whether a procedure is valid enough depend on how much new and unique information the data represent. If a procedure has the potential to add a piece of important information that will otherwise not be available, it may be worth using even if it has a low coefficient. On the other hand, it makes little sense to use a procedure that adds no new information even if it has a relatively high coefficient.

Ultimately, the point is to make good decisions. Every criterion-related procedure results in some errors. In screening for future reading problems, for instance, some individuals will be identified as future problems but turn out not to be; this type of error is called a *false-positive error.* Some individuals will not be identified as future problems but turn out to have difficulty learning to read; these are called *false-negative errors.*

The number of errors can be used as another way to look at the validity of the assessment and decision-making procedures. That is, computation of the number of correct predictions and the number of errors expressed as proportions provides another index of validity.

One major complication related to establishing criterion-related validity is the selection of appropriate criteria with which to correlate assessment data. For instance, what is the most appropriate criterion of school success or failure? Grades? Amount learned? Ability to apply what has been learned? Positive attitudes toward learning? Obviously, each is debatable. In choosing a criterion, four major qualities have been stressed: (1) relevance, (2) freedom from bias, (3) reliability, and (4) availability (Thorndike & Hagen, 1977).

Another complication is that the validation process requires a criterion measure that is highly reliable and valid. For the measurement of complex psychoeducational criteria, such measures simply do not exist. At best, what is available has moderate validity. Thus, the irony often is that researchers must use criterion data gathered by measures that have rather limited reliability and validity; this includes most of the procedures cited in this text.

A variety of other factors can confound the validation process related to criterion-referenced assessment. They need not be reviewed here. The point is that all these complications and confounding factors make it evident why so many of the available predictive and diagnostic assessment procedures should be used with great care and discretion.

In choosing such procedures, the question is not which will avoid making errors — they all make errors. The question is which will produce the smallest number of errors. And although the procedure that produces the smallest number of errors is the best that is available, it may not be good enough. Certainly, it will not be good enough for individuals for whom the findings are in error.

Finally, we note that there is a tendency to infer causation from criterion-related measures. For example, a test may predict failure, but this is not sufficient evidence that what the test measures is the cause of the failure. This jumping at conclusions reflects the common mistake of observing correlates and believing one is seeing cause and effect. The establishment of cause-effect connections requires construct validation.

Construct Validity

Construct validity refers to how well an assessment procedure measures something that is not directly observable, such as theoretical concepts or abstractions (intelligence, anxiety, perception, motivation). It also is used in theorizing about relationships among concepts and things that are observable (Nunnally, 1978).

The term *construct* is used to clarify that what we are trying to measure is a hypothetical idea *constructed* by scientists to help organize thinking about something that can't be seen directly. In effect, a construct is a myth that is found to be a useful and convenient way to understand and communicate about a theoretical notion. Of course, it is rarely discussed as a myth as long as enough scientists find it useful.

Because constructs are not directly observable,

they are not directly measurable. What then is measured?

Let's take intelligence as an example. Intelligence is an idea that has been constructed to reflect an attribute of people that many of us find interesting and important. Theories have been formulated to suggest the nature of this attribute and the behaviors that should be directly and indirectly associated with it. For instance, it has been suggested that one of the abilities that reflect intelligence is the ability to reason using verbal, graphic, and mathematical symbols. It also is argued that some groups of persons, such as the majority of university students, are likely to be more intelligent than others (for example, the majority of those who drop out of high school). Efforts to develop a test of intelligence will include — among other items — some that measure verbal reasoning. Efforts to determine the construct validity of the measure of intelligence, then, might involve comparing groups of university students and high-school dropouts as to their performance on tests of verbal reasoning ability. If the majority of university students are found to score higher, the findings will be seen as providing some evidence for the construct validity of the measure.

Obviously, no one set of findings is enough. Construct validation requires consistent findings from many different studies.

> Construct validity is established through a long-continued interplay between observation, reasoning, and imagination. . . . The process of construct validation is the same as that by which scientific theories are developed. (Cronbach, 1970, p. 142)

As with content and criterion-related validity, reasoning and judgment play an important role in construct validation. Also, as with content validity, there is no one correlation coefficient that describes how valid a construct measure is. However, unlike content validation, expert judgment alone cannot be used to validate a construct measure. Conclusions must be justified by an extensive body of research.

A major complication in the validation process is that constructs, such as intelligence, motivation, and self-concept, often are defined differently by those who develop the procedures used to measure the phenomena. Thus procedures that claim to be measuring the same construct may be very different from each other. This means the findings from validation studies using different measures often are not comparable. Therefore, even though many studies may have been done, it may not be appropriate to combine them as evidence for construct validity.

There is wide recognition of the difficulty of validating measures of constructs such as visual perception, psycholinguistic ability, and minimal cerebral dysfunctioning. Thus it is obvious that many assessment and decision-making procedures used in diagnosing such factors require a substantial amount of additional validation.

Norms and Standards

One of the most basic aspects of human behavior is that people try to make sense out of what they see. Complex things are observed and conclusions are made: the new neighbor appears to be wholesome and friendly; the person walking behind you in an unlit parking lot at night looks like a mugger or worse; students are judged by their teachers to be smart or not too smart; teachers are judged by students to be good or terrible.

What is the basis for such conclusions? Obviously people are influenced by the information available to them in a given situation. They also draw on past experiences. In addition, they may be influenced by some general ideas, theories, attitudes, values, and beliefs they have developed.

Because of differences in the information available and factors influencing how the information is processed, people often arrive at different conclusions about what seems to others to be the same phenomenon. In interpreting the same assessment data on an individual, one assessor may arrive at a diagnosis of learning disabilities, and another may conclude the person has no disability; among a group of students experiencing the same program, some may adore it, others may hate it, and the rest may think it's merely OK.

Given that people are seeing the same things, the differences in their conclusions probably reflect the use of different norms and standards in making judgments. For our purposes, the term *standard* refers to the use of values or a theoretical idea to make judgments about what has been assessed. The judgments often are about whether what is assessed is a problem, is "good" or "bad," or is consistent with some theory.

Norms are empirical standards. They are not value statements or theoretical statements. Formal norms are based on research and systematic observation. For example, a set of previous findings can be used as a set of norms in judging assessment data. Are the current findings higher, lower, or the same as the previous findings? How much higher or lower?

Assessment norms reflect data gathered on various research samples. The score for someone subsequently assessed is compared to the scores for the previous samples. The individual's score will be described in terms of how it compares to the average (mean or median) score for the research samples. It may be found to be above or below average or typical or atypical.

After norms are used, it is commonplace to apply some set of standards to make judgments. This can happen so quickly that it often is not apparent that judgments have been made. For example, a score above or below average may be quickly translated into a judgment that the performance was acceptable or unacceptable, passing or failing. This is understandable, especially with tests of achievement. However, it is important to understand that a value judgment—a standard—has been used. The use of norms by themselves does not lead to a judgment.

Why the distinction between norms and standards is important can be seen by taking a closer look at judgments based on commonplace assessments of behavior and performance. For example, we may have norms that show that an individual's activity level is well above the average found in research samples. On the basis of this information, should we conclude that the individual is highly active or hyperactive? The latter judgment carries with it the implication of a problem and pathology. Such a judgment may not be necessary based on the norms—especially if many of those studied previously who scored at the same level were not found to have problems. Thus the judgment of hyperactivity would reflect someone's standards (the assessor's standards based on theory). Somebody else might use the same findings and norms, but a different set of standards, and decide the individual is not hyperactive.

In general, the decisions that follow assessment activity usually are influenced by the norms and standards that have been used in making judgments about the meaning and significance of the assessment findings. Unfortunately, adequate norms are frequently unavailable, and the standards used in making judgments often are extremely controversial.

To illustrate the problem, we can look at the matter of norms for intelligence tests. The individual intelligence test for children developed by Wechsler is among the best assessment devices available to LD professionals. With regard to available norms, there is more data on this instrument than on almost any other major procedure. But, as we have suggested already, the statement "best available" should not be too readily interpreted as meaning that the instrument is unquestionably a "good" procedure. As published in 1949, the sample used to standardize and establish norms for the test included only white children. In the years prior to the test's 1974 revision, countless individuals were tested and decisions were made based on norms from this extremely narrow sample. The inadequacy of the norms (and apparent bias in the test's content) with regard to the types of youngsters included in the original samples led to enormous criticism, including judicial action. In an attempt to correct the situation, the 1974 and 1991 revisions gathered norms on samples representative of the population in the United States with respect to socioeconomic status, race/ethnicity, and geographical region distribution based on the most recent census data. For example, the 1991 revision used 1988 census data in selecting a validation sample consisting of 2200 children between ages 6 and 16, with an equal number of males and females. However, considerable criticism still is directed both at the content and the fact that the construct validity for many subgroups in the population remains to be established—including persons with learning disabilities. Furthermore, there is controversy over the widespread tendency to use IQ levels as standards for judging people as "good" or "bad" in a variety of contexts.

Summing Up

Understanding the concepts of reliability, validity, norms, and standards allows one to appreciate the current state of the art and the hurdles that must be overcome if psychoeducational assessment and decision-making practices are to improve. Such hurdles are not insurmountable. To do so, however, will be costly and require the talents of many.

On Teaching

III.1 Theories of Instruction and Models of Teaching

III.2 Enhancing Motivation and Skills in Social Functioning

III.3 Intrinsic Motivation and School Misbehavior

III.4 Learner Options and Decision Making to Enhance Motivation and Learning

III.5 Fernald's Techniques in Their Motivational Context

III.1   Theories of Instruction and Models of Teaching

Despite the long history of formal schooling, there is as yet no such thing as a comprehensive and widely accepted theory of instruction. There have been many efforts to weave ideas about learning and teaching into conceptual frameworks and models. A landmark effort was made in 1966 when Jerome Bruner published a work entitled *Toward a Theory of Instruction*; since then, there has been increasing interest in the development of such a theory.

The following material provides a glimpse at efforts to synthesize ideas about instruction and teaching. First, we focus on five individuals who can be viewed as providing a foundation for theory building; then, we outline the integrated set of ideas that Robert Gagné developed into a widely cited theoretical view of instruction; finally, we highlight Joyce and Weil's effort to categorize models of teaching.

Foundations for a Theory of Instruction

In exploring the foundations for a theory of instruction, Patterson (1977) cites (1) the Montessori Method, (2) Piaget's ideas on how the intellect develops, (3) Bruner's ideas on the processes of education and instruction, (4) Skinner's technological approach, and (5) Rogers's humanistic approach. Patterson's summary of each is abstracted here.

Montessori Method

Maria Montessori's Method (1964) offers a set of practices and principles based on the view that learning is a natural developmental process with sensitive periods to which teaching must accommodate. Patterson (1977) interprets Montessori's views as follows:

Since learning depends upon the natural development of the child, then the child should be allowed the greatest liberty or freedom within the limits of the freedom of others who are in association with her or him. The appropriate materials and resources must, of course, be made available to the child in a "prepared environment."

Respect for children, trust in their ability to grow and develop through use of and interaction with their environment, and patience in allowing them to progress at their own time and rate, are fundamental to the Montessori method. . . . (p. 45)

Montessori was concerned with the whole child . . . physical, social, emotional, and cognitive development. The attitudes of the teacher toward the child, and the relationship between the teacher and the child were recognized as important. (p. 61)

Piaget

Jean Piaget's (see Furth & Wachs, 1974) ideas on the origins of intellect have major implications for teaching. Piaget recognizes that the individual interacts with, rather than reacts to, the environment. Piaget discusses processes and structures in terms of such interactions. He sees development as an orderly, continuous process, progressing through stages, with qualitative individual differences appearing at each stage. Learning begins with the concrete and moves to the abstract; it is an active process that is facilitated by first allowing children to manipulate objects ("do") to experience ("see") a principle operating in their own actions. Then the perceptual and motor supports can be reduced.

Many of Piaget's implications for education are neither new nor unique. The work does provide support for the ideas of innovators such as Dewey and Montessori and is consistent with concepts such as discovery learning.

On the implications of Piaget's ideas for teaching, Patterson notes:

The contention, or perhaps better, the recognition, that thinking precedes the acquisition of language constitutes a challenge to education, which almost universally places emphasis upon language as the foundation for all education. Piaget emphasizes that thinking begins with, and is built upon, and grows out of sensorimotor activities. Thinking must begin with concrete objects and experiences before abstract or representational thinking can develop. The concept of cognition-as-action would radically change much of the instruction in school.

One of the most important of Piaget's ideas for education is his conception that the purpose of education is to facilitate the development of the thinking process. This is perhaps not original with Piaget; but heretofore there has been little basis for implementing it. Piaget provides a basis. With the information and knowledge explosion, it is becoming apparent that education cannot cram children with all they need to know; even if it could, much would be obsolete and useless by the time formal education was completed. The development of ability to think, not only in cognitive areas but in areas such as social and interpersonal relations, values, and morality and ethics, is certainly a priority in our current world.

With all its difficulties and deficiencies, the work of Piaget, in quantity and in quality, provides one of the best existing foundations for a theory of instruction. (pp. 129–30)

Bruner

Jerome Bruner (1966) has written cogently on the processes of education and instruction. Bruner sees formal education as a necessity in complex societies because young children cannot learn all they need to know as adults by observing and imitating others.

To facilitate instruction, Bruner stresses that we must know something about the predispositions in the learner that influence learning, about how to structure knowledge and present material, and about the role of rewards and punishments. He views people as natural learners — active, curious, seeking mastery and competence, with a "will to learn"; natural learning is seen as self-rewarding.

Problems are seen as arising in the artificial setting of schools because teaching emphasizes telling rather than doing and because natural "knowledge of results" is replaced with grades and other unnatural forms of feedback. Under such conditions, content often seems irrelevant and motivational problems arise.

Schools also seem to discourage intuitive (as contrasted with analytic) thinking. Intuitive thinking is seen in sudden insights and problem solutions. Bruner (1966) views such thinking as deriving from poetry, art, myth, and the humanities, and as providing fruitful hypotheses and creative ideas that can

be tested later by application of analytic thinking or scientific methodology. He sees the emphasis on giving correct answers as restricting intuitive thinking, while encouragement of risking a guess is seen as fostering it.

As Patterson notes, in summarizing the implications of Bruner's work on teaching:

Subject matter can be made interesting and still be presented accurately. The personalization of knowledge — making it meaningful and useful in relation to the child's thinking, attitudes, and feelings — creates interest. Learning is an active process, and the child should participate actively in the learning process. Activity promotes interest. The discovery method also engages the interest of the learner. The solving of real problems arouses interest. Curiosity, interest, and the urge toward competence and mastery lead to exploration, which is necessary for real learning and problem solving.

Bruner's dictum that any subject can be presented to a learner of any age in a form that is interesting and honest rests on the idea that any subject matter can be converted to a form appropriate for any level of cognitive development. This involves the structuring of subject matter in terms of basic themes, fundamental ideas, principles, issues, and relationships. These can be represented as a set of actions (enactive representation), by a set of images (ikonic representation), or by symbols (symbolic representation). Subjects can be presented sequentially in these modes, with the addition of detail and content, as students progress in school, thus constituting what Bruner calls the spiral curriculum. Later learning is easier when built upon earlier learning. Such structuring of subject matter or knowledge maintains the interest of the student. It also makes for economy in teaching and learning, and fosters retention and transfer, or generalization.

. . . Learning situations which are self-correcting are ideal; here the effects of actions become immediately apparent, as in experiments using apparatus such as balances. Extrinsic, external reinforcement does not foster continuation or persistence of learning. It may actually interfere with learning, by arousing too high a level of anxiety or by restricting attention and learning to the specific activities which are rewarded, thus discouraging transfer or generalization; and by weakening the satisfactions of intrinsic rewards through focusing the learner's attention on the "pay-off" or on satisfying the teacher. (pp. 180–81)

Skinner

B. F. Skinner's (1968) technology of teaching is based on a behavioral analysis of human functioning that contends that all behavior is shaped by environmental factors. Skinner sees teaching as a matter of establishing conditions by which desired behavior will be emitted and responses are then reinforced and shaped using appropriate types and schedules of reinforcement. He sees rewards as more powerful reinforcers than punishment.

For Skinner, inner states, such as thoughts and feelings, are simply covert behaviors that are learned in the same way overt actions evolve. They are not seen as causing behavior and thus don't have to be accounted for when environmental conditions are established to facilitate learning. Motivation is seen simply in terms of states of deprivation and use of related reinforcement contingencies.

Skinner criticizes education as currently being too artificial and irrelevant and as promoting conformity rather than diversity. He sees these problems as easily corrected through the appropriate technical use of behavioral principles.

Patterson summarizes Skinner's technological approach as having had three major applications:

1. In classroom management, the principles of behaviorism can be used to assure that children attend class, engage in those behaviors necessary for learning to take place, and do not manifest behaviors which are disruptive to learning. Discipline is achieved through the application of contingencies of reinforcement, emphasizing positive reinforcement. . . .

2. Programmed instruction utilizes principles of behavioral analysis in selecting and defining objective terminal behaviors which are desired as the outcome of learning, and then constructing a graded sequence of steps toward the objective, each of which is reinforced until it is established, at which time the next step is presented. Behaviors are elicited. . . [and] reinforced when they occur. . . .

3. Teaching machines are an efficient method of presenting programmed instruction. Programs can be constructed in advance. . . . Short steps which are necessary for some learners can be gone through rapidly by better students. Programs can be constructed at different levels. Delivery of reinforcements can be more systematic and immediate. Students are active in the learning process, constructing rather than selecting answers, and can progress at their own rate, and review if they wish. The teacher is freed for those activities which cannot be done by a machine. . . .

[In general, the approach] focuses on the specification of desired terminal behaviors and the process of achieving them through the application of the principles of programming. Technology increases the teacher's productivity and thus leads to a sense of accomplishment. (pp. 271–72)

Many behaviorists who advocate some of the approaches proposed by Skinner have added other ideas. In this respect, Patterson notes that for these neobehaviorists:

Behavior is not completely or automatically determined by its actual consequences. Consequences provide information which guides action. Consequences motivate behavior by representing possible outcomes which can be dealt with cognitively, so that the individual can decide to act or not in order to obtain or avert certain outcomes. Anticipated rather than actual consequences thus influence behavior. Behavior can also be influenced without direct experiencing of consequences by vicarious experience (observation of others), by reading about something, and by listening, activities which involve no objective stimulus, no overt response, and no contingencies or actual reinforcement.

Behavior is also influenced by social experiences. But in a social context, personal elements or standards also are involved: A person may eschew an external reinforcement because it is inconsistent with consequences for the self-concept.

Thus, it is increasingly being recognized that, while the principle of reinforcement is valid, it does not operate simply, automatically, or without the influence of internal affective and cognitive factors in much of human behavior. (p. 274)

Rogers

Carl Rogers's (1969) ideas reflect a humanistic approach. From his theories of personality and therapy, Rogers has attempted to evolve an approach to education and teaching. He begins with the view that people are basically good and rational. They are motivated toward actualizing their positive potentialities and only act badly as a defensive reaction to threats to their psychological well-being. That is, Rogers suggests that people, given the right opportunities, will develop into self-actualized or fully functioning persons.

In this approach, the goal of education is seen as the development of fully functioning or self-actualized persons. In defining what facilitates such development, Rogers stresses three key conditions that should be created in the teacher's interaction with others. These conditions involve conveying empathic understanding, respect (trust, positive regard), and genuineness. In general, the process of teaching is seen as requiring consistent commitment to providing opportunities for self-initiated, self-directed learning, for being genuine, and for conveying regard and empathic understanding in interacting with learners.

In summarizing Rogers's views on education, Patterson states:

> To educate toward a fully functioning person requires that education cease focusing on imparting facts, information, and knowledge, that it go beyond the objectives of development of the intellect or of thinking persons, to concern for the development of the affective, emotional, and interpersonal relationship qualities of individuals. The whole person must be educated.

Learning related to development of the whole person is significant learning, learning which is personal and experiential and which makes a difference in the person. The individual doesn't have to be motivated toward significant learning — the motivation is inherent in the drive toward self-actualization. Significant learning occurs when the learner perceives the subject matter as relevant for his or her own purposes. . . . learning is facilitated when external threats to the self are at a minimum. Freedom from threat enables the learner to explore, to differentiate, to try new ideas, to change. Significant learning is facilitated by experiential involvement with real problems. Initiation of the process and participation in it by the learner fosters significant learning. Self-evaluation rather than external criticism and evaluation fosters independence, creativity, and self-reliance. Significant learning, involving all these elements, is learning how to learn.

Learning also depends, of course, upon the learner. Motivation is a normal, natural characteristic of human beings if it has not been suppressed or destroyed by mistreatment. Stimulation by problem situations also occurs naturally in normal persons. Finally, the learner must perceive the facilitative conditions in the teacher, and here, also, individuals who have not been mistreated, deceived, conned, or turned off will be open to and recognize these conditions.

. . . The real teacher does not know everything and does not pretend to. He or she can admit mistakes. The teacher manifests prizing, acceptance, and trust by really listening to the student, without evaluating her or him, and by responding to what the student says — to the attitudes and feelings expressed as well as the content. Listening also evidences the attempt to understand, and responding attempts to communicate understanding. Teaching becomes a real, spontaneous, personal encounter with students.

The teacher also facilitates learning by building upon real problems in the lives and culture of students, by providing many easily accessible resources (including his or her own knowledge), by developing contracts with students through which they can develop their own learning programs, by providing programmed instruction units, by small group sessions and discussions or projects, by inquiry learning, by simulation learning, and by encounter-group sessions. (pp. 330–31)

Obviously, there are differences and commonalities among the five approaches reviewed. Ironically, one of the strong commonalities is that all five theorists propose views about the processes of learning and teaching that public schools have yet to adopt on any large scale.

The Conditions of Learning and Theory of Instruction

Robert Gagné (1985) has attempted to weave ideas about essential conditions for learning into a theory of instruction. He begins by clarifying his view of learning. Using an information-processing model, he conceives of learning as encompassing a set of nine processes: reception, expectancy, retrieval to working memory, selective perception, semantic encoding, responding, reinforcement, retrieval and reinforcement, and retrieval and generalization. To illustrate, he states:

> previously learned material in long-term memory is continually being retrieved to the working memory and to consciousness. There it may be rehearsed, not only in the sense of being repeated, but also *re-encoded* before being again returned to long-term memory. The process of encoding as it occurs in the working memory is continually influenced by inputs whose origins are external to the learner. These inputs have been processed initially by the sensory registers and by the kind of transformation we call selective perception. (p. 243)

Instruction is seen as the intentional arrangement of events in a learner's environment for purposes of making learning happen. To do this effectively requires arranging events that provide support to the internal processes of learning. A theory of instruction attempts to relate how the external events affect internal learning processes resulting in learning outcomes.

Gagné specifies three major themes for his theory of instruction:

1. Learning is conceived as the set of nine internal processes specified. These transform environmental stimuli into forms of information that progressively establish long-term memory states (learning outcomes) which, in turn, provide various performance capabilities.

2. Performance capabilities are practically oriented or theoretically based and can be grouped into five categories: intellectual skills, cognitive strategies, verbal information, attitudes, and motor skills. "These categories of human capability underlie distinctively different classes of human performance, which means that the effectiveness of the learning which produced them can be differentially assessed" (p. 245).

3. The specific operations involved in the events of instruction are different for each of the five categories of learning outcomes.

A sequence of nine instructional events are conceived to correspond to the nine internal learning processes. These events, related examples, and corresponding learning processes formulated by Gagné are:

1. gaining attention (for example, use of abrupt stimulus change) → reception

2. informing learners of the objective (for example, telling learners) → expectancy
3. stimulating recall of prior learning (for example, asking for recall) → retrieval to working memory
4. presenting the stimulus (for example, displaying the content with distinctive features) → selective perception
5. providing "learning guidance" (for example, suggesting a meaningful organization) → semantic encoding
6. eliciting performance (for example, asking learner to perform) → responding
7. providing feedback (for example, giving informative feedback) → reinforcement
8. assessing performance (for example, requiring additional learner performance, with feedback) → retrieval and reinforcement
9. enhancing retention and transfer (for example, providing varied practice and spaced reviews) → retrieval and generalization

Gagné stresses that his theory states that optimal learning will occur if each instructional event takes the form research has shown to be most effective (that is, the form shown to provide the greatest support for the internal learning processes). Moreover, the optimal form for some events—particularly 3, 4, 5, and 9—are viewed as differing for each of the five categories of learning outcomes (intellectual skills, cognitive strategies, verbal information, attitudes, and motor skills). He also stresses that with older, experienced learners not all nine instructional events are necessary because self-instruction comes into the picture once they learn how to learn (acquire learning strategies). Finally, Gagné notes three major assumptions underlying his theory, namely that (1) the learner will spend the necessary time on task, (2) the learner will be motivated to learn, and (3) instructional events will take into account individual differences in the learner's prior knowledge and "discourse comprehension" (ability to comprehend the stimuli presented).

Models of Teaching

Joyce and Weil (1986) take another approach to synthesizing ideas about instruction. They propose a framework for grouping 20 separate (but not mutually exclusive) teaching approaches or "models" into four families. As these authors have indicated previously, each approach has a great deal to say about the "kinds of realities admitted to the classroom and the kinds of life-views likely to be generated as teacher and learner work together" (1980, p. 1).

Joyce and Weil agree with Dewey that, at its core, the process of teaching involves the arrangement or creation of environments with which the learner is to interact. They elaborate this basic idea as follows:

> A model of teaching is a plan or pattern that we can use to design face-to-face teaching in classrooms or tutorial settings and to shape instructional materials—including books, films, tapes, and computer-mediated programs and curriculums (long-term courses of study). Each model guides us as we design instruction to help students achieve various outcomes. (1986, p. 2)

The four families, or models, of teaching are specified as (1) the information-processing family, (2) the personal family, (3) the social family, and (4) the behavioral systems family. At the outset Joyce and Weil emphasize that they do not view one model as superior for all purposes or as the best way to achieve a given objective. "However, we do find powerful options that we can link to the multiple educational goals that constitute a complete educational diet. The message is that the most effective teachers . . . need to master a range of models and prepare for a career-long process of adding new tools and polishing and expanding their old ones. . . . [C]ombinations of models can have a more dramatic effect on learning than any one could have alone "(1986, p. 5). Joyce and Weil's description of the models grouped under the four families is summarized in the following.

Information-Processing Family

These approaches emphasize ways to enhance efforts to acquire and organize data, sense problems and generate solutions, and develop concepts and language to convey them. The models in this family vary in emphasis: some provide information and concepts; others stress concept formation and hypothesis testing; a few focus on creative thinking; and a few others are meant to enhance general intellectual ability. All are seen as helping individuals improve their ability to acquire and use information and to think effectively. Many are seen as useful with respect to concerns about studying self and society in order to foster the personal and social goals of education.

Seven models are grouped under this family: (1) concept attainment, (2) inductive thinking, (3) inquiry training, (4) advance organizers, (5) memorization, (6) the developing intellect, and (7) scientific inquiry.

Personal Family

These approaches are oriented to the individual's capacity to function as an integrated personality. They focus on people learning to understand themselves (such as how individuals construct and organize their unique reality) and learning to take responsibility for learning. They encourage reaching for high quality lives through self-understanding, continuing growth, self-esteem, sensitivity, creativity, and productive relationships with their environments. "The cluster of personal models pays greater attention to the individual perspective and seeks to encourage productive independence, so that people become increasingly self-aware and responsible for their own destinies" (1986, p. 7). At the same time, these models are seen as producing positive interpersonal relationships and more effective information-processing capabilities.

Four models are included in this family: (1) nondirective teaching, (2) synectics, (3) awareness training, and (4) the classroom meeting.

Social Family

These approaches are oriented toward encouraging people to work together to generate collective energy or synergy. They emphasize cooperative study (working together on tasks, joint rewards) with a view to enhancing an individual's learning about and relationship with others or with society in general. They use processes by which reality is socially negotiated. Along with stressing social relations, there also is concern for cognitive (such as information acquisition and concept formation) and personal development.

Five models are included in this family: (1) group investigation (democratic processes as a source), (2) role playing (studying social behavior and values), (3) jurisprudential inquiry (clarifying public issues), (4) laboratory training (T-group model), and (5) social science inquiry.

Behavioral Systems Family

These approaches are oriented toward the processes by which human behavior is shaped and reinforced. Their roots are in behavior modification, behavior therapy, cybernetics, and social learning theory. "The stance taken is that human beings are self-correcting communication systems that modify behavior in response to information about how successfully tasks are navigated" (1986, pp. 11–12). Thus the emphasis is on organizing clearly defined tasks and methods for communicating feedback to make it easier for individual self-correction to take place. The intent is to change visible behavior rather than underlying psychological structure. Among the specific behaviors emphasized are basic academics, social and athletic skills, and relaxation to cope with anxiety. Common to behavioral models is the focus on turning learning tasks into a series of small, sequenced behaviors. Most rely on teacher control, but a few are based on the premise of self-directed learning.

Four models are included in this family: (1) mastery learning, direct instruction, and social learning theory, (2) learning self-control, (3) training for skill and concept development, and (4) assertive training.

In creating a learning environment, teachers can draw on models within a family and across families.

Summing Up

As Joyce and Weil stated in the preface to their 1980 edition,

> We believe the strength in education resides in the intelligent use of [the] powerful variety of approaches — matching them to different goals and adapting them to the student's styles and characteristics. Competence in teaching stems from the capacity to reach out to different children and to create a rich and multidimensional environment for them. Curriculum planners need to design learning centers and curricula that offer children a variety of educational alternatives.... The existing models of teaching are one basis for the repertoire of alternative approaches that teachers, curriculum makers, and designers of materials can use to help diverse learners reach a variety of goals.... We believe the world of education should be a pluralistic one — that children and adults alike should have a "cafeteria of alternatives" to stimulate their growth and nurture both their unique potential and their capacity to make common cause in the rejuvenation of our troubled society. (pp. *xxiii–iv*)

III.2   *Enhancing Motivation and Skills in Social Functioning*

Persons with learning disabilities and other learning problems often do not behave in ways others think they should. The behavior of such persons has been labeled behavior problems, misbehavior, adaptive behavior deficits, lack of social skills, and so forth. (Public Law 94-142 specifically requires assessment of "adaptive" behavior.) Recently, there has been a trend to view these behavior "problems" as an indication of immature social development, especially a lack of skills for interpersonal functioning and problem solving. This has led to a variety of "social skills training" programs.

How promising are programs for training social skills? Recent reviewers have been cautiously optimistic about the potential value of several proposed approaches. At the same time, there is concern that such skill training seems limited to what is specifically learned and to the situations in which the skills are learned. Moreover, the behaviors learned seem to be maintained for only a short period after the training. These concerns have been raised in connection with (1) training specific behaviors, such as teaching a person what to think and say in a given situation, and (2) strategies that emphasize development of specific cognitive or affective skills, such as teaching a person how to generate a wider range of options for solving interpersonal problems.

As with other skill training strategies, the limitations of current approaches seem to result from a failure to understand the implications of recent theory and research on human motivation. It is evident that many social skill training programs lack a systematic emphasis on enhancing participants' motivation to avoid and overcome interpersonal problems and to learn and continue to apply interpersonal skills to solve such problems.

In keeping with the ideas presented in Part 3, we have been exploring ways to engage a student initially in a variety of activities intended to overcome or minimize avoidance and enhance positive motivation for improving social functioning, especially the solving of interpersonal problems. The general assumptions underlying this work are discussed in Chapters 8 through 11. In addition, with regard to social functioning, we assume that

1. not all problems with social functioning are indications that a person lacks social skills
2. assessment of social skill deficiencies is best accomplished after efforts are made (a) to minimize environmental factors causing interpersonal problems and (b) to maximize a student's motivation for coping effectively with such problems
3. regular teaching and remedial strategies to improve skills for social functioning are best accomplished in interaction with systematic strategies to enhance motivation (a) for avoiding and overcoming interpersonal problems and (b) for continuing to apply social skills

The specific steps we have developed so far to address major motivational considerations in overcoming interpersonal problems are outlined in Feature 1. Steps in enhancing skills are outlined in Feature 2.

Because we have not addressed the topic of social skills in any depth in the text, a few words about the steps outlined in Feature 1 seem in order. The interest in training social skills has resulted in a rapidly growing body of literature specifying skills and procedures (see references at the end of Chapter 11). Although most social skills curricula await further evaluation, we have drawn upon available work to arrive at what appears to be a promising synthesis of "skills" and practices. Furthermore, our approach to teaching the skills uses a general problem-solving sequence. In essence, individuals are taught to (1) analyze interpersonal problem situations, (2) generate and evaluate a range of options and specific steps for resolving problems, and (3) implement and evaluate the chosen option, and then (4) if necessary, select another alternative.

These abilities can be practiced as lessons or when natural interpersonal problems arise in the classroom. For those who are interested and capable, the problem-solving framework itself can be taught. When formal lessons are used, small-group instruction is favored because it provides a social context for learning about social matters; however, individuals should be given private lessons when necessary. We propose that groups meet each day for 30–45 minutes over a period of about eight weeks.

For each step, three guidelines shape the choice of specific instructional objectives. Recognizing that both motivational and developmental readiness must be accommodated, the guidelines stress the following:

- Not teaching previously learned skills or those that the individual does not want to pursue currently.

(In such instances, scheduled lessons are replaced by enrichment activities; needed skills instruction is postponed until sufficient interest can be established.)
- Teaching the skills most needed in pursuing current relationships. (Lessons are not necessarily presented in the order listed in Feature 2.) Optimally, objectives are keyed to match the individual's current needs. Such needs are identified by the individual involved or by school personnel who have assessed the deficiencies by closely observing well-motivated attempts at solving interpersonal problems.)
- Developing missing prerequisites for learning and

Feature 1   Initial Steps for Enhancing and Maintaining Motivation to Solve Interpersonal Problems

Activities such as direct discussions, responding to direct questions, sentence completion, or Q-sort items, role playing, audiovisual presentations,* and so on are used as vehicles to present, elicit, and clarify

1. specific times when the individual experiences interpersonal problems (without assigning blame)
2. the form of the problems (again, no judgments are made)
3. the individual's perceptions of the causes of the problems**
4. a broader analysis of possible causes (the individual's thoughts about other possible reasons and about how other people might interpret the situation; intervener examples of other perceptions and beliefs)
5. any reasons the individual might have for wanting the interpersonal problems not to occur and for why they might continue
6. a list of other possible reasons for people not wanting to be involved in such problems
7. the reasons that appear personally important to the individual and why they are significant, underscoring the individual's most important reasons for wanting not to be involved in such problems
8. general ways in which the individual can deal

appropriately and effectively with such problems (avoid them; use available skills; develop new skills)
9. the individual's (a) general desire not to continue to experience interpersonal problems, (b) specific reasons for wanting this, and (c) desire to take some action
10. the available alternatives for avoiding problems, using acquired skills, and developing new skills
11. the available options related to activities and objectives associated with learning new skills (the specific activities and materials, mutual expectations, and so on)
12. specific choices stated as a mutually agreeable plan of action for pursuing alternatives clarified in steps 10 and 11.

Any step can be repeated as necessary (perhaps because of new information). Also, once the skill development activities are initiated, some of the steps must be repeated in order to maintain an individual's motivation over time.

*Videotapes are particularly useful to make points vividly (to portray others in comparable situations, to present others as models).
**Each step does not require a separate session (for example, steps 1 through 3 can be accomplished in one session).

Feature 2   Steps to Enhance Skills for Solving Interpersonal Problems

1. Presentation of examples of interpersonal problem solving (read by the instructor using visual aids or a videotape presentation).*
2. Group discussions of examples stressing (a) why the person in the example wanted to solve the problem, (b) the way the problem was analyzed, (c) possible solutions that were generated, and (d) the way in which pros and cons of solutions were considered, and choices made, implemented, and evaluated.
3. Presentation of an interpersonal problem and group discussion of why the person involved wants to resolve the problem and of how to analyze it.
4. Presentation of an appropriate analysis of a problem and group discussion and categorization of options.
5. Presentation of a range of options and specific steps for solving a problem; group discussion of pros and cons for evaluating which one should be pursued.
6. Presentation of a chosen alternative for solving a problem; group discussion of how to evaluate its effectiveness and to choose another option if necessary.
7. Presentation of a new problem with the preceding steps repeated as needed.

It is proposed that at least four problems be pursued in this fashion. By the fourth, the individual is to be able to do each facet of the problem-solving sequence during a given session. If not, up to three additional problems will need to be presented.

Evaluative feedback will underscore progress and satisfaction associated with accomplishment of program objectives and solving interpersonal problems at school. Consequences that the individual experiences when such problems are not solved appropriately also need to be highlighted.

*During any step, as appropriate, the discussion may include role playing, use of puppets with younger children, and so on. Initially, the intervener provides categories of ideas that may have been missed. All ideas generated during discussion are to be charted for subsequent reference.

performing needed skills. When necessary, individuals are involved in additional exercises to improve (1) communication, (2) divergent thinking, (3) recognition and understanding of individual differences, and/or (4) understanding the value of respect and concern for others.

Summing Up

Obviously, the ideas discussed here represent only a beginning. Given the growing interest in the areas of systematic enhancement of motivation and the training of social skills, we anticipate that programs for individuals with learning and behavior problems will increasingly incorporate procedures that reflect strategies for simultaneously enhancing motivation and skills.

III.3   Intrinsic Motivation and School Misbehavior

Too often learning problems and behavior problems go together. Because of this, it is essential to develop a perspective on school misbehavior. We want to highlight the importance of understanding the motivational underpinnings of school misbehavior. Our focus here is on the intrinsic motivation concepts of self-determination, competence, and relatedness.

An Intrinsic View of Motivation

The following discussion draws primarily on the work of Deci and his colleagues, because their theoretical ideas are consistent with a large amount of theory and research, and they consistently apply their work to schooling, clinical intervention, and special education populations (Deci, 1975, 1980; Deci & Chandler, 1986; Deci & Ryan, 1985; Ryan, Connell, & Deci, 1985). That perspective specifies three fundamental psychological needs motivating human activity—self-determination, competence, and relatedness. Deci and Ryan (1985) define self-determination as "a basic, innate propensity . . . that leads organisms to engage in interesting behaviors . . . out of choice rather than obligation or coercion, and those choices are based on an awareness of one's organismic needs and a flexible interpretation of external events" (p. 38). They define competence as the need people have to be effective. Relatedness is the need for warmth from and involvement with others (Deci & Chandler, 1986).

These needs are seen as the intrinsic motivating forces leading individuals to seek out challenges. And, seeking and conquering challenges are viewed widely as fundamental to development of the internal structures that guide subsequent action.

Besides growth-oriented behavior, intrinsic motivation theorists (Brehm & Brehm, 1981; Condry, 1977; Deci & Ryan, 1985; McGraw, 1978) also emphasize that individuals are especially vulnerable to events that (a) exert pressure and control, or (b) lead to repeated failure, negative feedback, or outcomes that are unpredictable or uncontrollable. Obvious examples are demands for conformity enforced with punishment for noncompliance. Less obvious examples are efforts to use material and social rewards to control behavior. For instance, even when students "shape up" to obtain an offered reward, they may perceive the situation as another effort to control them (limit their self-determination). Several research reviews concur that use of rewards, surveillance, deadlines, and other actions that exert pressure and control on an individual can undermine feelings of self-determination and lead to psychological reactance (Brehm & Brehm, 1981; Condry, 1977; McGraw, 1978; Deci & Ryan, 1985; Ryan et al., 1985). Psychological reactance is Brehm's term for the motivation to protect or restore options or freedoms (Brehm & Brehm, 1981). Such motivation is aroused when an option (freedom) that is important and believed to be available is removed or threatened.

It should be stressed, however, that it is the surrounding context, not events themselves, that is seen as determining whether external control produces negative effects. As Deci and Chandler (1986) point out:

> In the realm of education, both the general classroom context and the specific context for any given child seem to be determined primarily by the teachers' orientations and intentions. For example, when teachers offer rewards or impose deadlines with the intent of controlling the children's behavior—of getting the children to do what they want them to do—the rewards and deadlines have predicted negative effects (Deci, Nezlek, & Sheinman, 1981). On the other hand, when these events are presented as informative structures, as ways of acknowledging independent achievement or creative initiations, for example, they do not have negative effects. (p. 589)

From this perspective, a considerable amount of the motivation underlying school misbehavior can be understood in terms of a student's (1) growth-oriented activity stemming from psychological needs for self-determination, competence, and relatedness, and (2) reactions to threats to these three psychological needs. In the latter instance, degree of threat is dependent on how the student perceives events and their context.

Toward Categorizing Intrinsic Motivation for Misbehavior

Once we adopt an intrinsic view of motivation, the concepts can be applied in efforts to categorize intrinsic motivational underpinnings of devious and deviant behavior. Before illustrating the point with a working schema, however, we want to stress the basic context for such work—namely, the problem of describing school misbehavior.

Categorizing School Misbehavior

What makes a particular act at school deviant? Charles (1985) states classroom misbehavior "is behavior that the teacher judges to be inappropriate for a given time or place" (p. 4). That is, an act that bothers the teacher usually is seen as deviant. This is not to say the act *should* be identified as misbehavior or that the student should be seen as a discipline problem. It is simply a recognition that, as a representative of a powerful system, the teacher's perception generally prevails and is the starting point for intervention.

Similarly, any effort to categorize and classify troublesome school behavior is influenced by the rationale used by the classifier. One could, for example, simply categorize misbehavior in terms of designations used on behavior rating scales—arguing, high or low activity levels, crying, hitting and fighting, destroying things, not following rules and directions, not participating in class or not coming to school, lying, or cheating. (Such descriptive terms imply nothing about motivation.)

Most practitioners and researchers, however, are not satisfied with descriptive terms. They prefer to classify misbehavior with respect to its disruptive influence or postulated underlying pathology. For instance, some refer to acting out (as contrasted with withdrawn) students, using labels such as uncooperative, noncompliant, disrespectful, or inappropriately aggressive. These labels do not specify the motivational underpinnings for misbehavior, but the behavior commonly is explained in terms of youngsters' desires to "get attention," "flaunt authority," or "avoid doing the assigned work."

In contrast, some professionals see devious and deviant behavior as a manifestation of psychological and physiological disabilities. Thus, they use diagnostic labels such as attention deficit hyperactivity disorder, oppositional defiant disorder, depression, and so forth. One implication of this underlying-pathology view is that misbehavior is not always rationally motivated; another implication is that, although observers often infer rational intention, they may be in error. (Some interveners offer these implications as a basis for not considering rational motives for misbehavior; others are unconcerned about motives because their practices are not based on differential diagnoses of cause.)

One of the prerequisite tasks we have had to deal with in our efforts to explore motivational underpinnings for school misbehavior is that of categorically describing manifestations of such behavior. Because of the deficiencies related to current schemes for classifying children's problems, we have found it helpful for now to return to the use of basic dimensions to describe observable manifestations. The basic descriptive dimensions we use are (1) general type of behavior, (2) overtness, (3) energy level, (4) pervasiveness, and (5) frequency. That is, first we group the acts into two major categories, as highlighted by multivariate analytic studies (Quay & Werry, 1986): (a) acting-out behavior, and (b) withdrawal (physical and psychological). Second, we distinguish each category in terms of whether it is manifested overtly or covertly, whether the act is displayed in a highly intensive or passive manner, and whether it is seen in a narrow or broad range of situations. Then we rate its frequency of occurrence. We find this categorization provides sufficient descriptive differentiation among troublesome acts to allow us to proceed with exploring motivational underpinnings for such behavior.

Categorizing Motivational Underpinnings

As with learning problems, the largest proportion of devious and deviant behavior seen at school is not likely the result of internal pathology. Indeed, the majority of such behavior probably is motivated and rational. This position receives support from the prevalence with which misbehavior is characterized as an act of defiance, a diversion, revenge, an effort to deceive or manipulate, to be nonconforming or anticonforming, and so forth. (We do recognize that some behavior problems are an unintentional byproduct of efforts to cope without having acquired the skills for doing so appropriately. Purely unintentional misbehavior, however, seems most prevalent among young children who have not yet experienced a great deal of failure and frustration and among individuals with significant disabilities.)

In categorizing intentional misbehavior, a motivational perspective suggests the need to distinguish motivational subgroups. To begin, it is useful to differentiate proactive and reactive behavior. Proactive behavior is the individual's effort to seek out or establish conditions that produce feelings of satisfaction. In terms of misbehavior, this means the actions reflect an approach tendency. Reactive behavior is seen in efforts to cope and defend against conditions that produce unpleasant feelings (such as misbehavior reflecting an avoidance tendency).

Furthermore, as conceived by Deci and colleagues, the intrinsic motivational bases for most intentional behavior can be viewed as stemming from a desire to feel self-determining, competent, and related to others. From this theoretical base, a substantial portion of school misbehavior can be understood as students' attempts to act in ways that increase feelings of control, competence, and connectedness with significant others. That is, some misbehavior reflects proactive efforts to do things that lead to such feelings; other behavior reflects reactive efforts to deal with threats that interfere with such feelings (see Figure 1). For example, students often are compelled into situations in which they feel they cannot perform effectively and, under such circumstances, may react in negative or inappropriate ways to avoid or protest what is happening. Over a

period of time this reactive behavior, which was initially designed to defend against aversive situations, can become an established pattern of coping.

The same action may reflect proactive or reactive motivation and stem from a desire to feel self-determining, competent, or related to others. The misbehavior may take the form of overt or covert actions. Examples of the former include open and direct defiance and aggression, direct physical or psychological withdrawal, and nonconformity or conformity to deviant models; examples of the latter include manipulation, deception, passive withdrawal, and psychologically induced physical illness.

The importance of distinguishing the underlying motivation for misbehavior at school can be illustrated by thinking about six students who are noncompliant about following school rules.

Student A sets off the fire alarm in the hall. His action is based on a proactive effort to stir up some excitement. He is seeking the challenge of breaking the law and the feeling of competence that results from not getting caught.

Student B paints graffiti all over the bathroom wall. Her act also is proactive; but the behavior is intended to increase her acceptance by a subgroup of peers who she believes expect her to defy the rules (she is trying to conform to the standards set by deviant role models).

Student C proactively seeks to satisfy her need for self-determination by dressing according to her own view of what is best for her, rather than adhering to the school's dress code.

In contrast, Student D's action is reactive; he defiantly breaks the dress code as a direct protest

Figure 1   Motivational Underpinnings for Intentional Misbehavior at School

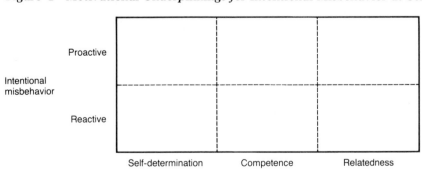

against what he views as a threat to his self-determination.

Student E's action is also reactive; she refuses to do classroom assignments as a way of diverting attention from the fact that she lacks the skills to perform competently in class.

Finally, Student F has been rebuffed in his efforts to establish a positive relationship with his teacher, and he reacts by withdrawing and giving her the silent treatment.

Summing Up

Obviously individuals misbehave for different reasons. However, this fact has often been ignored as school personnel and parents react to such behavior. In *Managing and Preventing School Misbehavior* (p. 422), we build on the preceding discussion by exploring the problem from an intervention perspective.

III.4   Learner Options and Decision Making to Enhance Motivation and Learning

If Mara dreams of being a musician and wants to spend time learning more about music, is this an option? If David's great passion is collecting baseball cards and memorizing facts and statistics about the game, can his program include a project focusing on baseball? James is curious about electronics, but he doesn't want to take a standard electric shop course because making buzzers and one-tube radios seems pretty far removed from television and computers. Can he have time to explore the topic in ways that uniquely interest him?

And if Mara, David, and James are allowed to pursue such content, what outcomes (skills, knowledge, and attitudes) and what level of competence (from budding awareness to moderate levels of mastery) should be expected from their activity?

Content and Outcome Options

From a motivational perspective, the answers to such questions are reasonably clear. Learners want to explore content that has personal value. In the process, they need help in pursuing outcomes and levels of competence that reflect their continuing interest and effort (Deci & Ryan, 1985; Stipeck, 1988).

Most individuals will find personal reasons for acquiring basic skills and information while exploring intrinsically valued content. For example, the more James pursues his interest in electronics, the more he will discover that he needs to improve his reading and math skills. Thus his ongoing exploration of electronics can indirectly lead to a personal desire to improve math and reading as he comes to view these skills as a means to his ends—rather than as something everyone else wants him to do.

There are three ways in which classroom content and outcomes can be readily expanded to provide a broad range of interesting options. The first involves expanding options to include a wide sampling of topics that are currently popular with the majority of the students (see Feature 1). The second way involves asking students, especially those who still

think there are too few positive options, to identify additional topics they would like to have included. Third, there are options the teacher identifies as important and worthwhile that can be introduced in ways that expand student interests.

The more severe the student's learning problem, the more it can be argued that variations from established content and outcomes are worth offering to mobilize and maintain the student's motivation. With a severe motivation problem, it may be necessary to include options not usually offered to such students (auto mechanics, video production, photography, work experiences).

Even more controversial may be the necessity to allow such students to "opt out" of certain content courses (reading, math) for a while. This occurs most frequently with students whose failures have led them strongly to avoid particular subjects.

Along with strong dislikes, students with motivation problems often have an area of strong interest that can be made the focus of their program. The intent is to allow a youngster to explore some intriguing area in depth and in ways that uniquely interest him or her.

Actually, such a comprehensive discovery-oriented project can be a useful option when any student wants to learn a great deal more about a topic. Projects give an intrinsic sense of form, direction, and immediacy to learning. (Any of the examples in Feature 1 may be undertaken as a project.)

Moreover, in pursuing comprehensive projects, students not only can discover more about a specific content area, they can also rediscover the personal value of improving reading, language, and a variety of other basic skills. After all, what makes certain skills "basic" is that they are necessary for pursuing many interests and tasks in daily living. When students come to understand this, they often develop a renewed interest in learning basic skills.

The many options illustrated here suggest that, rather than going "back to basics," it may be better to go "forward to basics" by enabling students to rediscover intrinsic reasons for learning such skills. While we're discussing the matter, we also should reemphasize that there has been a broadening of current views about what is and isn't a basic skill. There is more to coping with everyday situations than having competence to use the three Rs. Another prominent set of basic skills that students need, for instance, is the ability to interact positively in social situations. (A motivation-oriented program in this area is outlined in *Enhancing Motivation and Skills in Social Functioning,* p. 362.)

Calls for "back to basics" underscore the fact that there is always a conflict between required curriculum content and topics that have contemporary interest and are popular. From a motivational perspective, it would be nice if a way were found to achieve some sort of satisfactory balance. This might result in decreased time devoted to the established curriculum but it may also increase positive attitudes toward learning and school. Even if such a balance seems unnecessary for most students, it does appear justified in cases of learning problems, since the established curriculum has proved not to be effective.

Process and Structure Options

Content, of course, interacts with processes. An exciting presentation can make a topic really come to life. As with content and outcomes, there are three ways in which process options can be readily expanded—by adding procedures that are widely popular, by adding those of special interest to specific students, or by adding those newly identified by the teacher.

Feature 1   Popular Content Options

The following topics have been extremely popular with the majority of students with whom we work. Although the topic may be one that is regularly taught in schools, reference here is not to set curriculum. Students usually are interested in how a topic relates to the world as they know it, or they are intrigued with some exotic subtopic. They do not want to pursue a set curriculum.

- Animals—care, training, and breeding; incubating chickens; learning about prehistoric and exotic animals and about those that live in special climates
- Arts and crafts—expressive drawing and painting, constructing and building, exploring the work of others
- Career and vocation—adolescents, in particular, often want presentations about opportunities to observe jobs that may be worth pursuing
- Computers—basic uses, graphics, language and logic
- Consumer activity—comparing prices, learning about false advertising and advertising gimmicks, learning how to find a particular product
- Cooking to eat and sell—food planning, purchasing, and preparation keyed to specific interests of the students involved

- Creative writing—fiction and poetry
- Cultures of other peoples—comparing the way one lives with how others live (rituals, beliefs, music, food, dress, art, education)
- Design—graphics, drafting, architecture, construction
- Drama—writing plays; acting, staging performances; observing and criticizing TV, film, and stage productions; learning more about favorite people and current trends in theater, film, and TV
- Driving—most teens have a strong interest in preparing for driving
- Health and safety—first aid, CPR, personal care, sex education
- History—specific events, such as the invention of the automobile, space exploration, World War II; the background to a current event, such as the turmoil in the Mideast
- Math puzzles and measurement—number and graph puzzlers; how to handle money; how to keep records on material related to a hobby; how to measure in pursuing a particular interest, such as model building, wood construction, cooking, sewing, computers, video; how to compare sizes and weights; creative activities using math

Again we stress that students who have learning problems will have had negative experiences with a variety of instructional processes. Therefore, it is necessary to show them there are good alternatives to the procedures that led to their failures. For example, in pursuing projects, students with reading problems cannot be expected initially to rely heavily on reading. Visual- or audiovisual-oriented material, such as picture books and magazines, films and filmstrips, records, videotapes and audiotapes, field trips, teacher and other student presentations—all can be used. Products can include some written and some dictated material, along with artwork (drawings, graphs, model constructions, photographs, collages) and oral presentations.

James, for example, failed a seventh-grade social studies class and was scheduled to repeat it. The curriculum content for the course consists of specific historical, political, and cultural events and some basic geography. At the end of the course, students are expected at least to be able to identify the events and geographical features covered and to use source materials (atlas, almanac, encyclopedia, card catalogue) for finding additional historical and geographical material. More ambitiously, the intent is to equip students with the knowledge to analyze and discuss significant past events and relate them to life today.

The class James failed used the following procedures:

- Each week the teacher assigned a chapter to be read and questions to be answered and turned in; then, there was a multiple-choice, true-false test on the material at the end of the week.

- Motor trends—almost everything related to cars and motorcycles has proved to be of interest to one student or another
- Music—learning to play an instrument or sing, reading music, composing, learning more about favorite people and trends, reviewing and critiquing
- Newspaper and yearbook publication—all facets of planning, preparing, and distributing publications
- Photography—camera operations, picture composition, darkroom skills, creating interesting effects, displays
- Private enterprise/running a business—establishing and running a small business for profit at school, such as a small food service, or offering for sale products that are made on the premises
- Psychology—learning more about the views of others in the immediate environment, understanding why specific individuals and groups behave as they do
- Science—underwater creatures and plants, especially those that can be seen by scuba diving; electricity, especially as used in everyday life; chemical reactions; personal anatomy and biology; current events in science and medicine
- Space—other planets, space travel, constructing and flying rockets
- Sports—learning more about the present and past of favorite personalities, events, and equipment; learning to coach or referee
- Travel—learning what's interesting to visit locally and what's worth seeing in other countries, planning and taking trips, learning to use public transportation, learning about travel aids and skills such as map reading
- Video—writing, producing, acting, directing, camera work, editing
- Work experience—some students want to include work experience as part of their school program in order to earn needed money or to feel a sense of competence

A major concern in expanding options is that additional materials usually are needed. This concern can be minimized by asking those interested in the option to help gather the desired materials. (When topics are popular, several class members usually can be mobilized.)

- In class each day, the teacher spoke about the material covered in the text and had the students take turns sharing their answers to the assigned questions. Once a week they practiced looking up assigned material in atlases, almanacs, and so on.

Once a month they went to the library to learn how to use its resources.
- During the year, each student was to present four current events to the class on topics relevant to the material being discussed.

Feature 2   Offering Alternative Processes for the Same Content

A teacher using a topic exploration approach might proceed as follows:

- Rather than assign material, the teacher prepares ten varied topics covering the course content. He also identifies a long list of activities for pursuing such topics, each of which includes use of the desired basic research skills.
- At the beginning of the course, the teacher uses the first few classes to explain the ten varied topics and to help the students explore and choose from them.

He explains that each student can choose one or more topics and can choose from among a wide range of activities in learning about a topic. He also notes that each student can choose to work on a topic alone or in a small group. To help students get a good idea of the choices, he uses pictorial aids, an overhead projector, and filmstrips. The bulletin boards contain a variety of materials, such as pictures of other places and other times, historic newspaper clippings, and brief descriptions relevant to understanding the topics and activities being explored. There also are examples of what students have done in the past. A variety of pertinent reading material at different reading levels (magazines, pamphlets, fiction, and different texts) have been placed on the shelves with some opened for display. The teacher encourages the students to get up and look through the materials and to talk about the various alternatives. He answers questions as they arise. Finally, the teacher asks if any of the students have any relevant and feasible topics and activities they would like to have added. The one guideline he invokes is that groups have no more than four members.

- After aiding the students in choosing their topics and related activities, the teacher meets during class times with groups and individuals to assist and provide support and resources as they pursue their topics.
- Throughout the year, students share what they have learned about their topics with each other. (For example, one group studying how the effects of slavery are still felt in current race relations performs a play they have written. Another group studying the western movement in the United States forms a wagon train to experience the process and problems involved in undertaking such a trek [budgeting, buying supplies, dealing with changes in the weather, surviving harsh terrains]; they report their progress and adventures periodically to the rest of the class. One student, studying the development and forms of money used from ancient times to the present, reports on each historical stage. Another student, deciding to learn research skills by tracing her "roots," not only shares her family history with the class, but also is able to tell the others about a wide range of available historical resource material.)
- To link the material together and cover anything that might be missed, the teacher prepares a series of periodic presentations (lectures, films, video) and related supplementary reading and discussions.
- Each student turned in a written progress report summarizing what he or she had learned about the topic at the end of each month. Multiple-choice, true-false, and essay exams were given at midyear and at the end of the year. The reports and exams were used to evaluate how well the students had learned what the course was intended to teach. Students who had trouble reading or writing were given the exams orally. Grades were based on a combination of effort and performance.

- Three times during the school year, films were shown.
- Students who wanted extra credit could do a special term paper chosen from a list of topics the teacher had prepared or could choose three books from a prepared list and do reports on them.
- Grades were based primarily on test scores and extra-credit work. However, grades were lowered when current-event presentations or answers to the assigned reading questions were poor.
- When students like James were found to be having difficulty, the teacher recommended that parents spend more time helping with homework or find a tutor.

Because James failed the class, it seems reasonable to consider that the procedures were not a good match for him. In repeating the course, if he were confronted with the same processes, it would not be surprising for his behavior to reflect a lot of avoidance motivation. What would a set of alternative procedures look like? An example is provided in Feature 2 (see also Feature 3).

Besides specific processes, there is the matter of structure. Mara, David, James, and Matt need and want different amounts of support, direction, and external control (or limit setting) to help them learn.

They have each identified some things they can readily do on their own, but they know there are tasks and situations they will handle better with help. To have their changing needs matched, they must have the option of working alone or seeking support and guidance as often as is appropriate.

It is to be expected, of course, that those with the lowest motivation are likely to need the most support and guidance. At the same time, they are likely not to seek help readily. Moreover, those with avoidance motivation tend to react negatively to structure they perceive as used to control them.

In general, a greater range of options with regard to content, outcome, process, and structure are required for those with motivation problems. We will return to this topic after stressing the importance of options designed to enrich the experience of schooling and living.

Enrichment, Discovery, Inquiry, and Serendipity

As important as specific planning is, it is a mistake for school programs to overprescribe the specifics of what and how to learn. There must be time for sampling and exploring unscheduled topics and activi-

Feature 3   Different Processes, Different Outcomes

In recent years, there has been a major push for greater accountability in education. Everyone agrees that school programs should be more effective. But not everyone agrees with the extreme emphasis on highly specific objectives as advocated by some evaluators, especially when such evaluation ignores the processes used to reach desired objectives.

Some evaluators have even gone so far as to say they don't care what means are used as long as the ends are achieved. This extremist view ignores a simple fact: although two procedures may accomplish the same set of narrow objectives, they also may produce a variety of other, different outcomes.

Take the approach used with James and the one described in Feature 2, for example. A moti-

vational perspective suggests the two courses may lead to very different attitudes about the material learned. Lecture/text/test approaches tend to produce a distaste for social studies, history, geography, and similar subjects and for those who teach them. Teachers who teach in this way find little satisfaction in the process other than the sense of having pulled another group of students through.

In contrast, exploratory approaches lend themselves much better to personalization of learning and thus to the fostering and enhancement of intrinsic motivation along with the learning of specific content and skills. Students and teachers seem to find many personal satisfactions (valued learning and special friendships).

ties. This, of course, assumes there are interesting things available to investigate. The time for exploring can be viewed as an enrichment opportunity.

Some remedial programs are much too preoccupied with a student's problems and the tasks that must be pursued in remedying them. When this happens, enrichment experiences tend to be ignored and the learning environment takes on an air of pathology, drudgery, and boredom — all of which are contrary to enhancing motivation.

The model provided by programs for the gifted is a good example of the type of environment that may have a positive motivational impact on any learner. Such programs offer a rich set of learning centers that focus on topics such as those listed in Feature 1 and on many more. Enrichment activities are useful for enhancing motivation and reducing negative behavior and, of course, can lead to important learning.

Although enrichment activities may be seen as a frill for many students, they are important motivationally for students with learning problems. The richer the learning environment, the more likely students will discover a variety of new interests, information, and skills.

From a motivational perspective, enrichment options are not designed to teach specific information and skills. There are, of course, specific, and often predictable, outcomes that come from contact with any topic. However, almost by definition, an enrichment option produces many incidental and unpredictable (serendipitous) outcomes.

Furthermore, enrichment activities are not designed to operate as if everything a student learns is taught by the teacher. The hands-on nature of enrichment centers encourages independent exploration, experimentation, and learning. As questions arise, students can choose to use whatever information or help is available.

In the end, what students learn depends a great deal on their interests and effort. Some may decide to pursue a topic in great depth and to acquire a degree of mastery over it; others may simply dabble and gain a surface awareness, which they may or may not follow up.

As a general strategy, enrichment opportunities can be established by offering an attractive set of discovery and inquiry centers and helping the students explore the materials and ideas. Let's look at Mara's experience with an enriched program.

Mara's teacher explains that there are a variety of centers in the room that will change as the school year progresses. At the moment, there are centers dealing with electricity, tropical fish, computers, chemical reactions, African cultures, creative math, and many more. In order to offer a variety of centers each week, some are offered twice and some three times a week.

Mara is given a chance to sample the centers. She then is given the opportunity to choose one or two topics that really interest her. It is made clear that these are electives and that she can drop out at any time.

Mara is attracted to the tropical fish. She wants to know if it is hard to take care of them. She thinks she'd like to have some at home. Where do you buy them? Are they expensive? How long do they live?

The teacher answers a few of her questions and then points out that there is a group meeting on Monday, Wednesday, and Friday. They are learning all about where the fish come from, which can live with each other, how to breed them, and whatever else the group wants to explore about aquariums and fish.

Mara is intrigued but a little suspicious. She wants to know if the activity includes reading or other assignments and tests. The answer is an unequivocal no. She can come and learn whatever she wants, in the way that she wants, and no one will ask her to prove anything. It is her questions that are important — not the teacher's.

It is so inviting that Mara decides to give it a try. She finds that it's as good as it looks and sounds. As she attends regularly, it becomes evident to all who observe her that she is a bright, interested, and attentive learner whenever she is motivated by the topic. She remembers what she has learned and works well with others.

Not long after joining the group, her teacher noticed Mara had gone to the library and checked out picture books on tropical fish. A few days later, Mara approached her to ask for a little help in reading some of the captions.

Options for Those with Motivation Problems

The first step in working with such students involves exploration to find what the individual's interests are:

Sports? Rock music? Movies? Computer games? Such personal interests are used as a starting point. A student's interests are explored until he or she identifies a related topic—no matter how unusual—that he or she would like to learn more about (see Feature 4).

After identifying a topic, learning-activity options are reviewed to find those that are a good match with the student's needs, interests, and styles. For example, talkative students may prefer to work in small discussion groups. Other students will want a work area that is private and quiet. Students with high activity levels may choose to work with manipulable materials. Most will prefer to work on time-limited activities.

In accommodating a wider range of behaviors,

Feature 4   Options for Students with Motivation Problems

Harry comes to school with no intention of working on what his teachers have planned. He will spend as much time as he can get away with talking with his friends and looking for some excitement to make the time pass faster. He is frequently in the middle of whatever trouble is occurring. Everyone is waiting for him to do something bad enough that he can be removed from his present class.

There is an alternative to letting this tragedy run its course. Time can be spent helping Harry identify one area of personal interest that he would like to learn more about (pop culture, rock music, current teenage fashions). Then a personalized program can be developed based on a topic he would like to explore and ways he would like to explore it.

Approached in this way, most students like Harry will identify a topic and activities that interest them. However, one topic and a few activities won't fill up much time—perhaps an hour, maybe less. What then?

Well, Harry could be asked to pursue a regular program for the rest of the school day; but the odds are that he would simply resume his previous pattern of negative behavior. In the long run, this would probably defeat what the alternative program is trying to accomplish.

Our solution to the problem is as simple as it is controversial. We have students such as Harry attend school only for that period of time during which they have planned a program they intend to pursue. Our reasoning is twofold: (1) we know that students tend to work best when they are working on what they have identified as desirable, and (2) for students like Harry, it seems

likely the rest of the time is wasted, including getting into trouble. Obviously if they are not at school a full day, they are likely to get into less trouble. More important, the less we are in the position of coercing them, the less we are likely to cause the variety of reactive misbehaviors that characterize such students. Once we no longer have to do battle with them, many youngsters evolve an increasing range of academic interests, including renewed interest in becoming competent in the areas of reading and writing. The energy they had been devoting to fighting teachers and school may now be redirected to exploring what they are interested in doing for themselves. As Harry's range of interests increases, he will want a longer school day and is likely to make better use of it.

We recognize the many practical, economic, and legal problems involved in cutting back on the length of a student's school day. However, we think these problems must be contrasted with the costs to society and individuals of ignoring the fact that for certain students a lengthy school day interferes with correcting their problems. Indeed, in some cases, it only makes the problems worse.

For older students, of course, a shortened day paired with a parttime job or apprenticeship may be a most productive experience. Among the results of work experiences can be an increased feeling of self-worth and competence and enhanced intrinsic motivation toward overcoming learning problems. A job also can provide a student with a source of income, which may be needed, and can even help to establish career directions.

classroom rules and standards are redefined to accept behaviors such as nondisruptive talking and movement about the classroom. For some individuals, certain "bad manners" (some rudeness, some swear words) and eccentric mannerisms (strange clothing and grooming) may have to be tolerated initially.

The most basic process option, of course, is that of not participating at times or at all. There are times when David simply doesn't feel like working. He wants the option of drawing, playing a game, or resting for about an hour. There are days when Mara doesn't want to go to school. And there came a day when James concluded he was ready to drop out of school. Which, if any, of these should be offered as options? For whom?

At this point, you may think that such options are too inappropriate even to consider. However, as you reflect on what you have read in Part 3 and as you move on to read more about learner decision making, it will be clear that the type of options discussed are fundamental to addressing motivational differences.

Decisions about participation are the primary foundation upon which all other decisions rest (Adelman et al., 1984; Taylor et al., 1985). If the individual initially does not want to participate or subsequently comes to that point of view, all other decisions become highly problematic.

For students diagnosed as having learning disabilities, the decision process related to participation begins with the discussions about placement. Whether a student with problems is placed in a special program or maintained in regular classes, the immediate motivational concern always is whether the individual has decided that the program is right for him or her. Of course, even if the initial answer is yes, the student's perceptions of the situation may change. Thus decisions about placement must be continually reevaluated.

The next most basic decisions are those related to specific program options. The objective is to help the student pinpoint alternatives that match personal interests and capabilities. Again, initial decisions have to be modified in keeping with changes in the student's perceptions of what is a good match.

As the following discussion illustrates, the best decision-making processes include opportunities to explore and sample options physically. Thus all initial decisions can be seen simply as extended opportunities to investigate options.

In overcoming severe motivational problems, it appears important not to insist that a student continue to work in areas she or he wants to avoid. This strategy is intended to reduce the type of psychological and behavioral reactions that occur when individuals think they are being forced to do something they don't want to do. In particular, we don't want to increase avoidance, either in the form of withdrawal (including passive performance) or of active resistance (disruptive behavior).

Thus if a student initially indicates not wanting instruction in a specific area, it seems wise to hold off instruction temporarily—even in basic skills, such as reading or math. The time is better spent on activities that may eventually lead to renewed interests in the avoided area.

Withholding instruction as a step in renewing positive interest in an area seems to go against common sense. We recognize that this is a controversial and, for some, an alarming strategy. It is not one to be adopted lightly or naively—remember, it is a strategy to deal with motivation problems. From a motivational perspective, it is clearly rational to pursue areas of positive interest. To focus solely on positive interests may be the best way eventually to overcome motivation and skill problems related to reading and other basics.

Let's look at Mara in this context. Mara doesn't want reading instruction, and the teacher agrees to set it aside for now. If reading were completely ignored, the best outcome the teacher could expect is that Mara's avoidance motivation would not significantly increase. For many persons, this might be an acceptable outcome for art or music or other areas not seen as basic skills; it would not be acceptable to most people when it comes to the three Rs. Fortunately, what makes literacy skills basic is that most facets of daily living require them. Because they are designated as basic, they are a major focus of almost everyone in the society.

It is likely that most of what Mara chooses to learn at school, and much of her other experience, will lead frequently to situations that cause her to realize that she has a personal need for such skills. These daily encounters inevitably bring her into contact with people who convey to her their assumption that she already has or is in the process of acquiring such skills. These experiences affect her feelings and attitudes about acquiring basics.

As Mara's intrinsic awareness of the value of basic skills increases, she can be helped to learn any specific skills she identifies as needed in coping with daily life. Eventually Mara may arrive at a level of motivational readiness at which she will accept the teacher's offer to pick up with formal reading instruction. Equally important, if her intrinsic motivation has increased enough, the time she spends reading may be considerably greater than the time spent in formal instruction.

Appropriate decision processes can increase personal valuing and expectations of success, thereby enhancing motivation for learning and overcoming problems. By "appropriate" processes, we mean those that enable a student to self-select from desirable and feasible options. Besides improving motivation, such processes provide opportunities for strengthening a student's ability to make sound choices.

Students may differ greatly in their motivation and ability to make decisions (see Feature 5). That is why we believe learning to make decisions should be a basic focus of instruction and why it is so important to be ready to help youngsters with decision making.

Steps in Helping Students Make Decisions

In helping with student decision making, it is useful to view the process as a series of steps.

First, a student must understand the value of making her or his own decisions. Minimally, this means the student's knowing that the process provides opportunities for taking greater control over one's life and overcoming one's problems.

> "We want to work with you in ways you think are good, so we put together as many exciting learning ideas as we could. But you are the best judge of what you like. You might want to sample some of these options and see if any appeal to you, and you may want to suggest some other topics or activities. We only want to work with those you think are worth doing. We want you to have more control over your activities and program schedule than in the past. Would you like to take some time and see what's available?"

Second, the process must include ways for students actively to sample and select from available options and to propose others whenever feasible.

> "You can spend some time looking over the various options; feel free to watch other students who have chosen them. I'll be glad to answer your questions. We can also talk about other things you would like to learn about that may not be here yet. Let's try to find a topic that personally interests you. The important thing is that you get a chance to decide which things you want to spend your school time learning about."

Third, working out program details should be done as soon as choices are made. This is necessary so that the student is clear about the implications of following through on decisions. With such information, a student can either back off from a choice because it involves too much work or publicly commit to follow through.

> "Let's talk about your decision to learn to use a computer. That group meets each day for 10 weeks, an hour a day. Before you get to do graphics, you have to spend the first week learning basic computer operation. There is some reading material available; if you need help, some advanced students will be ready to explain the basics. If that sounds OK to you, write it on your posted schedule, and you can begin tomorrow."

Fourth, from the moment the student begins an activity, it is important to monitor motivation. If interest drops, the activity should be altered to better match the student; if it can't be modified, the student should have the option of changing activities. Such monitoring is discussed in Chapter 10.

Teacher frustration is a frequent problem in helping students to make decisions and to improve their ability to do so. Many of a student's initial decisions don't hold up well. For a variety of reasons, a student may quickly lose interest in a topic or activity. This may happen, for example, if a youngster has a disability or does not work hard enough. However, early in the efforts to help youngsters make effective decisions, such "blaming" conclusions about why a particular choice didn't work can be premature and harmful. In general, when early decisions must be altered, it is important both to avoid blaming the student and to help students avoid blaming themselves.

On the other hand, if the student manifests the common tendency to externalize blame (the activity is described as too hard or too boring), it may be useful at first simply to accept the reasons at face

Feature 5   Are Students with Learning Problems Competent to Make Good Decisions?

Making a sound decision involves having the necessary information about alternatives and about positive and negative outcomes. It also involves having the competence to evaluate available information. Not surprisingly, when someone is perceived as not competent to decide, they often are not given the information or opportunity to prove the perception is incorrect.

Who is competent to decide? This is one of the more difficult and controversial questions confronting professionals, parents, and society in general. Is it a matter of age? Education? Intelligence? If someone has a learning problem, are they less competent to make certain decisions than individuals without learning problems?

As yet, there are no satisfactory answers. There is, however, a rapidly growing body of research on the competence of youngsters with and without learning problems to participate in decision making (for example, Baumrind, 1978; Melton, 1983; Weithorn, 1983).

Findings to date suggest that many youngsters and their parents believe that children as young as 10 should participate in making decisions about everyday matters such as what clothes to buy and wear, what food to eat, what time to go to bed, and what friends to make. Parents and youngsters also generally agree that minors (13 and older) should participate in decisions regarding school programs and placements and physical and mental health treatment. Studies comparing youngsters' and adults' decisions as to treatment and research participation indicate that the decisions of children as young as 9 are similar to those made by adults; and by the time they're 14, minors seem able to think as competently as adults in weighing certain decision risks and benefits.

In contrast to this research, studies of practitioners' views of minors' competence tend to be less optimistic about youngsters' competence to decide. Unfortunately, research on practitioners' views of minors' competence to participate in decision making is sparse. In a survey of mental health professionals, we found that slightly less than half of those who were willing to respond indicated they asked clients under 18 to participate in the treatment decision. However, those who did ask, asked children as young as 12. Moreover, this group of professionals judge that 72 percent of those they asked did turn out to have the necessary level of competence for making the decisions. Of particular relevance to the ideas presented here, the reason most cited for why they asked children to participate in such decision making was to enhance the motivation for treatment (Taylor et al., 1985).

Despite the inadequacy of the available literature, findings to date support the importance of avoiding presumptions about students' lack of competence. Furthermore, classroom programs ought to be designed to facilitate and not delay development of increased levels of decision-making competence. Finally, we suggest that motivation often can be enhanced by encouraging students' participation in making decisions.

None of what has been said here is meant to imply that students will always make good decisions; nor will they always stick to a decision, nor should they. All we are proposing is that students (with and without learning problems) should be offered a wide range of learning options and should be helped to sample the options so that they have reasonable information upon which to base decisions. After they have experienced an activity for a while, they may decide that they made a mistake, and so all such decisions should be renegotiable. As we understand motivation and learning, such options and renegotiations are major factors in determining whether students want to follow through on decisions and whether they become good at making decisions.

value. By working on changes that reflect the individual's "alibis," in time it will become evident whether the student is merely making excuses.

Again, the point is that the ability to make good decisions is learned (see Baron & Brown, 1991). Making decisions and evaluating their outcomes can be a good process for developing this basic skill. However, if the process is contaminated by accusations and blame, motivation for decision making can be undermined. As with all areas of learning, interactions over time will clarify whether students who continue to make poor decisions do so because of developmental or motivational problems.

Dialogues with Students

As suggested already, decision processes that lead to positive student perceptions involve ongoing dialogue between student and teacher. One result is a series of mutual agreements about what is to be done and how to proceed.

The mechanism for carrying on the dialogue is called a conference, and the agreement is referred to as a contract. However, terms like *conference* and *contract* do not convey the full sense of what is involved, and at times have been interpreted in ways contrary to the meaning used here.

From a motivational perspective:

- Decisions must not be made for the student.
- Decisions must be modifiable whenever necessary.
- Dialogues should be designed to give, share, and clarify information seen as potentially useful to a student who is making a decision.
- Dialogues should involve not only conversational exchanges but also actual exploration and sampling of options.

The importance of the dialogue as a two-way process cannot be overemphasized. A conference should be a time for persons to say what they need, want, and hope for from each other. When problems exist, time should be devoted to problem solving. One conference often is insufficient for arriving at a major decision. Therefore, the dialogue is an ongoing formal and informal process.

Summing Up

Although the stress here has been on student decisions, good agreements are not one-sided. In general, the processes are meant to establish, maintain, and enhance a positive commitment on the part of both student and teacher toward working in a collaborative relationship. Such a relationship is fundamental to the correction of learning problems.

III.5   Fernald's Techniques in Their Motivational Context

Near the beginning of her classic volume *Remedial Techniques in Basic School Subjects* (1943), Grace Fernald states:

> Too often in present-day methods of teaching writing and spelling, voluntary activity is so limited from the start that even those children who have no special difficulty in learning do not like to write. The child may be required to sit in a certain position, conform to specific ways of making the details of his letters, and spell his words correctly. When finally he does all these things, he may be allowed to express an idea in written form. Usually, some adult will tell him what idea he should be eager to express. The result is that the little child who was bursting with ideas he wanted to put in writing has lost them in the formalities of learning to write and spell and at the same time has been negatively conditioned toward these activities. (p. 13)

As is clear from this statement, Fernald was concerned with far more than the "tracing" method, or VAKT techniques, that textbook writers tend to stress in reviewing her work. She was concerned with the learner's thoughts and feelings related to school activities and learning. VAKT techniques were to be used in a motivational context.

> Throughout the remedial work, projects suitable to the child's age and connected with his interests are made the basis of his writing and later of his reading.... The topics he chooses to write about depend upon his interests and aptitudes. (p. 94)

We do not mean to suggest that Fernald was unconcerned with other factors in the learning process. She obviously believed that the learning problems of some individuals were caused by defects in visual or auditory modalities and that "the hand-kinesthetic method ... serves to build up an adequate apperceptive background, which makes it possible for the child to use effectively such sensory cues as he has" (p. 32). However, she always stressed that her techniques for teaching included

much more than the "hand-kinesthetic method." In particular, she was interested in procedures by which each individual "not only learns rapidly but develops a positive emotional conditioning" (p. 13).

In keeping with the innovative spirit of Fernald's pioneering work, the staff at the Fernald Laboratory and Clinic at UCLA continued to explore new directions in dealing with learning problems until 1986. They were especially interested in systematic ways to address motivational considerations. One aspect of this work involved delineating the motivational context for what has become known as the Fernald Method (or Fernald Techniques).

Motivational Considerations

In efforts to develop a motivational context for instruction, a major focus is on three overlapping phases of motivation in learning and performance: (1) motivational readiness for instruction, (2) maintaining motivation during instruction, and (3) continued independent interest in the area for which instruction is provided. That is, during phase 1, the focus is on creating and enhancing motivational readiness for instruction. Phase 2 involves efforts to maintain and increase motivation during instruction. Phase 3 is concerned with ensuring that instruction doesn't undermine intrinsic motivation and that long-term intrinsic motivation is enhanced.

Throughout all three phases, the emphasis is on (a) clarifying intrinsic reasons for pursuing learning activities and overcoming problems, (b) providing meaningful opportunities to make personal and active choices from a variety of options, and (c) involving learners in evaluating how well their intrinsic objectives are met.

Phase 1: Motivational Readiness for Instruction

There is little need to point out that all individuals learn. It is also evident that an individual may not have the ability or interest to learn certain things at a given time. What is not so obvious to many people is the fact that an individual may have the ability and may want to learn something but may not be psychologically ready to accept instruction.

Students who misbehave at school clearly may be disturbed or hyperactive or have a variety of other pathological conditions. However, some misbehavior seems primarily to be a reaction to *demands* that students learn things they aren't interested in learning and to *required* participation in instructional activities when students don't want to be taught.

The first step in working with students who react against teacher and parental pressure is to find ways to establish readiness for instruction by reducing avoidance and increasing approach tendencies. This involves

- eliminating or at least minimizing transactions that lead to avoidance, such as activities students tend to see as coercive and aversive
- establishing procedures that increase student options and choices in terms of learning content, outcomes, and processes

The emphasis is on evolving a personalized learning environment. The program should be one in which instruction is not forced on students, many valued learning opportunities are presented, and help is offered and available at all times to aid students as they pursue desired learning outcomes.

The first aspect of establishing readiness for instruction, then, is to create a stimulating learning environment in which instruction is provided only *after* a student indicates that it is wanted. When instruction is sought, the emphasis shifts to the creation of a positive attitude (or "set") toward teaching processes and immediate outcomes. The intent is to convey to each student how well the program matches current interests and capabilities.

In the Fernald Method, the focus on motivational readiness for instruction begins with the teacher's clarifying that there is no intention of forcing the student to learn anything. This is particularly important for students who are reacting against teachers and instruction. In such cases, the initial focus is on exploring many topics and possible areas for learning until the student identifies an area of interest. Then, efforts are made to introduce a variety of independent learning activities in the area. The teacher remains interested and available to help at any time

the learner requests assistance but does not intervene, as long as the student is not disruptive.

The objective is to allow the individual to rediscover that there are intrinsic reasons for working with a teacher. In addition, as students have the opportunity to explore a wide range of learning interests and identify areas for self-improvement, they generally decide they need to improve basic reading, writing, and arithmetic skills. (What makes such skills basic is the fact that one finds the skills are necessary for pursuing so many interests and future goals.)

When students no longer resist instruction (when those with learning problems are ready to accept instruction), there remains the matter of maximizing motivational readiness. They need to be introduced to each instructional procedure in ways that maximize their expectations of success and their valuing of the opportunity to be taught. Fernald introduced students to the "hand-kinesthetic" method as follows:

> We start by telling the child that we have a new way of learning words, which we want him to try. We explain . . . that many bright people have had the same difficulty he has had in learning to read and have learned easily by this new method, which is really just as good as any other way. We let him select any word he wants to learn, regardless of length, and teach it to him by the method. (p. 33)

Thus, in introducing the method, she stressed the novelty of the approach, presented it as special in a positive sense, and had the student sample the process under fairly optimal circumstances, with an emphasis on student choice. She then moved on quickly to embed the method in what she called "story writing" and "special projects"; today these strategies are widely known as language experience and discovery approaches.

Fernald's efforts to provide a stimulating context for instruction reflected her concern with motivation. In this connection, over the years, we have continued to find that the best strategy usually is to introduce the tracing method and other remedial techniques within the context of a student's current interests. That is, we offer it as an aid to students as they pursue some chosen activity, such as personally identified writing activity (a story, poem, or newspaper article) or some discovery-oriented project of personal interest. Thus, rather than being limited by a specific technique's power to mobilize a student's interest, we are able to capitalize on a wide range of substantive and popular activities and topics in efforts to facilitate motivational readiness.

Phase 2: Maintaining Motivation During Instruction

Maintaining appropriate motivation depends on a student's continuing perception of instruction as a positive means to valued ends. The optimal situation for maintaining such motivation seems to be one in which

• a broad range of learner-valued content, outcome, and procedural options are available
• the learner is able to experience a high degree of self-determination in specifying learning content, outcomes, and processes
• support and guidance are varied in keeping with the learner's perceived needs
• the learner experiences a sense of satisfaction and competence from what is learned

This means, for example, that the learner (1) has chosen a personally meaningful context for learning skills, (2) has identified which skills (dealing with words, punctuation, facts, ideas) and how many will become the focus of instruction, and (3) has helped develop ways to structure and evaluate learning so that the activity results in feelings of personal satisfaction and increased competence.

With the Fernald Method, learners are provided opportunities to explore a wide range of options in story writing and special projects. Given a state of motivational readiness, they choose from what is offered or create their own context for learning. In either case, they draw on their own experiences and learn within a context that is personally meaningful and interesting. In addition, each student is encouraged to state what he or she wants to learn and practice each day.

For example, students are to specify whether they want to spend time on improving vocabulary (reading or spelling), the mechanics of English, handwriting, or whatever. They are encouraged to choose the specific words or skills to be learned and to specify the amount they want to learn at any given time.

Special care is taken not to underestimate the learner's range of interests and capability. As Fer-

nald stated in discussing the learning of reading and writing vocabulary:

> . . . remedial work is started by discovering some technique whereby the individual can learn to write any word he wishes to use. . . . The child is much more interested in writing and reading fairly difficult material that is on the level of his understanding than simpler material which is below his mental age level. In fact, the child who has never been able to read or write anything takes delight in learning difficult words. Our records show that these longer, more difficult words are actually easier to recognize on later presentations after the child has written them, than easier, shorter ones. (p. 44)

The steps devised by Fernald have evolved over the years (described in a subsequent section) and provide a framework for working out novel and personalized learning and practice activities. They demonstrate ways to provide structure (support and guidance) and feedback that maximize the type of learning and feelings of satisfaction and increased competence that are prerequisites to retaining what is learned.

The steps used for instructional purposes are designed to match the learner's motivation and capability. The steps for ongoing practice, review, and reteaching are designed to provide motivated practice. And motivated practice is necessary for maintaining what is learned and seems to be a necessary, if insufficient, prerequisite for generalization of learning.

Phase 3: Motivation After Instruction

If motivational concerns are properly attended to during instruction, the learner will continue to be interested in the area studied and have a positive attitude about the skills learned. Thus, the previous considerations are major determinants of later directions for learning (including maintenance and generalization). Given positive antecedent conditions, three ongoing conditions are necessary for continued and expanded use of what has been learned. These are

• *opportunities* to use what has been learned
• continuing *desire* to use and expand on what has been learned
• continuing *self-determination* and *supportive*

structure, when necessary, related to learning and performance

Opportunities may take several forms. For example, there can be free time at school to read, write, pursue projects, and so forth. There can also be structured enrichment activities at school and in the home and neighborhood designed to provide creative and exciting learning opportunities that are not tied to developmental and remedial objectives.

The desire to expand on what has been learned is a likely product of the learner's continued perception of personal choice and self-efficacy and the learner's feelings of self-determination and competence. Such perceptions and feelings are most likely to occur when an individual experiences control over fundamental decisions in the area of learning and has support and guidance as needed to prevent too much failure.

We have not stressed the use of extrinsic rewards and punishment as a way to establish, maintain, or enhance motivation. We know that the on-task behavior of many individuals can be increased to some degree through the systematic use of external reinforcement. However, we are also aware that such procedures can be counterproductive in establishing and maintaining the type of long-term behavior that is needed by most individuals if they are to meaningfully overcome their problems. Although Fernald did not specifically discuss this topic, the methods she developed avoid overreliance on extrinsics. It is likely she understood that overemphasis on extrinsics often is incompatible with maintaining and enhancing people's internal push to overcome their problems, and that it can interfere with their understanding that learning is something one does for oneself—not for others. Analyses of the procedures she developed show how much she tried to capitalize on students' personal interests, curiosity, and desire to feel competent and self-determining.

In the teacher's use of the Fernald Method, the following motivational considerations apply:

1. Motivational readiness for instruction, which involves
   • avoiding coercion
   • establishing valued options and choices
   • establishing positive "set" with regard to expectations of success and valued opportunities (processes and outcomes)

2. Maintaining motivation during instruction, which involves
   • the learner's valuing of the available content, outcome, and procedural options
   • the learner's perceptions of self-determination
   • support and guidance in keeping with the learner's perceived needs
   • feedback that stresses feelings of personal satisfaction, self-determination, and competence
3. Motivation after instruction, which results from
   • all of 1 and 2
   • continued opportunities for learning and performance
   • the learner's continued desire to use and expand on learning
   • continued self-determination and supportive structure as needed

Summary of Fernald Techniques: Stages and Steps

Over the years, we have amplified Fernald's ideas to capitalize on contemporary thinking about how to develop, maintain, and enhance student motivation. Thus the description that follows represents an amalgamation of Fernald's pioneering activity with recent thinking about motivation.

Fernald's original work and our subsequent efforts deal with a full range of school subjects and basic skills. To illustrate, however, here we emphasize only one facet of instruction designed to improve reading.

In working with severe learning problems, Fernald found it useful to begin with methods that involved a multisensory (tracing) approach for learning words. From this beginning stage, she moved systematically to procedures used widely in teaching anyone to improve vocabulary. In all, she delineated four overlapping stages through which she took individuals with reading problems.

All the stages are similar, in that each new word to be learned is identified by the student, usually in the context of intrinsically motivated activity. At any of the stages, words the student does not know are discovered as the individual reads and writes while pursuing a self-determined activity. The student is told to let the teacher know when encountering an unknown word while reading or when a word is needed for a written product. No effort is made to teach the words at this point; they are simply read to or written for the student. This is done to avoid disrupting the student's flow, enjoyment, and satisfaction in reading and writing. By agreement, a temporary record is made of those words the student wants to consider learning. (Obviously, the same type of strategy can be used to assess and plan instruction for a wide range of other skill deficiencies, like deficiencies in punctuation, capitalization, or grammar.)

The stages also are similar because they all call for simultaneously looking at (visualizing) and saying (vocalizing) the word that is being learned and because they prescribe immediate and subsequent practice and review.

The stages differ as follows:

Stage 1: Visual-auditory-kinesthetic-tactile — tracing words the teacher has written on tracing slips

Stage 2: Visual-auditory — no tracing but continued use of tracing slips with teacher-written words, then making the transition to teacher-written words on flashcards

Stage 3: Visual-auditory — use of words in print rather than teacher-written words

Stage 4: Independent learning — use of reference material, generalization, inference and other analytic and synthesizing skills to learn new words

Although Fernald specified four stages, these stages blend one into the other. Essentially, they form a continuum ranging from the extreme remedial strategy of stage 1 to the very general educational approaches used in stage 4.

The steps in each stage are described in the following sections.

Stage I

This stage is used with students who are motivationally ready for instruction and who are manifesting severe problems learning to read. There are seven basic steps:

1. At an appropriate time, the teacher sits down beside the student to facilitate the learning of new words. *Note:* The point of sitting next to the student is to convey committed interest and readiness to spend time helping, as well as to communicate a desire to minimize psychological distance and authoritarian transactions.)

2. The student looks over the list of words she or he has indicated an interest in mastering and chooses those to be worked on that day, including the order in which the words are to be learned.

3. With the student watching and listening, the teacher simultaneously says the first word aloud and writes it on a 4" × 11" tracing slip using a black crayon (see Feature 1). *Notes:* Black crayon is used because it produces a clear, dark, and textured stimulus. Newsprint is used for tracing slips because it is relatively inexpensive. In saying the word, the teacher reads it slowly and distinctly but without distorting it. In writing the word, the teacher uses large, neat, and well-formed letters to produce an oversized model that the student can easily trace and emulate. Unless the student can only print, cursive writing (script) is used because words written in script present a flowing, unbroken unit. For record keeping, the tracing slip can be dated in one corner.

4. The student takes the slip and, looking carefully at the word, says it aloud several times.

5. Next, using the writing hand, the student traces the word with the index or index and middle finger — maintaining good finger contact and flowing motion and saying the word clearly as it is traced. As a guideline, tracing and saying the word three times seems effective. How many times the word is traced usually is best left for the student to decide. *Notes:* For Fernald, the point of this step was to ensure that the student experienced simultaneous visual, auditory, kinesthetic, and tactile cues related to the word as a whole unit. However even if the student doesn't need multisensory cues and a whole word approach, this step has a number of nice motivational features. For example, it represents a novel strategy, and one that the student has not already failed at; it tends to capture a student's attention; it involves the student in active learning and practice.

6. After tracing and saying the word, the student turns the slip over and writes the word on the back, again saying it as it is written. If it is written incorrectly, what has been written is immediately blacked out (with the crayon) to limit confusion. Then, the student repeats steps 5 and 6 until the word is written correctly on the back of the slip or until the student decides not to bother with the word for now (see Feature 1).

7. Newly learned words are practiced on subse-

quent days and reviewed periodically. (See the discussion of practice and review at the end of this summary of stages and steps.)

Stage 2

Following the student's lead, the teacher can gradually phase out tracing from the learning process. Tracing slips are still used at the outset of stage 2. However, 3" × 5" flashcards are introduced as soon as the student indicates interest and the ability to use them effectively. Thus, for the student who is motivationally and developmentally ready to streamline the process, the steps will be as follows:

1–4. These steps remain the same. When the student moves to flashcards, the main change is that the words are written by the teacher with a pen or pencil that leaves a dark imprint.

5. The student learns the word by looking at it (in a concentrated way) and saying it several times.

6–7. These steps remain the same. Of course, when students have trouble with a particular

Feature 1   Tracing Slip

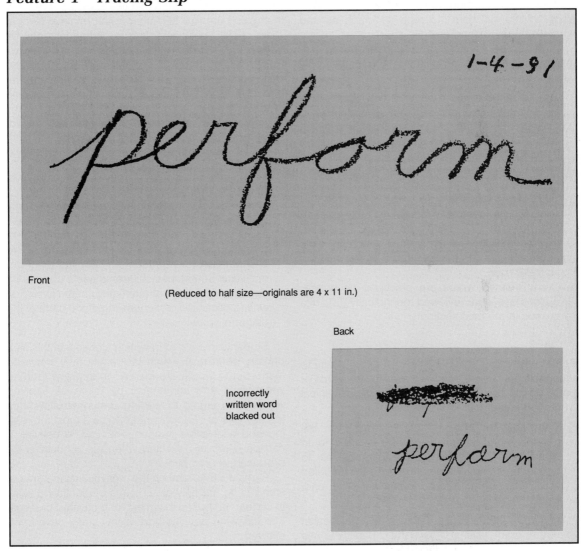

Front

(Reduced to half size—originals are 4 x 11 in.)

Back

Incorrectly
written word
blacked out

word, they may want to try the tracing procedures when they repeat step 5.

Stage 3

Again following the student's lead, the teacher can make a transition from stage 2 to 3. However, to do so, the student must not only be able to learn well using stage 2 but also must have learned how to look up words in a dictionary or other resource.

In stage 3, the individual sees a word in print that he or she wants to learn or looks it up in a dictionary or comparable reference resource. Fernald stressed that, by this stage, the students she worked with wanted to do a lot more reading, and she provided opportunities for them "to read as much as and whatever" they wished (p. 51).

At this stage, the student uses the following self-initiated steps, asking for help from the teacher only when necessary:

1. The student learns the word by looking at it (in a concentrated way) and saying it several times.
2. The word is written by the student on a 3 × 5 card using immediate recall rather than copying it. That is, the *original* source is put away and, as in other stages, the word is said as it is written from memory.
3. The word is checked against the original printed source. If it is incorrectly reproduced, it is crossed out and steps 1 and 2 are repeated (or the tracing method is used) until the word is written correctly or until the student decides not to bother with the word for now.
4. Newly learned words are practiced on subsequent days and reviewed periodically (as discussed in the next section).

Stage 4

Fernald described stage 4 as involving the ability to recognize new words from their similarity to words or parts of words already learned. From her clinical work, she found that:

> Soon after the child is able to learn from the printed word, he begins to generalize and to make new words from their resemblance to words he already knows. If the case is handled skillfully enough, the child is now eager to read. (p. 51)

At stage 4, students usually are reading at least at the fourth-grade level and have the capability to use analytic and synthesizing skills in reading new words. Equally important at this stage is a positive attitude toward reading. Subsequent improvements in vocabulary, comprehension, speed, and fluency will occur only if the student likes reading enough to do a great deal more than is involved in daily school instruction.

Subsequent Practice and Review Steps

The importance of spaced (distributed) practice and review is widely acknowledged. Often ignored by teachers and parents, however, is the importance of finding ways to increase the motivational aspects of practice activities. When practice activities in reading instruction are dull and boring, the minimal level of reading skill proficiency that is demanded may be acquired, but a dislike for reading may also be acquired. Thus a student may learn several hundred new words but may never become a good reader because he or she never voluntarily spends time reading.

Fernald devised several strategies for spaced, short-term, motivated practice and review. The essence of these strategies is seen in the "storywriting" approach. Fernald noted:

> Some children begin their writing with stories about their pets, their families, and other personal matters. Several of our cases with marked artistic ability started with sketches and paintings of things about which they later wrote. Most of the children liked to represent any subject diagrammatically. Sometimes children made elaborate diagrams of things that interested them. Their first writing consisted of the labeling of the parts of the diagram. (p. 94)

Students interested in writing stories use this as a primary context in which to identify new words to learn. Some words are learned to improve reading vocabulary, and some may be taken as spelling words. With regard to reading, a student often finds the story he or she has written to be a most interesting and accessible subsequent reading activity. It can be especially exciting when the product is reproduced in print (typed).

Fernald capitalized on the motivational features of storywriting not only as a means of identifying skills to be learned but as a context for motivated practice. The following practice and review steps have been evolved:

1. With the story written and new words chosen and learned (using one of the four stages described before), the student files the words in an alphabetical file for future reference. (Depending on the stage, either a 3 × 5 index file or one designed to handle tracing slips is used.)

2. The story is readied for typing. This preparation involves some basic editing and underlining of the words the student has chosen to learn (see Feature 2). *Note:* Since the student is encouraged to write freely and only a few new skills are focused on at any time, stories inevitably reflect skill deficiencies. Therefore the teacher edits the story to the extent of correcting basic punctuation, capitalization, and grammar errors. This is done so that what is subsequently read by the student is a reasonably good model but still is the student's own words. (The student should

Feature 2   Original Story

As written

(Writing reduced in size by 50%)

As edited by teacher

be consulted about how much editing is done and whether the teacher is to do it alone or with the student's involvement.)

3. The story is typed, usually within 24 hours, and returned to the student as a reading activity (see Feature 3). *Note:* Two typed copies are made—one for the student to take home if desired, the other for practice and review. In no special order, the underlined words are typed in a vertical list down the left side of the page under the typed story.

4. The practice and review copies of the story and the original handwritten product are placed in a folder facing each other so that the student can refer to both.

5. The student reads the typed story to the teacher. Any word that is not recognized is read to the student—unless the student has shown both motivational and developmental readiness to figure out words.

6. After reading the story, the student reads the list of chosen words typed beneath the story. A mark is placed after each word to indicate whether it was read correctly or incorrectly—for example, a + for correct, a 0 for incorrect. (Preferably the recordkeeping is done by the student.)

7. The next day, if the student has written another story, the process is repeated with the new story and word list. Whether there is a new story or not, the student again reads the list from the previous story. A second mark (+ or 0) is recorded.

8. The process of reading the separate words listed is repeated until a predetermined criterion is met. The criterion established over the years at the Fernald Laboratory and Clinic is three consecutive correct responses.

9. If a word is read incorrectly, the student is encouraged to pull the word from the word file and relearn it. *Note:* If the word is particularly troublesome, the student may choose to put it aside and spend the time more productively.

10. Periodic weekly or bimonthly reviews of all recently learned words can take a variety of forms. To maintain and enhance a student's motivation for such reviews, a variety of word games have evolved. In addition, progress can be charted by the student in a variety of ways (tallies, graphs).

Similar approaches have been worked out to provide motivated practice and review for learning words encountered in books and other reading material and for learning to spell. Furthermore, the same emphasis on motivated learning and practice can be found in Fernald's approaches to improving reading comprehension and speed and a wide range of other basic skills.

Feature 3   Typed Story

Maria

Jan. 4, 1991

Dance

Dance is good to learn. I'd like to go on stage and *perform*. I would like to dance with Barishnikov. I'd like to dance with him *because* he is *famous*.

	JAN. 5	JAN. 6	JAN. 9	JAN. 10	JAN. 11
dance	+	O	+	+	+
perform	O	O	*dropped*		
because	+	+	+		
famous	+	+	+		

Summing Up

Fernald stressed that the process of helping individuals with reading (and other) problems requires systematic and diligent effort on the part of both the learner and the teacher. Usually all parties begin the process with great enthusiasm, and significant success is common in the early stages. However, for a variety of reasons, the process may be cut short. Fernald lamented that in too many cases "the work is stopped at a stage when the individual still reads new material slowly and, if left to his own devices, word by word" (p. 55).

One reason for the frequent failure to overcome learning problems to the degree possible is that the motivational components of the learning process are not appropriately addressed. The methods attributed to Fernald, as well as all other remedial approaches, can be used in ways that maximize or undermine learner motivation. We suggest that in many cases, remedial procedures are ineffective because motivational considerations have not been planned systematically. When remedial procedures are effective, the positive results may be primarily due to motivational factors. Clearly the motivational impact and context of remedial practices is a matter deserving greater discussion and research.

On the Individual and Society

IV.1   Ethical Concerns About Negative Effects

IV.2   Whose Interests Are Being Served?

IV.3   Toward Services with an Informed Consumer Orientation

IV.4   Involving Parents in Schooling

IV.5   Social Control

IV.6   Cultural and Individual Differences as Barriers to Working Relationships

IV.7   Managing and Preventing School Misbehavior

IV.1   *Ethical Concerns About Negative Effects*

A variety of ethical concerns confront professional practitioners. Of particular concern are negative effects that can arise from diagnostic, treatment, and evaluation practices.

What negative effects? Among many others, there are

- mistaken diagnoses
- misprescriptions
- invasions of privacy
- self-fulfilling prophecies
- stigmatization of individuals
- overdependency on professionals

Just because a practice may have a negative effect is generally not an adequate reason for not using it. Many medications, for example, have side effects, but if people think they will help more than hurt, they use them. Most practitioners arrive at conclusions about whether a practice is ethical in just this way. If they think it is more helpful than harmful, it is seen as ethical.

What makes a practice more helpful than harmful? This question points up a basic problem in trying to resolve ethical issues. There is no easy answer. If there were, there would be far less controversy over what is and isn't ethical.

Although there is no simple answer, there are better ways to think about the matter than relying primarily on experience and intuition. Major concepts and principles provide an important foundation for thinking through ethical dilemmas. The following brief presentation may help clarify what we mean. (For a fuller discussion, see the references provided at the end of this selection.) Three topics are discussed: (1) costs versus benefits, (2) fairness, and (3) consent.

Costs versus Benefits

Professional practices are designed to provide benefits. Such benefits can be acquired only at a cost, in several senses of the term. Should we place a student in a special classroom? Should an individual be given remediation? Medication? Will the treatment correct the individual's problem? If so, will the benefits justify the financial expense, discomfort, stigmatization, and other potential negative effects persons may experience upon being labeled and treated as different from others?

Clearly, costs and benefits encompass more than financial considerations and often are not readily quantified. Besides finances, the costs and benefits most frequently discussed are psychological and physical, particularly those having to do with identification and subsequent interventions. Unfortunately, the sparsity of data on effectiveness and negative effects makes it difficult to specify benefits and costs, let alone determine net gains or losses. Reviewers find the validity of reported studies limited and inconsistent. As a result, the claim of positive benefits for persons with learning problems often is more hope than fact. Thus efforts to resolve ethical dilemmas by considering costs versus benefits for the individual must decide how heavily to weigh potential—but unproved—positive and negative effects.

From another perspective, it has been suggested that costs versus benefits also be analyzed with reference to the societal biases reflected in certain intervention practices. For example, children whose backgrounds differ from the dominant culture may be classified and treated as deficient primarily because their values and norms, and thus their actions and performance, are different from those of the dominant culture. In such situations, whether intentional or not, beneficial practices seem to have the effect of colluding with biases against certain subgroups.

The point is that ethical (and legal) perspectives can no longer remain oriented only to individuals. Concern over the use of IQ testing with minority students provides a dramatic illustration of this point. Litigants have argued that minority populations have been inappropriately served by most IQ tests and labeling (in California, *Diana v. State Board of Education,* 1970; *Larry P. v. Riles,* 1972). Court cases have stressed that intelligence testing should be "culture fair," including use of the individual's "home language," and that tests alone should not be used to classify students. Such litigation highlights the concern that the benefits of some identification practices for any individual may be considerably less than the costs to a particular subgroup of the society. In particular, there is concern about practices that may perpetuate racial injustices in the form of additional discrimination, stigmatization, and restriction of educational opportunities. What all this highlights is that harmful effects can go beyond individuals; the costs versus benefit for subgroups must also be considered.

A broader ethical perspective focuses on the overall negative effect professional practices can have on the entire culture. Some writers warn of a general loss of people's ability to cope with their problems. As a result of mystification about professional practices, people in modern societies are manifesting an ever-increasing, distressing, and unnecessary overdependence on professionals. With psychoeducational problems, this is illustrated by the large number of parents and students who simply accept labels, such as *learning disabilities* and *emotional disturbance,* and related special interventions, without question or understanding. Thus the suggestion has been made that professionals must judge the ethics of their activities not only in terms of the impact on an individual and on subgroups but also with regard to the impact on the entire culture.

Balancing costs against benefits is important, but the complexity of determining that costs outweigh benefits makes the application of this notion difficult. Even when the principle can be used effectively, it is still only one of the ethical guidelines to be considered. For instance, decisions that overemphasize utility (costs versus benefits) at the expense of equity and justice (fairness) have been especially criticized.

Fairness

Recent legal emphasis on "rights to treatment" and "right of all children to an education" also has highlighted the moral obligation to ensure that services are allocated fairly. If someone has a psychological or educational problem, it seems only fair that they be helped. In providing help, interveners are expected to be just and fair. The problem is, how do we decide what is fair?

The matter of fairness involves such questions as: Fair for whom? Fair according to whom? Fair using what criteria and what procedures for applying the criteria? Obviously what is fair for the society may not be fair for an individual; what is fair for one person may cause an inequity for another. To provide special services for one group's problems raises the taxes of all citizens. To deny such services is unfair and harmful to those who need the help.

Making fair decisions about who should get what services and resources and about how rules should be applied involves principles of distributive justice. For example, should each person be (1) given an equal share of available resources? (2) provided for according to individual need? (3) served according to his or her societal contributions? or (4) given services on the basis of having earned them (merit)? Obviously such principles can conflict with each other. Moreover, any of them may be weighted more heavily than another, depending on the social philosophy of the decision maker. For example:

> *Egalitarian* theories emphasize equal access to goods in life that every rational person desires; *Marxist* theories emphasize need; *Libertarian* theories emphasize contribution and merit; and *Utilitarian* theories emphasize a mixed use of such criteria so that public and private utility are maximized. (Beauchamp & Childress, 1989, p. 173)

Those practitioners who see themselves as "helping professionals" tend to emphasize individual need. That is, they tend to believe fairness means that those with problems should be given special aid. Indeed, the duty to serve those in need is seen as an ethical reason for classifying or labeling children.

Decisions based on the fairness principle often call for unequal allocation and affirmative action with regard to who gets the resources and how rules are applied. Thus, although they are intended to be just and fair, such decisions can be quite controversial, especially when resources are scarce.

There are always conflicting views as to which of many needs should be assigned highest priority. Are programs for the gifted more important than programs for students with learning disabilities? Should school athletic teams be funded at higher levels than vocational programs?

On a more individual level, parents, teachers, psychologists, and other practitioners consistently are confronted with the problem of applying rules differentially. For example, should different consequences be applied for the same offense when the children involved differ in terms of problems, age, competence, and so forth?

Some persons try to simplify matters by not making distinctions and treating everyone alike. It was said of Coach Vince Lombardi that he treated all his players the same—like dogs! We recall many instances in which teachers of problem populations have insisted on enforcing rules without regard to a particular student's social and emotional problems. They usually argued that it was unfair to other students if the same rule were not applied in the same way to everyone. In general, although a "no exceptions" approach represents a simple solution, it ignores the possibility that such a nonpersonalized approach may make a child's problem worse and thus be unjust.

Consent

In a society that values fairness and personal liberty, consent is a very important concept. Such a society has a strong commitment to ensuring personal autonomy for everyone. Children and individuals with problems often are treated in ways that diminish their autonomy. This occurs because of assumptions about their relative lack of competence and wisdom. Even when they are treated autonomously, their decisions may not be respected.

The idea that autonomy should be respected has made consent not only a legal but also a major moral concern. The legal and moral mechanism for maintaining autonomy usually is designated *informed consent*. Six major functions served by the consent mechanism are the promotion of individual autonomy, the protection of clients or subjects, the avoidance of fraud and duress, the promotion of rational decisions, the encouragement of self-scrutiny by professionals, and the involvement of the public in promoting autonomy as a general social value and in controlling professional practices and research.

The desirability of such outcomes seems evident. The problems and issues involved in appropriately eliciting consent have to do with such matters as: When is consent needed? When is it justified for one person to offer consent for another? Who decides when consent is needed and when one person can represent another? What information must be given

in eliciting consent? How can anyone be certain that consent has been voluntarily given? Each of these questions raises significant dilemmas for professionals.

To highlight major concerns associated with the concept of consent, we focus on (1) competence and paternalism as they affect decisions about when consent must be elicited and from whom, and (2) the nature of relevant information and voluntary consent.

The Question of Competence and the Problem of Paternalism

Competence in the context of consent refers to the ability to understand (the ability to receive and process information, make decisions, and choose from among alternatives). Criteria for deciding about the adequacy of these abilities are difficult to specify. Usually very general criteria are established, such as age and mental status.

Children—and those diagnosed as mentally retarded, autistic, or psychotic—usually are seen as incompetent in a legal sense and in need of surrogates (parents, guardians, and courts) to give consent. However, the basis for deciding what constitutes competence and when others should act remains controversial. The example of children's consent illustrates just how difficult the problem is. At what age should it be necessary to ask a child's consent before involving the child in a psychological or educational intervention (including testing)? With certain school assessment activity, the legal answer is that no individual consent is needed from either parents or child through the age period when attendance is compelled by the state. With regard to special psychological testing, special class placement, and therapeutic treatments, the common answer is that only the parents' consent is needed, and in some cases not even their consent is sought.

The question of competence is strongly related to the problem of paternalism. It comes as no surprise that professionals, parents, government agents, and many others in society have opinions as to what is good for children. Such opinions backed by the power to impose them may lead to excessive paternalism.

For example, the professional who tests a youngster who does not want to be tested is confronted with this problem. It is a paternalistic act whenever a child is made to undergo unwanted assessment, even though the activity is viewed as in the child's "best interests." Whether stated or not, when such actions are taken, the child's autonomy is made less important than the possible harm to the child or others if the child is not assessed or the possible benefits to be gained if the child is assessed.

Relevant Information and Voluntary Consent

Whenever consent is to be elicited, relevant information must be provided and decisions must be made voluntarily. Relevant information must be provided in an understandable manner—a requirement that is difficult to meet when complex psychoeducational practices are used. Cultural and language differences also may be barriers in making information understandable.

Providing relevant information does not guarantee that consent is given voluntarily. In many situations, consent is given because people feel they have no meaningful alternative. For example, children in special school programs and their parents may consent to additional assessment (therapy, medication, and so forth) because of fear that if they refuse they may be asked to leave the program.

When is voluntary consent needed? In addition to legal and ethical guidelines, voluntary consent is needed whenever the intent is to establish a helping relationship. Power relationships and situations in which influence is relied upon to elicit compliance do not involve the consent of participants. In contrast, helping relationships are based on voluntary consent. Thus, by definition, the obtaining of informed and voluntary consent defines whether the intent of an intervention is social control or helping.

When may consent be waived? The answer seems clearest when a problem is extremely threatening or an intervention is extremely unthreatening. For instance, persons who are seen as immediately dangerous to others or as unable to protect or care for themselves generally are accepted as likely candidates for waivers of consent.

Activities that are common to everyday living, such as much of the assessment and evaluation activity that permeates all our lives, provide another example. But they usually are not understood in terms of waived consent. They are, however, instances of de facto waived consent.

Although ethical concerns about waived consent are most likely to be raised in cases of extreme problems and dramatic interventions, consent that is waived in a de facto manner perhaps ought to be of equal concern. Many commonplace activities, such as routine achievement, intelligence, and interest testing in schools, can have life-shaping impact and are likely to have an effect on a large segment of the population. In instances in which consent is ignored, coercion is involved and needs to be justified.

Further Readings

For further information about costs, benefits, fairness, consent, the ethics of coercion, and other ethical considerations, see the following.

American Psychological Association (1981). Ethical principles of psychologists. *American Psychologist, 36,* 633–38.

Beauchamp, T. L. & Childress, J. F. (1989). *Principles of biomedical ethics.* New York: Oxford University Press.

Feinberg, J. (1973). *Social philosophy.* Englewood Cliffs, NJ: Prentice-Hall.

Keith-Spiegel, P. & Koocher, G. P. (1985). *Ethics in psychology: Professional standards and cases.* New York: Random House.

Rinas, J. & Clyne-Jackson, S. (1988). *Professional conduct and legal concerns in mental health practice.* Norwalk, CT: Appleton & Lange.

IV.2   Whose Interests Are Being Served?

The welfare of those with learning problems often depends on the ability of society (professionals, parents) to keep the difference between socialization and helping in perspective and to resolve conflicting interests appropriately.

Interventions for those with learning and behavior problems can be distinguished by whether the purpose is to serve the interests of the society, the individual, or both. At the root of this distinction, however, is the age-old inevitability of conflicts between individual and societal interests. It is this inevitable conflict that is at the core of so many legal and ethical dilemmas confronting those who intervene in the lives of others.

The problem of conflicting interests is reflected in the extensive concern raised about society's ability to exercise control through psychological and educational interventions. At one extreme, it is argued that there are times when society must put its needs before the individual rights of citizens by pursuing certain activities designed to maintain itself (involuntary socialization programs, compulsory testing). At the other extreme, it is argued that activities that jeopardize individuals' rights (coercion, invasion of privacy) are never justified. For many persons, however, neither extreme is acceptable, especially with minors.

Without agreeing or disagreeing with a particular position, one can appreciate the importance of the debate. It serves to heighten awareness that

- no society is devoid of some degree of coercion in dealing with its members (that is, no right or liberty is absolute), and that such coercion has been seen as particularly justifiable in intervening with minors
- interventions can be used to serve the vested interests of subgroups in a society at the expense of other subgroups (for example, to deprive minorities, the poor, females, and legal minors of certain freedoms and rights)
- informed consent and due process of law are central to the protection of individuals when there are conflicting interests at stake (for example, about who or what should be blamed for a problem and

be expected to carry the brunt of corrective measures)

Such awareness and greater sensitivity to conflicts among those with vested interests in interventions are essential if individuals in need of help are to be adequately protected from abuse by those with power to exercise control over them.

Conflicting Interests

The importance of understanding that a variety of persons and groups have vested and often conflicting interests in intervention practices has been recognized for many years. Strupp and Hadley (1977), for example, propose that there are three "interested parties" involved in intervention decision making: the client, society, and intervener. We contrast the interested parties by whether they are directly or indirectly involved. The former include persons or systems to be changed (individual referred because of a problem, an instructional program), interveners, and subscribers (parents, those who refer individuals to interveners, government or private agencies that underwrite programs). Indirectly involved parties include those whose influence has the potential to produce a major impact on the intervention (these parties range from other family members to those who lobby for, underwrite, study, evaluate, and teach about intervention). As to the different interested parties, a consistent problem arises as to who is the "client"—the person paying (parents, board of education, taxpayers, an insurance company) or the person with the educational or psychological problem.

Although it is not always articulated, each interested party has beliefs and values about the nature of identified problems and what should be done. It may be uncertain as to whose view should prevail.

James has been "acting out" at school and at home. His parents and teacher—and even he himself—agree that the behavior is inappropriate. However, each disagrees about the reason for the behavior and what needs to be done. The teacher and parents see the problem residing in James and want him treated to reduce the degree of inappropriate behavior and increase adaptation to social rules. While agreeing that James should be referred for treatment, the teacher and parents have different ideas about what type of intervention should be sought. Moreover, both viewpoints differ from that of a psychologist brought in for consultation—and from James's own perspective.

Interested in classroom order, the teacher has implemented a range of behavioral management strategies to curb James's classroom misbehavior. But they have not been effective, and so she suggests James be taken to a physician for evaluation of the need for medication to reduce his hyperactive behavior at school. Concerned for his long-term adjustment, James's parents want him to have individual psychotherapy to address his underlying emotional problems. The psychologist has a predilection for family systems theory and insists that the parents and James should be referred for family treatment. James says that he doesn't need treatment and indicates he would not have to fight with his teacher and parents if they would just "get off his back."

When there are conflicting interests, theory, philosophical principles, legislation, and legal precedents can provide broad guidelines for decision making. Decisions should be made with full recognition of the intent to help or to socialize. This includes considering the likely impact of proposed interventions on the individual (particularly potential negative effects). We suggest that an individual's best interests are not served when interventions designed to socialize (affect a youngster's social behavior through discipline, medication, skill training) are counterproductive to helping. From this perspective, decisions to pursue such interventions require specific justification that societal interests outweigh those of the individual. The bases for such a justification are found in social philosophical, legal, and psychological discussions, which we highlight after differentiating between helping and socialization interventions.

Helping versus Socialization Interventions

The key to differentiating helping from formal socialization interventions is found in whose best interests are to be served (see Figure 1). Helping interventions are defined in terms of a primary intention to serve the client's interests; socialization through formal intervention primarily seeks to serve the interests of the society.

How does one know whose interests are served? By definition, the individual's interests are served when she or he consents to intervention *without coercion* and has control over major intervention decisions. In contrast, socialization agendas usually are implemented under a form of "social contract" that allows society's agents to decide on certain interventions for the individual without asking for consent; in the process, society maintains control over intervention decisions.

When the intent is to serve the individual's interest but it is not feasible to elicit truly informed consent or ensure the individual has control, we are forced to operate in a gray area. This is quite likely to arise with young children and those with profound learning and behavior problems. In such cases, parents, guardians, or other surrogates are asked to become the individual's advocate until that person can act for himself or herself. We are also working in a gray area when intervening at the request of a surrogate who sees the intervention as in a person's best interests despite the individual's protests to the contrary.

Conflict over socialization versus helping can be expected whenever decisions deal with behavior the majority find disruptive or inappropriate. Such a conflict can arise in dealing with children who misbehave at school. School systems are established by society as socializing agencies (hence, compulsory education). When James misbehaved at school, the teacher's job was to bring the deviant and devious behavior under control. Interventions were designed to convince James he should conform to the prescribed limits of the social setting. His parents valued the school's socializing agenda, but also wanted him to receive special help at school for what they saw as an emotionally based problem. James, like most children, did not appreciate the increasing efforts to control his behavior, especially since he viewed his actions as an effort to escape such control. Under the circumstances, not only was there conflict among the involved parties, but it is also likely that the teacher's intervention efforts actually caused James to experience negative reactions.

Figure 1 Helping and Socialization Interventions

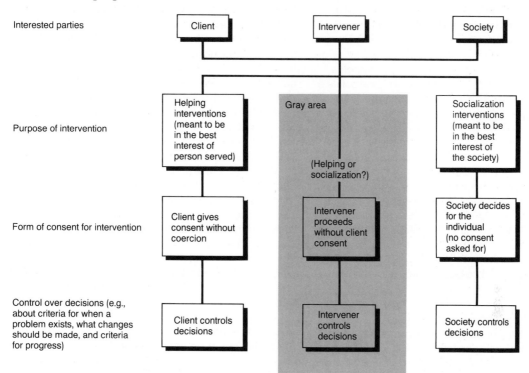

It is commonplace for practitioners to be confronted with situations where socialization and helping agendas are in conflict. Some resolve the conflict by clearly defining themselves as socializing agents. In such a context, it is understood that helping is not the primary concern. Others resolve the conflict by viewing individuals as "clients" and pursuing interventions that can be defined as helping. In such cases the goal is to work with the consenting individual to resolve learning and behavior problems (including, when appropriate, efforts to make environments more accommodative of individual differences). Some practitioners are unclear about their agenda or are forced by circumstances to try to pursue both agendas at once, and this adds confusion to an already difficult situation.

The problem of conflicting agendas is particularly acute for those who work in "institutional" settings such as schools and residential "treatment" centers. In such settings, the tasks confronting the practitioner often include both helping individuals over-

come underlying problems *and* controlling misbehavior to maintain the integrity of the social order. At times the two are incompatible. And although all interventions in the setting may be designated as "treatment," the need for social control can overshadow the concern for helping. Moreover, the need to control individuals in such settings has led to coercive and repressive actions.

Coercive Interventions

In the 1980s, the problem of coercive treatment of minors was illustrated by a series of court cases. As summarized by Melton and Davidson (1987),

in the case of *Milonas v. Williams* (1982) involving the Provo Canyon School in Utah, youth sent to the school were required to take polygraph examinations to prove they were obeying, among other rules, avoidance of "negative thinking," including a mere intent to say bad things about the school. Refusal of the polygraph examination resulted in punishment and failure to advance in the program or leave the school. Students' outgoing mail was censored, boys were required to rewrite "negative" letters, and therapists wrote comments like "manipulative" in the margins.

Other programs intended to "resocialize" troubled or troubling youth sometimes have resorted to holding youth incommunicado (see, e.g., *Doe v. Public Health Trust of Dade County,* 1983, on "no-communication therapy"), refusing to allow them to wear street clothes (see, e.g., *Wheeler v. Glass,* 1983), or keeping them in isolation for prolonged periods (see, e.g., *Mary & Crystal v. Ramsden,* 1980; *Santana v. Collazo,* 1983), or forcing them to wear self-derogatory signs, engage in other humiliation rituals (e.g., cleaning floors for hours with toothbrushes; see *Stare ex rel. K.W. v. Werner,* 1978), or submit to intense and prolonged group confrontation. (p. 174)

Not only do these cases illustrate coercive and repressive treatment, the rulings provide some guidelines as to the limitations of involuntary treatment for minors. At the same time, judicial cases raise concerns about the dangers involved in determining public policy and professional practice through litigation. Care must be taken not to conclude that judicial rulings provide satisfactory, never mind sufficient, guidelines for decisions about coercive treatment.

Given that there are limits, the question remains: When is coercive treatment appropriate? As suggested above, some practitioners argue that any type of involuntary psychoeducational intervention is unjustifiable. Others argue that various forms of majority-disapproved behavior (ranging from illegal acts through immoral and deviant behaviors to compulsive negative habits) produce enough social harm, offense, or nuisance to warrant compulsory treatment. Examples cited with respect to minors include substance abuse, gender confusion, truancy, aggressive behavior toward adults or peers, and low self-esteem.

Even when the focus is on the most dramatic psychosocial problems, serious ethical concerns are raised whenever compulsory treatment is proposed to socialize or "resocialize" individuals. When the need for coercive intervention is extrapolated from

dramatic cases to less extreme behaviors, such as classroom misbehavior and attention problems, the ethical concerns seem even more pressing. Ironically, in such instances the coercive nature of an approach may not even be evident, particularly when the activity is described as in keeping with appropriate socialization goals and as unlikely to be harmful.

For behavior that is illegal or in violation of organizational rules, it has been suggested that minors be compelled or at least "encouraged," to enroll in treatment rather than go to jail or be expelled from school. When treatment is offered as an alternative to punishment, the choice between the lesser of two evils may seem clear and devoid of coercion. A chronically truant or "incorrigible" youth might indeed express preference for a "diversion" program of treatment over juvenile detention. However, given a third nontreatment alternative seen as more desirable, treatment probably would not be chosen.

One moral basis for decisions to allow and pursue involuntary interventions is found in the philosophical grounds for coercion. As Feinberg (1973) and Robinson (1974) suggest, such decisions are informed by principles that address justifications for the restriction of personal liberty. These are:

1. To prevent harm to others, either
   a. injury to individual persons (the private harm principle), or
   b. impairment of institutional practices that are in the public interest (the public harm principle)
2. To prevent offense to others (the offense principle)
3. To prevent harm to self (legal paternalism)
4. To prevent or punish sin, i.e., to "enforce morality as such" (legal moralism)
5. To benefit the self (extreme paternalism)
6. To benefit others (the welfare principle) (Feinberg, 1973, p. 33)

As Robinson (1974) cogently states:

None of these justifications for coercion is devoid of merit nor is it necessary that any of them exclude the others in attempts to justify actions against the freedoms of an individual. . . . It is one thing to assert each of these justifications enjoys some merit but quite another to suggest that they are equally valid. And it is manifestly the case that they do not share equally in the force of the law. Yet, while not sharing equally, they have all, on one occasion or another, been relied on to validate a legal judgment. (p. 234)

Other related bases for decisions to allow involuntary interventions with children and adolescents are found in philosophical, legal, and psychological discussions of minors' competence (or lack thereof) to act in their own best interests. At one time, little doubt existed that minors lacked competence to act in their best interests, thus, treatment had to proceed without their consent. Currently, discussion has shifted to the question: At what age are minors competent to participate as equals or as sole deciders in decisions that affect them? The evolving answer to this question is reshaping views about when it is appropriate to pursue treatment without a minor's consent and is part of the larger concern for respect for the dignity of children (Melton, 1991).

For example, there is evidence that some minors at 14 years of age and even younger (including individuals manifesting psychoeducational problems) are competent to participate appropriately and effectively in making major intervention decisions — such as those made during individual educational program (IEP) planning (Taylor et al., 1985). Survey data indicate that a significant number of parents, professionals, and children take the position that individuals as young as 8 years old should play a greater role in decision making (Taylor et al., 1984; Tremper & Feshbach, 1981). In addition, a variety of benefits related to minors' decision making have been discussed, but there certainly also are risks (Melton, 1983).

Summing Up

Current theory and data are inadequate to resolve debates over age of competence and relative weighting of risks and benefits. The complexity of the problem is increased by the fact that risks and benefits vary with the type of decisions under discussion and developmental and motivational status of the decision maker. Little is known about whether intervention might improve decision making competence of younger children, thereby lowering the mean age at which competence is manifested and, perhaps, reducing risks and enhancing benefits (Tapp & Melton, 1983; Taylor & Adelman, 1986).

Ultimately, every practitioner must personally come to grips with what she or he views as morally proper in balancing the respective rights of the various interested parties when interests conflict.

IV.3   Toward Services with an Informed Consumer Orientation

David, James, Mara, Matt, Johnny, Mary, Jenny, you, your friends and family, us—much of the population of the world can be divided into those who are either directly involved or have significant indirect contact with learning and related problems. For our purposes here, anyone who has any degree of involvement is seen as a consumer. What are they consuming? Information and services about learning and related problems.

"What is dyslexia?" "How do I tell if my child has a perceptual-motor dysfunction?" "Where can I have my child tutored?" These and many similar questions are on the minds of those close to individuals who have learning problems. People want and deserve the best information available.

Answers should convey the type of information that clarifies rather than mystifies. We need appropriately cautious information to (1) put the matter into proper perspective, (2) look at general options for dealing with the problem, and (3) make decisions and follow through. Unfortunately, the hardest time for people to get information and sort things out for themselves seems to be when there is a pressing concern. Thus they may need help from others.

Help can come from various sources. Here, we group sources as (1) self-help resources (including help from acquaintances and friends) and (2) professional contact.

Self-Help

If so inclined, the interested party can use nonprofessional resources to find the information needed. The advantages in doing so are many, not the least of which is the money that may be saved. Three major types of nonprofessional resources are consumers' groups, parents' and self-help organizations, and media presentations such as popularized books and magazine articles.

Consumer information groups gather together and reproduce available information. A major resource for consumer information products is the Consumer Information Center (Department DD, Pueblo, CO 81009), an agency of the U.S. General Services Administration. It publishes a catalog listing booklets from almost 30 agencies of the federal government. Most of the booklets are free. Relevant available works include

- "Learning Disability: Not Just a Problem Children Outgrow"
- "Plain Talk About Children with Learning Disabilities"
- "Your Child and Testing"
- "Plain Talk About When Your Child Starts School"

The Foundation for Children with Learning Disabilities (FCLD) is a privately funded organization established in 1977 with one of its primary goals to promote public awareness of learning disabilities. The group publishes a resource manual entitled "The FCLD Guide for Parents of Children with Learning Disabilities." The guide provides basic information about learning disabilities (warning signs, guidelines for seeking help, children's rights, alternatives beyond high school), lists sources of information and help, and includes an annotated list of relevant books, periodicals, directories, and audiovisual materials. For a free copy, write FCLD, 99 Park Ave., New York, NY 10016.

The National Association of College Admissions Counselors publishes the "Guide for Learning Disabled Students," which lists schools that provide comprehensive programs for such students. To obtain a copy, write 9933 Lawler Ave., Suite 500, Skokie, IL 60077.

Higher Education and the Handicapped (HEATH) acts as a clearinghouse, providing information about secondary education for persons with learning disabilities. It offers fact sheets, lists of directories, and information about testing, types of programs, and organizations. Also available are bibliographies of recently published pamphlets and books about learning disabilities. Copies may be obtained by writing 1 Dupont Circle, NW, Washington, DC 20036.

Although the information in the materials cited here is presented clearly, not enough effort is made in these materials to clarify issues and consumer concerns.

Consumer advocate groups are more likely to provide the general public with critical as well as informative overviews of what to do and what not to do when faced with an educational, psychological, or medical problem. For example, an organization called Public Citizen (Health Research Group, 2000 P St., NW, Washington, DC 20036) has produced a number of booklets stressing consumer guidelines for careful selection of professional health services. Their approach provides information and instructs consumers in how to ask about and evaluate services to protect themselves when shopping for and using professional help. Although their work has not focused specifically on learning problems, it is still relevant because practitioners who work with learning problems often model themselves after the medical and mental health professions. Three examples of the Health Research Group's products are

- "A Consumer's Guide to Obtaining Your Medical Records"
- "Through the Mental Health Maze: A Consumer's Guide to Finding a Psychotherapist, Including a Sample Consumer/Therapist Contract"
- "Consumer's Guide to Psychoactive Drugs"

With specific reference to learning disabilities, an article by Worrall (1990) provides a ratings scale for differentiating between a promising intervention and a fraud that promises more than it can deliver.

With the rapid changes in laws, regulations, policies, and administrative mechanisms, legal resource networks have developed to provide information to parents and others concerned with individuals with special needs. Three major resources are the Parent Information Centers, Closer Look Information Project, and the Protection and Advocacy Network (see Feature 1).

Parents played a major role in establishing the LD field, and the organizations that parents established continue to play a major role. The obvious example is the Learning Disabilities Association of America (LDA, 4156 Library Road, Pittsburgh, PA 15234; or Kildare House, 323 Chapel, Ottawa, Ontario K1N 7Z2, Canada), with 50 state affiliates and more than 775 local chapters in the United States and abroad. Among its various functions, the organization serves as a referral center, publishes a newsletter, operates an LD literary depository, and provides general information about the field. It also sponsors an annual

Feature 1   Legal Resource Networks

As described by Massenzio (1983):

> The Parent Information Centers and the Closer Look Information Project were funded in the 1970s by the U.S. Office of Education. . . . From 1969 to 1972, a major focus of the Closer Look Project . . . was on the location and identification of existing special education facilities and resources. But between 1972 and 1975 . . . , the emphasis shifted to dissemination of the basic issues surrounding the right to education . . . judicial decisions, statutes, and regulations. . . . In 1978–79, the Closer Look Project added intensive training of potential parent-advocates to its activities. . . .
>
> Parent Information Centers dialogue with state and local officials often centered around issues of policy interpretations, provisions regarding IEPs, notice and due process, and the coordination of state plans and interpretations

> with federal requirements. Most importantly, information provided by Parent Information Centers has been of that finely tuned variety which could respond to more precise questions about timeliness, participants in meetings, due process, and the like. . . .
>
> . . . A growing number of the activities of state Protection and Advocacy Offices for developmentally disabled persons throughout the nation are concerned with special education issues. . . . In many localities, they represent an important source of information for all aspects of educational law . . . [and] policy matters. . . . The issues presented have recently required a broader knowledge of all aspects of special education implementation and a greater sophistication of analysis. . . . The offices tend not only to answer questions, but to define them as well. (pp. 274–75)

international conference. LDA prides itself in its breadth of concern for parent and self-help needs.

Adults diagnosed as LD are beginning to band together to help each other. In the United States there is the Association of Learning-Disabled Adults (PO Box 9722, Friendship Station, Washington, DC). Besides general information of use to interested parties, this organization has compiled a list of local self-help groups.

There are books and books and books—some useful, some questionable. There are many texts, journals, and works primarily for professionals. Books for the general public are fewer and have mostly focused on simple explanations and advice. They tend to stress descriptions of the problem and offer suggestions about what parents might do to help their child. A few examples follow:

- Bain, L. J. (1991). *A parent's guide to attention deficit disorders.* New York: Delta.
- Greene, L. (1984). *Kids who hate school: A survival handbook on learning disabilities.* Atlanta, GA: Humanitics.
- Osman, B. (1985). *Learning disabilities: A family affair.* New York: Warner Books.
- Painting, D. (1983). *Helping children with specific learning disabilities: A practical guide for parents and teachers.* Englewood Cliffs, NJ: Prentice-Hall.
- Rosner, J. (1987). *Helping children overcome learning difficulties: A step-by-step guide for parents and teachers* (rev. ed.). New York: Walker & Co.

Although there are many children's books with storylines designed to enhance youngsters' understanding of individual differences and learning problems, much rarer are nonfiction books aimed at providing information and suggestions to the student with a learning problem. One such book is

- Levine, M. (1990). *Keeping A head in school: A student's book about learning abilities and learning disorders.* Cambridge, MA: Educators Publishing Service, Inc.

While works for professionals have raised many issues and problems, popular books presenting a systematic critical look at the topic of learning disabilities have been rare. In one popular polemic entitled *The Myth of the Hyperactive Child and Other Means of Child Control* (Schrag & Divoky, 1975), the authors included an all-out assault on the concept of learning disabilities along with an attack on hyperactivity and treatments used with those given such diagnostic labels. In 1987 Gerald Coles's work *The Learning Mystique: A Critical Look at "Learning Disabilities"* took a much more detailed look at the field and its deficiencies.

Professional Contact

One would do well to gain a little consumer sophistication before contacting a professional resource—not because professionals are out to rip people off (although there are a few shady practitioners in any profession) but because the majority of professional services by their very nature have built-in biases and usually reflect prevailing treatment fads. Thus a specific practitioner may promote only one view of the problem and the needed treatment, and may also use confusing jargon or perhaps overly complex or unproved theories and practices.

With the need for caution in mind, let's quickly review a range of possibilities people may consider in contacting professionals for help. Keep in mind that in looking for help the consumer's problem is twofold—to identify feasible resources and then to evaluate their appropriateness.

As a first professional contact, the value of telephone "helplines" has been demonstrated. Well-designed, highly visible helplines can provide a means to inform and protect the public by providing ready access to information. In the 1980s, a national toll-free LD TEEN-LINE was tried by the Closer Look Information Project/The Parents' Campaign for Handicapped Children and Youth. Volunteer staff offered information and referrals to parents, teens, and educators. They covered matters related to educational advocacy, vocational and postsecondary education and training, vocational rehabilitation, community resources, and publications. Later in this reading we will describe another helpline service in detail. A note of caution: helplines can be abused. For example, besides the general problems of bias noted throughout the book, practitioners seeking clients may use the guise of a helpline primarily to solicit new customers.

For many parents, public schools and related public agencies provide the most natural and ongoing contact point for discussing a youngster's learning problems. Indeed, in the United States, federal guidelines stress the obligation of schools to identify learning disabilities and inform parents of their rights related to special programs (see Feature 2). Thus a very common and reasonable first referral involves directing people to a public-school counselor or psychologist for information.

As an alternative, local universities and colleges often have training or research programs focusing on learning and related problems. They may offer direct services, or at least can be a good source of information about reputable local resources. (Similarly, agencies and government departments for vocational rehabilitation may provide relevant services or referrals. Some public libraries also have established referral reference lists.) If public resources are not available or are not seen as appropriate, private practitioners may be considered. Private resources vary widely in terms of professional affiliation, available services, and competence. They range from referral, testing, and consultation services to training and remedial services in the form of tutoring and special schools; also very much part of the picture are the array of medical or medically related and psychological treatments discussed throughout this text.

Identification of public and private programs and practitioners can be done through the type of referral resources already described or by reference to any of a variety of referral directories available in public libraries.

Evaluating the appropriateness of a potential resource is not an easy task. As was noted in an early directory published by Academic Therapy Publications:

> We are frequently asked: How does one evaluate a facility or service to be sure it meets the needs of an individual? Clearly, the best way is to visit the facility and meet with its director and staff. A second avenue is to talk candidly with someone who has had a family member enrolled. If neither of the above strongly recommended practices is possible, then a letter of inquiry should be directed at the facility requesting a copy of its brochure and full information on the program, staff (credentials), fees, et cetera. At the same time, a descriptive statement on the child should be included so that the director of the facility can determine whether or not the program offered is appropriate. (p. *iv*)

Some referral services are designed to aid in the task of evaluating potential programs. However, the final judgment is always the consumer's. Thus, for visiting and evaluating a facility or service, the specific consumer's perspective is the most important frame of reference (see Feature 3).

If any single consumer-oriented guideline is to be emphasized, it is the importance of obtaining as clear a picture as possible about the competence of the individual(s) who will actually be working with the person to be helped. Brochures, written program descriptions, the charm of the person representing the program, fancy offices and material displays, and other such professional trappings are not completely irrelevant. They are simply much less important than the quality of the practitioners who are to spend the greatest amount of time with the person to be helped. Do these practitioners seem to know what they are doing? Are they willing to take the time to explain what it is they do and why? At the first meeting, how well do they do in trying to relate to the person to be helped?

Somewhere between self-help and turning the problem over to a professional is the expanding movement toward workshops and manuals designed to train parents and other nonprofessionals to work more effectively with youngsters. Currently most of these programs are designed to improve parenting in general, or to train parents of youngsters whose behavior is hard to handle and parents of very slow learners.

A Demonstration of Consumer-Oriented Services

To demonstrate a range of model services and to meet the need for information and referral to services, we developed (1) a community resource helpline, (2) a community resource referral system, and (3) an initial assessment and consultation program. These are briefly described next.

A Helpline for Learning Problems

Highly visible helplines provide one means of informing and protecting the general public. The specific intent of the demonstrated Learning Problems Community Resource Line was to clarify, guide, and demystify problems and appropriate services by providing the type of general information that can be given readily over the phone during a brief conversation. The service was for anyone experiencing a problem learning, anyone concerned about a friend or family member, and anyone who had questions about labels, tests, and remedial programs. The demonstrated program was staffed and implemented as follows.

Between 9 A.M. and noon, Monday through Friday, staff or supervised volunteers took calls from anyone with a question about learning problems. If the question could not be answered readily, expert resources were checked (library, professionals); then the person's call was returned, either to provide the information or to refer the caller to a resource better equipped to provide an answer.

Each person answering the phone was trained to provide basic information based on previous calls.

Volunteers had ready access to a staff member for consultation as needed. Also available was a catalogue of major referral sources (for example, the Community Resource System described next).

To advertise the availability of the helpline, flyers were sent to schools and social service agencies and posted on bulletin boards in libraries, markets, and so on. Announcements also were aired as public-service features on radio and television and in newspapers.

Data support general impressions about who calls and why. For example, mothers were most frequently involved in seeking help for their child, males were most often the focus of concern, and reading was the problem most frequently mentioned. The staff observed that a major benefit of the helpline was that it made it easier for consumers to

Feature 2   Parent Rights and Appeal Procedures

The following is a document prepared for parents by the Los Angeles Unified School District.

"I. General Rights
  - All handicapped children have the right to a free and appropriate public education.
  - Individuals have the right to privacy and confidentiality of all educational records including the right to see, review, and if necessary, challenge the records in accordance with the Family Educational Rights and Privacy Act of 1974.
  - Individuals have the right to request a copy of the education records prior to meetings.
  - All handicapped children have the right to placement in the least restrictive learning environment, to the program with least restrictive alternatives, and the right to enjoy the same variety of programs as are available to the nonhandicapped.
  - All individuals have the right to receive a full explanation of all procedural safeguards and rights of appeal.
"II. Rights Related to Assessment
  - The right to initiate a request for educational assessment.
  - The right to give or withhold written consent for any proposed activities.

  - The right to have 10 days in which to give or withhold consent.
  - The right to obtain an independent outside assessment. Procedures for obtaining such assessment shall be provided upon request.
  - The right to an assessment that is designed to be free of racial or cultural discrimination.
  - The right to have a description of the procedures and tests to be used and to be fully informed of the assessment results.
"III. Rights Related to Individualized Education Program
  - The right to be notified prior to, and to participate and/or be represented at, meeting(s).
  - The child's right to participate in the meeting(s) as appropriate.
  - The right to have the meeting within 35 school days from date of receipt of signed consent.
  - The right to have the meeting conducted in your primary language/communication mode.
  - The right to at least an annual review of the Individualized Education Program.
  - The right to appeal any decision of the Committee.

find help, and it encouraged them to do so earlier than might otherwise have been the case.

A Community Resource System

Referral practices tend to be taken for granted. Perhaps the most common practice remains that of the professional referral network (clients seeking referrals are given the names of one to three resources by a referral source). These names are seldom random choices. They tend to represent resources that the referrer has learned about through personal relationships (friends, colleagues), direct observation (brief visits), or through secondary sources (directories, brochures).

After an initial period of uncertainty and discomfort with their ability to match clients with services, most referrers begin to feel increasingly confident about their recommendations. This occurs despite the fact that there is little or no systematic evaluative information available on existing services; in particular, consumer feedback is virtually nonexistent.

It is widely assumed that referrers do have adequate and objective information and that prevailing referral practices do result in satisfactory referrals. Unfortunately, these assumptions often are untrue.

The appropriateness of a referral depends not on the referrer's perspective and preferences but on the match between the recommended service and the practical and psychological requirements of the client (financial costs, geographical location, program characteristics). Thus, even if professional referral networks could (and they can't) adequately and objectively evaluate and ensure the quality of

---

"IV. Rights Related to Appeals

"A. Informal Conference

- The right to have the informal conference within 10 days of receipt of written request for hearing.
- The right to be accompanied by a representative.
- The right to examine and have copies of any related educational documents.
- The right to referral to the fair hearing panel when the informal conference fails to resolve concerns.
- The right to be informed of available free or low cost legal or other relevant services.
- The right of the individual to remain in his/her present placement pending all appeals.

"B. Fair Hearing

- The right to a hearing held at a time and place of mutual convenience and within 45 days following receipt of written requests.
- The right to 10 days notice prior to hearing date, the notice to include date, time and place of hearing.
- The right to select one of the 3 panel members.
- The right to a decision within 10 days after appeal is heard.
- The right to request an administrative review of the decision of the fair hearing panel.

"C. Administrative Review by the Superintendent of Public Instruction

- The right to file a request within 20 days following the fair hearing panel decision.
- The right to be heard within 30 days following receipt of written request.
- The right to knowledge of all rights related to the administrative review.
- The right to be informed within 10 days of the date, time and place of administrative review.
- The right to a written decision within 15 days following the administrative review.
- The right to appeal the decision to a court of competent jurisdiction."

Source: Procedural Safeguards and Appeal Procedures for Individuals with Exceptional Needs, from Bulletin 23, Division of Special Education.

services to which they refer, they would still be confronted with the complex problem of determining that the service-client match will be a good one.

As a general approach, all services should be based on the view that the more they reflect consumer-oriented considerations, the greater the likelihood of appropriate decisions. For referrals to be consumer oriented, it is necessary to begin by clarifying consumer service needs (including the nature and scope of the problem as perceived by the client and the key characteristics of the services desired) and by clarifying the range of relevant options and basic information about each (cost, location, program rationale and features, and, where feasible, previous consumer evaluations).

Then, to aid the consumer in reviewing potential services, the options and information should be presented in an organized and comprehensible manner. To facilitate decision making, it is useful to help explore the pros and cons of the most feasible alternatives and to identify several promising possibilities. To encourage consumer self-protection, it is helpful to outline basic evaluative questions that consumers can ask of potential service providers before contracting for services.

In sum, in developing a consumer-oriented community resource system, the intent was twofold: (1) to provide consumers with ready access to information on relevant services, and (2) to minimize abuses in referral practices. At the same time, the hope was that the positive side effects of such an approach would prove to be a higher degree of client self-

Feature 3   Consumer Guidelines for Evaluating Potential School Placements

The emphasis here is on the student's evaluation. The reason for this is that youngsters' perspectives are so often ignored.

Before visiting the program, ask yourself the following five questions:

1. With what kind of teacher do I work best?
2. What things do I like to do in school?
3. What do I want to learn about?
4. What type of help do I like and need from the teacher?
5. What do I expect to get from my schooling? (What are my goals?)

You will want to keep your answers to these questions in mind as you try to find out what kind of teacher(s), activities, and support are available to you in the program you visit.

The following are things to ask and look for during a program visit:

Observe the class, noting:

1. Do the students seem interested in what they are doing?
2. Are there things you would like to do?
3. Do the activities and tasks seem like things you can do?

Interview the teacher or someone else such as a counselor, and

1. Tell what type of program you would like, especially the things you want and need from a program.
2. Ask how the program is run (rules, schedules, homework, grading, opportunity to pursue personal interests).
3. Ask about what you would be expected to do (behavior limits, skill level expectations).
4. Ask how hard it will be to make changes if parts of the program do not work out as you want them to.

Interview students in the program, and

1. Ask how they like it and why.
2. Ask if they can ask for and get help when they need it.
3. Ask what they would suggest you do to prepare for making this program a good one for you should you enroll.
4. Ask what they think is the most important thing you would need in order to do well in the program.

Find out what other types of help the program would have available for you (tutoring, counseling).

reliance in problem solving, decision making, and consumer awareness.

The six components of such a system are as follows.

1. Standardized information   Potential referral resources are actively sought and invited to become entries in the system. Each is asked to fill out a standard form to provide summary information for easy reference and comparison with other services. The information encompasses characteristics of clients served (type of problems, age, sex), general type of services offered and fees, brief statements regarding specific characteristics of the services (particular philosophical and/or theoretical orientation), and an indication of who to contact to initiate services. These sheets are dated and categorized in loose-leaf binder notebooks.

Separate books are kept for major geographical areas in the community. Each book is organized to distinguish types of services (tutoring, school programs, assessment and consultation, counseling and psychotherapy, medical services, full-service facilities, other services such as vocational training and recreation facilities serving problem populations). There is considerable cross referencing. All of this could be computerized.

2. Primary source material   Each service is asked to send all relevant descriptions and information (brochures, articles). These are dated, placed in sturdy plastic folders, and filed alphabetically in file cabinets. Information on each service is periodically updated.

3. Published directories   Several of the many available commercial directories are also provided. These are meant primarily for reference to services not yet catalogued in the system, as well as to those outside the geographical area.

4. System use information   This material explains the intent of the system and details steps for using each component. System users are directed to the binder notebooks, and it is suggested they first look at and compare services closest to home. Once they have identified several possible resources, the next step is to look at the additional filed information on each.

Then they are ready to make direct contact. In doing so, they are encouraged to review the consumer-protection guidelines provided. It is stressed that none of the services in the file has been evaluated by outside agencies, and thus their presence in the file is not to be viewed as an endorsement.

Because all efforts to catalogue resources are limited, a list is included of the type of general referral resources available in most communities (social welfare agencies, community mental health agencies, libraries, colleges, school coordinators). Clients who are unable to find what they need in such a resource file can proceed to contact these other referral resources. The information about general referral sources can be especially useful to consumers who live in distant communities.

5. Consumer protection guidelines   Handouts, *brief* abstracts of articles, and references to consumer-information material should be prominently displayed. Such handouts emphasize the types of questions a consumer might ask of a prospective service provider (about specific training and background of the individual who will actually provide the service, possible hidden costs, service benefits and risks of activities to be experienced, and so forth). The focus is on points such as those stressed by consumer advocates.

6. Consumer feedback   The main feedback emphasis is on the system itself. Users are encouraged to fill out suggestion cards describing ways in which the system might be improved. At a later date, data can be gathered on consumer evaluations of services used.

Over the years, clients were found to vary considerably in their readiness (in terms of motivation and skills) to use such a system. Some, of course, need little or no assistance. Others simply require a brief description by a receptionist. A few need help at each step. This latter group are likely candidates for an Initial Assessment and Consultation program.

Initial Assessment and Consultation

The increasing criticism of psychological and educational assessment and consultation services has underscored the need for new approaches. The focus of initial assessment and consultation is on general decisions about the types of services needed (special schooling, tutoring, psychotherapy) rather than detailed decisions about intervention steps (specific programming prescriptions).

Although most professional assessment and consultation can be seen as a form of problem solving, such problem solving may or may not be an activity professionals share with clients. The process demonstrated was meant to be one of shared or guided problem solving because the objective was to help consumers (students and parents together) arrive at their own decisions rather than passively adopting the professional's recommendations and referrals.

A consumer-oriented, guided problem-solving approach eliminates a number of problems encountered in prevailing approaches. The service costs about a tenth of what other assessment and consultation services charge; it avoids making "expert" and detailed prescriptions that go beyond the validity of assessment procedures; and it avoids referrals based on "old boy" networks by incorporating the type of community resource referral system already described.

As with all assessment involved in decision making, the assessment aspect of such a program has three major facets: (1) a rationale that determines what is assessed, (2) "measurement" or data gathering (in the form of analyses of records, observations, personal descriptions and perspectives, tests when needed), and (3) judgments of the meaning of what has been "measured."

The consultation aspect also has three major facets: (1) a rationale that determines the focus of consultation activity, (2) exploration of relevant information (including "expert" information), and (3) decision making by the consumers.

The specific procedures include:

- initial screening, usually via a phone conversation
- filling out of questionnaires by each concerned party (parents and child) regarding his or her perception of the cause of the referral problem and its correction
- gathering records and reports from other professionals or agencies in those cases in which the consumers agree that it might be useful
- analyzing—with the contribution of all interested parties—of questionnaires, reports, and records to determine whether there is a need to correct problems or verify their indications
- brief, highly circumscribed testing, if necessary and desired by consumers
- holding group conference(s) with immediately concerned parties to analyze problem(s) and in the process to determine whether other information is needed to complete the analysis
- if needed, additional brief and specific information gathering through testing, teaching, or counseling

- holding group conference(s) with the immediately concerned parties (1) to arrive at an agreement about how the problem will be understood for purposes of generating alternatives, (2) to generate, evaluate, and make decisions about alternatives to be pursued, and (3) to formulate plans for pursuing alternatives and for any support needed
- follow-up via telephone or conference to evaluate the success of each pursued alternative and determine satisfaction with the process

Problem analysis and decision making can be accomplished in one session. However, if additional assessment data are needed, one or two assessment sessions and a subsequent conference are planned.

Because some people have come to overrely on experts for diagnoses and prescriptions, a few individuals have been found to be a bit frustrated when they encounter an approach such as the one just described. They want professionals to give a battery of tests that will provide definitive answers, and they want decisions made for them. (They are convinced they cannot make good decisions for themselves.) These individuals may well reflect the negative side effects of professional practices that mystify consumers and make them feel totally dependent on professionals.

For more about the model services described above, see the following sources.

Adelman, H. S. & Taylor, L. (1984). Helping clients find referrals. *Remedial and Special Education, 5,* 44–45.

Adelman, H. S. & Taylor, L. (1984). A helpline for learning problems. *Journal of Learning Disabilities, 17,* 237–39.

Adelman, H. S. & Taylor, L. (1979). Initial psychological assessment and related consultation. *Learning Disability Quarterly, 2,* 52–64.

Adelman, H. S. & Taylor, L. (1983). *Learning disabilities in perspective.* Glenview, IL: Scott, Foresman.

Summing Up

The best consumer protection is a good professional. All professionals, of course, mean to do good. But what constitutes a "good" professional?

For consumer advocates, a consumer orientation is at the heart of the matter. Indeed, such an orientation is found in a set of professional guidelines formulated by the American Psychological Association. These guidelines state that members of a good profession:

1. Guide their practices and policies by a sense of social responsibility;
2. Devote more of their energies to serving the public interest than to "guild" functions and to building ingroup strength;
3. Represent accurately to the public their demonstrable competence;
4. Develop and enforce a code of ethics primarily to protect the client and only secondarily to protect themselves;
5. Identify their unique pattern of competencies and focus their efforts to carrying out those functions for which they are best equipped;
6. Engage in cooperative relations with other professions having related or overlapping competencies and common purposes;
7. Seek an adaptive balance among efforts devoted to research, teaching, and application;
8. Maintain open channels of communication among "discoverers," teachers, and appliers of knowledge;
9. Avoid nonfunctional entrance requirements into the profession, such as those based on race, nationality, creed, or arbitrary personality considerations;
10. Insure that their training is meaningfully related to the subsequent functions of the members of the profession;
11. Guard against premature espousal of any technique or theory as a final solution to substantive problems;
12. Strive to make their services accessible to all persons seeking such services, regardless of social and financial considerations. (APA, 1968, p. 10)

IV.4   Involving Parents in Schooling

Parent involvement in schools is a prominent item on the education reform agenda for the 1990s. It is, of course, not a new concern. As Davies (1987) reminds us, the "questions and conflict about parent and community relationships to schools began in this country when schools began" (p. 147).

A review of the literature on parents and schooling indicates widespread endorsement of parent involvement. As Epstein (1987) notes,

> the recent acknowledgements of the importance of parent involvement are built on research findings accumulated over two decades that show that children have an advantage in school when their parents encourage and support their school activities. . . . The evidence is clear that parental encouragement, activities, and interest at home and participation in schools and classrooms affect children's achievements, attitudes, and aspirations, even after student ability and family socioeconomic status are taken into account. (pp. 119–20)

With students who have learning problems, parent involvement has been mostly discussed in legal terms (participation in the IEP process). There has been little systematic attention paid to the value of, and ways to involve, the home in the efforts to improve student achievement. Our intent here is to highlight this matter from an intervention perspective. (Note: The term parent involvement, and even "family involvement," is too limiting. Given extended families and the variety of child caretakers, the concern would seem minimally one of involving the home. Thus, in the ensuing discussion, "parent" should be interpreted broadly.)

Barriers to Involvement

Research on barriers to home involvement primarily has focused on the participation of specific subgroups (parents from lower socioeconomic and ethnic minority backgrounds). Not surprisingly, the attitudes of a variety of familial, cultural, job, social class, communication, and school personnel have been implicated (Becker & Epstein, 1982; Comer, 1988; Davies, 1988; Dunst, Johanson, Trivette, & Humby, 1991; Epstein & Becker, 1982; Epstein, 1986, 1987; Klimes-Dougan, Lopez, Adelman, & Nelson, 1990; Pennekamp & Freeman, 1988; Tangri & Leitch, 1982). However, because the studies are correlational, causal relationships have not been established.

Minimally, barriers to home-school involvements may be categorized as institutional, personal, or impersonal. Furthermore, each type may take the form of negative attitudes, lack of mechanisms/skills, or practical deterrents—including lack of resources.

Institutional barriers encompass such concerns as inadequate resources (money, space, time); lack of interest or hostile attitudes toward parent involvement on the part of staff, administration, and community; and failure to establish and maintain formal parent involvement mechanisms and related skills. For example, there may be no policy commitment to facilitating parent involvement; provisions for interacting with parents when they don't speak English may be inadequate; no resources may be devoted to upgrading the skills of staff with respect to involving parents or enhancing their skills for participating effectively.

Similar barriers occur on a more personal level. That is, there may be a lack of interest or hostile attitude toward parent involvement on the part of specific individuals (administration, staff, parents, students); school personnel and/or parents may lack requisite skills or find participation uncomfortable because it demands their time and other resources. For instance, specific teachers and parents may feel it is too much of an added burden to meet to discuss student problems; others may feel threatened because they don't think they can make the necessary interpersonal connections because of racial, cultural, and language differences; still others do not perceive available activities as worth their time and effort.

Impersonal barriers to parent and staff participation are commonplace and rather obvious. For example, there are practical problems related to work schedules, transportation, child care; skill deficiencies related to cultural differences and levels of literacy; lack of interest due to insufficient information about the importance of parent involvement.

Overcoming barriers, of course, is a major concern in efforts to enhance parent involvement. However, the nature and scope of intervention is not limited to the problem of barriers.

Intervening to Enhance Parent Involvement

It is useful strategically to think of intervention to increase parent involvement as encompassing three sequential phases. The sequence begins with a broad focus; the first phase uses general, institutional procedures designed to facilitate participation of all who are ready, willing, and able. Then the focus narrows to those who need a bit more personalized contact (personal letters, phone invitations, highlighted information, contact and ongoing support from other parents) or a few more options to make participation more attractive. After this the focus narrows to parents who remain uninvolved and hard to reach (because of intense lack of interest or negative attitudes toward the school). This phase continues to use personalized contacts but adds cost-intensive special procedures.

The major intervention tasks to be planned, implemented, and evaluated can be conceived as (1) inviting involvement (outreach), (2) facilitating involvement, and (3) maintaining involvement.

Inviting Involvement

It is not uncommon for parents to feel unwelcome at school. The problem can begin with their first contacts. Many parents come to school mainly when they are called in to discuss their child's learning or behavior difficulties. Indeed, the only type of parent contact that interests some teachers is conferences designed to mobilize parents to deal with a student's learning and behavior problems.

Parents who feel unwelcome or "called on the carpet" cannot be expected to view the school as an inviting setting. Efforts to facilitate positive involvement must both counter factors that make the setting uninviting and develop ways to make it attractive to parents. This task can be viewed as the welcoming or invitation problem.

From a psychological perspective, the invitation problem is enmeshed with attitudes school staff, stu-
dents, and parents hold about involving parents. In most cases, involvement probably is best facilitated when attitudes are positive rather than neutral (or, worse yet, hostile). And, positive attitudes seem most likely when those concerned perceive personal benefits as outweighing potential costs (psychological and tangible).

Addressing the invitation problem begins with efforts to ensure that school personnel convey a welcoming tone. Informal interactions between personnel and parents can be expected to reinforce or counter the impact of formal contacts. Based on these assumptions, intervention designed to address the invitation problem should establish formal mechanisms that (1) convey a general sense of welcome to all parents, and (2) extend a personal invitation to those who appear to need something more.

Invitations to parents come in two forms: (a) general communications (flyers, newsletters, classroom announcements, form letters), and (b) special contacts (personal notes from the teacher; invitations a student makes and takes home; interchanges at school, over the phone, or during a home visit). For parents who do not respond to repeated general invitations, the next logical step is to extend special invitations and increase personal contact.

Special invitations can range from a note or a call to more cost-intensive processes, such as a home visit. They are directed at designated parents, intended to overcome attitudinal barriers, and can be used to elicit more information about persisting barriers. One simple approach is to send a personal invitation to designated parents for a specific event (a parent-teacher conference, a parenting workshop), or a request for greater involvement at home to facilitate their child's learning (providing enrichment opportunities or help with homework). If the parents still are not responsive, the next special invitation might include an RSVP and ask if there are any obstacles interfering with parental involvement.

For parents who do indicate obstacles, the problem moves beyond invitations. Overcoming barriers requires facilitative strategies.

Facilitating Involvement

General facilitation includes (a) sanctioning parent participation in any option to the degree each finds feasible (legitimizing minimal degrees of involvement), (b) accounting for cultural and individual diversity, (c) enabling participation of those with minimal skills, and (d) providing support to improve participation skills. In all these facilitative efforts, parents already involved could play a major role in helping to involve others.

If a parent is extremely negative, exceptional efforts may be required to present involvement as beneficial and to lead to a view of the school as supportive. In cases where a parent's negative attitude stems from skill deficits (doesn't speak English, lacks skills to help with homework), the option of a skill group is relatively easy to offer. This must be done in a way that minimizes stigma and maximizes intrinsic motivation. Some reluctant parents may be reached by offering them an activity designed to give them additional personal support, such as a mutual-interest group composed of parents with the same cultural background or a mutual support group (for a parent self-help group, see Simoni & Adelman, 1990). Such groups could meet away from the school at a time when working parents can participate. (The school's role would be to help initiate the groups and provide consultation as needed.)

Maintaining Involvement

As difficult as it is to involve some parents initially, maintaining their involvement may be even more so. Maintaining involvement requires (a) providing continual support for learning, growth, and success (including feedback about how involvement is personally benefitting the student), and (b) minimizing parents' feelings of incompetence and eliminating blame, censure, or coercion.

Summing Up

Interventions to enhance parent involvement in schooling might be built around creating a strong sense of community within the school, or at least within a specific classroom. The overarching intent of the intervention is to create a setting where parents, staff, and students want to and are able to interact with each other. To these ends, transactions that make parents feel incompetent, blamed, or coerced are weeded out and a setting is created that fosters informal encounters, information and learning opportunities, social interactions, shared decision making, and so forth. Parents need to be encouraged to drop in, be volunteers, participate in publishing a community newsletter, organize social events, plan and attend learning workshops, meet with the teacher to learn more about their child's curriculum and interests, help initiate parent social networks, share their heritage and interests, go on field trips, and so on and on. Creation of a sense of community encompasses finding ways to celebrate cultural and individual diversity in the school community.

IV.5   Social Control

Society's role in relation to problem populations has been widely discussed. As one writer nicely summarizes the matter:

> Society defines what is exceptional or deviant, and appropriate treatments are designed quite as much to protect society as they are to help the child. . . . "To take care of them" can and should be read with two meanings: to give children help and to exclude them from the community. (Hobbs, 1975a, pp. 20–21)

The topic of social control encompasses three concerns that increasingly appear to need attention. These can be discussed in terms of tendencies on the part of practitioners toward excessive use of (1) power, (2) limits, and (3) expert role-playing in relating to clients.

Power

As if dealing with the complexities of learning and learning problems were not enough, practitioners often find their work confounded by students' behavior problems. Students behind in their reading may also have trouble with peers, their family, and even with the law. Older students, in particular, often are involved with drug or alcohol abuse and truancy.

When confronted with behavior problems, practitioners experience the dilemma of trying to help and socialize at the same time. In order to help, they need the individual's cooperation; to gain cooperation, interfering behaviors must be brought under control. Because those who misbehave usually are not viewed as likely to control their own behavior, practitioners tend to see their only recourse as external pressure. Whether they are successful depends in part on the degree to which they can exercise real power in the situation.

Power stems from the political nature of the relationships between society and its citizens; among members of organizations, groups, families; and between professionals and their clients. In any situation, the source of power can be identified by clarifying who makes the decisions that have the

greatest influence over the most important processes and outcomes.

Most of us can easily identify situations in which decisions are made for us, and we feel coerced. It is more difficult to recognize situations in which we are coercive (see Feature 1). The use of power in efforts to control negative behavior raises concern about coercion and the loss of rights. Behavior modification, medication, screening, referral, placement, suspension, expulsion—all may be beneficial; but such procedures also may be used simply to force individuals to behave as others think they should. All may be misused in ways that deprive individuals of their rights.

Limits

In recent years, it has become clear that the limits imposed in order to control problem behavior in schools often conflict with helping. As one writer has noted, it would not be surprising to hear any student say to a teacher "If you are here to help me . . . why must I do everything your way?" (Weinberg, 1974, p. 15).

One of James's remedial teachers exercised control by insisting that students complete assignments exactly as prescribed, ask for permission before doing anything other than what they were directed to do, and not talk with each other or move around the class. James and most of the other students in the class hated the teacher and the program. Some rebelled and were punished, even to the point of expulsion; others simply did the minimum necessary to avoid severe punishments.

In contrast, the teacher who was most successful in helping David worked with each student to evolve a setting where they could talk quietly while working, move about as needed, and add personal experiences and interests to assignments as they desired. David and the others responded well to such an approach, and there was very little misbehavior.

Many writers have suggested that the overreliance on power and tight limits in many classrooms probably is short-sighted and counterproductive

(Deci, 1980; Dewey, 1938). Such tactics may have an immediate impact on some negative behaviors, but they may interfere with learning and even with the intended long-term socialization. A concern for the future is how to teach practitioners and parents to avoid an overemphasis on using power and tight limits to establish control and how to evolve helping procedures that can lead to cooperation and appropriate social functioning (see Feature 2).

Neither license nor naive permissiveness is an answer to concerns about excessive use of power and limits to control student behavior. What emerging approaches suggest is (1) to increase the range of valued options and realistic choices in classroom programs, and (2) to get rid of limitations that disrupt students' feelings of self-determination and appear to interfere with the establishment of helping relationships. The alternative to taking such steps seems to be a continuation of a large number of student and teacher dropouts, psychologically if not physically.

There's always an easy solution to every human problem — neat, plausible and wrong. (H. L. Mencken)

Expert Role-Playing

Tremendous pressures are exerted on professionals to provide immediate answers and services to the public. In meeting this pressure, cautious optimism, self-criticism, and professional standards often seem to give way to expert role-playing.

Overselling expertise by practitioners and researchers is a major concern in all fields. One facet of overselling expertise has been a trend toward large-scale use of procedures before their appropriate validation. In general, the tendency to overstate expertise appears to be highly related to the fostering of fads, panaceas, and mystical thinking (Frank, 1961; Illich, 1976). Such fads and panaceas reflect an uncritical acceptance of what are often very poor

Feature 1   Social Control in the Classroom

"I do not wish to refer to the traditional school in ways which set up a caricature in lieu of a picture. But I think it is fair to say that one reason the personal commands of the teacher so often played an undue role and a reason why the order which existed was so much a matter of sheer obedience to the will of an adult was because the situation almost forced it upon the teacher. The school was not a group or community held together by participation in common activities. Consequently, the normal, proper conditions of control were lacking. Their absence was made up for, and to a considerable extent had to be made up for, by the direct intervention of the teacher, who, as the saying went, 'kept order.' He kept it because order was in the teacher's keeping, instead of residing in the shared work being done.

"I am not romantic enough about the young to suppose that every pupil will respond or that any child of normally strong impulses will respond on every occasion. There are likely to be some who . . . because of previous experience, are bumptious, and unruly and perhaps downright rebellious. But it is certain that the general principle of social control cannot be predicated upon such cases. It is also true that no general rule can be laid down for dealing with such cases. The teacher has to deal with them individually. He or she cannot, if the educational process is to go on, make it a question of pitting one will against another in order to see which is the strongest, nor yet allow the untidy and non-participating pupils to stand permanently in the way of the educative activities of others. Exclusion perhaps is the only available measure at a given juncture, but it is no solution. For it may strengthen the very causes which have brought about the undesirable antisocial attitude." (Dewey, 1938, pp. 55–57)

"We like children who are a little afraid of us, docile, deferential children, though not, of course, if they are so obviously afraid that they threaten our image of ourselves as kind lovable people whom there is no reason to fear. We find ideal the kind of 'good' children who are just enough afraid of us to do everything we want, without making us feel that fear is what is making them do it." (Holt, 1964, pp. 167–68)

Feature 2   On Limits

Limits may be defined as the degrees of freedom or range of choices allowed an individual in any given situation. Stated differently, limits are the restraints placed on an individual's freedom of choice and action.

The concept of limits provides a basis for understanding the difference between permissiveness and license. The tendency is to use the term *license* when someone goes well beyond, or is encouraged to go well beyond, commonly accepted boundaries for behaving. If James completely ignores the limits that have been set for him and others like him, we see him as taking, or believing he has been given, license to behave very inappropriately.

When the term *permissiveness* is used, the tendency is to apply it to observed efforts to expand commonly accepted limits. If one agrees with such efforts, one may see them as a move toward establishing greater freedom and liberty; if one doesn't like the direction, it probably is seen as a step toward license and anarchy.

The diagram below graphically suggests that varying criteria may be used in establishing limits.

Every day you experience differences in the limits you are expected to stay within. As you go from one setting to another, you will observe that different criteria are used regarding what is acceptable behavior. What is appropriate at home is not appropriate at school. What friends expect is not usually the same as what parents expect.

In which situation do you experience the strictest limits?

For students with problems, schools and particularly special classrooms often are the places where the greatest sense of being controlled and losing freedom is experienced. Often the narrow limits imposed by their school program are much more restrictive than the students are likely to experience anywhere else, either currently or later in life. It has been suggested that this excessive control adds to their dislike of school and teachers (Koestner et al., 1984). What seems surprising is not that many rebel and misbehave under such circumstances but that so many accept as much control as they do.

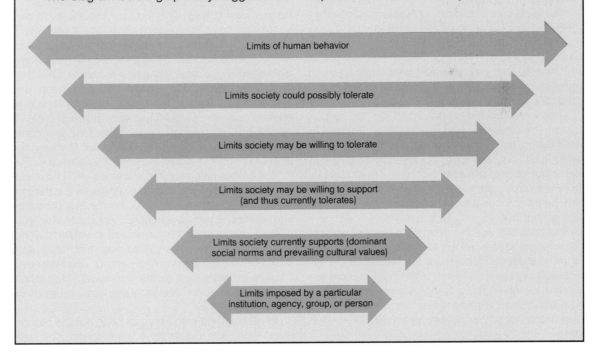

Limits of human behavior

Limits society could possibly tolerate

Limits society may be willing to tolerate

Limits society may be willing to support
(and thus currently tolerates)

Limits society currently supports (dominant
social norms and prevailing cultural values)

Limits imposed by a particular
institution, agency, group, or person

services. As the public is "burned" by many unfulfilled hopes and promises, they become disappointed, frustrated, and angry. The result often is a backlash in the form of malpractice suits, demands for greater accountability, and increasingly detailed government regulation.

We must increase efforts to demystify the general public. Key professionals in such activity are those who teach and write about learning disabilities, those who help shape policy, and those who provide services. The message we need to deliver is simple: Not only don't we know all the answers, we may not be asking some of the most important questions.

Schooling and Helping

Over the years, we have seen the number of students with learning problems increase well beyond the resources available to help them. At first our primary interest was in those who had learning disabilities. We wanted to understand their problems and help them, and thus demonstrate respect for rights, liberties, dignity, and worth. We saw our work as a way to serve society and perhaps improve the quality of education. Such straightforward motives were soon confounded.

We discovered that learning problems were often schooling and societal problems, and that it was impossible to limit our focus to any one subgroup of learning problems. We also found that schooling and helping are very complex phenomena, which sometimes are compatible but very often come into conflict.

These realities led us to reflect on the role of school environments and professional helpers in contributing to the cause of certain learning problems. It did not take long, however, to realize that blaming professionals was to miss the point; that is, there are circumstances that often make schooling and helping incompatible, especially for students who do not fit in.

Professionals working in schools struggle against horrendous odds in efforts to make programs work for most students. Many beat the odds and are remarkably successful. Even the most successful teacher, however, has a few problem students. And in some school districts there are large numbers of students for whom no one seems to know what to do.

One can debate who is at fault and what labels and definitions seem appropriate. Beyond debate, however, is that students in trouble at school need help.

Many school professionals who could provide such help, and who want to, indicate that conflicting societal priorities and pressures on school systems prevent them from doing so. They are asked increasingly to assume functions other than helping or educating, including a wide variety of activities related to caretaking, housekeeping, classroom management, recordkeeping to meet naive accountability demands, babysitting, and police work.

At times, teachers and other school personnel seem to be asked to solve some of society's most difficult problems—illiteracy, delinquency, racial prejudice, and poverty. And as the years go by without any solution for these complex problems, school professionals seem to be the target of society's frustration. In turn, some displace their frustration on those in need of help. This is such a common interpersonal dynamics problem experienced by those in the helping professions that it deserves a few comments before we conclude.

To the Rescue

So you want to help! That's a nice attitude, but it can sometimes lead to trouble—especially if you aren't aware of the interpersonal dynamics that can arise in helping relationships. Several concerns have been discussed in the psychotherapy literature. One that almost everyone has experienced has been described as a "rescue" (Karpman, 1968). A rescue is helping gone astray. Rescues encompass a cycle of negative interpersonal transactions that too commonly arise when one person sets out to intervene in another's life in order to "help" the person.

Think about a time when someone you know told you about a personal problem. Because the person seemed not to know how to handle the problem, you offered some suggestions. For each idea you offered, the person gave a reason it wouldn't work. After a while, you started to feel frustrated and maybe even a bit angry at the person. You may have thought or even said to the individual, "You don't really want to solve this problem; you just want to complain about it."

In rescue terms, you tried to help, but the person didn't work with you to solve the problem. The individual's failure to try may have frustrated you, and you felt angry and wanted to tell the person off. And that may only have been the beginning of a prolonged series of unpleasant interpersonal transactions related to the situation.

If you were ever in such a situation, you certainly experienced the price a person pays for assuming the role of rescuer. Of course, you know you didn't mean to become involved in a negative set of transactions. You wanted to help, but you didn't realize fast enough that the individual with the problem wasn't interested in working with you to solve it. And you didn't know what to do when things started going wrong with the process.

If you can't remember a time you were the rescuer, you may recall a time when someone tried to rescue you. Perhaps your parents, a teacher, or a good friend made the mistake of trying to help you in ways you didn't want to be helped. The person probably thought she or he was acting in your best interests, but it only made you feel upset; perhaps it increased your anxiety, frustration, anger, and maybe it even made you feel inadequate.

Rescue cycles occur frequently between teachers and students and parents and their children. Well-intentioned efforts to help usually begin to go astray because someone tries to help at a time, in a way, or toward an end the person to be helped doesn't experience as positive.

Let's take the example of a teacher, Ms. Benevolent, and one of her students, Jack. Ms. Benevolent is a new teacher who has just begun to work with a group of students with learning problems. She sees her students, Jack included, as handicapped individuals, and she wants so much to help them.

Unfortunately, Jack doesn't want to be helped at the moment. And when he doesn't want to be helped, Jack is not mobilized to work on solving his problems. Indeed, efforts to intervene often make him feel negative toward his teacher and even toward himself. For example, he may feel anger toward Ms. Benevolent and feel guilty and incompetent because of not working to solve his learning problem. Ironically, not only doesn't he see the teacher as a helper, but he also feels victimized by her. In response to these feelings, he behaves in a self-protective and defensive manner. Sometimes he even assumes the stance of being a helpless victim. ("How can you expect me to do that? Don't you know I have a learning handicap?")

Because Jack continues to respond passively, or in ways the teacher views as inappropriate, eventually she becomes upset and starts to react to him in nonhelpful and sometimes provocative ways. She may even have a tendency subtly to persecute Jack for not being appreciative of all her efforts to help him. ("You're just lazy." "If your attitude doesn't improve, I'm going to have to call your parents.")

The more the teacher pushes Jack to act differently and attacks him for acting (and feeling) as he does, the more likely he is to feel victimized. However, sooner or later he will probably become angry enough about being victimized that he reacts and counterattacks. That is, if he can, he shifts from the role of victim to the role of persecutor.

When interveners who see themselves as benevolent helpers are attacked, they may tend to feel victimized. Indeed, the experience of having been unsuccessful in helping may be sufficient to make some interveners feel this way. As Jack shifts to a persecuting role, Ms. Benevolent adopts a victim role. ("*After all I've done for you, how can you treat me this way?*" "*All I'm trying to do is help you.*")

Of course, interveners are unlikely to remain victims for very long if they can help it. If they do, "burnout" may well occur.

Sometimes, after the fighting stops, the parties make up, and the intervener starts to see the other person's behavior as part of the individual's problems and tries once more to help. However, if great care is not taken, this just begins the whole cycle again.

How can the cycle be avoided or broken? As we have stressed in Chapter 8, one of the essential ingredients in a good helping relationship is a person who wants to be helped. Thus it is necessary to be sure that the person is ready and willing to pursue the type of help that is being offered.

If the person is not ready and willing, interveners are left with only a few options. For one, the intervener can choose to give up trying to help. Or, if it is essential that the individual be *forced* to do something about the problem, the intervener can adopt a socialization strategy. Or effort can be made to explore with the individual whether he or she wants to think about accepting some help. This last approach involves trying to establish the motivational readiness discussed throughout this book.

IV.6   Cultural and Individual Differences as Barriers to Working Relationships

In working with individuals who have learning problems, we must be sensitive to a variety of human, community, and institutional differences and learn strategies for dealing with them. In working with students and their parents, differences will be encountered in

- sociocultural and economic background and current lifestyle
- primary language spoken
- skin color
- sex
- motivation for help

In addition, there are differences related to power, status, and orientation. Comparable differences are found among school personnel (clerks, teachers, nurses, psychologists, counselors, administrators).

Differences as a Problem

The range of differences may make it difficult to establish effective working relationships with students and others who affect them. For example, many schools do not have staff who can communicate effectively with students whose primary language is Spanish, Korean, Tagalog, Vietnamese, Cambodian, Farsi, or Armenian. Racial and ethnic differences between staff and students produce additional problems.

Workshops are often offered in an effort to increase specific cultural awareness. Unfortunately what can be learned in this way is limited, especially in a school of many cultures. Moreover, in the initial stages of increasing cultural sensitivity, there is a danger in prejudgments based on apparent cultural awareness. There are many reports of students who have been victimized by professionals so sensitized to cultural differences that they treat fourth-generation Americans as if they had just emigrated from their cultural homeland. Obviously the desired situation is to have language skills and cultural awareness, and to avoid overgeneralizations.

The objectives of accounting for relevant differences while respecting individuality can be successfully addressed, but accomplishing these objectives requires considerably more than consciousness raising. The fact of staff and student diversity must be used; that is, in building working relationships, we must learn to capitalize on the existence of individuals from diverse cultural and racial backgrounds. For example, differences among staff and students can be complementary and helpful, just as they are when staff from different disciplines work with and learn from each other. Students and parents who are bilingual and bicultural can also assist in a variety of ways.

Differences become a barrier to establishing effective working relationships among staff and to helping students when negative attitudes are allowed to prevail (see Feature 1). Generally the result is avoidance or conflict and poor communication. For example, differences in status, skin color, power, or orientation can cause people to enter a situation with negative feelings. Such feelings often motivate conflict. Many individuals who have been treated unfairly, been discriminated against, or been deprived of opportunity at school, on the job, and in society, use whatever means they can to seek redress or to strike back. Such an individual may promote conflict to try to correct power imbalances or call attention to a problem. However, power differentials are often so institutionalized that individual action has little impact.

It is frustrating to fight an institution. It is much easier, and may be more immediately satisfying, to fight with those who represent that institution. When this occurs in situations where individuals are supposed to work together, those with negative feelings may act in ways that produce significant barriers to a working relationship. Often the underlying message is, "You don't understand," or worse yet, "You probably don't want to understand." Or, even worse, "You are my enemy."

It is unfortunate when such barriers arise between students and those trying to help them; it is a travesty when such barriers interfere with staff working together effectively. Staff conflicts detract from accomplishing goals for students with learning and behavior problems and contribute in a major way to burnout.

Overcoming Barriers

When the problem is only one of lack of awareness and poor skills, it is relatively easy to overcome. Most motivated individuals can be directly taught ways to improve understanding and resolve conflicts that interfere with working relationships.

Inservice sessions, selected readings, and multicultural/interracial teaming allow staff to learn from each other. Students and their parents and community representatives can be tremendous resources for enhancing staff and student understanding and improving relationship skills.

There are, however, no easy solutions to over-coming deeply embedded negative attitudes. Certainly a first step is to understand that the problem is not differences per se, but negative perceptions stemming from the politics and psychology of the situation. It is these perceptions that lead to (1) negative prejudgments (one can't work effectively with a person because of an observed difference), and (2) the desire not to work with the individual.

Minimally, the task of overcoming negative perceptions that interfere with a particular working relationship is twofold. We need to find ways

1. to counter negative prejudgments (to establish the credibility of those who have been prejudged)
2. to demonstrate there is something of value to be gained from working together

Although the following excerpt is from an article specifically written about relations between blacks

Feature 1   Differences as a Barrier

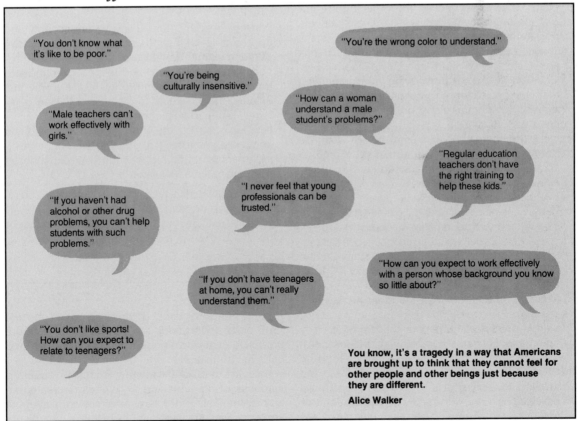

"You don't know what it's like to be poor."

"You're the wrong color to understand."

"You're being culturally insensitive."

"How can a woman understand a male student's problems?"

"Male teachers can't work effectively with girls."

"Regular education teachers don't have the right training to help these kids."

"If you haven't had alcohol or other drug problems, you can't help students with such problems."

"I never feel that young professionals can be trusted."

"How can you expect to work effectively with a person whose background you know so little about?"

"If you don't have teenagers at home, you can't really understand them."

"You don't like sports! How can you expect to relate to teenagers?"

You know, it's a tragedy in a way that Americans are brought up to think that they cannot feel for other people and other beings just because they are different.
Alice Walker

and whites, it has much relevance to interracial working relationships in general.

To grow up in contemporary society means to be bombarded by stereotypes, negative images, and misinformation that favor whites and degrade blacks. Therefore, we have all been exposed to and have incorporated some degree of racism. It would be remarkable to grow up nonracist given the racism in schools, on television and radio, in books, magazines, and newspapers, and given the absence of training for adults or children in how to tolerate, accept, and appreciate cultural differences. So we conclude that the first task in any interracial relationship is to acknowledge that we are all racist. . . .

The second task is for us to realize that racism takes different forms and that getting beyond racism requires a different process for a black than for a white person. A black person may need to discard the stereotypes of white women as exploitative, condescending, incompetent, silly, or untrustworthy. . . . Whites are more often in the position of needing information about blacks. . . . There is relatively little information about black arts, culture, and history in the mainstream press.

When we are no longer trying to be something that is impossible in this culture—nonracist—we are less vulnerable to guilt or defensiveness and it is easier to change. . . .

For an interpersonal [relationship] to work, we believe, the partners need both intention and commitment. These concepts operate politically as well as interpersonally.

Politically, . . . we need to be aware of the pervasiveness of institutional racism and its negative effects, and to work against that racism.

. . . Personally, we need to have good intentions in the [relationship] and commitment to the individual. . . . It is not acceptable to say, "I didn't mean to be offensive or hurt anyone," expecting to be let off the hook. On the other hand, good intentions also allow us to make some social blunders in the act of becoming less racist.

. . . Intention and commitment are inseparable. We must dedicate ourselves to change by actively pinpointing our own racist behavior and working to eliminate it." ("Women's Interracial Friendships," by Althea Smith and Stephanie Nickerson in *Women's Studies Quarterly, XIV,* Spring/Summer, 1986)

Building Rapport and Connection

To be effective in working with another person (student, parent, staff), you need to build a positive relationship around the tasks at hand. Necessary ingredients in building a working relationship are:

- minimizing negative prejudgments about those with whom you will be working
- taking time to make connections
- identifying what will be gained from the collaboration in terms of mutually desired outcomes—to clarify the value of working together
- enhancing expectations that the working relationship will be productive—important here is establishing credibility with each other
- establishing a structure that provides support and guidance to aid task focus
- providing periodic reminders of the positive outcomes that have resulted from working together

As to building relationships and effective communication, three things you can do are:

- convey empathy (the ability to understand and appreciate what the individual is thinking and feeling) and warmth (a sense of liking)
- convey genuine regard and respect (the ability to transmit real interest and to interact in a way that enables the individual to maintain a feeling of integrity and personal control)
- talk *with,* not *at,* the individual—active listening and dialogue (being a good listener, not being judgmental, not prying, sharing your experiences as appropriate and needed)

Ensuring confidentiality is also fundamental to building a positive working relationship.

Finally, watch out for ego-oriented behavior (yours and theirs). It tends to get in the way of accomplishing the task at hand.

Summing Up

In most situations, direct or indirect accusations that *"You don't understand"* are valid. Indeed, they are givens. After all, most people do not fully understand complex situations or what others are feeling.

In trying to build a working relationship, accusing someone of not understanding tends to create major barriers. This is not surprising, since the intent of such accusations generally is to make others uncomfortable and put them on the defensive.

It is hard to build positive connections with a defensive person. Avoidance of *"You don't understand"* accusations may be a productive way to reduce at least one set of major barriers to establishing working relationships.

Active steps toward building positive connections involve such fundamentals as conveying genuine empathy, warmth, regard, and respect. Self-criticism and self-disclosure can help create an atmosphere where defensiveness is minimized. Expressing appreciation for efforts in the right direction is also helpful. After a positive working relationship is established, it becomes feasible for the persons involved to help each other reduce inappropriate prejudgments and become increasingly sensitive to important differences related to culture, race, sex, age, professional orientation, and so forth.

Finally, it is essential to remember that accounting for individual differences is fundamental to working effectively with others. This point was poignantly illustrated by an event experienced by a school psychologist.

A Korean student who had been in the United States for several years and spoke comprehensible English came to the school psychologist seeking help for a personal problem. Trying to be sensitive to cultural differences, the psychologist referred the student to an Asian counselor. The student met with the counselor, but did not bring up his personal problem and did not return for a second scheduled session.

In a follow-up interview conducted by a non-Asian staff member, the student explained that the idea of telling his personal problems to another Asian was too embarrassing. Then why had he come in the first place?

Well, he did not understand he would be sent to an Asian. He had expected to work with the "blue-eyed counselor" a friend had told him about.

IV.7 Managing and Preventing School Misbehavior

Interventions to deal with misbehavior can be categorized in terms of phases, namely, efforts to prevent and anticipate misbehavior, actions to be taken during misbehavior, and steps to be taken afterwards. An understanding of intrinsic motivation in general, and reactive and proactive deviance in particular, has major implications for each of these intervention phases. For example, with respect to prevention, regardless of theoretical orientation most professionals recognize that social and school program improvements could reduce learning and behavior problems significantly. There is increasing acceptance that a primary preventive step involves normative changes in classroom programs. From the perspective of intrinsic motivation theory, such changes include designing classroom instruction to better match the broad range of differences in students' intrinsic motivation as well as their difference in capability. Such changes have been discussed as an essential prerequisite to individual intervention (Adelman, 1989; Adelman & Taylor, 1985a, 1986; Maher & Zins, 1987; Millman, Schaefer, & Cohen, 1981).

However, even if primary and secondary preventive steps are taken, there remains the necessity of intervening with individuals who continue to be troublesome. Discussions of practices for dealing with such students often are organized around the topics of discipline, classroom management, and student behavioral self-management. An appreciation of the role intrinsic motivation plays in deviant and devious behavior suggests approaches to such behavior that go beyond current disciplinary and management practices. Before discussing these matters, however, it is important to acknowledge the necessity of dealing with the impact of misbehavior and to highlight practical and research implications related to minimizing negative motivational and behavioral repercussions.

Discipline, Logical Consequences, and Recipient Perceptions

The first concern of school personnel is almost always with the impact of misbehavior, and rightly so.

Such behavior disrupts; it may be hurtful; it may disinhibit others. Thus, when a youngster misbehaves, a natural reaction is to want that youngster to experience, and other students to see, the consequences of misbehaving in hopes that consequences will deter subsequent misbehavior. Because the impact of misbehavior usually is the first concern, the primary focus of intervention usually is on discipline (Charles, 1985; Dreikurs, Grunwald, & Pepper, 1982; Hyman, Flanagan, & Smith, 1982; Knoff, 1987; Wolfgang & Glickman, 1986).

Given the primary role assigned to disciplinary practices, it is essential that their impact on intrinsic motivation be considered and investigated. Thus we highlight some motivational concerns as a stimulus for practice and research.

Discipline

Knoff (1987) presents three definitions of discipline as applied in schools:

> (a) . . . a punitive intervention; (b) . . . a means of suppressing or eliminating inappropriate behavior, of teaching or reinforcing appropriate behavior, and of redirecting potentially inappropriate behavior toward acceptable ends; and (c) . . . a process of self-control whereby the (potentially) misbehaving student applies techniques that interrupt inappropriate behavior, and that replace it with acceptable behavior. (p. 119)

In contrast to the first definition, which specifies discipline as punishment, Knoff sees the other two as nonpunitive—or, as he calls them, "positive, best-practices approaches." He appears to make this distinction because of the general recognition that punishment is an undesirable form of discipline and to be used only in an emergency.

Given current circumstances, school personnel often see punishment as the only recourse in dealing with a student's misbehavior. They use the most potent negative consequences available to them in a desperate effort to control an individual and make it clear to others that acting in such a fashion will not be tolerated. Such punishment takes the form of a decision to do something to the student that he or she does not want done. A demand for future compliance usually is made, along with threats of harsher punishment if compliance is not forthcoming, and the discipline may be administered in a way that suggests the student is seen officially as an undesirable person.

As with many emergency procedures, benefits produced by using punishment may be offset by a variety of negative consequences (increases in negative attitudes toward school and school personnel that often lead to other forms of misbehavior). Thus, as soon as the emergency is resolved, or in nonemergency situations, the emphasis often shifts from punishment to implementing logical consequences.

Logical Consequences and Recipient Perceptions

Guidelines for managing misbehavior generally emphasize the desirability of having discipline seen as reasonable, fair, and nondenigrating. Intrinsic motivation theory specifically stresses that "positive, best-practice approaches" are disciplinary acts recipients experience as legitimate reactions that neither denigrate one's sense of worth nor reduce one's sense of autonomy (Deci & Ryan, 1985). To these ends, discussions of classroom management practices usually emphasize establishing and administering logical consequences. This idea is evident in situations where there are naturally occurring consequences (if you touch a hot stove, you get burned).

In classrooms there may be little ambiguity about the rules; unfortunately, the same often cannot be said about "logical" penalties. Even when the consequence for a particular rule infraction has been specified ahead of time, its logic may be more in the mind of the teacher than in the eye of the student. Indeed, the distinctions made by Knoff reflect an observer's perspective of discipline. In the recipient's view, any act of discipline may be experienced as punitive (unreasonable, unfair, denigrating, disempowering).

Consequences involve depriving students of something they want or making them experience something they don't want. Consequences usually take the form of (a) removal/deprivation (loss of privileges, removal from an activity), (b) reprimands (public censure), (c) reparations (compensation for any losses arising from the misbehavior), and (d)

recantations (apologies, plans for avoiding future problems). For instance, teachers commonly deal with acting-out behavior by removing a student from an activity. To the teacher, this step (often described as "time out") may be seen as a logical way to stop the student from disrupting others by isolating, or the logic may be that the student needs a cooling-off period. It may be reasoned that (a) by misbehaving, students show they do not deserve the privilege of participating (assuming they like the activity), and (b) the loss will lead to improved behavior in order to avoid future deprivation.

Most teachers have little difficulty explaining their reasons for using a particular consequence. However, if the intent really is to have students perceive consequences as logical and nondebilitating, it seems necessary to determine whether the recipient sees a disciplinary act as a legitimate response to misbehavior. It is well to recognize the difficulty of administering consequences in a way that minimizes the negative impact on the recipient's perceptions of self. Although the intent is to demonstrate that the misbehavior and its impact are bad, students can too easily construe that they themselves are seen as bad.

Organized sports for young people provide examples of established and accepted sets of consequences that respect the recipient's perceptions. In these arenas, the referee is able to use the rules and related criteria to identify inappropriate acts and apply penalties; this is done with positive concern for maintaining the youngster's dignity as well as engendering respect for others.

For discipline to be seen as a logical consequence, it may be necessary to take steps to convey (a) that disciplinary responses are not personally motivated acts of power (authoritarian actions) and, at the same time, (b) that the social order has established rational reactions to a student's behavior when it negatively affects others. Also, if the intent of the discipline is a long-term reduction in future misbehavior, it may be necessary to take steps to help students learn right from wrong, to respect others' rights, and to accept responsibility. Towards these ends, motivational theorists suggest it may be useful to (a) establish a publicly accepted set of consequences to increase the likelihood that students experience them as socially just (reasonable, firm but fair), and (b) administer such consequences in ways that allow students to maintain a sense of integrity, dignity, and autonomy (Brehm & Brehm, 1981; Deci

& Ryan, 1985). These ends are probably best achieved under conditions where students are empowered (involved in deciding how to rectify the situation, avoid future misbehavior, and become positively involved in reputation building at school).

From a motivational perspective, it is essential to (a) gain a better understanding of recipient perceptions of discipline, and (b) develop disciplinary practices that minimize negative repercussions. These are both areas where there is a dearth of direct research.

Addressing Underlying Motivation

Beyond discipline, there is a need for research on interventions designed to address the roots of misbehavior, especially the underlying motivational bases for such behavior. Consider students who spend most of the day trying to avoid all or part of the instructional program. An intrinsic motivational interpretation of these youngsters is that it reflects their perception that school is not a place where they experience a sense of competence, autonomy, or relatedness to others. Over time, these perceptions develop into strong motivational dispositions and related patterns of misbehavior.

Relevant interventions for such problems begin with major changes in social and school programs. The aims of such changes with respect to motivational problems are to (a) prevent and overcome negative attitudes toward school and learning, (b) enhance motivational readiness for learning and overcoming problems that arise, (c) maintain intrinsic motivation throughout learning and problem-solving processes, and (d) nurture the type of continuing motivation that results in students engaging in activities away from school that can facilitate maintenance, generalization, and expansion of learning and problem solving. Failure to attend to these motivational concerns in a comprehensive, normative manner results in approaching passive and often hostile students with practices that can instigate and exacerbate many learning and behavior problems.

After accomplishing broad programmatic changes to the degree feasible, intervention with a misbehaving student involves remedial steps directed at specific factors associated with unintentional, proactive and/or reactive deviance. Because the concern here is with intentional behavior problems, the focus in the following sections is primarily on reactive and proactive misbehavior. First we highlight a few implications for counseling and consulting and then we discuss implications for general changes in school programs.

Counseling and Consulting

Understanding the motivational ideas just discussed can profoundly influence research and practice focused on counseling individuals who misbehave and consulting with their teachers and parents. For instance, with intrinsic motivation in mind, the following assessment questions arise:

- Is the misbehavior unintentional or intentional?
- If it is intentional, is it reactive or proactive?
- If the misbehavior is reactive, is it a reaction to threats to self-determination, competence, or relatedness?
- If it is proactive, are there other interests that might successfully compete with satisfaction derived from deviant behavior?

Answers to these questions may come from teachers, parents, or student. (To rule out a skill deficit, data also are needed on the youngster's abilities.) However, because of attributional biases, one can expect these interested parties to offer differing causal views (Jones & Nisbett, 1971; Miller & Ross, 1975; Monson & Snyder, 1975). Rather than viewing these differences as confounding assessment, such data can help clarify the student's underlying motivation and how others interpret that motivation. Both are central to planning corrective strategies aimed at affecting the student's intrinsic motivation. Differing perceptions can compound a problem by resulting in different analyses of what's wrong and what should be done. Awareness of differences in perceived cause enables interveners to explore how these differences are affecting the actions of each interested party and to clarify which perceptions may be counterproductive in resolving the problem.

Intrinsic motivational theory suggests that individual corrective interventions for reactive misbehavior require steps designed to reduce reactance and enhance positive motivation. For youngsters highly motivated to pursue deviance (those who choose to engage in criminal acts, for example), even more is needed. Intervention might focus on helping these youngsters identify and follow through on a range of valued, socially appropriate alternatives to deviant activity. From the theoretical perspective, such alternatives must be capable of producing greater feelings of self-determination, competence, and relatedness than usually result from the youngster's deviant actions.

To these ends, motivational analyses of the problem can point to corrective steps for implementation by teachers, clinicians, parents, or students themselves. If misbehavior is unintentional, the focus of intervention at school, in the clinic, and at home probably only needs to be directed at reducing stress and building skills. However, if the behavior is intentional, all interested parties probably should be encouraged to

- eliminate situations leading to reactivity and establish alternative ways for the student to cope with what cannot be changed
- establish activity options designed to redirect proactive misbehavior toward prosocial interests and behavior

For example, consultants might help teachers and parents understand motivational bases for a youngster's misbehavior and facilitate environment and program changes that account for the youngster's need to feel self-determining, competent, and related. Similarly, in direct counseling with students whose misbehavior is intentionally reactive, short-term work might stress increasing a student's awareness about how to work with others to produce circumstances that better match his or her psychological needs. Comparable counseling might be provided to those exhibiting proactive deviance; however, evidence from delinquent populations suggests short-term counseling in such cases is rather ineffective. Indeed, for both groups, it must be acknowledged that little is known about how effective even long-term psychotherapy or behavior-change strategies might be. Nevertheless, long-term intervention generally is described as providing the time frame necessary for dealing with students' affect, increasing their understanding of why they behave as they do, and exploring the possibility of change (Lambert, Shapiro, & Bergin, 1986). How well such outcomes can be achieved awaits appropriate evaluative research (Adelman, 1986; Maher & Bennett, 1984).

Motivationally, an appropriate test of the efficacy of long-term psychotherapeutic and behavior-change interventions for intentional misbehavior requires more than just specifying what we want youngsters to understand and do. Achievement of such objectives requires interventions that systematically address intrinsic motivation. To be specific, intervention must deal with the initial attitudes these youngsters are likely to bring to the counseling situation. They are unlikely to approach the process positively or even neutrally; there are negative attitudes to overcome. Assuming negative attitudes are overcome, the intervener must be able to (a) enhance the youngster's motivational readiness to develop a *working* relationship, and (b) maintain the youngster's positive intrinsic motivation for as long as intervention is needed. In terms of the motivational concepts discussed, the process should strive from beginning to end to stimulate feelings of self-determination, competence, and interpersonal relatedness. Finally, the intervention should focus on intrinsic motivation as an outcome objective. That is, the process should nurture the type of ongoing intrinsic motivation that results in the youngster's engaging in activities away from the intervention setting that facilitate maintenance and generalization of problem-solving behavior.

School Program Changes to Deal with Reactive Misbehavior

A student who perceives school personnel and activities as threats to self-determination, competence, and sense of relatedness to others may react in protective ways. For instance, a student who expects to do poorly on an assigned classroom task may misbehave as a way of protesting and avoiding the activity (Brehm & Brehm, 1981; Kaplan, 1980). If the teacher's reaction to the misbehavior is to threaten or apply punitive measures, the student may react in increasingly negative ways. The case of David provides an example.

Because of his many experiences of failure at school, David tends to perceive learning situations as threatening. Even before he knows much about a task, he expects to have difficulty coping. Thus, he feels vulnerable, fearful, and sometimes angry at being pushed into such situations. He would like to avoid them, and if he can't do so directly, he tries indirect ways, such as diverting the teacher to a discussion of other matters. When he can't manipulate the situation effectively, he engages in various acting-out behaviors, such as arguing, inciting the class to disruption, or regularly missing school. This often leads to a power struggle with the teacher, which ends with David sent to the principal or home. After a number of such experiences, he has developed rather strong negative expectations and attitudes about school and teachers and has learned a rather large range of behaviors to protect himself from what he perceives as bad situations. Unfortunately, the more he displays such behavior, the more those around him tend to think of him as uncontrollable and incorrigible.

A great deal of negative behavior by students such as David may reflect reactions to immediate school pressures. Those with long or intense histories of school problems may develop general expectations that most classroom experiences are hurtful. Given this expectation, a student may approach all classroom situations looking for the worst and thus perceiving it. Even when a teacher offers "exciting" new opportunities, the student may not perceive them as such.

If the intention is to address the motivational underpinnings for reactive misbehavior, two intervention process objectives seem fundamental: (1) to minimize external demands to perform and conform (eliminate threats) and (2) to explore learning activities with the student to identify which would be nonthreatening and interesting replacements (establish a program of intrinsically motivated activity). To these ends, intervention focuses first on assessing (if feasible) the nature of any perceived threats. Such an assessment is guided by motivational thinking about threats to perceived self-determination, competence, and relatedness. The data are then used to replace threatening situations and tasks with activity that produces positive perceptions with respect to identified psychological needs. Even if the specific areas of threat cannot be assessed, we can proceed to work with the student to eliminate and replace aspects of the program against which the student appears to be reacting.

In making changes, it is important to realize that students with extremely negative perceptions of teachers and school programs are not likely to be open to "new" activities that look like "the same old thing." There have to be vivid variations in alternatives offered for students to perceive differences. Several key elements of such interventions are summarized after the following discussion of proactive misbehavior.

School Program Changes to Deal with Proactive Misbehavior

Proactive misbehavior is aimed at directly producing feelings of satisfaction. That is, noncooperative, dis-ruptive, and aggressive behavior may be rewarding or satisfying to an individual because the behavior itself is exciting or because the behavior leads to desired outcomes (peer recognition, feelings of autonomy or competence). Intentional negative behavior stemming from such approach motivation can be viewed as the direct pursuit of deviance.

In practice, it is not easy to differentiate reactive and proactive misbehavior. For example, one student may proactively engage in decorating school walls with graffiti because it is interesting and exciting; another may do it to impress a peer group. Still another may reactively engage in such behavior because of anger toward school authorities. (Subsequently, this last student may acquire negative role models, such as gang members, and adopt their pattern of proactive misbehavior.) And, of course, students involved in deviant behavior inevitably come into conflict with school authorities and soon manifest additional reactive misbehavior.

Proactive misbehavior, such as staying home to watch TV or hang out with friends, participating with gangs, using drugs, and baiting authority, may be much more interesting and exciting to some students than any activity schools offer. That is probably why proactive misbehavior is so difficult to alter. From the perspective of intrinsic motivation theory, the fundamental objective of intervention in such cases is to establish a program of intrinsically motivated activity powerful enough to compete with the satisfaction gained from the misbehavior. This means the intervener must be able to explore options well beyond the norm to replace the student's current school program. Because such students are unlikely to give up their pursuit of deviance quickly, it may be necessary initially to accommodate a wider range of behavior than is typically accepted in schools; that is, if we want to recapture the interest of such students, we may have to increase tolerance temporarily for "bad manners" (some rudeness, some swearing), eccentric mannerisms (strange clothing and grooming), and temporary nonparticipation.

To be more specific, it may be necessary to begin by exploring with the student (a) topical interests (sports, rock music, movies and TV shows, computer games, auto mechanics), and (b) desired activities (working with certain individuals, use of nonstandard materials, special status roles). Such personal interests can be used as a starting point.

Exploring areas of interest may have to be continued until the student identifies a specific topic that he or she would like to learn more about. Concomitantly, the intervener may have to redefine rules and standards so that limits on behavior are expanded for such students (certain behaviors are tolerated and not treated as misbehavior). Failure to do so may account for the large proportion of these students who are pushed out or drop out due to constant conflict over misconduct.

The example of Harry, whom we mentioned earlier, suggests the extremes that may have to be attempted.

Harry would come to school, but he had no interest in working on what his teachers had planned. He spent much of the time talking to friends and looking for exciting ways to make the time pass. He was frequently in the midst of whatever trouble was occurring in class. He was unresponsive to threats of punishment. He readily accepted suspensions. It seemed clear that unless something dramatic were done he would be expelled from school. Rather than letting the tragedy run its course, it was decided to try an experimental intervention. The teacher set aside time to help Harry identify one area of personal interest that he would like to learn more about. After some discussion, he indicated he wanted to be a rock musician and would be interested in learning more about how people got into the field and in improving his musical skills.

Several interesting and realistic activities were identified that Harry agreed he would pursue, such as writing letters to musicians and agencies, setting up instrument instruction and practice time, and reading relevant publications. It was clear, however, that the one topic and the few activities would hold his interest for only 1 to 2 hours a day. Thus, it was easy to anticipate that he would simply fall into his pattern of misbehaving for the remainder of the day, and the experimental effort to counter his misbehavior by building an intrinsically motivating program would be defeated.

The solution devised for this problem was as simple as it was controversial. Harry was scheduled to come to school only for that period of time during which he had planned a program he intended to pursue. The reasoning was twofold: (1) It is clear that students such as Harry only work when they are working on what they have identified as desirable, and (2) they not only waste the rest of the time, they use it to pursue deviant behavior. If they are not at school a full day, they are less likely to get into trouble at school. More important, the less that school personnel are in the position of coercing and punishing them, the less likely the problem will be confounded by misbehavior that is a reaction to such practices. Moreover, when such students no longer are expending energy in misbehaving, they are in a better position to work with the teacher to evolve an increasing range of academic interests.

Indeed, it was a matter of only a few weeks before Harry indicated several additional areas of interest, including a desire to improve his reading. To accommodate his interests, his school day was expanded. Within a period of several months, he was regularly attending school all day, pursuing a combination of personally designated areas of interest and an increasing amount of the basic curriculum.

Clearly, there are many practical, economic, and legal problems involved in strategies such as cutting back on the length of a student's school day. However, we must consider the costs to society and individuals that derive from forcing certain students to be at school all day when it interferes with correcting their problems. It may be better to have a student's time at school temporarily reduced for positive reasons rather than as punishment (suspensions) or because of truancy. For older students, of course, a shortened day paired with a parttime job or apprenticeship already is an accepted and often productive strategy.

Summing Up

As stated above, it is important to realize that students with extremely negative perceptions of teachers and school programs may not respond to changes that look like "the same old thing." As suggested throughout this book, it seems necessary at least to make exceptional efforts to have students (a) view the teacher as supportive (rather than hostile and controlling or indifferent), and (b) perceive curricular and behavioral options as personally valuable and obtainable. Comprehensive, motivationally oriented intervention research is needed to clarify ways to produce major changes in students' perceptions about such matters.

In this brief discussion of interventions related to school misbehavior, we have only been able to touch upon a few major areas of practice. Table 1 is offered to provide a more comprehensive perspective on the nature and scope of needed intervention activity. An understanding of the intrinsic motivational bases for deviant and devious behavior generates profound implications for intervention research and practice. For example, such an understanding points to assessment questions, classification concepts, and corrective strategies that otherwise might be ignored. It also highlights the need for comprehensive research programs to develop and evaluate interventions that address motivational underpinnings of school misbehavior. Data from such research could shed considerable light on cause and correction with respect to all psychoeducational problems.

Table 1   Focus of Interventions for Dealing with Misbehavior

I. **Preventing misbehavior**

    A. Expand social programs

        1. Increase economic opportunity for low-income groups

        2. Augment health and safety prevention and maintenance (encompassing parent education and direct child services)

        3. Extend quality day care and early education

    B. Improve schooling

        1. Personalize classroom instruction (accommodating a wide range of motivational and developmental differences)

        2. Provide status opportunities for nonpopular students (e.g., special roles as assistants and tutors)

        3. Identify and remedy skill deficiencies early

    C. Follow up all occurrences of misbehavior to remedy causes

        1. Identify underlying motivation for misbehavior

        2. For unintentional misbehavior, strengthen coping skills (social skills, problem-solving strategies)

        3. If misbehavior is intentional but reactive, work to eliminate conditions that produce reactions (conditions that make the student feel incompetent, controlled, or unrelated to significant others)

        4. For proactive misbehavior, offer appropriate and attractive alternative ways the student can pursue a sense of competence, control, and relatedness

        5. Equip the individual with acceptable steps to take instead of misbehaving (options to withdraw from a situation or to try relaxation techniques)

        6. Enhance the individual's motivation and skills for overcoming behavior problems (including altering negative attitudes toward school)

II. **Anticipating misbehavior**

    A. Personalize classroom structure for high-risk students

        1. Identify underlying motivation for misbehavior

        2. Design curricula to consist primarily of activities that are a good match with the identified individual's intrinsic motivation and developmental capability

        3. Provide extra support and direction so the identified individual can cope with difficult situations (including steps that can be taken instead of misbehaving)

    B. Develop consequences for misbehavior that are perceived by students as logical (that are perceived by the student as reasonably fair, and nondenigrating reactions which do not reduce one's sense of autonomy)

III. **During misbehavior**

    A. Try to base response on understanding of underlying motivation (if uncertain, start with assumption the misbehavior is unintentional)

    B. Reestablish a calm and safe atmosphere

        1. Use understanding of student's underlying motivation for misbehaving to clarify what occurred (if feasible, involve participants in discussion of events)

        2. Validate each participant's perspective and feelings

        3. Indicate how the matter will be resolved emphasizing use of previously agreed upon logical consequences that have been personalized in keeping with understanding of underlying motivation

4. If the misbehavior continues, revert to a firm but nonauthoritarian statement indicating it must stop or else the student will have to be suspended
5. As a last resort use crises back-up resources
    a. If appropriate, ask student's classroom friends to help
    b. Call for help from identified back-up personnel
6. Throughout the process, keep others calm by dealing with the situation with a calm and protective demeanor

IV. **After misbehavior**

A. Implement discipline—logical consequences/punishment
    1. Objectives in using consequences
        a. To deprive student of something wanted
        b. To make student experience something not wanted
    2. Forms of consequences
        a. Removal/deprivation (loss of privileges, removal from activity)
        b. Reprimands (public censure)
        c. Reparations (damaged or stolen property)
        d. Recantations (apologies, plans for avoiding future problems)

B. Discuss the problem with parents
    1. Explain how they can avoid exacerbating the problem
    2. Mobilize them to work preventively with school

C. Work toward prevention of further occurrences (see I & II)

References

In most cases, references cited in full in other sections of the book are not repeated here. These include the brief bibliography to works on remedial methods cited at the end of Chapter 11, those on brain function and assessment at the end of Readings Section I.2 ("CNS Function and Assessment of Minor Dysfunction") and the references to specific assessment procedures provided at the end of Readings Section II.1 ("Procedures and Instruments for Assessing Learning Problems").

Abikoff, H. (1979). Cognitive training interventions in children: Review of a new approach. *Journal of Learning Disabilities, 12,* 123–35.

Adams, M. J. (1990). *Beginning to read: Thinking and learning about print.* Cambridge, MA: MIT Press.

Adelman, H. S. (1970–71). Learning problems, Part I: An interactional view of causality. *Academic Therapy, 6,* 117–23.

Adelman, H. S. (1971). The not so specific learning disability population. *Exceptional Children, 8,* 114–20.

Adelman, H. S. (1972). Teacher education and youngsters with learning problems, Part III: The problem pupil and the specialist teacher. *Journal of Learning Disabilities, 5,* 593–604.

Adelman, H. S. (1978). The concept of intrinsic motivation: Implications for practice and research with the learning disabled. *Learning Disability Quarterly, 1,* 43–54.

Adelman, H. S. (1986). Intervention theory and evaluating efficacy. *Evaluation Review, 10,* 65–83.

Adelman, H. S. (1989). Prediction and prevention of learning disabilities: Current state of the art and future directions. In L. Bond & B. Compas (Eds.), *Primary prevention in the schools* (pp. 106–145). Newbury Park, CA: Sage.

Adelman, H. S. (1992). LD: The next 25 years. *Journal of Learning Disabilities, 25,* 17–22.

Adelman, H. S., Kaser-Boyd, N. & Taylor, L. (1984). Children's participation in consent for psychotherapy and their subsequent response to treatment. *Journal of Clinical Child Psychology, 13,* 170–78.

Adelman, H. S., Lauber, B. A., Nelson, P. & Smith, D. C. (1989). Toward a procedure for minimizing and detecting false positive diagnoses of learning disability. *Journal of Learning Disabilities, 22,* 234–44.

Adelman, H. S. & Taylor, L. (1983a). *Learning disabilities in perspective.* Glenview, IL: Scott, Foresman.

Adelman, H. S. & Taylor, L. (1983b). Enhancing motivation for overcoming learning and behavior problems. *Journal of Learning Disabilities, 16,* 384–92.

Adelman, H. S. & Taylor, L. (1984). Ethical concerns and identification of psychoeducational problems. *Journal of Clinical Child Psychology, 13,* 16–23.

Adelman, H. S. & Taylor, L. (1985a). Toward integrating intervention theory, research, and practice. In S. I. Pfeiffer (Ed.), *Clinical child psychology: An introduction to theory, research, and practice* (pp. 57–92). New York: Grune & Stratton.

Adelman, H. S. & Taylor, L. (1985b). The future of the LD field: A survey of fundamental concerns. *Journal of Learning Disabilities, 18,* 422–27.

Adelman, H. S. & Taylor, L. (1986). *An introduction to learning disabilities.* Glenview, IL: Scott, Foresman.

Adelman, H. S. & Taylor, L. (1988). Clinical child psychology: Fundamental intervention questions and problems. *Clinical Psychology Review, 8,* 637–65.

Adelman, H. S. & Taylor, L. (1990). Intrinsic motivation and school misbehavior: Some intervention implications. *Journal of Learning Disabilities, 23,* 541–50.

Adelman, H. S. & Taylor, L. (1991). Early school adjustment problems: Some perspectives and a project report. *American Journal of Orthopsychiatry, 61,* 468–74.

Adelman, K. A. & Adelman, H. S. (1987). Rodin, Patton, Edison, Wilson, Einstein: Were they really learning disabled? *Journal of Learning Disabilities, 20,* 270–79.

Alberto, P. A. & Troutman, A. C. (1990). *Applied behavioral analysis for teachers. Influencing student performance* (3rd ed.). Columbus, OH: Merrill.

Alexander, J. F. & Malouf, R. E. (1983). Intervention with children experiencing problems in personality and social environment. In P. Mussen (Ed.), *Handbook of child psychology, Vol IV: Socialization, personality, and social development.* New York: Wiley.

Allen, V. L. (1976). *Children as teachers: Theory and research on tutoring.* New York: Academic Press.

Alley, G. & Deshler, D. D. (1979). *Teaching the learning disabled adolescent: Strategies and methods.* Denver: Love Publishing Co.

Altman, I. (1975). *The environment and social behavior.* Pacific Grove, CA: Brooks/Cole.

American Academy of Pediatrics (1982). The Doman-Delacato treatment of neurologically handicapped children. A policy statement of the American Academy of Pediatrics. *Pediatrics, 70,* 810–12.

American Psychological Association (1968). Psychology as a profession. *American Psychologist, 23,* 195–200.

Ames, L. B. (1983). Learning disability: Truth or trap? *Journal of Learning Disabilities, 16,* 19–21.

Archibald, D. A. & Newman, F. M. (1988). *Beyond standardized testing: Assessing authentic academic achievement in secondary schools.* Washington, DC: National Association of School Principals.

Arter, J. A. & Jenkins, J. R. (1977). Examining the benefits and prevalence of modality considerations in special education. *The Journal of Special Education, 11,* 281–98.

Arter, J. A. & Jenkins, J. R. (1979). Differential diagnosis — Prescriptive teaching: A critical appraisal. *Review of Educational Research, 49,* 517–55.

Association for Children with Learning Disabilities (1985). Definition of the condition of specific learning disabilities. *ACLD Newsbriefs, 158,* 1–3.

Ausubel, N. (Ed.) (1948). Applied psychology. In *A treasury of Jewish folklore.* New York: Crown.

Ayres, A. J. (1978). Learning disabilities and the vestibular system. *Journal of Learning Disabilities, 11,* 18–29.

Badian, N. (1988). Predicting dyslexia in a preschool population. In R. L. Masland & M. W. Masland (Eds.), *Preschool prevention of reading failure* (pp. 78–103). Parkton, MD: York Press.

Baily, D. B., Jr., Buysse, V., Edmondson, R. & Smith, T. M. (1992). Creating family-centered services in early intervention: Perceptions of professionals in four states. *Exceptional Children, 58,* 298–309.

Baker, D. (1980). The efficacy of the Feingold K-P diet: A review of pertinent empirical investigations. *Behavior Disorders, 6,* 32–35.

Bakker, D. J., Bouma, A. & Gardien, C. J. (1990). Hemisphere-specific treatment of dyslexia subtypes: A field experiment. *Journal of Learning Disabilities, 23,* 433–38.

Bandura, A. (1978). The self system in reciprocal determinism. *American Psychologist, 33,* 344–58.

Bank-Mikkelsen, N. E. (1968). Service for mentally retarded children in Denmark. *Children, 15,* 198–200.

Bank-Mikkelsen, N. E. (1976). Administrative normalizing. *S. A.-Nyt, 14,* 3–6.

Barclay, J. R. (1983). *Barclay Classroom Assessment System.* Los Angeles: Western Psychological Services.

Barkley, R. A. (1977). A review of stimulant drug research with hyperkinetic children. *Journal of Child Psychology and Psychiatry, 18,* 137–65.

Barnes, K. E. (1982). *Preschool screening: The measurement and prediction of children at-risk.* Springfield, IL: C. C. Thomas.

Baron, J. & Brown, R. V. (Eds.) (1991). *Teaching decision making to adolescents.* Hillsdale, NJ: Erlbaum.

Barsch, R. (1967). *Achieving perceptual-motor efficiency: A space-oriented approach to learning.* Seattle: Special Child Publications.

Barth, R. S. (1990). *Improving schools from within: Teachers, parents, and principles can make a difference.* San Francisco: Jossey-Bass.

Bartoli, J. S. (1990). On defining learning and disability: Exploring the ecology. *Journal of Learning Disabilities, 23,* 628–31.

Bartoli, J. S. & Botel, M. (1988). *Remedial/learning disability: An ecological approach.* New York: Teachers College Press.

Bashir, A. S. & Scavuzzo, A. (1992). Children with language disorders: Natural history and academic success. *Journal of Learning Disabilities, 25,* 53–65.

Bassuk, E., Rubin, L. & Lauriet, A. (1986). Characteristics of sheltered homeless families. *American Journal of Public Health, 76,* 1097–1101.

Baum, S. & Kirschenbaum, R. (1984). Recognizing special talents in learning disabled students. *Teaching Exceptional Children, 16,* 92–98.

Baumrind, D. (1978). Reciprocal rights and responsibilities in parent-child relations. *Journal of Social Issues, 34,* 179–96.

Beauchamp, T. L. & Childress, J. F. (1989). *Principles of biomedical ethics* (3rd ed.). New York: Oxford University Press.

Becker, H. J. & Epstein, J. L. (1982). Parent involvement: A survey of teacher practices. *The Elementary School Journal, 83,* 85–102.

Begley, S. (1988, February 19). How to tell if you're smart: See your brain light up. *Newsweek,* p. 64.

Benjamin, H. (1949). *The cultivation of idiosyncracy.* Cambridge, MA: Harvard University Press.

Berger, E. H. (1981). *Parents as partners in education: The school and the home working together.* St. Louis, MO: C. V. Mosby.

Berk, R. A. (1984). An evaluation of procedures for computing an ability-achievement discrepancy score. *Journal of Learning Disabilities, 17,* 261–66.

Berliner, D. C. (1984). The half-full glass: A review of research on teaching. In P. L. Hosford (Ed.), *Using what we know about teaching* (pp. 51–77). Alexandria, VA: Association for Supervision and Curriculum Development.

Berrueta-Clement, J. R., Schweinhart, L. J., Barnett, W. S., Epstein, A. S. & Weikart, D. P. (1984). *Changed lives: The effects of the Perry Preschool Program on youths through age 19.* Ypsilanti, MI: High/Scope Press.

Berwick, D. M. & Kamaroff, A. L. (1982). Cost effectiveness of lead screening. *New England Journal of Medicine, 306,* 1392–98.

Bijou, S. W. (1970). What psychology has to offer education—now. *Journal of Applied Behavior Analysis, 3,* 65–71.

Bijou, S. W. & Baer, D. M. (Eds.) (1967). *Child development: Readings in experimental analysis.* Englewood Cliffs, NJ: Prentice-Hall.

Biklen, D. (1978). Consent as a cornerstone concept. In J. Mearig & Associates (Ed.), *Working for children: Ethical issues beyond professional guidelines* (pp. 90–114). San Francisco: Jossey-Bass.

Biklen, D. & Zollers, N. (1986). The focus of advocacy in the LD field. *Journal of Learning Disabilities, 19,* 579–86.

Blankenship, C. S. (1985). Using curriculum-based assessment data to make instructional decisions. *Exceptional Children, 52,* 233–38.

Bloom, B. S. (1978). New views of the learner: Implications for instruction and curriculum. *Educational Leadership, 35,* 563–75.

Bloom, B. S. (1982). *All our children learning.* New York: McGraw-Hill.

Bloom, B. S., Englehart, M. D., Furst, E. J., Hill, W. H. & Krathwohl, D. R. (1956). *Taxonomy of educational objectives: Handbook I: Cognitive domain.* New York: McKay.

Bohlmeyer, E. M. & Burke, J. P. (1987). Selecting cooperative learning techniques: A consultative strategy guide. *School Psychology Review, 16,* 36–49.

Bond, L. & Compas, B. (Eds.) (1989). *Primary prevention in the schools*. Newbury Park, CA: Sage.

Bradley, G. W. (1978). Self-serving biases in the attribution process: A re-examination of the fact or fiction question. *Journal of Personality and Social Psychology, 36,* 56–71.

Brehm, S. S. & Brehm, J. W. (1981). *Psychological reactance: A theory of freedom and control.* New York: Academic Press.

Brickman, P., Rabinowitz, V. C., Karuza, J., Jr., Coates, D., Cohn, E. & Kidder, L. (1982). Models of helping and coping. *American Psychologist, 37,* 368–84.

Bromwich, R. (1981). *Working with parents and infants: An interactional approach.* Baltimore: University Park Press.

Bronheim, S. (1991). An educator's guide to Tourette syndrome. *Journal of Learning Disabilities, 24,* 17–22.

Brookover, W. B., Beady, C., Flood, P., Schweitzer, J. & Wisenbaker, J. (1979). *School systems and student achievement: Schools can make a difference.* New York: Praeger.

Brophy, J. & Good, T. L. (1986). Teacher behavior and student achievement. In M. Wittrock (Ed.), *Third handbook of research on teaching* (pp. 328–75). New York: Macmillan.

Brown, A. L. & Campione, J. C. (1986). Psychological theory and the study of learning disabilities. *American Psychologist, 14,* 1059–68.

Bruner, J. S. (1966). *Toward a theory of instruction.* Cambridge, MA: Belknap Press.

Burlington School Committee of the Town of Burlington Massachusetts v. Department of Education, 105 S.Ct., 1986 (1985).

Buros, O. K. (Ed.) (1974). *Tests in print II.* Highland Park, NJ: Gryphon.

Burton, W. H. (1962). *The guidance of learning activities.* New York: Appleton-Century-Crofts.

California Task Force to Promote Self-Esteem and Personal and Social Responsibility (1990). *Toward a state of esteem.* Sacramento, CA: California State Department of Education.

Campione, J. C. & Brown, A. L. (1987). Linking dynamic assessment with school achievement. In C. S. Lidz (Ed.), *Dynamic assessment: An interactional approach to evaluating learning potential.* NY: Guilford Press.

Caplan, G. (1964). *Principles of preventive psychology.* New York: Basic Books.

Caplan, G. (1970). *The theory and practice of mental health consultation.* New York: Basic Books.

Carnine, D. (1991). Curricular interventions for teaching higher order thinking to all students: Introduction to the special series. *Journal of Learning Disabilities, 24,* 261–69.

Carnine, D., Silbert, J. & Kameenui, E. J. (1990). *Direct instruction reading* (2nd ed.). Columbus, OH: Merrill.

Carnine, D. & Woodward, J. (1988). Paradigms lost: Learning disabilities and the new ghost in the old machine. *Journal of Learning Disabilities, 21,* 233–36.

Case, R. A. (1978). A developmentally based theory and technology of instruction. *Review of Educational Research, 48,* 439–63.

Chalfant, J. C. (1985). Identifying learning disabled students: A summary of the National Task Force Report. *Learning Disabilities Focus, 1,* 9–20.

Chalfant, J. C., Pysh, M. V. & Moultrie, R. (1979). Teacher assistance teams: A model for within-building problem solving. *Learning Disability Quarterly, 2,* 85–96.

Chalfant, J. C. & Pysh, M. V. (1983). Teacher assistance teams. In C. Collins (Ed.), *Keys to success* (monograph of the Michigan ACLD Conference). Garden City, NY: Quality Printers.

Chalfant, J. C. & Scheffelin, M. A. (1969). *Central processing dysfunctions in children: A review of the research* (Phase III, NINDS Monograph No. 9). Bethesda, MD: U. S. Dept. of Health, Education, and Welfare.

Chall, J. S. (1983a). *Learning to read: The great debate* (updated edition). New York: McGraw-Hill.

Chall, J. S. (1983b). *Stages of reading development.* New York: McGraw-Hill.

Chall, J. S., Jacobs, V. A. & Baldwin, L. E. (1990). *The reading crisis.* Cambridge, MA: Harvard University Press.

Charles, C. M. (1985). *Building classroom discipline: From models to practice* (2nd ed.). New York: Longman.

Chase, A. (1977). *The legacy of Malthus: The social costs of the new scientific racism.* New York: Knopf.

Chase, S. (1956). *Guides to straight thinking.* New York: Harper & Brothers.

Chieh, S., Chu, Y., Lu, S., Tang, T. & Wang, T. (1985). Application of the short DDST-R in urban districts of Shanghai: A preliminary report. In W. K. Frankenburg, R. N. Emde & J. W. Sullivan (Eds.), *Early identification of children at risk: An international perspective* (pp. 329–32). New York: Plenum.

Clark, R. W. (1971). *Einstein: The life and times.* New York: World.

Clements, S. D. (1966). *Minimal brain dysfunction in children: Terminology and identification.* Phase one of a three-phase project. NINDS Monograph No. 3. U. S. Public Health Service Publication No. 1415. Washington, DC: U. S. GPO.

Cohen, A. L., Torgesen, J. K. & Torgesen, J. L. (1988). Improving speed and accuracy of word recognition in reading disabled children: An evaluation of two computer program variations. *Learning Disability Quarterly, 11,* 333–41.

Cohen, J. (1986). Theoretical considerations of peer tutoring. *Psychology in the Schools, 23,* 175–86.

Colarusso, R. P. (1987). Diagnostic-prescriptive teaching. In M. Wang, M. Reynolds & H. Walberg (Eds.), *The handbook of special education: Research and practice.* Oxford, England: Pergamon Press.

Coles, G. (1978). The learning-disabilities test battery: Empirical and social issues. *Harvard Educational Review, 48,* 313–40.

Coles, G. (1987). *The learning mystique: A critical look at "learning disabilities."* New York: Pantheon Books.

Colletti, L. (1979). Relationship between pregnancy and birth complications and the later development of learning disabilities. *Journal of Learning Disabilities, 12,* 25–29.

Comenius, J. S. (1632). *The great didactic,* translated into English and edited by M. W. Kentinge. New York: Russell & Russell.

Comer, J. P. (1988). Educating poor minority children. *Scientific American, 259,* 42–48.

Compas, B. E. & Adelman, H. S. (1981). Clinicians' judgments of female clients' causal attributions. *Journal of Clinical Psychology, 37,* 456–60.

Compas, B. E., Adelman, H. S., Freundl, P., Nelson, P. & Taylor, L. (1982). Parent and child causal attributions during clinical interviews. *Journal of Abnormal Child Psychology, 10,* 77–84.

Condry, J. (1977). Enemies of exploration: Self-initiated versus other-initiated learning. *Journal of Personality and Social Psychology, 35,* 459–77.

Cone, T. E., Wilson, L. R., Bradley, C. M. & Reese, J. H. (1985). Characteristics of LD students in Iowa: An empirical investigation. *Learning Disability Quarterly, 8,* 211–20.

Conoley, J. C. & Conoley, C. W. (1990). *School consultation: Practice and training* (2nd ed.). New York: Pergamon.

Cook, V. J., Howe, G. W. & Holliday, B. G. (1985). Community psychology for clinical child psychologists: Perspectives and roles. In S. J. Pfeiffer (Ed.), *Clinical child psychology: An introduction to theory, research, and practice* (pp. 57–92). New York: Grune & Stratton.

Copeland, W. C. (1983). Strategies for special education in the 1980s: A conference epilogue. *Policy Studies Review, 2,* 243–60.

Cott, A. (1985). *Help for your learning disabled child. The orthomolecular treatment.* New York: Times Books.

Cowen, E. L. (1980). The wooing of primary prevention. *American Journal of Community Psychology, 8,* 258–84.

Cowen, E. L. (1986). Primary prevention in mental health: Ten years of retrospect and ten years of prospect. In M. Kessler & S. E. Goldston (Eds.), *A decade of progress in primary prevention* (pp. 3–45). Hanover, NH: University Press of New England.

Cowen, E. L. & Hightower, A. D. (1990). The Primary Mental Health Project: Alternative approaches to school-based preventive intervention. In T. B. Gutkin & C. R. Reynolds (Eds.), *The handbook of school psychology* (2nd ed., pp. 775–95). New York: Wiley.

Cronbach, L. J. (1970). *Essentials of psychological testing* (3rd ed.). New York: Harper & Row.

Cronbach, L. J. & Gleser, G. C. (1965). *Psychological tests and personnel decisions* (2nd ed.). Urbana, IL: University of Illinois Press.

Cruickshank, W. M. (1983). Straight is the bamboo tree. *Journal of Learning Disabilities, 16,* 191–97.

Cruickshank, W. M., Bentzen, F. A., Ratzeburg, F. H. & Tannhauser, M. T. (1961). *A teaching method for brain-injured and hyperactive children.* Syracuse, NY: Syracuse University Press.

Cruickshank, W. M., Morse, W. C. & Grant, J. O. (1990). *The individual education planning committee: A step in the history of special education.* Ann Arbor: University of Michigan Press.

Curtis, B. A., Jacobson, S. & Marcus, E. M. (1972). *An introduction to the neurosciences.* Philadelphia: Saunders.

Dalby, J. T. (1979). Deficit or delay: Neuropsychological models of developmental dyslexia. *Journal of Special Education, 13,* 239–64.

Dangel, H. L. & Ensminger, E. E. (1988). The use of a discrepancy formula with LD students. *Learning Disabilities Focus, 4,* 24–31.

Dao, M. (1991). Designing assessment procedures for educationally at-risk Southeast Asian-American students. *Journal of Learning Disabilities, 24,* 594–601, 629.

Darrow, H. F. & Van Allen, R. (1961). *Independent activities for creative learning.* New York: Teachers College Press.

Davies, D. (1987). Parent involvement in the public schools: Opportunities for administrators. *Education and Urban Society, 19,* 147–63.

Davies, D. (1988, Spring). Low-income parents and the schools: A research report and a plan of action. *Equity and Choice,* 51–57.

Deci, E. L. (1975). *Intrinsic motivation.* New York: Plenum.

Deci, E. L. (1980). *The psychology of self-determination.* Lexington, MA: Lexington Books.

Deci, E. L. & Chandler, C. L. (1986). The importance of motivation for the future of the LD field. *Journal of Learning Disabilities, 19,* 587–94.

Deci, E. L., Nezlek, J. & Sheinman, L. (1981). Characteristics of the rewarder and intrinsic motivation of the rewardee. *Journal of Personality and Social Psychology, 40,* 1–10.

Deci, E. L. & Ryan, R. M. (1985). *Intrinsic motivation and self-determination in human behavior.* New York: Plenum Press.

DeFries, J. & Decker, S. (1982). Genetic aspects of reading disability: A family study. In R. N. Malatesha & P. G. Aaron (Eds.), *Reading disorders: Varieties and treatments* (pp. 255–79). New York: Academic Press.

Delacato, C. H. (1966). *Neurological organization and reading.* Springfield, IL: Charles C. Thomas.

Deno, S. L. (1987). Curriculum-based measurement. *Teaching Exceptional Children, 20,* 41–42.

Deshler, D. D. & Schumaker, J. B. (1986). Learning strategies: An instructional alternative for low-achieving adolescents. *Exceptional Children, 52,* 583–90.

Designs for Change (1985). *The bottom line: Chicago's failing schools and how to save them.* Chicago: Author.

de Weerd, J. (1984). Introduction. In D. Assel (Ed.), *Handicapped Children's Early Education Program: 1982–83 overview and direction* (pp. *vii–xiv*). Technical Assistance Development System of Special Education Program, U. S. Department of Education. Washington, DC: Government Printing Office.

Dewey, J. (1938). *Experience and education.* New York: Collier Books.

Dewey, J. (1966). *Lectures in the philosophy of education, 1899.* R. D. Archambault (Ed.). New York: Random House.

Diana v. State Board of Education, No. C-70-37 (N.D. Calif. 1970).

Doman, G. & Delacato, C. (1968). Doman-Delacato philosophy. *Human Potential, 1,* 113–16.

Douglas, V. I. (1972). Stop, look, and listen: The problem of sustained attention and impulse control in hyperactive and normal children. *Canadian Journal of Behavior Science, 4,* 259–81.

Dreikurs, R., Grunwald, B. B. & Pepper, F. C. (1982). *Maintaining sanity in the classroom: Classroom management techniques* (2nd ed.). New York: Harper & Row.

Duane, D. (1986). Neurodiagnostic tools in dyslexic syndromes in children: Pitfalls and proposed comparative study of computer tomograph, nuclear magnetic resonance, and brain electrical activity mapping. In C. Pavlidis & D. Fisher (Eds.), *Dyslexia: Its neuropsychology and treatment* (pp. 65–86). New York: Wiley.

Duane, D. (1989). Commentary on dyslexia and neurodevelopmental pathology. *Journal of Learning Disabilities, 22,* 219–20.

Dudley-Marling, C. (1985). Perceptions of the usefulness of the IEP by teachers of learning disabled and emotionally disturbed children. *Psychology in the Schools, 22,* 65–67.

Duffy, F. H. & McAnulty, G. B. (1985). Brain electrical activity mapping (BEAM): The search for a physiological signature of dyslexia. In F. H. Duffy & N. Geschwind (Eds.), *Dyslexia: A neuroscientific approach to clinical evaluation* (pp. 105–122). Boston: Little, Brown.

Dunst, C. J., Johanson, C., Trivette, C. M. & Humby, D. (1991). Family-oriented early intervention policies and practices: Family-centered or not? *Exceptional Children, 58,* 115–26.

Edmonds, R. R. (1979). Effective schools for the urban poor. *Educational Leadership, 37,* 15–27.

Edmonds, R. R. (1981). Making public schools effective. *Social Policy, 12,* 28–32.

Ekstrom, R. B., Goertz, M. E., Pollack, J. M. & Rock, D. A. (1986). Who drops out of high school and why? Findings from a national study. *Teachers College Record, 87,* 356–73.

Elmore, R. F. & Associates (1990). *Restructuring schools: The next generation of educational reform.* San Francisco: Jossey-Bass.

Engelmann, S., Becker, W., Hanner, S. & Johnson, G. (1978). *Corrective reading program.* Chicago: Science Research Associates.

Engelmann, S. & Bruner, E. (1984). *Distar reading program.* Chicago: Science Research Associates.

Epstein, J. L. (1986). Parents' reactions to teacher practices of parent involvement. *The Elementary School Journal, 86,* 277–93.

Epstein, J. L. (1987). Parent involvement: What research says to administrators. *Education and Urban Society, 19,* 119–36.

Epstein, J. L. & Becker, H. J. (1982). Teachers' reported practices of parent involvement: Problems and possibilities. *The Elementary School Journal, 83,* 103–113.

Erikson, E. H. (1982). Psychoanalytical reflections on Einstein's centenary. In G. Holton (Ed.), *Albert Einstein — Historical and cultural perspectives.* Princeton: Princeton University Press.

Federal Register (1977). U. S. Office of Education. Education of handicapped children. *Federal Register, 42,* 65082–85.

Feinberg, J. (1973). *Social philosophy.* Englewood Cliffs, NJ: Prentice-Hall.

Feingold, B. F. (1976). Hyperkinesis and learning disabilities linked to the ingestion of artificial food colors and flavors. *Journal of Learning Disabilities, 9,* 551–59.

Feniak, C. A. (1988). Labelling in special education: A problematic issue in England and Wales. *International Journal of Special Education, 3,* 117–24.

Fernald, G. (1943). *Remedial techniques in basic school subjects.* New York: McGraw-Hill. (Reissued in 1988 by PRO-ED.)

Feshbach, N. D. (1984). Empathy, empathy training and the regulation of aggression in elementary school children. In R. M. Kaplan, V. J. Konecni & R. Novoco (Eds.), *Aggression in children and youth* (pp. 192–208). The Hague, The Netherlands: Martinus Nijhoff.

Feuerstein, R. (1979). *The dynamic assessment of retarded performers: The learning potential assessment device, theory, instruments, and techniques.* Baltimore: University Park Press.

Feuerstein, R. (1980). *Instrumental enrichment: An intervention program for cognitive modifiability.* Baltimore: University Park Press.

Feuerstein, R., Rand, Y., Jensen, M. R., Kaniel, S. & Tzuriel, D. (1987). Prerequisites for assessment of learning potential: The LPAD model. In C. S. Lidz (Ed.), *Dynamic assessment: An interactional approach to evaluating learning potential.* New York: Guilford Press.

Fewell, R. R. (1991). Trends in assessment of infants and toddlers with disabilities. *Exceptional Children, 58,* 166–73.

Finn, C. E. (1989, July 12). Made in Japan: Low-tech method for math success. *Wall Street Journal,* A14.

Finn, J. D. (1989). Withdrawing from school. *Review of Educational Research, 59,* 117–42.

Finucci, J. M. & Childs, B. (1981). Are there really more dyslexic boys than girls? In A. Ansara, N. Geschwind, A. Galaburda, M. Albert & N. Gartrell (Eds.), *Sex differences in dyslexia* (pp. 1–10). Baltimore: Orton Dyslexia Society.

Flavell, J. J. (1985). *Cognitive development.* Englewood Cliffs, NJ: Prentice-Hall.

Forness, S. R. (1988). Reductionism, paradigm shifts, and learning disabilities. *Journal of Learning Disabilities, 21,* 421–24.

Forness, S. R., Cantwell, D. P., Swanson, J. M., Hanna, G. L. & Youpa, D. (1991). Differential effects of stimulant medication on reading performance of boys with hyperactivity with and without conduct disorders. *Journal of Learning Disabilities, 24,* 304–310.

Forness, S. R. & Kavale, K. A. (1987). Holistic inquiry and the scientific challenge in special education: A reply to Iano. *Remedial and Special Education, 8,* 47–51.

Forness, S. R. & Kavale, K. A. (1988). Psychopharmacologic treatment: A note on classroom effects. *Journal of Learning Disabilities, 21,* 144–47.

Forness, S. R., Sinclair, E. & Guthrie, D. (1983). Learning disability discrepancy formulas: Their use in actual practice. *Learning Disability Quarterly, 6,* 107–114.

Forness, S. R., Swanson, J. M., Cantwell, D. P., Youpa, D. & Hanna, G. L. (1992). Stimulant medication and reading performance: Follow-up on sustained dose in ADHD boys with and without conduct disorders. *Journal of Learning Disabilities, 25,* 115–23.

Frank, J. D. (1961). *Persuasion and healing.* Baltimore: Johns Hopkins Press

Frankenberg, W. & Fronzaglio, K. (1991). A review of states' criteria and procedures for identifying children with learning disabilities. *Journal of Learning Disabilities, 24,* 495–500.

Frankenberg, W. & Harper, J. (1987). States' criteria and procedures for identifying learning disabled children: A comparison of 1981/82 and 1985/86 guidelines. *Journal of Learning Disabilities, 20,* 118–21.

Frankenburg, W. K., Emde, R. N. & Sullivan, J. W. (Eds.). (1985). *Early identification of children at risk: An international perspective.* New York: Plenum.

Fraser, B. J. & Walberg, H. J. (Eds.) (1991). *Educational environments: Evaluation, antecedents, and consequences.* New York: Pergamon Press.

Freund, J. H., Bradley, R. H. & Caldwell, B. M. (1979). The home environment in the assessment of learning disabilities. *Learning Disability Quarterly, 2,* 39–51.

Frostig, M. & Maslow, P. (1973). *Learning problems in the classroom.* New York: Grune & Stratton.

Fuchs, D. (1991). Mainstream assistance teams: A prereferral intervention system for difficult-to-teach students. In G. Stoner, M. R. Shinn, & H. M. Walker (Eds.), *Interventions for achievement and behavior problems* (pp. 241–67). Washington, DC: National Association of School Psychologists.

Fuchs, D. & Fuchs, L. S. (1988). Evaluation of the Adaptive Learning Environments Model. *Exceptional Children, 55,* 115–27.

Fuchs, D., Fuchs, L. S., Benowitz, S. & Barringer, K. (1987). Norm-referenced tests: Are they valid for use with handicapped students? *Exceptional Children, 54,* 263–71.

Fuchs, L. S. (1991). *Integrating curriculum-based measurement with instructional planning for students with learning disabilities.* Paper prepared for the Fifth Annual Rutgers Invitational Symposium on Education.

Fuchs, L. S., Hamlett, C. L., Fuchs, D., Stecker, P. M. & Ferguson, C. (1988). Conducting curriculum-based measurement with computerized data collection: Effects on efficiency and teacher satisfaction. *Journal of Special Education Technology, 9,* 73–86.

Fuerst, D. R., Fisk, J. L. & Rourke, B. P. (1989). Psychosocial functioning of learning-disabled children: Replicability of statistically derived subtypes. *Journal of Consulting and Clinical Psychology, 57,* 275–80.

Furth, H. G. & Wachs, H. (1974). *Thinking goes to school: Piaget's theory in practice.* New York: Oxford.

Gaddes, W. H. (1985). *Learning disabilities and brain function: A neuropsychological approach* (2nd ed.). New York: Springer-Verlag.

Gadow, K. D. (1986). *Children on medication (Vol. 1): Hyperactivity, learning disabilities, and mental retardation.* Austin, TX: PRO-ED.

Gadow, K. D. (1991). Psychopharmacological assessment and intervention. In H. L. Swanson (Ed.), *Handbook of assessment of learning disabilities: Theory, research, and practice* (pp. 351–72). Austin, TX: PRO-ED.

Gage, N. L. & Needels, M. C. (1987). *Criticisms of process product research on teaching: A review and response.* Stanford: Stanford University, Center for Educational Research at Stanford.

Gagné, R. M. (Ed.) (1967). *Learning and individual differences.* Columbus, OH: Merrill.

Gagné, R. M. (1985). *The conditions of learning and theory of instruction* (4th ed.). Fort Worth, TX: Holt, Rinehart and Winston.

Galaburda, A. M. (1985). Developmental dyslexia: A review of biological interactions. *Annals of Dyslexia, 35,* 21–32.

Galaburda, A. M. (1989). Learning disability: Biological, societal, or both? A response to Gerald Coles. *Journal of Learning Disabilities, 22,* 278–82.

Garner, R. (1987). *Metacognition and reading comprehension.* Norwood, NJ: Ablex.

Garrett, H. E. (1954). *Statistics in psychology and education.* New York: Longmans Green.

Gartner, A., Kohler, M. & Riessman, F. (1971). *Children teach children.* New York: Harper.

Gartner, A. & Lipsky, D. K. (1987). Beyond special education: Toward a quality system for all students. *Harvard Educational Review, 57,* 367–95.

Gerber, M. & Kauffman, J. M. (1981). Peer tutoring in academic settings. In P. S. Strain (Ed.), *The utilization of classroom peers as behavior change agents.* New York: Plenum.

Gerber, M. M. & Semmel, M. I. (1984). Teacher as imperfect test: Reconceptualizing the referral process. *Educational Psychologist, 19,* 137–48.

German, M. L., Williams, E., Herzfeld, J. & Marshall, R. M. (1982). Utility of the revised Denver Developmental Screening Test and the Developmental Profile II in identifying preschool children with cognitive, language and motor problems. *Education and Training of the Mentally Retarded, 17,* 319–24.

Getman, G. N. (1965). The visuomotor complex in the acquisition of learning skills. In J. Hellmuth (Ed.), *Learning disorders* (Vol. 1). Seattle: Special Child Publications.

Gibbs, J. T., Huang, L. N. & Associates (1989). *Children of color: Psychological interventions with minority youth.* San Francisco: Jossey-Bass.

Gillingham, A. & Stillman, B. (1966). *Remedial training for children with specific difficulty in reading, spelling, and penmanship* (7th ed.). Cambridge, MA: Educational Publishing Services.

Glass, G. V. (1983). Effectiveness of special education. *Policy Studies Review, 2,* 65–78.

Goldman, S. R. & Pellegrino, J. W. (1987). Information processing and educational microcomputer technology: Where do we go from here? *Journal of Learning Disabilities, 20,* 144–54.

Goldstein, D. & Myers, B. (1980). Cognitive lag and group differences in intelligence. *Child Study Journal, 10,* 119–32.

Goldstein, K. (1939). *The organism.* New York: American Book.

Goldstein, M. J. (1988). The family and psychopathology. *Annual Review of Psychology, 28,* 491–532.

Gonzales, M. L. (1990). School + home = A program for educating homeless students. *Phi Delta Kappan, 71,* 785–87.

Good, T. L. & Brophy, J. E. (1986). School effects. In M. C. Wittrock (Ed.), *Handbook of research on teaching* (pp. 328–75). New York: Macmillan.

Goodlad, J. I. (1984). *A place called school.* New York: McGraw-Hill.

Gracey, C. A., Azzara, C. V. & Reinherz, H. (1984). Screening revisited: A survey of U. S. requirements. *Journal of Special Education, 18,* 101–107.

Graden, J. L., Casey, A. & Christensen, S. L. (1985). Implementing a prereferral intervention system: Part I. The model. *Exceptional Children, 51,* 377–84.

Graden, J. L., Casey, A. & Bonstrom, O. (1985). Implementing a prereferral intervention system: Part II. The model. *Exceptional Children, 51,* 487–96.

Grant, W. V. & Lund, C. G. (1977). *Digest of educational statistics: 1976 edition.* National Center for Education Statistics No. 77-401. Washington, DC: U. S. GPO.

Greenfield, P. M. (1984). *Mind and media: The effects of television, video games and computers.* Cambridge, MA: Harvard University Press.

Guilford, J. P. (1956). *Fundamental statistics in psychology.* New York: McGraw-Hill.

Guralnick, M. J. (1991). The next decade of research on the effectiveness of early intervention. *Exceptional Children, 58,* 174–83.

Gutkin, T. B. & Curtis, M. J. (1990). School-based consultation: Theory, techniques, and research. In T. B. Gutkin & C. R. Reynolds (Eds.), *The handbook of school psychology* (2nd ed., pp. 577–611). New York: Wiley.

Hall, J. & Gallagher, J. J. (1984). Minimum competency testing and the learning disabled student. In J. D. McKinney & L. Feagans (Eds.), *Current topics in learning disabilities* (Vol. 1). Norwood, NJ: Ablex.

Halpern, A. (1992). Transition: Old wine in new bottles. *Exceptional Children, 58,* 202–11.

Hambleton, R. K. (1990). Criterion-referenced testing methods and practices. In T. B. Gutkin & C. R. Reynolds (Eds.), *The handbook of school psychology* (2nd ed., pp. 388–415). New York: Wiley.

Hammill, D. D. (1990). On defining learning disabilities: An emerging consensus. *Journal of Learning Disabilities, 23,* 74–85.

Hammill, D. D., Brown, L. & Bryant, B. R. (1989). *A consumer's guide to tests in print.* Austin, TX: PRO-ED.

Hammill, D. D. & Larsen, S. C. (1974a). The efficacy of psycholinguistic training. *Exceptional Children, 41,* 5–14.

Hammill, D. D. & Larsen, S. C. (1974b). The relationship of selected auditory perceptual skills and reading ability. *Journal of Learning Disabilities, 7,* 429–36.

Hammill, D. D., Leigh, J. E., McNutt, G. & Larsen, S. C. (1981). A new definition of learning disabilities. *Learning Disability Quarterly, 4,* 336–42.

Harackiewicz, J. M., Sansone, C. & Manderlink, G. (1985). Competence, achievement orientation, and intrinsic motivation: A process analysis. *Journal of Personality and Social Psychology, 48,* 493–508.

Haring, K. A., Lovett, D. L. & Smith, D. D. (1990). A follow-up study of recent special education graduates of learning disabilities programs. *Journal of Learning Disabilities, 23,* 108–113.

Haring, N. G. & Miller, C. A. (1969). *Minimal brain dysfunction: Educational, med-*

ical, and health related services. (Phase II, N & SDCP Monograph, Public Health Publication No. 2015.) Washington, DC: U. S. Dept. of Health, Education, and Welfare.

Haring, N. G. & Phillips, E. L. (1962). *Analysis and modification of classroom behavior.* Englewood Cliffs, NJ: Prentice-Hall.

Haring, N. G. & Whelan, R. J. (1965). Experimental methods in education and management. In N. J. Long, W. C. Morse & R. G. Newman (Eds.), *Conflict in the classroom.* Belmont, CA: Wadsworth.

Harris, K. R. & Pressley, M. (1991). The nature of cognitive strategy instruction: Interactive strategy construction. *Exceptional Children, 57,* 392–405.

Haslam, R. H. A., Dalby, J. T. & Rademaker, A. W. (1984). Effects of megavitamin therapy on children with attention deficit disorders. *Pediatrics, 74,* 103–111.

Havighurst, R. J. (1972). *Developmental tasks and education.* New York: David McKay.

Haywood, H. C., Brown, A. L. & Wingerfeld, S. (1990). Dynamic approaches to psychoeducational assessment. *School Psychology Review, 19,* 411–22.

Hebbler, K. M., Smith, B. J. & Black, T. L. (1991). Federal early childhood special education policy: A model for the improvement of services for children with disabilities. *Exceptional Children, 58,* 104–114.

Heller, K., Holtzman, W. & Messick, S. (1982). *Placing children in special education: A strategy for equity.* Report of the National Academy of Sciences' Panel on Selection and Placement of Students in Programs for the Mentally Retarded. Washington, DC: National Academy Press.

Heshusius, L. (1982). At the heart of the advocacy dilemma: A mechanistic world view. *Exceptional Children, 49,* 6–13.

Heshusius, L. (1986). Pedagogy, special education, and the lives of young children: A critical and futuristic perspective. *Journal of Education, 168,* 25–38.

Heshusius, L. (1989). The Newtonian-mechanistic paradigm, special education, and contours of alternatives. An overview. *Journal of Learning Disabilities, 22,* 403–415.

Heshusius, L. (1991). Curriculum-based assessment and direct instruction: Critical reflections on fundamental assumptions. *Exceptional Children, 57,* 315–28.

Hewett, F. M. (1968). *The emotionally disturbed child in the classroom.* Boston: Allyn & Bacon.

Hewett, F. M. & Taylor, F. D. (1980). *The emotionally disturbed child in the classroom: The orchestration of success* (2nd ed.). Boston: Allyn & Bacon.

Hobbs, N. (1975a). *The future of children: Categories, labels, and their consequences.* San Francisco: Jossey-Bass.

Hobbs, N. (1975b). *Issues in the classification of children* (2 vols.). San Francisco: Jossey-Bass.

Hobbs, N. (1980). An ecologically oriented, service-based system for the classification of handicapped children. In S. Salzinger, J. Antrobus & J. Glick (Eds.), *The ecosystem of the "sick" child* (pp. 271–90). New York: Academic Press.

Hobson v. Hansen, 269 F. Supp. 401 (D.D.C. 1967) aff'g sub nom *Smuck v. Hobson,* 408 F. 2d 175 (D.C. Cir. 1969).

Hodgkinson, H. L. (1989). *The same client: The demographics of education and service delivery systems.* Washington, DC: Institute for Educational Leadership, Inc./Center for Demographic Policy.

Hodgson, J. M. (1992). The status of metalinguistic skills in reading development. *Journal of Learning Disabilities, 25,* 96–101.

Hoffman, B. & Dukas, H. (1972). *Albert Einstein: Creator and rebel.* New York: Viking Press.

Holt, J. (1964). *How children fail.* New York: Pitman Publishing.

Holt, J. (1989). *Learning all the time.* Reading, MA: Addison Wesley.

Holton, G. (1971–72, Winter). On trying to understand scientific genius. *American Scholar,* 95–110.

Honig v. Doe, 484 U.S. 305,108 S.Ct. 592 (1988).

Horn, W. F., O'Donnell, J. P. & Vitulano, L. A. (1983). Long-term follow-up studies of learning disabled persons. *Journal of Learning Disabilities, 16,* 542–55.

Howard, K. I. & Orlinsky, D. E. (1972). Psychotherapeutic processes. *Annual Review of Psychology, 23,* 615–68.

Hoyt, C. S., III, (1990). Irlen lenses and reading difficulties. *Journal of Learning Disabilities, 23,* 624–26.

Hunt, D. E. & Sullivan, E. V. (1974). *Between psychology and education.* Chicago: Dryden Press.

Hurn, C. J. (1985). *The limits and possibilities of schooling: An introduction to the sociology of education* (2nd ed.). Boston: Allyn & Bacon.

Hyman, I., Flanagan, D. & Smith, K. (1982). Discipline in the schools. In C. R. Reynolds & T. B. Gutkin (Eds.), *The handbook of school psychology* (pp. 454–80). New York: Wiley.

Iano, R. P. (1987). The study and development of teaching: With implications for the advancement of special education. *Remedial and Special Education, 7,* 50–61.

Idol, L. & Ritter, S. (1987). Data-based instruction. Do teachers use it? *Teacher Education and Special Education, 10,* 65–70.

Illich, I. (1976). *Medical nemesis.* New York: Pantheon Books.

Illich, I. (1977). *Toward a history of needs.* New York: Pantheon Books.

Irlen, H. (1983, August). *Successful treatment of learning disabilities.* Paper presented at the 91st Annual Convention of the American Psychological Association, Anaheim.

Irlen, H. & Lass, M. J. (1989). Improving reading problems due to symptoms of scotopic sensitivity using Irlen lenses and overlays. *Education, 109,* 413–17.

Jakobson, R. (1982). Einstein and the science of language. In G. Holton (Ed.), *Albert Einstein — Historical and cultural perspectives.* Princeton: Princeton University Press.

Jansky, J. J., Hoffman, M. T., Layton, J. & Sugar, F. (1989). Prediction: A six-year follow-up. *Annals of Dyslexia, 39,* 227–46.

Jason, L. A., Betts, D., Johnson, J., Smith, S. et al. (1989). An evaluation of an orientation plus tutoring school-based prevention program. *Professional School Psychology, 4,* 273–84.

Jenkins, J. R., Pious, C. G. & Peterson, D. L. (1988). Categorical programs for remedial and handicapped students: Issues of validity. *Exceptional Children, 55,* 147–58.

Johnson, D. & Myklebust, H. R. (1967). *Learning disabilities: Educational principles and practices.* New York: Grune & Stratton.

Johnson, D. W. & Johnson, R. T. (1986). Mainstreaming and cooperative learning strategies. *Exceptional Children, 52, 247–52.*

Johnson, L. J. & Pugach, M. C. (1991). Peer collaboration: Accommodating students with mild learning and behavior problems. *Exceptional Children, 57,* 454–61.

Jones, E. E. & Nisbett, R. (1971). The actor and observer: Divergent perceptions of the causes of behavior. In E. E. Jones, D. E. Kanouse, H. H. Kelley, R. E. Nisbett, S. Valens & B. Weiner, *Attribution: Perceiving the causes of behavior.* Morristown, NJ: General Learning Press.

Joyce, B. & Weil, M. (1980, 1986). *Models of teaching* (2nd and 3rd eds.). New York: Prentice-Hall.

Kagan, S. L. (1990). *Excellence in early childhood education: Defining characteristics and next-decade strategies.* Washington, DC: Office of Educational Research and Improvement, U. S. Department of Education.

Kagan, S. L., Rivera, A. M. & Parker, F. L. (1990). *Collaborations in action: Reshaping services for young children and their families.* Yale University Bush Center on Child Development and Social Policy.

Kameenui, E. J. (1991). Toward a scientific pedagogy of learning disabilities: A sameness of message. *Journal of Learning Disabilities, 24,* 364–72.

Kamin, L. J. (1974). *The science and politics of I.Q.* New York: Wiley.

Kanfer, E. H. & Goldstein, A. P. (1990). *Helping people change: A textbook of methods* (4th ed.). New York: Pergamon Press.

Kaplan, H. B. (1980). *Deviant behavior in defense of self.* New York: Academic Press.

Karpman, S. (1968). Script drama analysis. *Transactional Analysis Bulletin, 7,* 39–43.

Kauffman, J. M. (1989). The Regular Education Initiative as Reagan-Bush education policy: A trickle-down theory of education of the hard-to-teach. *Journal of Special Education, 23,* 256–77.

Kaufman, A. S. (1981). The WISC-R and learning disabilities assessment: State of the art. *Journal of Learning Disabilities, 14,* 520–26.

Kavale, K. A. & Forness, S. R. (1983). Hyperactivity and diet treatment: A meta-analysis of the Feingold hypothesis. *Journal of Learning Disabilities, 16,* 324–30.

Kavale, K. A. & Forness, S. R. (1985). *The science of learning disabilities.* San Diego, CA: College-Hill Press.

Kavale, K. A. & Mundschenk, N. A. (1991). A critique of assessment methodology. In H. L. Swanson (Ed.), *Handbook of assessment of learning disabilities: Theory, research, and practice* (pp. 407–432). Austin, TX: PRO-ED.

Kazdin, A. E. (1984). *Behavior modification in applied settings.* Pacific Grove, CA: Brooks/Cole.

Kean, T. H. (1989). The life you save may be your own: New Jersey addresses prevention of adolescent problems. *American Psychologist, 44,* 828–30.

Keogh, B. K. (1986). Future of the LD field: Research and practice. *Journal of Learning Disabilities, 19,* 455–60.

Keogh, B. K. & Bess, C. R. (1991). Assessing temperament. In H. L. Swanson (Ed.), *Handbook of assessment of learning disabilities: Theory, research, and practice* (pp. 313–30). Austin, TX: PRO-ED.

Keogh, B. K., Major-Kingsley, S., Omori-Gordon, H. & Reid, H. P. (1982). *A system of marker variables for the field of learning disabilities.* New York: Syracuse University Press.

Keogh, B. K. & Pelland, M. (1985). Vision training revisited. *Journal of Learning Disabilities, 18,* 228–36.

Keogh, B. K., Wilcoxen, A. G. & Bernheimer, L. (1986). Prevention services for risk children: Evidence for policy and practice. In D. C. Farran & J. D. McKinney (Eds.), *Risk in intellectual and psychosocial development* (pp. 287–316). Orlando, FL: Academic Press.

Kephart, N. C. (1960). *The slow learner in the classroom.* Columbus, OH: Merrill. (2nd ed. 1971.)

Kibler, R. J., Barker, L. L. & Miles, D. T. (1970). *Behavior objectives and instruction.* Boston: Allyn & Bacon.

Kimball, W. H. & Heron, T. E. (1988). A behavioral commentary on Poplin's discussion of reductionist fallacy and holistic/constructivist principles. *Journal of Learning Disabilities, 21,* 425–28.

Kinsbourne, M. & Caplin, P. (1979). *Children's learning and attention problems.* Boston: Little, Brown.

Kirk, S. A. (1962). *Educating exceptional children.* Boston: Houghton-Mifflin.

Kirk, S. A. & Chalfant, J. (1984). *Developmental and academic learning disabilities.* Denver: Love.

Kirk, S. A. & Gallagher, J. (1979). *Educating exceptional children* (3rd ed.). Boston: Houghton-Mifflin.

Kirk, S. A. & Kirk, W. D. (1983). On defining learning disabilities. *Journal of Learning Disabilities, 16,* 20–21.

Kirst, M. W. (1991). Integrating children's services. *EdSource.* Menlo Park, CA: EdSource Publications.

Klimes-Dougan, B., Lopez, J., Adelman, H. S. & Nelson, P. (In press) A study of low income parents' involvement in schooling. *The Urban Review.*

Knoff, H. M. (1987). School-based interventions for discipline problems. In C. A. Maher & J. E. Zins (Eds.), *Psychoeducational interventions in the schools* (pp. 118–40). New York: Pergamon.

Koestner, R., Ryan, R. M., Bernieri, F. & Holt, K. (1984). Setting limits on children's behavior: The differential effects of controlling vs. informational styles on intrinsic motivation and creativity. *Journal of Personality, 52,* 242–48.

Kolligan, J. & Sternberg, R. (1987). Intelligence, information processing, and specific learning disabilities: A triarchic synthesis. *Journal of Learning Disabilities, 20,* 8–17.

Koppitz, E. (1973). Special class pupils with learning disabilities: A five year follow-up study. *Academic Therapy, 13,* 133–40.

Krathwohl, D. R., Bloom, B. S. & Masia, B. B. (1964). *Taxonomy of educational objectives: Handbook II: Affective domain.* New York: McKay.

La Buda, M. C. & DeFries, J. C. (1988). Genetic and environmental etiologies of reading disability: A twin study. *Annals of Dyslexia, 38,* 131–38.

Lakebrink, J. M. (Ed.) (1989). *Children at risk.* Springfield, IL: Charles C. Thomas.

Lambert, M. J., Shapiro, D. A. & Bergin, A. E. (1986). The effectiveness of psychotherapy. In S. L. Garfield & A. E. Bergin (Eds.), *Handbook of psychotherapy and behavior change* (3rd ed.). New York: Wiley.

Larry P. v. Riles, 343 F. Supp. 1306 (N.D. Calif. 1972).

Lazarus, R. S. (1991). Cognition and motivation in emotion. *American Psychologist, 46,* 352–67.

LeBanks v. Spears, 417 F. Supp. 169 (1976).

Lee, V. E., Brooks-Gunn, J., Schnur, E. & Liaw, F-R. (1990). Are Head Start effects sustained? A longitudinal follow-up comparison of disadvantaged children attending Head Start, no preschool, and other preschools. *Child Development, 61,* 495–507.

Lehr, C. A., Ysseldyke, J. E. & Thurlow, M. L. (1986). *Assessment practices in model early childhood education programs* (Research Report No. 7). Minneapolis: University of Minnesota, Early Childhood Assessment Project.

Leinhardt, G. & Pallay, A. (1982). Restrictive educational settings: Exile or haven? *Review of Educational Research, 52,* 557–78.

Lennard, H., Epstein, L. J., Bernstein, A. & Ransom, D. C. (1970). Hazards implicit in prescribing psychoactive drugs. *Science, 169,* 438–41.

Lepper, M. R. & Greene, D. (1978). *The hidden costs of reward.* Hillsdale, NJ: Erlbaum Press.

Lerner, J. W. (1988). *Children with learning disabilities* (5th ed.). Boston: Houghton-Mifflin.

Levine, R. J. (1975). *The nature and definition of informed consent in various research settings.* Washington, DC: National Commission for the Protection of Human Subjects.

Levinson, H. N. (1980). *A solution to the riddle dyslexia.* New York: Springer-Verlag.

Lichtenstein, R. & Ireton, H. (1984). *Preschool screening: Identifying young children with developmental and educational problems.* Orlando, FL: Grune & Stratton.

Lidz, C. S. (Ed.) (1987). *Dynamic assessment: An interactional approach to evaluating learning potential.* New York: Guilford Press.

Lindsay, G. A. & Wedell, K. (1982). The early identification of educationally "at risk" children revisited. *Journal of Learning Disabilities, 15,* 212–17.

Lindsley, O. R. (1964). Direct measurement and prothesis of retarded behavior. *Journal of Education, 147,* 62–81.

Linn, R. L., Baker, E. L. & Dunbar, S. B. (1991). Complex, performance-based assessment: Expectations and validation criteria. *Educational Researcher, 20,* 15–21.

Lipson, M. Y. & Wixson, K. K. (1986). Reading disability research: An interactionist perspective. *Review of Educational Research, 56,* 111–36.

Liscio, M. A. (Ed.) (1985). *A guide to colleges for learning disabled students.* Orlando, FL: Academic Press.

Litigation and special education (1986). *Exceptional Children, 52,* (4).

Lloyd, J. W. & Blandford, B. J. (1991). Assessment for instruction. In H. L. Swanson (Ed.), *Handbook of assessment of learning disabilities: Theory, research, and practice* (pp. 45–58). Austin, TX: PRO-ED.

Lloyd, J. W., Crowley, E. P., Kohler, F. W. & Strain, P. S. (1988). Redefining the applied research agenda: Cooperative learning, prereferral, teacher consultation, and peer-modulated interventions. *Journal of Learning Disabilities, 21,* 43–52.

Long, B. B. (1986). The prevention of mental-emotional disabilities: A report from the National Mental Health Association Commission. *American Psychologist, 41,* 825–29.

Lovitt, T. C. (1975a). Applied behavior analysis and learning disabilities—Part I: Characteristics of ABA, general recommendations, and methodological limitations. *Journal of Learning Disabilities, 8,* 432–43.

Lovitt, T. C. (1975b). Applied behavior analysis and learning disabilities—Part II: Specific research recommendations and suggestions for practitioners. *Journal of Learning Disabilities, 8,* 504–518.

Lovitt, T. C. (1989). *Introduction to learning disabilities.* Boston: Allyn & Bacon.

Lyon, G. R. (1985). Educational validation of learning disability subtypes. In B. P. Rourke (Ed.), *Neuropsychology of learning disabilities: Essentials of subtype analyses* (pp. 228–56). New York: Guilford.

Lyon, G. R. & Flynn, J. M. (1991). Assessing subtypes of learning abilities. In H. L. Swanson (Ed.), *Handbook of assessment of learning disabilities: Theory, research, and practice* (pp. 59–74). Austin, TX: PRO-ED.

MacMillan, D. L., Hendricks, I. G. & Watkins, A. V. (1988). Impact of Diana, Larry P., and P.L. 94-142 on minority students. *Exceptional Children, 54,* 426–32.

Maher, C. A. & Bennett, R. E. (1984). *Planning and evaluating special education services.* Englewood Cliffs, NJ: Prentice-Hall.

Maher, C. A. & Zins, J. E. (Eds.) (1987). *Psychoeducational interventions in the schools* (pp. 118–40). New York: Pergamon.

Mahoney, M. J. (1974). *Cognition and behavior modification.* Cambridge, MA: Ballinger.

Male, M. (1988). *Special magic: Computers, classroom strategies, and exceptional children.* Mountain View, CA: Mayfield.

Mangrum, C. T. & Strichart, S. S. (Eds.) (1988). *College and the learning disabled student: A guide to program selection, development, and implementation* (2nd ed.). Orlando, FL: Grune & Stratton.

Mann, L. (1971). Psychometric phrenology and the new faculty psychology: The case against ability assessment and training. *Journal of Special Education, 5,* 3–14.

Mann, L., Cartwright, G. P., Kennowitz, L. A., Boyer, C. W., Jr., Metz, C. M. & Wolford, B. (1984). The Child Service Demonstration Centers: A summary report. *Exceptional Children, 50,* 532–40.

Mann, V. A. & Brady, S. (1988). Reading disability: The role of language deficiencies. *Journal of Consulting and Clinical Psychology, 56,* 811–16.

Marshall v. Georgia. U. S. District Court for the Southern District of Georgia, CV 482-233, June 28, 1984.

Marston, D. (1987–88). The effectiveness of special education: A time series analysis of reading performance in regular and special education settings. *Journal of Special Education, 21,* 13–26.

Massenzio, S. (1983). Legal resource networks for parents and individuals with special needs. *Exceptional Children, 50,* 273–75.

Mastropieri, M. A., Scruggs, T. E. & Levin, J. R. (1985). Mnemonic strategy instruction with learning disabled adolescents. *Journal of Learning Disabilities, 18,* 94–99.

Mather, N. (1988). Computer-assisted instruction. In C. S. Bos & S. Vaughn (Eds.), *Strategies for teaching students with learning and behavior problems.* Boston: Allyn & Bacon.

Mattes, J. (1983). The Feingold diet: A current reappraisal. In G. Senf & J. F. Torgesen (Eds.), *Annual review of learning disabilities: Vol. 1. Journal of Learning Disabilities Reader* (pp. 127–31). Chicago: Professional Press.

McCann, S. K., Semmel, M. I. & Nevin, A. (1985). Reverse mainstreaming: Non-handicapped students in special education classrooms. *Remedial and Special Education, 6,* 13–19.

McGrath, J. H. (1972). *Planning systems for school executives: The unity of theory and practice.* Scranton, PA: Intext Educational Publishers.

McGraw, K. O. (1978). The detrimental effects of reward on performance: A literature review and a prediction model. In M. R. Lepper & D. Greene (Eds.), *The hidden costs of reward* (pp. 33–60). Hillsdale, NJ: Erlbaum.

McKinney, J. D. (1988). Empirically derived subtypes of specific learning disabilities. In M. C. Wang, H. J. Walberg & M. C. Reynolds (Eds.), *The handbook of special education: Research and practice.* Oxford, England: Pergamon Press.

McKinney, J. D. (1989). Longitudinal research on the behavioral characteristics of children with learning disabilities. *Journal of Learning Disabilities, 22,* 141–50, 165.

McLeskey, J. (1989). The influence of level of discrepancy on the identification of students with learning disabilities. *Journal of Learning Disabilities, 22,* 435–38, 443.

McLeskey, J. & Waldron, N. L. (1991). Identifying students with learning disabilities: The effects of implementing statewide guidelines. *Journal of Learning Disabilities, 24,* 501–507.

McNeil, J. D. (1990). *Curriculum: A comprehensive introduction* (4th ed.). Glenview, IL: Scott, Foresman/Little, Brown.

McNutt, G. (1986). The status of learning disabilities in the states: Consensus or controversy? *Journal of Learning Disabilities, 19,* 12–16.

Meichenbaum, D. (1977). *Cognitive-behavior modification—An integrative approach.* New York: Plenum.

Meichenbaum, D. (1983). Teaching thinking: A cognitive-behavioral approach. In *Interdisciplinary voices in learning disabilities and remedial education* (pp. 1–28). Austin, TX: PRO-ED.

Melaragno, R. J. (1976). The tutorial community. In V. L. Allen (Ed.), *Children as teachers: Theory and research on tutoring* (pp. 189–98). New York: Academic Press.

Melton, G. B. (1983). Children's competence to consent: A problem in law and social science. In G. B. Melton, G. P. Koocher & M. J. Saks (Eds.), *Children's competence to consent.* New York: Plenum.

Melton, G. B. (1991). Socialization in the global community: Respect for the dignity of children. *American Psychologist, 46,* 66–71.

Melton, G. B. & Davidson, H. A. (1987). Child protection and society: When should the state intervene? *American Psychologist, 42,* 172–75.

Melton, G. B., Koocher, G. P. & Saks, M. (Eds.) (1983). *Children's competence to consent.* New York: Plenum.

Mercer, C. D., Hughes, C. & Mercer, A. R. (1975). Learning disabilities definitions used by state education departments. *Learning Disability Quarterly, 8,* 45–55.

Metzger, R. L. & Werner, D. B. (1984). Use of visual training for reading disabilities. *Pediatrics, 73,* 824–29.

Meyen, E. L. (1982). *Exceptional children and youth* (2nd ed.). Denver: Love Publishing Co.

Meyers, J. (1981). Mental health consultation. In J. C. Conoley (Ed.), *Consultation in the schools: Theory, research, procedures.* New York: Academic Press.

Miller, A. (1981). Conceptual matching models and interactional research in education. *Review of Educational Research, 51,* 33–84.

Miller, D. T. & Ross, M. (1975). Self-serving biases in the attribution of causality: Fact or fiction? *Psychological Bulletin, 82,* 213–25.

Miller, S. R. & Schloss, P. J. (1982). *Career-vocational education for handicapped youth.* Rockville, MD: Aspen.

Millman, H. L., Schaefer, C. E. & Cohen, J. J. (1981). *Therapies for school behavior problems.* San Francisco: Jossey-Bass.

Mills v. D.C. Board of Education, 348 F. Supp. 366 (D.D.C. 1972).

Mirkin, P. K. (1980). Conclusions. In J. Ysseldyke & M. Thurlow (Eds.), *The special education assessment and decision making process: Seven case studies.* Minneapolis: University of Minnesota, Institute for Research on Learning Disabilities.

Mirkin, P., Marston, D. & Deno, S. L. (1982). *Direct and repeated measurement of academic skills: An alternative to traditional screening, referral, and identification of learning disabled students.* Research Report No. 75. Minneapolis: University of Minnesota, Institute for Research on Learning Disabilities.

Mitchell, A., Seligson, M. & Marx, F. (1989). *Early childhood programs and the public schools: Promise and practice.* Dover, MA: Auburn House.

Mnookin, R. H. (1985). *In the interest of children: Advocacy, law reform and public policy.* New York: W. H. Freeman.

Monson, T. C. & Snyder, M. (1975). Actors, observers, and the attribution process: Toward a reconceptualization. *Journal of Experimental Social Psychology, 13,* 89–111.

Montessori, M. (1964). *The Montessori Method,* trans. Anne E. George. New York: Schocken. First published in Italian in 1909 and in English in 1912.

Moos, R. H. (1979). *Evaluating educational environments.* San Francisco: Jossey-Bass.

Morrison, S. R. & Siegel, L. S. (1991). Learning disabilities: A critical review of definitional and assessment issues. In J. E. Obrzut & G. W. Hynds (Eds.), *Neurological foundations of learning disabilities: A handbook of issues, methods, and practices* (pp. 79–95). San Diego: Academic Press.

Morsink, C. V., Thomas, C. C. & Smith-Davis, J. (1987). Noncategorical special education programs: Process and outcomes. In M. C. Wang, M. C. Reynolds & H. J. Walberg (Eds.), *The handbook of special education: Research and practice* (Vol. 2, pp. 287–309). Oxford, England: Pergamon.

Munn, J., McAlpine, A. & Taylor, L. (1989). Kindergarten Intervention Program: Development of an early intervention mental health program based on trained volunteers. *School Counselor, 36,* 371–75.

Murphy, V. & Hicks-Stewart, K. (1991). Learning disabilities and attention deficit-hyperactivity disorder: An interactional perspective. *Journal of Learning Disabilities, 24,* 386–88.

Myers, P. I. & Hammill, D. D. (1990). *Learning disabilities.* Austin, TX: PRO-ED.

Myklebust, H. R. (1954). *Auditory disorders in children.* New York: Grune & Stratton.

Myklebust, H. R. (1968). Learning disabilities: Definition and overview. In H. R. Myklebust (Ed.), *Progress in learning disabilities.* New York: Grune & Stratton.

National Assessment for Educational Progress (1976). *Functional literacy: Basic reading performance.* Denver: NAEP.

National Association for the Education of Young Children (1983). Progress report on the Center Accreditation Project. *Young Children, 39,* 35–46.

National Association for Perinatal Research and Education (1989). *Perinatal addiction research and education update.* Chicago: Author.

National Association of School Psychologists (1986). *Rights without labels.* Washington, DC: Author. (Reprinted in *School Psychology Review, 18,* 1989.)

National Center for Educational Statistics Bulletin (1983). *High school dropouts: Descriptive information from high school and beyond.* Washington, DC: Author.

National Commission on Excellence in Education (1983). *A nation at risk: The imperative for educational reform.* Washington, DC: U. S. Department of Education.

Neisser, U. (1976). *Cognition and reality: Principles and implications of cognitive psychology.* San Francisco: W. H. Freeman.

Nichols, P. & Chen, T. (1981). *Minimal brain dysfunction: A prospective study.* Hillsdale, NJ: Erlbaum.

NJCLD (1989). *Letter from NJCLD to member organizations.* Topic: Modifications to the NJCLD definition of learning disabilities.

Nunnally, J. C. (1978). *Psychometric theory* (2nd ed.). New York: McGraw-Hill.

Obrzut, J. E. & Boliek, G. A. (1991). Neurophysiological assessment of childhood learning disabilities. In H. L. Swanson (Ed.), *Handbook of assessment of learning disabilities: Theory, research, and practice* (pp. 121–46). Austin, TX: PRO-ED.

O'Connor, P. D., Sofo, F., Kendall, L. & Olsen, G. (1990). Reading disabilities and the effects of colored filters. *Journal of Learning Disabilities, 23,* 597–603, 620.

Odden, A. (1990). Class size and student achievement: Research-based policy alternatives. *Educational Evaluation and Policy Analysis, 12,* 213–27.

Office of Policy Research and Improvement (1989). *Cocaine babies: Florida's substance-exposed youth.* Tallahassee: State of Florida Department of Education.

Okolo, C. M. & Sitlington, P. (1986). The role of special education in LD adolescents' transition from school to work. *Learning Disability Quarterly, 9,* 141–55.

Olson, R., Wise, B., Conners, F., Rack, J. & Fulker, D. (1989). Specific deficits in component reading and language skills: Genetic and environmental influences. *Journal of Learning Disabilities, 22,* 339–48.

Orton, S. T. (1937). *Reading, writing, and speech problems in children.* New York: Norton.

Orvaschel, H., Sholomskas, D. & Weissman, M. M. (1980). *The assessment of psychopathology and behavioral problems in children: A review of scales suitable for epidemiological and clinical research (1967–1979).* DHHS Publication No. (ADM)80-1037. Washington, DC: U. S. GPO.

Paget, K. D. & Barnett, D. W. (1990). Assessment of infants, toddlers, preschool children, and their families. In T. B. Gutkin & C. R. Reynolds (Eds.), *The handbook of school psychology* (2nd ed.). New York: Wiley.

Palincsar, A. S. & Brown, A. L. (1984). Reciprocal teaching of comprehension-fostering and comprehension-monitoring activities. *Cognition & Instruction, 1,* 117–75.

Palincsar, A. S., Brown, A. L. & Campione, J. C. (1991). Dynamic assessment. In H. L. Swanson (Ed.), *Handbook of assessment of learning disabilities: Theory, research, and practice* (pp. 75–94). Austin, TX: PRO-ED.

Parker, R. M. (1990). Power, control, and validity in research. *Journal of Learning Disabilities, 23,* 613–20.

PASE v. Hannon, 506 F. Supp. 832 (N.D. Ill. 1980).

Patterson, C. H. (1977). *Foundations for a theory of instruction and educational psychology.* New York: Harper & Row.

Patterson, G. R. (1986). Performance models for antisocial boys. *American Psychologist, 41,* 432–44.

Pelham, W. (1986). The effects of psychostimulant drugs on learning and academic achievement in children with attention-deficit disorders and learning disabilities. In J. K. Torgesen & B. Y. L. Wong (Eds.), *Psychological and educational perspectives on learning disabilities* (pp. 257–96). Orlando, FL: Academic Press.

Pennekamp, M. & Freeman, E. M. (1988, Summer). Toward a partnership perspective: Schools, families, and school social workers. *Social Work in Education,* 246–59.

Pennington, B. F. & Smith, S. D. (1988). Genetic influences on learning disabilities: An update. *Journal of Consulting and Clinical Psychology, 56,* 817–23.

Pennsylvania Association for Retarded Citizens (PARC) v. Commonwealth of Pennsylvania, 334 F. Supp. 1257, 343 F. Supp. 279 (E.D. Pa. 1971, 1972).

Phelps, L., Chaplin, C. & Kelly, A. (1987). A parents' guide to vocational education. *News Digest, 8,* 1–11.

Phi Delta Kappa (1980). *Why do some urban schools succeed?* Bloomington, IN: Author.

Pihl, R. O. (1975). Learning disabilities: Intervention programs in the schools. In H. R. Myklebust (Ed.), *Progress in learning disabilities* (Vol. 3). New York: Grune & Stratton.

Polatajko, H. J. (1985). A critical look at vestibular dysfunction in learning-disabled children. *Developmental Medicine and Child Neurology, 27,* 283–92.

Poplin, M. (1988). Holistic/constructivist principles of the teaching/learning process: Implications for the field of learning disabilities. *Journal of Learning Disabilities, 21,* 401–416.

Powers, S. I., Hauser, S. T. & Kilner, L. A. (1989). Adolescent mental health. *American Psychologist, 44,* 200–208.

Primary Intervention Program (1987). *Program development manual.* Los Alimitos, CA: Southwest Regional Laboratory for Educational Research and Development.

Pugach, M. C. & Johnson, L. J. (1989). The challenge of implementing collaboration between general and special education. *Exceptional Children, 56,* 232–35.

Purkey, S. C. & Smith, M. S. (1983). Effective schools: A review. *The Elementary School Journal, 83,* 427–52.

Purkey, S. C. & Smith, M. S. (1985). School reform: The district policy implications of the effective schools literature. *The Elementary School Journal, 85,* 353–89.

Quay, H. C. & Werry, J. S. (Eds.) (1986). *Psychopathological disorders of childhood* (3rd ed.). New York: Wiley.

Rabinovitz, R. D. (1959). Reading and learning disabilities. In S. Arieti (Ed.), *American handbook of psychiatry* (Vol. 1). New York: Basic Books.

Rabinovitz, R. D. (1968). Reading problems in children: Definitions and classification. In A. Keeney & V. Keeney (Eds.), *Dyslexia: Diagnosis and treatment of reading disorders.* St. Louis: C. V. Mosby.

Reed, S. & Sautter, R. C. (1990). Kappan special report—Children of poverty: The status of 12 million young Americans. *Phi Delta Kappan, 71,* K1–K12.

Reynolds, C. R. & Kaiser, S. M. (1990). Test bias in psychological assessment. In T. B. Gutkin & C. R. Reynolds (Eds.), *The handbook of school psychology* (2nd ed., pp. 487–525). New York: Wiley.

Reynolds, M. C., Wang, M. C. & Walberg, H. J. (1987). The necessary restructuring of special and regular education. *Exceptional Children, 53,* 391–98.

Rhodes, W. C. & Tracy, M. C. (1972). *A study of child variance: Intervention* (Vol. 2). Ann Arbor: University of Michigan Press.

Risley, T. R. & Baer, D. M. (1973). Operant behavior modification: The deliberate development of behavior. In B. M. Caldwell & N. N. Ricciuti (Eds.), *Review of child development research* (Vol. 3). Chicago: University of Chicago Press.

Rissman, M., Curtiss, S. & Tallal, P. (1990). School placement outcomes of young language impaired children. *Journal of Speech Language Pathology and Audiology, 14,* 49–58.

Robinson, D. N. (1974). Harm, offense, and nuisance: Some first steps in the establishment of an ethics of treatment. *American Psychologist, 29,* 233–38.

Robinson, G. L. W. & Conway, R. N. F. (1990). The effects of Irlen colored lenses on students' specific reading skills and their perception of ability: A 12-month validity study. *Journal of Learning Disabilities, 23,* 588–96.

Rogers, C. R. (1969). *Freedom to learn.* Columbus, OH: Merrill.

Rooney, K. J. (1991). Controversial therapies: A review and critique. *Intervention in School and Clinic, 26,* 134–42.

Rosenshine, B. V. & Stevens, R. (1986). Teaching functions. In M. Wittrock (Ed.), *Third handbook of research on teaching* (pp. 376–391). New York: Macmillan.

Ross, A. O. (1985). To form a more perfect union. *Behavior Therapy, 16,* 195–204.

Rossi, P. H. & Freeman, H. E. (1982). *Evaluation: A systematic approach* (2nd ed.). Beverly Hills, CA: Sage.

Rourke, B. P. & Strang, J. D. (1983). Subtypes of reading and arithmetical disabilities: A neuropsychological analysis. In M. Rutter (Ed.), *Developmental neuropsychiatry* (pp. 473–88). New York: Guilford.

Rumberger, R. W. (1987). High school dropouts: A review of issues and evidence. *Review of Educational Research, 57,* 101–121.

Rusch, F. & Phelps, L. (1987). Secondary special education and transition from school to work: A national priority. *Exceptional Children, 53,* 487–92.

Rutter, M. (1981, February 26–28). *School effects on pupil progress: Research findings and policy implications.* Paper prepared for the National Institute of Education, U. S. Department of Education.

Rutter, M. (1983). *Developmental neuropsychiatry.* New York: Guilford.

Rutter, M. & Giller, H. (1983). *Juvenile delinquency: Trends and perspectives.* New York: Guilford.

Ryan, R. M., Connell, J. P. & Deci, E. L. (1985). A motivational analysis of self-determination and self-regulation in education. In C. Ames & R. E. Ames (Eds.), *Research on motivation in education: The classroom milieu* (pp. 13–51). New York: Academic Press.

Ryan, W. (1971). *Blaming the victim.* New York: Random House.

Salvia, J. & Ysseldyke, J. E. (1991). *Assessment* (5th ed.). Boston: Houghton-Mifflin.

Sameroff, A. J. (1985). Environmental factors in the early screening of children at risk. In W. K. Frankenburg, R. N. Emde & J. W. Sullivan (Eds.), *Early identification of children at risk: An international perspective.* New York: Plenum.

Samuels, S. J. (1987). Information-processing abilities and reading. *Journal of Learning Disabilities, 20,* 18–22.

Sarason, S. B. (1971, 1982). *The culture of the school and the problem of change* (1st and 2nd eds.). Boston: Allyn & Bacon.

Sarason, S. B. (1990). *The predictable failure of educational reform: Can we change course before it's too late?* San Francisco: Jossey-Bass.

Sarason, S. B., Levine, M., Goldenberg, I. I., Cherlin, D. L. & Bennett, E. M. (1960).

Psychology in community settings: Clinical, educational, vocational, social aspects. New York: Wiley.

Sawyer, D. J. (1992). Language abilities, reading acquisition, and developmental dyslexia: A discussion of hypothetical and observed relationships. *Journal of Learning Disabilities, 25,* 82–95.

Schain, R. J. (1972). *Neurology of childhood learning disorders.* Baltimore: Williams & Wilkins.

Schlechty, P. C. (1990). *Schools for the twenty-first century: Leadership imperatives for educational reform.* San Francisco: Jossey-Bass.

Schrag, P. & Divoky, D. (1975). *The myth of the hyperactive child and other means of child control.* New York: Pantheon Books.

Schumaker, J. B., Deshler, D. D. & Ellis, E. S. (1986). Intervention issues related to the education of LD adolescents. In J. K. Torgesen & B. Y. L. Wong (Eds.), *Psychological and educational perspectives on learning disabilities* (pp. 329–66). Orlando, FL: Academic Press.

Schweinhart, L. J. & Weikart, D. P. (1989). Early childhood experience and its effects. In L. Bond & B. Compas (Eds.), *Primary prevention in the schools* (pp. 106–145). Newbury Park, CA: Sage.

Sclafani, A. J. & Lynch, M. J. (1989). *College guide for students with learning disabilities 1988–1989.* Miller Place, NY: Laurel Publications.

Scott, S. S. (1991). A change in legal status: An overlooked dimension in the transition to higher education. *Journal of Learning Disabilities, 24,* 459–66.

Scriven, M. (1981). *Comments on Gene Glass.* Paper presented at the Wingspread Working Conference of Social Policy and Educational Leaders to Develop Strategies for Special Education in the 1980's, Racine, WI.

Shapiro, E. S. & Derr, T. F. (1990). Curriculum-based assessment. In T. B. Gutkin & C. R. Reynolds (Eds.), *The handbook of school psychology* (2nd ed., pp. 365–87). New York: Wiley.

Shaywitz, S., Cohen, D. & Shaywitz, B. (1978). The biochemical basis of minimal brain dysfunction. *Journal of Pediatrics, 92,* 179–87.

Shaywitz, S. E., Cohen, D. J. & Shaywitz, B. A. (1980). Behavior and learning difficulties in children of normal intelligence born to alcoholic mothers. *Journal of Pediatrics, 96,* 978–82.

Shaywitz, S. E., Escobar, M. D., Shaywitz, B. A., Fletcher, J. M. & Makuch, R. (1992). Evidence that dyslexia may represent the lower tail of a normal distribution of reading ability. *The New England Journal of Medicine, 326,* 146–50.

Shepard, L. A. (1991). Interview on assessment issues with Lorrie Shepard. *Educational Researcher, 20,* 21–23, 27.

Shepard, L. A. & Smith, M. L. (1983). An evaluation of the identification of learning disabled students in Colorado. *Learning Disability Quarterly, 6,* 115–27.

Shepard, L. A., Smith, M. L. & Vojir, C. P. (1983). Characteristics of pupils identified as learning disabled. *American Educational Research Journal, 20,* 309–331.

Shinn, M. R. (Ed.) (1989). *Curriculum-based measurement: Assessing special children.* New York: Guilford.

S-I v. Turlington, Order on Motion to Dismiss, No. 79-8020-Civ-Atkins, U. S. District Court, Southern District of Florida, October 9, 1986.

Sieben, R. L. (1977). Controversial medical treatments of learning disabilities. *Academic Therapy, 13,* 133–48.

Siegel, L. S. (1989). IQ is irrelevant to the definition of learning disabilities. *Journal of Learning Disabilities, 22,* 469–89.

Silberman, C. E. (1970). *Crisis in the classroom: The remaking of American education.* New York: Vintage Books.

Silver, A. A. & Hagin, R. A. (1990). *Disorders of learning in childhood.* New York: Wiley.

Silver, L. B. (1987). The "magic cure": A review of current controversial approaches to treatment of learning disabilities. *Journal of Learning Disabilities, 20,* 498–504.

Silver, L. B. (1990). Attention deficit-hyperactivity disorder: Is it a learning disability or a related disorder? *Journal of Learning Disabilities, 23,* 394–97.

Simmons, D. C. (1992). Perspectives on dyslexia: Commentary on educational concerns. *Journal of Learning Disabilities, 25,* 66–70.

Simoni, J. & Adelman, H. S. (1990). *School-based mutual support groups for parents.* Unpublished manuscript.

Skager, R. W. & Weinberg, C. (1971). *Fundamentals of educational research: An introductory approach.* Glenview, IL: Scott, Foresman.

Skinner, B. F. (1968). *The technology of teaching.* Englewood Cliffs, NJ: Prentice-Hall.

Skinner, B. F. (1974). *About behaviorism.* New York: Alfred A. Knopf.

Slavin, R. E., Karweit, N. L. & Madden, N. A. (1989). *Effective programs for students at risk.* Boston: Allyn & Bacon.

Slavin, R. E., Madden, N. A., Karweit, N. L., Dolan, L., Wasik, B. A., Shaw, A., Mainzer, K. L. & Huxby, B. (1991). Neverstreaming: Prevention and early intervention as an alternative to special education. *Journal of Learning Disabilities, 24,* 373–78.

Slavin, R. E., Madden, N. A., Karweit, N. L., Livermon, B. J. & Dolan, L. (1990). Success for all: First-year outcomes of a comprehensive plan for reforming urban education. *American Educational Research Journal, 27,* 255–78.

Smith, C. R. (1991). *Learning disabilities: The interaction of learner, task, and setting* (2nd ed.). Boston: Allyn & Bacon.

Smith, S. D. (Ed.) (1986). *Genetics and learning disabilities.* San Diego: College-Hill Press.

Smith, S. D., Pennington, B. F., Kimberling, W. J. & Ing, P. S. (1990). Familial dyslexia: Use of genetic linkage data to define subtypes. *Academy of Child and Adolescent Psychiatry, 29,* 204–213.

Snart, F. (1985). Cognitive-processing approaches to the assessment of remediation of learning problems. An interview with J. P. Das and Reuven Feuerstein. *Journal of Psychoeducational Assessment, 3,* 1–14.

Snow, R. E. (1986). Individual differences and the design of educational programs. *American Psychologist, 41,* 1029–39.

Spreen, O. (1982). Adult outcome of reading disorders. In R. N . Malatesha & P. G. Aaron (Eds.), *Reading disorders: Varieties and treatments.* New York: Academic Press.

Stainback, S. & Stainback, W. (1984). A rationale for the merger of special and regular education. *Exceptional Children, 51,* 102–111.

Stake, R. E. (1967). The countenance of educational evaluation. *Teachers College Record, 68,* 523–40.

Stake, R. E. (1976). *Evaluating educational programs: The need and the response.* Paris: Organization for Economic Cooperation and Development.

Stanovich, K. E. (1991a). Cognitive science meets beginning reading: Commentary. *Psychological Science, 2,* 70, 77–81.

Stanovich, K. E. (1991b). Reading disability: Assessment issues. In H. L. Swanson (Ed.), *Handbook of assessment of learning disabilities: Theory, research, and practice* (pp. 147–75). Austin, TX: PRO-ED.

Stanovich, K. E. (1991c). Conceptual and empirical problems with discrepancy definitions of reading disability. *Learning Disability Quarterly, 14,* 269–80.

Stauffer, R. G. (1980). *The language experience approach to the teaching of reading* (2nd ed.). New York: Harper & Row.

Steinbeck, J. (1955). Like captured fireflies. *California Teachers Association Journal, 51,* 7.

Stephens, T. M. (1977). *Teaching skills to children with learning and behavior disorders.* Columbus, OH: Merrill.

Stephens, T. M. (1985). Personal behavior and professional ethics: Implications for special educators. *Journal of Learning Disabilities, 18,* 187–92.

Stevenson, H. W. & Stigler, J. W. (1992). *The learning gap: Why our schools are failing and what we can learn from Japanese and Chinese education.* New York: Summit Books.

Stipek, D. J. (1988). *Motivation to learn: From theory to practice.* Englewood Cliffs, NJ: Prentice-Hall.

Stoddard, K. (1991). The changing role of teachers: Refocus on the family. *LD Forum, 17,* 15–17.

Strupp, H. H. & Hadley, S. M. (1977). A tripartite model for mental health and therapeutic outcomes with special reference to negative effects in psychotherapy. *American Psychologist, 32,* 187–96.

Suran, B. G. & Rizzo, J. V. (1979). *Special children: An integrative approach.* Glenview, IL: Scott, Foresman.

Swan, W. (1980). Handicapped children's early education program. *Exceptional Children, 47,* 12–14.

Swan, W. (1981). Efficacy studies in early childhood special education. *Journal of the Division for Early Childhood, 4,* 1–4.

Swanson, H. L. (1987). Information processing theory and learning disabilities: An overview. *Journal of Learning Disabilities, 20,* 3–7.

Swanson, H. L. (1988). Toward a metatheory of learning disabilities. *Journal of Learning Disabilities, 21,* 196–209.

Swanson, H. L. (1991). Operational definitions and learning disabilities: An overview. *Learning Disability Quarterly, 14,* 242–54.

Swanson, H. L. (Ed.) (1991). *Handbook of assessment of learning disabilities: Theory, research, and practice* (pp. 265–84). Austin, TX: PRO-ED.

Swanson, H. L. & Watson, B. L. (1982). *Educational and psychological assessment of exceptional children.* St. Louis: Mosby.

Swanson, J. M., Cantwell, D., Lerner, M., McBurnett, K. & Hanna, G. (1991). Effects of stimulant medication on learning in children with ADHD. *Journal of Learning Disabilities, 24,* 219–30, 255.

Swift, C. & Lewis, R. B. (1985). Leisure preferences of elementary-aged learning disabled boys. *Research in Special Education, 6,* 37–42.

Szasz, T. S. (1969). Psychiatric classification as a strategy of personal constraint. In T. S. Szasz (Ed.), *Ideology and insanity.* New York: Doubleday.

Tallal, P. (1988). Developmental language disorders. In J. F. Kavanagh & T. L. Truss, Jr. (Eds.), *Learning disabilities: Proceedings of the national conference* (pp. 181–272). Parkton, MD: York Press.

Tallal, P. (1990). *A follow-up study of children with language disorders.* Paper presented at the March meeting of the New York Orton Dyslexia Society.

Tangri, S. & Leitch, L. M. (1982). *Barriers to home-school collaboration: Two case studies in junior high schools.* Final report to the National Institute of Education. Washington, DC: Urban Institute.

Tapp, J. L. & Melton, G. B. (1983). Preparing children for decision making. In G. B. Melton, G. P. Koocher & M. Saks (Eds.), *Children's competence to consent* (pp. 215–34). New York: Plenum.

Taylor, H. G. & Fletcher, J. (1983). Biological foundations of "specific developmental disorders": Methods, findings, and future directions. *Journal of Clinical Child Psychology, 12,* 46–65.

Taylor, L. & Adelman, H. S. (1986). Facilitating children's participation in decisions that affect them: From concept to practice. *Journal of Clinical Child Psychology, 15,* 346–51.

Taylor, L. & Adelman, H. S. (1990). School avoidance behavior: Motivational bases and implications for intervention. *Child Psychiatry and Human Development, 20,* 219–33.

Taylor, L., Adelman, H. S. & Kaser-Boyd, N. (1984). Attitudes toward involving minors in decisions. *Professional Psychology, 15,* 436–49.

Taylor, L., Adelman, H. S. & Kaser-Boyd, N. (1985). Minors' attitudes and competence toward participation in psychoeducational decisions. *Professional Psychology, 16,* 226–35.

Thorndike, R. L. & Hagen, E. P. (1977). *Measurement and evaluation* (2nd ed.). New York: Wiley.

Thurlow, M. & Ysseldyke, J. (1979). Current assessment and decision making practices in model programs for learning disabled students. *Learning Disability Quarterly, 2,* 15–24.

Tindal, G. (1985). Investigating the effectiveness of special education. *Journal of Learning Disabilities, 18,* 101–112.

Tjossem, T. J. (1976). *Intervention strategies for high risk infants and young children.* Baltimore: University Park Press.

Topics in Early Childhood Education (1990). *Mainstreaming revisited.* Austin, TX: PRO-ED.

Topping, K. J. (1986). *Parents as educators: Training parents to teach their children.* Cambridge, MA: Brookline Books.

Torgesen, J. K. & Wong, B. Y. L. (Eds.) (1986). *Psychological and educational perspectives on learning disabilities.* Orlando, FL: Academic Press.

Touwen, B. C. L. & Huisjes, H. J. (1984). Obstetrics, neonatal neurology, and later outcome. In C. R. Almli & S. Finger (Eds.), *Early brain damage: Vol. 1. Research orientations and clinical observations.* New York: Academic Press.

Tremper, C. & Feshbach, N. D. (1981, August). *Attitudes of parents and adolescents toward decision making by minors.* Paper presented at the meeting of the American Psychological Association, Los Angeles.

Tucker, J., Stevens, L. J. & Ysseldyke, J. E. (1983). Learning disabilities: The experts speak out. *Journal of Learning Disabilities, 16,* 6–14.

Tyack, D. B. (1979). The high school as a social service agency: Historical perspectives on current policy issues. *Education Evaluation and Policy Analysis, 1,* 45–57.

U. S. Department of Education (1988). *To assure the free and appropriate public education of all handicapped children.* Tenth annual report to Congress on the implementation of the Education of the Handicapped Act. Washington, DC: Government Printing Office.

U. S. General Accounting Office (1981). *Disparities still exist in who gets special education.* Washington, DC: Comptroller General of the United States.

Van Duyne, H. J., Gargiulo, R. & Allen, J. A. (1980). A survey of Illinois preschool screening programs. *Illinois Council for Exceptional Children Quarterly, 29,* 11–16.

Vellutino, F. R. (1987). Dyslexia. *Scientific American, 256,* 34–41.

Victoria L. v. District School Board, 741 F. 2d (11th Cir. 1984).

Vogel, S. (1985). *The college student with a learning disability: A handbook for college LD students, admission officers, faculty, and administrators.* Lake Forest, IL: Barat College.

Vogel, S. (1987). Issues and concerns in LD college programming. In D. Johnson & J. Blalock (Eds.), *Adults with learning disabilities* (pp. 239–75). New York: Grune & Stratton.

Vygotsky, L. S. (1978). *Mind in society: The development of higher psychological processes.* M. Cole, V. John-Steiner, S. Scribner & E. Souberman (Eds.). Cambridge, MA: Harvard University Press.

Wagner, R. K. & Torgesen, J. K. (1987). The nature of phonological processing and its causal role in the acquisition of reading skills. *Psychological Bulletin, 101,* 192–212.

Walberg, H. J. (1991). Improving school science in advanced and developing countries. *Review of Educational Research, 61,* 25–69.

Wang, M. (1980). Adaptive instruction: Building on diversity. *Theory into practice, 19,* 122–28.

Wang, M., Gennari, P. & Waxman, H. C. (1985). The adaptive learning environments model: Design, implementation, and effects. In M. Wang & H. Walberg (Eds.), *Adapting instruction to individual differences.* Berkeley, CA: McCutchan.

Wang, M., Peverly, S. & Randolph, R. (1984). An investigation of the implementation and effects of a full-time mainstreaming program. *Remedial and Special Education, 5,* 21–32.

Wang, M. & Walberg, H. (Eds.) (1985). *Adapting instruction to individual differences.* Berkeley, CA: McCutchan.

Wang, M. & Walberg, H. J. (1988). Four fallacies of segregationism. *Exceptional Children, 55,* 128–37.

Wasik, B. A. & Slavin, R. E. (1990, April). *Preventing early reading failure with one-to-one tutoring: A best-evidence synthesis.* Paper presented at the annual convention of the American Educational Research Association, Boston.

Wasserstrom, R. (1975). Lawyers as professionals: Some moral issues. *Human Rights, 5,* 1–24.

Wedell, K. (1970). Diagnosing learning disabilities: A sequential strategy. *Journal of Learning Disabilities, 3,* 311–17.

Weinberg, C. (1974). *Education is a shuck: How the educational system is failing our children.* New York: Morrow.

Weiner, B. A. (1980). *Human motivation.* New York: Holt, Reinhart & Winston.

Weintraub, F. J., Abeson, A., Ballard, J. & La Vor, M. L. (Eds.) (1976). *Public policy and the education of exceptional children.* Reston, VA: The Council for Exceptional Children.

Weithorn, L. A. (1983). Involving children in decisions affecting their own welfare: Guidelines for professionals. In G. B. Melton, G. P. Koocher & M. J. Saks (Eds.), *Children's competence to consent.* New York: Plenum Press.

Wender, P. H. (1976). Hypothesis for possible biochemical basis of minimal brain dysfunction. In R. M. Knights & D. J. Bakker (Eds.), *The neuropsychology of learning disorders: Theoretical approaches.* Baltimore: University Park Press.

Westman, J. C. (1990). *Handbook of learning disabilities: A multisystem approach.* Boston: Allyn & Bacon.

Whalen, C. K. (1989). Attention deficit and hyperactivity disorders. In T. H. Ollendick & M. Hersen (Eds.), *Handbook of child psychopathology* (2nd ed.). New York: Plenum.

White, K. (1985–86). Efficacy of early intervention. *Journal of Special Education, 19,* 401–416.

Whiting, P. (1985). How difficult can reading be? New insight into reading problems. *Journal of the English Teacher's Association, 49,* 49–55.

Wiederholt, J. L. (1974). Historical perspectives on the education of the learning disabled. In L. Mann & D. Sabatino (Eds.), *The second review of special education.* Philadelphia: JSE Press.

Wiener, J. (1986). Alternatives in the assessment of the learning disabled adolescent: A learning strategies approach. *Learning Disabilities Focus, 1,* 97–107.

Wiggins, G. (1989). A true test: Toward more authentic and equitable assessment. *Phi Delta Kappan, 70,* 703–713.

Willson, V. L. (1987). Statistical and psychometric issues surrounding severe discrepancy. *Learning Disabilities Research, 3,* 24–28.

Wissink, J. F., Kass, C. E. & Ferrell, W. R. (1975). A Bayesian approach to the identification of children with learning disabilities. *Journal of Learning Disabilities, 8,* 158–66.

Witte, J. F. & Walsh, D. J. (1990). A systematic test of the effective schools model. *Educational Evaluation and Policy Analysis, 12,* 188–212.

Wolfensberger, W. (1972). *The principle of normalization in human services.* Toronto: National Institute on Mental Retardation.

Wolfgang, C. H. & Glickman, C. D. (1986). *Solving discipline problems: Strategies for classroom teachers* (2nd ed.). Boston: Allyn & Bacon.

Wolpe, J. (1958). *Psychotherapy by reciprocal inhibition.* Stanford, CA: Stanford University Press.

Wong, B. Y. L. (1991). Assessment of metacognitive research in learning disabilities: Theory, research, and practice. In H. L. Swanson (Ed.), *Handbook of assessment of learning disabilities: Theory, research, and practice* (pp. 265–84). Austin, TX: PRO-ED.

Woodhead, M. (1988). When psychology informs public policy: The case of early childhood intervention. *American Psychologist, 43,* 443–54.

Worrall, R. S. (1990). Detecting health fraud in the field of learning disabilities. *Journal of Learning Disabilities, 23,* 207–212.

Wright, S. & Cowen, E. L. (1985). The effects of peer-teaching on student perceptions of class environment, adjustment, and academic performance. *American Journal of Community Psychology, 13,* 417–31.

Ysseldyke, J. E. & Algozzine, B. (1982). *Critical issues in special and remedial education.* Boston: Houghton-Mifflin.

Ysseldyke, J. E., Thurlow, M. L., O'Sullivan, P. & Bursaw, R. A. (1986). Current screening and diagnostic practices in a state offering free preschool screening since 1977: Implications for the field. *Journal of Psychoeducational Assessment, 4,* 191–201.

Zigler, E. (1987). Formal schooling for four-year-olds? No. *American Psychologist, 42,* 254–60.

Zigler, E. F., Kagan, S. L. & Muenchow, S. (1982). Preventive intervention in the schools. In C. R. Reynolds & T. B. Gutkin (Eds.), *The handbook of school psychology* (pp. 774–95). New York: Wiley.

Zill, N. & Schoenborn, C. A. (1990). *Developmental, learning, and emotional problems: Health of our nation's children, United States, 1988. Advance data from vital and health statistics;* no. 190. Hyattsville, MD: National Center for Health Statistics.

Zins, J. E., Curtis, M. J., Graden, J. L. & Ponti, C. R. (1988). *Helping students succeed in the regular classroom: A guide for developing intervention assistance programs.* San Francisco: Jossey-Bass.

Name Index

Aaron, P. G., 435, 457
Abeson, A., 297, 461
Abikoff, H., 317, 431
Achenbach, T. M., 342, 346
Adams, M. J., 186, 242, 431
Adelman, H. S., 42, 73, 82, 87, 91,
  93, 110, 112, 115, 117, 119,
  131, 137, 138, 141, 165, 173,
  205, 295, 299, 303, 323, 327,
  333, 335, 337, 342, 364, 376,
  399, 408, 410, 412, 422, 425,
  431, 432, 437, 447, 457, 459
Adelman, K. A., 335, 432
Albert, M., 440
Alberto, P. A., 320, 432
Alexander, J. F., 45, 432
Algozzine, B., 341, 348, 462
Allen, J. A., 325, 460
Allen, V. L., 110, 432, 451
Alley, G. R., 234, 318, 432
Almli, C. R., 460
Altman, I., 203, 432
Amatruda, C. S., 342, 346
American Academy of Pediatrics,
  311, 432
American Educational Research As-
  sociation, 90
American Psychological Association,
  90, 394, 409, 432
Ames, C., 455
Ames, L. B., 314, 342, 347, 432
Ames, R. E., 455
Ansara, A., 440
Antrobus, J., 444
Archibald, D. A., 75, 433
Arieti, S., 454
Arter, J. A., 71, 293, 336, 433
Assel, D., 435
Aukerman, R. C., 249
Ausubel, N., 167, 433
Ayres, A. J., 292, 311, 433
Azzara, C. V., 323, 443

Badian, N., 327, 433
Baer, D. M., 293, 434, 454
Baily, D. B., Jr., 320, 433
Bain, L. J., 402

Baker, D., 311, 433
Baker, E. V., 75, 448
Baker, T., 348
Bakker, D. J., 31, 433, 461
Baldwin, L. E., 242, 436
Ballard, J., 297, 461
Bandura, A., 21, 93, 158, 433
Bangs, T. E., 249
Bank-Mikkelsen, N. E., 57, 433
Barclay, J. R., 93, 433
Barker, L. L., 192, 447
Barkley, R. A., 307, 310, 433
Barnes, K. E., 327, 433
Barnett, W. S., 103, 323, 434, 453
Baron, J., 250, 379, 433
Baroody, A. J., 249, 344
Barringer, K., 341, 346, 441
Barsch, R., 292, 433
Bartel, N. R., 248
Barth, R. S., 107, 433
Bartoli, J. S., 242, 249, 295, 299,
  322, 433
Bashir, A. S., 259, 434
Bassuk, M., 278, 434
Bastone, M., 190
Baum, S., 148, 434
Baumrind, D., 378, 434
Beady, C., 105, 435
Beauchamp, T. L., 392, 394, 434
Becker, H. J., 410, 434, 439
Becker, W., 238, 439
Begley, S., 32, 434
Bellak, C., 344, 346
Bellak, S., 344, 346
Bender, L., 343, 346
Benjamin, H., 186, 434
Bennett, E. M., 455
Bennett, R. E., 425, 449
Benowitz, S., 341, 346, 441
Bentzen, F. A., 8, 437
Berger, E. H., 110, 434
Bergin, A. E., 425, 448
Bereiter, C., 238
Berk, R. A., 329, 434
Berliner, D. C., 105, 434
Bernheimer, L., 101, 447
Bernieri, F., 166, 447

Bernstein, A., 62, 448
Berrueta-Clement, J. R., 103, 434
Berry, M., 249
Berwick, D. M., 101, 434
Bess, C. R., 317, 344, 347, 447
Betts, D., 115, 445
Bijou, S. W., 293, 294, 434
Biklen, D., 113, 128, 434
Binet, A., 67
Black, T. L., 102, 444
Blalock, J., 460
Blandford, B. J., 93, 160, 449
Blankenship, C. S., 336, 434
Bley, N. S., 249
Bloom, B. S., 108, 192, 294, 434,
  448
Boehm, A. E., 343, 346
Bohlmeyer, E. M., 109, 434
Boliek, G. A., 32, 308, 344, 345, 347,
  453
Bond, L., 114, 431, 435, 456
Bonstrom, O., 119, 443
Bos, C. S., 450
Botel, M., 242, 249, 433
Bouma, A., 31, 433
Boyer, C. W., Jr., 297, 450
Bradley, C. M., 7, 437
Bradley, G. W., 82, 435
Bradley, R. H., 93, 345, 346, 441
Brady, S., 317, 450
Brehm, J. W., 180, 365, 423, 425,
  435
Brehm, S. S., 180, 365, 423, 425,
  435
Brickman, P., 142, 435
Bromwich, R., 101, 435
Bronheim, S., 63, 435
Brookover, W. B., 105, 435
Brooks-Gunn, J., 102, 448
Brophy, J., 105, 435, 442
Brown, A. L., 71, 72, 94, 109, 211,
  318, 343, 435, 444, 453
Brown, L., 345, 347, 443
Brown, R. V., 250, 379, 433
Bruner, E., 238, 320, 439
Bruner, J. S., 1, 12, 141, 165, 275,
  355, 356, 435

Bruning, R., 250
Bryan, T., 344, 346
Bryant, B. R., 345, 347, 443
Burke, J. P., 109, 434
Burks, H., 342, 346
Burns, P. C., 249
Buros, O. K., 79, 341, 435
Bursaw, R. A., 326, 462
Burton, R. V., 342, 348
Burton, W. H., 207, 435
Buysse, V., 320, 433

Caldwell, B. M., 93, 345, 346, 441, 454
California Task Force to Promote Self-esteem and Personal and Social Responsibility, 114, 435
Campbell, J. D., 342, 348
Campione, J. C., 72, 94, 343, 347, 435, 453
Canfield, J., 250
Cantwell, D. P., 309, 310, 440, 459
Caplan, G., 45, 116, 435
Caplin, P., 32, 447
Carnine, D., 71, 185, 212, 234, 238, 250, 435
Carroll, L., 329
Cartledge, G., 250
Cartwright, G. P., 297, 450
Case, R. A., 435
Casey, A., 47, 117, 119, 443
Cassel, R. N., 342, 346
Cattell, R., 344, 346
Cawley, J. F., 249
Cazden, C. B., 249
Ceci, S. J., 250
Chalfant, J. C., 7, 47, 117, 248, 273, 297, 303, 436, 447
Chall, J. S., 242, 307, 436
Chandler, C. L., 73, 166, 365, 438
Chaplin, C., 122, 454
Chapman, C. A., 307, 344, 346
Charcot, 19
Charles, C. M., 366, 422, 436
Chase, A., 82, 436
Chase, S., 19, 436
Chen, T., 100, 452
Cherlin, D. L., 455
Chieh, S., 326, 436
Childress, J. F., 392, 394, 434
Childs, B., 85, 440
Christensen, S. L., 47, 117, 345, 348, 443
Chu, Y., 326, 436
Clark, R. W., 334, 436
Clements, S. D., 7, 297, 436
Clyne-Jackson, S., 394
Coan, R., 344, 346
Coates, D., 435
Cohen, A. L., 112, 436
Cohen, D. J., 28, 278, 456

Cohen, J., 110, 436
Cohen, J. J., 422, 451
Cohen, M., 308
Cohn, E., 435
Cohrs, M., 342, 343, 346
Colarusso, R. P., 71, 436
Coles, G. S., 13, 32, 71, 75, 79, 84, 93, 137, 273, 303, 332, 344, 346, 402, 436
Colletti, L., 28, 436
Collins, C., 436
Comenius, J. S., 155, 184, 436
Comer, J. P., 410, 437
Compas, B., 82, 114, 431, 435, 437, 456
Condry, J., 365, 437
Cone, T. E., 7, 437
Connell, J. P., 365, 455
Conners, C. K., 342
Conners, F., 28, 453
Connolly, A. J., 249
Conoley, C. W., 114, 116, 437
Conoley, J. C., 114, 116, 437, 451
Conway, R. N. F., 309, 455
Cook, V. J., 45, 437
Cooper, E. J., 250
Cooper, M., 251
Copeland, W. C., 59, 88, 437
Cott, A., 311, 437
Cowen, E. L., 45, 102, 114, 348, 437, 462
Crane, M. M., 344, 346
Cratty, B. J., 249, 292
Croasmum, P. A., 344, 347
Cronbach, L. J., 70, 78, 352, 437
Crowley, E. P., 119, 449
Cruickshank, W. M., 8, 47, 291, 292, 294, 296, 316, 337, 437
Crumrine, B. M., 249
Curtis, B. A., 306, 437
Curtis, M. J., 116, 443, 462
Curtiss, S., 259, 455

Dalby, J. T., 85, 171, 311, 438, 444
Dangel, H. L., 329, 438
Dangel, R. F., 250
Dao, M., 120, 438
Darrow, H. F., 207, 438
Das, J. P., 457
Davidson, E., 348
Davidson, H. A., 397, 451
Davies, D., 410, 438
Davis, G., 250
Davis, K., 250
Davison, L. A., 308, 345, 347
Day, B. D., 250
Deci, E. L., 73, 165, 166, 168, 183, 216, 250, 365, 367, 369, 414, 423, 438, 455
Decker, S., 32, 435
DeFries, J., 32, 438, 448

De Hirsch, K., 343, 346
Delacato, C. H., 30, 292, 311, 438
Denckla, M. B., 307, 344, 346
Deno, S. L., 300, 336, 438, 451
Derr, T. F., 336, 337, 456
Deshler, D. D., 234, 250, 294, 318, 432, 438, 456
Designs for Change, 121, 438
de Weerd, J., 438
Dewey, J., 39, 360, 414, 438
Dinkmeyer, D., 251
Dinkmeyer, D., Jr., 251
Ditunno, P., 249
Divoky, D., 79, 137, 310, 402, 456
Dodds, J., 342, 343, 346
Dolan, L., 112, 457
Doman, G., 292, 311, 438
Douglas, V. I., 294, 317, 438
Downs, M. P., 344, 347
Dreikers, R., 422, 439
Duane, D., 32, 33, 439
Dudley-Marling, C., 337, 439
Duffy, F. H., 32, 344, 346, 439
Dukas, H., 334, 335, 445
Dunbar, S. B., 75, 448
Dunst, C. J., 410, 439

Edelbrock, C., 342, 346
Edison, T. A., 334
Edmonds, R. R., 105, 439
Edmondson, R., 320, 433
Einstein, A., 334, 335
Ekstrom, R. B., 25, 439
Elardo, P., 251
Ellis, E., 318, 456
Elmore, R. F., 105, 439
Emde, R. N., 323, 336, 441, 446, 455
Englehart, M. D., 192, 434
Engelmann, S., 238, 250, 320, 439
Ensminger, E. E., 329, 438
Epstein, A. S., 103, 434
Epstein, J. L., 62, 345, 346, 410, 434, 439
Epstein, L. J., 448
Erikson, E. H., 335, 439
Escobar, E. H., 273, 327, 456

Fandall, A., 342, 343, 346
Farran, D. C., 447
Feagans, L., 443
Federal Register, 6, 8, 324, 439
Feinberg, J., 394, 398, 439
Feingold, B. F., 311, 439
Feniak, C. A., 58, 440
Ferguson, C., 336, 441
Fernald, G., 211, 212, 239, 240, 242, 249, 291, 292, 316, 380–389, 440
Ferrell, W. R., 93, 461
Feshbach, N. D., 114, 399, 440, 460
Feshbach, S., 342, 346

Feuerstein, R., 72, 109, 343, 346, 440
Fewell, R. R., 75, 440
Finger, S., 460
Finn, C. E., 108, 440
Finn, J. D., 121, 440
Finucci, J. M., 85, 440
Fisher, D., 439
Fisk, J. L., 7, 308, 441
Flanagan, D., 422, 445
Flavell, J. J., 72, 440
Fletcher, J. M., 306, 456, 459
Flood, P., 105, 435
Flynn, J. M., 7, 273, 332, 449
Foote, F. M., 344, 346
Forness, S. R., 258, 275, 294, 295, 300, 303, 309, 310, 311, 322, 440, 446
France, A., 12
Frank, J. D., 414, 440
Frankenburg, W. K., 300, 323, 327, 342, 343, 346, 436, 440, 441, 455
Fraser, B. J., 93, 160, 345, 346, 441
Freeman, E. M., 410, 453
Freeman, H. E., 141, 262, 455
Freund, J. H., 93, 441
Freundl, P., 82, 437
Friel, J., 343, 347
Fronzaglio, K., 300, 440
Frostig, M., 291, 292, 316, 441
Fuchs, D., 47, 58, 109, 336, 341, 346, 441
Fuchs, L. S., 58, 109, 336, 341, 346, 441
Fuerst, D. R., 7, 441
Fulker, D., 28, 453
Fuller, W. W., 342, 346
Furst, E. J., 192, 434
Furth, H. G., 355, 441

Gable, R., 345, 346
Gaddes, W. H., 92, 306, 307, 441
Gadow, K. D., 310, 441
Gage, N. L., 104, 441
Gagné, R. M., 172, 227, 355, 358, 359, 441, 442
Galaburda, A., 32, 308, 440, 442
Gallagher, J. J., 8, 295, 443, 447
Gardien, C. J., 31, 433
Garfield, S. L., 448
Gargiulo, R., 325, 460
Garner, R., 72, 442
Garrett, H. E., 351, 442
Gartner, A., 58, 110, 442
Gartrell, N., 440
Gelzheiser, L. M., 250, 345, 346
Gennari, P., 109, 460
Gerber, M. M., 110, 325, 442
German, M. L., 326, 442
Geschwind, N., 308, 439, 440

Gesell, A., 342, 346
Getman, G. N., 292, 442
Gibbs, J. T., 120, 442
Giller, H., 25, 455
Gillingham, A., 212, 239, 442
Ginsburg, H. P., 250, 344
Glass, G. V., 58, 442
Gleser, G. C., 70, 437
Glick, J., 444
Glickman, C. D., 422, 462
Glover, J., 250
Goertz, M. E., 25, 439
Goethe, 244
Goffman, E., 63
Golden, C. J., 308, 345, 347
Goldenberg, I. I., 455
Goldman, S. R., 112, 442
Goldstein, A. P., 42, 56, 207, 446
Goldstein, D., 33, 442
Goldstein, E., 190
Goldstein, K., 291, 292, 316, 442
Goldstein, M. J., 45, 442
Goldston, S. E., 437
Gonzales, M. L., 278, 308, 442
Good, T. L., 105, 435, 442
Goodlad, J. I., 105, 281, 296, 443
Gracey, C. A., 323, 324, 443
Graden, J., 47, 116, 117, 119, 443, 462
Grant, J. O., 10, 47, 437
Grant, W. V., 443
Greene, D., 168, 448, 450
Greene, L., 402
Greenfield, P. M., 112, 443
Greer, J. G., 157, 342, 348
Gresham, F. M., 308
Grothe, C., 190
Grunwald, B. B., 422, 439
Guilford, J. P., 351, 443
Guralnick, M. J., 102, 443
Gustavson, J. L., 308
Guthrie, D., 300, 440
Guthrie, J., 347
Gutkin, T. B., 116, 347, 437, 443, 448, 453, 454, 456, 462

Hackett, M. G., 343, 347
Hadley, S. M., 254, 395, 458
Hagen, E. P., 95, 351, 459
Hagin, R. A., 102, 457
Hall, J., 295, 443
Hall, L. E., 308
Hallahan, D. P., 292
Halpern, A., 122, 443
Hambleton, R. K., 336, 337, 443
Hamlett, C. L., 336, 441
Hammill, D. D., 9, 238, 248, 293, 298, 299, 345, 347, 443, 452
Hanna, G. L., 309, 310, 440, 459
Hanner, S., 238, 439
Harackiewicz, J. M., 166, 443

Haring, K. A., 259, 443
Haring, N. G., 292, 294, 297, 319, 443, 444
Harper, J., 300, 441
Harris, A. J., 249, 444
Harris, D. B., 344, 347
Harris, K. R., 72, 338
Harris, T. L., 250
Hartlage, L. C., 308, 345, 347
Haslam, R. H. A., 311, 444
Hauser, S. T., 119, 454
Havighurst, R. J., 119, 444
Haywood, H. C., 72, 444
Heath, S. B., 249
Hebbler, K. M., 102, 444
Heller, K., 59, 88, 444
Hellmuth, J., 442
Hendricks, I. G., 59, 88, 449
Heron, T. E., 295, 322, 345, 347, 447
Hersen, M., 347, 461
Herzfeld, J., 326, 442
Heshusius, L., 141, 295, 303, 320, 322, 337, 338, 444
Heward, W. L., 345, 347
Hewett, F. M., 142, 294, 319, 320, 444
Hicks-Stewart, K., 35, 452
Hightower, A. D., 114, 437
Hill, W. H., 192, 434
Hiscock, M., 308
Hobbs, N., 13, 58, 59, 91, 135, 326, 413, 444
Hodgkinson, H. L., 25, 280, 445
Hodgson, J. M., 317, 445
Hoepfner, R., 190
Hoffman, B., 334, 335, 445
Hoffman, M. T., 327, 445
Holliday, B. G., 45, 437
Holt, J., 178, 197, 414, 445
Holt, K., 166, 447
Holton, G., 334, 445
Holtzman, W., 59, 444
Holubec, E. J., 251
Honzaki, E., 249
Horn, W. F., 259, 275, 303, 445
Hosford, P. L., 434
Howard, K. I., 141, 445
Howe, F., 99
Howe, G. W., 45, 437
Hoyt, C. S., III, 309, 445
Huang, L. N., 120, 442
Hufano, L., 190
Hughes, C., 300, 451
Huisjes, H. J., 28, 460
Humby, D., 410, 439
Hunt, D. E., 170, 445
Hunt, J. McV., 275
Hunter, R., 190
Hurn, C. J., 13, 445
Huxby, B., 457

Hyman, I., 422, 445
Hynd, G. W., 308, 344, 347, 452

Iano, R. P., 295, 322, 445
Idol, L., 445
Ilg, F. L., 342, 347
Ing, P. S., 28, 457
Illich, I., 42, 63, 90, 132, 414, 445
Ireton, H., 326, 327, 448
Irlen, H., 309, 445
Irwin, M. E., 249
Ishihara, S., 344

Jacobs, V. A., 242, 436
Jacobson, S., 306, 437
Jakobson, R., 334, 445
Jansky, J. J., 327, 343, 346, 445
Jason, L. A., 115, 445
Jaynes, J. H., 251
Jenkins, J. R., 58, 71, 238, 293, 336,
    433, 446
Jensen, M. R., 72, 440
Johanson, C., 410, 439
Johnson, D., 293, 316, 446, 460
Johnson, D. J., 344, 347
Johnson, D. W., 109, 251, 446
Johnson, G., 238, 439
Johnson, J., 115, 445
Johnson, L. J., 47, 92, 116, 117, 446,
    454
Johnson, R. T., 109, 251, 446
Jones, E. E., 81, 325, 424, 446
Joyce, B., 108, 141, 202, 227, 355,
    359, 360, 361, 446

Kagan, S. L., 102, 114, 123, 280,
    446, 462
Kaiser, S. M., 75, 454
Kamaroff, A. L., 101, 434
Kameenui, E. J., 184, 212, 238, 435,
    446
Kamin, L. J., 82, 446
Kanfer, F. H., 42, 56, 207, 446
Kaniel, S., 72, 440
Kanouse, D. E., 446
Kaplan, H. B., 425, 446
Kaplan, R. M., 440
Karpman, S., 416, 446
Karuza, J., 435
Karweit, N. L., 58, 102, 112, 457
Kaser-Boyd, N., 131, 431, 459
Kass, C. E., 93, 461
Kauffman, J. M., 58, 110, 248, 442,
    446
Kaufman, A. S., 329, 343, 446
Kaufman, N. L., 343
Kaufman, S. H., 250
Kavale, K. A., 258, 275, 294, 295,
    303, 309, 311, 322, 336, 341,
    347, 440, 446
Kavanagh, J. F., 459
Kazdin, A. E., 24, 447

Kazuk, E., 342, 343, 346
Kean, T. H., 280, 447
Keeney, A., 454
Keeney, V., 454
Keith-Spiegel, P., 394
Kelley, H. H., 446
Kelly, A., 122, 454
Kendall, L., 309, 453
Kenowitz, L. A., 297, 450
Keogh, B., 7, 101, 273, 300, 303,
    309, 317, 344, 347, 447
Kephart, N. C., 291, 292, 316, 447
Kessler, M., 437
Kibler, R. J., 192, 447
Kidder, L., 435
Kilner, L. A., 119, 454
Kimball, W. H., 295, 322, 447
Kimberling, W. J., 28, 457
Kinsbourne, M., 32, 308, 447
Kirk, S. A., 7, 8, 248, 291, 293, 298,
    316, 332, 344, 347, 447
Kirk, W. D., 332, 344, 347, 447
Kirschenbaum, R., 148, 434
Kirst, M. W., 280, 447
Klimes-Dougan, B., 410, 447
Knights, R. M., 461
Knoff, H. M., 422, 423, 447
Koestner, R., 166, 447
Kohler, F. W., 110, 449
Kohler, M., 119, 442
Kolligan, J., 295, 447
Konecni, V. J., 440
Koocher, G. P., 131, 138, 394, 451,
    459, 461
Koppitz, E., 33, 247, 343, 347, 448
Krathwohl, D. R., 192, 434, 448
Kuder, R., 344, 347

La Buda, M. C., 32, 448
Laing, R. D., 63
Lakebrink, J. M., 102, 448
Lambert, M. J., 425, 448
Langford, W. S., 343, 346
Larsen, S. C., 9, 293, 342, 348, 443
Lass, M. J., 445
Last, C. G., 347
Lauber, B. A., 112, 432
Lauriet, A., 278, 434
Lauter, P., 99
La Vor, M. L., 297, 461
Layton, J., 445
Lazarus, R. S., 110, 448
Lee, V. E., 102, 448
Lehr, C. A., 326, 448
Lehtinen, L. E., 292, 316
Leigh, J. E., 9, 443
Leinhardt, G., 58, 448
Leitch, L. M., 410, 459
LeMay, M., 307, 344, 346
Lennard, H., 62, 448
Leonard, K., 345, 346
Lepper, M. R., 168, 448, 450

Lerner, M., 310, 459
Lerner, J. W., 208, 209, 248, 291, 448
Levin, J. R., 250, 318, 450
Levine, M., 308, 402, 455
Levine, R. J., 128, 448
Levinson, H. N., 311, 448
Lewin, K., 41
Lewis, J. F., 342, 343, 347
Lewis, R. B., 147, 459
Liaw, F. R., 102, 448
Lichtenstein, R., 326, 327, 448
Lidz, C. S., 72, 94, 440, 448
Lindsay, G. A., 93, 333, 448
Lindsley, O. R., 294, 320, 448
Linn, R. L., 75, 448
Lipsky, D. K., 442
Lipson, M. Y., 327, 449
Liscio, M. A., 122, 449
Livermon, B. J., 112, 457
Lloyd, J. W., 93, 119, 160, 449
Lombardi, V., 393
Long, B. B., 114, 449
Long, N. J., 444
Lopez, J., 410, 447
Lovett, D. L., 259, 443
Lovitt, T. C., 238, 320, 449
Lu, S., 326, 436
Lund, C. G., 10, 443
Luria, A. R., 308
Lynch, M. J., 122, 456
Lyon, G. R., 7, 273, 332, 449

MacMillan, D. L., 59, 88, 449
Madden, N. A., 58, 102, 112, 457
Maher, C. A., 422, 425, 447, 449
Mahoney, M. J., 23, 449
Mainzer, K. L., 457
Major-Kingsley, S., 7, 273, 447
Majovski, L. V., 308
Makuch, R., 456
Malatesha, R. N., 435, 457
Male, M., 112, 449
Malouf, R. E., 45, 432
Manderlink, G., 166, 443
Mangrum, C. T., 122, 295, 449
Mann, L., 293, 297, 449, 450, 461
Mann, V. A., 249, 317, 450
Marcus, E. M., 306, 437
Marshall, R. M., 308, 326, 442
Marston, D., 118, 300, 450, 451
Marx, F., 102, 451
Masia, B. B., 192, 448
Masland, M. W., 433
Masland, R. L., 433
Maslow, P., 441
Massenzio, S., 401, 450
Mastropieri, M. A., 250, 318, 450
Mather, N., 112, 450
Mattes, J., 450
McAlpine, A., 114, 452
McAnulty, G. B., 32, 344, 346, 439
McBurnett, K., 310, 459

McCann, S. K., 61, 450
McCarthy, J. J., 344, 347
McGrath, J. H., 205, 450
McGraw, K. O., 365, 450
McIntosh, R., 251
McKinney, J. D., 7, 273, 443, 447, 450
McLeskey, J., 300, 329, 450
McNeil, J. D., 187, 192, 450
McNutt, G., 9, 300, 443, 450
McPartland, J. M., 345, 346
Mearig, J., 434
Meichenbaum, D., 294, 317, 451
Melaragno, R. J., 110, 451
Melton, G. B., 131, 138, 378, 397, 399, 451, 459, 461
Menken, H. L., 414
Mercer, A. R., 248, 300, 451
Mercer, C. D., 248, 300, 451
Mercer, J. R., 342, 343, 347
Messick, S., 59, 444
Metz, C. M., 297, 450
Metzger, R. L., 309, 451
Meyen, E. L., 89, 451
Meyers, J., 116, 451
Milburn, J. F., 250
Miles, D. T., 192, 447
Miller, A., 170, 451
Miller, C. A., 297, 443
Miller, D. T., 82, 424, 451
Miller, S. R., 122, 451
Millman, H. L., 422, 451
Milne, A. A., 266
Mirkin, P. K., 300, 341, 347, 451
Mirsky, A. F., 307
Mitchell, A., 102, 451
Mnookin, R. H., 127, 136, 138, 451
Monson, T. C., 82, 424, 452
Montessori, M., 234, 250, 355, 452
Moos, R. H., 93, 160, 452
Morrison, G. M., 299, 452
Morse, W. C., 47, 437, 444
Morsink, C. V., 58, 452
Moultrie, R., 47, 436
Muenchow, S., 114, 462
Mundschenk, N. A., 336, 341, 347, 446
Munn, J., 114, 452
Murphy, V., 35, 452
Mussen, P., 432
Myers, B., 33, 442
Myers, P. I., 238, 452
Myklebust, H. R., 291, 293, 316, 331, 342, 347, 446, 452, 454

National Assessment for Educational Progress, 121, 452
National Association for the Education of Young Children, 103, 452
National Association for Perinatal Research and Education, 278, 452

National Association of School Psychologists, 59, 331, 452
National Center for Educational Statistics, 25, 452
National Center for Health Statistics, 10
National Commission on Excellence in Education, 105, 452
Needels, M. C., 104, 441
Neisser, U., 67, 228, 452
Neisworth, J. T., 157, 342, 348
Nelson, P., 82, 112, 410, 432, 437, 447
Nevin, A., 61, 450
Newman, F. M., 75, 433
Newman, R. G., 444
Nezlek, J., 365, 435
Nichols, P., 100, 452
Nickerson, S., 420
Nisbett, R. E., 81, 325, 424, 446
Northern, J. L., 344, 347
Novak, J., 251
Novoco, R., 440
Nunnally, J. C., 351, 452

Obrzut, J. E., 32, 308, 344, 345, 347, 452, 453
O'Connor, P. D., 309, 453
Odden, A., 113, 204, 453
O'Donnell, J. P., 259, 275, 445
Office of Policy Research and Improvement, 278, 453
Ogilvie, V., 190
Okolo, C. M., 122, 453
Ollendick, T. H., 461
Olsen, G., 28, 309, 453
Olson, R., 453
Olson, S., 308
Omori-Gordon, H., 7, 447
Orlinsky, D. E., 141, 445
Orton, S. T., 30, 291, 292, 295, 316, 453
Orvaschel, H., 342, 345, 347, 453
Osman, B., 402
O'Sullivan, P., 326, 462

Paget, K. D., 323, 453
Painting, D., 402
Palincsar, A. S., 94, 109, 211, 318, 343, 347, 453
Pallay, A., 448
Parker, F. L., 280, 446
Parker, R. M., 309, 453
Patterson, C. H., 355, 356, 357, 358, 453
Patterson, G. R., 45, 453
Pavlides, G., 249, 439
Pelham, W., 310, 453
Pelland, M., 309, 447
Pellegrino, J. W., 112, 442
Pennekamp, M., 410, 453
Pennington, B. F., 28, 454, 457

Pepper, F. C., 422, 439
Peterson, D. L., 58, 446
Peterson, D. R., 342, 347
Peverly, S., 109, 461
Pfeiffer, S. I., 432, 437
Phelps, L., 122, 454, 455
Phi Delta Kappa, 105, 454
Phillips, E. L., 294, 319, 444
Piaget, J., 275, 355, 356
Pihl, R. O., 132, 313, 454
Pious, C. G., 58, 456
Plaistad, J. R., 308
Polatajko, H. J., 311, 454
Pollack, J. M., 25, 439
Polster, R. A., 250
Ponti, C. R., 116, 462
Poplin, M. S., 238, 295, 322, 454
Powers, S. I., 119, 454
Pressley, M., 72, 338, 444
Primary Intervention Program, 114, 454
Pugach, M. C., 47, 92, 116, 117, 446, 454
Purkey, S. C., 105, 454
Purkey, W., 251
Pysh, M. V., 47, 117, 436

Quay, H., 342, 347, 366, 454

Rabinovitz, R. D., 32, 454
Rabinowitz, V. C., 435
Rack, J., 28, 453
Rademaker, A. W., 311, 444
Rakic, P., 308
Rand, Y., 72, 440
Randolph, R., 109, 461
Ransom, D. C., 62, 448
Rapkin, B. D., 348
Ratzeburg, F. H., 8, 437
Ravens, J. C., 343, 347
Reed, S., 278, 300, 454
Reese, J. H., 7, 437
Reeves, G., 186
Reid, H. P., 7, 447
Reinherz, H., 323, 443
Reisman, F. K., 250
Reitan, R. M., 308, 345, 347
Reschly, D. J., 308
Reynolds, C. R., 75, 308, 347, 437, 443, 445, 453, 454, 456, 462
Reynolds, M. C., 58, 436, 450, 452, 454
Rhodes, W. C., 42, 454
Ricciuti, N. N., 454
Rie, E. D., 308
Rie, H. E., 308
Riessman, F., 110, 442
Rinas, J., 394
Risley, T. R., 293, 454
Rissman, M., 259, 455
Ritter, S., 445
Rivera, A. M., 280, 446

Rizzo, J. V., 42, 458
Robinson, D. N., 87, 137, 398, 455
Robinson, G. L. W., 309, 455
Rock, D. A., 25, 439
Rock, S. L., 345, 346
Rodin, A., 334
Rogers, C., 355, 357, 358, 455
Rogers, W., 269
Ronning, R., 250
Rooney, K. J., 312, 455
Rosenshine, B. V., 105, 455
Rosner, J., 402
Ross, A. O., 23, 455
Ross, M., 82, 424, 451
Rossi, P. H., 141, 262, 455
Rourke, B. P., 7, 273, 308, 441, 449, 455
Roy, P., 251
Rubin, L., 278, 434
Rudegeair, F., 343, 347
Rumberger, R. W., 25, 120, 121, 455
Rusch, F., 122, 455
Rutter, M., 25, 33, 105, 203, 455
Ryan, R. M., 164, 166, 183, 216, 250, 365, 369, 423, 424, 435, 447, 455
Ryan, W., 84, 166, 455

Sabatino, D. A., 461
Saks, M. J., 131, 138, 451, 459, 461
Salzinger, S., 444
Salvia, J., 73, 75, 92, 341, 345, 347, 455
Sameroff, A. J., 93, 455
Samuels, S. J., 295, 455
Sansone, C., 166, 443
Sarason, S. B., 105, 107, 115, 455
Satz, P., 343, 347
Sautter, R. C., 278, 300, 454
Sawyer, D. J., 317, 456
Scavuzzo, A., 434
Schaefer, C. E., 422, 451
Schain, R. J., 306, 342, 344, 345, 347, 456
Scheffelin, M. M., 297, 436
Schlechty, P. C., 105, 456
Schloss, P. J., 122, 451
Schnackenberg, R. C., 312
Schnur, E., 102, 448
Schoenborn, C. A., 10, 462
Schrag, P., 79, 137, 310, 402, 456
Schumaker, J. B., 234, 250, 294, 318, 435, 456
Schweinhart, L. J., 103, 434, 456
Schweitzer, J., 105, 435
Sclafani, A. J., 122, 456
Scott, S. S., 122, 456
Scriven, M., 227, 456
Scruggs, T. E., 250, 450
Seidel, H. M., 342, 347
Seligson, M., 102, 451

Semel, E. M., 249
Semmel, M. I., 61, 325, 442, 450
Senf, G. M., 450
Shapiro, D. A., 425, 448
Shapiro, E. S., 336, 337, 456
Shari, E., 190
Shaw, A., 457
Shaywitz, B. A., 28, 278, 456
Shaywitz, S. E., 28, 273, 278, 327, 456
Sheinman, L., 365, 435
Shepard, L. A., 7, 9, 90, 300, 337, 341, 348, 456
Shepherd, M. J., 250
Shinn, M. R., 336, 441, 456
Sholomskas, D., 345, 347, 453
Sieben, R. L., 63, 311, 312, 457
Siegel, L. S., 299, 452, 457
Silberman, C. E., 264, 457
Silbert, J., 212, 238, 435
Silver, A. A., 102, 457
Silver, L. B., 35, 63, 311, 457
Simmons, B. K., 171, 249, 457
Simmons, D. C., 457
Simoni, J., 410, 457
Sinclair, E., 300, 440
Sipay, E. R., 249
Sitlington, P., 122, 453
Skager, R. W., 349, 457
Skinner, B. F., 23, 293, 294, 355, 357, 457
Slavin, R. E., 58, 102, 110, 112, 251, 457, 461
Smith, A., 420
Smith, B. J., 102, 444
Smith, C. R., 170, 248, 457
Smith, D. C., 112, 432
Smith, D. D., 259, 443
Smith, K., 190, 422, 445
Smith, M. L., 7, 9, 300, 341, 348, 456
Smith, M. S., 105, 454
Smith, R. M., 157, 342, 348
Smith, S., 115, 445
Smith, S. D., 28, 454, 457
Smith, T. M., 320, 433
Smith-Davis, J., 58, 452
Solar, R. A., 250
Snart, F., 71, 336, 457
Snow, J. F., 308
Snow, R. E., 108, 457
Snyder, M., 82, 424, 452
Sofo, F., 309, 453
Soifer, R., 249
Sparta, S., 190
Spreen, O., 259, 457
Stainback, S., 58, 458
Stainback, W., 58, 458
Stake, R. E., 74, 260, 261, 262, 458
Stanovich, K. E., 242, 329, 344, 348, 458
Stauffer, R. G., 242, 249, 458

Stecker, P. M., 336, 441
Steinbeck, J., 223, 458
Stephens, T. M., 132, 320, 458
Sternberg, R., 295, 447
Stevens, L. J., 10, 300, 460
Stevens, R., 105, 455
Stevenson, H. W., 69, 77, 105, 276, 277, 458
Stigler, J. W., 69, 77, 105, 276, 277, 458
Stillman, B., 212, 239, 442
Stipek, D. J., 165, 180, 251, 369, 458
Stoddard, K., 278, 458
Stoner, G., 441
Strain, P. S., 119, 442, 449
Strang, J. D., 273, 308, 455
Strauss, A. A., 291, 292, 316
Strichart, S. S., 122, 295, 449
Strupp, H. H., 254, 395, 458
Sugar, F., 445
Sullivan, E. V., 170, 445
Sullivan, J. W., 323, 346, 436, 441, 455
Suran, B. G., 42, 458
Swan, W., 102, 458
Swanson, H. L., 10, 72, 88, 92, 295, 299, 308, 317, 347, 348, 441, 446, 447, 449, 453, 458, 459, 462
Swanson, J. M., 309, 310, 440, 459
Swift, C., 147, 459
Szasz, T. S., 42, 63, 459

Tallal, P., 259, 455, 459
Tang, T., 326, 436
Tangri, S., 410, 459
Tannhauser, M. T., 8, 437
Tapp, J. L., 399, 459
Taylor, F. D., 142, 320, 444
Taylor, H. G., 306, 308, 459
Taylor, L., 42, 73, 82, 85, 110, 114, 115, 119, 131, 137, 138, 141, 165, 205, 295, 299, 303, 323, 337, 376, 378, 399, 408, 422, 431, 432, 437, 452, 459
Telzrow, C. F., 308
Thomas, C. C., 58, 452
Thorndike, R. L., 95, 293, 351, 459
Thornton, C. A., 249
Thurlow, M. L., 325, 326, 341, 347, 348, 448, 451, 459, 462
Tindal, G., 73, 258, 459
Tjossem, T. J., 101, 459
Topics in Early Childhood Education, 459
Topping, K. J., 110, 460
Torgesen, J. K., 112, 275, 295, 303, 317, 436, 453, 456, 460
Torgesen, J. L., 112, 436, 450
Toro, P. A., 345, 348
Touwen, B. C. L., 28, 460

Tracy, M. C., 42, 454
Tranel, D., 308
Tranel, N. N., 308
Trapani, C., 250
Tremper, C., 399, 460
Trivette, C. M., 410, 439
Trout, B., 345, 346
Troutman, A. C., 320, 432
Truss, T. L., 459
Tucker, J., 10, 300, 460
Tyack, D. B., 13, 460
Tzuriel, D., 72, 440

U.S. Bureau of the Census, 25
U.S. Department of Education, 10, 121, 460
U.S. General Accounting Office, 85, 460

Valens, S., 446
Van Allen, R., 207, 438
van Duyne, H. J., 325, 460
Vaughn, S., 251, 450
Vellutino, F. R., 32, 460
Vitulano, L. A., 259, 445
Vogel, S., 122, 460
Vojir, C. P., 7, 456
Vygotsky, L. S., 275, 318, 460

Wachs, H., 355, 441
Wade, T., 348
Wagner, R. K., 317, 460
Walberg, H. J., 58, 59, 93, 104, 106, 108, 109, 160, 203, 345, 346, 436, 441, 450, 452, 454, 460, 461
Waldron, N. L., 300, 450
Walker, A., 419
Walker, H., 441
Wallace, G., 248, 342, 348

Walsh, D. J., 106, 462
Wang, M. C., 58, 59, 108, 109, 436, 450, 452, 454, 460
Wang, T., 326, 436, 460, 461
Wasik, B. A., 110, 457, 461
Wasserstrom, R., 132, 461
Watkins, A. V., 59, 88, 449
Watson, B. L., 88, 92, 459
Waxman, H. C., 109, 460
Wechsler, D., 353
Wedell, K., 93, 333, 448, 461
Weikart, D. P., 103, 434, 456
Weil, M., 108, 141, 202, 227, 355, 359, 360, 361, 446
Weinberg, C., 349, 413, 457, 461
Weiner, B. A., 446, 461
Weiner, F., 344, 348
Weintraub, F. J., 297, 461
Weithorn, L. A., 378, 461
Weissberg, R. P., 348
Weissman, M. N., 345, 347, 453
Wells, H., 250
Wender, P. H., 32, 461
Wepman, J., 291, 316
Werner, D. B., 309, 451
Werner, H., 291, 292, 316
Werry, J. S., 366, 454
Westman, J. C., 141, 235, 461
Whalen, C. K., 310, 461
Whelan, R. J., 294, 319, 444
White, K., 102, 461
Whiting, P., 309, 461
Wiederholt, J. L., 291, 461
Wiener, J., 72, 461
Wiggins, G., 75, 461
Wiig, E. H., 249
Wilcoxen, A. G., 101, 447
Wilkening, G. N., 308
Williams, E., 326, 442

Williams, R., 190
Willis, W. G., 344, 347
Willson, V. L., 329, 461
Wilson, L. R., 7, 437
Wingerfeld, S., 72, 444
Winnicott, D. W., 121
Wise, B., 28, 453
Wisenbaker, J., 105, 435
Wissink, J. F., 93, 333, 461
Witte, J. F., 106, 462
Wittrock, M., 435, 442, 455
Wixson, K. K., 327, 449
Wlodkowski, R. J., 251
Wolfensberger, W., 57, 462
Wolfgang, C. H., 422, 462
Wolford, B., 297, 450
Wolpe, J., 211, 462
Wong, B. Y. L., 72, 275, 295, 303, 453, 456, 460
Woodhead, M., 95, 462
Woodward, J., 71, 435
Worrall, R. S., 312, 401, 462
Wozniak, R. H., 250
Wright, S., 252, 462

Yarrow, M. R., 342, 348
Young, D. L., 249
Youpa, D., 309, 310, 440
Ysseldyke, J. E., 10, 73, 75, 92, 300, 325, 326, 341, 345, 347, 348, 448, 451, 455, 459, 460, 462

Zaragoza, N., 251
Ziai, M., 342, 347, 348
Zigler, E., 102, 103, 114, 462
Zill, N., 10, 462
Zins, J. E., 116, 422, 447, 449, 462
Zinsser, W., 249
Zollers, N., 113, 434

Subject Index

Accommodating individual
differences. *See*
Individualization; Personalization
Accountability, 253, 257, 258,
280–282, 337, 409
Achievement
age (AA), 331
discrepancy with potential, 324,
328–331
tests, 5, 330, 343
ACLD. *See* Learning Disabilities Association of America (LDA)
Activities for learning. *See* Intervention, methods, tools, and techniques
Adaptive behavior. *See* Misbehavior
Adaptive Learning Environments
Model (ALEM), 109
Adolescents, 119–123, 295
case examples, 148
life tasks, 119–120
postsecondary careers and education, 122, 295
rights of, 130–131, 133–136
service options for, 47–48, 58,
67–70
transition from adolescence,
119–120
Adults, 119–123, 295, 402
legislation. *See* Legislation
postsecondary careers and education, 122, 295, 400
service options for, 47, 122
Advocacy, 295–298
Age-appropriate life tasks. *See* Remediation
ALEM (Adaptive Learning Environments Model), 109
Allergies, 310–311
Alternative schools, 106
American Speech-Language Hearing
Association (ASHA), 296
Americans with Disabilities Act (PL
101-336), 297
"Animal school" parable, 186
Anoxia (oxygen deprivation), 32
Aphasia, 8, 297

Applied behavioral analysis, 237,
293, 294, 320, 357
Aptitude-treatment interaction (ATI).
See Match
Assessment, 49–53, 66–97, 253,
328–339, 341–348, 349–353.
See also Diagnosis; Evaluation;
Placement; Planning for
treatment; Screening
of achievement, 5, 330, 343
authentic, 75, 92
bias in, 68, 79–86, 325
of central nervous system
dysfunction, 77, 304–308, 330,
332
and classification. *See* Diagnosis,
and classification
and consultation, 46, 49, 91–92,
407–408
consumer's guide to tests, 345
curriculum-based, 237, 295, 315,
322, 336, 337
and decisions, 49–53, 70, 127–138
defined, 50
dynamic, 72, 93–94
of environment, 93, 345
errors of, 67, 90, 91, 151, 218,
329, 332–333, 351, 391
ethical concerns of. *See* Ethical
concerns
factors shaping, 67–75, 76
focal point for/focus of, 43–45, 76,
92–93, 146, 150–151
functions of, 50–53, 76, 323–339
for identification, 50–52, 67,
323–327, 328–333
improving, 90, 91–94, 150–151
interpretation problems with,
77–79, 349–353
interventionist, 93–94
for monitoring progress. *See* Monitoring, as a learning strategy
of motivation, 183, 199–202, 216,
379
negative effects of. *See* Negative
effects
and neurological signs, 7, 304–307

Assessment *(continued)*
neuropsychological, 305–307, 330,
344–345
norms used in, 78–79, 352–353
orientations to, 53–55, 70–72,
314–320, 329
performance assessment, 75, 92,
342–345
of person-environment interaction,
73, 93, 327
phases of, 76
and placement, 333–336
for planning programs and treatment, 50, 52, 67–75, 91–94,
217–219, 243–245, 336–338
portfolio, 75
and preassessment interventions,
91–92, 325
purposes and functions of, 50–53,
76, 323–339
reassessment, 49
reliability of, 78, 349
screening. *See* Screening
sequential approaches to, 91, 93,
151, 217–219, 333
standards used in, 78–79,
352–353
technical concerns, 78–79, 332,
349–353
test profiles and patterns in, 329
tests and other procedures in,
292, 293, 307, 329, 330,
341–348
transaction-oriented, 73, 93, 327
types of procedures, 76, 330,
341–348
validity and validity problems of,
78, 341, 349–352
Association for Children and Adults
with Learning Disabilities
(ACLD). *See* Learning Disabilities
Association of America (LDA)
Association of Learning Disabled
Adults, 401
At risk, 67, 99–102, 278, 323
Attention deficit disorder (ADD). *See*
Attention problems

Attention deficit-hyperactivity disorder (ADHD). *See* Attention problems

Attention problems, 7, 35, 63, 233, 236, 292, 309–311, 312. *See also* Misbehavior

Attitudes. *See* Motivation

Attribution bias and tendencies, 81–82, 201, 325

Backlash, 332, 416

Barriers to major changes, 281–282, 418–421

Basic psychological processes, 8, 9, 292–293, 299, 315–318, 329

Basic skills, 15, 149, 177, 184–187, 199, 241, 369, 381

Basics plus, 184–187, 193

BEAM (Brain electrical activity mapping), 32

Behavioral analysis, 237, 293, 294, 320, 357

Behavioral approach, 23–25, 55, 159, 237–238, 293–294, 318–322, 357, 360–361

Behavioral objectives, 54, 55, 257, 315, 318–320, 321, 337, 339. *See also* Curriculum-based assessment

Behaviorist classroom programs, 55, 237–238, 293–294, 357, 360–361. *See also* Applied behavioral analysis

Behavior management, 293–294, 315, 357

Behavior modification, 293–294, 357. *See also* Observable problems orientation; Reinforcement

Behavior problems. *See* Misbehavior

Bias
in assessment, 68, 79–86, 325
in attribution of cause, 81–82, 201, 325
in evaluation, 81–82, 201, 259, 264, 325
in referral, 68, 325

Biochemical insufficiencies or imbalances. *See* Central nervous system

Blaming the victim, 84, 303, 325

Brain electrical activity mapping (BEAM), 32

Brain functioning. *See* Central nervous system

Brain injury or trauma. *See* Central nervous system, function and dysfunction

Burlington School Committee v. Department of Education, 89

Burnout, 215, 417, 419

Career education, 122, 295, 298

Case management, 47. *See also* Multidisciplinary team diagnostic and placement decisions

Categorization of psychoeducational problems. *See* Diagnosis

Cause. *See also* Central nervous system, function and dysfunction
behaviorist perspective of, 23–25
continuum of, 22–23, 273–275
and correlates, 20–22
and effects, 19–20
of learning problems, 22, 24, 25, 27, 34, 171
locus of, 22
models of, 20–22, 93

CEC (Council for Exceptional Children), 295, 296

Central nervous system (CNS)
assessment of, 77, 304–308, 330, 332
biochemical insufficiencies in, 28, 29
endocrine deficiencies in, 29, 32
function and dysfunction, 8, 9, 12, 14, 27–34, 53, 273, 292, 297, 303, 304–308, 314–315, 332
genetic causes, 28, 32
minimal brain dysfunction and damage (MBD), 8, 306
neurological impulse transmission, 31–32
perinatal causes, 29
postnatal causes, 29
prenatal causes, 28
recovery from dysfunction, 31
theories of, 30, 32, 304–308
training, 30, 311

Cerebral
cortex, 304, 305
dominance, 7, 30, 304, 311
dysfunction. *See* Central nervous system, function and dysfunction
hemisphere, 304

Characteristics of learning disabilities, 6, 7, 298–299

Child-find programs, 45, 67, 323, 324–327

Children with Specific Learning Disabilities Act, 297

Children's assent and rights, 130–131, 393–394, 404

Child Service Demonstration Centers, 297

Choice, 198–199, 218, 235, 369–379, 393–394, 396–399, 404–405, 415, 425–427

Chronological age (CA), 331

Civil Rights Act, 296

Classification. *See* Assessment; Diagnosis

Classroom management, 294, 320, 357, 396, 414, 422–429

Class size, 61, 112–113, 204

CLD. *See* Council for Learning Disabilities

Clinical teaching, 56. *See also* Remediation

Closer Look Information Project, 401

CNS. *See* Central nervous system

Coercion. *See* Intervention, coercive

Cognition and cognitive functioning and behavior modification, 293, 294
prerequisites, 232–233, 243, 250
strategies. *See* Intervention, cognitive strategies for; Metacognition
tests of, 330, 343

College programs for LD, 122, 295, 400

Colored lenses, 309

Commitment and learning. *See* Motivation

Compensation and compensatory strategies, 24, 53, 54, 71, 172, 259, 315

Competence, 130, 192
in LD, 378
of minors, 130, 378, 393–394, 399
of professionals, 409, 413–417
striving for. *See* Motivation, intrinsic

Computerized tomography (CT-scan), 32

Computers, 108, 112, 337

Conferences and dialogues
case examples, 129–130, 201, 219–222
between learner and intervener, 199–202, 216, 379

Conflicts of interest. *See* Intervention, coercive

Consent for intervention, 127–131, 393–394, 396–399, 404–405. *See also* Ethical concerns

Consultation. *See also* Multidisciplinary team diagnostic and placement decisions; Prereferral intervention; Working relationships
with clients, 46, 49, 91–92, 407–408, 424–425
among professionals, 46–47, 91–92, 116–117, 275, 420

Consumer concerns and information, 70, 127–130, 345, 400–409

Consumer Information Center, 400

Continuum of alternative placements. *See* Placement

Continuum of programs, 15–16, 277–280

Contracts and agreements for learning, 199–202, 216, 219–222. *See also* Consent for intervention

Control, 133–138, 395–399, 413–417. *See also* Socialization
limit setting, 205–207, 413–414, 415
power to, 131–138, 422–424
rewards as. *See* Reinforcement
social, 82–86, 135–136, 255–256, 413–417

Cooperative learning, 109–110, 114, 235, 360

Costs vs. benefits. *See* Ethical concerns, cost–benefit analysis

Council for Exceptional Children (CEC), 295, 296

Council for Learning Disabilities (CLD), 295, 296, 299

Criterion-referenced objectives, 54, 55, 257, 315, 318–321, 336, 337. *See also* Curriculum-based assessment

Cross-age tutoring. *See* Tutorial Community; Tutoring

Cross-categorical and noncategorical approach to special education. *See* Regular Education Initiative (REI)

CT-scan. *See* Computerized tomography

Cultural factors, 8, 9, 13

Curiosity. *See* Motivation, intrinsic

Curriculum, 176–195, 356

Curriculum-based assessment, 237, 295, 315, 322, 336, 337

Cylert. *See* Medication and drugs

DCCD (Division for Children with Communication Disorders), 296

DCLD (Division for Children with Learning Disabilities), 295

Decision making. *See also* Control; Helping and helping relationships; Structure for learning; Working relationships
competence, 130, 378, 393–394, 399
conflicts, 133–136, 254–255, 395–399
in interventions. *See* Assessment, and decisions; Intervention, and decision making
by learner, 133–134, 187, 199, 369–379, 393–394, 396–399
in placements, 50, 52, 70, 127–131, 133–135, 333–336
politics of, 136–138, 254–255, 395–399, 404–405

Definitions of LD. *See* Learning disabilities

Delivery systems. *See* Placement, alternatives

Demystification, 131–133, 400–409, 416

Development. *See also specific areas of development*
areas of, 219
levels of, 219
matching of, 170–173
and performance differences, 172
and performance dimensions, 172
problems of, 229–230, 314–315
tasks, 119–120, 189–192
variations in and patterns of, 171

Developmental lag, 22, 32–34, 314, 327

Diagnosis. *See also* Assessment; Discrepancy between achievement and intellectual ability, formula; Negative effects; Placement; Screening
case example, 80, 331, 334–335
and classification, 51–52, 68, 95, 273–274, 329–332
differential, 273–274, 328, 333–335
and labels and labeling, 50, 51, 52, 58–59, 67, 256, 329–332, 391–392
and misdiagnosis, 67, 90, 91, 151, 329, 332–333, 391
posthumous, 332, 334–335
sex differences in, 85

Diagnostic teaching/diagnostic prescriptive model. *See* Underlying problems orientation

Dialogues. *See* Conferences and dialogues

Diana v. State Board of Education, 89, 391

Diet therapy. *See* Medically related treatments

Direct instruction, 55, 71, 108, 149, 229, 237–238, 293, 294, 295, 315, 318–320, 322, 336–337, 339. *See also* Observable problems orientation

Discipline, 44, 129–130, 422–424

Discrepancy between achievement and intellectual ability
case example, 331
criteria, 324, 328–331
formula, 6, 329, 331

Discrimination in placement, 70, 82–86, 88–90

Distar, 238, 320

Division for Children with Communication Disorders (DCCD), 296

Division for Children with Learning Disabilities (DCLD), 295

Division for Learning Disabilities (DLD), 296, 299

Doe v. Public Health Trust of Dade County, 398

Domains of learning, 189–192, 219

Dropouts, 120–121

Drug abuse, 278

Drug treatment, 62, 206, 309–310

Due process. *See* Parents, consent of; Procedural safeguards and due process

Dynamic assessment, 72, 93–94

Dynamic instruction, 109, 211, 318

Dyslexia, 8, 32, 242. *See also* Remediation, of reading problems

Early education, 101–104, 297

Early identification, 46, 67

Early intervention, 16, 99, 101–104, 278–279, 302, 323–324

Early school adjustment. *See* School, adjustment problems

East Harlem magnet schools, 106

Eclecticism, 55–56

Economic Opportunity Act, 296

Educational goals, 190–191

Educational reform, 104–113

Education for All Handicapped Children Act (PL 94-142), 8, 47, 127, 297, 298, 320, 323, 337, 362

Education of the Handicapped Act, 297

Education of the Handicapped Amendment Acts (PL 98-199 and PL 99-457), 323

Effective schools, 105–107

Electroencephalogram (EEG), 306

Elementary and Secondary Education Act of 1965, 296

Elementary education, 104–119

Eligibility criteria. *See* Learning disabilities, definition criteria and problems

Emotional functioning, 7, 8, 9, 34, 235, 240, 250, 295, 344

Endocrine deficiencies, 29, 32

Enhancing motivation, 164, 179–180, 362–364, 369–379, 382–383, 424–429

Enrichment for learning, 69, 148, 192–194, 373–374

Environment (physical and social), 21, 158, 159–161, 187, 203–204. *See also* System changes
assessment of, 93, 345
as cause of learning problems, 14, 22, 25–26, 99, 186, 273–275
as focus of change, 22, 43–46, 99, 101, 105–113, 150–151, 159–161, 170, 203–204, 217–218, 277–280, 425–429
and learning. *See* Learning, environment for; Transactional model

Environment (physical and social)
  (continued)
  levels of, 160
  variables for planning intervention,
    161
Ethical concerns, 62–63, 86–90, 280,
    391–394, 409
  cost–benefit analysis, 62, 391–392
  demystification, 131–133, 400–409,
    416
  fairness, 392–393
  informed consent, 127–131,
    393–394, 396–399, 404–405
  negative consequences, 87–90,
    391
  privacy, 62, 86–87, 391
Ethical guidelines, 90, 128, 132–133,
    409. *See also* Children's assent
    and rights; Parents, rights of
Ethnic diversity, 25, 88–90, 120,
    129–130, 391–392, 418–421
Evaluation, 51, 52, 73–75, 157,
    252–267. *See also* Assessment;
    Curriculum-based assessment;
    Feedback; Learning disabilities,
    and follow-up research
  behavioral objectives, 54, 55, 257,
    318–321
  behaviorist-oriented, 257, 318–321
  bias in, 81–82, 201, 259, 264
  comprehensive, 258
  definition of, 74, 262
  focus of, 256–258
  framework for, 260–261
  interested parties, 134–138,
    254–255
  of intervention programs, 259,
    315
  monitoring progress. *See* Monitor-
    ing, as a learning strategy
  negative effects of, 265
  phases of, 147
  processes, 258–265
  research, 259, 280–281
  standards used in, 260–261
  steps in, 262–265
Expectancies of success and failure,
    166–167, 179
Expectancy age (EA), 331
Extrinsic motivation. *See* Reinforce-
    ment, rewards and punishments

Facilitating learning. *See* Instruction;
    Intervention
Fads in intervention, 311–313,
    414
Family. *See* Parents
Family Educational Rights and Pri-
    vacy Act of 1974, 87, 404
FCLD. *See* Foundation for Children
    with Learning Disabilities

Feedback. *See also* Conferences
    and dialogues; Evaluation;
    Monitoring, as a learning strat-
    egy
  case examples, 129–130, 201,
    219–222, 371–373, 374
  in intervention, 168, 187, 364
  and motivation, 168, 187, 199–202,
    383
Fernald method. *See* Multisensory
    methods
Forward to Basics, 149, 184–187,
    369
Foundation for Children with Learn-
    ing Disabilities (FCLD), 400
Future directions, 15–16, 91–94, 152,
    270–283, 294–295, 299–303

General education. *See* Regular edu-
    cation
General Education Initiative, 58
Generalization of learning, 277, 338,
    357, 424
General learning strategies. *See*
    Learning strategies
Genetics, 28, 32
Goals of education, 190–191
Grade age (GA), 331
Grades and grading, 168–169

Handicapped Children's Early Edu-
    cation Programs (HCEEP), 297
Hard neurological signs. *See* Assess-
    ment, and neurological signs
Headstart. *See* Prekindergarten pro-
    grams
Health and safety, 16, 278–279
Hearing, 7, 8, 328
Helping and helping relationships,
    135–136, 255–256, 396–397,
    416–417
Helplines, 402, 403–405
Heredity, 28, 32
Hierarchical approaches. *See* As-
    sessment, sequential
    approaches to; Intervention, se-
    quential and hierarchical
    approaches to
Higher Education and the
    Handicapped (HEATH), 400
Higher order thinking. *See* Cognition
    and cognitive functioning
High risk. *See* At risk
Hobson v. Hansen, 89
Holistic view, 295, 322
Homelessness, 278
Home-school partnership. *See* Par-
    ents
Honig v. Doe, 89
Humanistic intervention and instruc-
    tion, 357–358, 360

Hyperactivity and hyperkinesis. *See*
    Attention problems

IARLD (International Academy for Re-
    search in Learning Disabilities),
    296, 299
Identification. *See* Assessment, for
    identification
IEP. *See* Individualized educational
    plan
IFSP. *See* Individual Family Service
    Plan
Immigrants, 25, 278
Impulsivity. *See* Attention problems
Incidence of LD. *See* Learning
    disabilities, incidence/prevalence
Inclusive education. *See* Main-
    streaming
Individual Family Service Plan, 297,
    320
Individualization, 73, 108–110, 147,
    170, 301
Individualized educational plan (IEP),
    47, 48, 177, 297, 320, 321, 336,
    337, 339, 398
Individuals with Disabilities Education
    Act (IDEA) (PL 101-476), 48,
    297
Information processing approaches,
    294–295, 358–359, 360
Informed consent. *See* Consent for
    intervention; Ethical concerns
Initial assessment and consultation,
    46, 49, 91–92, 407–408
Inservice education, 16, 116–118,
    278, 279
Instigating factors. *See* Cause
Institutes for LD research, 298, 318
Instruction, 154–155, 156–175,
    176–195, 196–225, 226–251,
    355–389. *See also* Helping and
    helping relationships;
    Intervention; *specific areas for
    instruction*
  activities for. *See* Intervention,
    methods, tools, and techniques
  case examples, 59–60, 148, 201,
    219–222, 245–246, 319,
    371–373, 374, 375, 376,
    395–396, 427
  competence of teachers for, 228
  content of, 219
  curriculum for, 176–195, 356
  direct. *See* Direct instruction
  domains of, 189–192, 219
  dynamic, 109, 211, 318
  environment and context of, 11,
    21, 105–113, 114, 158, 159–161,
    187, 203–204, 217–218
  humanistic approach, 357–358,
    360

Instruction *(continued)*
improvement of, 104–113, 141–152, 163–174, 177–194, 197–224, 275–280, 355–389
individualization of, 73, 108–110, 147, 170, 301
information on progress. *See* Monitoring, as a learning strategy
least-intervention teaching, 214–215
as a matching process. *See* Match
and models of teaching, 359–361
Montessori Method, 355
and motivation. *See* Motivation
objectives and goals of, 164, 190–191, 202, 215, 237, 257, 360–361
personalization of. *See* Personalization
sequential and hierarchical approaches to. *See* Intervention, sequential and hierarchical approaches to
society as context for, 13, 135–136, 255–256, 413–417
techniques, 184, 207–214, 248–251, 315–320, 380–389
theories of, 355–361
trial and appraisal teaching, 145
Intelligence tests and IQ, 5, 6, 330, 331, 343, 353, 391–392
Interaction of learner and environment. *See* Transactional model
Interagency Committee on Learning Disabilities, 298
Interfering factors, 188, 217, 218, 235, 236, 241, 242, 276, 365–368
International Academy for Research in Learning Disabilities (IARLD), 296, 299
International Reading Association (IRA), 296
Interpersonal relationships. *See* Social and interpersonal behavior
Intervention
activity continuum, 16, 279
assent for. *See* Consent for intervention
and assessment. *See* Assessment; Reassessment
behaviorist classroom. *See* Behaviorist classroom programs
case examples, 59–60, 129–130, 148, 201, 219–222, 245–246, 319, 371–373, 374, 375, 376, 395–396, 427
coercive, 131, 135, 136–138, 395–399. *See also* Control
cognitive strategies for, 71–72, 109, 117, 234, 250, 317–318

Intervention *(continued)*
comprehensive approaches, 15–16, 277–280
consent for. *See* Consent for intervention
continuum of, 16, 272–280
controversial, 303, 309–313
coordination of, 277–280
and decision making, 49–53, 70, 127–138, 187, 199, 235, 254–255, 369–379, 393–394, 396–399, 404–405
defined, 42–43
at an early age, 16, 99, 101–104, 278–279, 302, 323–324
and early identification, 46, 67
efficacy of. *See* Evaluation
for environment change, 22, 43–46, 99, 101, 105–113, 159–160, 203–204, 217–218, 277–280, 281–282, 425–429
ethical concerns of. *See* Ethical concerns; Procedural safeguards and due process
evaluation of. *See* Evaluation
evolving trends. *See* Future directions
expanding, 41–49, 123, 146–151, 301–302, 428–429
focal point for/focus of, 43–46, 146–151, 158–163
guidelines for, 90, 128, 132–133, 151, 404–405, 409
humanistic, 357–358, 360
improving, 141–152, 270–282
integration of, 280
interested parties, 134–138, 254–255, 395–396
least needed. *See* Least intervention needed
levels of, 217–219, 241–242
match. *See* Match
medical. *See* Medically related treatments
methods, tools, and techniques, 184, 207–214, 248–251, 315–320, 380–389
models of, 141–143, 355–361
and motivation. *See* Motivation
negative effects of. *See* Negative effects
object or focus of, 43, 146–151
orientations to. *See* Learning strategies; Observable problems orientation; Underlying problems orientation
outcomes. *See* Instruction, objectives and goals of
phases of, 146, 147
placements. *See* Placement
preassessment, 91–92

Intervention *(continued)*
prereferral. *See* Prereferral intervention
rationale for, 141–142, 146–151, 254–256
readiness. *See* Prerequisite skills and attitudes
and referral. *See* Referral
remediation. *See* Remediation
and rescues, 416–417
screening for. *See* Screening
sequential and hierarchical approaches to, 91, 93, 142, 143, 151, 217–219, 243–245, 362–364, 428–429
services. *See* Placement
societal approach to. *See* Society as context
staffing. *See* Inservice education
tasks of, 45–49
theory and research, 141–146, 236–237, 297–298, 299–301, 327, 332
Intrinsic motivation. *See* Motivation
IRA (International Reading Association), 296

Journal of Learning Disabilities, 291, 299
Judicial decisions, 89, 91, 391, 397, 398

Kindergarten Intervention Program (KIP), 114
Kinesthetic approach. *See* Multisensory methods

Labels and labeling. *See* Diagnosis, and labels and labeling
Language and psycholinguistic area, 232, 243
approaches, 249, 292–293
tests, 293, 307, 330, 343
Language experience approach to reading. *See* Reading, approaches to
Larry P. v. Riles, 89, 91, 391
Laterality, 7, 30, 311
LD field, 291–303
concerns of, 294–303, 312–313
consumers in. *See* Consumer concerns and information
future of, 299–303
history of, 291–303
legislation. *See* Legislation
organizations in, 8, 295–296
research and theory status, 297–298, 299–301
research institutes, 298, 318
training in, 297, 302–303
trends in, 294–295

Lead poisoning, 101
Learner, 158–159, 197–202
    attitudes. *See* Motivation
    capacities, 21, 158, 162, 171
    current states of being and behav-
        ing, 21, 158, 162
    mobilization of, 197–214
    perceptions, 160, 173–174,
        179–184, 197–201, 202, 206,
        216, 275, 423–424
Learning. *See also* Match; Motivation;
    Personalization; Society as
    context; Transactional model
    arrested, 22, 158, 162
    case examples, 59–60, 148, 201,
        219–222, 374, 375, 376, 427
    conditions of, 358–359
    context. *See* Instruction, environ-
        ment and context of; Instruc-
        tion, society as context for
    cooperative, 109–110, 114, 235,
        360
    delayed, 22, 158, 162
    deviant, 21, 158, 162
    disrupted, 22, 158, 162
    enhanced and optimal, 22, 158,
        162
    environment for. *See* Instruction,
        environment and context of; In-
        struction, society as context for
    facilitation. *See* Instruction
    productive factors for, 105–106
Learning disabilities. *See also* LD
    field; Learning problems
    advocacy, 295–298
    approaches to. *See* Instruction;
        Intervention; Remediation
    assessment of. *See* Assessment
    causes of. *See* Central nervous
        system, functions and
        dysfunctions; Underlying prob-
        lems orientation
    characteristics of, 6, 7, 298–299
    definition criteria and problems, 7,
        9, 10, 11, 298–299, 300,
        328–329, 331
    definitions of, 8–10, 298–299
    diagnosis of. *See* Diagnosis
    and exclusionary criteria for diag-
        nosis, 9, 328
    and follow-up research, 259
    heterogeneity in. *See* Type I, II,
        and III problems
    identification of. *See* Screening, for
        early identification
    incidence/prevalence of, 10, 121,
        272, 300
    interventions for. *See* Intervention
    as a learning problem. *See*
        Learning problems

Learning disabilities *(continued)*
    misdiagnosis. *See* Diagnosis, and
        misdiagnosis
    orientations to. *See* Learning
        strategies; Observable problems
        orientation; Underlying problems
        orientation
    in perspective, 11–13, 271–275
    popularization of, 8
    prevalence/incidence of, 10, 121,
        272, 300
    and psychological processes, 8, 9,
        292–293, 299, 315–318, 329
    referral sources for. *See* Referral
    research. *See* Research status
    and sex differences, 85
    subtypes of, 7, 273, 301, 332
    symptoms of, 6, 7, 298–299,
        304–307
Learning Disabilities Association of
    America (LDA), 8, 9, 295, 296,
    298, 299, 401
Learning Disability Quarterly, 295,
    299
Learning Disabled Adult Committee,
    295
Learning Potential Assessment De-
    vice, 109
Learning problems
    behavioral view of, 23–25
    causes and instigating factors of,
        22, 24, 25, 27, 34, 171, 366–367
    as context for understanding learn-
        ing disabilities, 11–13, 271–275
    continuum of, 22–23
    and cultural factors, 8, 9, 13
    and economic factors, 8, 9, 13, 25,
        107, 120–121, 278
    and emotional overlay, 3, 4
    interactional/transactional view of.
        See Transactional model
    and political factors, 13, 277–280,
        303, 395–399, 413–417
    types of. *See* Learning disabilities;
        Type I, II, and III problems;
        Types of problems
Learning quotient (LQ), 331
Learning strategies, 55, 71–72, 109,
    234, 250, 294, 315, 317–318.
    See also Intervention, cognitive
    strategies for; Metacognition
Least intervention needed, 56–57,
    59–60, 187, 217, 275, 339
Least-intervention teaching, 214–215
Least restrictive environment (LRE),
    57, 59–60, 275, 333, 339. *See
    also* Mainstreaming
Le Banks v. Spears, 89
Legal resource networks, 401
Legislation, 102, 297, 323

Legislation *(continued)*
    Americans with Disabilities Act (PL
        101-336), 297
    Children with Specific Learning
        Disabilities Act, 297
    Civil Rights Act, 296
    Economic Opportunity Act, 296
    Education for All Handicapped
        Children Act (PL 94-142), 8, 47,
        127, 297, 298, 320, 323, 337,
        362
    Education of the Handicapped Act,
        297
    Education of the Handicapped
        Amendment Acts (PL 98-199
        and PL 99-457), 323
    Elementary and Secondary Educa-
        tion Act of 1965, 296
    Family Educational Rights and Pri-
        vacy Act of 1974, 87, 404
    Individuals with Disabilities Educa-
        tion Act (IDEA) (PL 101-476), 48,
        297
    PL 88-164, 296
    PL 93-380, 297
    Rehabilitation Act of 1973, 297
    Rehabilitation Amendments Act of
        1986 (PL 99-596), 297
    Social Security Act, 323
Life skills, 119–120
Life tasks. *See* Development, tasks;
    Remediation, of age-appropriate
    life tasks
Limits on behavior, 205–207,
    413–414, 415. *See also* Control;
    Socialization
Listening, 8, 9, 214, 232
Literacy, 121
Litigation, 89, 91, 391, 397, 398
Locus of causality, 22
Logical consequences, 422–424

Magnetic resonance imaging (MRI),
    32
Magnet schools, 106
Mainstreaming, 57–58, 62, 69, 236,
    275, 334. *See also* Regular Edu-
    cation Initiative (REI)
Maintenance of learning, 277, 338,
    424
Marker variables, 272–273
Marshall v. Georgia, 89
Mary & Crystal v. Ramsden, 398
Mastery learning, 108, 237. *See also*
    Direct instruction
Match, 73, 157–174, 177–183,
    216–219
    concept of, 160–163
    development and, 170–173, 187,
        188, 216–219

Match *(continued)*
  motivation and, 163–170, 187, 188, 216–219
  options and. *See* Options
  personalization and. *See* Personalization
  person and environment, 20–23, 44–45, 150–151, 157–158, 160–162
  and strengths and weaknesses, 148, 172
Materials. *See* Intervention, methods, tools, and techniques
Math, 8, 9, 232, 249
Maturational lag or delay, 22, 32–34, 314, 327
MBD (minimal brain dysfunction), 8, 306
Medically related treatments, 62–63, 309–313, 335
Medical model, 22, 327
Medication and drugs, 62, 206, 309–310
Megavitamin therapy. *See* Medically related treatments
Memory, 7, 233–234, 307, 317–318
Mental age (MA), 331
Mental retardation, 8, 9
Metacognition, 71–72, 109, 117, 234, 250, 294, 317–318. *See also* Cognition and cognitive functioning
Methods. *See* Intervention, methods, tools, and techniques
Methylphenidate. *See* Medication and drugs
Mild–moderate problems, 217–219, 243–245
Mills v. Board of Education of the District of Columbia, 89
Milonas v. Williams, 397
Minimal brain dysfunction or damage, 8, 306
Minority groups. *See* Ethnic diversity
Misbehavior, 35, 182, 235, 236, 293–294, 365–368, 422–429
  proactive, 182, 367–368, 422, 424, 426–427
  reactive, 182, 367–368, 422, 424, 425–426
Missing prerequisites. *See* Prerequisite skills and attitudes; Remediation
Mixed dominance and laterality problems, 7, 30, 304, 311
Mnemonic instruction. *See* Memory
Modality training. *See* Sensory, modalities
Modeling and guided change, 117–118

Models of teaching, 359–361
Monitoring, as a learning strategy, 9, 199–202, 234, 319. *See also* Conferences and dialogues; Feedback
Motivated practice, 187, 202, 212–214, 369–377, 382, 386–388
Motivation, 73, 156–175, 177–184, 235, 250–251, 295, 320, 356, 358, 362–364, 365–368, 369–379, 380–389, 422–429. *See also* Personalization
  assessment of, 183, 199–202, 216, 379
  avoidance, 166, 180–183, 184, 197, 198, 366–368, 380
  case examples, 148, 167, 201, 219–222, 371–377
  as cause of learning problems. *See* Learning problems, causes and instigating factors of
  continuing, 164, 382–383, 424
  decision making and, 187, 199, 369–379
  expectancy x value (E x V), 179
  expectations and, 166–167, 179
  extrinsic. *See* Reinforcement, rewards and punishments
  feedback and, 168, 187, 199–202, 383
  intrinsic, 110, 165–166, 179–180, 197, 200, 235, 275, 295, 356, 358, 365–368, 422
  and learning, 163–165, 180, 183, 187, 197–214, 275–277, 362–364
  match concept and, 163–170, 187, 188, 216–219
  as outcome of intervention, 164
  practice and. *See* Motivated practice
  as a primary concern, 163, 197, 243, 275–277, 365–368, 369–379, 380–383
  problems of, 177, 180–183, 229, 235, 365–368, 374–377, 380–389, 424–427
  processes and strategies to enhance and maintain, 164, 179–180, 362–364, 369–379, 382–383, 424–429
  as a readiness prerequisite. *See* Prerequisite skills and attitudes
  reinforcement. *See* Reinforcement
  subgroups, 181, 182, 366–368
  underlying factor for behavior problems, 180–184, 365–368, 424–427

Motivation *(continued)*
  undermining of, 167–170, 182, 357, 358
  valuing and, 165–166, 179, 206
Motor functioning. *See* Perceptual-motor area
MRI (magnetic resonance imaging), 32
Multidisciplinary team diagnostic and placement decisions, 47, 324, 329, 337
Multisensory methods, 238–240, 292, 380–389
Mystification and demystification, 131–133, 392, 400–409, 416

National Advisory Committee on Handicapped Children, 7, 297
National Association of College Admissions Counselors, 400
National Association of School Psychologists, 296
National Health Interview Survey of Child Health, 10
National Joint Committee for Learning Disabilities (NJCLD), 9, 296, 298–299
Negative effects, 62–63, 86–90, 310, 323, 391–394. *See also* Ethical concerns
  of assessment, 86–90
  of evaluation, 265
  of intervention, 62–63, 127, 391–392
  invasion of privacy, 62, 86–87, 391
  of labeling, 58–59, 331
  minimizing, 90
  self-fulfilling prophecies, 62, 391
  for society, 90
  stigmatization, 62, 88, 391
Neurofibromatosis, 28
Neurological impulse transmission. *See* Central nervous system, neurological impulse transmission
Neurological soft signs. *See* Assessment, and neurological signs
Neuropsychological assessment, 305–307, 330, 344–345
NJCLD. *See* National Joint Committee for Learning Disabilities
Norms, assessment, 78–79, 352–353
Nutrition. *See* Medically related treatments
Nystagmus, 306

Objectives, of instruction and intervention. *See* Instruction

Observable problems orientation, 54, 55, 71, 237–238, 293–294, 295, 315, 318–320, 336–337, 339, 341
Observation as an assessment process. *See* Assessment, tests and other procedures in
Oculomotor functioning, 306, 307. *See also* Vision training
One-to-one instruction. *See* Tutorial Community; Tutoring
Open classroom, 206
Operant conditioning. *See* Reinforcement
Options, 127–138, 198–199, 216, 218, 369–379
  in interventions, 187, 216, 369–379
  for learning, 16, 198–199, 216, 369–379
Organizations in the LD field, 8, 295–296
Orientations to intervention. *See* Learning strategies; Observable problems orientation; Underlying problems orientation
Orton Dyslexia Society, 295, 296
Overreliance on professionals, 62–63, 392, 414

Parent Information Centers, 401
Parents
  consent of, 127–130
  involvement in schooling of, 129–130, 410–412
  rights of, 127–130, 393–394, 404–405
Parents' Campaign for Handicapped Children and Youth, 402
PASE v. Hannon, 89
Paternalism, 131, 393–394
Peer consultation. *See* Prereferral intervention
Peer tutoring. *See* Tutorial Community; Tutoring
Pennsylvania Association for Retarded Citizens v. Commonwealth of Pennsylvania, 89
Perception, 33, 243
  auditory, 307
  kinesthetic, 231, 306, 307
  tactile, 231, 306, 307
  visual, 100, 307, 309
Perceptual-motor area, 8, 78, 231, 243, 307
  approaches, 231, 249, 292, 293
  tests, 292, 330, 343
Performance dimensions, 172
Perinatal causes of problems, 29, 100, 278
Perry Preschool Project, 103

Premature birth, 29, 99
Personalization, 73, 110, 149, 173–174, 188, 215–223, 275–277
  assumptions of, 216
  definition of, 173–174
  elements of, 216
  remediation and, 188, 215–223
  steps toward, 222–223
PET. *See* Positron emission tomography
Phonics and phonology. *See* Reading
Placement, 47–48, 50, 51, 52, 57–58, 67–70. *See also* Least intervention needed; Least restrictive environment
  alternatives, 47, 57–58
  and assessment, 333–336
  case example, 59–60
  consumer guidelines and. *See* Consumer concerns and information
  continuum of alternatives and, 57–58
  decision making and, 50, 52, 70, 127–131, 133–135, 333–336
  discrimination in, 70, 82–86, 88–90
  and due process. *See* Procedural safeguards and due process
  sequential approaches to, 143
  service options and settings for, 47
  single vs. multi-stage, 93
Planning for treatment, 50, 51, 52, 143, 146, 147, 183, 336–338. *See also* Individualized educational plan (IEP)
Political factors. *See* Learning problems, and political factors
Positron emission tomography (PET), 32
Postnatal causes of problems, 29
Postsecondary education, 122, 295, 400
Potential/achievement discrepancy. *See* Discrepancy between achievement and intellectual ability
Poverty, 8, 9, 25, 107, 120–121, 278
Practice and learning. *See* Motivated practice
Preacademic learning. *See* Prerequisite skills and attitudes
Precision teaching. *See* Applied behavioral analysis; Behaviorist classroom programs
Prekindergarten programs, 16, 99–104, 278–279, 297
Prenatal causes of problems, 28, 100, 278

Prenatal exposure to drugs, 278
Prereferral intervention, 45, 46–47, 91–92, 117, 275, 337
Prerequisite skills and attitudes, 110, 120, 164, 177–188, 197, 231–236, 242, 243, 276, 315, 319, 336–337, 363, 380–382, 383, 424, 425
Preschool children and preschooling. *See* Prekindergarten programs
Prevalence of learning disabilities, 10, 121, 272, 300
Prevention, 16, 45, 99–101, 104, 277–280, 302, 422, 428
Primary Intervention Program, 114
Primary Mental Health Project, 114–115
Privacy, 62, 86–87, 391, 395
Problem solving
  as a basic skill, 114, 362–364
  case example, 219–222
  interpersonal, 235, 362–364
  steps in, 144–145
Procedural safeguards and due process, 127–130, 404–405. *See also* Ethical guidelines
Productive learning factors, 105–106
Program evaluation. *See* Evaluation
Project Intervention, 107
Projects for learning, 369–377, 381
Protection and Advocacy Network, 401
Protective reactions, 182. *See also* Misbehavior, reactive
Psycholinguistics. *See* Language and psycholinguistic area
Psychological bias, 81–82, 201, 325
Psychoneurological assessment. *See* Assessment, neuropsychological
Psychotherapy. *See* Helping and helping relationships; Intervention, methods, tools, and techniques; Underlying problems orientation
Public Citizen, 401
Public Laws. *See* Legislation
Punishment. *See* Reinforcement
Pursuit of deviance, 182

Questionnaires, use of in assessment. *See* Assessment, tests and other procedures

Rating scales, use of in assessment. *See* Assessment, tests and other procedures
Rationale for intervention, 141–142, 146–151, 254–256
Reading, 8, 9, 186, 232. *See also* Dyslexia

Reading *(continued)*
    approaches to, 238, 239–241, 242,
        380–389
Readiness to learn. *See* Prerequisite
    skills and attitudes
Reasoning, 9, 234, 250
Reassessment, 49
Reciprocal determinism, 21, 93. *See
    also* Transactional model
Reciprocal teaching, 211, 318
Recordkeeping. *See* Monitoring, as a
    learning strategy
Referral, 68, 405–407
    bias in, 68, 325
    case example, 59–60
Regular education, 104–113
Regular Education Initiative (REI), 58
Rehabilitation Act of 1973, 297
Rehabilitation Amendments Act of
    1986 (PL 99-596), 297
Reinforcement
    overreliance on extrinsics,
        167–170, 357, 358, 365
    rewards and punishments, 44,
        129–130, 165, 320, 357,
        358–359, 422–424
Relatedness. *See* Motivation, intrinsic
Relationship building. *See* Working
    relationships
Reliability of assessment, 78, 349
Remediation, 44, 142–143, 146–147,
    177, 180–183, 187–189,
    226–251, 276, 314–322,
    365–368, 374–377, 380–389.
    See also Helping and helping
    relationships; Instruction; Inter-
    vention
    of age-appropriate life tasks, 188,
        217, 218, 241, 276, 315
    approaches to, 53–55, 70–72, 188,
        229–230, 236–251, 315
    of attention. *See* Attention prob-
        lems
    of basic skills, 149, 177–178,
        184–187, 199, 241, 369, 381
    case examples. *See* Instruction,
        case examples
    of cognitive prerequisites, 233,
        243, 250
    compensatory strategies, 24, 53,
        54, 71, 172, 259, 315
    content focus for, 231–236,
        249–251
    contrasting orientations. *See*
        Learning strategies; Observable
        problems orientation; Underly-
        ing problems orientation
    criteria for, 229–231
    distinguished from regular prac-
        tices, 227–229

Remediation *(continued)*
    effectiveness of, 259
    emotional problems and, 235, 250,
        295
    hierarchical approaches to. *See*
        Assessment, sequential
        approaches; Intervention, se-
        quential and hierarchical
        approaches
    of interfering factors, 188, 217,
        218, 235, 236, 241, 242, 276,
        365–368
    in language and psycholinguistic
        area, 232, 243, 249, 292–293,
        316–317
    learning strategies and. *See* Learn-
        ing strategies
    levels of, 188, 241–242
    materials for. *See* Intervention,
        methods, tools, and techniques
    of math problems, 232, 249
    of memory problems, 233,
        317–318
    methods. *See* Intervention, meth-
        ods, tools, and techniques
    of missing prerequisites, 188, 217,
        218, 231–236, 242, 243, 276,
        315, 319, 336–337, 363,
        380–382, 383, 424, 425
    motivation problems and. *See* Mo-
        tivation
    need for, 227, 229–231, 276,
        328–338
    negative effects of. *See* Negative
        effects
    observable problems orientation.
        See Observable problems ori-
        entation
    orientations to. *See* Learning
        strategies; Observable problems
        orientation; Underlying problems
        orientation
    in perceptual-motor area, 231, 243,
        249, 292, 316–317
    and personalization, 188,
        215–223
    of prerequisite skills and attitudes,
        188, 217, 218, 231–236, 242,
        243, 276, 315, 319, 336–337,
        363, 380–382, 383, 424, 425
    prevailing approaches. *See* Learn-
        ing strategies; Observable prob-
        lems orientation; Underlying
        problems orientation
    processes and techniques for. *See*
        Intervention, methods, tools, and
        techniques
    psychological impact of, 228
    of reading problems, 232, 238,
        239–241, 242, 249

Remediation *(continued)*
    of reasoning problems, 234, 250,
        317–318
    sequential strategies for. *See* Inter-
        vention, sequential and hierar-
        chical approaches to
    of social problems, 235, 236, 250,
        362–364
    of underlying problems. *See*
        Underlying problems
        orientation
Rescue dynamics, 416–417
Research status, 141–146, 236–237,
    259, 297–298, 327, 332
Resource concept, 118–119
Restructuring schools, 105–113
Reteaching, 217, 244, 245
Reversals, 100
Rewards. *See* Reinforcement
R-H factor, 28
Rights related to LD. *See* Children's
    assent and rights; Parents, rights
    of
Risks vs. benefits. *See* Ethical con-
    cerns, cost–benefit analysis
Ritalin. *See* Medication and drugs

Santana v. Collazo, 398
School. *See also* Educational reform;
    Effective schools; Instruction;
    Intervention; Placement;
    Postsecondary education; Regu-
    lar education; Special educa-
    tion
    adjustment problems, 100,
        113–116, 278, 279
    characteristics of, 105–106
    climate/culture, 105
    dropouts, 120–121
    misbehavior at. *See* Misbehavior
    restructuring, 105–113
    staffing patterns, 61
    staff–student ratio, 61, 112–113,
        204
Scotopic sensitivity, 309
Screening, 45–47, 50, 51, 52, 67, 68,
    91, 323–327. *See also*
    Assessment; Diagnosis
    and diagnosis, 324
    for early identification, 46, 67
    errors and misdiagnosis, 67, 68,
        90, 91, 151, 323, 324
    for lead poisoning, 101
    limitations of, 67, 323–327
    procedures for, 323–327
    sequential approaches in, 143,
        217–219, 243–245
Self-concept and self-esteem, 114
Self-determination. *See* Motivation,
    intrinsic

Self-evaluation. *See* Monitoring, as a learning strategy
Self-fulfilling prophecies. *See* Negative effects
Self-help resources, 400–402, 412
Self-monitoring. *See* Monitoring, as a learning strategy
Self-regulation. *See* Monitoring, as a learning strategy
Sensory. *See also* Perception
    intake, 53, 210–211
    integration, 231, 238–241, 305
    modalities, 231, 238–241
    systems, 9
Sequential strategies. *See* Assessment, sequential approaches to; Intervention, sequential and hierarchical approaches to
Services. *See* Placement
Severe problems, 217–219, 243–245
Sex differences and sex role bias, 85, 88, 100
Signs and symptoms. *See* Assessment, and neurological signs
Simultanagnosia, 306
S-I v. Turlington, 89
Skill hierarchies and sequences, 142–143, 319, 336
Social and interpersonal behavior skills and functioning, 235, 250–251, 295, 360, 362–364
    social competency, 114, 301
    tests, 330, 344
Social control. *See* Control, social
Socialization, 135–136, 255–256, 396–397. *See also* Control; Limits on behavior
Social Security Act, 323
Societal bias, 82–86
Society as context, 13, 86, 135–138, 255–256, 277–280, 413–417
Soft signs. *See* Assessment, and neurological signs
Special education, 57–58, 61–62. *See also* Placement
Speech, 7, 8, 9, 232, 307
Spelling problems, 8, 9, 232
Spiral curriculum, 356

SQ3R technique, 152–153, 287
Staff development. *See* Inservice education
Stages of development. *See* Developmental tasks
Standardization of tests, 341, 349–353
Standards for making judgments. *See* Assessment, standards used in; Evaluation, standards used in
Stare ex rel. K.W. v. Werner, 398
Stimulant medication. *See* Medication and drugs
Strephosymbolia, 7
Structure for learning, 198, 202, 205–207, 370–373
Student-teacher conferences. *See* Conferences and dialogues
Substance abuse, 273
Success For All, 112–113
Survival skills, 49
System changes, 16, 43–45, 150–151, 277–280, 281–282, 425–429

Task analysis, 238
Teacher assistance team, 47, 117. *See also* Prereferral intervention
Teaching. *See* Instruction; Intervention; Remediation
Techniques. *See* Intervention, methods of
Tests and test batteries. *See* Assessment; Diagnosis
Theories of instruction, 355–361
Therapy-oriented practices. *See* Helping and helping relationships; Intervention, methods, tools, and techniques; Underlying problems orientation
Tools and techniques for intervention. *See* Intervention, methods, tools, and techniques
Tourette's syndrome, 63
Transactional model, 20–23, 24, 35, 43, 45, 93, 150, 157–163, 174, 273–275, 295

Transition phases of intervention
    transition in, 48, 115–116
    transition out, 49
Transition services, 48–49
Treatment. *See* Helping and helping relationships; Instruction; Intervention; Remediation
Trial and appraisal teaching. *See* Instruction
Tutorial Community, 111–112
Tutoring, 47, 61, 69, 110–112, 114
Type I, II, and III problems, 13–15, 19, 22–23, 24, 25, 27, 35, 43, 59, 61, 99, 104, 106, 141, 188, 189, 271–274, 276
Types of problems, 11–15. *See also* Type I, II, and III problems

Underachievers and underachievement, 6
Underlying problems orientation, 53, 54, 71, 188, 229, 230, 238–240, 292–293, 295, 314–318, 315, 329, 336, 339, 341. *See also* Assessment, orientations
Underlying psychological processes. *See* Basic psychological processes

VAKT. *See* Multisensory methods
Validity, assessment, 78, 341, 349–352
Valuing, motivation and, 165–166, 179, 206
Vestibular treatment, 311
Victoria L. v. District School Board, 89
Vision and visual acuity, 33, 328
Vision training, 309
Vitamin deficiencies, 29
Vocational education, 122, 295, 298
Volunteers. *See* Tutoring
Vulnerabilities, 101, 180

Wheeler v. Glass, 398
Working relationships, 116–118, 202, 206, 207, 418–421, 425
Written language problems, 8, 9, 232